The Texas Rangers

Illustrated with Drawings by Lonnie Rees
and with Photographs

FOREWORD BY LYNDON B. JOHNSON

UNIVERSITY OF TEXAS PRESS, AUSTIN

The Texas Rangers

A CENTURY OF FRONTIER DEFENSE

by WALTER PRESCOTT WEBB

The title page picture is from a painting by Tom Lea, *Ranger Escort West of the Pecos*. The original work is a gift to the state of Texas from C. R. Smith, chairman of the board of American Airlines. Governor John B. Connally accepted the painting in 1965 for permanent display in the governor's office. It is used here with the permission of Tom Lea and Governor Connally. The two men in the foreground are Colonel George W. Baylor, *left*, and Sergeant J. B. Gillett, two illustrious figures in the colorful history of the Texas Rangers.

International Standard Book Number 0-292-73400-x (cloth);
0-292-78110-5 (paper)
Library of Congress Catalog Card Number 65-23166

Printed in the United States of America

Second Edition
Thirteenth Printing of the University of Texas Press
Cloth Edition, 1991
Second Printing of the University of Texas Press
Paperback Edition, 1991

The paper used in this publication meets the minimum requirements of American National Standard for Information Sciences—Permanence of Paper for Printed Library Materials, ANSI Z39.48-1984.

PUBLISHER'S NOTE

This edition of *The Texas Rangers* is identical with the first edition published by Houghton Mifflin in 1935 with the exception of the front matter from which the publishers have eliminated two poems, adding the Foreword by President Johnson. The text is printed from the plates of the 1935 edition.

Discussing a possible new edition of *The Texas Rangers* with the publishers shortly before his death, Dr. Webb indicated that there were a number of changes which he would like to make before its publication, since some of his points of view and interpretations of facts had been altered by the passage of three decades. He also hoped that the story of the Rangers could be brought up to date, either by him or by another writer. But he had made no changes at the time of his death and we cannot presume to make them for him; the story of the latter-day Rangers must remain to be told by someone else in another book.

THE UNIVERSITY OF TEXAS PRESS

FOREWORD

THE American Frontier cannot properly be described in the past tense. The influence of the Frontier has been great upon our political institutions, our social patterns, our values and aspirations as a people, and, especially, upon the democratic character of our society. The influence of the Frontier as a molding force in our system is far from spent.

A century after the heyday of our Frontier settlement—with all the legends that still live so vividly in our national life—the vastness, openness, and opportunity of the American West continue to assert a powerful influence upon our Nation. Our present westward movement of population is a factor requiring as much reckoning now as in the latter half of the nineteenth century—perhaps more. The development of resources and opportunity in the still new and underdeveloped regions of America continues after a century to shape and stimulate our economy. The Frontier in America is neither dead nor dormant—it lives as a source of our national vigor.

Historically the Frontier is not narrowly defined. All of our land has been, at one time or another, a part of the American "West"—Pennsylvania, Kentucky, Ohio, as much as Colorado, California or Texas. When Abraham Lincoln came to the White House from Illinois he came as a Westerner from the prairie states. "The West" is not so much a geographic place as it is a symbol—a symbol of America's confidence that on beyond the moment, on beyond the present terrain, the world will be brighter, the future better.

Dr. Walter Prescott Webb was a son of the American West and lived to become one of its two or three greatest historians and analysts. His contemporaries in the learned fields recognized him for the giant that he was, and I was privileged to know him for the man that he was—unassuming, enthusiastic, confident always that this Nation would find fulfillment of its democratic ideals as we fulfilled the opportunity and promise of the American West.

Were Dr. Webb still living I am sure he would find great satisfaction and thrill in the devotion Americans today are manifesting for the heritage drawn from the symbolic West of our history. As we become a more populous and far more urbanized nation, an instinct develops—a right and just instinct—to preserve the heritage of open country, clear skies, clean streams. More importantly another instinct develops—an instinct to preserve the equality of opportunity, the dignity of the individual, the commitment to justice for all that derive from the spirit of the Frontier era. Our affluence, our abundance, our strength and power have not dulled the values experience taught us through the challenge of opening the Frontier.

The Frontier—and the West—are synonymous in our minds with adventure, courage, bravery, independence, and self-reliance. Yet still another essential is not to be overlooked. Adventuresome and individualistic as they were, America's western pioneers never left far behind the rule of law. They risked much and sacrificed much to win opportunity. But they turned unfailingly to respect for the law to assure that those gains would not be meaningless.

Dr. Webb memorialized one of the most storied, yet most truly effective, law-enforcement organizations in this book, *The Texas Rangers*. I am happy that the University of Texas Press is republishing this monumental work, on which Dr. Webb spent fourteen years of his life. The individual episodes he recounts are a rich part of our thrilling national heritage. But the significance of the Texas Rangers is greater than the sum of these individual stories.

The never-ending quest for an orderly, secure, but open and free society always demands dedicated men. The Rangers—and Dr. Webb, himself—were just such men. Their influence was worked not by recklessness or foolhardiness, but by the steadiness of their purpose and performance—and by the sureness, among both the law-abiding and the law-breaking, that thought of self would never deter the Ranger from fulfilling the commitment of his vows as an agent of law, order, and justice.

One of the stories Dr. Webb related to me which I have repeated most often through the years stems from a figure in this volume, Captain L. H. McNelly. Captain McNelly was one of the most effective of the Texas Rangers, yet he was thin as a bed slat, weighing hardly 135 pounds, consumptive, in many ways the very opposite of the prototype of a Ranger. But Captain McNelly repeatedly told his men that "courage is a man who keeps on coming on." As Dr. Webb would explain to me, "you can slow a man like that, but you can't defeat him—the man who keeps on coming on is either going to get there himself or make it possible for a later man to reach the goal."

In the challenging and perilous times of this century, free men everywhere might profitably consider that motto. We cannot be sure that in our own time we will reach and fulfill the goals of our society or the ideals on which our system stands. But we can, by dedication and commitment, be the kind of people who "keep on coming on."

LYNDON B. JOHNSON

May, 1965

ACKNOWLEDGMENTS

I AM indebted to innumerable persons for assistance on this work and cannot hope to call all by name. Among the adjutant generals who have given direct or indirect help are Thomas D. Barton, W. D. Cope, W. W. Sterling, and Carl Nesbitt. Among the Ranger captains are June Peak, J. H. Rogers, Tom R. Hickman, W. L. Wright, C. J. Blackwell, J. B. Wheatley, Frank Hamer, and R. W. Aldrich. To Captain Aldrich I am indebted for the opportunity of visiting the Ranger camps and meeting the men in their work.

Miss Edith Heiligbrodt, former archivist in the adjutant general's office, made transcripts from the records for my use. Miss Winnie Allen and Mrs. Mattie Austin Hatcher, of the University Archives, assisted in many ways. Miss Ione Spears rendered invaluable aid as research assistant in checking references, preparing bibliography, and in reading the entire manuscript critically. Members of the History Staff of the University of Texas who contributed are Professor Eugene C. Barker, Professor Charles W. Ramsdell, and Mr. J. Evetts Haley. To Lonnie Rees, the artist, I am deeply obligated for the pencil sketches and oil paintings which enliven the pages. The artist's devotion to the task was in itself an inspiration. I have not forgotten that Charles Armstrong rode halfway across Texas to give me the records of his father, John B. Armstrong, or that William Callicott, when practically blind, wrote the best account of Captain McNelly that has been done, or that Harbert Davenport was never too busy to answer any question about the lower Rio Grande, or that Raphael Cowen told me how his grandfather, John S. Ford, got the name of Rip Ford in the Mexican War, or that Captain J. B. Gillett of Marfa has written generous letters from time to time encouraging me to complete the task. Nor shall I forget Arch Miller of the Big Bend whose originality of expression puts the writer to shame. Jane and Mildred, wife and daughter, have borne patiently the unpleasantnesses that emanate from one who writes a book. They have stood up well under the first drafts and insisted that the work go on. The completion of the task was facilitated by a grant from the Bureau of Research in the Social Sciences at the University of Texas.

W. P. W.

THEY RODE STRAIGHT UP TO DEATH

A PREFACE

IN 1835 the Texas Rangers were organized and given legal status while Texas was in the midst of revolution against Mexico. Their almost continuous service to 1935, when they were absorbed in a larger organization, indicates that the need for them has been persistent while their changing functions reflect the evolution of the society they protected from its primitive beginning as a frontier community to a commonwealth of five million people. Though his duties have varied from decade to decade, the Ranger has been throughout essentially a fighting man.

It was Eugene Manlove Rhodes who suggested that the Western man—he was speaking of the cowboy—can be understood only when studied in relation to his work. And so it is with the Ranger. When we see him at his daily task of maintaining law, restoring order, and promoting peace—even though his methods be vigorous—we see him in his proper setting, a man standing alone between a society and its enemies. When we remember that it was his duty to deal with the criminal in the dangerous nexus between the crime and the capture, when the criminal was in his most desperate mood, we must realize that neither the rules nor the weapons were of the Ranger's choosing. It has been his duty to meet the outlaw breed of three races, the Indian warrior, Mexican bandit, and American desperado, on the enemy's ground and deliver each safely within the jail door or the cemetery gate. It is here recorded that he has sent many patrons to both places.

As strange as it may seem in some quarters, the Texas Ranger has been throughout the century a human being, and never a mere automaton animating a pair of swaggering boots, a big hat, and a six-shooter all moving across the prairies under a cloud of pistol smoke. Surely enough has been written about men who swagger, fan hammers, and make hip shots. No Texas Ranger ever fanned a hammer when he was serious, or made a hip shot if he had time to catch a sight. The real Ranger has been a very quiet, deliberate, gentle person who could gaze calmly into the eye of a murderer, divine his thoughts, and anticipate his action, a man who could ride straight up to death. In fatal encounter—the last resort of a good officer—the Ranger has had the unhurried courage to take the extra fraction of a second essential to accuracy which was at a premium in the art and the science of Western pistology. The smoke from such a man's hand was a vagrant wisp and never the clouds read of in books written for those who love to smell powder smoke vicariously.

The method of telling the story of the Rangers at work has the added merit of revealing the relative stature of the workman. From the records emerge in successive chapters the dominant figures who have shaped the tradition and made the story what it is by their achievements.

Because of two destructive fires the official records for the early period are scant, but the records for the period since the Civil War are abundant. Though manuscript and printed sources form the basis, other records have been used freely. With assiduity I have sought out the veterans and heard their accounts. Men in active service have given me their *frijoles* and bread and black coffee. They have suffered me to share their camp, ride their best horses, fire their six-shooters, and to feel the companionship of men and horses when the saddle stirrups touch in the solitudes. They are masters of brevity when they speak of themselves—as economical of words as of pistol smoke. 'We had a little shooting and he lost' was the way one told the story of a personal encounter. They do not respond to direct questions of a personal nature, and it is best not to ask them. 'I have been accused once,' responded one whose exploits would fill a book. 'We were camped out on the Pecos. A norther came up, I pulled the cover off, and he froze to death.' From the official records I have obtained the official facts, but from the living men I have, I trust, caught something of the spirit of an institution.

W. P. W.

Austin, Texas
September 16, 1935

CONTENTS

ILLUSTRATIONS

ILLUSTRATIONS

ILLUSTRATIONS

I

TEXAS: A CONFLICT OF CIVILIZATIONS

Of this far-famed corps — so much feared and hated by the Mexicans — I can add nothing to what has already been written. The character of the Texas Ranger is now well known by both friend and foe. As a mounted soldier he has had no counterpart in any age or country. Neither Cavalier nor Cossack, Mameluke nor Moss-trooper are like him; and yet, in some respects, he resembles them all. Chivalrous, bold and impetuous in action, he is yet wary and calculating, always impatient of restraint, and sometimes unscrupulous and unmerciful. He is ununiformed, and undrilled, and performs his active duties thoroughly, but with little regard to order or system. He is an excellent rider and a dead shot. His arms are a rifle, Colt's revolving pistol, and a knife.

GIDDINGS, *Sketches*

I. TEXAS: A CONFLICT OF CIVILIZATIONS

1. THE LAND

THE organization commonly known as the Texas Rangers may be defined as a fighting force which had its origin in a three-cornered racial and cultural conflict. The history of this conflict, which constitutes a unique chapter in American life, is a little less than the history of the Texas frontier and a little more than the history of the Texas Rangers.

To understand the conflict it is necessary to consider the land on which it occurred. Texans frequently speak of the great area of their state or hear it spoken of by others. Large as it is, Texas constitutes but a part of that long slope which descends from the foothills of the Rocky Mountains to the Mississippi and the Gulf. From the upper side of this tilted plain many rivers flow southeasterly in almost parallel courses. The Red River, which is the largest, forms the northern boundary of Texas as far west as the hundredth meridian, while the longest river, the Rio Grande, separates Texas from Mexico for almost a thousand miles. Between these two streams are the Sabine, Neches, Trinity, Brazos, Guadalupe, San Antonio, Nueces, and their tributaries. Farther west the Pecos, a tributary of the Rio Grande, deserves especial mention, because it sets off a desert region, the Trans-Pecos country, which with much of the Rio Grande valley constitutes a semi-desert environment.

The casual observer of the map might think that the natural geographic divisions of the state north of the Rio Grande would consist of a series of river valleys or hydrographic basins, more or less parallel, with a general descent to the southeast. While these valleys exist, they do not furnish the dominant feature of the land, and not one of them presents the character of a homogeneous environment. For example, if one should start at the mouth of the Trinity, the Brazos, or the Colorado and traverse the stream to its source, he would find himself passing from a heavily timbered and well-watered country into a level prairie region — the blackland belt — which was covered originally with tall grass and scanty trees — and thence onto a high, subhumid plain of the purest type known on this continent. This transition from the forests to the plains is approximately marked by the ninety-eighth meridian which bisects Texas into almost equal parts. The ninety-eighth meridian separates the Eastern Woodland from the Western Plains; it separates East Texas from West Texas. East Texas is but the southwestern corner of the Great Eastern Woodland which covers the right half of the United States; and West Texas is but the southern and eastern section of the Great Western Plains which occupy the left half of the country.

Between the Eastern Woodland and the Western Plains nothing is so striking as the contrasts, and these must be considered carefully by one who seeks to understand the social and cultural problems of the people.[1] Interesting as the subject may be, we cannot here consider the contrasts between the two great environments, but must confine our attention to that part of each region which lies in Texas.

East Texas — like the whole Eastern Woodland — is a land of plenteous rainfall, ranging from fifty inches on the Louisiana side to thirty inches along the western. The topography and the vegetation of East Texas arise directly from the climatic factor of rainfall. The land is deeply eroded and the top soil has in many places been washed away to lay bare rolling red hills. Upon these hills and in the numerous valleys grow forest trees of all sorts — walnut, hickory, sweet gum; long leaf, short leaf, and loblolly pine, offering shade in summer and shelter in winter to both animal and human life. The only part of East Texas that is not forested is the narrow coastal plain along the Gulf shore and the region south of Matagorda Bay. East Texas is not different in general appearance, in climate, or in vegetation from Mississippi, Georgia, or other southern states.

In West Texas the rainfall nowhere exceeds thirty inches and in the higher and western part, it falls to fifteen or in some places to ten inches, approaching in spots the true desert.[2] Because of scant rainfall,

[1] For a description of these two larger environments see *The Great Plains*, Chapters I, II.

[2] The reader should not get the notion that all West Texas is a true plain. There are subdivisions which differ in character one from another. The whole Rio Grande valley is desert-like and requires irrigation. The region west of the Pecos, known in Texas as the Trans-Pecos, is truly desert, the wildest and most picturesque part of the state. The High Plains constitute the most striking feature. They cover a large portion of the Panhandle and break off on the south at about the thirtieth parallel. They are a mesa-like tableland rising above the general level of the country from ten to eighty feet. This irregular precipice which forms their fringe is called the Cap Rock. The High Plains exhibit every characteristic of the true plains. Originally they were heavily carpeted with grass, which, with a light rainfall, prevented erosion. For a description of the High Plains see Willard D. Johnson, 'The High Plains and their Utilization,' *Twenty-First and Twenty-Second Annual Report of the United States Geological Survey*.

forest trees do not grow in this western half. The mesquite — a scrubby gnarled tree with a mighty root system — is found from the ninety-eighth meridian westward for some two hundred miles. Along the streams the hackberry, cottonwood, and willow make ribbons of foliage which wind over the Plains towards the foothills of the Rockies.

The western half of the state was the grasslands. There grew the tall grasses of the prairie region, the needle and wheat grasses, and the curly mesquite which has in it enough of the distilled spirit of the vast sun and the sweet rain of the dry country to make wild broncs out of old horses in a month's grazing. Farther west and to the north — in the Panhandle — was the buffalo grass, a coarse bunch grass which gave sustenance to the wild herds whose millions of hoofs thundered across the Plains for unknown thousands of years.

To the southwest — beyond the Pecos and in the upper valley of the Rio Grande — the scene changes from that of the grasslands to the desert, where rainfall is less than fifteen inches on an average. Instead of level or rolling plains mantled with grass, one sees the wild forms of desert topography, battlement and mesa, fault and escarpment, chimneys and towers, surviving fragments of an older plain which has been worn down not so much by rain as by wind and sun beating upon a bare surface. The vegetation is the cactus in a thousand species and varieties, the greasewood, and the sage.

2. *THE INDIANS OF TEXAS*

It would have been strange indeed if the conditions of the land, as set forth above, had not been reflected in the life, the culture, and the character of the Indians. Because the Indians lived close to the land, they were finely adapted to it — were truly its children. 'The earth is our mother and the sun our father,' was their way of expressing the truth. As Texas was divided into a forest and a plain, so were the Indians divided into forest tribes in East Texas and Plains tribes in West Texas. They were two peoples whose respective ways of life, whose culture, differed as much as their homeland, as the grassy rolling plains differ from the tree-clad hills, as a wigwam from a tipi or a log cabin from a soddie. The eastern tribes, for example, were sedentary and agricultural; they lived in permanent villages, built their wigwams of bark and tree, made and used pottery, and supplemented the game they killed with corn, squash, and bean. The western Indians were nomadic wanderers who knew little or nothing of agriculture. They lived among the millions of buffalo, and from the clumsy animal they supplied practically every necessity of life save water. From the hides they made their clothes and their tipis; from the bones their crude tools; from the tendons thread; from the hoofs glue; while the meat served as almost their sole article of food. On the whole, the lot of the Plains Indians was harder than that of the timber tribes because the Plains dwellers had to wander about in search of subsistence. While all Indians were more or less warlike, the Plains tribes were by their wild habits of life fierce and ungovernable. They were constantly shifting about, fighting for possession of land and water, and for social distinction.

The location of the Texas Indian tribes as they were in the first quarter of the nineteenth century now concerns us. Among the Woodland Indians the Caddo stock, or confederacy, was the most important. From their original home in Louisiana, they spread into Texas. Their traditions do not lead back to the time when they were not agricultural. When they emerged from the underworld, there came first an old man carrying in one hand fire and a pipe and in the other a drum, then came his wife with corn or maize and pumpkin seed. The absence of weapons and the presence of corn and pumpkin seed are indicative of their dispositions and inclinations. They were farmers and not warriors primarily.

The Caddo Indians spoke of their confederacy as *texas*, *texias*, or *techas*. The word in the narrow sense meant 'allies' and in a broader sense it meant 'friends,' an appropriate name because these tribes were usually friendly with the European peoples.

Along the coast, in the vicinity of Matagorda Bay, dwelt the ferocious Karankawa, who were not numerous enough to stand long before the white races. By 1860, under the repeated blows of the Europeans, they had perished.

In the transition region between the forests and Plains dwelt several transitional tribes exhibiting a culture, half plains and half forest. In the south were the Lipans, an offshoot of the Apaches, separated from the main tribe by a Comanche wedge, and northward were the Tonkawas, Tawakonis, Wacos, and the Wichitas. Some of these Indians cultivated the soil to a limited extent, but all made regular excursions after the buffalo. They were not strong, but they were dangerous and troublesome. They may be called the semi-plains or prairie tribes.

Farther west, ranging the Plains from southern Texas to Kansas, were the fierce Comanches of Shoshone stock who had come but recently from the mountains of the northwest to take the southern

Plains. West of them, in the foothills of the Rockies and along the Pecos were the principal Apache groups. South of the Rio Grande in what is now Mexico were numerous small bands, but these played an insignificant part in Texas Indian problems and may therefore be disregarded.

The Indian situation as just described was disturbed in the first third of the nineteenth century by the migration of tribes from the eastern and southern United States. The most important among the newcomers were the Cherokees who, under their leader Colonel Bowl, came to Texas about 1824 and settled on a tract of land along the Angelina, Neches, and Trinity rivers, where they remained for fifteen years. The expulsion of the Cherokees in 1839 constitutes one of the many tragic episodes in American Indian relations. Other, though smaller, bands, such as the Kickapoos, Coshattas, and Seminoles, came to or through Texas, running like frightened game before the devastating fire of the American frontier. Some of the fugitives stopped in Texas, many sojourned there, and some went into Mexico and settled along the Rio Grande where they could depredate in Texas when they considered such an adventure feasible.

From the above sketch of the Indian situation in Texas during the early part of the nineteenth century, it should be apparent that the first permanent settlers — Anglo-Americans from the United States — would find a complicated and troublesome Indian problem to solve before they could hold their land in peace. It should be equally obvious that more than half their difficulties would come from the Plains, mainly from the Comanche and to a less extent from the Apache, Tawakoni, Lipan, Wichita, and Waco bands.

3. THE COMING OF THE SPANIARDS

The essential facts about the Spanish frontier are that it advanced on Texas from the south and that it finally came to rest on the Rio Grande, the southwest border of the state. With Mexico City as a center, the Spaniards began early in the sixteenth century to conquer and incorporate the native population and push the frontier line farther and farther northward. In 1601, Santa Fe was established and in the latter part of the century missions and presidios were set up in East Texas adjacent to the French in Louisiana. More important, however, for our purpose was the planting of a permanent Spanish stronghold in San Antonio in the year 1718. Santa Fe and San Antonio constituted the strongest northern outposts of the Spanish Mexican frontier until the end of the Spanish régime. Between these two outposts lay that part of Texas occupied and stubbornly defended by the Comanches and Apaches.

Many reasons have been advanced for Spain's failure to extend or even hold this northern line, but they are general reasons, applicable to the whole frontier line and to all Spanish possessions; and while they are, in a measure, true, they are not needed to explain Spain's failure between San Antonio and Santa Fe. The important factor on that segment of the frontier was the Plains Indians.

The scope of this work does not permit a narrative of what went on between the Spaniards and these Indians. The general theme of the story would be one of continuous war in which tragedy and disaster dogged the Spaniards. On the east side the Comanches slaughtered all the priests at San Saba, signally defeated Parilla on Red River, broke up the settlement at Bucareli, and terrorized the troops and citizens at San Antonio; on the west side the Apaches did their work equally well. Father Garces declared that he did not write of them for want of paper, a stock of which would be required to tell of the troubles with the Apaches.

One fundamental reason why Spain failed to cope successfully with the Plains Indians was that Spain attempted to subdue them with the same methods and the same frontier agencies which had been used successfully with an entirely different *kind* of Indian. Spain's frontier institutions were made in the West Indies and further developed in the fertile Mesa Central around Mexico City, where the Indians were civilized, sedentary, agricultural, and, as compared with the nomads of the Plains, as docile as sheep.

Among these tribes Spain went with three agencies: the *conquistador* to conquer, the religious to convert, and the *encomendero* to exploit. This machine worked with marvelous effectiveness and speed in the rich and humid Mesa Central, but as it advanced northward into the arid country, it began to fail. Naturally the economic part of it broke down first — broke as soon as it ceased to show a profit, and the *encomienda* system was abandoned in 1720, though its failure had been evident long before it was acknowledged. Two agencies now remained, the religious and the military, to uphold the frontier. Spain established a string of missions from Louisiana to California and continued with royal support the effort to advance northward. The labors of the holy fathers were at best wholly negligible for the Indians and often disastrous to the missionaries. The wild Comanche and Apache were not amenable to the gentle philosophy of Christ nor were they tamed by the mysteries and elaborate ceremonials of the church. The war-whoop was sweeter to them than evening vespers; the crescent bow was a better symbol of their desires than the holy cross; and it was far more joyful, in their eyes, to chase the shaggy buffalo on pinto ponies than to practice the art of dry-farming under the direction of a black-robed priest.

In 1772, Spain tacitly admitted that the church had failed by abandoning the missions on the northern frontier. Thereafter sole dependence for further advance was the citizen and the soldiers. At the time the missions were abandoned, the frontier was pulled back from the Plains and the soldiers were established in a line of fifteen presidios, only two of which — Santa Fe and San Antonio — lay north of the Rio Grande. Later events caused Spain and Mexico to abandon these two positions, and in 1848 the boundary between Texas and Mexico was permanently established. The Rio Grande, occupied by a Latin-Indian race, constituted one side of the cultural triangle. Thus it was that Spain turned the southern Great Plains back to the Comanches and Apaches who became bolder and more aggressive than ever. They carried the war into Mexico with the result that at the end of the Spanish-Mexican régime they were more powerful and in possession of more territory than they were at any time before. The task of subduing them remained for the Americans who were making their way into the Plains from the east.

4. THE COMING OF THE AMERICANS

With the coming of the Americans the three races or cultures which were to struggle for supremacy were all present in Texas. The Americans, slow, powerful, inexorable, made their way westward, coming at length into conflict with the Mexicans along the Rio Grande and with the Indians of the Plains. Out of the three-cornered conflict has come the unique character of Texas with its dramatic history and peculiar institutions.

When the United States purchased Louisiana from Napoleon in 1803, the American political frontier made a long stride westward, leaving the frontier of occupation far behind. For twenty years the pioneers moved rapidly forward over a broad front only to find the Spanish province of Texas directly in their path. The movement of the pioneers was apparently as blind, instinctive, as the migratory progress of the cutworms or locusts, and even a poor prophet could see that the horde would not stop at a political boundary. Those first independent spirits who entered Texas without any sort of official sanction from either government concerned are called filibusters, a polite name for freebooters and international trouble-makers. Such men as Peter Ellis Bean and Philip Nolan came to catch wild horses, to trade, and to spy out the country. Like the first teal of the season, they were the forerunners and heralds of thousands of swift followers.

The legal and more orderly occupancy of the Spanish province by the Anglo-Americans was initiated in 1820 by Moses Austin and was successfully carried out after his death by his talented young son, Stephen. The Austins began their negotiations for a grant of land in Texas under auspicious circumstances. For one thing, they had lived in Missouri when Missouri was Spanish territory and therefore they could approach the officials as patriots who wished to resume their former relationship as subjects of the Spanish crown. Even when Mexico revolted from Spain and in 1821 established a republic, the cause of Austin's colony prospered because Mexican officials looked with favor on the American form of government and likewise on Americans. Notwithstanding such providential favors, Stephen F. Austin needed all the tact and sound common sense that he possessed to carry him through the trying years when he was attempting to plant an American colony in a Mexican territory and struggling to harmonize the interests of a self-willed and cocksure group of Americans with the vague desires of a conglomerate Latin-Indian population.

With that good judgment which ever characterized him, Austin chose the most desirable portion of Texas for his colony — the country that lies between the Colorado and the Trinity rivers. The soil and climate there were similar to much of that in the United States from whence the settlers were to come. There were few Mexicans in that part of the province; the Indians in the immediate vicinity were neither numerous nor unfriendly; the Comanche and the Apache were far enough west to offer no immediately serious problem. Therefore the colony flourished and grew with no more difficulties than usually attended such pioneer movements.

The movement of Americans to Texas was greatly accelerated when in 1825 Mexico passed a general colonization law designed to encourage foreign emigration. By 1830 the American population of Texas numbered thirty thousand; it was larger than the population of Mexicans and Indians combined.

Mexico became alarmed at the rapid influx of Americans, and in 1830 passed a law closing the door which had five years before been so generously opened to foreigners. It was not without cause that

Mexico did this, for the Americans had been both turbulent and troublesome. Some of them had set revolutionary movements on foot in Texas, and many more were always ready to join such adventures. From 1830 to 1835 there was constant and increasing friction between the American colonists and the Mexican government. The Texas Revolution began in 1835; complete independence was declared on March 2, 1836, and in the following month it was made secure by the decisive victory on the field of San Jacinto where Santa Anna was captured and made to acknowledge that Texas was free.

5. *INDIAN WARRIOR, MEXICAN VAQUERO, AND TEXAS RANGER*

By the opening of the Revolution the three races that were to struggle for supremacy were all present in Texas. The Indians held undisputed possession of the Plains; the Mexicans held the southwest with their line of occupation resting on the Rio Grande; and the Anglo-Americans, henceforth called Texans, had virtual possession of the timbered portion of the then Mexican province. Since the three races were to wage constant war one with another, it was necessary for each to produce its representative fighting man. The Comanche had his warrior brave and the Mexican his *caballero*, *ranchero*, or *vaquero*. To meet these the Texans created the Ranger, who, since he was the latest comer, found it necessary to adapt his weapons, tactics, and strategy to the conditions imposed by his enemies. In spite of the fact that each of these fighters influenced the others, each remained the true representative of the customs and ideals of his respective race, a symbol of the fighting genius of his group.

The Indian warrior, first in the field, was out of a nomadic people whose ideals and purposes never harmonized with those of their European foes. It is not the purpose here, or anywhere in this volume, to praise the Indian or to condemn him, but rather to understand him and to see his way of life as he saw it. His home was the wild prairie and the broad high plain where roamed millions of buffalo and countless droves of deer, and smaller game. He loved these things with devotion and fought for them with all his ferocious cunning. His tactics in war were in thorough keeping with his primitive nature. He knew nothing of the white man's code of war, of his so-called humanity. He could not take prisoners for the simple reason that he had no prison to hold them and no food to sustain them. He killed the

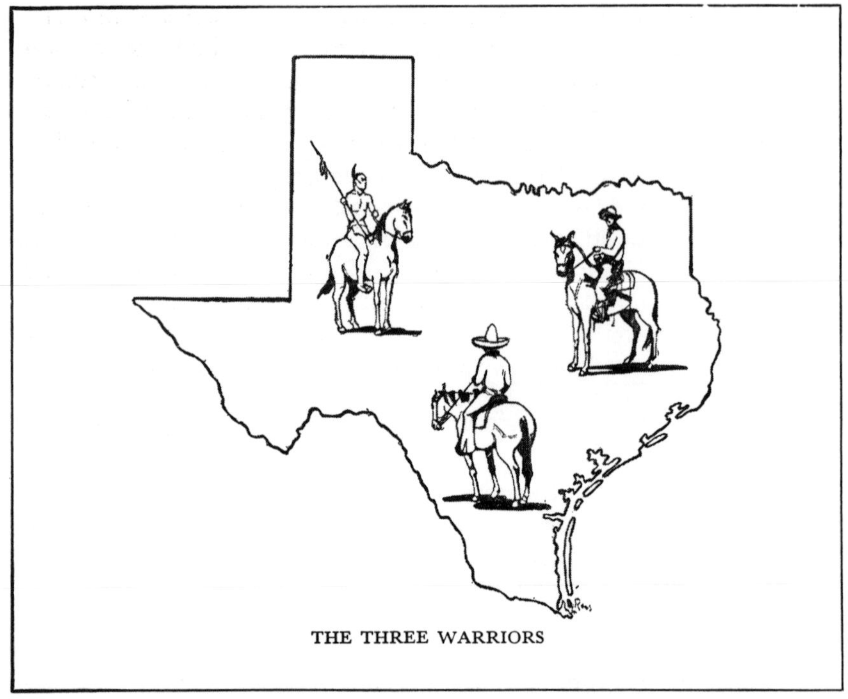

THE THREE WARRIORS

men, took the women, and adopted into the tribe the children who were too young to run away. The Indian's religion was to the white man mere superstition and his education would not merit the name in the white man's vocabulary. Yet both were well suited to the red man's purposes. His religion taught him that the earth was his mother and the sun his father, that the Giver of all good was the Great Mystery, that it was his duty to be courageous — after the Indian fashion — to be generous to his friends and faithful to his comrades in arms. Had the Indian and not the white man written history, he would have filled it with true stories of the hazardous feats of warriors in carrying their slain or wounded comrades off the field of battle. It was a part of the Indian's religion to save his comrades from the enemy and give him a decent burial with his scalp where nature placed it.

The Indian's education — by which is meant preparation for life — was not found in books, but in nature and in tradition which was for him nåture's lore. The movement of wild animals, the flight of birds, the bent twig, and the tracks by the water holes told the Indian stories that the white man has all but forgotten. All the red man's education was based on primary sources.

War was the end and aim of the Indian's life. His arms were therefore of major importance to him. They consisted originally of the bow and arrow, and though the tomahawk was found among the timber tribes, it played a much smaller part in the forays of the Plains folk. In the later period, the Indians used firearms to some extent, but they kept the bow and arrow until the end of the chapter.

The most singular factor in Indian warfare in Texas, and in all the Plains country, was the horse. The Spaniards brought horses with them to the New World, and in the sixteenth century some of these horses escaped from Coronado, DeSoto, and others, to run wild, to multiply, to spread northward, to supply the lowly pedestrian-nomads of the Plains with mounts. Steam, electricity, and gasoline have wrought no greater changes in our culture than did horses in the culture of the Plains Indians. When the cultural anthropologist tells us that the horse did not introduce new culture traits among the Plains Indians but rather emphasized and accentuated those already present, he gives us a glimpse of the meaning of the horse to these people, tells us that they were ready and waiting for the horse to come. The horse made the Plains Indians more nomadic, less inclined to agriculture, greater raiders, better hunters, and more dangerous warriors than they had ever been. The horse enlarged the tipi but did not change its material, shape, or structure, increased the quantity of wealth without affecting the variety, and enabled the chief to take more wives because he could provide more food and clothing for them.

The horse was not the first beast of burden, for the Indians were using the dog and *travois* when the horse arrived. The Indian merely made his dog harness larger, lengthened the poles of his *travois*, and, as an indication of appreciation of the boon which had been conferred upon him, named the horse the God-dog. It was the horse primarily that enabled the Plains Indians to extend their power southward, to beat back the Spaniards and Mexicans for more than a century, to fight the Texans over a thousand-mile frontier, and to contend, ofttimes successfully, with the American army from the Mexican border to the Canadian line, over a belt of country twenty-five hundred miles long and more than a thousand miles wide. These mounted warriors of the Plains, led by Quanah Parker and Lone Wolfe of the Comanches, Geronimo of the Apaches, Little Wolf of the Cheyennes, and Sitting Bull of the Sioux and many other lesser ones have come to typify *the* American Indian.

The Mexican *caballero*, whose complex character is more difficult for us to understand than is that of the Indian warrior, now passes before us. The Mexican nation arises from the heterogeneous mixture of races that compose it. The Indian blood — but not Plains Indian blood — predominates, but in it is a mixture of European, largely Latin. The result is a conglomerate with all gradations from pure Spanish to pure Indian. There are corresponding social gradations with grandees at the top and peons at the bottom. The language is Spanish, or Mexican, the religion Catholic, the temperament volatile and mercurial. Without disparagement it may be said that there is a cruel streak in the Mexican nature, or so the history of Texas would lead one to believe. This cruelty may be a heritage from the Spanish of the Inquisition; it may, and doubtless should, be attributed partly to the Indian blood. Among the common class, ignorance and superstition prevail, making the rabble susceptible to the evil influence of designing leaders. Whatever the reasons, the government of Mexico has ever been unstable, frequently overturned by civil war, and changed but seldom improved by revolution. This constant political ebullition has made any governmental policy, however good it might be, impossible of realization, and transitory.

The Mexican warrior, like the Indian, was a horseman, and in the northern part of the country mainly a *ranchero.* He loved gay attire, both for himself and horse; the braided trousers, the broad sombrero, the gay *serape*, the silver spurs, and the embossed and inlaid saddle exhibit a facet of his character.

He carried the lance for show, and was most skillful and devastating with the knife. As a warrior he was, on the whole, inferior to the Comanche and wholly unequal to the Texan. The whine of the leaden slugs stirred in him an irresistible impulse to travel with rather than against the music. He won more victories over the Texans by parley than by force of arms. For making promises — and for breaking them — he had no peer.

The Texan, who composed the third side of this cultural triangle, was a transplanted American, an outrunner of the American frontier. His qualities are too well known to warrant description. The mountains of Tennessee, the turbulent society of Missouri, the aristocracy of Virginia contributed their adventurous elements to his composition. These outriding frontiersmen were farmers primarily, woodsmen, riflemen, and fighters. They were Protestant in religion, democratic in politics and social life, individualists in all things, following only such leaders as could stay out in front. These early Texans knew nothing of Mexican character, had never seen the Plains, and had no knowledge of fighting Indians on horseback. They had used horses for transportation, but they were not habitual horsemen, and their weapons were unsuited to mounted warfare. They were intelligent, cool, calculating, and capable of sustained endurance and suffering. For weapons they carried the long rifle, which they used with unerring precision; the horse pistol and the knife constituted their side arms. Finding none of these weapons suitable for use on horseback, they later adopted and improved the revolver which became their own sweet weapon.

The Texas Rangers represented the Texans in their conflict with Plains warriors and Mexican *vaqueros* and *caballeros* and in the fighting that followed they learned much from their enemies. In order to win, or even to survive, they combined the fighting qualities of three races. In the words of an observer a Texas Ranger could ride like a Mexican, trail like an Indian, shoot like a Tennessean, and fight like a devil.

II

OUT OF THE REVOLUTION

The stars have gleamed with a pitying light
On the scene of many a hopeless fight,
On a prairie patch or a haunted wood
Where a little bunch of Rangers stood.

They fought grim odds and knew no fear,
They kept their honor high and clear,
And, facing arrows, guns, and knives,
Gave Texas all they had — their lives.

W. A. PHELSON

II. OUT OF THE REVOLUTION

1. FAINT BEGINNINGS IN AUSTIN'S COLONY

WHEN the Anglo-American society was first established in Texas, institutions were as yet unformed and needs but vaguely felt. These Americans of Texas had been on the frontier long enough to know that neither fine theories of government nor nicely adjusted institutions would endure unless they were suited to conditions. These men were 'practical' in a narrow sense to the uncompromising necessities of wilderness life, alert to every event, ready to adapt themselves to the immediate situation and to the solution of the immediate problem.

If the Indians gave trouble, the Texans banded together under a local leader and went forth to war. When the expedition was over, the organization broke up and the men returned to their homes and farms. These early experiences taught the Texans how to act in emergencies, gave them training, developed their fighting technique, and brought forth by degrees leaders who were qualified to meet the foe, Mexican or Indian. These early fighters were not Rangers in the sense that they bore that name or that they constituted a permanent organization or a profession. With this explanation, a few of these early episodes may be related to show why and how some of them became Rangers.

Stephen F. Austin was the first Texan to be captured by the Comanche Indians. Austin had brought a few settlers to Texas in 1821. In order to adjust a misunderstanding with the Mexican government about the location of the colonists, Austin found it necessary early in the following year to go to Mexico City. He left San Antonio in March, going by way of Laredo and Monterey. Near the Nueces River he and his two companions were captured by the Comanches who seized all their belongings. While these Indians were very hostile towards all Mexicans, they had as yet but little experience with the Americans, and were friendly towards them. This fact probably saved Austin's life.

The Comanches released him and his companions and restored all their property save four blankets, a bridle, and a Spanish grammar.[1]

While Austin was absent, the Indians caused the few settlers some trouble. The Karankawas of the coast were accustomed to preying on the shipping that came into Texas harbors. Because of these hostilities, the settlers became discouraged, and Baron de Bastrop, who had charge in Austin's absence, appealed to the Spanish governor, Trespalacios, who ordered the enlistment of a sergeant and fourteen men to be stationed near the mouth of the Colorado. These men entered the service in May, 1823; they were poorly equipped and unpaid, but evidently accomplished some good as Austin asked that they be continued in the service. These men were similar to the later Rangers in that they were irregular, wore no uniforms, and were neither militia nor regular. There is no record, however, that they were called Rangers, and we do not know whether they were composed of Mexicans or Americans.

The use of the word 'Ranger' occurs in 1823, when Austin employed on his own account and at his own expense ten men to serve as Rangers. We know nothing further of this organization.[2] A little later, however, when the Tonkawas persisted in stealing, and finally made a raid on the Colorado settlements, Austin raised thirty men and followed them. He compelled the chief to give up the horses and to whip the braves that stole them. The Texans insisted on helping with the whipping, and, according to the account, proved much more thorough than did the Indian chief in applying the lash. Austin ordered the chief to leave the settlements alone, and threatened to shoot instead of whip in the future.

Professor Barker estimated that nine-tenths of the fatal encounters with Indians during the first three years of the colony — that is, up to 1824 — took place with the numerically weak but bloodthirsty Karankawas. In June of 1824 these Indians came into the settlement on the Colorado, and were caught skinning a calf. The Texans rallied under Captain Robert Kuykendall, of the militia, and fought a skirmish. Austin sent the militia in pursuit and killed five Indians. The result of the expedition was a treaty in which the Karankawas agreed not to come east of the San Antonio River.[3]

With the Wacos and Tawakonis Austin also had trouble, and as these were prairie Indians and stronger than the Tonkawas and Karankawas, the problem with them was more serious after 1824. The tribes

[1] Eugene C. Barker, *The Life of Stephen F. Austin*, pp. 45–46.

[2] *Ibid.*, p. 102.

[3] *Ibid.*, pp. 105–106.

in 1824 had between two and three hundred warriors, but they lived nearly two hundred miles to the west of the settlements and did not often disturb them. However, these prairie Indians hated the Tonkawas, and in 1824 a band of nearly two hundred penetrated the settlements on a Tonkawa hunt. To avoid future trouble, Austin sent commissioners to make a treaty with these Indians. The village was found on the site of the present city of Waco, and a treaty of peace was made. Because of his tact and good judgment, Austin had little or no trouble with the wild tribes. He realized the importance of this friendship of the Comanches for Americans and undertook to preserve it until the colony was strong enough to stand upon its own feet. He did this, even though the Comanches were raiding and pillaging the Mexican towns of San Antonio and Goliad.

The word 'Ranger' appears in the record of Austin's colony when in 1826 the Tawakonis came into the settlements hunting Tonkawas and stealing horses. Captain James J. Ross, with thirty-one men of the militia, attacked sixteen Indians, killing eight and wounding five. Austin now proposed an aggressive campaign against them and their neighbors the Wacos. He proposed to use the friendly Cherokees, Shawnees, and Delawares as allies, but the Mexican commandant, Ahumada, forbade the alliance and ordered a suspension of the campaign until help could be obtained from the interior of Mexico. In the interval of waiting, Austin called a meeting of the representatives of the six militia districts to provide for defense. At this conference it was agreed to keep a permanent force of from 'twenty to thirty Rangers in service all the time.' Each landowner was to serve or furnish a substitute, one month, for every half league of land that he owned. Whether this force ever took the field we do not know.[4]

2. *RANGERS OF THE REVOLUTION*

Not until the outbreak of the Texas Revolution in 1835 do we find much evidence of the existence of an irregular corps of fighters called the Texas Rangers. While this is not the place to discuss the Texas Revolution, some mention must be made of its causes in order to show the situation of the Texans. Fundamentally, the Texans differed too much from the Mexicans to live long or amicably under Mexican rule. The differences were to be found in race, language, religion, and in governmental ideals. If there was little friction in the early years —

[4] Barker, *The Life of Stephen F. Austin*, pp. 165–166.

from 1821 to 1830 — it was owing more to the remoteness of Texans from Mexico and to the tact and skill of Stephen F. Austin than it was to the compatibility of the two races. From the first the Texans exhibited a disposition to do only what pleased them. They nominally became Catholics — as required by law — but remained Protestant. They came to a land where slavery was prohibited by the constitution, but they brought their slaves and kept them. When in 1828 the Mexican government sent an able officer, General Manuel Terán, to inspect the province, he noted with alarm the strength, independence, and the swaggering arrogance of the Americans. He declared that they had slight respect for Mexican law, and that each one carried his political constitution in his pocket, assumed that he was a sovereign in his own right. As a result of Terán's report, the Mexican congress passed the law of April 6, 1830, which undertook to shut off further immigration from the United States and to tighten a control which had been salutarily neglectful. The attempt to put into effect the provisions of this law precipitated a series of events which culminated in a struggle for supremacy between the two races and resulted finally in victory and independence for the Texans.

The Texans conducted their revolution after the pattern which their fathers had used sixty years earlier. They formed local committees of safety and correspondence, and by August, 1835, every municipality, precinct, or jurisdiction had such a committee. Through these committees a call was issued for a general convention, or consultation. An election was called for October 5 to elect delegates to a general consultation of October 15. Events were moving so rapidly that before the general consultation met, war was inevitable. Austin had returned from his long imprisonment in Mexico converted to the cause of war. He took charge of the local committee at his capital San Felipe, and assumed direction of the revolutionary movement. Feeling that this committee, which was merely the local committee of correspondence, lacked authority to act for the whole people, he urged the sending of delegates from each municipality to form a temporary body with power to act until the consultation met. This body was called the 'permanent council.' On October 11 it organized with a president and secretary, and assumed authority to direct the affairs of the Revolution. In the meantime hostilities had begun, and when the consultation met, it lacked a quorum, and adjourned until November 1. The permanent council then invited the members of the consultation to meet with it, and a number of them did so. This permanent council sat for twenty-one days, and kept a journal from October 11 to 26.

On October 17, 1835, Daniel Parker offered a resolution creating a corps of Texas Rangers. Silas M. Parker was authorized to employ and direct the activities of 'twenty-five Rangers whose business shall be to range and guard the frontiers between the Brazos and Trinity rivers.' Garrison Greenwood was to establish ten Rangers on the east side of the Trinity; D. B. Frayar with twenty-five Rangers was to patrol the country between the Brazos and Colorado. These men were designated as 'superintendents,' and not captains. It seems that Isaac W. Burton was also a captain, though perhaps by a later appointment.

The committee of five, appointed to consider the resolution creating the Texas Rangers, recommended that the superintendents of the Rangers operating between the Colorado and Brazos and between the Brazos and Trinity should rendezvous at the Waco village on the Brazos. The company operating east of the Trinity should have its headquarters at Houston.[5]

From this date until the end of the Revolution, it is possible to trace through the journals and minutes of the revolutionary bodies the existence of the Texas Rangers whose business seems to have been mainly to guard against the incursions of the Indians on the west.

When the consultation met on November 1, it received a report from the permanent council, the temporary body already described, of what had been done. The permanent council reported among other things the authorization of the volunteer Rangers to protect the frontier.[6] On November 6 a resolution was offered providing that the 'route of the Rangers employed, or may be employed, to protect our frontier, be extended from the Colorado River to the Guadalupe.' A committee made a favorable report on November 9, and commissioned G. W. Davis to raise twenty men for this new service.[7]

Having affirmed and approved what had been done, the consultation turned to the future. It provided for a complete military establishment to consist of the regular army, militia, and a corps of one hundred and fifty Rangers. These last were to be divided into three detachments, and when called into the field were to form a battalion under the commander-in-chief.[8]

The consultation was succeeded by the general council which it had created. The ordinance providing for a corps of Texas Rangers was read for the third time on November 24, 1835, and passed. It provided for three companies of fifty-six men, each company officered

[5] Eugene C. Barker (Editor), 'Journal of the Permanent Council,' *The Quarterly of the Texas State Historical Association*, Vol. VII, pp. 249–262.

[6] Gammel, *Laws of Texas*, Vol. I, p. 513.

[7] *Ibid.*, pp. 526–527.

[8] *Ibid.*, pp. 543–544.

by a captain and a first and second lieutenant. The major in command was subject to the orders of the commander-in-chief. The privates were enlisted for one year and given $1.25 a day for 'pay, rations, clothing, and horse service.' The Rangers were to be always ready with a good horse, saddle, bridle, and blanket, and a hundred rounds of powder and ball. The officers were to receive the same pay as officers in the dragoons of the United States service, and in addition the pay of privates in the ranging corps.[9]

The officers of this ranging corps were elected on the night of November 28. The captains were Isaac W. Burton, William H. Arrington, and John J. Tumlinson. R. M. Williamson and James Kerr were nominated for the office of major. Williamson was elected.[10]

On December 17, a resolution was offered asking for a 'special ranging company of ten men,' to range on the headwaters of Cumming's and Rabb's creek. The request was refused. Silas M. Parker, still in the field, wrote to the council inquiring about the employment of a surgeon, but the committee was of the opinion that the Rangers would need no other than the regular army surgeons.

In these rather tedious details we find the rudiments of what later became the established tradition. The Rangers were an irregular body; they were mounted; they furnished their own horses and arms; they had no surgeon, no flag, none of the paraphernalia of the regular service. They were distinct from the regular army and also from the militia.

By January the Revolution was approaching its climax, and to make matters worse for the Texans, dissension had arisen within the revolutionary government. The provisional governor, Henry Smith, had fallen out with the council, and the quarrel culminated in the deposition of the governor by impeachment. James W. Robinson, provisional lieutenant governor, now became acting governor. On January 14, he delivered his first message to the general council, reviewing the situation of the Texans and offering suggestions for the solution of the problems. He stated that the defenseless situation of the country called for speedy relief. He set forth vividly the situation of the Texans: The Texans were confronted on one side by hordes of merciless savages, brandishing the tomahawk and scalping knife, recently red with human gore, while on the other side were 'the less merciful spear and ruthless sword of the descendants of Cortez, and his modern Goths and Vandals.' The acting governor recommended the raising of the detachments of

[9] For a copy of the ordinance, see Gammel, *Laws*, Vol. 1, pp. 924–925.

[10] 'Proceedings of the General Council,' November 28, 1835, Gammel, *Laws*, Vol. 1, pp. 600–601.

Rangers from the inhabitants of the frontier where they are designed to range.

There is no evidence to indicate that the Texas Rangers distinguished themselves during the Revolution. Events were a little too big for this small corps of men who had been sent out to the western frontier to watch for Indians while the regular army and the militia, almost every available man, went to meet the Mexicans. On March 2 the convention declared Texas free; on March 6 the Alamo fell under the blows of Santa Anna; and on April 21 Santa Anna himself was defeated and captured on the field of San Jacinto. The Texas Rangers had little or nothing to do with these dramatic events, though a number of men who later became important members of the Rangers participated in them. As a matter of fact, there is no evidence to indicate that the Indians caused any trouble during the Revolution. The Texans took every precaution to placate and pacify the Indians in order that they might have their hands free to fight the Mexicans. Commissioners were sent to treat with the Cherokees in East Texas. On January 17, the general council passed a resolution providing that five commissioners be appointed to make a treaty of amity and commerce with the Comanche Indians, and five hundred dollars was to be appropriated for the expense of making the treaty. Thus did the Texans extend the olive branch to the Cherokees on the one hand and to the Comanches on the other.

It was noted above that Isaac W. Burton was made a captain of Rangers by the general council in 1835. It seems that General Rusk ordered Burton with twenty men to scour the country along the Gulf coast and keep a lookout for a Mexican approach by water. Burton and his Rangers were concealed on the beach when on the early morning of June 3 they sighted a vessel in the bay of Copano. The men signaled the vessel to send a boat ashore. Five Mexicans came ashore and were promptly captured. Sixteen Rangers now entered the boat and succeeded in capturing the Mexican vessel, the *Watchman*, loaded with supplies for the Mexican army. The Rangers started with the *Watchman* to Velasco, but were detained by contrary winds. Meantime two other vessels, the *Comanche* and *Fanny Butler*, anchored off the bar. The Rangers compelled the captain of the *Watchman* to decoy the officers of the other two boats aboard, and in this way they got possession of all three ships with supplies worth twenty-five thousand dollars. The ships were taken into the port of Velasco and the supplies turned over to the Texas army. Because of this feat, Captain Burton's Rangers received the name of the 'horse marines.'[11]

[11] Yoakum, *History of Texas*, Vol. II, pp. 180–181.

III

THE RANGERS AND THE REPUBLIC

The white man and the red man cannot dwell in harmony together. Nature forbids it.

President M. B. LAMAR

So, the government provided for their protection as best it could with the means at its disposal, graciously permitting the citizens to protect themselves by organizing ... ranging companies.

NOAH SMITHWICK

The river and its banks now presented every evidence of a total defeat of our savage foe. The bodies of men, women, and children were to be seen on every hand wounded, dying, and dead.

Colonel JOHN H. MOORE

III. THE RANGERS AND THE REPUBLIC

1. HOUSTON AND LAMAR

THE Republic lasted from 1836 until Texas joined the Union in the latter part of 1845 or the early part of 1846. This was on the whole a turbulent period in which the policy towards the Indians and Mexicans, and therefore towards the Rangers, was in large measure determined by the military views of the president.

Sam Houston, the hero of San Jacinto and the first president of the new republic, was without doubt one of the most original characters in Texas, an enigma to his friends and a sore trial to his enemies for whom he had small compassion. Houston was friendly to Indians. He had reason to regard them, for he had partaken of their hospitality, had lived their life, and, it is said, had become like an Indian in the interval between his disappearance in Tennessee and his appearance in Texas. Houston favored a policy of strict economy which influenced him to reduce the Texas military establishment to a minimum. Mirabeau Buonaparte Lamar's administration intervened between Houston's first and second terms. The contrasting character and antagonistic policy of these two strong-willed men were reflected in the frontier affairs.

Houston, favoring a policy of economy and of friendship for the Indians, did not augment the military organization. In fact, we hear little of Rangers during his first administration. Early in December, 1836, we find that congress passed a law 'to protect the frontier.' This law provided that the president was required to raise a battalion of mounted riflemen, two hundred and eighty men, for the protection of the frontier. Each man was to furnish a serviceable horse, a good rifle, and a brace of pistols if they could be procured. The same law provided that the president should cause to be erected such blockhouses, forts, and trading houses as he deemed necessary to prevent Indian depredations. It authorized the president to make treaties with the Indians and to appoint agents to reside among them, and to distribute presents among them not to exceed in value twenty thousand dollars.[1] The question may arise as to whether 'mounted riflemen' were Rangers. The answer is found, apparently, in another law, passed five days later, specifying the pay of 'Mounted Riflemen, now and hereafter in the ranging service on the frontier.' It was retroactive and made provision for all officers and soldiers 'who have been actually engaged in the ranging service since July, 1835.'[2]

In June of the next year, 1837, congress passed a joint resolution authorizing President Houston to leave the capital for thirty days 'to organize and set on foot the corps of mounted gun men' authorized by congress for the protection of the northern frontier.

An act providing for the 'better protection of the northern frontier,' approved June 12, provided for a corps of six hundred 'mounted gun men,' rank and file. They were to be raised by voluntary enlistment for a period of six months. Each man was to furnish a substantial horse, well shod all round, extra horseshoe nails, a good gun, two hundred rounds of ammunition, and other provisions and equipment except beef. Each six men were to furnish themselves a pack-horse. The corps was to be divided into three divisions, and if practicable, each division was to have attached to it a company of friendly Indians — Shawnees, Cherokees, Delawares, or some others — to serve as spies. The Indian spies were supplied with provisions and given such pay as might be agreed upon between them and the president. They were to be 'paid in goods.' It is quite obvious that this corps was intended for the Indian service, but the men are not spoken of as Rangers.[3]

On May 15, 1838, Houston approved a bill providing for a 'Corps of Regular Cavalry' of two hundred and eighty men. The enlistment was to be from one to three years as the president might determine. The troops were to be used to protect the southwestern frontier from the approach of the Mexican forces.[4]

Lamar became president on December 10, 1838, and proceeded to reverse every policy that Houston had adopted. Where Houston pursued peace, Lamar, like his two namesakes (for his name was Mirabeau Buonaparte), favored war. Houston loved Indians, if he loved anything; Lamar hated them, but his hatred for Indians was probably secondary to his hatred for Houston.

[1] Gammel, *Laws of Texas*, Vol. 1, pp. 1113–1114. The law was approved by Houston on December 5, 1836.

[2] *Ibid.*, p. 1134. The law was approved December 10, 1836.

[3] *Ibid.*, pp. 1334–1335. The act was approved June 12, 1837. Evidently Houston signed the joint resolution authorizing him to absent himself from the capital to organize this corps before he signed the bill creating it.

[4] *Ibid.*, pp. 1480–1481. The law was approved May 15, 1838.

Lamar, in his message to congress, set forth his determination to handle the Indians with steel and lead. He stated that the proper policy to pursue towards them was one of absolute expulsion. 'Nothing short of this will bring us peace or safety.' The Indians could not be handled by treaty or by a policy of moderation and forbearance. The United States had pursued that policy in vain. 'The white man and the red man cannot dwell in harmony together. Nature forbids it.' The strongest of antipathies of color and modes of thinking separate them. 'Knowing these things, I experience no difficulty in deciding on the proper policy to be pursued towards them. It is to push a rigorous war against them; pursuing them to their hiding places without mitigation or compassion, until they shall be made to feel that flight from our borders without hope of return, is preferable to the scourges of war.'[5]

In preparation for this war, Lamar turned to the regular military establishments. He recognized that war was expensive, but he thought it was most commonly successful in proportion to judicious expenditures, and that it seldom succeeded under the guidance of 'those who would value gold above liberty and life above honor.'[6] Lamar's advocacy of the regular and militia arms implies that the irregular force which was coming to be called Texas Rangers would for a time be in abeyance or in eclipse.

An act approved December 21, 1838, provided for a regiment of eight hundred and forty men, for a term of three years, for the protection of the northern and western frontier. There were to be fifteen companies of fifty-six men officered by a captain, a first and a second lieutenant. The regiment was to be divided into eight detachments and stationed in regular army posts along the line of the frontier from Red River to the Rio Grande.

The full provisions of this law were never carried into effect. Colonel William G. Cooke made an expedition to the Red River, and established one post near the Cross Timbers, but his expedition exhausted the appropriation, which amounted to three hundred thousand dollars, and nothing further was done.[7] That this regiment was intended to form a part of the regular service is indicated by the long enlistment, the permanent location in forts, the fact that a part of the force was infantry, and the elaborate provision for a staff of officers.

On December 29, 1838, Lamar approved a law for the 'further protection of the Frontier against the Comanches and other Indians.'

[5] Harriet Smither (Editor), *Journals of the Fourth Congress of the Republic of Texas, 1839–1840*, Vol. I, pp. 14–15.

[6] *Ibid.*, p. 11.

[7] Gammel, *Laws of Texas*, Vol. II, pp. 15 ff.

This law provided for eight companies of mounted volunteers for six months. The regiment was to receive the same pay as the mounted riflemen who were called into the ranging service under the law of December 10, 1836. The regiment was to have a colonel, a lieutenant colonel, and a major. These men may be called Rangers.[8] In the following January a law was passed providing for one company of fifty-six Rangers to range on the frontier of Gonzales County.[9] Eight days later three similar companies were provided for Bastrop, Robertson, and Milam counties. The term of service was six months.[10] The next day, January 24, a law was approved appropriating a million dollars for the protection of the frontier. The president was authorized to discharge all men in the military service save the regiment for the protection of the northern and western frontier, and the ordnance staff.[11] This did not mean that the president was to discharge the Rangers, as the law provided that he could use the money for the defense of the country, and to carry into effect the act passed by the congress then in session. Two days later a law was signed providing for two companies of Rangers for the protection of the counties of San Patricio, Goliad, and Refugio.[12]

Two laws that may have some significance were passed and approved by David G. Burnet, during the absence of Lamar, in December, 1840. One provided for the transportation of ammunition to the post at San Antonio, and for the 'purchase of three Spy Horses' at that place. The second law authorized the president to appoint and commission three persons to raise fifteen men each to act as spies on the northern and western frontier.[13] It is probable that these companies were commanded by John T. Price, Henry W. Karnes, and John C. Hays. Prior to this, however, congress passed a law providing for three hundred volunteers for three months to make a campaign up the Brazos against the hostile Indians. The men were to be armed and mounted as usual, but the term Ranger does not appear in the records.

The above provisions bring us to the end of Lamar's term of office. Despite his liberal provisions for the regular military establishment, the ranging service continued. To be sure, it is often difficult to draw the line between Rangers and regular soldiers and militia. It is easy to see, however, that the Rangers were much more economical and they were probably more effective. Where a regular army, enlisted for from one to three years, required an expenditure of a million dollars,

[8] Gammel, *Laws of Texas*, Vol. II, pp. 29–30. [9] *Ibid.*, p. 44.

[10] *Ibid.*, p. 78. [11] *Ibid.*, pp. 84–85. [12] *Ibid.*, p. 93.

[13] *Ibid.*, pp. 474–476. The first act was approved December 24, and the second, December 26, 1840.

a corps of Rangers could be raised for three months or six at small expense. Thus it was that the financial situation of Texas made a regular military establishment, a large force, impossible, and in spite of the attitude of the president, made the Rangers necessary. There was a vitality in the poverty of Texas which served to institutionalize the irregular partisan Texas fighter.

Houston's policy during his second administration was a reversal of Lamar's and a return to one of peace. Houston appointed agents and sent them to the frontiers to 'talk' with the various tribes. Not only that, he disbanded the regular army, as he had practically done by furlough in his first term, and sold the navy, but he could not suspend entirely the corps of Indian fighters. He approved a law on January 29, 1842, providing for a company of mounted men to 'act as Rangers' on the southern frontier.[14] On July 23 he was authorized to accept the services of one company on the Trinity and Navasoto. The men were to equip themselves and prepare for a 'tour of not less than two months.' The same act provided for two companies to range on the southwestern frontier. Small appropriations were made for both forces.[15]

Houston's opposition to a large military force is indicated by a law of January 16, 1843, providing for the organization of the Texas militia with a full corps of officers. Houston vetoed this bill, and it was passed over his veto.[16] On the same day, however, he approved a bill for a company of mounted men to act as spies on the southwestern frontier until the militia bill could be put into effect.[17]

The law of January 23, 1844, brings us to the emergence of a leader in the force. This law authorized John C. Hays to raise a company of mounted gunmen to act as Rangers on the western and southwestern frontier, from the county of Bexar to the county of Refugio and westward. This was evidently the company that made such a reputation for John C. Hays, whose activities will be noted elsewhere.[18] On December 14, 1844, H. L. Kinney was authorized to raise a company for the protection of Corpus Christi.[19] In February of 1845 (during the administration of Anson Jones) a law was passed extending Hays's authority. He was to have charge of a long frontier extending from Refugio and Goliad counties to Robertson and Milam. Hays was to command at Bexar. Ten men under a lieutenant were to be stationed in Robertson and Milam; fifteen men under a lieutenant in Travis county; thirty men under Hays as captain in San Antonio; and fifteen men under a lieutenant in Refugio and Goliad. The officers were to

[14] Gammel, *Laws of Texas*, Vol. II, p. 746. [15] *Ibid.*, p. 816.
[16] *Ibid.*, p. 846 ff. [17] *Ibid.*, p. 865.
[18] *Ibid.*, pp. 943–944. [19] *Ibid.*, p. 1049.

be instructed 'to scour the frontiers of their respective counties, protect them from incursions, and when concentrated in emergencies, to be under the command of Captain Hays.' Provisions, horseshoes, and medicines were to be furnished by the government, not to exceed ten dollars for a man. The same law authorized Henry L. Kinney to raise, or continue, a company of forty men for the protection of Corpus Christi.[20] The last law pertaining to the Ranger service passed by congress appropriated $405.55, the sum Hays had spent for horseshoeing and the repair of arms during the year 1844.[21] Thus ends the legal history of the Ranger force during the Republic. Though the story is tedious, it shows that the Rangers were always needed.

2. *IN THE WAKE OF REVOLUTION*

For the activities of the Texas Rangers — if they might be so-called — during the Revolution there remain to us but few accounts. It has already been noted that on the night of November 28, 1835, the general council elected R. M. Williamson as major of three companies of Rangers and selected Isaac W. Burton, William H. Arrington, and John J. Tumlinson, or Tumblinson, as captains. Noah Smithwick served under Tumlinson and R. M. Williamson, and has left us some account of what these Rangers did. Texas had an army of five or six hundred men, and was preparing to invade Mexico. The Indians took advantage of the situation and began to raid the frontier and murder the citizens. 'So,' says Smithwick, 'the government provided for their protection as best it could with the means at its disposal, graciously permitting the citizens to protect themselves by organizing and equipping ranging companies.' Since Smithwick's account gives such an excellent idea of the nature of the Rangers' work in this early period, it is given in his own words, as follows:

'Captain Tumlinson was commissioned to raise a company on the Colorado, and early in January, 1836, he reported for duty with a company of sixty mounted men, myself included. We were assigned to duty on the head waters of Brushy Creek, some thirty miles northwest of the site of the present capital, that city not having been even projected then. The appointed rendezvous was Hornsby's station, ten miles below Austin on the Colorado, from which place we were

[20] Gammel, *Laws of Texas*, Vol. II, pp. 1124–1125. This is the last important law made by the Republic pertaining to the Rangers and frontier protection.

[21] *Ibid.*, p. 1147.

to proceed at once to our post, taking with us such materials as were necessary to aid us in the construction of a blockhouse. We were on hand at the appointed time and, just as we were preparing for our supper, a young white woman, an entire stranger, her clothes hanging in shreds about her torn and bleeding body, dragged herself into camp and sank exhausted on the ground. The feeling of rest and relief on finding herself among friends able and willing to help her, so overcame her overtaxed strength that it was some little time before she could give a coherent explanation of her situation. When she at length recovered, she told us that her name was Hibbons; that, in company with her husband, brother and two small children, she was journeying overland up to their home on the Guadalupe, when they were attacked by a band of Comanches; the two men were killed, the wagon plundered, and herself and children made prisoners; she being bound onto one of their mules and her little three-year-old boy on the other.

'The other child was a young babe, and the poor little creature, whose sufferings the mother could not allay, cried so continuously that at length one of the Indians snatched it from her and dashed its brains out against a tree.

'The scene of the attack being a lonely spot on a lonely road, the cunning redskins knew there was little risk of the outrage being discovered till they were beyond the reach of pursuit; so, when a cold norther met them at the crossing of the Colorado about where the city of Austin stands, they sought the shelter of a cedar brake and lay by to wait for it to subside. Confident that Mrs. Hibbons could not escape with her child, and trusting to her mother's love to prevent her leaving it, the Indians allowed her to lie unbound, not even putting out guards. It was bitterly cold, and, wrapping themselves in their buffalo robes, they were soon sound asleep. But there was no sleep for Mrs. Hibbons. She knew, as did her captors, that there was small hope of rescue from the discovery of her murdered relatives, and, realizing that the only hope lay in herself, she resolved to escape and to rescue her child. There was no time to lose, as another day's travel would take her so far beyond the reach of the settlements that it would be impossible for her to procure help before the savages reached their stronghold; so she waited until assured by their breathing that her captors were asleep, then, summoning all her courage, she carefully tucked the robe about her sleeping child and stole away, leaving him to the mercy of the brutal barbarians.

'She felt sure the river they had crossed was the Colorado, and knew there were settlements below; how far down she had no idea, but that seeming to offer the only means of escape, she made straight for the river, hiding her tracks in its icy waters, hurried away as fast as the darkness would permit.

'Once she thought she heard her child call, and her heart stood still with fear that the Indians would be awakened and miss her. She momentarily expected to hear a yell of alarm, and, not daring to leave the shelter of the bottom timber, she meandered the winding stream, sometimes wading in the shallow water along the edge, and again working her way through the brush and briers, tearing her clothing and lacerating her flesh, never pausing in her painful journey till late in the afternoon, when she came upon the first sign of civilization in some gentle cows feeding in the river bottom.

'Perceiving that they were milk cows, she felt that she must be near a white settlement, but she dared not attempt to call assistance lest the Indians be in pursuit; so she secreted herself near the cows, which she surmised would soon be going home, and waiting till they had finished their evening meal, followed them into the station, having spent nearly twenty-four hours in traveling a distance of only ten miles on open ground.

'Fortunate, beyond hope, in finding the Rangers there, she implored us to save her child, describing the mule he rode, the band of Indians, and the direction they were traveling.

'Hastily dispatching our supper, we were soon in the saddle, and with a trusty guide (Reuben Hornsby), traveled on till we judged that we must be near the trail, and fearful of crossing it in the darkness, we halted and waited for daylight. As soon as it was light enough, our scouts were out and soon found the trail, fresh and well defined as if the marauders were exercising neither haste nor caution in their retreat; having no doubt spent a good portion of the previous day in a fruitless search for their escaped prisoner. They did not seem to be at all alarmed as to the consequence of her escape, and it was about 10 o'clock in the morning when we came upon them, just preparing to break camp. Taken completely by surprise, they broke for shelter of a cedar brake, leaving everything except such weapons as they hastily snatched as they started. I was riding a fleet horse, which, becoming excited, carried me right in among the fleeing savages, one of whom jumped behind a tree and fired on me with a musket, fortunately missing his aim. Unable to control my horse, I jumped off him and gave chase to my assailant on foot, knowing his gun was empty. I fired on him and had the satisfaction of seeing him fall. My blood was up and, leaving him for dead, I ran on, loading my rifle as I ran, hoping to bring down another. A limb knocked my hat off and one of my comrades, catching a glimpse of me flying bareheaded through the brake on foot, mistook me for a Comanche

'I WAS RIDING A FLEET HORSE...'

and raised his gun to check my flight; but, another Ranger dashed the gun aside in time to save me. The brave whom I shot, lay flat on the ground and loaded his gun, which he discharged at Captain Tumlinson, narrowly missing him and killing his horse; when Conrad Rohrer ran up and, snatching the gun from the Indian's hand, dealt him a blow on the head with it, crushing his skull.

'The other Indians made good their escape into the cedar brake, where it was worse than useless to follow them; but, we got all their horses and other plunder, and, to crown our success, we achieved the main object of the expedition, which was the rescue of the little boy, though the heedlessness of one of our men came near robbing us of our prize in a shocking manner. The Indians, careful of the preservation of their little captive — they intended to make a good Comanche of him — had wrapped him up warmly in a buffalo robe and tied him on his mule preparatory to resuming their journey. When we rushed upon them they had no time to remove him, and the mule, being startled by our charge, started to run, when one of our men, not seeing that the rider was a child, gave chase and, putting his gun against the back of the boy, pulled the trigger. Fortunately the gun missed fire. He tried again with like result. The third time his finger was on the trigger when one of the other boys, perceiving with horror the tragedy about to be enacted, knocked the gun up, it firing clear, sending a ball whistling over the head of the rescued child. Providence seemed to have interposed to save him. The boys held an inquest on the dead Indian and, deciding that the gunshot would have proved fatal, awarded me the scalp. I modestly waived my claim in favor of Rohrer, but he, generous soul, declared that, according to all rules of the chase, the man who brought down the game was entitled to the pelt, and himself scalped the savage, tying the loathsome trophy to my saddle, where I permitted it to remain, thinking it might afford the poor woman whose family its owner had helped to murder, some satisfaction to see that gory evidence that one of the wretches had paid the penalty of his crime. That was the only Indian I ever knew that I shot down, and, after a long experience with them and their success at getting away wounded, I am not at all sure that that fellow would not have survived my shot, so I can't say positively that I ever did kill a man, not even an Indian.

'The scene of the rescue was on Walnut Creek, about ten miles northwest of Austin. Gathering up our booty, which was inconsiderable, we started on our return, and late in the afternoon rode into the station in triumph. There was a suspicious moisture in many an eye long since a stranger to tears, when the overjoyed mother clasped her only remaining treasure to her heart, and I could not help stealing a glance at Rohrer, and trying to imagine what his feelings would have been had not his gun refused to obey his murderous behests. The little one was too much dazed and bewildered by the many strange scenes through which it had passed so rapidly, to even know its mother....

'We went on up to our appointed station, where we built the old Tumlinson blockhouse, making it our headquarters till the invasion of Santa Anna necessitated our recall, after which it was burned by the Indians and never rebuilt. And, save this old dismantled hulk, there is not, to my knowledge, one of those old Tumlinson Rangers now living.'[22]

The Tumlinson Rangers were called into Bastrop early in March when Santa Anna was marching on San Antonio where he was to raze the garrison at the Alamo and make of it the shrine of Texas liberty. All military forces, including the Rangers, were ordered to concentrate at Gonzales, leaving the frontier unprotected. The run-

[22] Noah Smithwick, *The Evolution of a State*, pp. 118–123.

away scrape was on, and the Rangers were ordered to cover the retreat of those people fleeing from Bastrop. Major Williamson took command of the Rangers, relieving Captain Tumlinson and Lieutenant Jo Rodger, who went to look after their own families.

In order to guard the rear, Noah Smithwick was put in charge of eight men and sent to spy out the approach of the Mexicans along the San Antonio road. Before this squad arrived at its post a courier came flying with a note saying that the Alamo had fallen, the garrison had been put to the sword, Houston was in retreat, and the whole population fleeing towards the Sabine over which waved the Stars and Stripes. It was decided that all men should go back save two who were to serve as pickets to bring warning of danger. Most of the men had families and were anxious to return and carry them to safety. Smithwick said he had neither kith nor kin, was young, active, well armed, and well mounted. 'Well, boys,' he said, 'you hear the order. I've got to stay. Now who is going to stay with me?' No one responded, and finally, as the Ranger expressed it, 'up spoke brave Horatius' in the person of Jim Edmundson, a boy of sixteen: 'By gumie, Cap, I ain't afraid to stay with you anywhere.' So Jim Edmundson and Smithwick remained for two days on guard. Both had good horses, and Smithwick said he knew that with a fair start no Mexican plug could catch them. They took a position on a high point overlooking the road and the country and settled down for their vigil. Sharply they scanned the distance for enemies, either Indian or Mexican. They left their horses saddled, slipped the bridles, gave them corn, and ate the cold food they had, not daring to strike a fire. For two nights Smithwick kept watch 'with ear and eye,' not daring to trust a growing boy to keep awake, but neither Indians nor Mexicans appeared. The man and boy then set out for the settlements, but when they rode into Bastrop they found the town depopulated save for the company of twenty-two Rangers. After sinking all the boats the Rangers started down the east side of the stream, but were ordered to return and get as many cattle across the river as possible. The river was up and the cattle could not be crossed, but the Rangers remained around Bastrop until one morning they discovered a large band of Mexicans on the west bank. This was a signal for a general retreat.

The Rangers had become careless and had only one sentry on guard, Uncle Jimmie Curtice. Smithwick rushed to Major Williamson, saying, 'You ain't going to leave Uncle Jimmie on guard, are you, Major?' 'Good God! No,' replied the Major and he ordered Smithwick to go call in Uncle Jimmie. The old man was found sitting on a log with a bottle of whiskey beside him.

'Hello, Uncle Jimmie,' cried Smithwick, 'mount and ride for your life. The Mexicans are on the other side and our men all gone.'

'The hell they are! Light and take a drink,' said Uncle Jimmie.

'There's no time for drinking. Come — mount and let's be off. The Mexicans may swim the river and be after us any moment.'

'Let's drink to this confusion,' insisted the old Ranger, and the younger one, thinking it the quickest way to start him, took a drink. As they rode off after the retreating squad, Uncle Jimmie prided himself on the fact that they were the last to leave the field.

The route of the Rangers lay through a pine forest, and the country was so wet that the force could not leave the road for fear of bogging down. Major Williamson went ahead, leaving the command in charge of Lieutenant George M. Petty. At Cole's settlement, now Brenham, the Rangers found a note from Major Williamson informing them of the massacre of Fannin's men. The Rangers now had a band of Mexicans behind them, and they thought there was another between them and Houston's retreating army. 'With two of our men flat afoot and several others not much better off, the enemy close upon us in the rear and the Brazos river booming full in front, there was nothing for us but to try and keep out of the way.' When the scouts went out that night, they discovered a band of moving figures which they thought to be Mexicans. This report caused the Texans to go up the river to the crossing at Tinoxtitlan, where they fell in with Colonel Bain and Captain Bob Childress, who, with their Rangers, had been convoying the refugees from the country. Two of these Rangers were without horses, and the four dismounted men constructed a raft and started down the river, two of them getting drowned on the way. The main squad of Rangers arrived within hearing of the guns of San Jacinto, but, owing to the detour at Washington, were too late for the fight. Smithwick declared that it was his turn to swear, and even though he was proficient in English and knew some Spanish 'cuss words' to boot, he could not do justice to his feelings.

The Rangers had followed in the wake of the Runaway Scrape, and the sight that met their eyes was one they could never forget. 'The desolation of the country through which we passed beggars description. Houses were standing open, and beds unmade, the breakfast things still on the table, pans of milk moulding in the dairies. There were cribs full of corn, smoke houses full of bacon, yards full of chickens that ran after us for food, nests of eggs in every fence corner, young corn and garden truck rejoicing in the rain, cattle cropping the luxuriant grass, hogs, fat and lazy, wallowing in the mud, all abounded. Forlorn dogs roamed around the deserted homes, their doleful howls adding to the general sense of desolation. Hungry cats ran mewing to meet us, rubbing their sides against our legs in token of welcome.'

Then the Rangers rode onto the field of San Jacinto where the Mexicans lay dead in piles. Smithwick said the buzzards and coyotes gathered to the feast, eating the horses but refusing the Mexicans because of their peppery skins. Finally the human carcasses dried up and fell apart, and the cows chewed the bones and spoiled the milk until the people buried the Mexican remains in self-defense.

3. *AFTER SAN JACINTO*

After the battle of San Jacinto, Captain Tumlinson left the service and was succeeded by Captain Coleman, who was ordered to build a fort near Austin. Coleman's Fort, rude log huts surrounded by a stockade, was erected on Walnut Creek six miles below, and to the east of, Austin. There are few records to indicate the sort of services rendered by these men. A later writer declared that before they came the settlers complained that the Indians killed their children, but after they came they only complained that the Rangers killed their hogs.[23]

Captain Coleman did not remain long in command. He was not popular and was dismissed from the service when one of his subordinate officers tied a drunken Ranger to a tree where he choked to death.

Captain Andrews was appointed to the command, and while he was captain the Rangers had a brush with the Comanches near Austin. In the spring of 1837 the men were sitting around camp, smoking, spinning yarns, and playing the fiddle when their attention was attracted by the flare of a camp fire on the opposite side of the Colorado. In response to a call for volunteers, Lieutenant Nicholas Wren and fifteen of the best-mounted men crossed the river and spent the night in the brush. As they were approaching the camp about daylight, they came suddenly upon a *caballado* of horses and mules which set up a great commotion, but even the snorting horses and braying mules failed to arouse the Indians who had not taken the precaution to place a sentinel. Apparently they had been on a horse-stealing excursion, and, having ridden hard out of the settlements, considered themselves beyond danger. When the birds began to twitter as heralds of dawn, a sleepy tawny brave raised himself to a sitting posture and commenced to sing his matin lay, 'Ha ah ha, ha ah, ha.' Some of the Rangers who

[23] *Telegraph and Texas Register*, July 8, 1840.

had gone too close to the Indian camp for comfort now withdrew and the Indian, hearing the noise, sprang to his feet with every sense alert. Joe Weeks planted a ball in the Indian's back, probably about at the point where a white man's suspenders cross. The firing became general, the Indians stampeded to a ravine, and in the firing Joe Martin was killed. The Rangers captured all the Indians' horses and camp equipage, and returned to Fort Coleman with their dead Ranger. The Indians soon retaliated. The Rangers had again become careless and had not mounted a guard. Early in the morning, the Indians rushed upon the horse herd which was grazing on the creek near by. They came blowing whistles and yelling like demons, and drove off the horses so quickly that but one shot was fired by the Rangers. Fortunately some of the horses broke away from the herd, and the Indians did not tarry to get them. Felix McClusky, a wild Irishman, had his horse in camp and Smithwick secured his and the two started after the loose horses that had escaped the Indians and run towards Hornsby's settlement on the Colorado where lived Isaac Casner. Isaac was out early this morning, and when he heard horses running and saw the two bareheaded men in pursuit, he put spurs to his horse and dashed for home. The humor of the situation was too much for the Irishman who let out a blood-curdling yell which sped the two-hundred-pound Casner on his way.

'Be Jasus,' said Felix, 'look at him run!' The people at Hornsby's fort, hearing the noise, threw open the gate of the stockade just as Casner dashed in, yelling 'Injuns.' The horses passed by but were soon turned by the Rangers and driven into the fort. When Smithwick took the Irishman to task for yelling, that son of Erin declared, 'I was tryin' to stop him.' With the recovered horses the Rangers now followed the Indians towards the Plains, but after three days they came into the mustang country on the head of the San Gabriel where the trail was obliterated by pony tracks. In this raid the Indians recovered some of the same horses that the Rangers had taken from them in the daylight raid on their camp already described.

Early in the summer of 1837, two Comanche chiefs and six warriors came into Fort Coleman with a white flag, and requested that a commissioner be sent among them to make a treaty of peace and put an end to the constant war. Though the white people did not trust the Indians, they were desirous of peace and permitted the Indians to select a commissioner. Their choice fell on Smithwick who gave up the life of a Ranger for that of an emissary of peace. During his stay with the Comanches there was little trouble with them on the frontier.

Captain Andrews retired from the command of the Rangers, and was succeeded by Captain William Eastland. Andrews had been very successful in dealing with his men, allowing them the liberty that frontiersmen demanded. Eastland had different ideas, and attempted to exercise more rigid discipline. The result was that the men marched out, stacked their arms, told him to go to hell and they would go home. Eastland yielded gracefully, and held the respect of his men.

On October 13, 1837, Lieutenant A. B. Van Benthusen of the mounted gunmen and Captain Eastland left Fort Smith on Little River in pursuit of horses stolen from the Colorado. The company moved up the Colorado, and on November 1, Van Benthusen separated from Eastland, thus reducing his force to eighteen men. On November 3 the party met some Cherokees, with Keechi guides, on the Brazos. One of the Keechis was killed, but the Cherokees came up and asserted their friendship for the Texans and their enmity for the Comanches. The Texans continued in a northeast direction on the Indian trail through a country 'full of Muskit prairies, and very well watered.' On November 10 the gunmen fell in with a large body of Indians on the headwaters of the Trinity in latitude 33½° north.

The Texans took a position on a mound and waited the Indian attack. The story of the fight is related by Lieutenant Van Benthusen. 'I stood at the top of this mound until I saw about one hundred and fifty mount their horses and come towards us. I then ran down and stationed my men in a point of timber; the Indians immediately charged upon us, uttering the most savage yells. They soon surrounded our little party of eighteen men, and for about two hours a severe fire was kept up on both sides without ceasing, most of the time they were not farther than fifteen or twenty steps; they were led on by a chief who was most splendidly mounted; our men shot this forward chief down, when the savages ceased firing and fell back for some distance; I thought the battle was over; but I was mistaken, for in about fifteen minutes the Indians again advanced upon us, led by another chief. At this time I had lost but four men and six horses. Presently we discovered a smoke rising around us, the Indians had made a ring of fire completely around our position, the fire was advancing rapidly, our only alternative was to leave our remaining horses and charge the savages on foot. The charge lasted about ten minutes; six more brave men fell in routing the Indians.... We then commenced our retreat on foot.'

The retreat with the wounded men required seventeen days, ending at the Sabine on November 27, after an absence of fifty-eight days.[24]

In the winter of 1837 or 1838, Captain Henry W. Karnes, who was

[24] Lieutenant A. B. Van Benthusen, *Telegraph and Texas Register*, August 4, 1838.

stationed at San Antonio, sent for Captain Eastland to bring his Rangers in to join Karnes's men and be present at a treaty. Instead of coming for a treaty, the Comanches made a raid, killing a Mexican vaquero and stealing all the Rangers' horses. Smithwick says the company of Rangers at Fort Coleman was disbanded in 1838.[25]

4. CAPTAIN JOHN H. MOORE'S FIGHTS WITH THE COMANCHES

(February 15, 1839)

On January 25, 1839, three companies of volunteers organized in the upper settlements of the Colorado for an expedition against the Comanches. They were placed under the command of Colonel John H. Moore with William M. Eastland and Noah Smithwick as captains. There were sixty-three white men and sixteen Lipan and Tonkawa Indians under Castro, the Lipan chief. Other members of the party were the young Indian brave, Flacco, and Andrew Lockhart who had a daughter held as captive in the Comanche camp.

The party set out from LaGrange on February 26, and marched directly up the Colorado River. The Indian spies who had been sent ahead when the party reached the mouth of the Llano, returned on February 13 and reported that the Comanches were camped on Spring Creek in the valley of the San Saba. The next day the Rangers continued towards the Indian encampment. They cached their baggage and moved under cover of the timber until near sunset which found them within ten miles of the village. After nightfall the men stole silently on until within a mile of the Indians, where they dismounted preparatory to an attack at daybreak. Captain Eastland's company formed the right wing, the Bastrop boys under Smithwick the center, and the Lipans commanded by Castro the left. At the moment of discovery, the Rangers and their Indian allies charged into the village, 'the men throwing open the doors of the wigwams or pulling them down and slaughtering the enemy in their beds.' The former peaceful scene now became one of pandemonium. Women and children were screaming, dogs barking, men — red and white — yelling, and doubtless swearing, and guns cracking. Noah Smithwick said that just at this exciting juncture, and for some unexplained reason, Colonel Moore ordered a retreat. Moore said in his report that he did it because smoke had made it too dark to shoot, that his men in their excitement had emptied their guns and had to retire to re-

[25] The above account is taken from Noah Smithwick, *The Evolution of a State*.

load. Smithwick declared that Castro was so disgusted that he withdrew his men and set out for home. Juan, son of Castro, had been detailed to run off the Indians' horses and to continue with them on to the settlements. He succeeded in getting only a part of them, but the Indians slipped around and ran off half of the Texans' horses. The Rangers retired to the place where they had left their horses, and the Indians sent a Lipan woman with a flag of truce (said to be the one President Houston had given them the previous year), whose purpose seemed to be to arrange an exchange of prisoners, but whose real purpose was to spy out the damage done to the Rangers. Juan Sies lied glibly to the spies, saying that not a man was scratched. Joe Martin was mortally wounded and begged Smithwick to shoot him or to give him a gun with which to shoot himself. The wounded were placed on litters and the sorry cavalcade set out for the settlements. Since the seventy-nine men had lost forty-six horses, more than half of them had to go on foot, for Juan was far away with the horses he had taken from the Indians.[26]

In October of 1840 Colonel Moore made a better showing against the Indians. On Monday, October 5, he broke camp on Walnut Creek near Austin, marched up the Colorado through the mountains until he passed the headwaters of the San Gabriel, then bore to the northwest, crossed the Colorado and scoured the country to the San Saba. He traveled up the San Saba two days and crossed to the Concho. There were heavy rains and a norther, and one of the men, Garrett Harrell, was buried on the Concho on October 16. The expedition then turned back to the Colorado, striking it at a beautiful and fertile spot that offered many inducements for settlements. Here Moore found a trail and followed it up the Red Fork of the Colorado. On Friday, October 23, he found that the Indians had been cutting pecan trees to get the nuts, and the sign indicated that they were near. Colonel Moore placed his men in a sheltered position to protect them from the severe norther and sent two of his most expert Lipan spies on the best horses to find the Indians. The spies returned in the late afternoon with the information that the Comanches — sixty families and about one hundred and twenty-five warriors — were encamped in the bend of the Colorado. The Rangers tied their packhorses in a hollow to conceal them, and at break of day advanced on the Indian encampment. Captain Thomas J. Rabb took the right, Lieutenant Owen with fifteen mounted men the center, and Lieutenant

[26] Colonel Moore's report of this fight, made March 10, 1839, may be found in *Journals of the Fourth Congress of the Republic of Texas*, Vol. III, pp. 108–110; other accounts are in Smithwick, *The Evolution of a State*, Chapter XVI; John Henry Brown, *The Indian Wars and Pioneers of Texas*, pp. 74–75.

Nicholas M. Daw (or Dawson) the left. When within two hundred yards of the encampment, the horsemen under Owen passed to the left and the entire command charged upon the unsuspecting Indians. The Indians fled for the river, which formed a half-moon about their camp, while the Texans dismounted in the middle of the village and poured their rifle fire upon them. Many were slain before they were able to reach the river, in which they took refuge, and others were drowned. Those who crossed were followed by the mounted men and cut down on the prairie. 'The river and its banks now presented every evidence of a total defeat of our savage foe. The bodies of men, women and children were to be seen on every hand wounded, dying, and dead.... The pursuit ceased at the distance of four miles from the point of attack, and finding that the enemy was totally overthrown, I ordered my men to the encampment.'

Thirty-four prisoners were brought in, but seven of these escaped during a stampede of the horses on a dark night. It was estimated that forty-eight Indians were killed on the ground and eighty killed and drowned in the river. Two of the Texans and two horses were wounded.

By ten o'clock the little army had assembled at the Indian encampment. A fire was made in which all the Indian homes, a hundred saddles, and a large number of skins of various kinds were destroyed. Five hundred horses were captured and brought into the settlements.

Colonel Moore estimated that this battle took place three hundred miles from Austin, and according to the opinion of himself and his Indians, more than halfway to Santa Fe. He described the country between the Concho and the Colorado, where the distance is about sixty miles, as of unexampled fertility.[27]

5. *BIRD'S FIGHT ON LITTLE RIVER*

(May 26, 1839)

The Indian depredations of 1839 led to a petition for succor from people dwelling on the upper courses of the Brazos, Colorado, and Trinity, with the result that congress called for several companies of three months' Rangers to give protection to these settlements. Thirty-four men were recruited in Houston under command of Lieutenant W. G. Evans, and marched into Fort Milam two miles from the present

[27] Colonel John H. Moore to Branch T. Archer, Secretary of War, November 7, 1840, *Telegraph and Texas Register*, November 18, 1840.

town of Marlin on April 3, 1839. On April 21, a company of fifty-nine men was raised in Austin and Fort Bend counties under the command of Captain John Bird. This company reached Fort Milam on May 6. Captain Bird assumed command of the united force, and on May 20 set out with fifty men for another fort on Little River farther in the Indian country, where they arrived on Friday, May 24. On the morning of the twenty-sixth, while Bird and Brookshire were absent, Indians ran a herd of buffalo through the Ranger camp and discovered the Rangers. When Captain Bird reached camp, preparations were made for pursuit of the Indians which was begun at one o'clock with thirty-five men, leaving a camp guard of two. The Rangers soon came in sight of twenty-seven well-mounted Indians who were pursued for three miles with no success. Bird then ordered a retreat, and was pursued and soon surrounded by forty Indians, 'hurling their arrows upon us from every direction.' The Rangers took refuge in a ravine and the Indians retired to the top of a hill three hundred yards off, where they were joined by reinforcements of two hundred, making two hundred and forty Indians against thirty-five Rangers. The Indians drew up in line of battle, and, letting out a warwhoop which went from one end of the line to the other, they charged the barricaded white men furiously, but were beaten back with considerable loss. After dark they marched off, 'throwing up in the air a composition of something that had the appearance of lightning, which was supposed to be a signal for retreat,' uttering as they went their peculiar guttural howl with which the Indians bewail the dead. About nine o'clock the Rangers secreted their seven dead men, including Captain Bird, and marched down the ravine towards Fort Smith, carrying three wounded men with them. Captain Nathan Brookshire assumed command and the decimated squad reached Fort Smith at 2 A.M. Sunday night. On Monday the retreat was continued to Camp Nashville. This battle, often spoken of as 'Bird's Victory,' was Pyrrhic, and further served to set the Indians in commotion for more depredations on the frontier.[28]

6. THE MEXICAN PLOT DISCOVERED

Four events of the year 1839 and 1840 are tied together by cause and effect more clearly than are most of the episodical events of the

[28] Captain Nathan Brookshire's report in *Journals of the Fourth Congress of the Republic of Texas*, Vol. III, pp. 110–111; John Henry Brown, *Indian Wars*, pp. 70–73; *Telegraph and Texas Register*, June 5, 1839. The newspaper report gives no mention of Bird's death.

frontier. These are the killing of Manuel Flores, and the discovery of a Mexican plot to unite the savages in a war on the Texans; the fight with the Cherokees, and their expulsion from Texas; the Council House Fight in San Antonio in which a large number of Comanche Indians (mainly the chiefs and head men) were killed; the raid on Linnville by the Comanches in retaliation for the slaughter of the chiefs, and the defeat of the Comanches as they returned from the Linnville raid in the battle of Plum Creek, near the town of Lockhart. This series of warlike enterprises may be considered best as a sort of post-graduate course in Indian warfare from which the real leaders, such as Ben McCulloch and Jack Hays, emerged.

It was fortunate for the Texans that Mexico had too much trouble at home to send any considerable force to Texas for several years after the defeat of Santa Anna at San Jacinto. The Centralist party was still in power in Mexico, but it had to struggle for its precarious existence with the Federalist party, which was always ready to strike for what it called freedom. Mexico was also involved in foreign trouble, and in 1838 the French sent an ultimatum to Mexico, demanding a large indemnity in settlement of some claims which the distracted and bankrupt Mexican government had failed to pay. The Federalist party took advantage of the French disturbance to revolt, but the movement failed and the usual shooting of the generals in charge followed.

These turbulent conditions in Mexico freed Texas from attack by large Mexican forces. The Centralists, however, undertook to stir up the Indians and the Mexican residents of Texas to make a general war along the frontier until such time as the Mexicans would be prepared to make good their claims to the struggling young republic. There were many mysterious happenings on the Texas frontier, all more or less connected with the Mexican policy of fomenting trouble.

On May 18, 1839, Lieutenant James O. Rice and seventeen men of Captain M. Andrews's Company of Texas Rangers attacked a party of twenty or thirty Indians and Mexicans on the San Gabriel fork of Little River twenty-five miles from Austin, killing three men and capturing six hundred pounds of powder and lead, one hundred and fourteen horses and mules and camp equipage. Judged by its results this is probably one of the most important Indian fights that ever took place in Texas. One of the three men killed was Manuel Flores, a Mexican, who had on his person papers revealing the plot to unite all the Indians on the frontiers of Texas for a general war which was to be aided by a simultaneous attack by a large army from Mexico.

This idea of an alliance between Indians and Mexicans for a war on Texas was not new, nor was it out of keeping with the practices of warfare. As early as 1836 such a plan had been set on foot. It was known that between 1836 and 1838 the Cherokees had visited the Mexicans at Matamoros and negotiated and discussed with the officials the possibilities of a conquest of Texas. As a part of the plan, the Indians were to be given and guaranteed possession of their hunting grounds in Texas; a sort of Indian buffer state was to be set up between the Mexican nation and the Americans of the United States.

The plan of a united attack assumed more definite form and more ambitious proportion in 1837. Indians were to rendezvous north of the San Antonio road between San Antonio and Nacogdoches, as soon as the leaves put out. A Mexican force of five thousand men was to cross the Rio Grande and advance from the west to meet the Indians when they were assembled and ready. Texans were to be exterminated or expelled, and the Indians were to have the territory, to divide among the various bands that had participated in the war. Anthony Butler claims that he, having secured this information, made a special trip to Texas to lay it before General Houston in order that the Texans might make preparations to protect themselves. Whatever the reasons, this plan was not carried out in 1837, but seems to have been kept alive.

The papers found on the dead body of Manuel Flores revealed that at least the Indians' part in the destruction of the Texas frontier was to be carried forward in 1839. It seems that the plot was in the hands of Valentin Canalizo of Matamoros. In a letter of instruction to Flores he informed the Indians of their duties. They were to cease making excursions into the settlements, but were to hang on the border, and harass the Texans, destroy their trade, break up their commerce, burn their homes, and divide the spoils, according to Indian custom.

If large bodies of Texans did concentrate, then the Indians were to hang on their flank and rear, to hold them together, while other bands plundered distant settlements from which the men had been called by the cry of war. Flores was also instructed to communicate with Cardova, who had gathered a band of insurgents at Nacogdoches. In this plot the Cherokees of East Texas were fatally entangled. In a letter from Cardova to Flores, it was stated that the Cherokees and other tribes had promised to unite in the common undertaking.

The Indians were further implicated when some citizens living near Red River killed Don Pedro Julian Miracle on August 20, 1838. The don had a diary running from May 29 to August 11 which showed that he had been to Nacogdoches and in touch with the Cherokee chiefs and with Cardova. From Matamoros he made his way northward, hiding from all Texas parties and meeting with the Indians wherever he could. He bore instructions from Vicente Filisola, predecessor of Canalizo at Matamoros, to incite the Indians to war. There is ample evidence that he was attempting it and some evidence of a measure of success.[29]

[29] For documentary sources on this episode, see a report of the Secretary of State containing correspondence relative to the encroachment of the Indians of the United States upon the territory of Mexico in *Senate Executive Document* No. 14, Thirty-Second Congress, Second Session, Serial No. 660. An account may also be found in Brown, *Indian Wars*, pp. 62–66.

IV

FROM CHEROKEE TO COMANCHE

Commissioner: 'Where are the prisoners you promised to bring into this Council?'

Comanche Chief: 'We have brought in the only one we had; the others are with other tribes. How ... do you like the answer?'

'The Indians... approached... the town... riding very nearly at full speed, and in the shape of a half-moon.... The citizens... had to flee to the bay where most of them were saved by getting into a lighter.'

WILLIAM H. WATTS

'Many of the arms, and most of the saddles and baggage were left. We ate, drank and rested for a moment; I then had a bon-fire made of most of the Indian trumpery.'

Captain J. R. CUNNINGHAM

IV. FROM CHEROKEE TO COMANCHE

1. EXPULSION OF THE CHEROKEES

(July 15–25, 1839)

THOUGH the papers found on the dead Manuel Flores hastened the ruin of the Cherokees in Texas, there is a lack of evidence that the Cherokees did more than listen with Indian politeness to the warlike proposals of the Mexican agents. The Indians had been in Texas since about 1820, had remained at peace with the anxious Texans during the Revolution, were living an agricultural life, and had never depredated to any extent on the people. Bowles, the chief, was a sensible man, wise enough to know that peace was preferable to war with the Texans. The land of Bowles and his people was good land; it lay far inside the settled limits of the state — a red island in a white sea. But the presence of such people was intolerable to the Anglo-Americans whose consistent policy was to roll the Indians back.

The auspices of the destruction of the Cherokees were favorable. Lamar had declared a policy of war, and besides, the treaty of peace with the Cherokees had never been ratified by the congress, albeit made in good faith and at a time when the Texans were in great danger from all quarters and eager for peace with Indians on almost any terms. When the Flores papers were taken by Price's Rangers and sent by General Edward Burleson to Albert Sidney Johnston, secretary of war, indignation flamed high and it was determined at once to drive the Cherokees out. Nearly all the forces of the regular army were set moving towards their forest-girdled home, while a pacific gesture was made by sending commissioners to negotiate with them for complete removal from the state. The story of these negotiations with Bowles and the ensuing events is one of tragedy and pathos. Bowles received the commissioners — David G. Burnet, A. S. Johnston, Hugh McCloud, and Thomas J. Rusk — with great dignity and with a gravity that betokened the seriousness of the situation to him and his people. The commissioners were authorized to pay the Indians for their improvements, but not for the land which they were required to vacate. Bowles said that he could not accede to the request and gave reasons why he considered that he had, or should have, title to the land. He said further that *he* knew that war was futile for him, that the Indians would be destroyed, but that he could not convince his tribe, and would have to abide by their decision even though it meant his death and the destruction of his people. He asked the commissioners to postpone the crisis until the Indians could gather their crops, but this request was refused, and the various bodies of troops, under the command of Brigadier General Kelsey H. Douglas of the Texas Militia, began a concerted movement on the Indians. In his command were Edward Burleson, commander of the regular troops, who was first on the field, and two volunteer companies, which perhaps could be classed as Rangers, under Captains James Ownsby and Mark B. Lewis. The fighting began on July 15, 1839, and lasted for two days. At the end of that time the Indians had been routed and Bowles killed in a brutal manner. Pursuit of the Indians went on until July 25. The Texans not only drove out the Cherokees, but also Delawares, Shawnees, Caddos, Kickapoos, Boloxies, Creeks, Muscogees, and Seminoles. Douglas recommended that a force be sent east to destroy the villages and corn of all the Indians left in that section.[1] It is extremely doubtful if history will justify the measures adopted by the Texans against the Cherokee Indians, and it is quite evident that Chief Bowles is the hero of the whole episode, for he acted nobly throughout and died like a gentleman. To justify the Texans in any measure, we must bear in mind that they had war on the whole western frontier, that the papers of Flores had implicated the Cherokees, and that since their lands were coveted, their removal or destruction was inevitable.

The remnant fled to the Cherokee tribes in Arkansas and other parts of the United States. In August the papers reported that as the fugitives approached Red River they fell in with some hunters who gave them a farewell shot and killed four.[2]

In December, while Colonel Edward Burleson with a body of regulars and some Tonkawa scouts and a few volunteers was scouting the upper Brazos and Colorado in search of wild Indians, he came upon a trail of horses and cattle leading southward. He followed the trail and on Christ's natal day overtook the fugitives on the west bank of the Colorado about three miles below the mouth of the San Saba. As Burleson

[1] *Lamar Papers*, Vol. III, pp. 45-47. *Annual Report of the Secretary of War*, November, 1839, pp. 35-40.

[2] *Telegraph and Texas Register*, August 28, 1839.

approached the camp, the Indians sent a messenger to ask him for a parley. The Indians proved to be a remnant of the Cherokees who were trying to make their way to Mexico where they hoped to establish a permanent home. The party was led by The Egg, second to Colonel Bowles, and by John Bowles, son of the dead chief. According to the report, the Indians opened fire on the Texans because their messenger was detained, Burleson demanding the surrender of the Indians. The Indians were driven from the field, leaving seven dead, including The Egg and John Bowles. All the camp equipage, all the horses and cattle, one man, five women, and nineteen children fell into the hands of the Texans. Among the captives were the mother, wife, three children, and two sisters of John Bowles. The Texans lost one Tonkawa and a captain of the volunteers.

The expulsion of the Cherokees and other tribes from East Texas practically brought to an end the Indian troubles within the settled portion of the state. There were still Wacos, Tawakonis, and Wichitas in middle Texas, but all of these were not as formidable as the wild Comanches who dwelt farther out and whose courage and ferocity were unsurpassed by red or white anywhere. The Indian battle line henceforth is the western frontier.

2. *THE COUNCIL HOUSE FIGHT AND THE SLAUGHTER OF COMANCHE CHIEFS*

No sooner had the Indian problem in the east been solved than the situation became acute with the Comanches. On January 9, 1840, three Comanche chiefs rode into San Antonio where they sought a conference with the red-haired Texas Ranger, Henry W. Karnes. The Indians stated that eighteen days previously the tribe had held a council, and had agreed, among themselves, to ask the Texans for peace. Colonel Karnes told the chiefs that no treaty was possible unless the Comanches would bring in all white prisoners. The Indians replied that they had agreed in their council to do this very thing. The conference ended with the understanding that the Comanches would return in twenty days with the prisoners for the purpose of signing the treaty.

Colonel Karnes at once wrote a long letter to General Albert Sidney Johnston, secretary of war, in which he related what had happened, and added his own recommendations as to what should be done. Karnes said he had no faith in an Indian's promise, which had been broken too many times, that he did not keep the three Indian emissaries as hostages because their number was too inconsiderable to guarantee the future. He suggested that commissioners be sent to San Antonio with authority to treat with the chiefs when they returned, and that a strong body of troops be sent to give protection, and, if necessary, to hold the Indians who came to the council as hostages until all white captives were delivered. Karnes said that he had to go to New Orleans on business, and could not be present, but he urged that men be sent who would act with promptness and decision. It is not difficult to see that these recommendations were in full keeping with the vigorous policy adopted by Lamar, and they were accepted almost *in toto* by the government. Three companies of infantry were sent under Lieutenant Colonel William S. Fisher.

On March 19 three Indian runners appeared, announcing the arrival of the Comanches. The Indians, among whom were many chiefs, came to the place appointed, bringing a little girl with them. The captive was Matilda Lockhart, a very intelligent child, who told the Texans that she had seen several other prisoners whom the Indians planned to bring one at a time in hopes of getting a better price. Orders were immediately given for the soldiers to march to the council house and surround it.

The chiefs were then called together; among them was Muk-war-rah, the bald-headed medicine man of the tribe with which Smithwick had lived.

'Where are the prisoners you promised to bring into this talk?' asked the commissioner.

'We have brought in the only one we had; the others are with other tribes,' replied Muk-war-rah.

A pause ensued, and the Indian broke the silence with an impudent question: 'How do you like the answer?'

At this point a company of soldiers was ordered into the room and the talk was resumed. The Indians acknowledged that they had broken previous pledges, but insolently demanded that their new ones be accepted. Finally, when the soldiers were stationed, the chiefs were informed that they were prisoners, and would be held until the other captives were delivered. For a Comanche to surrender thus was unheard of. One made a dash for the back door, and being blocked by the sentinel, stabbed him. Others drew their knives and strung their bows, and the fight became general. It raged in the council house, in the yard front and rear. A few savages broke through the line and were pursued and slain by waiting horsemen. Thirty-five Indians, including practically all the head men, three women and two children, were killed, and twenty-seven were captured. One renegade Mexican escaped. Over a hundred horses and a large quantity of buffalo robes and peltries were taken. The Texan loss was seven killed, including citizens, and eight wounded. The Texans now sent a squaw, mounted on a good horse, back to the Plains to bear the saddest news that had ever come from the Texans, and to demand that the other prisoners be sent in. The Indian woman promised to return in four days, but nothing more was heard of her.[3] Unfortunately, the same thing cannot be said for the Comanches who from this time forward for nearly forty years observed no peace with the Texans. Six months later they took a terrible revenge in the raid on Linnville.

3. THE COMANCHE RAID ON LINNVILLE
(August 8, 1840)

The Comanche Indians, after the slaughter of their chiefs in San Antonio, withdrew far out on the Plains to bewail their dead and plan a revenge. Several months went by and the Texans were lulled into the belief that the Indians had been punished so severely that they would henceforth let the settlements alone. August came with its intense heat, and some time during that month a cavalcade of Comanches set out for the seacoast, but not to enjoy the aquatic sports or to seek relief from the tropical heat. Despite the fact that the Comanches were going on a raid, they carried, as was their custom, women and probably some children. The number in the party was estimated variously from a few hundred to one thousand.

This vast body moved south and east just west of the settlements and in an open country. They were first heard of on August 5 when a band of twenty-seven came upon Dr. Joel Ponton and Tucker Foley of the Lavaca settlement, now Hallettsville, en route from Columbus to Gonzales. The Indians chased the two men three miles, killed Foley and wounded Ponton who reached home and spread the alarm. Adam Zumwalt immediately started on the Indian trail with thirty-six men. At about the time this was happening the mail carrier, en route from Austin to Gonzales, crossed the trail going southward and reported the fact at Gonzales, saying that he crossed the trail near

[3] For the official account of the Council House Fight, see *Journals of the House of Representatives of the Republic of Texas*, Fifth Congress, First Session, Appendix, pp. 133 ff. The accounts by Smithwick, Brown, and others are based on these reports.

Plum Creek. Ben McCulloch, whose name will figure largely in later accounts, sprang to his saddle, gathered twenty-four men and hastened to the Big Hill neighborhood, which lies on a divide between the tributaries of the Guadalupe and those of the Lavaca. Here McCulloch and Zumwalt united and started south on the trail on August 6, and soon fell in with a company from DeWitt County, under the Indian fighter, John J. Tumlinson from Cuero and Victoria. Captain Tumlinson now assumed the command of the force of one hundred and twenty-five men, and took up the march to Victoria.

The Indians were already at Victoria. There they killed thirteen people, including Pinkney Caldwell, a German, seven negroes, and a Mexican. The next day, August 7, they bore off towards the coast, taking between fifteen hundred and two thousand head of horses. On the way they captured a Mrs. Crosby, said to be a granddaughter of Daniel Boone, and her infant child, and would have added a Frenchman to the list of nationals had he not climbed a tree and hid in the long moss that festoons the great oaks of that region.

The Indians struck Linnville, a small port, early on Saturday, August 8. A vivid description of their approach to and activities in Linnville was written by William H. Watts, whose brother was killed in the raid.

'The Indians made their appearance on the Victoria road on the morning of Saturday the 8th instant, about eight o'clock, and were discovered by some of the citizens while they were yet about two miles from the town; but not having heard, or not believing that a body of Indians would venture so low down the country, or could approach so near without some intelligence of the fact, we were careless and supposed they were Mexican traders with a large caravan, nor were we undeceived until they approached very near to the town, which they did riding nearly at full speed, and in the shape of a half-moon for the purpose of surrounding the place. The citizens then had no other alternative but to flee to the bay where most of them were saved by getting into a lighter....

'The Indians appeared to be perfectly contented, and remained in town till after dark, burning one house at a time. They destroyed nearly all the goods and all the houses; also, a large number of cattle and calves, which they drove into pens and burned, or cut to pieces with their knives and lances.

'The citizens remained in sight of the town all day witnessing the shocking scene of the destruction of their property without being able to make any resistance, having no guns or any means of defence. Some of the citizens returned next morning and buried the dead, the

'THE INDIANS APPROACHED THE TOWN RIDING NEARLY AT FULL SPEED'

remainder continued on to the Pass [Aransas Pass], where they were kindly treated....'[4]

In Linnville the Indians killed two negroes and three white men, including Major H. O. Watts, collector of customs, and brother of the writer of the letter from which the above extract was taken. They carried off as captives Mrs. Watts and a negro woman and her child. After looting the wholesale houses and stores, the Indians proceeded to 'adopt the white man's clothing' with grotesque effects. The warriors put on the coats, the chiefs the tall hats, and they plaited the bright ribbons and calicoes from the warehouses into their horses' manes and tails, making gay streamers as the riders dashed about in the stiff sea breezes of the coast.

Thus far they had killed and captured not less than twenty or twenty-five people, and they must have felt that the murder of the chiefs in San Antonio had been avenged. They withdrew from the town after nightfall of August 8, returning to their western haunts by the broad trail they had made coming down. They carried with them between two and three thousand horses and mules, many of them loaded with the plunder of Linnville. This greed for plunder probably spelled their doom, encumbering them too much.

[4] H. M. Watts to *Austin City Gazette.* Letter published in *Telegraph and Texas Register,* September 3, 1840.

4. THE VICTORY AT PLUM CREEK

(August 12, 1840)

By the time the Comanches left Linnville, or shortly after, the border was aflame and the Texans were rallying to the warwhoop of their own leaders. As already stated, Tumlinson, Zumwalt, and McCulloch were on the trail, and by the time the Indians started the northward journey, the white men were approaching Victoria. Another body was being organized some miles farther up the country between Gonzales and Lockhart. The important question for the Texans was whether the Indians would return by their downward trail, or go west and scatter into small bands to meet at some designated point far out on the Plains beyond the settlements. It is probable that their heavy booty and the great herd of horses, together with the absence of vigorous opposition, led them to attempt to return by the downward trail. This important fact was soon ascertained and spread by courier to all the clans of every river valley of the border.

The Tumlinson party met the returning Indians on August 9 on a prairie south and east of Victoria, where some desultory fighting took place in which one Texan was killed. The Texans had only one hundred and twenty-five men; there was some hesitancy among the leaders. McCulloch wanted to charge, but Tumlinson did not give the needed order and as a result of indecision the Indians slipped away, and this party of Texans, excepting four men, never saw them again.

In the meantime things were moving rapidly farther up the trail. Lafayette Ward left the Lavaca settlements on the night of August 7 with twenty-two men, riding hard for Gonzales, where Captain Matthew Caldwell joined him with thirty-seven men. The united party traveled hard, and on the morning of August 10 was at Seguin. Until this time the Indian fighters were of the opinion that the savages would return on the west side of the Guadalupe, but now a courier arrived 'on foaming steed' and informed them that the Indians were still following their old trail, and were being pursued by the party from below. Caldwell decided to meet the Indians at Plum Creek, and his party marched all day, camping that night at the San Antonio crossing of the San Marcos. The march was continued over a burned prairie through flying ashes that blinded and stifled men and horses, and camp was pitched on Plum Creek. Recruits continued to come in. Captain James Bird arrived from Gonzales with about thirty men. Ben McCulloch and three companions, angered at Tumlinson's failure to precipitate a fight near Victoria, had made a killing ride, warned the settlers, passed the Indians, and joined the forces that were to meet the marauders on Plum Creek. Early in the morning the pickets had dashed in before daylight and reported that General Felix Huston, of the militia, had arrived, and at the suggestion of Matthew Caldwell, Huston assumed supreme command. Caldwell was a far better man in an Indian fight, and most of the Texans were dissatisfied with the choice, but did not oppose it.

Before daybreak on the morning of August 12 the Texas sentinels reported the Indians about three miles off. As the command prepared to move, another courier arrived saying that Colonel Edward Burleson with eighty-seven men and thirteen Tonkawa runners were only three or four miles off, coming at a gallop despite the fact that the Tonks were on foot. While the Texans waited for these reinforcements the Indians appeared, moving diagonally across the prairie that stretches out to the west from Plum Creek, and, as yet, oblivious to their enemies concealed in the brush along Plum Creek.

When the Texans rode out to meet the cavalcade, the Indians at once formed for battle. Both Indians and Texans now began to feint by exhibitions of horsemanship. The Indians were particularly conspicuous, curveting about on horses adorned with the bright ribbons and calicoes of Linnville. While this exhibition was in progress, the herders were pushing the great *caballado* forward, and it became apparent to the experienced Indian fighters that they were seeking to delay the Texans until they could get their booty out of reach, as had happened at Victoria. Burleson, Ben McCulloch, Caldwell, and others were anxious for a charge. Finally a Comanche chief rode forth with an enormous headdress and put on an exhibition of his prowess, exposing himself to the aim of the long riflemen. Instantly he fell, and Caldwell exclaimed, 'Now, General, is your time to charge them! They are whipped.' The charge was ordered, the horse herd stampeded, and so did the Indians. It was estimated that between sixty and eighty Indians were killed and Huston reported that bodies were found concealed in thickets, sunk in the river, or on the prairie as high up as the San Antonio road. Of the four prisoners taken at Linnville, one, Mrs. Crosby, was killed and three were recovered. Both Mrs. Watts and the negro woman were wounded, but the negro boy was unhurt.[5]

[5] For official reports of General Felix Huston, see *Journals of the House of Representatives of the Republic of Texas*, Fifth Congress, First Session, Appendix, pp. 141 ff. See *Telegraph and Texas Register*, August 19, 26, and September 3, 1840. John Henry Brown, who was a participant, has given a careful and accurate account in *Indian Wars*, pp. 78–82. Z. M. Morrell, a Baptist preacher of the frontier, also participated and gave his account in *Fruits and Flowers*, pp. 124–131. Victor M. Rose tells of McCulloch's part in his *Life of Ben McCulloch*, pp. 55 ff. Practically every history dealing with this period gives some attention to this fight.

One who has followed the previous accounts of Indian fights, as related above, must surely see a new spirit exhibited by the Texans, both at San Antonio and at Plum Creek. There was at Plum Creek no bungling, though Felix Huston would have bungled had he not been advised by the best Indian fighters in Texas who were at his elbow, ready at a moment's notice to take matters into their own hands. Among these were Edward Burleson, who was ever ready to raise the warwhoop, Matthew Caldwell, familiarly and affectionately known as Old Paint, a young man who had not been much heard from in Texas, John Coffee Hays, and Ben McCulloch and his three companions, Alsey S. Miller, Archibald Gibson, and Barney Randall. These bloody engagements were developing some real leaders, men who could go into an Indian fight and not bungle.

The battle of Plum Creek was a severe blow to the Indians, and never again did they send a large body into or below the settlements, never again did they undertake to wipe out a town. Henceforth they came in small bodies, stealing horses, killing women and children, and fighting the larger bodies of citizens and soldiers only when they had to do so. This does not mean that their nature was changed, or their ferocity in any sense modified; it means that the character of the war was different.

The following episode is illustrative of less important fights with the Indians. On July 4, 1840, Captain J. R. Cunningham, in charge of nineteen volunteers, met a party of twenty Indians between the Frio River and the Leona. Captain Cunningham's report of this pursuit and battle gives such an excellent idea of trailing, that the account is given in his own words.

'We followed it [the trail] for about six miles, when we came to the Indian camp. The sign was still hot, and showed that they had made an acquisition of six to their numbers. I dispatched Antonio, the Tonkawa, ahead — we followed at a brisk pace. The trail crossed the Frio to the west bank in about five miles, and struck above the river, rather bearing towards the Leona, into the prairie.... We neglected to supply ourselves with water. The trail gradually led us from water, until it was too far to return. The suffering of the men and horses was immense for nine hours in the heat of the day; and what made it worse for us, we knew we had to fight before we could get water, as the Indians, in all probability, would encamp on the first they came to. Between five and six P.M., the Tonkawa brought us the welcome news of Indians and water, stating that they numbered about twenty.... Four men, with the Tonkawa, were detailed to stampede the *caballado*;

the others were dismounted and proceeded on foot. They were instructed strictly, in both languages, not to fire without the signal for a charge. All went well; the front files had advanced opposite the center of the camp, within twenty paces of the Indians, where I halted them, waiting for the rear files to close up. We were still undiscovered, as the Indians were busily engaged in saddling up their horses for the evening's march. I was rejoicing at the certainty of the game, when one of the rear files, becoming alarmed at the proximity of his dangerous enemy, either intentionally or through fright, discharged his piece — unfortunate! The Indians broke; I ordered charge! fire! The surprise... was complete; all shot upon the wing.... We kept up the charge for some six hundred yards through the thicket, with brisk fire and yell.... Towards the close of the action, but three Indians were left to cover the retreat. This they did nobly, under the fire of ten or twelve as good shots as ever cocked a rifle. One of the three had his thigh broken.... He fell upon his horse's neck, and all put out for a more agreeable place. The men were too much fatigued and too thirsty to pursue horsemen farther on foot; I ordered their return to water and the Indian camp. Abundance of meat — buffalo, horse, cow and venison — was found. Many of the arms, and most of the saddles and baggage were left. We ate, drank and rested for a moment; I then had a bon-fire made of most of the Indian trumpery.'

When the charge was ordered, Captain Cunningham missed some of his men. He later learned that a Welshman named Davis had quit the fight to pillage the Indian camp and had been rewarded by finding a quantity of double eagles which the Indians had taken from a Mexican wagon train. The Welshman's punishment was in keeping with the vigorous practices of the time. Captain Cunningham said: 'I had him properly punished. He was stripped of his shirt, his back and arms painted, his head covered with a red flannel cap, with flowers, and rode, with his face to the rear of a no-tailed mule through the public square and principal streets of town [San Antonio], the company marching, in silent procession, behind. The guilty scamp was then turned loose in the center of the square. He has left by the light of the moon.'[6]

[6] Report of Captain J. R. Cunningham, *Journals of the House of Representatives of the Republic of Texas*, Fifth Congress, First Session, Appendix, pp. 151–153.

V

THE CAPTAIN COMES: JOHN C. HAYS

The Indians ... fought under great disadvantage but continued to struggle to the last, keeping up their war songs until all were hushed in death.

JOHN C. HAYS

Me and Red Wing not afraid to go to hell together. Captain Jack heap brave; not afraid to go to hell by himself.

FLACCO OF THE LIPANS

You may depend on the gallant Hays and his companions; and I desire that you should obtain his services and co-operation.

President SAM HOUSTON

The Ranger and inventor met in the Store of Samuel Hall ... and became great friends. The veteran Indian and Mexican fighter told Colt that ... his pistols ... were far too light and flimsy for the work demanded of them upon the frontier ... (and that) it was all but impossible for a man on horseback, riding 'hell-for-leather' to load them.... About a month later ... a new model Colt, the Walker revolver, was put upon the market.

ROY C. MCHENRY

V. THE CAPTAIN COMES: JOHN C. HAYS

1. EARLY SERVICE IN TEXAS

THUS far there had developed no well-recognized and permanently established corps of Rangers. There were no captains, apart from the regular military establishment, who were looked to for protection, who were always ready to ride on the Indian trail. There were a number of men fitted to do this, chief among them perhaps being Matthew Caldwell and Edward Burleson, but both belonged to the army. When Houston became president, he practically abolished the regular military force in the name of economy. There was one point, however, that always needed some sort of military force, and that was San Antonio. Every Mexican force that entered Texas struck or hoped to strike that place, and it had to be guarded constantly. The man who was finally selected to perform this task was John Coffee Hays.

John C. Hays, known in Texas as Jack Hays, was born at Little Cedar Lick, Wilson County, Tennessee, on January 28, 1817. He was from the same section of the country as the McCullochs, Sam Houston, and Andrew Jackson, and was the same adaptable sort of person. It is said that Jackson purchased the Hermitage from Jack Hays's grandfather, John Hays, who served with Jackson in some of his Indian wars, and who built Fort Haysboro. Jack's father, Harmon Hays, also fought with Jackson and named his son for General John Coffee, one of Jackson's trusted officers.

Hays came to Texas in 1837 or in the early part of 1838 — then about twenty-one years of age — and took up his residence at San Antonio. Some accounts say that he joined the Texas Rangers and fought Indians and Mexicans under Deaf Smith and Henry W. Karnes. In February, 1840, a group of San Antonio citizens recommended him to President Lamar as one competent to survey the boundary of Travis County in which Austin, the capital, had just been located. 'He is a gentleman of purest character and of much energy and ability. He is by profession a surveyor, and has been employed as such in this

COLONEL JOHN COFFEE HAYS

county for the two last years and has shewn himself fully competent to any work in his line.' [1] The first record of military service was his participation in the Plum Creek fight, but there is nothing to indicate that he distinguished himself there. He must have shown much courage and ability, however, for in 1840 he became a captain of a company in San Antonio and below. Captain John T. Price, in charge of a spy company, or Rangers, was sent to the Nueces in January, 1841, to watch the movements of Canales, Vasquez, and Variel, who were operating in that region. Price wrote that he reached the Nueces on January 9, where 'I met with Capt. Hays, who had passed down that river from the mouth of the Frio.' [2] Evidently Hays received his appointment in 1840, under the administration of Lamar. He held it continuously until after the Mexican War, and under his leadership the best tradition of the Texas Rangers was established.

While the Texans were exterminating Cherokees and waging relentless war with Comanches, conditions were getting very bad on the Mexican border. Northern Mexico has always been the rallying point for revolutionists, for the party out of power. The constant rumors of invasion kept the southwestern border, and especially San Antonio, in constant apprehension. These were the conditions which sent John T. Price and John C. Hays to the Nueces early in 1841.

The first expedition that Hays made as captain was to Laredo. Here he acted with his characteristic boldness and judgment. He entered the town, captured some horses, intimidated the Mexican soldiers, and then withdrew to a camp on the outskirts. The next day Hays returned the horses and told the Mexicans that he had not taken them with a view of carrying them off, but merely to let the Mexicans know that the Texans would retaliate on them for any raids or robberies they committed.[3]

In the next expedition, made in April, 1841, Hays took more vigorous measures. A considerable trade had sprung up on the Mexican border between the Texans and Mexicans. The traders brought into San Antonio beans, sugar, flour, leather, shoes, and saddles, to exchange for calico, bleached and unbleached, tobacco, and American hardware. Early in 1841 two of these traders left San Antonio with a heavy cargo and were attacked by a band of freebooters under Agaton. Hays

[1] C. Van Ness to Lamar, February 15, 1840, *Lamar Papers*, Vol. v, pp. 409 f.

[2] John T. Price to Branch T. Archer, January 23, 1841, *Journals of the House of Representatives of the Republic of Texas*, Fifth Congress, First Session, Appendix, p. 444.

[3] President M. B. Lamar collected material preparatory to writing a history of Texas. Among the notes are sketches by various characters, including one by Hays. It is stated here that Hays served with Henry W. Karnes in 1839 in the spy service. It is also stated that Price's and Hays's spy companies were organized in the spring of 1840 because of rumors of Indian and Mexican invasions. *Lamar Papers*, Vol. IV, Part I, pp. 231 ff.

set out immediately with twelve Americans, including himself, and thirteen Mexicans under Captain Antonio Perez, a daring Indian fighter and citizen of San Antonio. On their way down, they stopped at Antonio Navarro's ranch to bury two Mexicans killed by the Comanches a day or two before. On the third day out, an express rider passed post-haste in the night carrying the news from San Antonio that the Texans were coming. The result was that the Rangers were met ten miles from Laredo on April 7 by Captain García with a party of about thirty-five men who had come out to capture the gringos. They rode up to the Texans sounding a bugle, made an attack, crying out to Hays and his men to surrender or they would be overwhelmed by superior forces. Some shots were exchanged, and the Mexicans withdrew, leaving one dead on the field. The six-shooter, which enabled men to fight on horseback, was not yet in use, and in the fight that followed, the Texans would dismount, charge the Mexicans, then mount and follow. Finally, the Mexicans dismounted and made a stand, the Texans charged, drove them from their position, and captured their horses. The Mexicans grounded their arms and called for quarter, with the exception of the captain and three wise men who remained on horseback. The Rangers found three dead and three wounded on the field, took twenty-five prisoners and twenty-eight horses with saddles and bridles. Captain García carried the news of his defeat to Laredo with the result that consternation prevailed and many of the residents 'jumped the river.' The *alcalde* came with a white flag to beg that the Texans spare the town and to accede to any demand that might be made. Hays told him that all he wanted was Agaton and protection for the traders to San Antonio. The Rangers, who had received no injuries, then set out for San Antonio with their prisoners.[4]

Hays was equally effective against Indians, as is illustrated by the story of an expedition he made in the summer after Indians who had been committing depredations and stealing horses around San Antonio. Gathering a force of thirty-five men, fifteen Americans and twenty Mexicans, Hays set out for the Indian country. The Indian trail led towards the mouth of Uvalde Canyon, and when within two miles of that place the Rangers came upon a party of ten Indians, which they had located by the flock of buzzards that always hung over an Indian camp. Hays and a Mexican crept up close and found the strength and situation of the Indians. The Rangers attacked and the

[4] The above account is based on two accounts found in Ford's Memoirs (MS.). One is Hays's report to Branch T. Archer, secretary of war, dated April 14, 1841, which Ford says was published in *The Austin Sentinel*, April 22, 1841; the other is by P. L. Buquor, said to have been published in *The Floresville Chronicle*.

Indians fled to a thicket. What happened in the thicket we have in Hays's own words: 'The Indians had but one gun, and the thicket being too dense to admit their using their arrows well, they fought under great disadvantage but continued to struggle to the last, keeping up their warsongs until all were hushed in death. Being surrounded by horsemen, ready to cut them down if they left the thicket, and unable to use their arrows with much effect in their situation their fate was inevitable — they saw it and met it like heroes. They were twelve Indians — ten were killed — and two taken prisoners; one of them being desperately wounded and the other a squaw.' [5]

Returning to San Antonio, Hays increased his force to fifty men and enlisted Flacco and ten Lipan warriors and again started in pursuit of the main tribe of Indians. This expedition resulted in what is known as the Battle of the Llano. Hays came upon the encampment just as the Indians were preparing to march, the approach of the Rangers having been reported to them. With twenty-five men Hays attacked about one hundred warriors, who had placed themselves between the Rangers and the women and pack-horses. In the running fight that ensued, the Indians had several killed, which they bore off the field. It was in this battle, the date of which is unknown, that Hays's horse ran away with him, carrying him entirely through the Indian lines. Flacco, who was a great favorite with the Texans, dogged Hays's heels, and now set out after him thinking he was making a charge. The result was that Ranger captain and Indian chief went flying through the Indians' lines and came out on the other side, rode around the flank and joined their comrades. Flacco remarked, after the excitement was over, that he would not be left behind by anyone, but that Capitan Jack, as the Indians called him, was 'bravo too much.' [6]

Following the battle of Plum Creek, the Indian troubles, though ever present, assumed minor importance in comparison with events on the Mexican front. Between June, 1841, and September, 1842, Texas sent two expeditions into Mexico and Mexico sent two into Texas.

The first, most ambitious, and ill-advised of these was the Santa Fe Expedition which left its rendezvous on Brushy Creek near Austin about June 20, 1841, bound for New Mexico. The Texans sanguinely hoped to take over Santa Fe by negotiation and open a trade from Texas similar to that flowing across the Plains to Missouri. There was

[5] Hays's notes in *Lamar Papers*, Vol. IV, Part I, pp. 233–234. A similar account is in the Caperton manuscript. Hays's official account of the fight, dated July 1, 1841, is in Ford's Memoirs, purported to be copied from *The Austin Sentinel*.

[6] *Lamar Papers*, Vol. IV, Part I, pp. 234–235; Caperton, Sketch of John C. Hays, Texas Ranger (MS.).

hardly a settlement between Austin and Santa Fe save wild Indians of the Comanche and Apache breed. Part of the country is a desert, and water was scarce over several hundred miles of it. Not a Texan in the party had ever been to Santa Fe and not one knew more about its location than that it lay across the Plains to the northwest. Thus poorly equipped and prepared, the Texans set out on what Andrew Jackson in a letter to Sam Houston later called 'The wild-goose campaign to Santa Fe.' After many trying adventures and much suffering, the Texas reached their destination, broken, dispirited, desperately hungry, and almost dying with thirst. The Mexicans received them with open arms — *à la Mexicano*, threw them in prison and sent them to the interior. Occasionally one was shot, but the survivors gradually made their way back to Texas.[7]

In retaliation Mexico sent General Rafael Vasquez to capture San Antonio in March, 1842. At the time Hays was in the neighborhood with about one hundred men, mostly from Gonzales. Vasquez remained in San Antonio only two days when he withdrew and marched back to the Rio Grande, followed by Hays, who had not sufficient strength to attack him.

In July, James Davis, commanding two hundred volunteers, including a company of gunmen under Captain Ewen Cameron, was attacked near Lipantilican by General Canales with a force of two hundred regulars and five hundred volunteers or *rancheros*. The Mexicans, after twenty minutes of fighting, withdrew leaving three dead on the field.[8]

The capture of San Antonio in March and the clash with Canales in July should have warned the Texans to expect further trouble and caused them to increase the military force, but the poverty of the Republic drove relentlessly in the direction of economy and military insufficiency. All the forces were disbanded save 'the few spies under Capt. John C. Hays at post San Antonio.' Hays was ordered to increase his force to one hundred and fifty men and to keep them constantly and actively employed as spies and Rangers between the San Antonio River and the Rio Grande. Again poverty ruled. Hays could not increase his force because the men were too poor to arm and equip themselves and the state was too poor to pay those already in the service.

In commenting on the situation the secretary of war said: 'Those

[7] For a full account, see George Wilkins Kendall, *Narrative of the Texan Santa Fe Expedition.* For a definitive study of the route of the Texan Santa Fe expedition see H. B. Carroll, 'The Route of the Santa Fe Expedition,' MS., University of Texas Archives.

[8] Adjutant General James Davis to G. W. Hockley, secretary of war, July 7, 1842, *Journals of the House of Representatives of the Republic of Texas*, Seventh Congress, Appendix, pp. 14–15.

who were willing to enlist, were for the most part utterly destitute of means to fit themselves for the field — the government was equally so — it could neither furnish the means to equip and mount a force, nor sustain them for any length of time in the field. The consequence was a second surprise of San Antonio.' [9]

Hays learned on September 10 that General Adrian Woll was approaching the city with a large force and would enter it on the next morning. Apparently Hays had but few men with him, but he called the citizens together, made the best arrangements he could for the protection of the town, and with five men set out to find Woll's army. He failed to find the enemy who had left the roads to approach the town through the hills, but when he returned to San Antonio about daylight on the eleventh he found it surrounded by a force estimated at thirteen hundred. He wrote from Seguin on September 12: 'I have examined the camp and numbers, I think, correctly. I staid around town all day of the 11th, and have left spies behind, and if I can I will try and watch their approach to this river. All information will be reported every opportunity.' [10]

Hays and other couriers spread the word that San Antonio had fallen, and that the district court in session there had been captured. This warcry raised the citizens *en masse*, and soon many detachments under various local leaders were concentrating on Bexar. Matthew Caldwell raised the warwhoop and brought eighty-five men; he arrived, as usual, among the first, and was elected to command the two hundred and twenty-five men who had assembled.

Woll advanced to the Salado with two hundred cavalry and six hundred infantry, and a general engagement was brought on. On Sunday, September 17, Caldwell wrote that they had fought all day until the enemy retreated, carrying off their dead. 'The enemy are all around me on every side; but I fear them not. I will hold my position until I hear from reinforcements. Come and help me — it is the most favorable opportunity I have ever seen. There are eleven hundred of the enemy. I can whip them on my own ground without any help, but I cannot take prisoners. Why don't you come? — Huzza! huzza for Texas.' In spite of this heroic note the Texans were not without their tragedy. Captain Nicholas Dawson came from LaGrange with fifty-three men and attempted to join Caldwell. He was cut off and surrounded by the Mexicans, who kept out of rifle range and turned the artillery on the Texans. Dawson raised the white flag, but it was

[9] 'Report of the Secretary of War and Marine,' November 12, 1842, *Journals of the House of Representatives of the Republic of Texas*, Seventh Congress, Appendix, pp. 30–31.

[10] Hays to the secretary of war, September 12, 1842, *Journals of the House of Representatives of the Republic of Texas*, Seventh Congress, Appendix, p. 16.

fired upon. Only fifteen of the men escaped, many of them being cut down after they had surrendered.[11] The Mexicans had sixty killed, including Cardova who had figured in the Cardova rebellion and in the plan for the Indian uprising.

Woll now began his retreat, followed by the Rangers and by Caldwell's force. By this time a company had been organized for Hays with Henry McCulloch as lieutenant; Ben McCulloch also had arrived and was attached to Hays's company. Hays was described at this time by one of his men as follows: 'Captain Jack Hays, our intrepid leader, five feet ten inches high, weighing one hundred and sixty pounds, his black eyes flashing decision of character, from beneath a full forehead, and crowned with beautiful jet black hair, was soon mounted on his dark bay war-horse and on the war-path.' [12] It is said that General Woll offered five hundred dollars for the head of this youth of twenty-five who hung on his flank and anticipated his movements, who constantly tantalized the Mexicans by drawing them out after him and then driving them back.

When the Mexicans began their retreat, the Texans followed on their heels and finally Hays attempted to take the cannon which was used to protect the Mexican rear. This attempt was described by a participant as follows:

'At length the shrill, clear voice of our captain sounded down the line — "Charge!" Away went the company up a gradual ascent in quick time. In a moment the cannon roared, but according to Mexican custom overshot us. The Texas yell followed the cannon's thunder, and so excited the Mexican infantry, placed in position to pour a fire down our lines, that they overshot us; and by the time the artillery hurled its cannister the second time, shot-guns and pistols were freely used by the Texans. Every man at the cannon was killed, as the company passed it.' [13]

When General Woll had withdrawn beyond the Rio Grande, many of the Texans returned home, but a number of them remained around San Antonio to launch the most disastrous expedition that ever went from Texas into Mexico — the so-called Mier Expedition.

The movement on Mexico was initiated and officially sanctioned by President Houston when on October 3, 1842, he wrote to Brigadier General A. Somervell instructing him to establish a rendezvous on the southwestern frontier and organize a force for an invasion of Mexico — provided he thought it could be made successfully. 'Our greatest reliance,' said Houston, 'will be upon light troops and the celerity of our

[11] Yoakum, *History of Texas*, Vol. II, pp. 364–365, *note*.

[12] Morrell, *Fruits and Flowers*, pp. 168–169. [13] *Ibid.*, pp. 176–177.

'THE TEXAN YELL SO EXCITED THE MEXICAN INFANTRY THAT THEY OVERSHOT US'

movements.' Houston, knowing the character of the Texans, warned Somervell to enlist no men who were not willing to cross the Rio Grande if ordered to do so. 'If you cross the Rio Grande you must suffer no surprise, but be always on the alert. Let your arms be inspected night and morning, and your scouts always on the lookout.'

In conclusion Houston commended Hays and his men: 'You may rely upon the gallant Hays and his companions; and I desire that you should obtain his services and co-operation, and assure him and all the brave and subordinate men in the field, that the hopes of the country and the confidence of the Executive point to them as objects of constant solicitude. Insubordination and a disregard of command, will bring ruin and disgrace upon our arms. God speed you.' [14]

The material out of which Somervell recruited his army could hardly have been worse. The sturdier and more reliable men had left, but a rabble of adventurers and self-willed individuals assembled in the hope of participating in any excitement but with little expectation of subordinating their impetuous desires to the general good. After much confusion and some dissension, seven hundred and fifty men left San Antonio about November 18 and arrived at Laredo on December 8. The following day a number of soldiers plundered the

[14] *Journals of the House of Representatives of the Republic of Texas*, Seventh Congress, Appendix, pp. 3 f.

town and when Somervell returned the plunder to the *alcalde* and arrested a number of stragglers, two hundred men withdrew, and returned home. The remaining force moved down the river, crossed it, and took Guerrero. Here it was decided to mount all the men and a requisition was made on the town for one hundred horses. Soon all semblance of discipline was gone and the men openly and boldly expressed their contempt for their commanding officer. General Somervell, unable to control the men, decided to abandon the enterprise and ordered the return to Gonzales on December 19. Five captains and a large number of other officers and many men refused to obey and decided to continue the expedition. Among these were Ewen Cameron, William N. Eastland, Samuel H. Walker and Big Foot Wallace, men whose later reputations as Rangers reached not only through Texas but through the United States as well. Major Hays and Ben McCulloch returned with Somervell. We will leave Hays and his men and follow the fortunes of the three hundred whose exploits, adventures, and tragedies are known under the name of the Mier Expedition.

The day after Somervell set out for the interior of Texas, the Three Hundred elected William S. Fisher as commander, and pushed down the Rio Grande, until they arrived opposite Mier, a desolate adobe town set in a desert south of the Rio Grande. The Texans attacked the town, but not before the Mexican troops arrived. The Texans made a desperate struggle, but in the confusion that ensued from the wounding of Fisher, they were led to surrender with the understanding that they were to be treated as prisoners of war and kept near the northern border. Instead they were now marched to Matamoros, and thence to Monterey. On February 2, 1843, they were started to Saltillo, where they found some of the Texans who had been captured at San Antonio in September. Here they were turned over to an officer named Barragan and driven a hundred miles west to Hacienda Salado. For some time they had been planning to escape, and now they put their plan into execution.

At sunrise, February 11, Captain Cameron, a powerful Scotchman, gave the word, and with the aid of Samuel Walker seized and disarmed the guard, captured the ammunition stores, drove the cavalry from the yard, and made the infantry surrender. Here five Texans were killed and several wounded. Holding their prisoners as hostages, the Texans stipulated that their wounded should be cared for as prisoners of war; they then liberated the Mexicans they had captured and set out on the desperate journey for the Rio Grande. It was a venture which had little prospect of success, for the region between

Saltillo and the Rio Grande is a desert waste and no man among them knew the road. For a time they kept to the main highways, and should have continued to do so, depending on their fighting ability to carry them through. They abandoned the road after they passed Saltillo, and were soon lost in a limitless desert, without food and without water. They were in a wild, rugged, and arid country, fugitives, hunted like wolves. They threw away their arms to lighten their load, ate snakes and grasshoppers, burrowed in the earth for moist dirt to wet tongues which had swollen so that they could not close their mouths. In their desperation for water, they drank their urine with effects too ghastly to be described. Finally the Mexicans located them, sent out the cavalry, and brought them in. Five died of starvation, four reached Texas, three were never heard of, and the remainder were recaptured, and returned to Salado in irons.

Santa Anna, who was in power, first decreed that all should be shot, but such a vigorous protest was launched by American and British ministers that the decree was modified. Every tenth man was to die. A pitcher was presented to them containing one hundred and fifty-nine white beans and seventeen black ones. The men drew one by one and learned their fate. Big Foot Wallace said he noticed that the black beans were poured in on top of the white ones, and when he reached his big hand (almost too big to get into the mouth of the pitcher) he 'dipped deep' and came up with a white bean. Captain Ewen Cameron drew a white bean, though he had led the expedition and the break for freedom. He had, however, incurred the enmity of Canales by fighting him at Lipantilican. Canales now insisted that Cameron be shot, and Santa Anna issued the order to have it done.

The Texans were confined in Mexico City and in Perote prison to the east on the Vera Cruz road. They were horribly mistreated, but all were liberated in one way or another before the Mexican War when Big Foot Wallace, Samuel Walker, and many others, returned to Mexico at the head of a victorious army. In justice it must be said that the scores, if not perfectly balanced, were made less unequal by them and their comrades in 1846 and 1847.[15]

In the early part of this volume it was stated that the Texans had to fight. They could not surrender to the Indians, especially to a Comanche or an Apache, and certainly they were learning by this time that they could not surrender to a Mexican. The important fact here is that a certain tradition was developing which was to mould the character and determine the fiber of a Texas Ranger.

[15] The most authoritative account of the Mier Expedition is that of Thomas J. Green, *Journal of the Texan Expedition Against Mier*. See also John C. Duval, *Big Foot Wallace*.

2. *LIFE OF THE EARLY TEXAS RANGERS*

Major Hays, acting upon orders from the secretary of war, returned from the Rio Grande and took up his duties at San Antonio. Never again did an armed Mexican force set foot in the town, and therefore we hear little of activities against the Mexicans until the outbreak of the Mexican War. In the intervening period, 1842–1845, Houston's pacific policy towards the Indians seemed to exert some influence. Though occasional raiding parties entered the settlements, there were no such affairs as Linnville or Plum Creek. This did not mean that Hays could relax his vigilance. He gathered about him a distinguished group of men, and scoured the frontier wherever danger or the signs of it appeared. These men were professional Rangers who had been tried, who through long experience and constant elimination by resignation, by discharge, by Indian arrow, and by Mexican spear had come down to a small group who combined a knowledge of Indian and Mexican character which made them formidable to any enemy. It is the purpose now to leave the chronological narrative, and devote a section to the life and services of the Texas Rangers of this first period.

When Stephen F. Austin stated that he needed Rangers to give protection from the Indians in 1823, he evidently used the term as a common noun, certainly in a sense which the term Texas Ranger does not convey today. The word was almost synonymous with rover, a free lance who ranged over a wide area and who acted without very much supervision — a use of the term which continued for many years. The contemporary literature reveals that these early Indian fighters — for such they were in the beginning — did not speak of themselves as Rangers. The laws that created these early forces designated them as 'mounted volunteers,' 'mounted gunmen,' 'spies,' and 'rangers.' Occasionally the law stated that these forces were 'to act as rangers' on a certain frontier, or were 'to range' over a certain area. It is true that much later, men who had served with Hays or even before him wrote of their experiences as Rangers. It was not until the Mexican War that contemporary writers recognized the existence of an institution specifically known as Texas Rangers.

The character of the Ranger is to be found in his function, his method, his dress, and equipment. An examination of the laws creating these early forces of Indian fighters, and of the contemporary accounts of their activities, reveals clearly that these mounted volunteers, gunmen, spies, or Rangers, had well-defined and highly specialized duties.

They were entirely distinct from the soldiers of the regular army, from the militia, and from the local police. The organization was simple, almost primitive, something like the band of Comanche braves who followed their chief, or the *posse comitatus* of the early Germans. The term of service was short, either three or six months. At first there was nothing like a *permanent force*, such as Hays had later at San Antonio. Another characteristic of these early organizations, and this applies to every force that has borne the name, was the absence of formal discipline. The simplicity of the organization and the small size of the force and the character of the work made military rule of the formal sort impossible. Furthermore, the very qualities necessary for a Texas Ranger made him impatient of discipline. The natural turbulence and independence of the frontiersman made obedience distasteful to him.

It follows that no man could lead or control these Indian and Mexican fighters simply because some political authority had given him an appointment to do so. The leaders had to *emerge* from the group, and all that the state could do was to confirm and legalize a fact. Hays was made a Ranger captain after he had proved his leadership. The same sort of ability made McCulloch and Sam Walker, and many others, even the droll and whimsical Big Foot Wallace, officers. It is not too much to say that a Ranger captain had to prove his leadership every day, in every battle, and in every campaign. The price of failure at any time was death to his prestige and supremacy. This demand for *real* leadership, for superiority of both physique and intelligence, became a tradition in the force and that tradition is as potent today as it was when Hays was captain.

To speak of courage among Texas Rangers is almost a superfluity. They all have it to a high degree, and the man who lacks it cannot long remain a private. A captain not only had courage, which may be a purely emotional thing, but he had what is better, a complete absence of fear. For him fear and courage are unknown; he is not conscious of either. This means that he is free, with every faculty about him, to act in complete accord with his intelligence.

The main requisite of the Ranger captain is intelligence. He is all mind, and his mind works, not only in emergencies, but ahead of them; he anticipates the contingency and prepares for it. As a part of this intelligence, he must have judgment, and it must be almost unerring. He must use it not only in handling the enemy, but in handling his own men. Many a man can succeed in a battle and fail completely in camp because he cannot judge the character of his men, does not know, almost by instinct, how to deal with them. It is this judgment that enabled the successful officer to associate with his men every day, sleep with them at night, suffer with them on campaigns, and yet retain their respect. The barrier separating the leader from the follower is one of quality and not of clothes, stripes, and chevrons. So far as the records show, no great Ranger captain has ever been loquacious. Hays has been described as having a sad, silent face, McCulloch was noted for his taciturnity, McNelly for his quietness, John B. Jones for his refined elegance, and John H. Rogers for his meditative religious nature bordering on mysticism.

A Ranger captain, to be successful, must combine boldness with judgment. Once he has decided to strike, having always only a small group, he must strike with such force as to devastate or completely demoralize his enemy. It is not his size but his speed that gives him momentum.

Finally, a leader of Rangers, if we are to draw conclusions from cases, must have youth. Hays was a captain at twenty-three, a major at twenty-five, a colonel at thirty-one, and his services in the force ended at or before he was thirty-four. McCulloch was the same age as Hays; Sam Walker was thirty-two at the time of the Mier Expedition and was killed at thirty-five; McNelly was dead at thirty-three. The roll of the force would probably show that every important man from Jack Hays to Frank Hamer entered the service and made his name while young. One reason for this, perhaps, is that a leader of such men must have strength and endurance. He does not direct his men, but he *leads* them.

The story of the Rangers thus far shows that all of them were mounted. Horses were of the utmost importance to them, and when a man presented himself for enlistment, the captain not only examined him but his horse as well. It is said that Hays would not accept a man who did not have a horse worth a hundred dollars. Since the men were at war constantly with mounted Indians and mounted Mexicans, their horses had to be the best. Furthermore, the vast distances of Texas could not be covered rapidly or at all except on horseback. There is a saying among the Rangers, or was until the coming of the automobile, that a Ranger was no better than his horse. A Ranger wanted to be first in advance; he had no desire to be last in retreat. The Indians realized the importance of horses, and in practically every collision each side tried to stampede the *caballado* of the other. Many an expedition had to be abandoned because the horses were broken down and no others could be had. Up to the time of Hays it was not unusual for the Indians to set the Rangers afoot.

Since the warfare of the Texas border had to be conducted or horseback, it follows that the Rangers needed weapons suited to such warfare. Such weapons the Texans did not have until the time of Jack Hays. They were first equipped with the long rifle, the shotgun, and the single-barreled pistol which the Americans brought with them from the United States. These weapons were all developed for use on the ground and in the forests. The Americans, having never been in contact with mounted Indians, having never faced a mounted foe, had no weapons suited to horseback fighting. If the reader will review the early battles described thus far in this volume, he will see that there is no instance where the Texas Rangers fought either Mexicans or Indians on horseback. They would dismount, leave a guard with the horses, and attack, or receive the attack, on foot. The Mexicans followed somewhat the same procedure, though they used lances to some effect on horseback. Not so with the Indians. They could ride and discharge their arrows with remarkable effect and with great rapidity. Their favorite game was to draw the fire of the Texans, and when the guns were empty they would charge the dismounted men before they could reload. The Texans met this situation by firing in platoons so that some of the men would have ready weapons at all times. The thing that saved the Texans from the Indians in these early days was that an Indian was extremely skittish of danger. He did not fancy an open charge where somebody was sure to be killed. It was not until the invention of the Colt revolver and its adoption by Hays that the Rangers, or any Texans, changed their old woodland tactics. The story of this revolution in border warfare, which took place in Hays's company, will be related in another place.

In the early days, when the Rangers made an expedition after the enemy, they were likely to carry any sort of equipment that struck their fancy, or that they possessed. After the force became somewhat perfected under Hays's leadership, the equipment, while not standardized, was more uniform, but in general it may be said that it consisted of the barest necessities. Caperton has described the equipment of the early day as follows:

'Each man was armed with a rifle, a pistol, and a knife, and with a Mexican blanket tied behind his saddle, and a small wallet in which he carried his salt and his ammunition, and perhaps a little *panoln* [*sic*], or parched corn, spiced and sweetened, a great allayer of thirst, and tobacco, [with these] he was equipped for months; and the little body of men, unencumbered by baggage wagons or pack trains, moved as lightly over the prairie as the Indians did, and lived as they did, without tents, with a saddle for a pillow at night, blankets over them, and their feet to the fire. Depending wholly upon wild game for food, they of course sometimes found a scarcity of it, and suffered the privations which are known to all hunters. Sometimes there was a necessity of killing a horse for food, when all else failed. The men were splendid riders, and used the Mexican saddle, improved somewhat by the Americans, and carried the Mexican *riata*, made of rawhide, and the lariat, used to rope horses with.' [16]

The Ranger's campaign method and technique have been described by one of the men as follows:

'He would put a layer of grass, or small brush, beneath his pallet, to avoid being chilled by the cold ground, and to prevent his blankets from becoming saturated in case of rain. His gum coat was placed over his saddle and rigging; his gun was by his side; his coat, boots and pistols were used as a pillow; his rations were fastened to his saddle; his head was to the north, and his feet to the fire, if he dared to have one. Generally he slept with most of his clothes on — ready to spring up and fight at a moment's notice. The least noise — of an unusual nature — would wake him, and in an instant he would be in fighting trim. In the warfare of those days it was victory or death. The Ranger would give quarter, but he never asked it.... It was a rule of the Rangers to camp on the south side of a thicket — in summer he had the advantage of the south breeze, and in winter it afforded protection against the "northers." Running streams were passed at once, to avoid the possibility of a sudden rise and consequent delay. When he reached a swollen stream he improvised a ferry in various ways; one was in the construction of a raft; another by tying stake-ropes together, stretching [it] from bank to bank, putting a stirrup on the line, attaching ropes thereto on either side. A "rig" was made to hold whatever had to be crossed, and the loaded rig was suspended from the stirrup and drawn over the stream. A third [way] was by making a kind of sack of rawhide, in which the baggage was deposited, and pulled across by means of a rope; a log or two to which it was lashed would keep it from sinking.

'Rangers swam by the side of their horses, and guided them. No kind of weather precluded them from crossing rivers. They did so during "northers," and while snow and sleet were falling. The one idea ruled — make a rapid, noiseless march — strike the foe while he was not on the alert — punish him — crush him! With many there was a vengeful spirit to urge them on. Mothers, sisters, fathers, brothers, had been inhumanly butchered and scalped. Loved relatives had been captured, enslaved and outraged, and the memory of the cruel past rose up before the mind's eye, and goaded them into action.

[16] John C. Caperton, Sketch of Colonel John C. Hays, Texas Ranger (MS.).

They fearlessly plunged into the thickest of the fight, and struck for vengeance. Braver men never pulled a trigger or wielded a blade.' [17]

On the frontier there were few roads, and these the Rangers often did not care to use in case they were spying. They traveled by course, by the stars, the sun, and the Texas streams. At night they rode by the north star, or by the procession of stars that rolled like a giant ferris wheel from east to west. Many of the early leaders had engaged in surveying, were good woodsmen who found it easy enough to travel by the course of the streams. The men knew that all the rivers tended southeast. They usually traveled on the divides between two river basins, and could tell in this way about where they were, and which direction they were going. The contemporary writers spoke of settlements as being 'on the Colorado,' or 'on the Brazos,' or 'on the Trinity.' These river valley settlements were almost like independent states, and there was a close feeling of unity between the people in each river valley. Farther west, the rivers rose to higher and more arid land, and the distinction between different valleys disappeared in the monotonous level of the broad plains.

The men did not spend all of their time in the Indian chase. Occasionally they would go into San Antonio to recruit, rest their horses, and enjoy a little amusement. At that time San Antonio was inhabited almost wholly by Mexicans, and the Americans there had to be always on their guard. The favorite amusements were chicken fights which were held, Mexican style, on Sunday. Everybody participated, even the *padres*. 'The priests, after celebrating mass would go out and heel a chicken; the best heeler they had was the *padre*.' The Rangers loved the *fandango* which was the great event, and it is said that the Rangers were constant attendants and that Hays himself might be seen whirling around with some fair *señorita*.

The Rangers always had good horses, and some of them had blooded race stock brought in from Kentucky or other states that love the royal animal and the sport of kings. Shortly before annexation a horse race was arranged in San Antonio near San Pedro Springs, in which Rangers, Mexicans, and Indians participated. This was long before the American cowboy was heard of, yet these Rangers, Mexican *caballeros*, and Comanche warriors performed about all the feats that are now seen in the standardized rodeos.[18]

[17] Victor M. Rose, *The Life and Services of General Ben McCulloch*, pp. 84 f. Rose attributes the quotation to John S. Ford. Ford probably published the tribute in some newspaper.

[18] For a description of this contest see John C. Duval, *Early Times in Texas*, Chapter v, and Josiah Wilbarger, *Indian Depredations in Texas*, pp. 290 ff.

3. *SOME GOOD MEN AND TRUE*

It is perhaps worth while at this point to introduce some of the young men who gathered around Hays and distinguished themselves in the service. Ben McCulloch was at one time lieutenant in Hays's company, though his services with the company were by no means continuous. He was born in Tennessee, a neighbor of David Crockett with whom he and his brother, Henry, planned to come to Texas. After Crockett's political defeat, that worthy would not wait for the McCulloch boys, so anxious was he to go 'where the bullets fly,' and he reached Texas in time to die in the Alamo. The McCullochs arrived a few days later, and Ben had command of artillery at San Jacinto. He made his home at Gonzales, and in time of trouble was always the first to call the clan together to follow either Indians or Mexicans. McCulloch was one of the leading spirits in the defeat of the Comanches at Plum Creek, and there performed a feat indicating his ability as Indian fighter and Ranger. He was also with Hays at San Antonio when it was taken by General Woll.

Ben McCulloch had every quality of a partisan Ranger. His special ability lay in the fact that he could go inside the enemy's lines, get information, and escape with his life. So much will be said of him in relating the history of the Rangers in the Mexican War as to make further discussion unnecessary.

Samuel H. Walker was from Maryland, where he was born about 1810. It is said that he participated in the Indian wars in Florida in 1836 while the Texas Revolution was in progress. He joined Hays's company at San Antonio and soon distinguished himself for courage and coolness. Samuel Walker's name is indissolubly linked with that of Colonel Samuel Colt and the six-shooter which became the Rangers' favorite weapon. In 1831, Samuel Colt, a lad of sixteen, while bound for Calcutta as a sailor, whittled out a model for a revolving pistol. Upon his return to the Western world he took out patents in the United States and in England. On the night of February 26, 1836, young Colt sat in the Indian Queen Hotel's cheapest room in Washington and examined his first American patent which bore the signatures of Andrew Jackson and Benjamin Butler. Back in New York Colt sold stock, took out a charter, and constructed his first factory at Paterson, New Jersey. In a short time after the lathes and drills began to turn, Colt placed before the directors his first manufactured gun, a six-shooter of .34 caliber with a four-and-one-half-inch octagon barrel and a concealed trigger which dropped into view when the gun was cocked. There was no trigger guard, and when the pistol was being loaded it had to be taken into three pieces. Other weapons were made ranging in size from .22 to .50 caliber.

All accounts agree that Colt found a poor market for his new weapons, including a revolving rifle. In some manner a few of the revolvers found their way to Texas and fell into the hands of Jack Hays and his Rangers at San Antonio. One account has it that they were brought to Texas by S. M. Swenson, a merchant who was a friend of Sam Houston. Another account states that 'two arms dealers from Texas happened along, snapped up almost the whole lot and took them back West' where they sold for as much as two hundred dollars apiece. All we know of a certainty is that the guns fell into the hands of the Texas Rangers who found them admirably adapted to the needs of a man who had to fight on horseback. Because of the rather extensive use of the weapons in the young republic, the first Colt was named the 'Texas.'

In the meantime Colt was making every effort to have his weapons accepted by the Federal Government, but without success. Colt could not know that his ultimate success would come from Texas. While he was meeting failure in the North, Samuel H. Walker and his comrades were sitting by the campfires or in the shade of mesquite and huisache bushes of Southwest Texas and discussing the faults and merits of the Texas Colt. Finally Samuel H. Walker was sent to New York to purchase arms for the new republic.

'The Ranger and the inventor met in the store of Samuel Hall, the leading gunsmith and arms dealer in the city at that time, and became great friends. The veteran Indian and Mexican fighter told Colt that, while his pistols were the best arms of the sort that had been produced, they were far too light and flimsy for the work demanded of them upon the frontier. Among other defects, it was all but impossible for a man on horseback, riding "hell-for-leather" to load them, for the barrel had to be taken off to allow the empty cylinder to be replaced with a full one and the rider had to hold on to all three parts, the loss of one of which rendered the arm useless.

'The Ranger captain went back to Paterson with Colt and spent several days at the factory. About a month later, when he had returned to Austin, a new model Colt, the Walker revolver, was put upon the market. It was a great improvement over any that had preceded it. The frame was much heavier and stronger. The grip was of a more convenient shape, coming more naturally to the hand to give a steady hold.' The springs were made simpler, the disappearing novelty trigger was replaced by a visible one and protected by a trigger guard, the cylinder was made longer to take a heavier charge, and the caliber was first .44 and later .47. The increased weight and perfect balance made the firearm an effective club with which to buffalo some recalcitrant person who hardly deserved shooting. 'The feature which must have appealed most to Captain Walker was a neat lever rammer, attached below the barrel, which accurately seated the bullets in the chamber without removing the cylinder.... Colt at once applied for a patent on the rammer, which was granted him on August 29, 1839.' [19]

This Walker Colt was perfectly adapted to the men who had helped design it. They now began to fight Comanches and Mexicans without dismounting. We cannot be sure where it was that they first tried out the new weapons, but some accounts state that the encounter occurred on the Pedernales, probably in what is now Kimball County.

But the recognition of the Colt revolver in Texas could not save the inventor. Colt went into bankruptcy in 1842, and though he was able to save his patents, he saved nothing else and for five years he lived in penury.

When the Mexican War began in 1846, Jack Hays was made colonel of a regiment of Texas Rangers. The heart of this force was the handful of men who had followed him for five years around San Antonio. These men doubtless had their tried Walker Colts, and it was but natural that all others of the command wanted to be armed as were the veterans.

Samuel H. Walker was sent to New York to look up Samuel Colt and give him an order for one thousand six-shooters, two for each Texas Ranger. Colt had no models and advertised in the New York paper for them without success. He designed another gun, now known as the 'Old Army Type,' and had the Whitney gin people manufacture the weapons according to specifications. These weapons reached the Texas Rangers soon after they landed at Vera Cruz, and their distribution was recorded by Rip Ford. The story of how the Rangers used them, and of the impression that the heavily armed Texans made on all observers will be told later in the narrative.[20]

One of the most original characters in Texas was W. A. A. Wallace. Everybody in Texas knew him as 'Big Foot' Wallace, and so he shall be called in this narrative. He was born in Rockbridge County,

[19] Roy C. McHenry, 'Hand-Gun History,' *The American Rifleman*, August 15, 1923; Webb, *The Great Plains*, pp. 167–179.

[20] For a more complete account of the influence of the revolver in American history, see Webb, *The Great Plains*.

Virginia, in 1817, came to Texas in 1837, and later joined Hays in San Antonio. His giant stature and childlike heart, his drollery and whimsicalness endeared him to the frontier people. His inexhaustible fund of anecdotes and a quaint style of narrative, unspoiled by courses in English composition, made him welcome by every fireside. He went on the Mier Expedition, and many stories are told of his strange antics. When the Texans took a building at Mier, they found a baby which the Mexicans in their haste had left behind. At some risk to himself — which he never hesitated to take when necessary — he raised the baby over a protecting wall, dropped it in the yard, and yelled to the Mexicans to come and get it. He drew a white bean at Salado by 'dipping deep,' and was sent to prison in Mexico City. While there the Mexicans put him and the other Texans to work on the streets, making them haul dirt in carts to which they were harnessed like horses. In spite of his size, Big Foot was not a good work horse. He often ran away, upsetting the cart, running over all in his path, and knocking corners off the adobe houses. Returning to Texas, he attached himself to Hays's company and was made a captain in his regiment in the Mexican War. Going back over the familiar ground where he had been imprisoned, starved, and mistreated, Big Foot, it is feared, took revenge by proxy. He always resided on the frontier where his strong arm ever shielded the settler. He, like Ben McCulloch, never married. When the stage line was opened to California, he drove the stage from Austin to El Paso, a distance of seven hundred miles through the Indian country. He had an eye for the dramatic, and made a romantic figure as he entered the little towns with his team at a high gallop. Though often attacked by the Indians, he managed to live until 1899 and to die a natural death. He is buried in the state cemetery at Austin, his grave marked by a small stone engraved with a just and classic epitaph.

Big Foot Wallace

Here Lies He Who Spent His
Manhood Defending The Homes
of
Texas

Brave Honest and Faithful

Born April 3, 1817
Died Jan. 7, 1899

VI

THE TEXAS RANGERS IN THE MEXICAN WAR

Here we constructed our tents — constructed, we say, because the government never furnished us, during our whole term of service, with a patch of canvas large enough to keep out a drop of rain, or shield us from a ray of the scorching sun.... The consequence was, that wherever we were encamped for any length of time, we were obliged to construct rude shelters out of poles, cane, rushes, or any other material which the vicinity afforded. And the Rangers' camp frequently looked more like a collection of huts in a Hottentot hamlet, or a group of rude wigwams in an Indian village, than the regular cantonment of volunteers in the service of the United States.

SAMUEL C. REID

Riding singly and rapidly, they [the Rangers] swept around the plain under the walls, each one in a wider and more perilous circle. Their proximity occasionally provoked the enemy's fire, but the Mexicans might as well have attempted to bring down skimming swallows as those racing daredevils.

GIDDINGS, *Sketches*

The departure of the Rangers would have caused more regret than was generally felt, had it not been for the lawless and vindictive spirit some of them had displayed in the week that elapsed between the capitulation of the city [of Monterey] and their discharge.... The commanding general took occasion to thank them for the efficient service they had rendered, and we saw them turn their faces toward the blood-bought State they represented, with many good wishes and the hope that all honest Mexicans were at a safe distance from their path.

GIDDINGS, *Sketches*

Hays's Rangers have come, their appearance never to be forgotten. Not any sort of uniforms, but well mounted and doubly well armed: each man has one or two Colt's revolvers besides ordinary pistols, a sword, and every man a rifle.... The Mexicans are terribly afraid of them.

General ETHAN ALLEN HITCHCOCK

VI. THE TEXAS RANGERS IN THE MEXICAN WAR

The entrance of Texas into the Union in 1845 was calculated to relieve the state of all responsibility for its frontiers. Required to bring no dowry of lands and chattels, Texas generously gave Uncle Sam two large and fierce frontiers, one occupied by a miscellaneous collection of Indians, and the other by several million irate Mexicans. For all these the United States accepted full responsibility. The rejoicing over annexation into the Union had hardly ceased before the roll and throb of fife and drum could be heard in the distance as the American army came by land and sea to meet a Mexican army on the new border. It was in full keeping with the turbulent past that Texas entered the Union to the accompaniment of war.

The drums of Zachary Taylor's army ceased to roll at the mouth of the Nueces in July, 1845; here the army remained and grew for nine months. South of the Nueces was disputed ground; Mexico claimed this river as the boundary of Texas; Texas and the United States claimed the Rio Grande.

While on Corpus Christi Bay, Taylor mustered several companies of Hays's Texas Rangers into the national service, leaving them in their respective locations to guard the frontier. He accepted them reluctantly, to keep the Texans' hearts in the game.[1] By April, Taylor had crossed the disputed region beyond the Nueces and taken a position on the Rio Grande opposite Matamoros. Here he found himself some twenty-five miles from his base of supplies at Point Isabel and surrounded by a chaparral thicket and Mexican enemies; here he felt the need of men familiar with the country and the character of the inhabitants; here he called for two companies of Texas mounted men to keep open his communication and relieve the regular cavalry of a service which they found oppressive and difficult.[2] When sixty of his dragoons were captured while on a scout on the river Taylor wrote to Washington that 'hostilities may now be considered as com-

[1] Taylor to Adjutant General, August 5 and September 1, 1845. *House Executive Document* No. 60, Thirtieth Congress, First Session, pp. 83; 106–107. Serial No. 520.

[2] Taylor to Adjutant General, April 15, 1846. *House Executive Document* No. 60, Thirtieth Congress, First Session, pp. 138–139. Serial No. 520.

CAPTAIN BEN McCULLOCH

menced,' he asked the governor of Texas for four regiments — two mounted and two foot.[3]

This was the call — to fight Mexico on equal terms — that the Texans had long waited for. Their response was expressed in the song —

[3] Taylor to Adjutant General, April 26, 1846. *House Executive Document* No. 60, Thirtieth Congress, First Session; Governor J. P. Henderson, April 26, 1846, *The Texas Democrat*, May 6, 1846.

IN THE MEXICAN WAR

Then mount and away! give the fleet steed the rein —
The Ranger's at home on the prairies again;
Spur! spur in the chase, dash on to the fight,
Cry vengeance for Texas! and God speed the right.

1. SAMUEL H. WALKER'S SCOUTS

The first Texas Ranger to perform noteworthy service for Taylor was Samuel H. Walker who was with Taylor in May, and was authorized to raise a company. He established his camp between Point Isabel and Taylor's main force. Having secured information that the Mexicans were crossing the river with the intention of severing the line and isolating Taylor, Walker set out on April 28 with seventy-five men to carry the news to Taylor. Twelve miles from Point Isabel he encountered fifteen hundred Mexican cavalry, and in the fight that followed his inexperienced men were dispersed and pursued almost to the Point. Walker was missing and reported killed, but he came in, asked for volunteers, and with six men carried the message to Taylor in spite of the many Mexicans along the road.[4]

As Taylor marched down the river the Mexicans crossed it behind him. The booming of guns told him that the garrison under Brown was being attacked; and Walker told him that a Mexican force was lying on the road to cut off relief. Taylor sent Walker with six men to communicate with Brown. An escort of dragoons accompanied Walker across the prairie to the edge of the chaparral that concealed the Mexicans. There the dragoons waited while Walker went forward into the brush.[5]

Walker had carried to Major Brown news that Taylor was safe at Point Isabel and coming soon to his rescue, and he had brought back to Taylor word that Fort Brown would hold out until help arrived.[6] He had rendered this service where others, less experienced, would probably have failed, a service significant in many respects of the sort that the Texas Rangers were to contribute throughout the war; it set an example for other Texas Rangers to emulate; and it spread the name of the Texas Ranger for the first time beyond the limits of Texas.

[4] Taylor to Adjutant General, May 3, 1846. *House Executive Document* No. 60, Thirtieth Congress, First Session, pp. 289–290. Serial No. 520.

[5] Brown to Bliss, May 4, 1846. *House Executive Document* No. 60, Thirtieth Congress, First Session, pp. 293–294. Serial No. 520.

[6] Taylor to Adjutant General, May 5, 1846. *House Executive Document* No. 60, Thirtieth Congress, First Session, pp. 292–293. Serial No. 520.

At three o'clock on May 7, Taylor with twenty-three hundred men and a long wagon train drew out of Point Isabel. 'If the enemy oppose my march, in whatever force, I shall fight him,' said the general. The next day he met the Mexicans at Palo Alto Prairie, a vast, level, grass-covered plain, in the first battle of the war, and again at Resaca de la Palma on May 9. Arista's army, shattered and disorganized, withdrew south of the Rio Grande, and Taylor marched on to find the flag still high over Fort Brown, though its defender, Major Brown, had been mortally wounded. Arista set out for Monterey, more than one hundred and sixty miles away, and the summer passed before Taylor was ready to follow him.

Taylor had a choice of two routes to Monterey, chief city of the north: one by way of Linares, the route of the retreating Mexicans, and the other by way of the Rio Grande and San Juan River. The next important service of the Texas Rangers was to determine which of these routes the American army should follow.

2. *A REGIMENT OF TEXAS RANGERS*

In response to Taylor's call for four Texas regiments, only three were raised and these formed a division under Governor J. Pinckney Henderson. The two mounted regiments were commanded by Colonel John C. Hays and Colonel George T. Wood.

Wood's men, from the interior and eastern part of Texas, may be called the East Texas Rangers. Hays's regiment comprised the frontiersmen of the first tier, Westerners, experienced Mexican and Indian fighters and others attracted by Hays's fame and the prospect of stirring adventure.

Hays's regiment did not come to the Rio Grande in a body, but by companies and as individuals. Walker was followed closely by Price, and on May 19, Ben McCulloch's company arrived at Point Isabel and reached Matamoros by May 23. R. Addison Gillespie's company came overland by Laredo and Mier and did not report until July.[7]

Among these companies Ben McCulloch's, raised among the Indian and Mexican fighters on the banks of the Guadalupe River, was exceptional. A member of the company wrote: 'This company was perhaps the best mounted, armed, equipped and appointed corps

[7] Taylor to Adjutant General, June 24, 1846. *House Executive Document* No. 60, Thirtieth Congress, First Session, p. 307; July 31, p. 321; August 3, p. 402. S. C. Reid, *Scouting Expeditions*, pp. 40–41.

that was out in the ranging service; and from the time of its arrival at headquarters until after its disbandment at Monterey, enjoyed more of the trust and confidence of the commanding general than any other volunteer company of the invading army.' [8]

McCulloch, a man of bold features, prominent forehead, straight nose, and deep-set blue eyes, was an ideal partisan leader. His face a mask and his features under such control as to give no clue to his feelings, or emotions, or intentions, it was as natural for Ben McCulloch to remain calm in danger as it was to breathe. Sudden emergencies served to quicken his faculties, rather than to confuse them. His courage may best be described as a complete absence of fear.

McCulloch's camp, which was established before Matamoros on May 22, 1846, has been described by one of his men as follows:

'Here we constructed our tents — constructed, we say, because the government never furnished us, during our whole term of service, with a patch of canvas large enough to keep out a drop of rain, or shield us from a ray of the scorching sun. Whether it was because they thought the Texan troops were accustomed to, and could endure more hardships than any other troops in the field, we do not know.... We were left to shift for ourselves, wholly unprovided with tents, camp equipage, or cooking utensils.... The consequence was, that wherever we were encamped for any length of time, we were obliged to construct rude shelters out of poles, cane, rushes, or any other material which the vicinity afforded. And the Rangers' camp frequently looked more like a collection of huts in a Hottentot hamlet, or a group of rude wigwams in an Indian village, than the regular cantonment of volunteers in the service of the United States.' [9]

McCulloch's first duty was to examine the territory between Taylor's army at Fort Brown and the Mexican army at Monterey in order to determine the most practical route for the invading army. His first scout was made towards Linares in the wake of Arista's retreat. With forty picked men McCulloch rode forth on June 12 in the afternoon. Instead of striking directly for Linares on the trail of the retreating army, the Rangers rode up the river to the Rancho de Guadalupe, where they camped and feasted on the fruits, melons, roasting ears, and vegetables of the season. The next morning they continued towards Reynosa, still up the river, but once out of sight of the *rancho* they turned sharply to the left and rode through the brush to intercept the Linares road. On the third day out they encountered their first adventure. The Rangers habitually camped off the road but near

[8] Reid, *Scouting Expeditions*, p. 38.

[9] *Ibid.*, pp. 42–43.

enough to command it. In the early dawn the sentinel heard a body of horsemen approaching, and hailed them.

'Quien vive?' challenged the *ranchero*.

'Amigos,' answered McCulloch, riding forward.

'Nuestros Amigos — los malditos Americanos!' shouted the Mexican, bringing his bell-mouthed *escopeta* to position. But he was too late, for McCulloch was flying towards him with a half-dozen Rangers at his heels. The Mexicans fled to the chaparral, leaving guns, pistols, spurs, and horses. The party was led by Blas Falcon, *ranchero*, chief, robber, and the reputed murderer of Colonel Cross.

The action was characteristic of McCulloch and of all able Ranger captains. It was to strike like a bullet, suddenly and with little warning. It was in this whirlwind manner that he took the villages and *ranchos* which he could not avoid. 'It would be difficult to picture the astonishment and alarm at the different *ranchos*, as the Rangers entered them; or the consternation of those upon whom we came suddenly upon the road. By forced night marches, our commander frequently got upon the other side of some of the settlements, and rode into them, as if direct from Monterey or Linares, and going towards Matamoros. By doubling and twisting about, they were thrown completely off the scent, and were willing to answer any questions with a readiness which showed that life or death depended upon their alacrity.' [10]

In their hurried march southward the Rangers were guided by trail and map. Arista's trail was easily followed. His camp grounds were marked by worn-out rags, castoff shoes, broken sandals, and dirty cards dropped from some gambler's *monte* pack. The map presented a graphic picture of the country in great detail, the trails, roads, and most important of all, the water holes.

By June 20, McCulloch was within sixty miles of Linares. From some *pastores* he heard that there was no more water on the route. The map, however, indicated water ten miles away. McCulloch sent Lieutenant John McMullen with ten men to ascertain the fact. McMullen found the water hole dry, but pushed on until within thirty miles of Linares, finding no water anywhere.

Having learned that the Linares route was impracticable, lacking in subsistence and water, and that Arista had moreover moved on to Monterey, McCulloch decided to go no farther. Instead of returning to Matamoros, he cut through the brush northwest in the hope of meeting General Canales, the 'Chaparral Fox,' who was reported to be on the Monterey road recruiting *rancheros*. Canales had a long and bloody record on the border, and the Texans had scores to settle

[10] Reid, *Scouting Expeditions*, p. 45. Quoted from George Wilkins Kendall.

BEN McCULLOCH AFTER THE MEXICAN WAR

with him. 'To strike the "Chaparral Fox" in his own hills — slaughter his band, and take "reynard" himself captive, was a thing above all others McCulloch most desired to do.' [11] The men rode all day — the longest of the year — through an arid and desolate country. By night they were almost mad with thirst, threatening to kill the Mexican guide unless he led them to water. Just before darkness fell they were rewarded by a joyous cry of discovery. Horses were spurred forward, but McCulloch, always well mounted, reached the precious spot first, dismounted, and with drawn gun declared he would shoot the first man who rode into the stagnant pool. The men dismounted, drank, filled their canteens, and then watered their horses.

The summer solstice was marked that night by a flood of rain. An incident of the night is worth relating for the light it throws on the character of the men who rode with McCulloch. Samuel Reid was sleeping with an old Texan veteran of San Jacinto known as the Major, now a private. Reid became conscious of a rivulet finding its way under his blankets, but the major slept soundly. Finally the young man aroused the older one to suggest a shift of quarters. The major admonished him to lie down and go to sleep. 'Don't you see that we have got this puddle of water warm now, and if we move, we shall only get into another and take cold.'

On the next day, June 22, the Rangers intercepted the Monterey road. Finding Canales gone and his trail cold, McCulloch turned towards Reynosa on the river — above Matamoros — to which point Taylor had advanced a small force. The garrison was expecting an attack from Canales, and when the Rangers appeared suddenly from the direction of Monterey, they created as much excitement among the Americans as they had among the Mexicans of the *ranchos*.

McCulloch's men had spent ten days in the interior of the enemy country, traveling not less than two hundred and fifty miles. From the time they left Matamoros until they reached Reynosa, they never took off their coats, boots or spurs. They had brought back information which caused General Taylor to decide that the direct route to Monterey was impracticable, either in wet weather or in drought.[12]

At Reynosa the Texas Rangers set up their camp, first in the open, then in some abandoned sheds, and finally in an old gin house which sheltered both men and horses. Here they remained until July 9, a period of comparative idleness during which the Rangers began to build a reputation as trouble-makers. They had no love for Reynosa,

[11] Reid, *Scouting Expeditions*, pp. 46–47.

[12] *Ibid.*, pp. 43–52; Taylor to Adjutant General, July 2, 1846, *House Executive Document* No. 60, Thirtieth Congress, First Session, pp. 329–332. Serial No. 520.

while their feelings for the rough border characters there were of a positive nature. It was in Reynosa that the Mier prisoners were so inhumanly treated in 1842. Some of these former prisoners were now Rangers; their presence did not add to the peace of the community nor to the safety of those they recognized or assumed to recognize as former enemies and persecutors.

'Our orders were most strict,' wrote one of them, 'not to molest any unarmed Mexican, and if some of the most notorious of these villains were found shot, or hung up in the chaparral,... the government was charitably bound to suppose, that during a fit of remorse and desperation, tortured by conscience for the many evil deeds they had committed, they had recklessly laid violent hands upon their own lives! *Quien sabe?*' [13]

General Taylor confessed that he could not stop the Texans. 'I have not the power to remedy it.... I fear they are a lawless set.' Later he stated that if they would be subordinate, they would be the best soldiers among the volunteers, 'but I fear they are and will continue [to be] too licentious to do much good.' [14] Taylor was no master of diction, and his word 'licentious' may not express the meaning he meant to convey. On the other hand, he may have had in mind the celebration of July 4, when two horse-buckets of whiskey slightly diluted with water and sweetened with loaf sugar were used to wash down a dinner of Mexican pigs and chickens which the Rangers accidentally killed while firing salutes in honor of the day! [15]

Not only did they observe American holidays, but they participated in the *fiestas* and *fandangos* of the Mexicans for miles around. In Mexico, San Juan's day, June 24, is observed by riding contests which resemble the jousts and tourneys of medieval times. One game required a horseman to take a chicken from one point to another some two miles distant. The entire body of Mexicans were his opponents, who pursued and captured the chicken if they could. The Rangers entered this contest, and because of the better quality of their horses, they possessed an advantage. Clinton DeWitt took the first chicken and set out at breakneck speed, followed by a band of yelling Mexican horsemen. Riding down all opponents he could not dodge, DeWitt had just gained the open when a finely mounted horseman charged on him from behind a house and seized the chicken. The horses were running side by side, and DeWitt, seeing his advantage, seized the Mexican by the neck, stopped his own horse short, threw his opponent to the ground,

[13] Reid, *Scouting Expeditions*, p. 53.

[14] Taylor to Wood, July 7, 1846, Governors' Letters. Hereafter referred to as G.L.

[15] Reid, *Scouting Expeditions*, p. 61.

and bore his prize to the goal with a yell of triumph. The race was repeated until the Mexicans were compelled to confess that there were '*No mas Gallenas in Reynosa.*' [16]

The *fandangos* were often disturbed by the presence of Rangers. One night Lieutenant John McMullen led twenty men silently out and informed them that they were going far into the country to a *fandango* which Canales was supposed to be attending. The place was surrounded, and McMullen with a few men at his heels walked boldly into the group of dancers. Women screamed and the men bolted for the open spaces only to find the way blocked by bearded Texans who looked coolly and somewhat longingly at them down a gun barrel. Failing to find Canales, McMullen did not inform the Mexicans of his purpose, but told them that in passing he heard the noise, and came by for a visit.

On July 9, Taylor's army moved forward to Camargo, from which place the Rangers made an important scout up the San Juan valley. The American army, coiling about Camargo, with its tail stretching down the sinuous stream to Point Isabel, was preparing to strike Monterey, more than a hundred miles south, the Rangers' scout to determine the path of the stroke. McCulloch first reconnoitered the western or China route, influenced somewhat perhaps by a report that Colonel Juan N. Seguin, a former Texan patriot who had gone over to the side of the Mexicans in 1842, was operating out of China with a band of irregulars.

The Rangers moved cautiously, and did not reach China, sixty miles from Camargo, until their second night out. They took the town on the morning of the third day, although McCulloch had already learned from a prisoner that Seguin was gone. Captain Ben was deeply chagrined, and rode into town with the rim of his hat turned up, a sure sign that he was not pleased and in no mood for familiarity. By dawn of August 6, the Rangers were in their saddles and on their way back to Camargo, where McCulloch reported unfavorably on the China route.[17] For the second time he had rendered valuable service, and he had added to the record that Samuel H. Walker had made in the first days of the fighting. It was as General King said: 'He [Hays] and his officers and men were not only the eyes and ears of General Taylor's army, but its right and left arms as well.' [18]

Taylor now sent McCulloch's and Gillespie's Rangers, accompanied

[16] Reid, *Scouting Expeditions*, Chapter VI.

[17] *Ibid.*, pp. 78 ff. Taylor to Adjutant General, August 10, 1846. *House Executive Document* No. 60, Thirtieth Congress, First Session, p. 408. Serial No. 520.

[18] W. H. King, 'The Texas Ranger Service,' in Dudley G. Wooten, *Comprehensive History of Texas*, Vol. II, p. 338.

by Captain Duncan and Lieutenant Wood, artillery and engineering officers, respectively, to reconnoiter the Mier route. McCulloch became ill and remained at Mier, and the command continued in charge of Captain Duncan. This movement was as much an advance as a reconnaissance, as evidenced by the fact that Duncan demanded the surrender of Cerralvo, which was made a military depot.

Duncan returned to Camargo on August 19, and two days later General T. J. Worth, at the head of the Second Division, moved south along the beautiful San Juan River. The invasion of the interior had begun at last. All along there was movement, slow, deliberate, steady, always forward. By September 10, the army had drawn itself about Cerralvo, its tail lengthened by seventy miles. The Rangers were busy continually, here, there, everywhere, the East Texas men doing escort duty while McCulloch's and Gillespie's men served as spies and scouts under the immediate orders of the commanding general.[19]

Hays at the same time was advancing with the major portion of his regiment from Matamoros by another route. He left Matamoros on August 5 and reached China twenty days later, 'buying' mules as he went. Quartermaster Henry Whiting called on the *alcaldes* of the towns to furnish mules at twenty dollars each. 'This call,' he wrote, 'might have been ineffectual, had not a Texan mounted regiment (Colonel Hays's) been moving into the quarter whence we expected these mules. A regiment will make that possible which might otherwise be deemed impossible.' [20] Texas Rangers were competent mule buyers.

Hays's Rangers reached San Fernando, beautifully situated on a river of that name, on August 13. This might have been a Capua to the Rangers, as one of the men reported that he was domiciled with an aristocratic Mexican family and found himself in such pleasant company that he could hardly realize that he was there through the circumstance of war. But Jack Hays did not leave his Rangers idle long enough for them to be Capuaized by the Mexicans. He probably ascended the Rio San Fernando and crossed the divide to China, where he arrived on or about August 25, just as the main army was concentrating at Cerralvo across San Juan valley.[21]

The move on Monterey was begun on September 13 by two parallel or converging columns. The main army moved from Cerralvo with McCulloch and Gillespie leading the advance, and went by Papagallos

[19] Taylor to Adjutant General, August 25, 1846. *House Executive Document* No. 60, Thirtieth Congress, First Session, pp. 412 ff., and August 31, 1846, pp. 322–323. Serial No. 520.

[20] H. Whiting to Thomas S. Jessup, August 6, 1846. *House Executive Document* No. 60, Thirtieth Congress, First Session, p. 676. Serial No. 520.

[21] Taylor to Adjutant General, August 25, 1846, *ibid.*, pp. 412–413; Special Orders No. 129, August 27, 1846, *ibid.*, p. 526.

and Marin. The regiment of Rangers under Hays moved from China by way of Caderita. The first blood was drawn by McCulloch's men on September 14, when thirty-five of them attacked and drove from the town of Ramos two hundred Mexican cavalry, wounding two.[22]

The two columns were united at San Francisco on September 17. That night six thousand men slept in sight of the lofty Saddle Back and Miter Mountains which guard Monterey. Every man knew that Monterey would be reached the following day and that fighting would surely follow. Taylor ordered the Texas mounted troops under Major J. Pinckney Henderson 'to form the advance of the army tomorrow,' and to move at sunrise.[23]

3. THE RANGERS AT MONTEREY

The Texas division arrived before Monterey in advance of the other troops. General Taylor was present, accompanied by members of his staff, and surrounded by McCulloch's Texas Rangers. A twelve-pound cannon ball, thrown from a near-by fort, tore up the dirt near the advance, while a party of Mexican cavalry made a sortie to observe or to draw out the Americans. Many of Taylor's men, moved by curiosity, left the ranks and approached the city in 'the general desire to see that as yet unseen biped, a Mexican soldier,' while the squads of Rangers rode forth to exhibit their feats of horsemanship which they had learned on the plains of Texas in their contests with Comanches and Mexicans.

'Like boys at play on the first frail ice with which winter has commenced to bridge their favorite stream, those fearless horsemen, in a spirit of boastful rivalry, vied with each other in approaching the very edge of danger. Riding singly and rapidly, they swept around the plain under the walls, each one in a wider and more perilous circle than his predecessor. Their proximity occasionally provoked the enemy's fire, but the Mexicans might as well have attempted to bring down skimming swallows as those racing daredevils. While the marvelous ring performances of that interesting equestrian troupe was in progress, the artillerists of the citadel amused themselves by shooting at the spectators on the hills.'[24]

[22] Henry, *Campaign Sketches*, p. 182.

[23] Taylor to Adjutant General, Order No. 119, September 17, and No. 120, September 18, 1846. *House Executive Document* No. 60, Thirtieth Congress, First Session, p. 506. Serial No. 520.

[24] (Luther Giddings), *Sketches of the Campaigns in Northern Mexico*, pp. 143–144.

'THEY SWEPT AROUND THE PLAIN UNDER THE WALLS'

After a time Taylor gave orders for the play to cease, and directed that the army encamp at a spring at Walnut Grove, the picnic ground of fashionable Monterey. Taylor, finding that the eastern approach to the city was well guarded by forts and fortification, conceived the plan of sending a part of his force around the city to cut off retreat towards Saltillo, and to take the city in reverse. The movement was to begin the next day under General Worth. The Hays Rangers were to accompany Worth while the East Texas men under Henderson and Wood were to remain with Taylor at Walnut Grove. Under the spreading branches of Walnut Grove the campfires flickered, the Rangers and soldiers polished their weapons, told stories, thought of home, which some would see no more, and slept to be awakened before day by a drizzling rain; the campfires still burned, revealing weird figures guarding the Mexican prisoners brought in during the night.

It was Sunday, September 20. By nine o'clock the rain ceased, and the clouds broke and tumbled about the mountains or drifted down the deep valleys, revealing the heights, rain-washed and clean in the brilliant sunlight of an autumn morning. By two in the afternoon, Worth's column was ready to move. The general, sitting a splendid horse, reviewed his men with a stern, grave countenance, yet he inspired them with confidence by his very bearing.

General Worth's instructions were to detour to the right, find the Saltillo road, block it, cut off supplies, and if possible take the heights that guarded the entrance to the city.[25] All of this he was to do, and more.

But what of this column of men upon which his success depended? The division consisted of two brigades, one under Lieutenant Colonel Staniford and the other under Brigadier General Persifer F. Smith. At the head of the column — always at the head — were the heavily armed, ununiformed, sun-tanned Texans, whose faces were hidden behind handle-bar mustaches and flowing beards. Young men, desperately courageous, singularly careless of their own lives, singularly concerned with the life of their enemies, sat astride their restless, steel-muscled ponies, patiently awaiting action.

Down the Marin road, to the right through cornfields sere with autumn sun, and into the chaparral they plunged; by six o'clock the advance was six miles from Taylor, almost in reach of the Saltillo road, nearly under the guns hidden on Independence Hill. In front of the Rangers a spur of hill extended down from the right, pushing the road to the left and quite under the fire of the enemy's batteries. Worth with thirty Rangers ascended the hill to view the fortifications, unconscious of some dismounted cavalry concealed in the cornfield to the left. As he returned, the Mexicans ran forward to cut him off, opening a rattling fire as they came. The Rangers at the foot of the hill were thrown into confusion and the horses became unmanageable. One man was thrown to the ground, but John McMullen picked him up without dismounting; another was knocked from the saddle, but clung to leather and mane for a hundred yards before righting himself. Worth and his small party retired in good order and unharmed.[26]

Nightfall and camp near humble *jacales*. Pigs and chickens in the yard — food for the Rangers. Corn for the horses. Darkness, rain, and the chill of tropical mountains. At nine General Worth scrawling a note in the cornhouse by the light of burning shucks, asking for a diversion the next day in his favor. A Ranger riding through the night with the message. Rangers lying in fitful sleep on the wet ground or among the shucks. Saddled horses making little noises with nostril

[25] Worth to Bliss, September 28, 1846. *House Executive Document* No. 4, Twenty-Ninth Congress, Second Session, p. 102. Serial No. 497.

[26] Worth to Bliss, September 28, 1846, as cited. Reid, *Scouting Expeditions*, pp. 153 ff.; Ripley, *War with Mexico*, Vol. 1, p. 203.

and hoof and saddle leather, crunching now and then a vagrant grain of corn. A captain and private sleeping together on a board. Tomorrow war.

Worth's column moved at six o'clock. When the Texas Rangers turned the angle of a hill by which lay the *hacienda* of San Jeronimo, they found themselves facing a body of mounted lancers supported by infantry. The opposing forces stood motionless, taking each other's measure. In splendor of equipment, the Mexicans excelled. Their nimble and spirited horses, their richly embossed saddles, brilliant uniforms, and bright poised lances made an imposing contrast to the tatterdemalion Texans. At the head of the Mexican force rode a trooper with long black mustache and splendid military bearing, Lieutenant Colonel Najera.

McCulloch and his men in front failed to get the order to dismount and moved swiftly to meet the advancing enemy. Mexican and Texan horse struck head on with terrific impact and for a moment friend and foe were intermixed, fighting desperately with swords, knives, pistols, and lances. McCulloch, once completely cut off from his men, put spurs to his horse, rode down all in his path, and came back to his command unscratched. The Mexicans were soon fleeing towards the Saltillo highway while the dismounted Rangers picked them off with rifles and Duncan raked them with artillery. More than a hundred dead Mexicans, among them the handsome Najera, were the only obstacles between Worth and the Saltillo road.[27]

The view of Monterey from the road was picturesque and inspiring. On either hand, in the foreground, rose two high hills fortified and crowned by palace and fort, natural gateposts of the city, between which passes the Santa Catrina River and the Saltillo highway, and between them — between palace and fort — had to pass Worth's army.

Beyond and below the hills the Santa Catrina takes an easterly course for about two miles, and then makes an elbow turn to the left. Within the crooked arm of the river lay the city of Monterey. The Saltillo road, parallel to the river, becomes the Calle de Monterey, a principal street. Far beyond this scene, on the east and north in Walnut Grove, were the tents and camps of Taylor's army.

Though Worth had gained the Saltillo road, he was eight miles from the main army with four days' provisions, with all communication severed, a superior force in front of him, and the unknown dangers

[27] Worth to Bliss, September 28, 1846, *House Executive Document* No. 4, Twenty-Ninth Congress, Second Session, pp. 102 ff., Serial No. 497; Smith, *War with Mexico*, Vol. I, p. 243; Reid, *Scouting Expeditions*, pp. 156–158.

of an enemy country behind. In order to guard the approach from Saltillo, he dispatched Major Brown and a body of Rangers to secure the rear, which was done by taking a stone mill where the road and the river break through a mountain pass some three miles out.

Ordinarily a rash man, Worth was now calm, collected, and decisive. He would storm Federation Hill first. It lay on his right, and across the river from him. It is oblong, with its axis parallel to the stream. On its western end, facing Worth, the Mexicans had planted a battery which commanded the approaches from Saltillo. Six hundred yards away, on the opposite end, Fort Soldado overlooked the city.

From his headquarters in an old sugar house Worth directed the operations. He sent the attacking forces forward in three divisions, or waves, with intervals between. The advance was commanded by Captain C. F. Smith and comprised four artillery companies acting as infantry and six companies of dismounted Texas Rangers.

The advance force moved from the sugar house at noon. The Rangers led off down the road, turned into the bush on the right, emerged into some cornfields, plunged waist deep into the rapid current, and, though under fire of shot and grape, clambered out without loss, and sought a brief rest and shelter at the base of their objective. The Mexicans were swarming along the hillside above, arranging themselves in favorable positions as sharpshooters. General Worth, perceiving this show of resistance, sent forward the second party under Captain D. S. Miles, and perceiving numerous reinforcements coming from the city, he dispatched the third division obliquely up the hill towards Fort Soldado. Meantime the Rangers and regulars had gained the height, taken the gun, and turned it on the Mexicans who were fleeing to the shelter of the fort.

A mad race began among the different organizations to see who should first reach the fort. Down the ridge they went, artillery, infantry, Louisiana volunteers, and the Texas Rangers yelling like Comanches. Captain R. A. Gillespie, of the Rangers, was the first to mount the enemy's works, closely followed by soldiers of the Fifth and Seventh Infantry. Soon the regimental flags were fluttering above the fort, disturbed only by shrieking shells which came from the batteries at the Bishop's Palace.[28] Most of the storming force remained at the fort and on the hill during the night, but the Rangers were sent back to care for their horses and prepare for the attack on the opposite hill the following day. General Worth moved his quarters forward,

[28] Worth's Report, September 28, 1846, *House Executive Document* No. 4, Twenty-Ninth Congress, Second Session, pp. 102 ff., Serial No. 497; Reid, *Scouting Expeditions*, pp. 161–165; Smith, *War with Mexico*, Vol. 1, pp. 244–246; Ripley, *War with Mexico*, Vol. 1, pp. 219–222.

and the main army bivouacked in a gorge at the foot of the captured hill as the night was ushered in by a terrific autumnal storm. Black clouds, shot through with chain lightning, rolled in turmoil over the peaks of the Sierra Madre, or fell down the valley of the Santa Catrina, so low at times that the Americans and Mexicans on the tops of the opposing peaks looked at each other over them. Artillery fire crowned each hill with a white cap of smoke, and sent a thousand sharp echoes laughing from rock to rock at the sullen thunder. The storm burst with torrents of rain while darkness finally cut off the view and put an end to the cannonade. With arms in their hands the hungry Rangers slept in the pelting rain, but they were not unhappy, for they had won their objective, and were to move at three o'clock in the morning against Independence Hill and the Bishop's Palace.[29]

The plan of attack on Independence Hill was similar to that used against Federation Hill. There were three companies of artillery, dismounted, three of infantry and seven companies of Texas Rangers under the joint command of Colonel John C. Hays and Lieutenant Colonel Samuel H. Walker. The attacking party numbered more than four hundred and fifty of whom two hundred were Rangers.[30]

Independence Hill, parallel to Federation, is a truncated oval mesa tilted towards the city. On the lower end, overlooking Monterey, stands the Bishop's Palace; on the upper or western end fortifications commanded the palace in one direction and the approach from Saltillo in the other. The Mexicans, considering this approach impracticable, had posted no guards upon it; here Worth determined to strike. At three o'clock two columns advanced, one to the right and one to the left of this declivity, their progress timed so that they would converge at the summit near daylight. Lieutenant Colonel Childs, accompanied by Hays's Rangers, led the right; Captain Vinton and Walker's Rangers took the left. So difficult and slow was the ascent that dawn found the forces but halfway up, when a gun blazed above, telling them that they were discovered. Not an American rifle cracked until they were within twenty yards of the top when with a wild yell they sprang towards the summit. The struggle was desperate and brief. 'The Mexicans fled in confusion, some towards the Palace, while others ran headlong down the hill.' The Americans were too exhausted to give chase, nor were they able to prevent the Mexicans from carrying off one of their two cannon. The Stars and Stripes were run up, and cheer after cheer rolled from the throats of the victors, was answered from

[29] Worth's Report of September 28, as cited; Reid, *Scouting Expeditions*, p. 168.

[30] Reid, *Scouting Expeditions*, p. 181. Justin H. Smith explains that in the Mexican War most of the 'artillery' served as infantry. *War with Mexico*, Vol. 1, p. 497, *note*.

Federation, echoed from camp in the gorge, and returned by Taylor's men on the opposite side of the city. 'It was a glorious sight,' said one of these, 'and quite warmed up our chilled bodies.' [31]

The success in gaining possession of the upper end of Federation Hill enabled General Worth to concentrate his forces for the final attack on the Bishop's Palace. By noon a thousand men were ready and a howitzer began throwing shells against the walls and through the windows, producing what Worth described as a 'visible sensation.' The Mexicans were in the meantime sending reinforcements from the city, as if determined to drive the Americans from the height. As the Mexicans seemed to be preparing to take the offensive, the Americans laid a trap for them. The Texas Rangers were divided into two parties, concealed in a forward position, with Hays on the right and Walker on the left. Behind the Rangers were five companies of regulars; before them Blanchard's Louisianians occupied the center and were alone visible to the enemy.

The Mexican preparations were made with elaborate ceremony. 'Battalions of infantry formed in front of the Palace, their crowded ranks and glistening bayonets presenting a bold and fearless front, while squadrons of light-horsemen, with lances bright and fluttering flags, and heavy cavalry, with scopets and broadswords gleaming in the sun, richly contrasting with the gaudy Mexican uniforms, made a most imposing sight.' [32]

In view of this spectacular array, the Louisiana troops fell back, the Mexican bugles sounded, and the Mexicans advanced, steeds prancing, swords rattling, and leather creaking. Before them they saw only Blanchard's retreating men. Suddenly, twenty yards in front of them, on right, on left, came the quick shuffling of many feet, a gliding movement like that of sliding doors, and the Mexican way was blocked by a wall of bayonets. In an instant there was a crash of rifles, front and flank, from the Rangers and regulars, and the order 'Charge!' The Mexicans broke and fled, some into the Palace gate, some to the city below. The Palace gate swung to, but the howitzer pounded it open and the Americans poured into the yard. The entire garrison, save about thirty prisoners, was soon in full flight down the hill.[33]

General Worth moved his headquarters to the Bishop's Palace. His situation was not a happy one and his peace of mind was not improved by bad news from front and rear. Taylor's 'diversion' on the

[31] Ripley, *War with Mexico*, Vol. 1, pp. 224–225; Reid, *Scouting Expeditions*, pp. 182–183; Henry, *Campaign Sketches*, p. 204.

[32] Reid, *Scouting Expeditions*, pp. 185–186; Worth's Report, September 28, 1846, *House Executive Document* No. 4, Twenty-Ninth Congress, Second Session, pp. 102 ff. Serial No. 497.

[33] *Ibid.*

east had been unsuccessful and all but disastrous, and it was reported that large Mexican forces were approaching from Saltillo. Soon, however, Taylor began his attack on the east, and when Worth heard the cannon he interpreted it as an order for him to commence action.[34]

Two columns advanced by parallel streets into the city. Hays and his Rangers led the right by the Calle de Monterey, while a similar force advanced by the Calle de Iturbide with Walker at the head. Lieutenant George B. Meade and Ben McCulloch had reported that the Mexicans had withdrawn as far as Campo Santo, or Cemetery Plaza, and it was here that the Americans met the first obstinate resistance. Every house and block had to be taken by force. Rangers and light infantry fought under cover of the houses, and with picks and crowbars they tunneled through the walls while sharpshooters mounted the roofs and worked their guns from the housetops as the artillery swept the streets. Axes crashed against doors, timbers fell, rifles cracked, and men shouted in anger, triumph, or in pain. The firing on Taylor's side ceased, permitting the Mexicans to concentrate against Worth. The advance was checked, withdrawal would have been easy, and more reasonable than Taylor's withdrawal across town; but no retreat was sounded, none was wanted.[35]

Sunset closed the operations, but the Texans and regulars were firing from the roofs by daylight on Thursday, September 24. During the night several men crossed the street and picked a hole in the very masonry of a large building. They now crossed over, threw explosives into the building, and as the occupants dashed out, they were killed by Texans firing from the post-office and housetops. Before active operations were well begun, Worth received orders from Taylor to suspend the advance until a conference could be had and a concerted plan of action agreed upon, but before any common plan was effected, the Mexicans came to parley.

Colonel Moreno appeared before Taylor with a flag of truce and a letter from Ampudia proposing to evacuate the city.[36] The details of

[34] Worth's Report, September 28, as cited; Reid, *Scouting Expeditions*, p. 193.

[35] Justin H. Smith gives an interesting account of Hays's part in this operation. He states that the Texans pushed forward because Hays wanted to sleep in the post-office where he had once been a prisoner. 'Colonel Hays, a shy man with a broad forehead, a Roman nose, restless hazel eyes, and the courage of twenty lions packed in his delicate frame, had been a prisoner in the Monterey post-office once, and had sworn a great oath to sleep this night in the post-office or in hell, and nothing could stop him. By dark the Americans were only a square from the market place and the Colonel had the postal accommodations at his command.' *War with Mexico*, Vol. I, p. 258. This is an excellent story which might have been true, but is not. Hays had never been a prisoner in Mexico. On the Mier Expedition he turned back at the Rio Grande.

[36] Ampudia to Taylor, September 23, 1846, *House Executive Document* No. 4. Twenty-Ninth Congress, Second Session, pp. 79–80. Serial No. 497.

the capitulation do not concern the Texas Rangers, whose part was to be the first in action, the last out; to fight, not to parley. The Mexicans were permitted to retire with the honors of war and provision for an eight weeks' truce, terms so liberal as to call down on Taylor a storm of protest and criticism.[37] The Texans who had overstayed their enlistment quit and went home, riding north on October 2, a week after the surrender. Taylor granted them a discharge with alacrity; the prospect of living in Mexico with one thousand idle Texas Rangers was one which even Old Rough and Ready could not contemplate with equanimity.[38]

4. FROM MONTEREY TO BUENA VISTA

'The departure of the Rangers,' said an officer, 'would have caused more regret than was generally felt, had it not been for the lawless and vindictive spirit some of them had displayed in the week that elapsed between the capitulation of the city and their discharge.... Gifted with the intelligence and courage of back-woods hunters, well-mounted and skilled in arms, they were excellent light troops. Had they remained and given their whole attention to the guerillas, they might have been exceedingly useful. The commanding general took occasion to thank them for the efficient service they had rendered, and we saw them turn their faces toward the blood-bought State they represented, with many good wishes and the hope that all honest Mexicans were at a safe distance from their path.' [39]

While these Rangers were without doubt 'gifted with the intelligence and courage of back-woods hunters,' they were not back-woodsmen in the sense that they were wholly crude and ignorant. In McCulloch's company were lawyers, doctors, poets, surveyors, and legislators. Many a night these men sat around their campfires and enlivened their discussions and reinforced their arguments with quotations from the Greek and Latin writers. Their desire to return home is understandable when we consider that those homes were exposed to Indian depredations.

Five months elapsed from the fall of Monterey until the victory of

[37] Articles of Capitulation of the City of Monterey, *ibid.*, pp. 80–81. See Justin H. Smith's *War with Mexico.*

[38] Taylor's Orders No. 124, October 1, 1846, *House Executive Document* No. 60, Thirtieth Congress, First Session, p. 508. Serial No. 520. McCulloch's and Gillespie's companies were discharged earlier.

[39] (Luther Giddings), *Sketches of the Campaign in Northern Mexico*, pp. 221–222.

Buena Vista. In the meantime, political motives combined with military considerations to change the fortunes of war and the movements of commanding generals. When Taylor learned that the government disapproved the truce, he notified Santa Anna that offensive operations would be resumed on November 13. Three days later his army occupied Saltillo. About the middle of December he moved a portion of his force to Victoria, midway between Monterey and the coast town of Tampico. While he was here General Winfield Scott came to the Rio Grande, and finding Taylor far in the interior, sent a message after him designed to paralyze his further movement and place him on the defensive with a skeleton organization. Nine thousand of his best troops were to be taken from him to go with Scott to Vera Cruz for the purpose of launching a campaign against Mexico City. Too much success on the part of a Whig general was not desired by a Democratic administration. Taylor was ordered to take a position at Monterey and not to advance beyond that place. In great dejection he made his way thither to take stock of his depleted forces. On January 27 he wrote that he evidently no longer held the confidence of the government and expressed regret that he had not been relieved of his command.

There is something pathetically heroic and half humorous about this old man, when, stripped of his veteran troops and exasperated beyond measure, he assumed the offensive in violation of his orders and struck the best Mexican army assembled a blow from which Mexico could not recover.[40]

Meantime the absence of Texans to serve as scouts and guides and to carry messages resulted in many disasters, and actually altered the course of military events. Couriers were killed, dispatches intercepted, and reconnoitering parties were cut off and captured.[41] Among these disasters, that of Lieutenant John A. Richey was fraught with the gravest military consequences. When Scott found Taylor absent from the Rio Grande, he sent his famous order of January 3 to Taylor, who was then at Victoria, by Lieutenant Richey. At Villa Gran, in the vicinity of Linares and McCulloch's successful scout, Richey was set upon by Mexican *vaqueros*, lassoed, and put to a brutal death. Scott's orders were captured, revealing to Santa Anna the fact that Taylor was to be left at Monterey with a skeleton force. This

[40] On January 26, 1847, Scott ordered Taylor not to advance beyond Monterey. *House Executive Document* No. 60, Thirtieth Congress, First Session, p. 864, Serial No. 520; Stevens, *Campaigns on the Rio Grande*, p. 41.

[41] Wool to Taylor, reports of January 27 and 29, *House Executive Document* No. 60, Thirtieth Congress, First Session, pp. 1106 and 1108; Serial No. 520; Smith, *War with Mexico*, Vol. I, p. 371.

information caused Santa Anna to attempt to crush Taylor, and resulted in the battle of Buena Vista.[42]

Ben McCulloch, in keeping with his promise to return to Mexico upon the resumption of hostilities, set out for Taylor's army, and on January 1, 1847, rode into Monterey with twenty-seven Rangers at his heels. McCulloch moved on to Saltillo, where he met Taylor who was just back from Victoria. Taylor, finding his force dispirited, refused to fall back to Monterey as he had been ordered to do, and was making active preparations to advance to Agua Nueva. When the Rangers arrived, McCulloch's men refused to enlist for the war, or even for twelve months, but Taylor was in such need of their peculiar service that he violated the regulations and took them on their own terms.[43]

On January 28, Santa Anna, acting on the information furnished by the captured Richey dispatches, left San Luis Potosi and arrived at Encarnacion, just across a thirty-five-mile desert from Taylor, on February 17, with more than fifteen thousand men. It was the first duty of McCulloch and his Rangers to cross the desert, which had swallowed up Borland and Heady of the main army, and spy out the Mexican forces.

McCulloch chose sixteen men to accompany him on his first scout, which reached the vicinity of Encarnacion about eleven o'clock on the night of February 16. Here he came upon the advance guard of a cavalry force which he routed by his usual bold measures. The Rangers returned to headquarters before day, having triumphed where others had failed.[44]

Taylor still had no assurance of the enemy's plan or knowledge of the size of his force. On February 20 he sent Lieutenant Colonel May to La Hedonia and sent McCulloch back to Encarnacion.[45]

Riding in the dark, the Rangers reached the Mexican pickets at midnight, went inside the lines, and from the dimensions of the camp, McCulloch calculated almost exactly the size of the Mexican force. Five men under Lieutenant Fielding Alston were sent back to Taylor while McCulloch and one man remained to see what daylight would reveal. As dawn approached, reveille sounded and the drowsy camp sprang to life. The Mexicans built their fires of green wood which

[42] Scott to Taylor, January 3, 1847, *House Executive Document* No. 60, Thirtieth Congress, First Session, pp. 848–850. Serial No. 520. See also Smith, *War with Mexico.*

[43] Taylor to Adjutant General, June 8, 1847, *House Executive Document* No. 60, Thirtieth Congress, First Session, p. 1176. Serial No. 520. 'I determined to accept them for the period of six; trusting that the peculiar necessity for their services would justify this departure from the prescriptions of the law.'

[44] Reid, *Scouting Expeditions*, p. 235; Taylor to Adjutant General, March 6, 1847, *Senate Executive Document* No. 1, Thirtieth Congress, First Session, p. 132.

[45] J. H. Carleton, *Battle of Buena Vista*, pp. 12–17.

caused a dense smoke to rise and almost obscure the soldiers. The Rangers rode slowly and deliberately out between Mexican pickets, and when clear of danger they hurried away to Taylor at Agua Nueva to report that Santa Anna had twenty thousand men.

The information brought by Alston's squad caused Taylor to withdraw to an impregnable position behind the pass of Angostura or narrows near the *hacienda* of Buena Vista, a position that could not be flanked or turned. Taylor was waiting to hear McCulloch's story, and when he had done so, he said, 'Very well, Major, that's all I wanted to know. I am glad they did not catch you,' and with his staff Old Zach rode towards Buena Vista.

Not until Santa Anna arrived near Taylor's camp did he learn of the American retreat which he misconstrued to his own grief. Lured on by it he struck Taylor in his chosen position. It was as ever before, Taylor fought with the courage of a lion and the good luck of a novice. The Mexican army was beaten and hurled back across the desert in a most disastrous retreat. 'The great want of Mexico,' said Stevens, 'was a victory and the restoration of her moral power.' Success here would have enabled Santa Anna to meet Scott at Vera Cruz with a victorious army supported by a united nation. That Ben McCulloch contributed much to the American victory no one can doubt. If Taylor had made mistakes, the Texas Rangers had helped him to escape their consequences.[46]

Taylor's work in Mexico was now done — enough to make him president. McCulloch's Rangers served six months and went home; others came to take their places, and there was no time probably when Taylor did not have a few Rangers on his line. With inactivity, however, they again became troublesome. Taylor wrote that 'the mounted men from Texas have scarcely made one expedition without unwarrantably killing a Mexican.' He earnestly requested that no more Texas Rangers be sent to his column.[47]

[46] Taylor wrote on June 8: 'The services rendered by Major McCulloch and his men, particularly in reconnoitring the enemy's camp at Encarnacion, and advising us certainly of his presences there, were of the highest importance.' *House Executive Document* No. 60, Thirtieth Congress, First Session, p. 1176. Serial No. 520.

Giddings says: 'General Taylor was induced, by the information brought him by that trusty and accomplished scout, Captain McCulloch, to change his ground from Agua Nueva to the gorge of Buena Vista.' *Sketches*, p. 287.

[47] Taylor to Adjutant General, June 16, 1847. *House Executive Document* No. 60, Thirtieth Congress, First Session, p. 1178. Serial No. 520.

5. *FROM VERA CRUZ TO MEXICO CITY*

General Winfield Scott landed his army at Vera Cruz in March, 1847, and after reducing that place, advanced towards Mexico City. Fighting at Cerro Gordo, Contreras, and Churubusco, Molina del Rey, and Chapultepec, his army entered the capital September 14, 1847. Very few, if any, Texas Rangers reached the Vera Cruz line until after Scott's army was well on its way to Mexico City. It is evident that the Rangers did not render the service to Scott that they did to Taylor. Scott did not seem to need them for advance troops and spies; he preferred to base his plans on reports of engineers rather than on those of frontier soldiers such as the Rangers were.

What, then, was their task on the Vera Cruz line? The answer requires a brief consideration of Scott's situation. A glance at the map of Mexico indicates that Scott's route took him through a broken, mountainous country where the ranges of the Sierra Madre converge towards the south to an abrupt point below the capital. The country is a succession of gorges and peaks, narrow passes and defiles, thickets and forests — a land as dangerous as it is mysterious and beautiful. The Mexicans could not check Scott's progress towards the capital. 'Mexico has no longer an army,' wrote the commanding general in April. 'Thence to the capital hardly a show of resistance is to be expected. Yet we cannot, at once, advance in force. We are obliged to look to the rear.... Deep sand, disease and bands of exasperated *rancheros* constitute difficulties.' [48]

The Mexicans had invoked guerrilla warfare in extreme form. They plundered Scott's line, cut it, and slew isolated parties wherever found. As the American line lengthened, the danger and difficulty of protecting it grew correspondingly greater. In April the guerrilla leader J. C. Robelledo captured ten wagons loaded with supplies. In June Brevet-Colonel McIntosh lost one-fourth of his wagon train and a number of men in passing from Vera Cruz to the head of the army. In July General Pierce lost a hundred men out of a thousand; Captain Wells followed with two hundred and lost forty. Only large parties attempted to go through.

The efforts of the inexperienced soldiers to cope with the guerrillas or to punish them ended in disasters. The record of a soldier's diary for four days tells a bloody story.

[48] Scott to Taylor, April 24, 1847 (from Jalapa). *House Executive Document* No. 60, Thirtieth Congress, First Session, p. 1171. Serial No. 520.

On Thursday several parties went out after *pollitos* and *carne*, 'fell in with some rancheros or guerrillas.... The result was... that several of our men were killed.' On Friday the Illinois company went out after *carne* and guerrillas; they came back without dead guerrillas but with two dead soldiers. Saturday two men belonging to the Illinois regiment and one from the New York regiment were killed by guerrillas. Sunday morning more Illinois men went out to avenge the death of their companions. Later in the afternoon they returned. Two of their men had been lassoed, dragged on the ground at full speed, and speared to death.[49]

Into this situation came Captain Samuel H. Walker, first with Scott as he had been first with Taylor. Though he held a commission now as captain of mounted rifles in the regular army, he was looked upon as a Texas Ranger and was so referred to by contemporaries. He remained a Ranger in tactics and methods, and for these reasons we may follow him to his tragic end. Walker reached Perote, about one-third the distance between Vera Cruz and Mexico City, on May 25, just at the time so many misfortunes were befalling the regular troops. 'This morning,' wrote Oswandel, '... Gen. Twiggs' division and a large train... arrived in Perote city. Among them I noticed Col. Harvey and his regiment of dragoons, and Capt. Samuel H. Walker, the Texas Ranger, with two companies of mounted riflemen, mounted on fine spirited horses. They are all fine, strong, healthy and good looking men, nearly every one measured over six feet; they took up their quarters in the Castle Perote.... I learn they are to remain with us to keep the National Road open between this castle and the city of Jalapa. So guerrillas, *robadors* (robbers), take warning... for the renowned Capt. Samuel H. Walker takes no prisoners.' [50]

The expectations with reference to Walker were fully realized. He remained at Perote throughout the summer, scouting the roads and feeding the guerrillas their own medicine. He sometimes brought in booty, captured horses, ammunition, and all sorts of supplies, but there is no record of his bringing captives. When he left the city on June 29, Oswandel wrote: 'Should Capt. Walker come across the guerrillas God help them, for he seldom brings in prisoners. The Captain and most all of his men are very prejudiced and embittered against every guerrilla in the country.' [51] He struck them at Las Vegas on June 20 and at La Hoya Pass later in the morning, routing them and

[49] J. J. Oswandel, *Notes on the Mexican War*, pp. 147–153.

[50] *Ibid.*, pp. 171–172.

[51] *Ibid.*, p. 198.

capturing their flag bearing skull and bones and the words 'No Quarters.'[52]

Walker's presence at the castle of Perote had a significance for him and for the Mexicans. His recollections of a long imprisonment there, with Big Foot Wallace, Thomas J. Green, and other Mier prisoners, were as vivid as they were unpleasant. It was at Perote that a number of the Texans had effected their escape by digging up the stone floor and tunneling under the massive walls of the castle. A story went the rounds among the soldiers that Walker while a prisoner had made a prophecy that the American flag would some day fly from the castle turret, and when the Mexicans made him and other prisoners dig a hole in the yard and erect a flagpole, Walker placed an American dime under the pole, promising to return as a victor and claim it. The prophecy had been fulfilled; the American flag was flying above the castle, and Walker dug up the dime and exhibited it to his companions.[53]

In August, when Scott moved against Mexico City, he left twenty-two hundred men under Colonel Childs at Puebla. No sooner was Scott away than bandits and guerrillas began to pour in, putting Colonel Childs under virtual siege. On September 14, Scott's army entered the capital. Santa Anna, hoping to retrieve his failing fortunes, gathered about five thousand men, who, while nondescript in character, were sufficient, he thought, to take care of the sick Yankees at Puebla. Childs stubbornly held on, cheered by news of Scott's victories around the capital and encouraged by word that General Jo Lane was coming to raise the siege. With Lane was Jack Hays, and his regiment of Texas Rangers, who had come to guard the American line.

On October 4, Lane reached Perote, where he found Samuel H. Walker. A game of hide-and-seek now took place between Santa Anna and Lane, Hays and Walker. Santa Anna's purpose was to prevent Lane and the Rangers from reaching Childs at Puebla; Lane and the Texas Rangers hoped not only to go to Childs, but to capture Santa Anna. Santa Anna started to the mountain pass El Pinal, where he hoped to block the Americans, and on the way he left a garrison and some guns at Huamantla. Hearing of this through a spy, Lane decided to strike the force and capture the supplies and guns. On October 8, with eighteen hundred men, he set out. At the front of the band rode 'a rather short, slender, spare, slouchy man, with reddish hair, small reddish beard, mild blue eyes and a quiet kindly manner,'

[52] For accounts of Walker and Wynkoop's fights at Las Vegas and La Hoya, see Wynkoop to Scott, June 23, 1847, and Walker to Wynkoop, June 21, 1847. *Senate Executive Document* No. 1, Thirtieth Congress, First Session, pp. 21–25. Serial No. 503; Oswandel, *Notes*, pp. 188–193.

[53] Oswandel, *Notes on the Mexican War*, pp. 176–177.

CAPTAIN SAMUEL H. WALKER

who for five months had been scourging the guerrillas in that vicinity. It was no other than Samuel H. Walker whose experience made him the natural leader of the expedition. On the afternoon of October 9, these mounted men, led by the curly-haired Ranger, swept into the streets with sabers flashing and guns firing. Santa Anna came up with his full command and the fighting was desperate. Then came Lane and his full force, to support the advance; the Mexicans fled; the guns were captured. Samuel H. Walker lay dead upon the field, shot through the head and chest.[54]

Walker's men burst into tears when they saw him in death. A soldier wrote that it had never been his fortune to meet a grander and nobler soldier. 'He was brave, faithful and obedient to his superior in rank and kind to his men. He was, without doubt, one of the bravest officers in the army.' His commanding officer said: 'This victory is saddened by the loss of one of the most chivalric, noble-hearted men that graced the profession of arms — Captain Samuel H. Walker, of the mounted riflemen. Foremost in the advance, he had routed the enemy when he fell mortally wounded.' [55]

Samuel H. Walker had fallen five days after Jack Hays and his regiment of Texas Rangers arrived. Hays and his men caught up the task that Walker had laid down, and carried it on with a vengeance. It was President Polk himself who had designated Hays as the proper man to send to Mexico to clear the road of guerrillas.[56] His men were real Texas Rangers as distinguished from Walker's company. Their uniforms were an outlandish assortment of long-tailed blue coats and bob-tailed black ones, slouched felt hats, dirty panamas, and black leather caps. Most of them wore long bushy beards. Their horses were all sizes and breeds, Texas ponies, and American thoroughbreds, but they were without exception, tough, mettlesome, and quick. The arms of this particular band of Rangers excited the admiration and wonder of all. Each Ranger carried a rifle and four pistols, two old-style single-shooters and two brand-new six-shooters, which they had received just out of Vera Cruz. They also carried a short knife, hempen ropes, rawhide riatas, or hair lariat. They carried anything else they chose to tie to their saddles.[57]

[54] Smith, *War with Mexico*, Vol. II, pp. 177–178. Lane to Adjutant General, October 18, 1847, *Senate Executive Document* No. 1, Thirtieth Congress, First Session, pp. 477 ff., Serial No. 503; (Anonymous), *General Taylor and his Staff*, pp. 185 ff.

[55] Oswandel, *Notes on the Mexican War*, p. 351; General Joseph Lane to Adjutant General, October 18, 1847, *Senate Executive Document* No. 1, Thirtieth Congress, First Session, p. 479. Serial No. 503.

[56] Polk's *Diary*, July 17, 1847, Vol. III, pp. 90 ff.

[57] Albert G. Brackett, *Lane's Brigade*, pp. 173–174; Ford, Memoirs. (MS.) Ford gives a long and detailed account of the progress of Hays from Vera Cruz to Mexico City and back.

The leader of this band was as remarkable for shyness, modesty, and inconspicuity as his followers were for the lack of these attributes. 'I shook hands with him, and could scarcely realize that this wiry-looking fellow was the world-renowned Texas Ranger. Jack was very modest.... He was very plainly dressed, and wore a blue roundabout, black leather cap, and black pants, and had nothing about him to denote that he belonged to the army, or held any military rank in it. His face was sun-browned; his cheeks gaunt; and his dark hair and dark eyes gave a shade of melancholy to his features; he wore no beard or moustache; and his small size — he being only about five feet eight — made him appear more like a boy than a man.' [58]

Lane and Hays moved to Puebla, and drove off the besiegers that surrounded Colonel Childs. From this place Lane's brigade marched in November against Matamoros, killed sixty Mexicans, captured twenty-one American prisoners, mounted them at the expense of the Mexicans, and restored them to service. They took three pieces of artillery, twelve tons of shot, and a large number of muskets, sabers, and other war material. On the return with a train loaded with plunder, Hays's advance was attacked in a mountain pass near Galaxara by a superior force. The Rangers emptied their guns and were compelled to fall back on the main force while their retreat was covered by Hays himself.[59]

Soon after this event the Rangers moved on to Mexico City, their coming recorded by no less a personage than General Ethan Allen Hitchcock. 'Hays's Rangers have come,' he wrote on December 6, 'their appearance never to be forgotten. Not in any sort of uniform, but well mounted and doubly well armed: each man has one or two Colt's revolvers besides ordinary pistols, a sword, and every man a rifle. All sorts of coats, blankets, and head-gear, but they are strong athletic fellows. The Mexicans are terribly afraid of them.' [60] When they brought in some prisoners, Oswandel confided to his diary that 'This is one of the seven wonders... for they generally shoot them on the spot where captured.' [61]

'Our entrance into the City of Mexico produced a sensation among the inhabitants,' wrote Ford. 'They thronged the streets along which we passed. The greatest curiosity prevailed to get a sight at "Los Diabolos Tejanos" — The Texas Devils.' When the Rangers arrived,

[58] Brackett, *Lane's Brigade*, pp. 194–195.

[59] Lane to Adjutant General, December 1, 1847, *House Executive Document* No. 1, Thirtieth Congress, Second Session, pp. 86–89. Serial No. 537.

[60] *Fifty Years in Camp and Field*, p. 310. Ford also gives the date of entry as December 6.

[61] Oswandel, *Notes on the Mexican War*, p. 398.

THE RANGERS ENTER MEXICO CITY

many Americans were being killed within the City of Mexico, but now men had come who took eye for eye, tooth for tooth. The Mexicans called them *los Tajanos sangrientes*. A sneak thief stole one of their handkerchiefs, was detected, refused to stop. 'A six-shooter was levelled upon him and discharged. The Mexican dropped lifeless to the pavement. The Ranger recovered his handkerchief, and went his way as if nothing had happened.' Another threw a stone at a Ranger. The Texan's hand fell to his holster, a shot rang out, and the Mexican fell dead. A waiter at the inn of the National Theater on learning that his guests were Texas Rangers dropped his tray and fled the place. When Adam Allsens of Robert's company was murdered in a part of the city called by the Texans 'Cutthroat,' the Rangers took a bloody vengeance. The Mexicans carried in their dead on a wooden litter. 'At breakfast time they had brought in fifty-three corpses.... In the evening the captain reported more than eighty bodies lying in the morgue.... They had been shot in the streets and left lying.' Complaint was made to General Scott. He called in Hays and questioned him. Hays boldly defended the Rangers, telling the General that no one could impose on them. Scott passed the matter over, but found work for the Rangers outside the capital.[62]

The Rangers were sent on many expeditions after guerrillas and Mexican forces, usually as a part of General Jo Lane's command. On January 21, 1848, a mixed force of three hundred and fifty men set out for Tehuacan where Santa Anna was reported to be with a hundred cavalry and an indefinite number of guerrillas. When about forty miles from the place, the party met a coach with an escort of ten men. The occupant of the coach produced a pass, or safe-conduct, signed by Brigadier General Persifer F. Smith. Lane had no alternative but to restore the men their arms and let the carriage pass. Hays protested vigorously.

'Do you know, Colonel Hays,' asked General Lane, 'the penalty for violating a safe-conduct? It is death.'

'That's all right,' responded Hays, 'I'll take the chances.'

'I'd rather you would set him at liberty,' said Lane.

'If you order me to do so, General, of course I shall obey.'

'Well, then, if you prefer it in that form, Colonel Hays, I order you to let the Mexican re-enter his carriage and go undisturbed on his way.'

The column moved to one side and the carriage passed into the darkness. No sooner was it out of sight than a messenger was sent from the Mexican party to warn Santa Anna, probably saving him from capture.[63]

After an all-night march the Americans arrived before Tehuacan at four in the morning. The story of what happened is best told by one of the participants, John S. Ford.

'The enemy was found. No noise was heard but the thunder of our horses' hoofs on the stone pavement, and the rattling clang of scabbards. All was silent. Not a living thing was in sight. Men and animals had disappeared, or were in deep sleep.

'We entered the deserted apartments [of Santa Anna]. There was a long table in a very long room. The cloth was still laid, and candles were burning. It was not yet daylight. The writer went into a long room off the dining-hall. A candle had been turned over burning, and had gone out, leaving a line of melted wax across the green covering of the writing desk. An ink-stand of crystal, with a silver top by its side, had been upset over a white satin mat, tied with pink ribbons,

[62] Ford, Memoirs. (MS.)

[63] Ford in his Memoirs gives the story as coming from Dr. David Wooster of San Francisco, California. According to Ford the account was published in *The Vidette* at Washington, probably in 1886. For the official report of General Lane, February 10, 1848, see *House Executive Document* No. 1, Thirtieth Congress, Second Session, pp. 89 ff. Serial No. 537.

leaving a broad black stain across its middle, not yet dry.... Everything betokened the haste and hurry of flight. Seventeen packed trunks were left in a room adjoining the patio.... In the same room was a great bedstead, a state affair, with posts to the ceiling, all of burnished brass.

'And now began the sack of the trunks. They contained everything, from a tiny slipper from the tiny foot of Donna Santa Anna to full court toilette; dresses by the hundreds, which General Lane gallantly had forwarded to Donna Santa Anna with the expressed hope that when next he found her dresses he would find her in them. A coat of Santa Anna's, by actual test, weighed fifteen pounds, so much was it embroidered and embossed with solid gold. This was given to the State of Texas. There was a resplendent gold bullion sash of immense proportions and weight. This was sent to some other state....

'But marvel of all, a Texas lieutenant, and perhaps some privates, drew from the bottom of a trunk a long, tapering, green velvet-covered case. This was quickly opened, and from its satin cushions was taken a cane.... Its staff was of polished iron. Its pedestal was of gold, tipped with steel. Its head was an eagle blazing with diamonds, rubies, sapphires, emeralds — an immense diamond in the eagle's beak, jewels in his claws, diamonds everywhere. The cane was a marvel of beauty.

'The Texans cried out with one accord: "Give it to Colonel Jack!"

'The finders instantly assented, and joined the chorus: "Give it to Colonel Jack!"'

Though Hays accepted the cane, Major William H. Polk, brother of the President, expressed the desire to send it to his brother. Hays gave it to him, telling him to say that it was from the Texans.[64]

According to Ford, the Rangers had an opportunity to see Santa Anna before they left Mexico. The war was practically over, and Santa Anna was leaving the country on a safe-conduct. The Rangers were near Jalapa and it was necessary for Santa Anna to pass them on his way out. The following account is Ford's.

'One day news came that Gen. Santa Anna was on his way out of the country and would stop for dinner... about four miles above us in the direction of the City of Mexico. This intelligence produced considerable excitement. Col. Hays and a few other officers left camp with a view to meet Gen. Santa Anna and pay their respects to him.

[64] Ford, Memoirs. (MS.) Dr. Wooster in *The Vidette*. Wooster says he is writing thirty-five years after the events happened; his account agrees in substance with the official report of this expedition.

Major Alfred Truitt and the writer concluded they would ride into Jalapa, and witness the demonstration of the Mexicans in honor of their great general. We had not been in the city very long before a couple of Rangers came in with a request for us to return to camp — "the men say they are going to kill Gen. Santa Anna when he reaches there." We mounted and rode in haste.

'On reaching camp we discovered everything at a white heat.... Revenge was the ruling passion of the hour. We knew the men we had to deal with. No attempts to exercise the authority of officers were made — no threats of punishment were let fall. We appealed to reason and to honor. What was said may be summed up in this wise. The men said Gen. Santa Anna had waged an inhuman and unchristian war upon the people of Texas — had murdered prisoners of war in cold blood. We knew many in the crowd around us had lost relatives in the Alamo, [at] Goliad and elsewhere. To this it was replied, "Yes, that is admitted, but did not the world condemn Gen. Santa Anna for his cruel butchery of prisoners? That was a stain upon his reputation as a soldier.... Will you not dishonor Texas and yourselves by killing him?" To the last question the response was: "Gen. Santa Anna is not a prisoner of war." "He is virtually a prisoner of war. He is in his own country, and is traveling under a safe-conduct granted by our commanding general; to take his life would be an act the civilized world would brand as assassination. You would dishonor Texas!" They answered, "Then we will not do it."

'The men then wanted to talk to Santa Anna, but were advised to remain silent. They were stationed on the side of the road.

'The line was formed.... A courier came down the road, at a brisk gallop, and informed us that Gen. Santa Anna was nearby. Every eye was in the direction of the anticipated passer. He, his wife, and daughter, were in a carriage, which appeared to be an open one. All had a fair view. The writer was of the opinion that the old warrior's face blanched a little at the sight of his enemies of long standing. He might have thought of the bitter recollections these bronze and fearless men had garnered up from the past, and how easy it would be for them to strike for revenge and for retribution. He sat erect, not a muscle of his face moved — if his hour had come he seemed resolved to meet it as a soldier should. His wife was pretty. She bowed frequently, and a smile played upon her countenance. Miss Santa Anna resembled her father — had a rather long nose and was undemonstrative.

'The "ununiformed" representatives of Texas stood motionless and silent — not even a whisper disturbed the air.... The carriage passed on — the Mexican guard of honor marched by in good order. There were no salutations, no ungraceful remarks.... The Texans broke ranks and returned to camp.' [65]

The Mexican War ended with the Treaty of Guadalupe Hidalgo. The army evacuated the country in time for all the generals to run for office: Taylor, Scott, and Hitchcock for the presidency, and General Jo Lane for vice-president. Taylor's luck held out and he was elected, while all the others were defeated. The Texas Rangers returned to their native state to resume an humbler rôle as guardians of the frontier.

[65] Ford, Memoirs. (MS.) Lane and Hays had a fight with guerrillas at Sequalteplan on February 25, 1848. This was probably the last conflict of the war. For reports of it, see *House Executive Document* No. 1, Thirtieth Congress, Second Session, pp. 98 and 102, Serial No. 537, and Ford's Memoirs. It was in the Mexican War that Ford gained the title of 'Old Rip' or 'Rip' Ford. He entered the army as a physician, and it was his duty as surgeon and adjutant in Hays's regiment to make out the death certificates for those killed in battle. Feeling that some formality was necessary in such serious documents, Ford would write on each, 'Rest In Peace.' As time went on, he economized by using the initials of these three words after his signature, thus: 'John S. Ford. R.I.P.' The soldiers began calling him Rip, and the name stuck for the remainder of his long and eventful life. The authority for this story is Ford's grandson, Raphael Cowen, of Brownsville, Texas.

VII

FIRST YEARS IN THE UNION

It appears . . . that they think that the general government employs me to herd the horses of the citizens generally, when the fact is that I have not a single soldier under my control, and am not charged with the defense of the frontier against Indian depredations. . . . I can only act as a civil magistrate to execute the Indian Laws and Treaties.

ROBERT S. NEIGHBORS, *Indian Agent*

But the Indians, unfortunately, 'no comprende' annexation, 'no comprende' paper treaties, 'no comprende' why his war parties are to hang up their shield and spears and bows.

The Texas Democrat

They [the Comanches] must be pursued, hunted, run down, and killed. . . . They must be punished even to the captivity of their women and children. . . . Harney can take the dragoons along with him, but for the light work he must have Texas Rangers.

GEORGE WILKINS KENDALL

VII. FIRST YEARS IN THE UNION

1. THE CONFUSION OF NEW MASTERS

THE entrance of Texas into the Union changed all relationships on the frontier and resulted in confusion and uncertainties that did not end until long after the civil war and reconstruction. In this chapter we are concerned with the confusion of the period between the close of the Mexican War and the opening of the Civil War when the Texans and the Indians were adjusting themselves, or refusing to adjust themselves, to new masters, the agents of Uncle Sam.

The Texans had very definite ideas as to how Indians should be treated. Their psychology was fixed, and they refused to yield their views to the more lenient policies of the federal government. Out of the maelstrom of the past and its many bitter experiences they had come with hard and relentless methods. Their independent existence for ten years had fostered self-reliance and created new institutions suited to the circumstances, and produced in them a spirit that could not be cast off lightly. Theoretically they were quite willing to turn the task of protecting the frontier over to the federal government, but practically they were unwilling to accept the federal plan; they soon demanded that the work be done through their institutions and leadership — at federal expense. They easily convinced themselves, for example, that the Texas Rangers knew best how to whip Mexicans and exterminate Indians, and their impatience with the clumsy methods and humanitarian policy of the United States Army was colossal. The Texans demanded that the United States should muster the Rangers into federal service, pay them with federal money, and let them run all the Mexicans into the Rio Grande and all the Indians into Red River.

Naturally, the United States could not deal with Texas in such a special way. When the United States extended its sovereignty over Texas, its Indian policy was well established and its system of Indian control complete. It considered the Texas frontier merely as an extension of its own frontier, and could do no other than apply the same control in Texas that was used elsewhere in the Indian country.

The new masters — new to Texas — that were sent to handle the Indians were soldiers for war and agents for peace. The soldiers were established in posts extending from the Rio Grande to Red River to form a line which separated the Indian country from the white man's but which in no sense separated Indians and white men. The posts were too far apart, the garrisons were too small, and often composed of infantry who were useless in pursuit of mounted warriors. The soldiers were circumscribed by many limitations that the Texans could not tolerate with patience. Soldiers could not kill Indians because of their mere presence. On the contrary, it was their duty to protect them. The Texans were wont to look upon them as game wardens and not warriors, and the Texans wanted an open season on all Indians. The army was further limited because it was dealing with Indians in a *state* rather than in a *territory*. It was generally assumed — and in most cases correctly — that by the time a state entered the Union, the Indians would have been removed, but this was not true in Texas, which, because of its size and the contrasting character of its eastern and western parts, was half white and half red, half civilized and half savage. Legally the soldiers had no more authority over the white inhabitants than they had over the people of the seaboard states. It was the state's business to regulate intercourse among citizens, traders, and Indians, but this the state was impotent to do.

The Indian agents were federal civil magistrates whose business it was to execute the Indian laws and the terms of Indian treaties; and like the soldiers, they had less authority in Texas than elsewhere because Texas was a state. In reality the Indian agent had no power stronger than persuasion with which to control his charges. The Texans were almost as impatient with the agents as they were with the soldiers, and constantly accused them of protecting the Indians in their deviltry and shielding them after their raids. It was such a charge that led Major Robert S. Neighbors, the ablest Indian agent in Texas, to write: 'I have not a single soldier under my control, and am not charged with the defense of the frontier against Indian depredations.... I can only act as a civil magistrate.... I have no more power to defend the citizens, make war, or defend the frontier than any other citizen.'[1]

With the Indians, as with the Texans, the problem was largely psychological. They too had a past, memories, mores, ideals of conduct, and institutions; and they knew just enough history to confuse them. They remembered a blessed state of independence when they could

[1] Robert S. Neighbors to Governor H. R. Runnels, January 20, 1858. G.L.

devote themselves to chasing the buffalo and to fighting among themselves, and now they found themselves cribbed in on every side. They might have understood the federal system — agents for peace and soldiers for war — but the relations incident to the entrance of Texas into the Union were beyond their comprehension. The Texans had long been their enemy, the United States their friend — at a distance. Peace with the Great Father at Washington should not impose on them peace with their enemies in the river valleys of Texas. To them the people of each river valley were a separate people. To make matters worse, the Great Father now told the Comanches and Apaches that they could no longer raid in Mexico, a thing that the Texans had never discouraged. They had raided in Mexico for two centuries, a good custom which yielded many Mexican ponies.

A contemporary observer said that it was a simple matter to make a treaty with Mexico, draw a line on a map in Washington, and say to the Indian: 'Shinny on your side, Mr. Indian.' 'But,' he continued, 'the Indian, unfortunately, "no comprende" annexation, "no comprende" paper treaties, "no comprende" why his war parties are to hang up their shields and spears and bows. It is all, from beginning to ending, ridiculously absurd to him.' [2]

The Indians did not hang up their bows and spears, but used them assiduously on every favorable occasion. The Texans expected the federal government to deal with Indians as they would have done; in fact they probably expected more of the federal government than they would have been willing to do for themselves. There was misunderstanding all around, and it became plainly evident that Texas was none too happy over the results of union. The editors who loved a matrimonial simile likened Texas to the fair bride whose hand had been sought by many suitors, and who had at last yielded to the gentle blandishments and liberal promises of the gentleman in tall hat and striped breeches; and without stopping to consider the polygamous implications, the editors accused Uncle Sam of being a deceiver whose efforts to please ceased the moment he got past the altar. In this strain the editor of the *Gazette* wrote: 'No bride ever joined her fate to that of her lover with a holier, more pure, and less selfish zeal than that with which Texas has joined herself to the United States. No lover has ever treated his bride with more cruelty, cold-heartedness, and less feeling, than the United States have treated Texas. The want of protection, the scornful look, *and the efforts to rob her of her dowry* — all mark the faithlessness and deception of the lover.' [3]

[2] *The Texas Democrat*, August 4, 1849.

[3] *Texas State Gazette*, October 6, 1849.

It will be observed that this disillusionment was complete by 1849, only a year after the Mexican War. The complaint was that the United States was not protecting the frontier, not sending enough soldiers to Texas, and not permitting the Texans to protect themselves by employing the Rangers. While Zachary Taylor was President it was charged that he was prejudiced against Texas before he set foot in it, that he was opposed to the Mexican War, and that he did everything he could 'to degrade our gallant Rangers.' Proof was found in the fact that he had sent thirty-two companies of troops to Florida to take care of six or seven hundred Indians, and had left Texas, plagued by fifteen thousand warriors (a palpable exaggeration) with only four or five hundred troops. The editor flayed Taylor as he would have flayed a Comanche, saying that he neglected Texas because Texas voted for a better man in the last election.[4]

There was a constant plea for mounted men and endless complaint at the use of infantry which were as much out of place in Texas, one editor declared, as 'a sawmill on the ocean.' Because the government would not place the Rangers in the field, it was charged that the officials at Washington were indifferent to the Indian atrocities, and that the life of a Texan was held in no more regard at Washington than a kit of codfish.[5]

The opinion of the Texas people was well expressed by George Wilkins Kendall, who gained ample knowledge of Plains Indians on the Santa Fe Expedition. From Brussels he wrote: 'I see that the Comanches are still continuing their forays upon the Texas borders, murdering and carrying off defenseless frontier settlers who had been granted protection.... They [the Comanches] must be pursued, hunted, run down, and killed — killed until they find we are in earnest. ... If Harney can have his own way, I cannot but believe he will call in Hays, McCulloch, and all the frontier men, and pursue the Comanches to the heads of the Brazos, the Colorado, and even up under the spurs of the Rocky Mountains — they must be beaten up in all their covers and harassed until they are brought to the knowledge of ... the strength and resources of the United States. Harney can take the dragoons along with him, but for the light work he must have Texas Rangers — without them even he ... can effect but little.'[6] The Texans agreed with Kendall that the Comanches should be killed and the Rangers employed as executioners.

For ten years after the Mexican War the Texas Rangers were little more than a historical expression. Theoretically there was no place

[4] *Texas State Gazette*, October 20, 1849; January 12, 1850; May 20, 1850.

[5] *Ibid.*, August 21, 1852.

[6] *Ibid.*, September 1, 1849.

for them because the United States had agreed by treaty to protect the frontier. Though they were called frequently in emergencies, they were never permitted to remain long in service, usually three or six months. If Texas called them, it demanded that the United States pay them, and this the government consistently refused to do for any length of time. It could not make them a permanent institution without admitting that the army was incompetent, and this it was not willing to do. For the most part the Rangers were inefficient, the service ragged, and able leadership almost wholly lacking. They were kept alive by a great need which, while not continuous enough to give them permanence, was too recurrent to let them die. Before attempting to follow their intermittent activities, we may consider the work of the Indian agents in Texas.

2. *THE WORK OF THE INDIAN AGENTS*

Among the new masters in Texas were the federal Indian agents, chief of whom was Major Robert S. Neighbors, who had served the Republic in a similar capacity. He was assisted by John H. Rollins, John H. Rogers, and Jesse Sturm. A fifth man, who seems to have represented the state, was H. G. Catlett.

The Indian agents had no sinecure, for theirs was a mission of peace among people who had a love for war and a genius for stirring it up. The agents, always on or beyond the frontier, and without physical force to support them, had to rely on tact and diplomacy in handling their refractory charges. To be effective, yea, even to preserve their own lives, they had to gain the friendship and hold the confidence of the Indians; and because they did this they often incurred the ill will of the whites.

Their task was made more difficult by unscrupulous trading-house factors who sold the Indians liquor and firearms, and frequently thwarted the efforts of the agents to bring the Indians into councils to be held elsewhere than at the trading house. The most troublesome trader in Texas was George Barnard whose famous establishment was on the upper Brazos near Fort Spunky in what is now Hood County. In the autumn of 1850, Rollins and Catlett were undertaking to bring the Comanches into a council on the Llano. Suddenly a rumor spread along the frontier that an Indian war was impending, that Barnard had abandoned his trading house, was falling back on the settlements, and bringing in all his stock. Catlett exclaimed: 'Things must be squalley and danger certain when Barnard will admit it.' Rollins made a different report, but it was even less favorable to Barnard's character and designs. He said that Barnard had wrecked the council on the Llano because it was not to be held near his trading house, that he had no fear of the Indians, and that if he were falling back on the settlements it was because he feared the authority of the United States. Rollins hoped that Barnard would come in and save him the trouble of removing him, 'and that in haste.' [7]

As a matter of fact Barnard's position was impregnable. He was safe in the confusion of new masters. General Brooke wanted to remove him, but he was powerless to do so because the federal government had no authority over Texas citizens. General Brooke asked Governor Bell to call him in, but the governor replied that he was powerless because there was no state law governing the relations of citizens and traders with the Indians.

The laws of the Republic had been repealed by the admission of Texas to the Union, and 'the intercourse laws of the United States are the only ones to govern and direct.' The governor added that he had no objection to the removal of all Indian traders.[8] The important fact is the revelation of a hopeless tangle which left George Barnard and others as unscrupulous as he sitting high on the Texas border beyond the reach of Indian agents, federal soldiers, and state laws.

The Texas agents found their task further complicated by the varied status of the Indians with whom they had to deal. Some of the tribes or bands had been in Texas from time immemorial. Those considered as native sons were Comanches, Coshattas, Karankawas, Tonkawas, Wacos, Lipans, and two or three minor groups. Another class was composed of bands that had migrated from the United States and had made Texas their adopted home. Among those adopted sons were Delawares, Shawnees, Caddos, Ionies, Anadarkos, Wichitas, and Kickapoos. The third group was composed of visitors or sojourners: Seminoles, Creeks, Cherokees, Osages, and parties of Delawares, Shawnees, Toways, and Kickapoos.[9]

Naturally the agents' problem with each group differed. They had

[7] H. G. Catlett to Dr. S. G. Haney, September 14, 1850; John H. Rollins to General Brooke, September 25, 1850; October 4, 1850. G.L. For an account of Charles Barnard, see Thomas T. Ewell, *History of Hood County*, pp. 52 ff.

[8] General George M. Brooke to Governor Bell, October 6, 1850; Brigadier General Harney's Orders No. 34, April 22, 1851; Harney to Bell, April 22, 1851; Bell to Harney, May 5, 1851. G.L.

[9] Two lists of the Texas Indians are in the Bell papers. One list is in a letter, H. G. Catlett to Governor Bell, May 3, 1851; the other is attached to a treaty made by John H. Rollins with the Comanches and other tribes on Spring Creek near the San Saba, December 10, 1850. Both lists omit the Lipans, a fragment of the Apache tribe.

to maintain the natives, tolerate the permanent residenters, but their constant purpose was to make the sojourners unwelcome and their visits short. Among the visitors the Seminoles deserve especial attention.

We should know little of the Seminoles in Texas but for their remarkable leader, Coacoochie — better known as Wild Cat. Of him the agents never tired of talking and writing. John Rollins met him on the Llano in May, 1850, at the head of 250 Seminoles and Kickapoos. Wild Cat told Rollins that he had left Florida because the United States had promised to give him a country west of the Mississippi, but when he arrived at this place the government set him down among the Creeks, who gave him no voice in the management of affairs. Wild Cat complained to no effect, and now, as a last resort, he had decided to be done with Creeks and seek a permanent and more pleasant home in Mexico. He would pay for his new home by defending the Mexicans against the wild tribes of the United States. If his services were accepted by Mexico, he would return to the Indian territory, gather his people — and all others who would join him — and lead them to the south bank of the Rio Grande.

Wild Cat was not disturbed by the fact that a large party of Seminoles had sojourned long enough on the Llano to have a corn crop growing. He casually alluded to the corn by saying that the Indians would remain in Texas until it was ripe. His negotiations in Mexico were so successful, however, that Wild Cat called the Indians to the Rio Grande before the corn was ripe and had them transported into Mexico at the expense of the Mexican government.

Flushed with success, Wild Cat returned to the Llano in September and announced that he was on his way to the Indian territory to gather the balance of his people and conduct them to Mexico. On his way north he visited the Caddos and endeavored in many talks to induce them to join him in Mexico. To them he told another story of his warlike intentions: he would not make war on the wild Indians, the Comanches, but on the Texans; and for this purpose he would combine all tribes and punish those that refused to join him. He made similar talks to the Comanches and Wacos. The peaceful Caddos were so frightened by the dilemma that they broke into small parties, and passed down the Brazos where they hoped to remain until the Wild Cat had led his Seminoles southward.

On the last day of October Rollins wrote that the Indians had not put in their return appearance, but they were expected at any time, and under Wild Cat's leadership they would create a serious problem. 'I attach more importance to the movements of this man than to all of the Indian reports and intrigues of the day. Indeed it is *the intrigue* of the times when a single chief boldly enters upon the execution of a plan that, unless speedily frustrated, must end in a general war with possibly all of the Indian tribes.' [10]

The sub-agent, Marcus Duval, picks up the story of Wild Cat where the Texas agent lays it down. Wild Cat approached the Indians north of Red River with a plausible and lying tongue. He told them that he had found an ideal and permanent home for them, 'a country just suited to their wants,' on *this* side of the Rio Grande, and that all who desired, of whatever tribe, would be welcome to go there with him and remain there forever. Duval attempted to discredit the story by telling the Indians that it was false, that Wild Cat owned not a foot of land in Texas, and that the Texans wanted as few Indians as possible, but many of the Seminoles believed Wild Cat and prepared to follow him.

Wild Cat, instead of confining his activities to his own people, proceeded to stir up trouble with the lower Creeks for whom he had no love. On the night of October 19, he set out to talk to the upper Creeks, for whom he had some regard, but he turned back when he heard that the principal chief of the Creek nation had called out the light horse of the lower Creeks to arrest him. Wild Cat did not appreciate this news, and tried to express his displeasure to Agent Duval, whom he met. The conference was not a success because Duval had no interpreter and Wild Cat had too much liquor, but the Indian returned the next day better prepared for conversation, and told the agent that if the Creeks wanted trouble they could have it. Within three days' travel were Tawakonis, Caddos, and Keechies, ready to come to him at a moment's notice, and to come fighting. The Comanches in Texas were also his allies and he had sent runners to them. He would be ready for the lower Creeks, but if fighting started he did not want the whites, or the upper Creeks, to mix in it, but to stand aside and permit him and his enemies to fight it out Indian style. Would Agent Duval take this word to the upper Creeks and tell them that Wild Cat would not disturb their country, but would remain south of the Canadian where he could be found by those who wanted to meet him?

What would happen when this scheming Wild Cat's followers found that they had been deceived about the move to Texas? He would simply lie himself out of his difficulty by saying that the Texans had deceived him, and would then have a body of infuriated Indians at his heels with which to harass the border, plunder the California immigrants, and rob the wagon trains. 'I do not know such to be his

[10] John H. Rollins to Governor Bell, October 30, 1850. G.L.

intention, but he is a bold, restless, ambitious chief, and is not likely to be kept still by force or fear,' said Duval.

Nor was this all. Wild Cat was a liberator of slaves ten years in advance of Abraham Lincoln. In 1849 he had conducted a large number of runaway slaves to Mexico and settled them just across the line. Other negroes continued to run away — 150 to 200 within two months. They were ranging, said Duval, in bands of from forty to eighty, on the western borders of Texas, and would probably wait for Wild Cat to come south. Some of them belonged to whites, some to Seminoles, and some to Creeks. They would constitute a 'formidable band' in Texas where they would secrete, protect, and guide all runaway slaves who made their way to the Texas plains.

There was no doubt that Wild Cat was directing the flight of the slaves, but he skillfully concealed the fact, even from his own people, by pretending that the negroes fell in with him by chance, as happened on the Brazos. Having no authority over them, he could not prevent their going along with him to Mexico. Once in Mexico they would act as auxiliaries to Wild Cat on his incursions into Texas. Wild Cat had actually induced many Seminoles to join him by telling them that their negroes had already fled, and would be waiting for their masters on the Rio Grande. Duval enlightened them with the information that negroes were free in Mexico.

To Agent Duval these slaves were of great importance. He thought they should be arrested regardless of whether they came out of Texas or out of the Indian country. Did the governor have any force within fifty or eighty miles of Austin that could be used to catch them? The Indian owners would pay fifty dollars a head for every slave captured. Mr. George Aird was being sent to San Antonio to learn whether the negroes were to be arrested. 'There being such a number of them, mostly women and children [and therefore easily captured], it might be made of interest to a number of men or a company of Rangers to enter into their capture as a speculation; as it will pay if they only get one hundred.'

Agent Duval now revealed that he was not above using the Texas Rangers and the federal soldiers for his personal gain. In fact, as a subtle schemer, he ranks next to Wild Cat. Among the negroes who had fled the winter before were eighteen that had belonged to Duval's brother, and of these, twelve were supposed to be with Wild Cat. In the meantime the brother had died, and though Marcus Duval does not state it, we may assume that his interest in his dead brother's negroes was a thing apart from the duties of a Seminole sub-agent. A Mr. George Aird was bringing a list of the names of the negroes to

San Antonio, and it would be entirely agreeable for the governor and the military authorities to aid in capturing the property at the rate of fifty dollars a head.[11]

Governor Bell fell into the trap and suggested to General Brooke that the troops assist in capturing the negroes. General Brooke, evidently a northern man, and certainly one conscious of both law and propriety, replied in his usual courteous manner. He pointed out that Wild Cat was not in Texas, but in Mexico, on lands assigned him by the Mexican government, and that he had proved his prowess and fidelity to the Mexicans by whipping their enemies from the United States on two occasions. General Brooke readily admitted that Wild Cat had some negroes with him, but they might be Seminole slaves. The ownership of negroes was hard to determine, a matter of great delicacy. Moreover, Mr. Duval had not sent names nor the usual legal proof required. As for using the army to arrest fugitive slaves, that was unusual; the general could not recollect a single instance when either the regular army or the volunteers had been employed for that purpose. He had, however, issued orders to prevent negroes whose status had not been determined from passing into Mexico. The Comanches were to be instructed in council by Judge Rollins not to permit the passage of negroes through their country. They were to be told that if they found any blacks and delivered them to Fredericksburg they would receive fifty dollars for each one, but if they found a negro and did not deliver him they might expect trouble with the Great Father, the President of the United States.[12] There is no record that any of Wild Cat's negroes were delivered by federal troops, by Texas Rangers, or by Comanche Indians.

Wild Cat with his Seminoles, Kickapoos, and negroes found a permanent home by the Rio Grande near the Mexican town of Piedras Negras opposite Eagle Pass, Texas. Their descendants dwell there to this day in about the same state of civilization as their ancestors had in 1850. After the Civil War, the Seminoles composed a company of scouts in the federal army and rendered valuable service to Colonel R. S. Mackenzie in the last campaigns against the wild tribes of the plains.[13]

The Indian agents exercised such influence as they could over the native and resident Indians through councils and treaties. Making a treaty with a tribe, or several tribes, was a task that tried the patience

[11] Seminole Sub-Agent M. Duval to Governor Bell, October 20 and 21, 1850. G.L.

[12] General George M. Brooke to Governor Bell, November 12, 1850. G.L.

[13] For a brief account of Wild Cat and the Seminoles, see Cora Montgomery. *Eagle Pass, Life on the Border.*

of the agents sorely; and getting either the whites or the Indians to observe the treaty was even more difficult. In fact an Indian treaty was as big a farce as a modern international agreement. The intrigue, expressions of high regard, the concealment of the real purpose, the lying and cheating, and the general effort at face-saving were the same in the forests of Texas as they are at Portsmouth or Paris or London.

The preliminary procedure of an Indian treaty was about as follows: The agent, acting under orders, would decide that a treaty was desirable. He would then go into what he called the wilderness — the term hardly applied to a Plains country, yet there is no other word — and visit with the Indians. He would tell those whom he met that he hoped to see them at a certain time and place, on the Llano, or the Brazos, or by some other stream, probably in the vicinity of a trading house, give a few presents and more promises, and send dependable Indians to other tribes with the news and propaganda. If the Indians agreed to come in — and some of them would always agree — preparations were made for the assembly. Quantities of beads, hatchets, mirrors, and fine combs, of which the Indians were very fond and doubtless in great need, would be provided. A company of soldiers would be present, also some Texas Rangers if they were available, commissioners to make the treaty for Texas and the United States, and the agents. By the date set, the council ground would be a place of some activity, but in all probability no Indians would be there, save a few friendly ones who hoped by an early arrival to secure more than their share of the spoils of Indian treaties. A real Indian rarely kept an appointment on time; to do so sacrificed some measure of his independence. Some bands, usually of the Comanches, would not come at all, having no confidence in white men or in their own ability to out-tongue them in council.

Finally the council would assemble. Matters were conducted with much gravity, on the part of the white men in order to impress the Indians, and on the part of the Indians because gravity in council was in keeping with their nature. The chiefs and commissioners, captains, head chiefs, and old men occupied the center of the circle; behind each group stood the respective warriors, armed cap-a-pie. The peace pipe was passed from lip to lip in silence, and then the commissioner made a talk in which he stated the purpose of the council, expressed his love for the red man, and implied the overwhelming power of the Great Father. Then the Indians spoke, always with simplicity, and often with impressive eloquence and beauty. It was on a cloudy day in the middle of November, 1845, that a Wichita chief addressed himself to the Texans.

'I am a chief,' he said. 'You can stand and look at me and see what sort of man I am. I cannot see the sun, but the Great Spirit will look down and see me shake hands with my white Brothers.... I have now seen you myself and my heart beats for peace. I will go back and tell my warriors what I have seen. The Great Spirit hears me, the mother earth hears me and knows that I tell the truth. There is no use to talk too much, for men who do so may tell lies.'

Such speeches were not unusual among the Indians, though not all revealed the keen insight of the Wichita. After both the Indians and the whites had talked too much, and told a good many lies, the treaty was drawn and signed by the white men; the Indians made a mark opposite their names, which were phonetically written by white men, presents were distributed, and the council broke. The red men returned to their buffalo tipis and the whites to their cabin homes, but neither had any confidence that the other would do what had been promised. They were not unlike John W. Gates's description of the attitude of one stock manipulator towards another:

The tarantula jumped on the centipede's back
And chortled in ghoulish glee,
'I'll poison that murderous son-of-a-gun,
If I don't, he'll poison me.'

It is not practicable to follow in detail the activities of the Texas Indian agents as they pursued the thankless task of dealing with fickle, irresponsible, and primitive people. They might work for months to bring the Indians into a council and have all their efforts thwarted by some wild rumor set afloat by an unscrupulous trader. If the Lipans came into council they would report that the Comanches were hostile and preparing for war. The agents knew that the Lipans feared and hated the Comanches, that they wanted to join the Texans in war on them, partly to take revenge on their enemies and partly to have the opportunity of visiting San Antonio and other towns.

It was in the fall of 1850 that the agents undertook a series of councils with all the Texas tribes. After many preliminary conferences, the agents set the date November 15, 1850, for a general council with all the tribes. The Indians who came to the treaty grounds were Buffalo Hump's Comanches, the Caddos, Lipans, Quapas, Tawakonis, and Wacos. After the accustomed delay, and much deliberation, the treaty was signed on December 10, 1850.

Among the solemn agreements were the following: The United States should have the sole and exclusive right to regulate trade and would protect authorized traders. The Indians were to remain at peace with the United States and with all nations with whom the country was at peace, including the Indians of the north. The Indians were to give up criminals, surrender captives, both white and black, stop the passage of negroes through their country, return all stolen animals, stop the practice of horse theft, and deliver all young men who went on unauthorized raids to Fort Martin Scott for trial, and not come below the line of posts without written permission. The government would maintain trading houses, prohibit liquor, and send among the red men blacksmiths, school teachers, and preachers to administer their respective services to the tribes.

This frontier compact was signed by John H. Rollins, agent and commissioner, Captain H. W. Merrill of the army, Captain J. B. McGown of the Texas Mounted Volunteers (Rangers), by John Connor and Jesse Chisholm, interpreters. The proper scrawls were made by Buffalo Hump and eleven other Comanches, including Small Wolf, Never Stops, Pole Cat, and Rifle Breech, by six Caddos, four Lipans, five Quapas, four Tawakonis, and four Wacos. Among these signatories were such personages as Short Tail, Double-Barreled, and Hollow.

That the treaty was a fraud on the part of the whites was revealed in a letter which General Brooke wrote to Governor Bell on December 25, 1850. General Brooke sent a printed copy of the document to Governor Bell, but reminded the governor that the treaty was not binding: it was incomplete, made without instructions or authorization from the general government, and lacked the approval of the Senate, the reef of many and better treaties. It was of some value as an expression of friendship and of a desire for peace. He added that the Indians could not carry out their part of the agreement unless they were given annuities of food and clothing. The government should also send them farmers, blacksmiths, schoolmasters, and missionaries as an expression of its interest in their welfare. In short, the highest federal military commander in Texas informed the governor that both had co-operated in making a treaty that was binding only on the Indians, and that the terms were such that the Indians could not comply with them. Despite his candor, the general complained in less than sixty days that 'The Indians have not complied with a single article of their stipulations whilst we have complied with all.' They had used the treaty of December 10 as a *ruse de guerre* to secure the liberation of a Comanche boy. As soon as the grass rose he would send six companies against them, and would probably remuster the volunteers, known as Rangers.[14]

We have no record of what Buffalo Hump, Pole Cat, Small Wolf,

[14] Brooke to Major General R. Jones, Adjutant General, Washington, February 5, 1851. Copy to Governor Bell marked 'Confidential.' G.L.

and Short Tail were saying among themselves out on the plains. They were doubtless, in their simple way, congratulating themselves on having wrangled out of the white men some powder and lead with which to hunt the big game that they pestered and some fine combs with which to capture the smaller forms of life that pestered them, on having acquired the quantities of five-cent calicoes of bright colors with which to adorn themselves and the ten-cent mirrors to reflect their adornment. With sardonic mien they doubtless spoke of the fact that their promises would lull the white fools into repose which would enable ambitious warriors to raid deep into the settlements in search of blood-red scalps and bright bay horses.

3. FRAGMENTS OF WAR, 1848–1858

When the federal government assumed responsibility for the protection of the Texas frontier, it theoretically put the Texas Rangers out of business. Actually the institution survived as a flickering flame with little legal status and less financial support. Under the circumstances it could not develop able leaders, and did not conduct a single well-planned military campaign prior to 1858.

The story of the Rangers for the period is one of a struggle upward from the low state to which admission to the Union had reduced them. Each of the five governors pushed the Rangers a little higher than his predecessor had left them. Governor Wood ordered them from the sidelines only upon requisition of the United States military authorities; Governor Bell called them in emergencies and demanded that the federal government accept and pay them; Governor Pease went further in authorizing local companies with the pious hope that the federal government would refund the state's expense; Governor Runnels created an efficient state organization and with it waged successful war on both the Indian and the Mexican frontiers. Sam Houston returned to the executive chair with a far more vigorous policy, where Indians were concerned, than he had ever pursued as president of the Republic, but his use of the Rangers was mysterious and his purpose adroitly concealed. We know that he had in mind a grandiose scheme, a bold ambitious one, in which the Texas Rangers were to play the greatest rôle in their history. The activities of the Rangers from 1848 to 1858 will be followed in the remainder of this chapter. The fights they engaged in were what the frontiersmen call scrimmages, fragments of war Their more respectable achievements under Runnels and the grand plan formulated for them by Houston will be considered in later chapters.

On August 11, 1849, General George M. Brooke called on Governor George T. Wood for three companies of Rangers who were to establish headquarters at Corpus Christi and range the country from Goliad to the Rio Grande for six months. These companies were called because of Indian depredations. H. L. Kinney reported that thirty-six people had been killed, captured, or wounded, and 1353 head of horses had been stolen in Nueces and San Patricio counties. H. Clay Davis, tycoon of Rio Grande City, reported that several hundred families had been driven into Mexico, and so many captured that he had offered fifty thousand dollars for their return. Conditions were no better at Brownsville, from whence the citizens had sent a representative to induce the Washington authorities to raise a 'battalion of Texas Rangers to exterminate the Indians.' [15] Before the close of 1850 General Brooke had called for five companies of 79 Rangers each. The commanders were John S. Ford, Big Foot Wallace, J. B. McGown, Henry McCulloch, and R. E. Sutton. These men were tried soldiers and Rangers, and had they been continued in service, might have built up an efficient organization and performed much excellent service. The Ranger tradition prevailed, in that each Ranger was to furnish his own horse, saddle, bridle, halter, and lariat; the government supplied a percussion rifle, pistol, and ammunition.[16]

One of the earliest reports of these Rangers had to do with their bad conduct on the Mexican border. It seems that from Matamoros to Guerrero large quantities of merchandise were being smuggled across the river into Mexico. The duties were so heavy that the merchants found it more economical to bribe the Mexican officials than to pay the duty. The rivalry among the three ports of entry — Matamoros, Camargo, and Mier — for the favor and the dollars of the smugglers was very keen; and when the Camargo officials agreed to permit a cargo to cross for a fee of twenty-five per cent, the Mier officers contented themselves with 'a much less sum,' and got the business. When the merchants crossed near Mier they were met and captured by thirty-seven Mexican soldiers from Camargo. For the consideration of two thousand dollars a party of Texas Rangers and mustang hunters crossed and recaptured the cargo. Not only did they bring the new merchandise back, but they added to it the pants, shirts, and guns of the Mexican

[15] *Texas State Gazette*, August 29, September 1, October 20, December 29, 1849; January 26, May 11, 1850.

[16] Brooke to Bell, January 30, March 10, August 10, 1850, October 10, October 15, 1850. G.L.

soldiers. General Brooke reported the episode to the governor, expressed surprise that the Texas Rangers had conducted themselves in such an unbecoming manner, and declared that if the reports proved to be correct, he would disband them and oppose their further use.[17]

On January 14, 1850, Captain John J. Grumbles started in pursuit of a party of Indians that had ambushed and murdered Major Bryant near Goliad. The Rangers followed the Indians to the Woll road, fifteen miles from Fort Inge, but were forced to come into Fort Inge for provisions. Grumbles reported that with a fair start he could have diminished the number of ruthless murderers. 'As it was,' wrote the captain in the grand manner of the day, 'I was doomed to disappointment, and the war path that we followed with all the fury of revenge burning in our bosoms, we were compelled to retrace, sad, weary, and dejected.' [18]

The manner in which a company of Texas Rangers came into being is well illustrated in a report made by Captain R. E. Sutton of Goliad. On May 14, 1849, the Indians struck the upper settlements of Goliad County on the west side of the San Antonio River fifteen miles above the town, drove off all the horses of the neighborhood, and killed a horse and colt belonging to Colonel Hodges. A party of citizens pursued the Indians to the Calviers ranch, where they lost the trail. On June 2, the Indians returned and took the horses from Refugio mission, and on the following night they raided the Carlos ranch eighteen miles below Goliad, taking all the horses they could find and killing several head of cattle for Morgan O'Brien. On June 4 they relieved Sutton of six horses and the Hillyer ranch of two. Near Goliad they came upon a farm attended by two negroes. They stripped the negroes of their clothing, took all the food, ripped open the feather beds, and announced that they were going on to Goliad to whip the Americanos.

By this time the Americanos were on their trail under the leadership of J. W. Johnson and R. E. Sutton. They struck the Indians at eleven o'clock at night and dispersed them, capturing their buffalo robes, saddles, bridles, and shields.

The governor mustered this band of Indian fighters into the Ranger service on July 7 with Johnson as captain and R. E. Sutton as first lieutenant, and the company went into camp above Goliad on the San Antonio River. Having secured this much recognition, they hurried to

[17] P. W. Humphrey to Major George Deas, November 24, 1849; Colonel Henry Wilson to Deas, November 24, 1849; General George M. Brooke to Governor Bell, December 23, 1849. G.L.

[18] Captain John J. Grumbles to Governor Bell, January 30, 1850. G.L.

San Antonio to offer their services to the federal government, only to find that other companies — evidently those of Ford, Grumbles, and McGown — had been received. At the suggestion of the governor, they continued in service, depending on the governor (in case he were re-elected) to secure their pay from the state. Shortly after their return to Goliad, Captain Johnson was killed in an affray and the command passed to Lieutenant Sutton.[19]

Captain Henry McCulloch, who was guarding the Corpus Christi country, reported some excitement in his sector during the Christmas holidays of 1850. On December 12 he left his camp for a scout to Copano, Black Point, and Corpus Christi, passing over a country which he described as a barren waste of hogwallow prairie, with little timber and water and no inhabitants. Returning to camp on December 24, he learned that five squads of Rangers were out searching for Indians whose trail had been discovered. On December 26, Lieutenant King struck the trail going up the divide between the Madio and Aransas rivers. The Rangers came upon an encampment of Lipans on the east branch of the Madio within four miles of the Ranger headquarters. In the skirmish Lieutenant King was wounded and two Indians were supposedly killed. By daybreak the next morning McCulloch was on the trail which he followed for twenty-five miles. He reported that the chase now began in earnest, 'the Indians flying for life and I pursuing with all possible speed.' Robes, saddles, blankets, bridles, lariats, meat, and broken-down horses and mules marked the path of the red men for fifteen miles. The chase ended at a chaparral thicket where the Indians quit their horses and took to the brush on foot.[20]

This promising organization of Texas Rangers in the federal service was broken up in the fall of 1851 by order of General Brooke, and the responsibility for such protection as they were giving was thrown upon the governor.[21]

In August, 1852, the governor ordered the adjutant general, James S. Gillett, to muster three companies into service and station them along the Rio Grande. Gillett mustered one company at San Antonio under Captain Owen Shaw, one under G. K. Lewis at Corpus Christi, and a third under H. Clay Davis at Rio Grande City.[22]

Before these Rangers had built a campfire on the Rio Grande, Governor Bell dispatched one of his long-winded letters to President Millard Fillmore, demanding that they be taken over by the federal

[19] R. E. Sutton to Governor P. H. Bell, January 7, 1850. G.L.

[20] H. E. McCulloch to Major George Deas, January 4, 1851, copy to Governor Bell. G.L.

[21] Brooke to Bell, February 7, 1851. G.L. [22] Gillett to Bell, October 1, 1852. G.L.

government. The attempt of the Texas governor to dictate the policy at Washington brought a sharp and spirited reply from C. M. Conrad, Secretary of War, who stated that the Indians were generally peaceful and the reports of Indian atrocities had slight foundation. He reminded the governor that most of the troubles came from private malefactors who were subject only to state laws. If Texas could not defend its citizens against robbers and murderers, it surely should not 'expect the United States to *pay* the expences of the proceedings.' He added that the Texans had helped bring on the trouble by mixing in 'the criminal enterprises of Caravajal in violation of the laws of their country.' If these vagabonds and outlaws were driven from Mexico, and sought to indemnify themselves by raids in Texas, Texas must look after them. Conrad further incensed the Texans by intimating that the Texas Rangers were more expensive and less efficient than the regular soldiers. Though Conrad's letter contained much truth, it did not placate the Texans or induce them to maintain a state constabulary to control the outlaws and brigands of the magic valley.[23]

The meager reports from Governor Bell's Rangers do not indicate that they performed any heroic service on the Rio Grande. On September 15, 1852, Captain Owen Shaw, stationed at Laredo, received an express from Hamilton P. Bee, informing him that the Indians had crossed the river twenty-five miles above town and sacked the ranches as far down as Roma. Shaw intercepted their trail and overtook the Indians on September 17 in their camp on the San Roque, thirty miles northwest of Fort Ewell. The Indians issued from an arroyo in skirmish line and opened fire with rifles, arrows, and one six-shooter. From a distance of seventy-five yards the Rangers used their long rifles with telling effect. The Indians were driven from the arroyo by a charge, only to be cut down by mounted men on the prairie. Nine Indians were killed, eleven wounded, and one escaped; twenty-three horses and mules, with saddles, bridles, and arms were captured. Shaw did not name the tribe or give the number of Rangers engaged.[24]

This little victory called forth the following eulogy from the *Gazette*: 'Shaw has distinguished himself by this well-fought engagement and has proved to the people that he is worthy of the confidence placed in him by Governor Bell. He is, in my opinion, the very personification of a tip-top Ranger. Heat, rain, nor hunger — in fact, nothing can back him. His company too is one of the best ever called into service.'[25]

[23] C. M. Conrad to Governor Bell, September 10, 1852.

[24] Captain Owen Shaw to Governor Bell from Camp Bee, 15 miles above Laredo, September 22, 1852. G.L.

[25] *Texas State Gazette*, October 2, 1852.

'THE RANGERS USED THEIR LONG RIFLES WITH TELLING EFFECT'

That the Rangers were well pleased with themselves is indicated by a letter written by a member of the force from Camp San Francisco: 'Matters have changed very much since our arrival here. The citizens now feel perfectly secure... whereas before our arrival they were afraid to leave Laredo. There have been no Indians seen in this region since our fight with them.' [26]

H. Clay Davis, at Rio Grande City, was just as well pleased. Though no redskins had been seen, he kept fifteen or twenty men scouting and ranging with as much energy as had been exhibited by the most assiduous Texans of the past. His Rangers were, he said, like Mohawks; they struck terror to the Indian's soul, and made him prefer a cave in the mountains to the risk of 'encountering the rifles of those I have the honor to command.' [27]

The border was fairly quiet from 1852 to 1855, partly because the United States was undertaking to establish the Indians on a reservation in Texas, but during the last two years of Governor Pease's adminis-

[26] Unsigned letter from a member of Owen Shaw's Rangers, dated November 13, 1852, published, *Texas State Gazette*, November 27, 1852.

[27] H. Clay Davis to Governor Bell, December 12, 1852, from Camp del Monte. G.L.

tration there was considerable activity. Governor Pease called out at least six companies of minute men or Texas Rangers, one in 1855, one in 1856, and four in 1857.

The first company, commanded by J. H. Callahan, was ordered to range on the Guadalupe and later in Medina and Bexar counties. As the state treasury was empty, the men took the field with the understanding that they should furnish arms, horses, and ammunition, and await the act of a future legislature for pay. The evil consequences of such a system became evident in a short time. On September 4, 1855, Callahan left Bandera Pass in pursuit of a party of Lipans, who crossed the Rio Grande near Eagle Pass. Before Callahan's Rangers reached Eagle Pass, they fell in with a band of men under an adventurer named W. R. Henry, who had established a camp on the Leona in July and issued a call for volunteers to assist him in overthrowing the Mexican government. Henry claimed to have been a former Texas Ranger and to have been engaged by the federal government in an Apache campaign. Before leaving the federal service, he wrote the Governor of Chihuahua asking employment in fighting Indians in Mexico. He seemed to be willing to fight on either side of the Rio Grande and for any country that needed his services.

When Callahan came through on the Indian trail, it was only natural that Henry and his crowd should join in the chase. Their combined force, numbering 111 men, crossed the Rio Grande at Eagle Pass on October 2, and on the following day marched towards San Fernando, where the Indians were encamped. They were met in battle by a large body of Mexicans and Indians, and lost four men killed and seven wounded. At nightfall the Mexicans retired towards San Fernando and the Texans returned to Piedras Negras, which they captured on October 4. Callahan informed the Mexicans that he would hold the town until the Indians had been delivered or defeated, and he appealed to the Texans to come to his aid. He mentioned the Seminoles and Mescaleros, a thousand strong under Wild Cat and other celebrated leaders.

In spite of his bold talk, Callahan and Henry found it impossible to hold Piedras Negras in the face of the growing Mexican forces, but they found retreat to Texas dangerous because the Rio Grande had risen to cut them off. In order to escape from their situation, or to cover their plundering in the Mexican town, they set fire to Piedras Negras and crossed the river under the protection of the flames. The burning of Piedras Negras was wholly unwarranted and resulted in the dismissal of Callahan from the Ranger service. There can be little doubt that he was led on by Henry, and there is some evidence that he was actuated by a desire for plunder. The episode illustrated the danger of sending

Texas Rangers into the field with no provision for their maintenance and without assurance of payment for their services.[28]

In 1857 the use of the minute men was greatly extended. Governor Pease appointed at least four officers and stationed them at strategic points along the western frontier. John H. Connor was to protect Brown and San Saba counties; Thomas K. Carmack was to guard Erath and Palo Pinto; Neill Robinson was to scout the upper Guadalupe and Blanco valleys; and Thomas C. Frost was to pitch his camps in the bosques of Coryell and Comanche.[29]

Not one of these companies distinguished itself. Robinson, Neill, and Carmack left practically no record of their presence on the frontier, while Connor and Frost left but little to their credit. Connor managed to find a small party of Indians, but was completely deceived and worsted by them. When they first appeared 'driving a cavyyard of horses leasurely along,' he thought they were white men; when he saw that one had on a hat, he thought they were Caddos; when they 'razed the war hoop,' and shot his horse in the neck, he learned that they were Comanches. While Connor's horse bucked him off, the Indians charged his two companions, wounding one and dismounting the other.[30] Connor had proved by every rule of the frontier that he was not competent to carry a Ranger's commission: he could not see, ride, or shoot, and when Rip Ford took charge of the Rangers he promptly dismissed Connor from the service.

Thomas C. Frost made no better record than Connor, but did succeed in arousing the ire of the irascible Major Neighbors by his ill-advised reports. After reporting various Indian depredations in Comanche and adjoining counties, Frost expressed the opinion that the atrocities were committed or instigated by the Indians from the Texas reservations. He added, on hearsay, that when the people appealed to Major Neighbors for relief, they received curses, threats, and renewed outrages.[31]

No man could bring false charges against Major Neighbors without having to face them. Governor Runnels, who had succeeded Pease, sent the Frost letter to the military commander at San Antonio, who in turn passed it on to Neighbors. The agent wrote a scorching letter

[28] A detailed study of the Callahan raid is in preparation by Mr. Ike Moore to whom I am indebted for the above account. A complete list of sources will appear in Mr. Moore's study. Brief accounts of the episode may be found in Jesse Sumpter's Life, MS., University Archives, and in Olmsted, *A Journey Through Texas*, pp. 506–507.

[29] Letters and instruction of officers, dated November 23, 1857, signed by Governor E. M. Pease; Pease to Thomas C. Frost, December 7, 1857. G.L.

[30] Captain John H. Connor to Governor E. M. Pease, December 11, 1857. G.L.

[31] Thomas C. Frost to Governor H. R. Runnels, January 8, 1857. G.L.

to the governor branding all that had been said of him as 'absolutely false in every particular.' He took the governor to task for circulating the letter, and requested that a copy of his own letter be sent to Frost. Neighbors gave the facts about the raid conducted by six Comanches, and declared that had Frost spent as much energy in pursuit of Indians as he had in making a lengthy report, he might have overtaken the Indians and given them the punishment and the frontier the protection that he was employed to give.[32]

In the autumn of 1857 Governor Pease anticipated the future and present use of the Texas Rangers in civil disturbances by authorizing Captain G. H. Nelson to raise an 'emergency' company for the purpose of stopping the Texans of Karnes and adjoining counties from making war on Mexican teamsters who were driving freight wagons between Port Lavaca and San Antonio.

Captain Nelson recruited his men in San Antonio, New Braunfels, and San Marcos, and by October 20 was encamped on the Cibolo awaiting the wagon train which he escorted through Karnes County amidst considerable excitement. On the return trip, the Rangers passed near Helina a down train which belonged to G. L. Pyron of San Antonio and was in charge of William Pyron, the owner's brother. On November 21 — the day after Nelson had passed the train — when Pyron's cartmen went out to round up their oxen, two of them were killed and two others fled on foot for San Antonio. Pyron loaded the dead bodies into a wagon and drove to the Cibolo, where he buried the Mexicans and waited for the Rangers. The presence of the Rangers improved conditions so much that no further trouble was reported, and in December the 'emergency' company was disbanded.[33]

Though Governor Pease had advanced the Ranger force by calling several minute companies, he gave neither continuity nor able leadership to the service, but he foreshadowed the future by calling an emergency company for the suppression of civil disturbances. The next governor, Hardin R. Runnels, advanced the Rangers to a higher position and gave them the leader that was needed — John S. Ford. Whereas Pease sent the Rangers into scrimmages — fragments of war — Runnels sent them fighting over a thousand-mile frontier.

[32] Robert S. Neighbors to Governor H. R. Runnels, January 20, 1858. G.L.

[33] John Withers to Governor Pease, October 14, 1857; Captain G. H. Nelson to Governor Pease, November 14, 28, December 17, 1857. G.L.

VIII

THE BLOODY YEARS, 1858–1859

You may withdraw every regular soldier ... from the border of Texas ... if you will give her but a single regiment ... of Texas Rangers.

SAM HOUSTON

He [Iron Jacket] was followed by warriors and trusted for safety to his armor. The sharp crack of five or six rifles ... and in a few moments the chief fell riddled with balls.

JOHN S. FORD

I send you ... a small part of the Comanche Chiefs Coat of mail, it covered his body and each piece lapped over like shingles on a roof. It is all I could get as it was eagerly taken and divided by the boys.

Ranger ROBERT COTTER *to Governor* RUNNELS

I have this day crossed all the Indians out of the heathen land of Texas and am now out of the land of the Philistines. If you want to have a full description of our Exodus, read the 'Bible' where the children of Israel crossed the Red Sea. We have had about the same show, only our enemies did not follow us to Red River.

ROBERT S. NEIGHBORS

VIII. THE BLOODY YEARS, 1858–1859

1. *RIP FORD'S CAMPAIGN*

GOVERNOR HARDIN R. RUNNELS entered the executive office in January, 1858, determined to give protection to the frontiers. Under the aegis of his resolve the fires that had been smouldering since Texas entered the Union burst into the flames of war and the Texans' rifles roared from the Indian tipis north of Red River to the Mexican *jacales* south of the Rio Grande. There was more fighting and bloodshed in Texas in the two years, 1858–1859, than in any other similar period save only that of the Revolution in 1836.

Having despaired of federal aid, the legislature, immediately after assembling, passed a law for the better protection of the frontier. The governor approved the law on January 27, 1858, and on the following day sent a commission to the experienced Ranger, John S. (Rip) Ford, appointing him to the supreme command of all state forces with the title of Senior Captain. Ford was authorized to call a hundred additional men and instructed to establish headquarters at some suitable point on the frontier. He was told to co-operate with the federal authorities and Indian agents, but to brook no interference with his plan of operation from any source. 'Your position,' wrote the governor, 'will be one of some delicacy, but I hope your sense of duty, your desire to be useful to the State, and your judgment will be sufficient to steer you through any difficulty.'

And as to Indians: 'I impress upon you the necessity of action and energy. Follow any and all trails of hostile or suspected hostile Indians you may discover, and if possible, overtake and chastise them, if unfriendly.' [1]

The governor's choice of Ford as supreme commander was a wise one. In fact, no better man could have been found in Texas to execute such bold designs as were now on foot. Ford left Austin for the frontier in February and made his first report from Brown County on the

[1] Copy of Ford's commission, dated January 28, 1858; Governor H. R. Runnels to Ford, January 28, 1858, and February 13, 1858. G.L.

MAJOR JOHN S. (RIP) FORD

twenty-seventh of that month. The published accounts of the Indian depredations there had not been exaggerated. Many settlements were deserted, property loss had been great, and a feeling of insecurity had paralyzed business. If he were to go over the whole line, he would need twenty-five more men. There was some question in his mind as to whether the minute men (under Connor, Carmack and Frost) who were on the frontier should continue in service. His own Rangers were in high spirits, cheerful, and anxious for a fight.[2]

The governor replied that Ford must use his discretion as to new men, but warned him not to exceed the state appropriation for the expedition. Whatever was to be done must be done quickly, declared the executive. Public opinion and the state demanded it. It was hoped that the 'most summary punishment would be inflicted on the enemy.'[3]

In the meantime Ford had exercised his authority as Senior Captain to order John H. Connor and his minute men out of service on March 1. Connor began pulling political wires which resulted in a barrage of protesting letters to the governor, who in irritation wrote Ford on March 10 telling him not to be influenced by 'the howlings of corrupt and designing bad men.' Said he: 'I have seen the letter of the old *vagabone* written to the *Intelligencer*.... I suspect some puppy now in the pay of the State and living on supplies furnished for the substance of the men in the service to have done this thing and if I had proof of it I would order him dismissed the service.... If you call out any more men I shall object to Connor or one-eyed Indians as commanders.... You will have the right to pick your men. This you must attend to. I have nothing to do with giving men the preference nor have you, because they have been in the service, or because they have contracted debts expecting to be kept in service.... Dispense with any portion of the men whenever you are satisfied they are no longer needed and consider this your order for doing so. *I am responsible.*'

Warming to his subject, the governor declared that a thousand men on the frontier would not satisfy everybody, and that the dismissal of any would raise just such a row as that voiced by 'The Hells hounds who are noising about Connor and his men being dismissed.' The thing to be reckoned with now was public opinion, and what with such a large force on the frontier the people would want to hear of some action, 'to hear of Indians and their being whipped.' True, frontier people were a little unreasonable. If they lose 'a cow or a Jackass occasionally,' it is because they place themselves where such losses may be expected. In reality the state could better afford to pay for cow or jackass than to spend

[2] Ford to Runnels, February 27, 1858. G.L.

[3] Runnels to Ford, March 7, 1858. G.L.

ten times their price for troops, but since the troops were out they could only justify themselves by getting results. 'If something is not done the people who have the bill to foot will regard the whole affair as humbug gotten up for the benefit of a few croakers whose wish is to live from the public crib and those of us who have lent a willing ear to reports as dupes only.' Ford was told to move quickly and quietly, and to remember that his own and the governor's reputation depended upon some immediate and drastic action.[4]

Before this challenging letter had reached him, Ford had broken his command into four detachments which swept the country from Brown County to the Brazos Reservation in parallel routes. Lieutenant Edward Burleson moved by the Camp Colorado road; Nelson by Palo Pinto; Tankersley by Comanche and Buchanan (now Stephens); and Pitts, accompanied by Ford, moved by way of Eastland and Buchanan.

Ford reached the Reservation on March 19, where plans were made to induce the Reserve Indians to join the expedition. Captain L. S. Ross, the agent, called the chiefs to council where their war spirit was stirred against their age-old enemies, the Comanches. A hundred warriors volunteered, and spies were immediately sent running up the tongue of Cross Timbers to locate the camps of the enemy north of Red River. Forsooth the Texans were going now to meet the Comanches on their own hunting ground, even beyond the Texas border.[5]

In each letter to the governor, Ford expressed the greatest confidence in his ability to accomplish his mission. On April 7 he answered the governor's letter already alluded to, and accepted its challenge. He was writing from the Brazos Reserve with the Indians around him. The chiefs had assembled a hundred men who had placed themselves under Captain Shapley P. Ross, son of the agent. Tomorrow the Indians would dance and hold high carnival and Ford would be present among them. They were pretty good Indians, had cut loose from the wild tribes, were farming, and becoming civilized. They had fields of wheat and corn. Near him were wagons drawn by oxen and driven by red men; in the fields the women and children were dropping corn. There were eleven hundred of these simple folk, and if some of them had not killed somebody's cattle or stolen a few horses, they were better than an equal number of people in the settlements, said Ford.

All was in readiness for the expedition which would move on April 20. The whereabouts of the Comanches was known and the expedition would move directly, swiftly upon them. Ford would consider anything short of a telling victory a disastrous failure; he wanted to assume

[4] Runnels to Ford ('Private and Confidential'), March 10, 1858. G.L.

[5] Ford to Runnels, March 31, 1858. G.L.

full responsibility and to take all the blame for failure. 'I am anxious to save you harmless in case of misfortune. You may rest assured the apprehensions of our not being able to meet the enemy, beat them, and justify the expediency of the expedition, are few and far between.'[6]

On April 22 a cavalcade consisting of one hundred and two men, two wagons, an ambulance, and fifteen pack-mules left Camp Runnels, near the Reservation, and toiled northward over the rolling plain. At Cottonwood Springs the army was augmented by Captain Shapley P. Ross and his one hundred and thirteen braves from the Brazos Reserve. Ford had hoped to receive twenty more white men here, but these had fallen under the influence of John R. Baylor, who was by this time assuming his sorry rôle as trouble-maker, which he played consistently and with little credit.[7]

On April 29, Ford crossed Red River and marched up the north bank, making frequent stops, and sending out spies and small detachments to gather information. On May 7, he left Red River for the Washita, a branch of which he reached the next day. He was now well outside the limits of Texas and in the enemy's country. On May 10, the spies killed a buffalo from which they extracted two Comanche arrowheads, and on the following day they saw some Indians running and killing buffalo. The direction taken by the Indians' meat-laden ponies told the Rangers the direction in which their objective lay.

Observing every precaution of stealth, Ford's two hundred and fifteen men left camp at two o'clock on the afternoon of May 11. At the intersection of the Fort Smith and Santa Fe road, they spied Indians in a valley beyond the divide, apparently unconscious of their proximity to a dangerous foe. The Rangers and their allies advanced cautiously by ravine and draw while the Keechi trailer went to locate the exact position of the Comanche camp.

The attack on the Indian camp was planned for seven o'clock on the morning of May 12. The Rangers came first on five lodges which were demolished by the Tonkawas who took some prisoners, and mounted themselves on Comanche horses. Two Comanches escaped toward the Canadian, and were followed at full speed by the whole body of Rangers and their red auxiliaries. After a run of three miles the pursuers topped out on a hill from which they saw the conical white skin tipis of the main village three miles distant on the Cherokee side of the Canadian.

The Comanches, warned by the flying couriers from the first camp, were ready for the attack. Their chief was none other than Iron

[6] Ford to Runnels ('Private'), April 7, 1858. G.L.

[7] Ford to Runnels, April 26, 1858; John R. Baylor to Runnels, April 23, 1858. G.L.

Jacket whose name and reputation for invulnerability were both derived from an old coat of mail which had inexplicably come down to him from some illustrious Spaniard. After the first clash, Iron Jacket appeared in gorgeous array, shingled, as it were, in overlapping pieces of steel, and bore down on the Rangers' red allies.

'He was followed,' wrote Ford, 'by warriors and trusted for safety to his armor. The sharp crack of five or six rifles brought his horse to the ground, and in a few moments the chief fell riddled with balls. Our Shawnee guide, Doss, and Jim Pockmark the Anadarco Captain, claim the first and last wounds. The fight was now general, and extended very soon over a circuit of six miles in length and more than three in breadth. It was, in fact, almost a series of single combats. Squads of Rangers and Indians were pursuing the enemy in every direction. The Comanches would occasionally halt and endeavor to make a stand... their efforts were unavailing [and] they were forced to yield ground in every instance. The din of battle had rolled back from the river — the groans of the dying, cries of frightened women and children, mingled with the reports of firearms, and the shouts of men as they rose from hill top, from thicket, and from ravine.

'The second chief had rushed into the conflict with the friendly Indians. A shot from the Shawnee Captain, Chul-le-qua, closed his career. The Comanches between the camp and the river were all killed or driven from the field, and our red allies sent up a wild shout of triumph.'

The Rangers and friendly Indians continued the pursuit until their horses could stand no more. It was now high noon and the victors began to round up the captured camp, the horses, prisoners, and trophies, always the *desideratum* in border wars. Meanwhile another Indian encampment some three or four miles up the Canadian had heard the din of battle, embodied, and were now threatening to charge the Rangers. There followed one of those marvelous exhibitions of savage warfare of the plains which has ever been the theme of those fortunate enough to observe it. Ford's description of it would do credit to Parkman.

'They [the Comanches] were evidently playing for an advantage and their maneuvers induced our Indians to believe them very strong. Our allies proposed to draw them out and requested me to keep my men in line to support them, if necessary. The Comanches descended from the hill to accept their professed invitation. With yells and menaces, and every species of insulting gesture, and language, they tried to excite the Reserve Indians into some act of rashness by which they could profit. A scene was now enacted beggaring description. It re-

'THE COMANCHES DESCENDED FROM THE HILL'

minded one of the rude and chivalrous days of Knight-errantry. Shields and lances, and bows, and headdresses — prancing steeds and many minutiae were not wanting to complete the resemblance. And when the combatants rushed at each other with defiant shouts, nothing save the piercing report of the rifle varied the affair from a battlefield of the middle ages. Half an hour was spent in this without much damage to either party. A detachment of Rangers advanced to reinforce the friendly Indians, and the Comanches quitted the field, and the imposing pageant vanished from view, like a mimic battle upon the stage.'

The fighting again became general and lasted until two o'clock. Every conflict resulted in victory for the Rangers. Though Buffalo Hump was reported to be twelve miles away with a large force, he was not molested because horses and men were completely exhausted by seven hours of fighting.

Ford estimated that he had engaged three hundred warriors. The Texans had killed seventy-six Indians, captured over three hundred horses, and eighteen prisoners, 'mostly women and children.' The Texans had two killed and two wounded.

Ford commended warmly the services of the youthful Shapley P. Ross who led the Reserve Indians and paid tribute to his four captains whose names have been mentioned. 'They behaved under fire,' he said, 'in a gallant and soldier-like manner and I think they have fully vindicated their right to be recognized as Texas Rangers of the old stamp.' Captain Nelson, in a separate report, declared that 'The only distinction in the ardour of the entire command was the relative speed of their horses.'

On the day following the battle, Ford took up the return march to Texas, arriving at Camp Runnels on May 21, after an absence of some thirty days. The difficulty of the march is indicated by the fact that both his wagons and the ambulance broke down and were abandoned. Ford sent the governor a map showing his line of march, which, unfortunately, cannot be found in the records.

In Ford's eyes the campaign was of much importance. It had demonstrated that the Indians could be followed, found, and defeated in their own country; it proved that the buffalo ranges beyond Red River could be penetrated and held by white men. Ford might have added — and he may have had it in mind — that what was most needed for such undertakings was a leader with brains and courage. Texas had not lacked men to follow; what it had lacked for ten years or more was a Texas Ranger with brains supported by a governor with enough internal fortitude to back him up. Ford and his men had rescued an ideal.[8]

Ford participated in no more fighting at this time on the upper Indian frontier, but he did procure information about the Indians that probably influenced the policy of the United States and perhaps led indirectly to the campaign and victory of Van Dorn. On July 1, Captain L. S. Ross invited Ford to come to the Brazos Agency for a conference. Ford remained there until July 5, when Jim Little One, a Caddo, and Anadarko Jim, returned from a spying trip north of Red River where they had been sent to determine the identity of raiders in Jack County. The reports brought by these two Indians were not reassuring for the future. At the Keechi and Kickapoo villages they found all the men absent — on a buffalo hunt, the women said. At the Caddo village they found an American horse which they asked

[8] Ford wrote his official report to Governor Runnels on May 22, the day after he reached Camp Runnels. The first two pages of this original letter were found in the governor's papers in the state library and the remaining pages were found in the adjutant general's office some six years later. In addition to Ford's report there is one by Lieutenant A. Nelson, May 21, 1858. The fate of Iron Jacket's coat of mail is revealed in an undated letter from Robert Cotter, a first sergeant, to the governor. 'I send you... a small part of the Comanche Chiefs Coat of mail, it covered his body and each piece lapped over like shingles on a roof. It is all I could get as it was eagerly taken and divided by the boys.'

Chief Chic-ah-he to account for. The chief said that the horse had been 'found' in the Wichita Mountains. The horse, an iron gray with the letter 'S' on the right hip, a sunken scar on the left side near the last rib, and split ears, was delivered. Chic-ah-he now asked if this were the only horse they were seeking. The Indians answered, 'No. There are others.' The Keechi then told them there were three more in the Wichita camp — also 'found' in the mountains.

Away went Anadarko Jim and Jim Little One to examine the three horses at Arbuckle. The commanding officer asked the two spies to remain there until the Kickapoo and Keechi hunting parties returned — perhaps their hunt had resulted in 'finding' more horses. But this invitation was diplomatically declined. The spies heard that a small band of Comanches had in their possession some American property — a bob-tailed mare, a dun American mule, a black vest and some other garments. The Kickapoo trader told them that the hunting parties were not bringing furs and peltries, but horses which they claimed to have won from the Comanches.

Ford was of the opinion that all these civilized Indians were in alliance with the Comanches. These Indians had recently held a council and agreed to consolidate the seven bands under Chief Pa-ha-yo-co. They had made a treaty with the tribes east of Red River. While one band had gone into the Creek country with all the women and children, the other six were to continue the war, and if crowded, were to fall back on that refuge and gain allies.

Ford said that if he were continued in service he would not hesitate to move on the head chief, punish him, and all others who interfered with his movements or aided his enemies. He would also punish the traders who were growing rich from the bloody traffic. What was needed was a strong force and a winter campaign.[9]

While Ford was writing his report, the governor was preparing a letter ordering him to disband his command because the regiment bill in Congress was doomed. At the same time, General D. E. Twiggs wrote to his superior officer recommending a drastic change of federal policy in Texas, saying that for ten years 'we have been on the defensive.' A regiment should be sent into the Indian country, to follow the Indians summer and winter, to give them something to do at home in taking care of their families.[10] To Governor Runnels he wrote that he had always considered the federal force too small to give protection, and that the best way to protect Texas was to send a mounted

[9] Ford to Runnels, July 5, 1858. G.L.

[10] General D. E. Twiggs to Lieutenant Colonel L. Thomas, July 6, 1858. G.L.

force into the Indian country. 'As long as there are wild Indians on the prairie, Texas cannot be free from depredations.' [11]

General Twiggs asked permission to send three or four cavalry companies into the Indian country and at the same time Governor Runnels poured two hot letters broadside into John B. Floyd, Secretary of War, and James Buchanan, President.[12] He incorporated Ford's arguments and information, Twiggs's recommendations, and the statements of Major Neighbors, and intimated that unless some action were taken, Texas would take some bold steps. The result of this agitation was Van Dorn's campaign and signal victory of October 1, 1858.

On August 9, the War Department ordered four companies of cavalry and one of infantry to march from Fort Belknap on September 15 and establish a depot on Otter Creek, west of the Wichita Mountains, in the present state of Oklahoma. From this base scouting parties were to scour the country between Red River and the North Fork of the Canadian and from meridian 100 to 104 east and west.[13]

The details of Van Dorn's march from Belknap are not known. He left on September 15 with four companies of the Second Cavalry and one of the Fifth Infantry. He was also accompanied by L. S. Ross and one hundred and twenty-five friendly Indians from the Reserve. He marched northwest, and established his depot as directed. On September 29 his spies brought him word that the Comanches were in force at a point ninety miles east of him. Taking his cavalry and Indians Van Dorn made the march in thirty-seven hours, and a little after daybreak on the morning of October 1 he charged the camp of one hundred and twenty lodges, which housed over five hundred Indians. The battle lasted for thirty minutes, 'during which there were many hand-to-hand engagements.' Fifty-six Indian warriors were left dead on the field, all the lodges were burned, three hundred horses were captured, and the surviving Indians were dispersed among the mountains. General Twiggs declared that this was 'a victory more decisive and complete than any recorded in the history of our Indian warfare.' This may be true, but if it is true, it only serves to show the magnitude of Ford's victory five months earlier in which he killed more Indians with fewer men and less loss. On this occasion five men,

[11] Twiggs to Runnels, September 9, 1858. G.L.

[12] General D. E. Twiggs to Lieutenant Colonel L. Thomas, July 27 and August 4, 1858; Runnels to John B. Floyd, August 9, 1858; Runnels to President James Buchanan, September 17, 1858. G.L.

[13] A. M. Dunkard, Acting Secretary of War, to Governor H. R. Runnels, August 28, 1858. G.L.

including two officers, were killed; both Van Dorn and Ross were wounded along with eight or nine others.[14]

With the Van Dorn victory we come to the end of the aggressive military campaign, on the northern border of which it is not too much to say that John S. Ford had been the prime mover. The Comanches had been followed beyond the limits of Texas and defeated first by Ford's Texas Rangers on the Canadian and again by Van Dorn's regulars. In both campaigns the Reserve Indians of Texas had rendered good and honorable service. The story of their sorry reward will be related in the following section.

2. *THE RESERVE INDIANS*, 1855–1859

When Ford and Van Dorn pursued the Comanches beyond the Red River and practically annihilated those they found in what is now Oklahoma, they turned a page in the story of the Texas frontier. The Indians never again attacked the people of the Texas frontier with the confidence which they had exhibited hitherto, because they had learned that they had no retreat safe from the Rangers or from the United States soldiers south of the Red. But before the Texans were free from the wild Indians who were their avowed enemies, they turned on those left in the state who had professed friendship by settling on reservations and had proved it by joining the expeditions against the Comanches.

As early as 1852 it was well known that many of the Indians in Texas were destitute. Agent John Rollins had said they had to choose between stealing and starving; General Brooke declared that they could not observe the treaties they made without subsistence and clothing; and even the Texas newspaper editors conceded as early as 1853 that their condition was deplorable. A waspish editor jumped on the United States Government for giving the Indians glittering and gorgeous trinkets instead of food. Their need was for bacon, corn, and farming tools.[15]

The advantages of gathering the Indians on reservations where they could be guarded, fed — and protected — were not considered by the Texans prior to 1853. In that year Jefferson Davis became Secretary of War, and brought to the office an intense interest in all

[14] General D. E. Twiggs's printed report, October 19, 1858, Indian Depredations Papers State Library.

[15] *Texas State Gazette*, February 26, 1853.

that pertained to the West. On September 19, 1853, Davis wrote to Governor Bell that the protection of the frontier was the most difficult problem facing the army, and 'nowhere has it been found more difficult, than on the Western frontier of Texas.' The vast extent of the Texas plains and their proximity to Mexico, where the Indians could find a safe retreat while they formulated new plans, made it impossible for the force at the disposal of the army, or any force in proportion to that required elsewhere, to give the security expected by the people of Texas. The trouble arose from the fact that the Indians had the right to roam in Texas, but the troops did not have the right to molest them unless they committed an outrage. If Texas would give the Indians a defined territory, a reserve, the government could restrict them to it and the military could take control of them if they were found elsewhere. The United States had adopted such a policy with success, and Texas might imitate the nation by setting aside a reserve.[16]

Six months later, Governor Pease sent Davis a law which the legislature had passed providing for the Indian reserves within Texas.[17] The law, approved February 6, 1854, provided that twelve leagues of land should be set aside in three separate reserves for the Indians. No reserve was to be placed farther than twenty miles within the line of posts which separated the Indian range from the settlements.[18] The government appointed Captain Randolph B. Marcy of the army and Robert S. Neighbors to make the surveys. These two men met at Fort Belknap, in Young County, and set out to locate the land. They called in the chiefs of the Anadarkos, Caddos, and Wacos, who lived on the Brazos below Fort Belknap, and asked them where they preferred to make their permanent homes. These Indians expressed their willingness to live anywhere *below* Fort Belknap, but feared to live north or west of it, where they would be subject to the fury of the Comanches and Kiowas who would not even permit them to hunt on the western range. The commissioners promptly selected four leagues of land below the fort and surveyed it in the presence of the Indians who were to occupy it. This reservation was located about twelve miles below Fort Belknap, on the Brazos, and was commonly called the Brazos Reserve. The more docile Indians were congregated here, and remained throughout their residence faithful to the whites.[19]

Having finished this part of their task, Marcy and Neighbors turned

[16] Jefferson Davis to Governor P. H. Bell, September 19, 1853. G.L.

[17] Governor E. M. Pease to Jefferson Davis, March 13, 1854. Military Papers, S.A.

[18] Gammel, *Laws of Texas*, vol. III, pp. 149 f.

[19] A concise statement of facts concerning the Reserve Indians, together with a bibliography, may be found in Virginia P. Noel, *The United States Indian Reservations in Texas, 1845–1859*. M.A. Thesis, University of Texas.

to the southern Comanches. These Indians, cut off from their northern brethren and caught between the whites and the wild tribes of the Plains, were for the time being ready to accede to the wishes of the Great Father. They had lost their primitive Comanche vigor without losing their desire for gain or their aversion for work. They were truthful enough to say that they had never planted corn, but were deceptive enough to agree to the experiment, if the Great Father would send some white farmers to teach them the art. The sequel will show that they yielded only to the point of observing the operation.

For this sorry remnant of the Comanche nation, Marcy and Neighbors surveyed four leagues of land on the Clear Fork of the Brazos, about forty miles southwest of Fort Belknap, in what is now Shackelford and Throckmorton counties. It was reported to be a good country, abounding in wood and water; corn was already growing there to prove the fertility of the soil. These two reservations were designed to meet the needs of all the willing Indians of central Texas. To the far west, in the deserts of the Trans-Pecos, were the Mescalero Apaches and their kinsmen the Lipans. For them four leagues of land were surveyed adjacent to the Ionie-Anadark-Waco Reserve on the Brazos. The commissioners expressed the opinion, however, that these Trans-Pecos bands would not come to central Texas to live, but would prefer to remain where they were.[20]

The next task — that of rounding up and bringing in the Indians — devolved almost wholly on Robert S. Neighbors, who was indefatigable where Indians were concerned. Many difficulties attended his efforts, enough to exhaust the patience of a less conscientious and persistent person, but he met and surmounted most of them.

As already noted, some of the Indians were camped at or roaming in the vicinity of the Brazos Agency. These Indians — Caddos, Ionies, Wacos, Tawakonis, and others — were left in charge of Major Neighbors's assistant, George Hill. The first obstacle the agents met was government delay. The Indians were destitute, and dependent on the whites for home and food, but neither was available. Hill reported that he found the Comanches dying of starvation; those living were preparing to eat their horses and remain friends of the whites. Hill's troubles were further increased by the circulation of alarming rumors. A German named Lyendecker created consternation among the Indians by reporting that the white people were gathering them to the reservation for convenience in exterminating them. Sanaco, the Comanche chief, immediately cleared out for higher altitudes and purer

[20] Robert S. Neighbors and Randolph B. Marcy to George Manypenny, Fort Belknap, September 30, 1854. Indian Affairs Papers, S.A.

air, taking with him eight hundred followers. It was thought that he would join the northern Comanches.[21]

The United States soldiers also caused their share of trouble. Major Neighbors reported that three companies of dragoons were encamped near the Brazos Agency with the avowed purpose of making war on the Texas Indians. The settlers now became alarmed, fearing that an indiscriminate war would follow in which the friendly Indians would be involved. Neighbors dryly observed that while one department was busy trying to settle the Indians and turn them toward peace, another department was inciting them to war.

Even Neighbors's assistants added to his difficulties by their incompetence and bungling. George Howard had collected some two hundred and fifty Tonkawa Indians on the Nueces near Fort Inge, but the commander of Fort Inge would not permit them to come within the line of forts, even temporarily. Neighbors immediately went over the petty officer's head in an appeal to General Persifer F. Smith for protection and a change of policy, and purchased wagons, probably in San Antonio, to transport Howard's Indians' baggage over the several hundred miles of arid country separating Fort Inge on the Nueces from the Reserve on the Brazos.[22]

Howard then reported that he was unwell, and Neighbors himself set out for Fort Inge to bring in the Indians, but when he arrived there on April 5, he found them all gone. A citizen named Saunders, at the head of an armed band of citizens, had come down upon them for the purpose of running them off and taking their ponies. The Tonkawas managed to stand off the white men, but became alarmed at what might follow, and stampeded to parts unknown.[23] Neighbors blamed Howard for the fiasco, and expressed the opinion that the service would improve if Howard were retired.

While Neighbors was in the far west, Hill was making some progress on the Brazos. He reported that he had assembled his Indians and had started farming operations. But even these were attended with difficulties, both historical and providential. The farmers had made a late start and a drought was on — no rain had fallen for nine months, not since the previous June. In the face of this, some corn was being planted.

The Comanches offered a different problem where farming was in question. For one thing, Sanaco and his band had fled. Ketumseh's band was there, and runners had been sent to the fugitive Sanaco who

[21] George Hill to R. S. Neighbors, Fort Belknap, January 25, 1855. I.O.L.R.

[22] Robert S. Neighbors to George W. Manypenny, San Antonio, Texas, April 2, 1855 I.O.L.R.

[23] R. S. Neighbors to George W. Manypenny, San Antonio, April 17, 1855. I.O.L.R.

had left in January. Word had come that Sanaco's Comanches were destitute, naked, without ammunition, had already eaten their dogs and started on their horses. Two renegade Mexicans had told Sanaco's Indians that Ketumseh and George Hill were eating together at the Brazos Reserve, and that Ketumseh's followers were full of food and contentment. Upon hearing this, the Indians fell upon Sanaco and other chiefs and captains with abusive language, accusing them of possessing hearts of women. The band divided: some went north, some came into the Reserve; and Sanaco, declaring that the hearts of his people had forsaken him, set off to see the Santa Fe New Mexicans.

The truth of the matter was that all was not beer and skittles with Ketumseh's Comanches at the Reservation. The agent urged them to plant corn, but they declared that they preferred to wait until they could do it on their own land. They did not wish to have anything to do with corn planting until then, but were willing to 'look and learn.'

By June 10, 1855, Neighbors reported that the Comanches were on their own reserve — two hundred and forty-nine of them, and others were expected.[24] John R. Baylor, their agent, made a favorable report on them, saying that if their progress continued they would in a few years be a happy and contented people. On January 1, 1856, Baylor reported four hundred and fifty present, and warned that too much should not be expected of these wild people. He was still of the opinion that they could be fed cheaper than they could be whipped.[25] John R. Baylor may have made a truthful report, but the venomous attitude which he exhibited after his dismissal from the Indian service, and his constant conspiring to bring on the destruction of his former charges and to wreck all of Major Neighbors's plans, arouse some doubt as to his sincerity here and his reliability in general.

In June Major Neighbors reported that five hundred and fifty-seven Indians were at the Brazos Reserve, and two hundred more were expected by July 1, among them the Tonks, who were assembled at Fort Clark, near the Rio Grande. On August 27, Neighbors and Hill went through the formality of holding a general Indian council. The agents wrote the treaty and the Indians signed it without reservation and with little knowledge of its contents. Among the signers was Ketumseh.[26]

It would seem that Major Neighbors's efforts had been rewarded with a large measure of success. He had gathered in practically all the Indians save the northern Comanches and Kiowas, and he held their

[24] R. S. Neighbors to George W. Manypenny, Fort Belknap, June 10, 1855. I.O.L.R.

[25] See Baylor's letters dated October 7 and 31, 1855; also his report, January 1, 1856. I.O.L.R.

[26] R. S. Neighbors to George W. Manypenny, Fort Belknap, June 10, 1855; Neighbors to Charles E. Mix, Brazos Agency, September 5, 1855. I.O.L.R.

unbounded confidence. We have seen that on two occasions the Indians proved their allegiance to Texas by furnishing valuable auxiliaries for destructive expeditions against the northern Indians. Two years went by in comparative peace; then the storm which swept the Reserve Indians beyond the borders of Texas, and cost Major Neighbors his life, broke. Neighbors had proved his ability to handle the red men and, to some extent, protect the settlers; the task of controlling the whites and protecting the Indians proved insuperable for him.

The situation of the Reserve Indians was nevertheless a precarious one. Their petty domiciles had been located directly in the path of that migratory horde of whites who had now come to the very edge of the Plains. On the other side, to the north and west, were the wild Comanches and their untamed allies. Between these two devastating forces the weak bands of the reservation could make no choice that would not bring them to the same end.

The Comanches had good cause for their bitterness. They had not forgotten that these government pets had come with Ford's Rangers and Van Dorn's regulars to kill their chiefs and warriors, burn their tipis, and capture their squaws, papooses, and ponies. Their scorn for an Indian who would attach himself to white men was exceeded only by their hatred of one who would fight with white men against Indians. Though they dared not make an open attack on either the Reserve Indians or the whites, they took their revenge on both. They came into Texas in small bands, skulking along the streams, traveling by moonlight, and lying up in the day until they found the settlers' cabins. Then they mounted themselves on good fast horses, killed whom they could, took scalps where they found them, and made a trail that any Texan could follow to the front door of the Reservations. There they would scatter, leaving little more trail than the crows above them, and permitting their pursuers to form their own conclusions. By such adroitness they led the frontiersmen, who were ever ready to believe the worst about any Indian, to conclude that their troubles were coming from the Reserves of the Clear Fork and the Brazos. In that case the only course for them was to exterminate the Reserve Indians or drive them from Texas.

Between the Reserve Indians and the infuriated Texans stood the resolute figure of Robert S. Neighbors. He realized that the Reserve Comanches under Ketumseh could not be controlled as long as the northern Comanches were roaming, and asked for federal troops and state troops to protect both the Indians and the settlers. At the same time, he asserted that the reports of harm done by the Reserve Indians were exaggerated. He pointed out that while the Indians could not

MAJOR ROBERT S. NEIGHBORS

protect themselves, they were then willing to act as auxiliaries to any force sent against the wild tribes. Though the Texans knew full well that this was true — it had been proved by both Ford and Van Dorn — the performances of the red allies did not allay the wrath of the Texans.

Meantime John R. Baylor, the first agent of the Reserve Comanches, had been discharged from the service; he now assumed the rôle of trouble-maker which he played with rare gift. In a public letter Baylor claimed that he was still sincerely in favor of feeding the Reserve Indians, but he wanted them to behave themselves while eating government provender. His special animus was directed against his own former charges, the Comanches of whom he had once given good reports. He now reversed himself and could find in them nothing but evil. The agents were also at fault. They should either confine the Comanches to the Reserves or drive them from Texas.

Shortly after Baylor was dismissed, a mass meeting of the citizens was called on the Brazos. Baylor apparently dominated the affair, making full use of what prestige his recent official position in the Indian service had given him. He contrived to present his case against the Indians, made charges against Neighbors, and fanned the emotions, passions, and prejudices of his hearers like a true demagogue. At least one man in the group penetrated his motives and recognized his tactics for what they were. He said that Baylor lied about Neighbors, about having authority to sign the names of absent men to the petition, and about a conversation he claimed to have had with Ketumseh. Baylor claimed that Ketumseh had admitted to him that some of the Indians who had been killed while depredating were Reserve Indians. The man said this could not be true because, at the time the conversation was supposed to have taken place, Ketumseh had quit speaking to Baylor!

Major Neighbors was intelligent enough to recognize the hopeless situation of his Indians, and, on March 29, 1858, he recommended that the Comanche Reserve be abandoned and the Comanches moved north of Red River. In May, Neighbors went to Washington for the purpose of acquainting the government with the conditions that surrounded him in Texas, and as a result of his efforts Thomas J. Hawkins was sent to make an investigation of the whole Indian trouble. In the meantime Captain John S. Ford was sent with his Texas Rangers to investigate for the state. Ford took a position at the mouth of Hubbard's Creek on the Clear Fork of the Brazos and proceeded to gather information. He found many rumors afloat about the Indians and learned that even his officers were prejudiced against them. On April 15 a meeting of the officers was called at Camp Runnels and a plan was set on foot to have the Indians watched and reported on. It was determined to send out parties of reconnaissance, and, as an indication of the tensity of the situation, every man present was oath-bound to secrecy.

Ford found that some of the men were determined to fasten guilt upon the Reserve Indians regardless of the facts. One of the men said, 'If a trail can be traced from the point where a depredation has been committed to the Comanche Reserve, then there can be no doubt as to their complicity.'

'That thing can be managed — the trail can be made,' said Captain Allison Nelson.

This was too much for Rip Ford, and he replied: 'No, Sir, that will not do; I am responsible to the State, and to public opinion, and I will take no step in the matter, unless I am backed by facts of such a character as to justify me before the public. I am willing to punish the Comanches, if they are found guilty; but I am not disposed to do so unjustly and improperly.' [27]

This same Allison Nelson was sent out to investigate, and despite his obvious desires to do so, he found nothing implicating the Comanches. Ford now called on the citizens to submit their charges in writing, but not a charge was made.

Nelson seemed determined to bring on trouble, and broke his oath of secrecy by conspiring with the citizens. He preferred charges against Major Neighbors and entertained a movement to have himself appointed in Neighbors's place. When Ford had written his report, he gave it to Nelson to mail to Governor Runnels. Nelson sent the report to Washington instead and accompanied it by a letter assailing the three Indian agents — Neighbors, Ross, and Leeper. Ford commended all three of these men, withdrawing a bad opinion which he had previously expressed against Leeper. Of Major Neighbors he said, 'The ordeal through which Major Neighbors has passed endorses him. He needs no commendation from any quarter.' [28] Thus matters stood until the end of the year.

It was two days after Christmas. Seventeen Indians from the Brazos Reserve were encamped in the bend of the Brazos where Keechi Creek enters the larger stream. They had been there for some time and had been visited by the whites in their neighborhood. They were the peaceful Caddos and Anadarkos. Their agent, Shapley P. Ross, was in Waco, and the agency was in charge of the farmer of the Brazos Reserve, J. J. Sturm.

According to Sturm's account, the Indians were asleep when the white men stole upon their camp and fired upon them, killing four men and three women. Sturm went at once to the scene of the murder, and reported on his return that he never expected to see a more horrible sight. There in their beds lay the bodies of seven of the best, most inoffensive Indians on the Reserve, 'Their countenances indicating that they passed from calm sleep to the sleep that knows no waking.' Sturm named six men who did the deed. The leader was Captain Peter Garland, and one of the men was a Dr. McNeill.

[27] Ford, Memoirs. (MS.)

[28] Ford to Thomas J. Hawkins, affidavit, November 24, 1858. I.O.L.R. See Noel, pp. 124–127, for copy of Ford's report.

W. W. McNeill also sent a report — probably to Ford — which varied from Sturm's. He said that some citizens were trailing some thieves and came upon the Caddo camp. A friend in the rear had no gun, and becoming alarmed, shouted to the others to look out, for the Indians were about to fire on them. The fight then commenced. News of the atrocity reached Major Neighbors at Austin, and he immediately wrote Governor Runnels, urging prompt action. He then proceeded to make an investigation with the purpose of bringing the murderers to justice in the courts.

Ford's company of Rangers was in Comanche County at a place known as Camp Leon near Cora. Judge N. W. Battle of the Nineteenth Judicial District deputized Ford to arrest the men accused of murdering the seven Indians. Ford declined to accept the duty, basing his refusal upon the fact that he was a military officer and not subject to the orders of civil officials. He has set forth in his Memoirs a lengthy and well-reasoned defense, but without doubt his decision was dictated somewhat by caution.[29]

Ford's refusal aroused in Major Neighbors a feeling of deep resentment which he expressed in strong terms. Neighbors expressed the hope that Ford's Rangers would be recalled, and declared that the captain had pandered in a contemptible manner to the prejudice of a band of lawless men against the very Indians who led him to victory over the Comanches the spring before.[30]

The situation of the Reserve Indians was now desperate. Baylor and his helpers kept the frontier aflame with rumors. Agent Ross wrote, 'I also hear that he [Baylor] is prowling around the reserve with a body of armed men with the avowed object of taking scalps.' Captain Plummer of the United States Rifles was on hand to protect the Indians, but this did not deter Baylor, who informed Captain Plummer that he had determined to destroy the Indians if it cost the life of every man in his command. The Indians now prepared to defend themselves and were hovering near the Baylor crowd. According to one report an old Indian was induced to approach the citizen army and was captured, dragged away by a rope, killed, and scalped. Fifty or sixty Indians followed the Texans, exchanging shots with them. The fight was kept up until dark, when the Indians returned, reporting that they had killed five of Baylor's men and had one of their own killed. This was on May 23.

On June 11 orders came for the removal of the Indians to the reserve

[29] Ford's Memoirs.

[30] Neighbors to Denver, February 14, 1859. *Senate Executive Document* No. 2, Thirty-Sixth Congress, First Session, pp. 603–605. Serial No. 1023. Noel, pp. 132 ff.

THE REMOVAL OF THE INDIANS FROM TEXAS

north of Red River. Neighbors reported that the Reserves were already virtually broken up, that all work was suspended, and that the Indians could not cultivate their gardens. In order to preserve peace, the governor of Texas sent John Henry Brown with a company of Texas Rangers to the vicinity of the Reserves. Brown was a less able man than Ford, and was soon in conflict with Neighbors. Neighbors wanted to send the Indians out to gather their stock. Brown insisted that a white man accompany them, and offered to furnish an escort. This offer Neighbors refused, and the result was that the Indians were compelled to leave without having an opportunity to gather their stock. Finally the cavalcade set out for Red River with their belongings loaded on wagons. Major Neighbors, with an escort of United States soldiers, made the last march with his charges. On September 1 he turned the Indians over to Agent Blain, discharged the employees, and then set out for San Antonio to make his final report. He had been in the Indian service since the days of the Republic, and had always performed his duty with unflinching nerve. His last trip with his charges must have been a sad one. In a letter to his wife — the last one he wrote her — he said:

'I have this day crossed all the Indians out of the heathen land of Texas and am now out of the land of the Philistines.

'If you want to have a full description of our Exodus out of Texas — Read the "Bible" where the children of Israel crossed the Red Sea. We have had about the same show, only our enemies did not follow us to R[ed] River. If they had — the Indians would have — in all probability sent them back without the interposition of Divine providence.' [31]

Some sort of providence was to put an end to the life of the man who had given that life in the service of the Indians. His work was done, for now no Indians resided legally in Texas. All were henceforth outlaws. Major Neighbors returned to Texas and stopped at Fort Belknap. He had made many enemies, and these had evidently now turned against him the animosity they felt against the Indians. He was shot in the back by Ed Cornett, a man whom he did not know. France Peveler has told the story that the Rangers went after Ed Cornett, and brought him to justice without the aid of judge or jury.

The closing of the Reserves marks an important point in the tragic annals of the Texas tribes and the record of the bloody Texas frontier. The creation of the Reserves represents the most important attempt that was made to deal tolerantly with the native people. In perspective the Reserves seem to have been but a convenient corral in which the human cattle could be rounded up preparatory to the long drive from which there would be no returning. The removal of these Indians cleared up all impractical theories about the friendly Indians and amicable relations between the two races. Prior to the event there was always some chance that the Indian hunters might kill a friend, but with the breaking up of the Reserves there was no longer any chance for such a mistake. No Indian had any business in Texas. If he came now, it was at his own peril, and it was the duty of any Texan to kill him and then inquire as to his intentions. The Indians continued to come in spite of the danger, but they walked more circumspectly than ever along the borders where Texas Rangers stood to greet them.

[31] R. S. Neighbors to Mrs. Lizzie A. Neighbors, August 8, 1859. Neighbors Papers, University of Texas Archives.

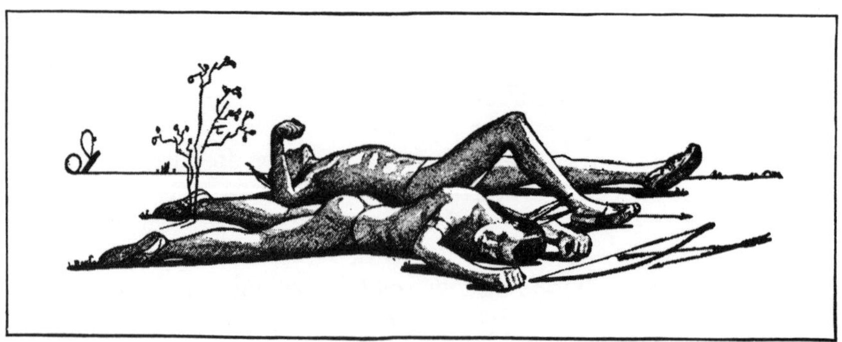

IX

THE CORTINAS WAR ON THE RIO GRANDE

¡Viva Cheno Cortinas! ¡Mueran los Gringos! ¡Viva la República de México!

The Mob

We have careered over the streets of the city in search of our adversaries... our personal enemies shall not possess our lands until they have fattened it with their own gore.

JUAN N. CORTINAS

They rushed upon the Mexicans, six-shooter in hand, rolled them up on the center, and routed them. The fleeing Mexicans were pursued by the Texans.

JOHN S. FORD

IX. THE CORTINAS WAR ON THE RIO GRANDE

1. THE RISE OF CHENO CORTINAS

WHEN General Zachary Taylor led his army to the Texas border in April, 1845, he established Fort Brown on the river opposite the Mexican town of Matamoros. Around the fort the city of Brownsville grew up to become the principal city of the lower Rio Grande valley. At the time of the Cortinas War it had a population of more than two thousand people composed largely of Mexicans but dominated and controlled by Americans. Since the majority of the voters were ignorant Mexicans, called 'cross-mark patriots,' machine politics developed at an early date and has continued for the same reason to the present time. The two factions found it expedient to adopt color symbols in order that the voter would always know which side he was on by the color of the ribbon on his shirt. One faction was the Blues and the other the Reds. The leaders on both sides were Americans, often men of considerable wealth and influence. Stephen Powers of the Blues had enjoyed the confidence of Martin Van Buren and under him had served as minister to Switzerland. Among the Reds were Charles Stillman, father of the New York banker, James Stillman, and Samuel A. Belden, an able lawyer. Richard King and Mifflin Kennedy, who were building their fortunes and laying the foundations of their great ranches, lent their sympathies if not their money to the Reds.

As elections approached, the Blues and Reds developed their organizations under *comisionados*, and held their voters in ranks by pinning on them the red and blue emblems of their political faith. On these occasions the humble Mexicans were treated with utmost consideration. Promises of all kinds were made to them, but scarcely were they made until they were broken. An active participant in politics declared that 'The elections... were a combination of force, fraud, and farce and the smartest "fishers of men" like the apostles of old gained the day.' [1]

Not only were the Mexicans bamboozled by the political factions,

[1] William Neale, *The Evening Ranchero*, July 5, 1876. Quoted in Lieutenant W. H. Chatfield, *The Twin Cities of the Border*, p. 14.

but they were victimized by the law. One law applied to them and another, far less rigorous, to the political leaders and to the prominent Americans. The Mexicans suffered not only in their persons but in their property. The old landholding Mexican families found their titles in jeopardy and if they did not lose in the courts they lost to their American lawyers. The humble Mexicans doubted a government that would not protect their person and the higher classes distrusted one that would not safeguard their property. Here, indeed, was rich soil in which to plant the seed of revolution and race war.

High and low were ready to support a champion of Mexican rights, one who would throw off American domination, redress grievances, and punish their enemies; and just such a champion arose in the person of Juan Nepomuceno Cortinas.

His father was Trinidad Cortinas, an uneducated and wholly undistinguished *ranchero*, but in the veins of his mother coursed the best blood that Spain contributed to the New World. Juan Nepomuceno, born May 16, 1824, was the black sheep of his mother's otherwise commendable flock. Though his brothers and sisters were cultured and educated, Juan was impervious to all good influences. He successfully resisted education, did not learn to read, and only learned to sign his name after he became governor of Tamaulipas. By choice a member of the *vaquero* class, he kept himself surrounded by a gay and roistering group of congenial fellows. Prior to 1859 his military experience was inconsequential. His enemy, Adolphus Glavaecke, records that during the Mexican War Cortinas murdered his employer, stole his mules, and sold them to the United States Army. Later he captured Charles Stillman's freighting carts and took the goods to Mexico, but in 1852 he was back in Texas stealing horses and killing sheep. Glavaecke claims that he in 1858 followed Cortinas into Mexico and brought back some of his own horses and others belonging to John S. Cross and J. Mallett. Glavaecke adds, 'I had him indicted for his numerous Robberies, and since then he has been seeking my life.' The indictment charges Cortinas with the theft of 'one black steer and one dun colored cow.' What Adolphus does not tell is that the same grand jury indicted him for receiving stolen cattle.[a] Though indicted on more than one count, there is no evidence that Cortinas was ever prosecuted; certainly he was never convicted.

[a] Affidavit of Adolphus Glavaecke, January 16, 1860. A copy of the indictment of Cortinas is in the Governor's Letters. For a Mexican estimate of Glavaecke see *Reports of the* [*Mexican*] *Committee of Investigation*, p. 160. 'Adolpho Glavaecke, who had a band of robbers on his ranche for the purpose of stealing horses from Mexico, and who subsequently speculated in cattle stolen in Texas.' With him was mentioned William D. Thomas, alleged to have been a 'horse thief in Mexico, and a cattle thief in Texas.'

JUAN N. CORTINAS

In 1859 he was living on his mother's ranch on the Texas side some six or seven miles west of Brownsville. Then in the prime of manhood he bore a striking appearance. He was of medium size, fair in complexion, fearless in manner, self-possessed and cunning. His brown hair, green-gray eyes, and reddish beard set him apart among his people. He had inherited personal charm and acquired from his little mother excellent manners. These qualities, combined with a flair for leadership, the disposition of a gambler, an eye for the main chance, and a keen intuitive insight into the character of the Mexicans, made him a man of destiny.[3]

It was the custom of Juan Nepomuceno to ride from his *rancho* into Brownsville for his morning coffee. While Cheno — as he was then

[3] The description is based partly on Ford's Memoirs, but largely on information furnished by Harbert Davenport.

called — was in the coffee house on July 13, 1859, the city marshal, Robert Shears, arrested a drunken Mexican who had previously been Cheno's servant. The unnecessary brutality of the marshal caused Cortinas to remonstrate, mildly enough in the beginning. Shears, exasperated at his interference, answered with an insult which called for action. Cortinas promptly shot the marshal in the shoulder, took the Mexican behind him and galloped out of town in the grand style of an American cowboy or a Mexican *vaquero* on a holiday. This episode had about it all the dramatic qualities that any rising young bandit — or hero — could desire. Cheno, popular member of the wealthy class, a Mexican, had shot a representative of American law, rescued the humblest member of Mexican society, and carried him boldly away to a safe retreat on his mother's Santa Rita Ranch.

The whereabouts of Cortinas for sixty days after the shooting cannot be determined. Adolphus Glavaecke asserted that Cortinas held a captain's commission to raise a hundred men to assist the Federals in Tampico, and that the money to pay the men was secured from Matamoros. Glavaecke worked through Miguel Tijerina, commander of the Mexican cavalry and cousin to Cortinas, to get Cortinas away from the border, but the effort was unsuccessful, for Cortinas continued to delay his departure, and proved himself, as his cousin remarked, 'a desperate contrary fellow.'

That Cortinas was planning some move was indicated by the fact that he was gathering horses and men, sometimes in Texas and sometimes in Mexico. Thus things went along until the early morning of September 28. On the night before, a fashionable ball was held in Matamoros and attended by many from the Texas side of the river; there was much noise and merrymaking by belated parties who were returning to their homes, and consequently, when at about three o'clock in the morning, wild yells and screams awoke the citizens of Brownsville, they thought little of it until they heard above the clamor and hoofbeat of horses such sounds as '¡Viva Cheno Cortinas! ¡Mueran los Gringos! ¡Viva la República de México!'

By daylight Cortinas with his hundred men had complete possession of the town. He came to kill the Pole, Adolphus Glavaecke, and Robert Shears, whom he called the 'squinting sheriff.' Though both of these escaped, he killed three Americans whom he described as 'wicked men, notorious among the people for their misdeeds.' He killed one Mexican for shielding one of the Americans. Part of his band broke open the jail, liberated ten or a dozen prisoners, and killed the jailer. Others took possession of Fort Brown which had but recently been evacuated by United States troops who had gone to the Reservation war. The Mexicans attempted to break open the magazine where one hundred and twenty-five barrels of powder were stored. They tried to hoist the Mexican flag over the fort, but failed for want of tackle. During this time the Americans dared not appear on the street with arms or to gather in groups while Cortinas continued to search for his personal enemies. Finally, through the influence of Miguel Tijerina and General Caravajal, Cortinas was induced to gather his followers and move out of the city without doing more damage. 'Thus was a city of from two to three thousand inhabitants occupied by a band of armed bandits, a thing till now unheard of in the United States,' wrote Major S. P. Heintzelman to Colonel Robert E. Lee.

Taking refuge on his mother's ranch, Cortinas issued his first proclamation in which he said 'we have careered over the streets of the city in search of our adversaries.' He spoke of Adolphus Glavaecke and lawyers who were bent on taking the Mexicans' lands. He would not injure the innocent, but would strike for the emancipation of the Mexicans. 'As to land,' he said, 'Nature will always grant us sufficient to support our frames.... Further, *our personal enemies shall not possess our lands until they have fattened it with their own gore.*' [4] In response to his bold and ringing call the Mexicans flocked to Cortinas's camp.

The thrill was no less for the Americans than for the Mexicans, though quite different in quality. They sent urgent calls for help to the commanding officer at San Antonio, to Governor Runnels, and to President Buchanan. Immediate steps were taken to protect the town until help could arrive. In their desperation the citizens appealed to the Mexican troops, who came under Caravajal, and for a time American citizens witnessed the sorry spectacle of seeing themselves protected on their own soil by Mexican soldiers quartered in a United States fort. An American apologized for the flattering attention given the Mexican soldiers by saying 'we are over a bed of coals, and care is necessary to get off from so dangerous a position.' A citizen guard of twenty-five was organized to patrol the streets at night. 'For God's sake,' wrote the American, 'urge the government to send us relief. Let the great guns again watch over our dear sister Matamoros, and the soldiers of Uncle Samuel keep marauders here in check, or practically the boundary... must be moved back to the Nueces.' [5]

[4] Cortinas's Proclamation of September 30, 1859. 'Difficulties on Southwestern Frontier,' *House Executive Document*, No. 52, Thirty-Sixth Congress, First Session, pp. 70–72, Serial No. 1050.

[5] Unsigned letter to New Orleans *Daily Picayune*, said to have been written by F. W. Latham, Deputy Collector of Customs of the Brazos Santiago District. 'Difficulties on Southwestern Frontier,' pp. 39 ff.

While events were stirring in Texas, Cortinas was becoming a lion in Matamoros. If he had any intention of remaining quiet, he gave it up when word came to him that the Americans had captured his lieutenant, the sixty-five-year-old Thomas Cabrera. Cortinas sent a merchant messenger to demand the release of Cabrera and to tell his captors that unless Cabrera was liberated Brownsville would be laid in ashes. The demand was refused and Cortinas crossed the river, but dared not enter the town on account of a guard that had been organized to patrol the town.

This guard, composed of about twenty men under W. B. Thompson, was known as the Brownsville Tigers. It was decided to make a drive on Cortinas while he was on the Texas bank. The Tigers were joined by some forty Texas-Mexicans and by Colonel Loranco of Matamoros. The combined force had two small cannon, one from Fort Brown and one from Mexico. The history of the expedition might be given from the official sources, but the true spirit of it is best given by William Neale in the *Evening Ranchero* of July 5, 1876.

'And after a little drilling, they sallied forth under the command of Captain Thompson to seek the enemy. They took with them two pieces of brass artillery, and I believe they meant mischief, for my old friend, Henry... made his will just before he marched. Now, mind, I will not state positively... but I think the facts are that the Brownsville Tigers... got as far as Mr. Glavaecke's ranch, situated about three miles from here, in four days; and proceeding on at the same rate, they got to Santa Rita, seven miles from Brownsville, in a week; and there, sure enough, they found the enemy, or perhaps, more properly speaking, the enemy found them. Which one found the other is a question never yet fully decided; consequently, I give the honor to the Tigers.... A halt was called. The Tigers made a firm stand, and immediately preparations were made for some movement. Much discussion ensued, and much difference of opinion prevailed among the officers... and that means the main body, for they were nearly all of them colonels, captains or majors — I say much difference of opinion prevailed, as to the propriety of fighting after dinner.

'The sheriff — then acting in a military capacity and mounted on a beautiful white steed — in vain reiterated the words of command, "Come along, boys!" The "boys" wouldn't come. They made a firm stand — at a respectful distance too, from the enemy's line, or where they suspected the line to be, for only a few straggling Mexicans could be seen, as they dodged in and out of the chaparral....

'Either by intent or accident, some firing commenced. The Tigers made a desperate charge — for home — leaving their cannon in possession of the enemy, and though it had taken a week to get to Santa Rita, they made much better time in getting back. I was personally acquainted with one of the officers in that famous expedition, who, though a cripple, has since frequently declared to me that he got home on that occasion in less than forty minutes! and I believe he did.'[6]

This whimsy does not conform in all details to the official report, but the results are the same. Both the Mexicans from Matamoros and Captain Thompson lost their cannon, and returned to Brownsville in headlong flight which even an official report does not conceal. Major Heintzelman said that the rout became general, all being anxious to reach Brownsville first, and added, apparently with unconscious humor, that the Mexicans brought up the rear. The expedition started out on October 22 and 'returned' on October 24.

Following the fight at Santa Rita, Cortinas became bolder and his prestige correspondingly greater. Each morning at six o'clock he informed his enemies of his presence by firing salutes from the captured cannon. On October 26 he wrote a friend in Brownsville telling him that he had heard that Brownsville was barricading the streets and preparing to fight him. He declared that he did not wish to wage war on the town because he had many friends there, but he asserted that he had sufficient artillery to batter down the houses and would do it unless four of his enemies were delivered to him. Among his friends were Mayor Stephen Powers and Sheriff James Browne; among his enemies were Glavaecke and Marshal Shears, the 'squinting sheriff.' Beyond the city limits Cortinas did as he pleased. He intercepted the mail and held Francis Campbell prisoner for ten days to read it to him. He subsisted upon the country and laid it waste, but in many respects he acted with restraint. After reading the mail he would reseal the letters, hang the mail bag on a tree and send the Americans word where it might be found. When his men drove eighty or ninety beeves belonging to Sheriff Browne into his camp, he killed eleven, penned the others in corrals near Matamoros, and sent the sheriff word where to find his cattle along with a due bill for those he had appropriated.

The first outside aid to reach Brownsville was a body of Texas Rangers under Captain W. G. Tobin of San Antonio. On the whole these men were a sorry lot, and their conduct for the remainder of the war reflects no credit on the organization. Harbert Davenport dryly remarks that Tobin had one good man, but unfortunately, he fell off a carriage and broke his neck soon after reaching the city. Shortly

[6] *The Evening Ranchero*, July 5, 1876. Quoted in W. H. Chatfield's *The Twin Cities of the Border*, p. 15. See also letter from Mayor Stephen Powers to Governor Runnels, October 23, 1859, G.L.

after Tobin arrived, Thomas Cabrera was taken from prison by a 'lawless mob' and hanged. Major Heintzelman implies and Ford asserts that the deed was done by Tobin's men. Shortly after this event, Tobin sent Captain Littleton towards Point Isabel to meet Captain Donaldson of the United States Army, who was on his way to Brownsville. Littleton missed Donaldson, fell into an ambuscade near Palo Alto Prairie, and left three dead Rangers and one captive in the hands of the Mexicans. Thus did Cortinas revenge the death of Thomas Cabrera.

Tobin's next move was to lead an expedition to attack Cortinas at Santa Rita. Tobin's force had grown by recruits and by the addition of Captain M. Kennedy's Brownsville volunteers — perhaps the Tigers themselves — until it numbered about two hundred and fifty men. The Rangers found Cortinas, just as the Tigers had a month earlier, and met him in about the same fashion and with similar results. They did manage to get the little twenty-four-pound howitzer, which they had borrowed from the United States ordnance officer, back to Brownsville, and in this respect proved the superiority of the Tobin Rangers over the Brownsville Tigers in the handling of artillery. Major Heintzelman said in his report that the decision of the Rangers to withdraw was a wise one because the Rangers were so demoralized that an engagement would have resulted in Tobin's defeat. The return to Brownsville was effected on November 25. Major Heintzelman wrote:

'Cortinas was now a great man; he had defeated the "Gringos," and his position was impregnable; he had the Mexican flag flying in his camp, and numbers were flocking to his standard. When he visited Matamoros he was received as the champion of his race — as a man who would right the wrongs the Mexicans had received; that he would drive the hated Americans to the Nueces, and some even spoke of the Sabine as the future boundary.'[7]

Emboldened by his repeated successes over city marshals, municipal corporations, Brownsville Tigers, and a combined force of Mexican troops and home guards, Cortinas had, on the day before he met Tobin's Rangers, issued from Rancho del Carmen a proclamation in which he set forth the grievances of the Mexicans and announced the enlargement of his program. Up to this point he seemed actuated by a desire to do away with his enemies, but now he proposed to put himself at the head of a society for the improvement of the unhappy condition of the Mexican residents. The rules of this society were written in

[7] Major S. P. Heintzelman's Report to Colonel Robert E. Lee, March 1, 1860, in 'Troubles on Texas Frontier,' *House Executive Document*, No. 81, Thirty-Sixth Congress, First Session, pp. 2 ff. Serial No. 1056. Ford's Memoirs. (MS.)

The Great Book' about which was drawn the veil of impenetrable secrecy. The Texans assumed that Cortinas proposed to restore the country from the Rio Grande to the Nueces to Mexico or set it up as an independent state, but there is nothing in this proclamation to substantiate this view. In fact, Cortinas stated specifically that the Mexicans reposed confidence in Governor-elect Houston, and expected him to give them legal protection when he came into office.

Cortinas reminded the Mexicans of their sufferings, and referred to the flocks of vampires in the guise of men who came to the settlements without any capital save corrupt hearts and perverse intentions.

'Some, brimful of laws, pledged to us their protection against the attacks of the rest; others assembled in shadowy councils, attempted and excited the robbery and burning of the houses of our relatives on the other side of the river Bravo; while others... when we entrusted them with our titles,... refused to return them under false and frivolous pretexts; all, in short, with a smile on their faces, giving the lie to that which their black entrails were meditating. Many of you have been robbed of your property, incarcerated, chased, murdered, and hunted like wild beasts, because your labor was fruitful, and because your industry excited the vile avarice which led them.... There are to be found criminals covered with frightful crimes...; to these monsters indulgence is shown, because they are not of our race, which is unworthy, as they say, to belong to the human species....

'Mexicans! Is there no remedy for you?...

'Mexicans! My part is taken; the voice of revelation whispers to me that to me is intrusted the breaking of the chains of your slavery, and that the Lord will enable me, with powerful arm, to fight against our enemies, in compliance with the requirements of that Sovereign Majesty, who, from this day forward, will hold us under His protection. On my part, I am ready to offer myself as a sacrifice for your happiness....

'Mexicans! Peace be with you!'[8]

This stirring appeal, supported by repeated victories, brought more recruits to Cortinas's camp. Among those who came for liberty or plunder was Santos Cadena with forty men from Agua Leguas in Nuevo Leon. They stayed until they were loaded with plunder, and then returned. Sixty convicts broke prison at Victoria, Tamaulipas, armed themselves, and marched triumphantly to Cortinas's camp. Thus things stood until the second outside American force arrived under Major S. P. Heintzelman on December 5.

[8] The proclamation was written from Rancho del Carmen, dated November 23, 1859. Cortinas's sister was named Carmen, and he was probably at her ranch. The proclamation is to be found in 'Difficulties on Southwestern Frontier,' pp. 79–82.

On December 14, Major Heintzelman left Fort Brown with one hundred and sixty-five men of the regular army and one hundred and twenty of Tobin's Rangers for Cortinas's camp, which lay nine miles up the river. Half an hour before day the troops were within less than two miles of where the bandit was supposed to be with about three hundred and fifty men. The Rangers were asked to reconnoiter, but said Heintzelman, 'they were so thoroughly stampeded by their previous expedition that it was only after much difficulty and delay that I could get any of them to go.' The camp was found deserted, the signs indicating that it had not been occupied for a week. The barricades of ebony logs, dirt, and brush were cleared and the army advanced three miles when a flag was sighted six hundred yards away. A burst of smoke and a round shot informed the Americans that the enemy had been found and that he would fire on the United States troops. The Americans returned the fire and captured the camp, but Cortinas had escaped. Eight Mexicans were killed and one Ranger and two regulars were wounded, the Ranger mortally.[9]

2. *THE COMING OF RIP FORD'S RANGERS*

While the battle of La Ebronal — so called from the barricade of ebony logs — was in progress, Major John S. Ford with fifty-three Rangers was close enough to hear the cannon. After ending his rather inglorious activities around the Reserves, Ford returned to Austin, where in November it was reported to him that Corpus Christi had been burned and that Cortinas was laying waste the lower country. Ford hastened to spread the alarm; he met Forbes Britton, senator from Nueces, on Congress Avenue, told him the story, but added that he doubted that all of it was true. As luck would have it, Governor Runnels came along just then and Senator Britton relayed the story of the supposed destruction of his home town, emphasizing his agitation with dancing eyes, trembling voice, and quivering chin. Governor Runnels was deeply affected — for Britton was a senator — and exclaimed, 'Ford, you must go; you must start tonight, and move swiftly.' And the governor appointed the Ranger major in command of all state forces on the Rio Grande. The next afternoon Ford led his army down Congress Avenue, ferried the Colorado River at the foot of the street, and headed south for a ride of more than five hundred miles to

[9] Major S. P. Heintzelman to Colonel Robert E. Lee, March 1, 1860, 'Troubles on Texas Frontier,' pp. 2–14; Ford's Memoirs. (MS.)

the scene of the Cortinas War. The army was not imposing. It numbered eight men on horseback; it carried one or two guns, a few pistols, and perhaps a little grub lashed to the saddles. It did not have one dollar of public money, for the simple reason that the treasury was empty. In this easy manner were the Texas Rangers sent upon their missions.

Fortunately the army gathered recruits as it advanced. At Goliad some funds were procured, and somewhere *en route* the Rangers picked up an ambulance and wagon for conveyance of baggage and supplies. When, in the early morning of December 14, Major Heintzelman and Captain Tobin attacked Cortinas's camp at La Ebronal, Ford and his fifty-three well-armed and mounted men were close enough to hear the firing. Ford's Rangers put out at a gallop, followed by the wagon and ambulance. As they clattered through Brownsville they created a commotion among the home guards, who thought for a time that Cortinas was upon them, but fortunately the guards discovered the identity of the Rangers and cheered them lustily as they passed through the town and out by the river road to the scene of conflict. They arrived too late for the fighting, but found Major Heintzelman's army resting in camp after its labors.

The story of the Cortinas War from the time of the fight at La Ebronal on December 14 to the final dispersion of the Mexican forces is one of continual victory for the Americans and continual retreat of Cortinas up the river. Immediately after the fight there were many rumors as to Cortinas's whereabouts and purposes, and some time was spent in fruitless investigation of these reports. Finally, however, it was learned that he had established himself at the Barstone in the W. P. Neale home, which he had fortified. On December 21, one hundred and fifty regulars and one hundred and ninety-eight Rangers and Texans set out for this place. They arrived two days later to find the Neale home sacked, fences, corrals, and *jacales* burned, and the enemy gone. Cortinas then retired to Edinburg, plundered the custom house and post office, but when Heintzelman and Ford entered the place on Christmas Day, Cortinas was farther up the river in a canebrake, and when they got to the canebrake he was elsewhere.

On the night of December 26, the American forces camped near Las Cuevas and while there they learned that Cortinas was eighteen miles up the river at Rio Grande City or Ranch Davis, as the Mexicans called it.

Rio Grande City is no more than a hamlet, or at best a village, which sprawls between a hill and the river. Its main street is an infinitesimal point on the long river road that runs from Brownsville to El Paso.

Major Heintzelman and Ford formed a plan to trap Cortinas here by sending the Rangers on a circuitous route through the hills to intercept the road above the town and cut off the further retreat of Cortinas. The troops made a night march with the Rangers in advance, but Cortinas had disposed his men in such a manner that it was impracticable to pass around him. Consequently the Rangers halted a short distance from the Mexican pickets and awaited the coming of day and the arrival of Major Heintzelman's troops. As Ford states, 'every man held his bridle in his hand and got what sleep he could.' Just before day the rumble of artillery carriages notified the Rangers that the regulars were approaching.

Cortinas had prepared to meet his enemies by stationing his left wing on the hill near the cemetery, his right wing near the river, while his center, supported by the artillery, held the road. The American plan was for Tobin's Rangers to strike Cortinas's left wing while Ford struck the center for the purpose of clearing the way for the use of artillery. The Rangers advanced at a gallop, struck the enemy, and for a time the fighting was furious. The Mexicans opened fire with their artillery, and their bugles sounded a charge which was answered with a withering fire that sent many Mexican horses away with empty saddles. At this point the Mexicans saw the regular troops with their white-topped wagons rise the ridge back of the town, and they gave way precipitately. Cortinas abandoned his provisions, half-cooked breakfast, and baggage, but took the cannon with him. The Rangers pursued the Mexicans along the river road towards Roma. Four or five miles out they captured one piece of artillery and nine miles out they found the other. Cortinas quit the road with his bodyguard and made his way into Mexico. It was reported the day after the battle that he was at Guerrero, and later he was heard of at Mier, Camargo, and Reynosa. Major Heintzelman moved the regular troops to Roma, where he encamped, while the Rangers set up headquarters at Rio Grande City.

It is obvious from the official reports that the regular troops never got into battle. The best evidence of this is the list of casualties. Sixteen Rangers were wounded and not a single United States soldier was scratched. The Mexicans had sixty killed.[10]

No sooner had the Rangers established a permanent camp at Rio Grande City than trouble developed among them. It was a custom among volunteer troops to elect their own officers, and it seems to have

[10] In his field report to the adjutant general on the day of the battle, Major Heintzelman says: 'Major Ford led the advance, and took both his [Cortinas's] guns, ammunition wagons, and baggage. He lost everything.' 'Difficulties on Southwestern Frontier,' pp. 97–98. But in his general report to Colonel Robert E. Lee, dated March 1, Heintzelman is less generous. 'Troubles on Texas Frontier,' pp. 2–14.

been understood that an election was to be called to choose a major notwithstanding the fact that Governor Runnels had appointed Ford to that office before he left Austin. Captain Tobin, whose record of inefficiency runs through the story from the time of the death of Cabrera until Tobin's dismissal, aspired to the supreme command of the Texas Rangers. By courting favor with the privates and making bargains with some of the officers, Tobin won the election by six votes over Ford, who made no canvass. With the election over, Ford called the Rangers together in the hay lot of Ringgold Barracks and read his official report of the battle which they had just fought. He commended the men, mentioned them by name, and offered no criticism of anyone. His justice and consideration led some of them to say that had he read the report before the election, the result would have been different.

Ford now withdrew from the organization, and accompanied by some of his men, set out for Brownsville. Tobin remained temporarily at Ringgold Barracks, where he continued to add to his poor record. His discipline was notoriously weak and his men began to depredate on the citizens. One man reported that Tobin's Rangers burnt up his fences and pens for firewood and a horse by accident, that they used a few of his hogs and goats and fifty barrels of his sweet potatoes. 'I estimate,' he said, 'the value of the property taken by Cortinas at fully two hundred dollars, and the value of the property destroyed by Tobin's command at fully one thousand dollars.' [11]

When Ford reached Brownsville he found two commissioners, Angel Navarro and Robert H. Taylor, who had come with authority from Governor Houston to restore order among the state troops. On January 12 they ordered Major Tobin to come to Brownsville immediately to be mustered out of service, and without waiting for him to arrive, organized two companies with Ford and John Littleton as captains. Ford states that the reorganization took place on January 20 and that the men were enrolled for twelve months unless sooner discharged. These two companies were placed under the command of Major Heintzelman, who had by this time returned from Roma.[12]

In the lull following the fight at Rio Grande City, the steamboat *Ranchero*, King and Kennedy line, undertook to make its way from Rio Grande City to the mouth of the river with a cargo valued at two or three hundred thousand dollars, including sixty thousand in specie.

[11] F. M. Campbell to Captain J. B. Ricketts, January 28, 1860, 'Troubles on Texas Frontier,' p. 19. See also Ford's account in his Memoirs.

[12] See Angel Navarro to Governor Houston, February 15, 1860, 'Difficulties on Southwestern Frontier,' pp. 120–122. Ford, Memoirs. (MS.)

The boat carried a few passengers, a small squad of United States troops under Lieutenant Loomis L. Langdon, and the two cannon taken from Cortinas at Rio Grande City. Around this steamer occurred the fight of La Bolsa on February 4, 1860.

La Bolsa Bend, which lies about thirty-five miles above Brownsville, was really a great loop in the river shaped thus ⊂ with the mouth or open part facing Mexico. On the Mexican side was the *rancheria* of La Bolsa, and here Cortinas had established himself, improvised some fortifications on the river bank, and sent depredating parties into Texas. On January 24 a party of his raiders had captured the mail rider, carried him to La Bolsa and held him prisoner until the fight of February 4. There was much talk in the camp of taking the *Ranchero* as it attempted to make La Bolsa Bend. In short, Cortinas was about to turn river pirate.

On February 4 the *Ranchero* approached La Bolsa, escorted or accompanied by Major Tobin's Rangers. Meantime Major Heintzelman had sent two companies of cavalry and the two newly organized companies of Texas Rangers scouting up the river. The result was that Ford and Tobin met at La Bolsa and both of them took a hand in the fighting around the *Ranchero*.

Ford states that the fighting started when a detachment of his men under Corporal Milton A. Duty reached Zacatal in the Bolsa and discovered Mexicans taking some plunder from Texas. In this skirmish Ranger Woodruff was mortally wounded and some of the property was recovered. Tobin's men arrived about this time and the *Ranchero* also came into view. It was fired on by the Mexicans, a bullet passing through the flag on the masthead, but Lieutenant Langdon turned the cannon on the Mexicans and saved the boat from immediate capture.

A messenger was sent to find Ford, who came on the scene with the main body of his men at about three o'clock. To Langdon's inquiry as to whether he proposed to cross into Mexico, Ford answered, 'Certainly, Sir.' Before crossing he wrote Major Heintzelman: 'There is a numerous force lying in wait along the Mexican side to capture the boat, or at least attempt it. I shall pass over this evening afoot, and beat the brush in the neighborhood. Tomorrow morning I will pass over my horses, and, with the whole force under my command, go down upon the Mexican side, keeping as near the boat as possible.' On its way down the river this letter passed through the hands of Captain George Stoneman, who had some cavalry at 'Old Camp.' At eight o'clock Stoneman wrote that he was leaving at once to meet the steamer.[13]

[13] Letters of Langdon, Ford, Stoneman and Heintzelman may be found in 'Troubles on Texas Frontier,' pp. 63–64.

With the aid of the steamer Ford crossed thirty-five of his own men and ten or eleven under Major Tobin. The Rangers formed under the protection of the bank, and moved upstream until they had come within thirty yards of the picket fence or stockade behind which Cortinas had formed his lines. The fighting now began in earnest. Ford told his men to fire slowly, aim well, and waste no ammunition. One or two men became demoralized and one 'made the steamer at race horse speed,' but Ford restored morale by stating that there was plenty of ammunition and that the next footrace would be ended by a Texas bullet.

While the fight was in progress Captain Martin swung the *Ranchero* about and moved upstream to permit Lieutenant Langdon to turn the cannon on the Mexicans. The Rangers continued to advance along the embankment until the head of the column passed the line of picket fence; they had flanked the Mexican left.

The Rangers led by Ford and another officer now charged up the bank, firing when possible. 'They rushed upon the Mexicans, six-shooters in hand, drove them, rolled them up on the center, and routed them. The fleeing Mexicans were pursued by the Texians,' wrote Ford. The skirmish, which lasted more than an hour, was constantly broken by the yells and cries of the contestants. The Mexicans shouted frequently, but occasionally, above the din and rattle of rifle and six-shooter, the Texas yell rose clear and distinct; such a cry, remarked a spectator on the *Ranchero*, as Mexican lungs could not produce.

It was estimated that Cortinas had between two and four hundred men, including sixty cavalry. The cavalry, drawn up on his right, were the first to quit the field, and the infantry followed. The red-bearded Cortinas was the last to go. After failing utterly to rally his men, he turned on the Texans and emptied his revolver, and though three Rangers were ordered to concentrate their fire on him, he spurred his horse from the field without injury. The Mexicans reported that the bullets struck his saddle, hit his belt, and clipped off a lock of his hair. 'But for obscurity,' says Ford, 'it being almost dark, the frontier pirate would have been killed.' The Rangers had one man killed and four wounded. The Mexicans were reported to have lost twenty-nine killed and forty wounded.[14] It would be pleasant to end the story of how forty-five or fifty Rangers defeated and put to flight more than four times their number of enemies without recording some act of unnecessary violence, but it must be told that some of the Texans set fire to the *jacales* occupied by Mexicans. Ford states that the deed was

[14] The account is based on Ford's Memoirs and on official documents in 'Troubles on Texas Frontier,' pp. 63–70.

AT LA BOLSA

'The red-bearded Cortinas was the last to go... he spurred his horse from the field without injury.'

done without his orders, but Heintzelman goes further and states that it was done contrary to Ford's orders and by men not of his party. This can only mean that it was done by Tobin's men.[15]

After the fight the Rangers returned to Texas and Tobin set out for Brownsville, leaving the situation in the hands of Ford and of Stoneman. The next morning, February 5, Ford took forty-seven men and horses and crossed back into Mexico with the purpose of marching down the Mexican bank abreast the steamer. At Las Palmas, two or three miles below La Bolsa, they found much commotion among the Mexicans who were fleeing in terror from the 'Reengers.' Ford sent an unsealed note in Spanish among them assuring them that they would not be harmed. About this time a heavy force of Mexicans appeared, accompanied by the Prefect of Las Palmas, who came to protest the presence of the Texans in Mexico. Ford told the Mexicans that he had authority from the General García to wage war in Mexico on Cortinas. The Prefect asked for time to communicate with headquarters, and

[15] 'Troubles on Texas Frontier,' p. 12.

since the *Ranchero* had grounded on a sandbar and could not be got off for some hours, Ford agreed to wait.

He now inquired as to the identity of the miscellaneous assemblage of *rancheros*, soldiers, and bandits — eight hundred of them — drawn up near his forty-seven Rangers. He was told that some were rural police and some were *rancheros*.

'To what corps do the two hundred belong drawn up on our right?' he asked. The Mexican shrugged suggestively and answered, '*Quien sabe.*' Ford felt sure they were Cortinas men and believed that if trouble started he would have to fight the entire force. The Rangers passed the night in anxiety with sentinels on guard. The next morning, February 6, the Mexican officials were on hand early for an interview with Ford and Stoneman. Ford explained why the troops had crossed, warned the Mexicans against permitting depredations, and intimated that if war should come, it would be accompanied with disastrous consequences to them. The Mexicans urged the Texans to return to their side of the river and gave assurances that the *Ranchero* should not be harmed on its way to the Gulf. The boat had in the meantime got off the bar, steamed down the river and anchored to await the results of the conference. The Rangers returned to Texas and the *Ranchero* went through to the Gulf without further molestation.[16]

After the fight at La Bolsa, Cortinas retired to the Burgos Mountains in the interior. Ford's Rangers and Stoneman's cavalry continued to scout the border and made a number of raids into Mexico. Ford states that they went to La Mesa on March 17 on a report that Cortinas was there. After a short fight, some of the Rangers dragged from under a bed a Mexican major who began to call loudly for 'El Coronel' Ford. The major informed Ford that an attack had been made on the Mexican national guard. Turning to Stoneman, Ford exclaimed, 'Well, Captain, we have played Old Scratch, whipped the Guardia Nacional, wounded a woman, and killed a mule.' Unfortunately the woman died, along with four or five men. Lieutenant Nolan took the blame for killing the mule, but excused his act by saying that it was dark and he mistook the mule for a Mexican. Ford estimated that the Mexicans had six hundred men, and it was his opinion that a part of them belonged to Cortinas.[17]

[16] The account of what happened in Mexico is from Ford's Memoirs. The main facts are given in Major Heintzelman's report of February 10, 'Difficulties on Southwestern Frontier,' pp. 114–115. Heintzelman commended Ford and commented on the fact that on this occasion the inhabitants were not disturbed.

[17] For official account of incident see joint report of Ford and Stoneman, dated Camp on Rio Grande, March 18, 1860, 'Troubles on Texas Frontier,' pp. 80–81. In these official reports La Mesa is spelled the Mera. For the Mexican account see *Reports of the* [Mexican]

The town of Reynosa was also treated to a visit by the Texas Rangers, the first it had known since the Mexican War. Ford and Stoneman heard that Reynosa had offered to pay a reward of thirty thousand dollars to the troops who would enter their town as they had entered La Mesa. Stoneman kept his regulars on American soil near Edinburg, but agreed to come over if a fight started. On April 4 the Texas Rangers swept into the town in three detachments on parallel streets. Ford led one party, Captain Littleton one, and Lieutenants Nolan and Dix the third. The Texans reached the plaza, where they were surrounded on all sides by armed Mexicans. The crack of a single gun would have started a fight, and Ford states that the Rangers dropped their Sharps rifles in hopes that one would discharge and open the shooting. In the parley that ensued, the Mexicans inquired why their town had been invaded. 'To get the thirty thousand dollars,' Ford replied. Then he told the Mexicans that he had come to demand the surrender of the Cortinas men. The Mexicans denied the presence of Cortinas men among them, and the Rangers withdrew, accompanied to the river by Mexican officials.[18]

These raids that Ford and Stoneman were making into Mexico were brought to an end by the arrival of a very distinguished gentleman whose title and name were Colonel Robert E. Lee, the new commander of the Department of Texas, succeeding Colonel D. E. Twiggs. Lee came with specific instructions from Secretary of War Floyd to stop Mexican depredations, and, if necessary, to pursue Mexicans beyond the limits of the United States. Floyd commended Lee to Governor Houston as 'an officer of great discretion and ability.'

Colonel Lee arrived at San Antonio late in February and on March 15 left there for the border. He reached Fort Duncan on March 20, and on the following day started down the river to traverse the entire scene of the Cortinas War. He reached Rio Grande City on April 2, met Ford — just back from Reynosa — on April 7, and arrived at Fort Brown on April 11. As he came down the river he addressed firm but courteous notes to the Mexican officials, civil and military, telling them exactly what was expected of them.

Lee was not deceived into thinking that all the damage in the valley had been done by Cortinas. After reporting that most of the *ranchos* from Rio Grande City to Brownsville had been destroyed or abandoned, he added: 'Those spared by Cortinas have been burned by the Texans.'

Committee of Investigation, pp. 195 ff. The Mexican account has the fight taking place on March 16, one day earlier than the American account.

[18] For the Mexican account, see *Reports of the* [Mexican] *Committee of Investigation*, pp. 196 ff. Francis Lepeda, President of Reynosa, addressed a letter to Colonel Robert E. Lee on April 8, in which he gave an account of Ford's entrance into Reynosa.

When Ford told him of the Reynosa raid, Lee's only comment was: 'You should have sent a courier to inform them who you were.' Colonel Lee could not know that the success of the Texas Rangers was owing largely to the fact that they never send heralds of their approach to an enemy.

Of his meeting with Colonel Lee and his impression of him, the Texas Ranger wrote:

'Lieut. Col. Lee arrived, and pitched his camp a mile or so above Edinburg. The writer had reported to him; and rode out and called to pay his respects. He was received with great courtesy, met where he alighted from his horse, and invited to take supper....

'His [Lee's] appearance was dignified, without hauteur, grand, without pride, and in keeping with the noble simplicity characterising a true republican. He evinced an imperturbable self-possession, and a complete control of his passions. To approach him was to feel yourself in the presence of a man of superior intellect, possessing the capacity to accomplish great ends, and the gift of controlling and leading men.'

Though the Cortinas War was at an end, its evil consequences lived after it. Fifteen Americans and eighty friendly Mexicans had lost their lives; Cortinas was supposed to have lost one hundred and fifty-one men. The valley was laid waste, damage claims by American citizens alone aggregating $336,826.21. Cortinas was still at large, well on his way to fame and fortune. He became a brigadier general of the Mexican army and later governor of Tamaulipas. He amassed a fortune estimated at half a million, and continued to sponsor depredations in Texas until the end of his long life.[19]

[19] For an account of the later career of Cortinas see *Reports of the* [Mexican] *Committee of Investigation*, pp. 148 ff.

X

SAM HOUSTON'S GRAND PLAN

I have not painted an imaginary character [of Colonel R. E. Lee]. ... As he is a 'Preux chevalier, sans peur et sans reproche'... he would not touch anything that he would consider vulgar filibustering.... You would find him well fitted to carry out your great idea of a Protectorate.

A. M. Lea *to* Governor Houston

On the 12 instant Mrs. Houston presented me with another son. ... so you will think I have had a *protectorate* at home.... No, the Bond Holders are the men to whom we are first to look.... I will write today to ... Ben McCulloch. Ben will do for a very 'Big Captain.'

Sam Houston *to* Colonel Mann

I am for some work if it is undertaken. We look on it as a mission of mercy and humanity.... It must be to elevate and exalt Mexico....

Sam Houston *to* Ben McCulloch

took the executive chair he found the tame Indians removed from the state and the wild Indians so beaten up that they had withdrawn far to the northward. The almost complete absence of savages from Texas practically predetermined the nature of the Indian troubles during Houston's short term. It meant that the raiding parties into Texas would come either from the Reserve Indians who had been removed or from the wild Indians who had been pursued and harried by Ford and Van Dorn. Such raiding parties did come to Texas to steal horses, to burn cabins, to murder hapless citizens, and to avenge in every way known to a savage real and imagined wrongs.

Houston had a choice of two methods in dealing with the situation. The first, and more logical one under the circumstances, would have been to establish Ranger guards along Red River and the western border to prevent the raiders from entering Texas and to discover and pursue them if they did. Such a policy would have been in keeping with Houston's traditional Indian policy. The second method would have been to emulate Runnels and send bands of Texas Rangers north of Red River to destroy or chastise the Indians on their hunting grounds. In case this course were adopted, however, it would have been necessary to determine whether the raiders came from the Reserve Indians or from the Comanche bands. The citizens were inclined to fasten the guilt on the Reserves, but Houston was of the opinion that the wild Indians and evil white men were largely responsible, and he once stated that he could not protect the settlers from 'white Indians.' Moreover, it was almost certain that an expedition north of Red River would end in failure. If the Rangers went after Reserve Indians, they would have to pursue people who were under the direct protection of the federal government; if they went after Comanches, who were now on the alert, they would have to go into a wild, desert-like country where all the advantages would be with the enemy, where chances of success were indeed slim. The fact that Houston, for the first time in his life, adopted a vigorous policy towards the Indians and sent an expedition north of Red River presents a problem that requires reflection. The failure of the expedition, which Houston made no serious effort to prevent, leads us to seek his motive.

There was little in Houston's inaugural address to indicate that he would deal vigorously with the Indians. He did describe the frontier situation and advocate its protection by Texas Rangers, but he also spoke of moral influence, councils, treaties, and annuities — things which, he asserted, gave security under the Republic and would do so again. 'The extent of our frontier,' he said, 'stretching as it does, from the Red River to El Paso, on the Rio Grande, and from thence to the mouth of that river, comprises a distance of but little short of two thousand miles. One half of that distance is exposed to Indian depredations, and the other bordering upon Mexico, which is in a state of anarchy.' He added that Indian depredations were so common as to cease to excite sympathy in the interior. The federal troops were unfit for Indian service. The best protection would be provided by a force of Texas Rangers who understood Indian warfare and whose horses could subsist on grass. These Rangers should be placed in federal service.[1]

Houston was wise enough to know that he could not wait on the action of the federal government, and five days after his inaugural he wrote to Captain W. C. Dalrymple inviting him to Austin for a conference. 'I wish to take immediate steps for giving protection to the frontier,' he said. Four days later he authorized Dalrymple to raise a company of eighty-three men, rank and file, but on January 5 he reduced the number to sixty men.[2] Two other companies were called under Edward Burleson and John H. Connor on January 7 and 9, respectively.[3]

On January 20–21 Houston issued his 'Orders to Ranging Companies.' Dalrymple was to establish his camp to the north in Cooke County between Fish Creek and Big Wichita. Connor was to occupy a middle position on the San Saba and Burleson was to locate his quarters on the Nueces to the south. The Ranger stations were to be five miles beyond the settlements, the forces were to be divided into detachments and so placed as to give the maximum protection to the greatest area, and patrols were to move from one detachment to another at regular intervals. The officers were to permit no horse-racing, gambling, or drinking among the men.

A more singular provision, however, was that each captain should employ 'six good Mexican guides.' It was quite reasonable for Burleson on the Nueces to employ Mexicans, but it is difficult to see how Connor in middle Texas and Dalrymple on Red River could use them when few Mexicans or none lived within a hundred miles of their camps.[4] Early in February, Houston called three additional companies of twenty men, each under a lieutenant, and on March 5 he ordered Peter Tumlinson to raise a seventh company of forty-seven men. The exact location of these smaller companies is not important. They

[1] Houston's inaugural address, December 21, 1859.

[2] Houston to W. C. Dalrymple, December 26, 1850; December 30, 1859; January 5, 1860. G.L.

[3] Houston to Burleson, January 4; Connor, January 9; J. M. W. Hall, January 19, 1860. G.L.

[4] Houston to Captains of Ranging Companies, January 20–21, 1860. G.L.

doubtless formed a part of the line between Dalrymple on Red River and Burleson on the Nueces.[5]

Houston further increased the military force on the Indian front by calling out minute companies. On March 9 he ordered the chief justice of each exposed county to organize a company of fifteen men which could be increased in emergencies to twenty-five. Twenty-three counties were designated, and among them were Burnet, Bosque, San Saba, Lampasas, Eastland, Erath, Comanche, Hamilton, Palo Pinto, Jack, Young, and Coryell.[6]

By the end of March, Houston had on the Indian frontier an active force of five hundred and seventeen men and a potential force of eight hundred and sixty-three men. In a letter to Secretary of War Floyd he stated that seven hundred and thirty men were operating against the Indians.[7] If we add to this the force under Ford and Tobin on the Rio Grande, we have a total of a thousand or more Texas Rangers in active service, probably the largest force that Texas ever had in the field at one time. In the light of the fact that the Cortinas War had practically ended and that the Indians had been driven out of the state, the great military force needs some explanation, and especially so since Houston had always favored a pacific Indian policy and a small and economical corps of Indian fighters.

Houston's military preparations did not end with his call for Rangers. He made most strenuous efforts to procure arms for three times as many men as he had in the field. On March 8 he ordered Colonel William J. Herbert to collect all the arms and ammunition he could get within the state and called in all the six-shooters that had been loaned to the counties on the ground that he had to arm the people of the frontier. On the same day he wrote to the Secretary of War requesting that the government furnish Texas two thousand percussion rifles, one thousand Sharps, three thousand Colt revolvers, and one thousand cavalry accouterments. In the same letter he offered to raise for the service five thousand Texas volunteers.[8] He declared, 'Texas is ready for the emergency and will act at a moment's warning. Texas needs, to repel invasion both from the Indians and Mexico, an immediate supply of arms.'

[5] Houston to Peter Tumlinson, March 5, 1860. G.L.

[6] Circular, March 9, 1860, signed Sam Houston, Commander in Chief; Houston to J. M. W. Hall, May 5, 1860. G.L.

[7] Houston to A. G. Walker, March 10, 1860; Secretary of War John B. Floyd, April 14, 1860. G.L.

[8] Houston to Colonel William J. Herbert, March 8, 1860, G.L.; John B. Floyd, March 8, 1860, 'Difficulties on Southwestern Frontier,' *House Executive Document*, No. 52, Thirty-Sixth Congress, First Session, pp. 138; 145–146, Serial No. 1050.

The federal government did not feel that it needed five thousand Texas Rangers or that Sam Houston was entitled to receive for Texas such liberal quantities of percussion rifles, Sharps carbines, Colt six-shooters, and cavalry accouterments. Floyd told Houston that 2651 federal soldiers were already in the state and that 842 more were coming from New Mexico. As to arms, Texas was entitled to 169 muskets which number might be doubled by anticipating the next year's supply. The double quota would amount to $5000, whereas the governor of Texas had requested, at the lowest estimate, almost $100,000 worth of arms!

To be sure Houston could point to the Cortinas War as an excuse for raising a military force, but it must be remembered that he did nothing to put Cortinas out of Texas. In fact while he was complaining to the federal government about invasions from Mexico, he was sending an officer to the Rio Grande to muster out the Rangers. At no time did he send a soldier to Ford's assistance, and he was quick to dismiss him at the first opportunity. We may recall also that Cortinas considered Houston as a friend, and stated in his proclamation of November 23, 1859, that when Houston became governor the Texas-Mexicans would receive the protection to which they were entitled.

Houston's policy towards the Indians was more mystifying than that towards the Mexicans. He magnified the Indian depredations to the federal government and at the same time he condemned the use of federal troops in putting down the troubles he complained of. He wrote to Secretary Floyd in April, saying that there was no prospect of a cessation of Indian barbarities soon. He stated that the regular army was incapable. In the first place, the regulars detested the Indian service. In the next place, the Indians made their forays on horseback, moved with wonderful celerity, and the regulars, being mostly infantry, could not pursue; and if they did, they would only furnish a subject of ridicule and amusement to the Indians. Garrisons were useless unless the Indians were fools enough to march up to them and be shot down. The cavalry were also inadequate. Their fine American horses could not chase Indians a single day without becoming tender-footed; moreover, these horses were grain-fed, and there was no grain on the Indian frontier. Houston believed that the Texas Rangers would fulfill all the requirements. Ten companies could patrol and protect the frontier. He set forth with eloquent plausibleness their superb fitness for the work in Texas.

'It is evident to my mind that Texas Rangers stand pre-eminent on the score of economy and usefulness.... They are excellent horsemen, accustomed to hardships, and the horses of Texas, having been raised on grass, can perform service without requiring grain to subsist them.... The Texans are acquainted with Indian habits, and also their mode of warfare. They are woodsmen and marksmen. They know how to find the haunts of the savages, and how to trail and make successful pursuit after them.

'They, too, have their families, their kindred, and their neighbors to protect. They have the recollections of a thousand outrages committed upon those dear to them by the savage, to impel them onward; and if, in pursuit of the foe, they get out of rations, they can subsist on game, being dexterous hunters. What are privations, suffering and danger to them, in comparison with the plaudits of their fellow citizens...? They are accustomed to the heat of the prairies, and the severe northers to which we are subject. They need no tents to shelter their hardy frames from the night winds, but are content with the earth for a bed and a blanket for a covering. Such a force as this, continually on the alert, will be a terror to the savage.' [9]

Houston marshaled much evidence to show how serious the Indian depredations were, and made much of the fact that the federal soldiers could not even protect their own horses. From Eastland and Palo Pinto counties he had news of the murder of three men and two boys. The German settlements on the Medina were being ravaged. Within four months the savages had killed fifty-one persons, raped two women, shot two ministers, carried away several captives, and stolen eighteen hundred head of horses, including seventy animals belonging to the cavalry at Camp Cooper! [10]

We need not depend on Houston and the Texans alone for accounts of the Indian depredations. Colonel Robert E. Lee wrote General Winfield Scott that the troops on the frontier were insufficient to keep out the Indians, that the cavalry horses were so reduced by constant service, want of food and grass, that they 'fall in pursuit and sometimes perish.' The horses belonging to the residents around Camp Cooper were driven off on February 3, and on February 17 someone broke into the mule-yard at Camp Cooper and drove off the whole herd of sixty-six animals. Only twenty-three were recovered. The following night all the animals were driven from the Indian Agency two or three miles from Cooper. Colonel Lee was of the opinion that the thieves were not Comanches.[11]

Though these Indian troubles were annoying, they were by no means

[9] Houston to Floyd, April 14, 1860. G.L.

[10] Houston to Floyd, April 14, 1860. G.L. March 12, 1860, 'Difficulties on Southwestern Frontier,' pp. 139–142.

[11] Colonel Robert E. Lee to General Winfield Scott, March 6, 1860, 'Difficulties on Southwestern Frontier,' pp. 135–136.

serious enough to justify the calling of a thousand Rangers, or the demand on the federal government for such large quantities of arms. On the other hand, Houston did not use the men he had effectively. At first he permitted each company to operate independently, or directly under his orders. At last he sent an expedition into the Indian country under Middleton T. Johnson, but he took no pains to equip it properly. It was mismanaged from the first, and Houston knew that it was mismanaged, yet he made no great complaint. It seems quite probable that he did not want a Ford or any efficient officer to move against the Indians, that he neither expected nor desired the Johnson expedition to succeed, and that his purpose in sending Johnson out was to hold the Rangers together until he was ready to use them in another way.

There is one explanation which will make all of Houston's strange military activities intelligible, consistent, and rational, and that is that from first to last he cared little about either the Cortinas troubles or the Indian depredations. What he had in mind was the boldest and most daring filibustering expedition that his fertile brain ever conceived, namely, to lead ten thousand Texas Rangers, supported by Indians and Mexicans, into Mexico, establish a protectorate, with himself in the leading rôle, and incidentally perhaps so dazzle the Americans that they would forget their factional quarrel over slavery and come to his support. At one stroke he would save the Union, expand the national domain, and perhaps receive as his just reward the Presidency of the United States.

To Houston the scheme was no chimera. He had every reason to believe that he could repeat what he had once done. He was a leader in the Revolution of 1836 which freed Texas from Mexico. He was influential in annexing Texas to the Union, an act which led to the Mexican War and the acquisition of all the Southwest, an area greater than Mexico. Houston had already held every high political office save one within the gift of the people; he had been governor of two states, twice President of the Republic he had helped to create, member of the United States Senate. Such were his rewards for San Jacinto, the capture of Santa Anna, and the emancipation of Texas. If the conquest of a part of Mexico gave him these honors, why should not the conquest of all of it send him to the White House?

Sam Houston was fully conscious of the possession of superior talents, but it is doubtful if his conceit ever caused him to overestimate his ability. He was bold and intelligent, a finished master of guile and deception. He was always a diplomat and in crises he was much of a statesman and never a scoundrel. Though he was not a conspirator, he had the ability to listen attentively to the plans of those who would make him a champion. His tongue was mobile and persuasive and his pen facile and compelling in its logic, but his gift of silence — which often passed for consent — amounted to genius. He was all things to all men; Indian to Indians, frontiersman to frontiersmen, and spokesman of the people, general to soldiers, a political seer, and a talented actor who knew how and when to wear an Indian blanket, lion-skin coat, or a dress suit. Whether we like him or not in no way alters the fact that Sam Houston was no ordinary man.

Sam Houston never let his left hand know what his right was about. He had no great confidence in any man, though he inspired those who served him with an implicit faith in himself. His letters show that he would send one man on an important mission, and set two or three others to watch and report on him. He was capable of carrying on a series of mutually independent enterprises all tending to an end which he alone could see, and no better example of this habit and policy can be found than in his military and political activities while governor of Texas. To outward appearances there was no relation between what he did on the Indian frontier and what he did not do on the Rio Grande. His threats to the President to invade Mexico to stop invasion seem inconsistent with his failure to send soldiers to suppress Cortinas. If we put together his military acts, his talk, threats, and Indian intrigue, they seem to be inconsistent and without order. But once we perceive, or assume, his purpose — the conquest of Mexico and the establishment of a protectorate — every act, threat, and intrigue becomes an integral and harmonious part of that ambitious plan.

SAM HOUSTON

Ambassador to the Cherokees | Governor of Texas | United States Senator

Houston's dream of such a conquest goes back to his last days in the United States Senate when he was littering the floor of the upper chamber with soft pine shavings. On February 16, 1858, he introduced a bill providing that the United States establish a protectorate over Mexico. Evidently such blatant imperialism was too much for a country that has always made its conquests with sanctimoniousness. Congress, as then composed, could not tolerate the expansion of cotton and potential slave territory.

When Houston returned to Texas to become governor in 1859, he brought the dream with him. The time to move against Mexico had come, all was propitious, and if the United States would not accept the call of manifest destiny, he would. There is unmistakable evidence that he began at once to discuss the protectorate with close personal friends, or permitted them to discuss it with him. He admitted as much when in February he wrote Secretary of War Floyd that matters new and startling were afoot, that he might not only feel it his duty to repel invasion 'but to adopt such measures as will prevent the recurrence of similar inroads upon our frontiers.' He added that 'Texas can and will if appealed to muster into the field ten thousand men who are anxious... to make reclamation on Mexico for all her wrongs.' [12] He frankly stated that he had been solicited to establish a protectorate over Mexico, and had been assured of men, money, and arms. 'To these overtures,' he said, 'I made no favorable response, though, as an individual, I might have co-operated with them, by placing myself beyond the jurisdiction of the United States.' Houston declared that he had remained 'tranquil and silent' in the hope that the United States would consummate a policy which would prevent the destruction of the miserable inhabitants of Mexico, a policy which 'must and will be achieved by someone.' Fully conscious of the proprieties, Houston assured the President, through the Secretary of War, that he would do nothing *officially* to embarrass the administration. He made it clear that he would not violate his oath or do anything that was dishonorable. I never have, nor will I ever perform an official act that is not intended for my country's advancement.' [13] Houston evidently meant that he would resign the governorship or remove himself from the United States or do both before he launched his filibustering expedition. If he moved against Mexico, he would go as an individual at the head of a group of volunteers. That he would not scruple to build his military organization out of American material and on American soil is clearly revealed by later developments.

[12] Houston to Secretary of War Floyd, February 13, 1860. G.L.

[13] *Ibid.*, March 12, 1860, 'Difficulties on Southwestern Frontier,' pp. 139–142.

In fact, while dealing so candidly with the War Department, he was casting about for able men to assist him. On the same day that he wrote his February letter to Floyd, he wrote another to Ben McCulloch in Washington, stating that there would be stirring times on the Rio Grande ere long. For Ben a hint from Sam Houston, his Tennessee neighbor and Texas comrade, was sufficient. More of Ben later.

The most startling phase of the plan in its early stages was the effort to enlist the support of Colonel Robert E. Lee and to give him a leading rôle in the enterprise. This effort — and its failure — is revealed by the correspondence of one A. M. Lea with Robert E. Lee and Governor Sam Houston. Colonel Robert E. Lee had been ordered to Texas to take command of the eighth military district at San Antonio with special instructions to put an end to the Cortinas trouble. The future southern general landed at Indianola late in February and was met there by P. L. Lea, who managed to receive an introduction to the Virginian, and to ride with him from Indianola to Victoria. At this point P. L. Lea gives way to his brother, A. M. Lea, who had already commended Robert E. Lee to Houston, and who seems to have been Houston's contact man.

Without delay A. M. Lea set out to bring Colonel Robert E. Lee and Governor Houston together for a conference. On February 24 he wrote to each of them and he wrote Colonel Robert E. Lee again on each of the two succeeding days.

The pertinent part of his letter to Governor Houston is as follows:

> Col. R. E. Lee, whom I mentioned in my note of Saturday last, passed up to San Antonio, that day, to take command of this Military Dept. My brother P. L. was introduced to him at Indianola, and came up with him to Victoria. On the way, they had much conversation, and my brother was greatly impressed with his whole bearing....You will find that I have not painted an imaginary character. If you invite him to a conference about the defense of the frontier, you will find true all I have said of his manners and ability. As he is a 'Preux chevalier, sans peur et sans reproche,' he is very careful to do nothing that may cast a slur upon his name. He would not touch any thing that he would consider vulgar filibustering; but he is not without ambition, and, *under the sanction of Govt.* might be more than willing to aid you to pacificate Mexico; and if the people of the U. States should recall you from the 'Halls of Montezumas' to the 'White House' at Washington, you would find him well fitted to carry out your great idea of a Protectorate. He is well informed in matters of state, honest, modest, brave and skillful.[14]

Here indeed was a grand plan which envisaged Sam Houston as President of the United States and Robert E. Lee as Protector of Mexico.

[14] A. M. Lea to Governor Sam Houston, Golidad, February 24, 1860. G.L. This letter is remarkable in that it pays such high tribute to a man who was not yet well known.

The three letters which A. M. Lea wrote to Colonel Robert E. Lee are not available, but Colonel Lee's answer, written from San Antonio on March 1, reveals their purpose. The reply is so courteous that one must read it carefully, and with a knowledge of what was on foot, to realize that Robert E. Lee was even conscious of the subtle measures being taken to ensnare him through an appeal to his ambition. The significant portion of the letter reads:

> I feel that I owe to your kindness rather than to my merit your recommendations to Govr. Houston. I am aware of his ability, and first became acquainted with him upon my entrance into the Military Academy. He was President of the Board of Visitors that year and the impression he made has never been effaced. I have followed with interest his career since, and have admired his manly qualities and conservative principles. His last position in favor of the Constitution and Union elicits my cordial approbation. Should military force be required to quiet our Mexican frontier, I have no doubt that arrangements will be made to maintain the rights and peace of Texas, and I hope in conformity to the Constitution and laws of the country. It will give me great pleasure to do all in my power to support both.[15]

Lea sent Colonel Lee's letter to Houston with a note marked 'Private' written below the signature on the last page. He said:

> This letter from Col. Lee arrived only last night. Although it is plain from his allusion to the 'Constitution and the Laws' that he wd. not participate in any movement upon Mexico not properly sanctioned by the Government, yet his expressions towards yourself are so justly complimentary that I thot you wd. be glad to see them, coming as they do from a man of high intelligence and sincerity. You see, indeed, that they are designed for no eye but mine.[16]

From March or April until August no records have been found dealing specifically with Houston's plan to 'pacificate' Mexico. The records do reveal that Houston was industriously working with his many seemingly unrelated or even conflicting enterprises. That they were all related transpires through two letters which he wrote in August. Before quoting the letters it may be well to reconstruct the case by summarizing Houston's activities until August, 1860.

We have noted that in January, February, and March he called out seven companies of Texas Rangers, stationed them on the Indian frontier, and required them to enlist 'six good Mexican guides.' In March he authorized twenty-three frontier counties to call out companies of fifteen minute men each which number could be increased to

[15] R. E. Lee to Albert M. Lea, Engineer, San Antonio, March 1, 1860. G.L.

[16] R. E. Lee to A. M. Lea, San Antonio, March 1, 1860. A. M. Lea's note to Governor Houston is dated Aransas, April 3, 1860. G.L.

His Excy. Gen. Houston, Goliad, Texas,
Austin, Texas; 24 Feb. '60.

Dear Sir,

Col. R. E. Lee, whom I named in my note of Saturday last, passed up to San Antonio, that day, to take command of this Military Dept. My brother P. L. was introduced to him at Indianola, & came up with him to Victoria. On the way, they had much conversation, and my brother was greatly impressed with his whole bearing. It seems that he was with Gen. Wool in his march from San Antonio via Parras to Saltillo, & was ordered thence to join Gen. Scott on the line via Vera Cruz. You will find that I have not painted an imaginary character. If you invite him to a conference about the defence of the frontier, you will find true all I have said of his manners and ability. As he is a "Preux Chevalier, sans peur et sans reproche", he is very careful to do nothing that may cast a slur upon his name.

A. M. LEA TO GOVERNOR HOUSTON, FEBRUARY 24, 1860

He would not touch any thing that he would consider vulgar fillibustering; but he is not without ambition, and, under the sanction of the Govt. might be more than willing to aid you to pacificate Mexico; and if the people of the U. States should recall you from the "Halls of the Montezumas" to the "White House" at Washington, you would find him well fitted to carry out your great idea of a Protectorate. He is well informed in matters of State, honest, modest, brave and skillfull.

you see that Providence is guiding you on to the consummation of your grand conception of the Protectorate almost in spite of yourself.

With respectful regards to Mrs. H. I am,

Very truly, Your friend & servt.,

A. M. Lea

A. M. LEA TO GOVERNOR HOUSTON (*continued*)

San Antonio, Texas
1 March 1860

Albert M. Lea Esqr
Engineer

Dear Sir

I am very much obliged to you for your friendly letters of the 24th, 25th & 26th Ult which arrived together by the last mail. I feel that I owe to your kindness rather than to my merit your recommendations to Govr Houston. I am aware of his ability & first became acquainted with him upon my entrance into the Military Academy. He was President of the Board of Visitors that year & the impression he made has never been effaced. I have followed with interest his career since, & have admired his manly qualities & conservative principles. His last position in favour of the Constitution & Union elicits my cordial approbation.

Should military force be required to quiet our Mexican frontier, I have no doubt that arrangements will be made to maintain the rights & peace of Texas, & I hope in conformity to the Constitution & laws of the Country. It will give me great pleasure to do all in my power to support both.

COLONEL R. E. LEE TO A. M. LEA, MARCH 1, 1860

very truly yours

R E Lee

To His Excy.

(Private)

Gen. Sam Houston,
Austin, Tex.

Arenosos, Tex.
3d April 1860.

Dr. Sir,

This letter from Col. Lee arrived only last night. Although it is plain from his allusion to the "Constitution and the Laws" that he wd. not participate in any movement upon Mexico not expressly sanctioned by the Government, yet his expressions towards yourself are so justly complimentary that I thought you wd. be glad to see them, coming as they do from a man of high intelligence and sincerity. You see, indeed, that they were designed for no eye but mine. You will be gratified to see also how anxious he expresses himself as to the repression of Indian depredations.

Respectfully,
A M Lea

COLONEL R. E. LEE TO A. M. LEA (*continued*) AND
A. M. LEA'S NOTE TO GOVERNOR HOUSTON

twenty-five. It should be noted also that, in spite of the large force he had in service, he did nothing to help put down the Cortinas trouble on the Rio Grande. On the contrary, he mustered Ford's Rangers out of service. It may be mentioned also that Cortinas stated in his proclamation of November 23, 1859, that when Sam Houston became governor, the Texas-Mexicans would receive the protection to which they were legally entitled. Houston also asserted in his letter to Floyd of February 13, 1860, that large Mexican forces would join him if he invaded Mexico. On March 8, Houston ordered Colonel William J. Herbert to collect all the arms and ammunition he could get and called in all the six-shooters that had been loaned to the counties. On the same day he requested Secretary of War Floyd to furnish Texas enough arms to equip three thousand men, including a thousand cavalry — forty times the quota allowable in one year. He proposed in addition to raise five thousand men for service in Texas.

Houston's Indian policy was more mysterious than his military. His first move was to write Major S. A. Blain, trusted Texan in charge of the Indian Reserves north of Red River, to send him Jacobs and five other experienced Indian guides; he would employ them for a season and treat them like gentlemen, but he gave no hint as to how or where he would use them. Though it was not like Houston to cry for war against Indians, he now did so, and within two months put nearly one thousand Texas Rangers on the Indian frontier, and in March he sent Middleton T. Johnson from Austin with orders to make a campaign into the Indian country.

While the Johnson expedition was moving with warlike attitude into the Indian country, Houston was sending secret agents among the Indians for the ostensible purpose of securing information, but what their real purpose was we can only suspect. This much we do know, that the agents made their reports to Houston rather than to the military commander in the field. It is certain that they passed through Johnson's camp and reported its mismanagement directly to Houston.[17]

While Johnson's army was moving on the Indians with the sword and the agents among them with secret purposes, Houston was undertaking to persuade the federal government to turn over the management of the Indian tribes of Texas and the Southwest to him and two others *named by him.* On February 17, 1860, he wrote Jacob Thompson, Secretary of Interior, suggesting that the Indians of the Southwest be established in an agency within Texas where annuities could be distributed. On the same date he wrote privately to President Buchanan, suggesting that the treaty conference be held in April or in May on the

[17] Houston to S. F. Jones, August 6, 1860; P. D. Turner to Houston, July 10, 1860. G.L.

Wichita and that he and two others named by him be appointed commissioners to hold the council. He assured Buchanan that he would sacrifice his personal comfort in order to make the treaty.[18] The government declined Houston's suggestions and denied itself his services with a cautiousness which indicates that his designs were clear to the officials at Washington.

Let us view Houston's acts upon the assumption that he was planning an aggressive war against Mexico. In such a move the 'six good Mexican guides' would be invaluable and the large force of Texas Rangers, who had so little to do in the West, would form the nucleus of the army of conquest and the hundred thousand dollars' worth of arms and cavalry accouterments furnished by the federal government, together with the six-shooters collected in Texas, would arm the force. If Houston could make a treaty with the Indians by which he could induce them to come to Texas and settle on a reservation, he could as easily persuade them to accompany him to Mexico. Jacobs and the five Indian spies would certainly find employment for a season and be treated like gentlemen. The Cortinas War would furnish a pretext and arouse the fighting spirit among the Texans and cause them to swarm into his camp at the bugle call. Cortinas himself might be enlisted in the enterprise. Houston believed, or stated, that many Mexicans would join him. Moreover, Houston doubtless felt that the rumpus he would kick up in Mexico would cause the people of the United States to forget their factional and sectional quarrel about slavery and come in large numbers to his support in Mexico as they had come to him in Texas in 1836. The above picture, though based on circumstantial evidence, has about it a harmony which is almost convincing.

The one essential lacking to make the picture complete was that indispensable prerequisite of any warlike enterprise — money. The August letters show that Houston had not overlooked the money. His plan was to obtain it from the London financiers who held the depreciated bonds of Mexico. In the furtherance of his purpose he arranged for Colonel Mann, John Hancock of Georgetown, and Ben McCulloch to meet a representative of the London bondholders in New York for the purpose of persuading the bondholders to back the Mexican expedition. He was prepared to show the bankers how they could recover their losses and compound their gains by coming to his aid. Because

[18] Houston to Jacob Thompson, February 17, 1860; to Buchanan, February 17, 1860. Thompson replied to Houston on July 19, and explained his delay by stating that he had been waiting the action of Congress. He declined to accept Houston's service because of the law of February 27, 1851, which provided that only 'officers and agents of the Indian Department' could make treaties with the Indians. G.L.

of the disturbed conditions in Mexico the bonds which they held had depreciated one third or more. If the London bankers could be induced to send good money after bad, support Houston until he could 'pacificate' Mexico, they would be repaid in full and receive face value and interest for their old bonds within five years. With the funds thus obtained, Ben McCulloch could purchase ten thousand rifles made according to the specifications sent him by Houston, the Texas Rangers would be armed, and the warcry would ring again on the Rio Grande.

Houston's letter of August 27, 1860, furnished instructions for the interview with the representative of the London bondholders and that of August 28 instructed Ben McCulloch to make preliminary arrangements for the purchase of arms.

AUSTIN, *August* 27, 1860

MY DEAR COLONEL [MANN]:

I have now the pleasure of thanking you for two letters. When the first arrived I was so situated that I could not write. The second came two days since and I reply at my first leisure. On the 12th instant Mrs. Houston presented me with another son, of course a fine child in midwife parlance. Since then she has been so unwell that for ten nights I was not undressed, so you will think I have had a *protectorate* at home to claim my attention.

Well, you will have received a letter ere this reaches you from Hon. John Hancock, than whom there is no more worthy gentleman and he is fully reliable. You may say to him everything, as well as anything. All the talk about raising funds in the United States is gammon. If the Bond Holders cannot be approached, it would take years to raise a reliable force to achieve any glorious result. I know of no one more competent to consider and mature the manner as well as the subject than yourself.

The judge has from correspondence of Mr. Richardson to me, long since written to him to see the company and has written them to send an agent to New York and will meet him there, and of course yourself, and if they the Bond holders will go into it, to know on what terms with mutual guarantees for the performance of obligations. To moot this subject in the United States would awaken and interpose obstacles to success, if not defeat the project. No, the Bond Holders are the men to whom we are first to look. It is stated here that they the B. H.... offered their Bonds at 33 1/3 pr cent discount and even less than that. If this project succeeds, no matter under whose direction they could if wisely and ably managed realize every dollar of the principal as well as the interest of their debt in five years. This I believe but will they think so? Will men in London trust any man so far from home? But we can see and try.

As to the plan of operation that is a small matter, and if we have the sinews, without which no man can move it will be an easy matter to give motion to the achievement in the right direction....

I will write today to Genl Ben McCulloch, you can let him see my letter. Ben will do for a very 'Big Captain' as my Red Brothers say.

Mrs. Houston unites with me in regards and benedictions to yourself and son.

Devotedly Thine
SAM HOUSTON

MANN

The letter to Ben McCulloch states the high purpose of the enterprise, and gives detailed specifications as to the kind of guns that Houston wanted.

AUSTIN, *August* 28*th*, 1860.

MY DEAR GENERAL:

Today I have written to our friend Colonel Mann, and advised that you should see the contents. You will see by it that I am for some work if it is undertaken. We look on it as a mission of mercy and humanity and must not sink into the character of spoil and robbery. It must be to elevate and exalt Mexico to a position among the nations of the world.

A friend of yours and mine wishes to know how long it would take Colonel Morse, or whoever may be the manufacturer to make seven or ten thousand of his rifles, and what they could be furnished at all complete? If this question should be asked and get out, it would do no good and might create a thousand foolish or silly rumors. So it is best to keep it *Sub Rosa*.

I wish to obtain one of these rifles and I will now describe it to you.... Let it be three feet long in the barrel bore 60 ball to the pound, from the end of the cartridge to the muzzle rifled, the chamber smooth surface. The rifles, or the threads to be straight and the rifling and grooving to be so made as to prevent the least possible friction. No twist in the rifles, *perfectly straight*. You will not approve of this plan, and yet I feel assured that it is the best ever conceived by man. Were we together I could convince you of its truth. Have you suggested the improvement in the cartridge? I wish the gun to weigh from 7 to 8 pounds, and I wish it eight inches from the butt to become gradually thin to the muzzle, leaving it thick enough at the muzzle not to dent or mash.

Now please see if such a gun can be made, and what a plain one of good material will cost. I am thus particular because I want one gun to my liking... and it is my wish too, Ben, to economize, for the 12th inst. Mrs. Houston presented me with another son....

Salute all my friends. Oh Ben, on my honor, I forgot to tell you that I am out of the scrape for President. I am arms folded, and will stay so unless some malice is squinted at me.

Mrs. Houston and the children unite in regards to you. Don't get married.

Thine Truly,
SAM HOUSTON [19]

BEN MCCULLOCH

[19] The entire correspondence, including the Lee-Lea letters, was found in the Governor's letters in the State Library at Austin. Apparently these letters have escaped the notice of the historians. It is probable that letters from Ben McCulloch and others are held by Houston's heirs.

The records showing the results of the conference in New York are not available, but it is a safe guess that the London bondholders had about as many Mexican bonds as their portfolios could carry.

Moreover, the Civil War was too close now to be averted. Winter was at hand, a winter of four months for the season, of four years for the nation, and of thirty for the South. But winter is the season when old men like to sit by the fireside and dream.

In the winter of 1860–61 a grim and wonderfully wise old man must have sat many evenings in the governor's mansion before a wide hearth on which a great fire danced and laughed at the fantastic shadows which kept perfect time on the walls and high ceiling. But these shadows were no more fantastic than the old governor's dream. From the north and for the future he saw civil war, and predicted with prophetic vision its outcome. To the south he saw what might have been, and that was more pleasant to him. He saw a column of ten thousand men at the head of which rode 'a very big Captain,' who had proved at Monterey and Buena Vista what the Texas Rangers under his lead could do in Mexico. Behind Ben McCulloch rode all the Texas Rangers drawn from the Indian frontier. The 'good Mexican guides' would be the right men in the right place now. A Mexican contingent, led perhaps by that valiant freebooter Cortinas, would grow in numbers as the column advanced into Mexico. Forward and on flank a thousand swarthy Indians — Kickapoos, Creeks, Cherokees, Kiowas, and Comanches — would go to scout, trail, and spy. Thus would Sam Houston go like Alexander the Great carrying American civilization southward as the Macedonian had borne Greek culture eastward. For Mexico peace, for the United States unity, for Sam Houston fame and glory. This was the dream into which every part of Governor Houston's military policy fits. Had the opportunity come to Houston ten years earlier, he might have carried his plan through with success. His correspondence reveals that he proposed to assume full responsibility for his acts, and in no way to entangle the United States.

XI

THE STATE POLICE

The war is not yet over. I tell you there has been a slow civil war going on here and has been since the surrender of the Confederate armies.

Governor E. J. DAVIS

If Texas is lawless, Governor Davis encourages that lawlessness by promoting and rewarding the lawless; if our state abounds in murders, it is because Governor Davis receives and honors the blood-stained.

Flake's Daily Bulletin

The state police don't earn their salt... but devote all their time and talents in hunting up imaginary Ku Klux Klans.

Texas State Gazette

The police law is abolished over the Governor's veto. Glory to God in the highest; on earth peace, good will towards men.

JOHN HENRY BROWN

XI. THE STATE POLICE

THE conflict of the Civil War caused the Texas Rangers to sink into insignificance as a fighting force. The Indians of the Plains, overawed by the magnitude of the great war, drew back from the settlements, hoping perhaps that the white men would kill one another to the last man and leave the country to them. On the other hand, the white men sought to placate the Indians in order that they might have a free hand in killing one another. Both the North and the South sent military forces into the Indian country for the purpose of controlling the Indians, or enlisting them in the regular service. The Confederate Government, hard pressed on all sides, could not devote much attention to the Texas frontier, and was little inclined and less able to maintain a military force there for any length of time.

The chief factor tending to subordinate the Rangers as an effective fighting force was the desire of every fighting man to see more active service. Though many companies of Rangers were sent to the frontier, they were almost as frequently drawn off to the regular armies. Toward the end of the struggle, it was generally felt that men went into the border service only to escape the greater dangers that might be found with Lee or Johnston.

This all but total eclipse of the Ranger service is reflected in the scarcity of Ranger records in the adjutant general's papers in Austin. So much attention was given to the Confederate, and so little to the border, service that it is practically impossible to follow the activities of the so-called Texas Rangers. If the story is ever told, it will be fragmentary, and will not reveal a single character distinguished for his deeds as a Ranger during this period.

For nine years after the Civil War, the Texas Rangers were nonexistent. The Federal Government refused to permit a state to organize bodies of armed men for any purpose, and the task of keeping back the Indians was assumed, if not performed, by the regular army. For a time Texas was under strict military control, but in 1869 E. J. Davis was elected as a Republican carpetbag governor, and in January, 1870, he took office.

In no sense was Davis a representative of the people of Texas. His election had been made possible by disfranchising the Confederates and those in sympathy with them and enfranchising their former slaves. The governor, being a sagacious politician, realized that he would need extraordinary instruments of control with which to maintain himself, and in order to secure these he recommended the creation of a large body of state militia and a state police. It is with the state police that we are concerned.

1. THE ORGANIZATION OF THE STATE POLICE

The state police force was organized on July 1, 1870, and continued to operate until the last of April, 1873. At the head of the force was Adjutant General James Davidson, whose character was revealed when he quit his office with thirty-four thousand dollars of public funds. As first organized, the state police had four captains, eight lieutenants, twenty sergeants, and one hundred and twenty-five privates. In addition to these, every local peace officer was enrolled as a member and made subject to the orders of the adjutant general.[1]

The first captains were M. P. Hunnicutt, E. M. Alexander, Jack Helm, and L. H. McNelly, but only the last two were ever heard from. Helm became notorious for his conduct and McNelly distinguished for his later services in a better organization. Among the lieutenants were two negroes and four white men, while the privates could be described as a light and dark mixture, but whether light or dark they were of about equal merit.

The organization was launched with great *éclat* by the governor and the adjutant general, and if one may believe the official reports, it accomplished much good. Governor Davis had prepared the way for the force by proclaiming that Texas was a state filled with desperate characters. At the end of the first month it was announced that the officers had arrested forty-four murderers and felons, five of whom they had killed for resisting arrest. The *Journal* praised the force and advised any rascals who were still running loose to seek a cooler climate. The adjutant general compiled a list of 2780 fugitives and criminals in one hundred and eight counties, and on December 31, 1870, he re-

[1] For a detailed account of the state police, see William Curtis Nunn, 'A Study of the State Police During the E. J. Davis Administration.' An M.A. thesis, University of Texas, 1931.
The history of the Police Act may be traced in the *Daily State Journal* files from 1870 to 1873. The *Journal* was the official organ of the Reconstruction Government in Texas, but despite this fact it is a valuable source.

ported that 973 of them had been arrested and property valued at thirty thousand dollars had been returned to the rightful owners.[2]

The governor was so well pleased that he asked the legislature, in a message of January 18, 1871, to increase the regular force and to authorize the appointment of twenty special policemen in each county. These were to be paid by the county when in actual service. The law of May 2 increased the number of commissioned officers by one third, and increased the pay by allowing twenty dollars a month for horses, and mileage at the rate permitted to sheriffs. All railway conductors, baggage masters, and other officials might be enrolled as state policemen without compensation.[3] If this law did not improve the conduct of the resident Texans, it did enable the carpetbag government to build up its political machine and to feed a few more of its followers out of the public funds.

The career of the state police affords a story of official murder and legalized oppression. The force never had the slightest chance to succeed, because it was bitterly opposed by the most substantial element in the state. Even though it had been efficient, which it was not, and even though it had done commendable work, which it did not, the people would have denied it any claim to success. No fault of the police was overlooked, no mistake excused.

2. *THE RECORD OF THE STATE POLICE*

Though space does not permit a complete story of the activities of the state police, a few illustrative incidents may be narrated. The first account records the murder of the Kelley boys in DeWitt County. It seems that Jack Helm, one of the first four captains, was responsible for the bitter feeling engendered in DeWitt County against the police. B. J. Pridgen, member of the legislature, said that the people believed that Governor Davis had conferred on the police captain absolute authority over the lives and property of the citizens. The captain was described as a man ignorant of the law and of the rights of the citizens. He was making arrests without legal authority and was levying contributions. He was reckless and indiscreet, and kept himself constantly in the saddle, 'swinging to and fro over the country,' insulting and terrifying the people. The results Pridgen described thus: 'Commu-

[2] *Report of the Adjutant General of the State of Texas for the Year 1870*, p. 11.

[3] Gammel, *Laws of Texas*, vol. VI, pp. 972–74.

nities were dissolved and society broken up from the fact that neighbors were afraid to let their families visit for fear that something might be said in social conversation that would be improperly construed against Helm and his men and magnified into mischief.'[4]

This was written about a month after the Kelley boys were killed on August 26, 1870. The reason for the killing is not clear, but it seems to have been connected with the Sutton-Taylor trouble. The story here is from the sworn statement of Mrs. Amanda Kelley, wife of Henry.

When the Kelleys arose on this August morning, they saw three men waiting on their horses near the yard gate. They recognized two of them as Doc White and John Meador. The third man was a stranger, a state policeman. The visitors invited Henry Kelley to 'step out here a few minutes,' and when he did so they told him that they wanted him to go with them to Hallettsville, thirty-five miles away. Kelley, accompanied by one of the men, fetched his horse and went into the house for his hat and gun. It was not until he appeared with the six-shooter, scabbard and belt that he was informed that he was a prisoner; at the request of his captors, he left the six-shooter on a block between the door and gate.

Mrs. Kelley now asked her husband if she might accompany the party as far as her father's home. Without waiting for Mrs. Kelley, the party of four men set out for the home of William Kelley, a quarter of a mile distant. Mrs. Kelley became apprehensive, was made more so by hearing two shots, and hurried on after the men. When she came up with them, she found that the party had captured William Kelley and had been joined by William Sutton.

When the party came to a trail, they ordered the prisoners to take it, but the women were in a buggy and had to travel the road. Amanda Kelley became more suspicious of the intentions of the men, left the buggy, passed through the brush and climbed a hill where she could command a view of the trail. She saw the men in a small clearing some fifty yards away, apparently engaged in conversation. Both the Kelleys were mounted and William was cutting tobacco and filling his pipe. Then he dismounted, and knelt to strike the match on the sole of his boot. As he did so, the woman saw one of the men point his gun downward at the kneeling figure and fire. Another gun fired and Henry Kelley fell from his horse to the ground. The firing now became general and smoke enveloped the scene to hide the actors from the terrified woman on the hill. She screamed and ran forward, only to find both the Kelleys dead. The state policeman and his companions

[4] *Daily Austin Republican*, November 1, 1870.

had ridden away.[5] Though Jack Helm was dismissed from the police force, no indictments were found.

In December, 1870, two negroes were murdered near Clifton in Bosque County and two young men of Hill County, Sol Nicholson and James Gathings, were charged with the crime. Lieutenant W. T. Pritchett was sent to Colonel J. J. Gathings's home, where the accused were supposed to be concealed. When Colonel Gathings learned that the officer had no warrants, he said, 'You cannot search my house with your damned negro police.' Pritchett paid no attention to this protest and ransacked the house without finding the men. As Pritchett was leaving, he and some of his men were captured by twelve or fifteen citizens who represented themselves to be officers of the law. The trial of the policemen was held at Hillsboro. Armed men had crowded into the courtroom and filled the streets. The justice of the peace fixed the bond of the policemen at five hundred dollars, whereupon Colonel Gathings, at the head of what the policemen termed a mob, rushed to the judge's bench with clenched fist and swore that 'By God, if the bond is not made strong and substantial, I will rearrest him [Pritchett] and hold him until the day of his trial.' Pritchett was released under bond, which he forfeited, on the ground that he was held only in order that the young men accused of slaying the negroes might make good their escape.

On January 12, 1871, Adjutant General Davidson left Austin for the scene of the trouble with fifty state guards. He declared martial law in Hill County, issued orders for the arrest of Colonel Gathings and seven other men. The *Waco Examiner* stated that the arrested men were taken to the courthouse, from which all save officers and the prisoners were excluded. The military authorities informed Gathings that he and his friends could escape court martial only by paying one hundred dollars for each day that martial law was in force. Gathings replied that he could not pay this, and thereupon Davidson told him that three thousand dollars in currency 'would satisfy him.' Gathings was further informed, according to the story, that if he failed to pay, the troops would be quartered on the people and that he would be tried and sent to the penitentiary before he could appeal his case. He was refused counsel and given fifteen minutes to make his decision. In the meantime the warrants against the state policemen were demanded and given up. Gathings was able to raise $2765 which Davidson accepted.

[5] Affidavit of Mrs. Amanda Kelley, October 15, 1870, published in the *Daily Austin Republican*, November 1, 1870.

This done, the officer raised the martial law decree, which had been in force two days, and returned to Austin.

A Waco editor exclaimed: 'Here we behold the melancholy and humiliating spectacle of an officer engaged in plundering a citizen of his property by aid of military power.... It is a robbery which is not sustained nor covered by Radical legislation.'[6]

The establishment of martial law in Walker County was brought about under the following circumstances: A negro named Sam Jenkins testified before a grand jury that he had been flogged by some white men. A few days later his body was found bearing evidence that he had been murdered. Captain L. H. McNelly was sent with a squad of state police to ferret out the crime, and in a short time he arrested four men and brought them for preliminary examination before Judge J. R. Burnett. The trial lasted three days, was attended with the greatest excitement, and resulted in the discharge of one man and orders to hold the others for trial at the next term of court. Captain McNelly was instructed to return three of the men to jail to await the next term of court.

Through the aid of friends the prisoners had obtained and concealed on their persons 'at least two six-shooters each.' These were now brought into action and McNelly and one of his men, Tom Keese, were wounded. The prisoners bolted for the streets, where they met friends and confederates with shotguns and other weapons and all rode out of town firing and yelling like savages.

On February 15, 1871, Davis declared martial law, and on February 27, Davidson convened a military commission for the trial of some twenty persons. Some of these were fined and one was sent to the penitentiary for five years. The expense of the proceedings was paid by a levy of twenty-five cents on the hundred dollars on all taxable property in the county.[7]

Norman Kittrell declared that the people did not resist martial law because they had been dominated for five years by the carpetbagger, scalawag, and negro, and were completely cowed. From memory he wrote: 'As I look back upon the day when I, but a little more than a youth, went with a committee of citizens to protest against the tax levy and martial law, and explain that they had done nothing to merit such treatment, I recall how contemptuously the petty tyrant Davidson

[6] *Waco Examiner*, quoted in *Texas State Gazette*, January 25, 1871; Davidson's Report, *Daily State Journal*, February 10, 1871.

[7] E. W. Horne to Governor E. J. Davis, *Daily State Journal*, February 10, 1871. For a list of the men arraigned, see Nunn, *State Police*, p. 111.

treated the committee. I wonder that the people had not risen in a body and wiped him and his roving band of buccaneers off the earth. I have always regretted that they did not.'[8] While Captain McNelly was convalescing from his wounds, he was interviewed by a reporter from the *Galveston News*. McNelly declared that the sheriff could have prevented the trouble by searching the people who entered the courtroom. He declared that martial law was not necessary, as shown by the fact that eight or ten men were collecting the tax, and he intimated that it was imposed for the money it would bring.[9]

Perhaps the most vicious application of martial law was made in Limestone and Freestone counties in October, 1871. On September 30, a group of citizens entered Clark's saloon in Groesbeck for a social drink and among them was D. C. Applewhite. In the saloon were four state policemen, Mitchell Cotton, a yellow man named Johnson, and two others. Cotton approached Applewhite in a threatening attitude, and when the white man asked the negro if he were armed, Cotton and his companion both fired. Applewhite ran from the saloon, crossed Waco Street, and fell off the sidewalk apparently dead. Mitchell Cotton followed him and fired two more shots into his body.

The four state policemen took refuge in the mayor's office, where they barricaded themselves, fired into the street and defied arrest. Later they were reinforced by twenty associates, and the combined party secured horses and rode out of town, threatening the people and firing their weapons as they went.

Mayor A. Zadek made every effort to handle the situation in an orderly manner. He organized two forces, one mounted to pursue and arrest the guilty person, and the other to patrol the streets. At midnight the sheriff of Limestone County arrived and secured warrants for the arrest of the murderers, who were now protected by more than one hundred armed negroes. Though armed citizens were riding in from all parts of the country, they did not create any disorder.

Judge J. W. Oliver came to Groesbeck on October 4 to warn the citizens against doing anything that would bring martial law; and, as a result of his advice, the people placed themselves under the command of Captain George W. Farrow of the state police. They went further and drew up a petition, containing seventy signatures, praying the legislature to save them from military rule. In part the petition ran: 'Everything done by us was at the command of the officers of the law and for our own protection from the threats and menaces of a mob of

[8] Norman G. Kittrell, *Governors Who Have Been, and Other Public Men of Texas*, p. 53.

[9] *Daily State Journal*, March, 17, 1871.

infuriated men. We would therefore appeal to you... to stand by us in this darkest hour of our history, and avert the evils and calamitous consequences which would be visited upon us by a declaration of martial law and a suspension of the writ of habeas corpus and right of trial by jury.' Davis disregarded all pleas, and on October 9, proclaimed martial law in Limestone and Freestone counties and assessed a penalty of fifty thousand dollars, which was paid by a three per cent tax.[10] Though the legislature was radically Republican, it denounced Davis for declaring martial law and demanded the withdrawal of the military forces.[11]

3. *PUBLIC OPINION OF THE STATE POLICE*

Enough has been said to show that the state police had little support from the people. Even where they were in the right, their efforts often ended disastrously for themselves. Governor Davis was always warm in his support of them. In a public address, he declared that lawlessness was increasing in Texas. Formerly, he said, one could travel from Galveston to Austin unarmed, but now it was not safe to do so. He asserted that there were seven or eight hundred homicides a year in Texas while in New York City there were only seventy or eighty. 'The war is not over yet. I tell you there has been a slow civil war going on here and has been ever since the surrender of the Confederate armies.' He proposed to end this by the militia bill and the police bill.

Flake published Davis's speech and added: 'It is difficult to comment upon a dispatch like this with any degree of calmness, for if the Governor used the language set down to him therein there is no word within the lids of Webster Unabridged to be used in reply but one — it is a lie.... If Texas is lawless, Governor Davis encourages that lawlessness by promoting and rewarding the lawless; if our state abounds in murderers, it is because Governor Davis receives and honors the blood-stained, as if they were decorated with medals of honor and distinction.' [12] Flake wrote a protest to Horace Greeley, comparing the state police to the *gens d'armes* of France and Austria. Davis, he said, had transplanted the Austrian system to Texas. 'He exercises universal espionage over the people of this State. His administration is inquisitorial. The cook that prepares our food, the servant who ministers to our personal com-

[10] For proclamation see the *Daily State Journal*, October 11, 1871. B. F. Baldridge to Adjutant General Davidson. A.G.P.

[11] *Appleton's Cyclopedia*, vol. IX, p. 732.

[12] *Flake's Daily Bulletin*, July 1, 1871.

fort, the confidential employee... may be... the hired spy of his Excellency, the Governor.'[13] At the same time the citizens of the state drew up a desperate petition praying Congress to deliver them from the tyranny that they feared, but Congress apparently took no heed of their pleas.[14]

The Davis paper, the *State Journal*, defended the police and claimed that they were performing much good work. It printed long lists of those arrested and it pointed out that several policemen had been killed in the performance of duty.

The most serious charge lodged against the state police was that of killing prisoners with the excuse that they were attempting to escape. The story will show that *la ley de fuga* has been invoked at times by the Texas Rangers in order to put away some criminal who was particularly obnoxious to the people. In most cases the Rangers have been supported in such acts by public opinion, but behind the state police was no supporting public opinion.

'Killed in attempting to escape.'

'Killed while resisting arrest.'

'These are two expressions,' said an editor, 'that are fast coming to have a melancholy and terrible significance to the people of Western Texas. They furnish the brief epitaph to the scores who have fallen and are falling victims to the ignorance, the arrogance, or the brutality of those charged with the execution of the law.'[15]

The *State Gazette* declared: 'The State police don't earn their salt. They never trouble themselves in pursuing real offenders, but devote all their precious time and talents in hunting up imaginary Ku Klux Klans.... If a negro is caught in the act of robbing a hen roost and soundly thrashed by some ex-Confederate, the whole police force would be forthwith ordered out on the ex-parte statement of the thieving black.'[16]

On April 11, 1873, the *State Journal* published a 'Roll of Honor,' the names of twelve policeman killed in service. By way of reply, D. M. Prendergast, member of the legislature, published a 'Roll of Horror,' a list of seventeen men who had been murdered by the police. 'These,' he said, 'are some of the men who compose the roll of horror. God save the mark!'[17]

The most effective weapon used against the state police was ridicule. The lower ranks of the force never had any standing, and when the

[13] *Flake's Daily Bulletin*, July 8, 1870.

[14] *Daily Austin Republican*, July 27, 1870.

[15] Editorial in the *Victoria Advocate*, reprinted in the *Austin Daily Republican*, October 10, 1870. This editorial was evidently brought forth by the murder of the Kelley boys in DeWitt County.

[16] *Texas State Gazette*, July 26, 1871.

[17] *Daily Democratic Statesman*, April 17, 1873.

head of it, the adjutant general, absconded with thirty-four thousand dollars of the people's money, he added no luster to the name of the force. Charges had been made earlier, by ex-members of the force, that the higher-ups had defrauded the privates and exploited them. The editor of the *Daily Democratic Statesman* described the way a policeman was made. The adjutant general, he said, would pick up some poor devil who was not worth a dime and fit him out with mount and gear. For a broken-down horse worth ten or twenty dollars he would charge fifty or a hundred and fifteen; for a shoddy uniform worth twelve dollars the recruit would pay twenty; for a thirty-dollar Winchester carbine he paid forty; and for a badge worth a dollar he paid three. 'And now we have a new-made policeman, fully equipped for the service in the holy work of reducing Texas to a sublime state of peace and order — but we don't have him long.' As soon as his outfit is paid for, he is forgotten and told that the treasury is empty.

The *Journal*, rankling under the ridicule, denied the charges and challenged any person to prove their truth. The editor gave the contract price for the supplies furnished the policeman; and while admitting that there was a 'stoppage' of three dollars for the badge, he claimed that the amount was returned when the policeman surrendered this emblem.[18]

Even Morgan C. Hamilton, who had been an extreme Radical Unionist, and writing as a United States Senator from Texas, joined in the ridicule of the police. 'As a class they are the most wolfish-looking set of men that have ever been employed on any public duty in this country,' he said.[19]

Ridicule gave way to burlesque in the *State Gazette*.

'They were all armed with terrible deadly ninety-nine shooting rifles — mitrailleuses, and they let our boys look at them....

'And they were filled up with good old copper distilled, and they had a coppery appearance about the nose, and a watery look out of the eyes, and were men of exceeding great stature, two of them laid end to end would have measured two and a quarter yards....

'And they were of the cavalry breed, mounted outside the ribs of sway-back double-barreled mustangs of an exceedingly fine stock — so fine that they did hardly cast a shadow; whose hip bones did protrude mightily, whereon these valiant warriors were wont to hang their massive felt helmets when they sought their pillows at night....'[20]

As soon as the state legislature became Democratic, the state police force was doomed. The bill for repeal passed both houses, was vetoed

[18] *Daily State Journal*, October 1, 1871.

[19] *Flake's Daily Bulletin*, August 24, 1871.

[20] *Texas State Gazette*, December 19, 1870.

by the governor, returned to the legislature, and on April 22 passed over the executive veto. On the same day and for several days there was much rejoicing. The *State Gazette's* editor reminded the people that the worst class of negroes in Texas had been enlisted and sent forth to redress the imaginary grievances of their race. 'The police system is a failure and a disgrace to our State, and should be swept from the statute book without ceremony,' he said. The editor of the *Dallas Herald* became so excited by the good news that he mixed his metaphors hopelessly but made his meaning clear. 'The people of Texas,' he exclaimed, 'are today delivered from as infernal engine of oppression as ever crushed any people beneath the heel of God's sunlight. The damnable police bill is ground beneath the heel of an indignant legislature.' The legislators were no less excited than the editors. John Henry Brown, who had sponsored repeal, rushed to the telegraph office and sent this exultant message to his home paper: 'The police law is abolished over the Governor's veto. Glory to God in the highest; on earth peace, good will towards men.' And up at Denton the people spent the entire night in shooting anvils in celebration of the news.[21]

[21] *Texas State Gazette*, April 22, 1873; *Norton's Union Intelligencer*, May 3, 1873.

XII

McNELLY AND HIS MEN IN SOUTHWEST TEXAS

I reported to the sheriff that the enemy had crossed the river . . . gone to the La Parra and gathered these beeves, that I had found them at the marsh, they had fought, and that I would now place him in charge of their bodies.

L. H. McNelly

That showed the kind of love Captain McNelly had for his men, and he did not have a man in his company that wouldn't have stepped in between him and death.

Bill Callicott

XII. McNELLY AND HIS MEN IN SOUTHWEST TEXAS

1. THE DeWITT COUNTY FEUD

In 1874 the legislature created two distinct military forces for the protection of the frontier and the suppression of lawlessness. The Frontier Battalion, commanded by Major John B. Jones, was designed to control the Indian front on the west. What was known as the Special Force of Rangers was sent to Southwest Texas with the primary purpose of suppressing the bandit troubles on the Mexican border. The commander of this force was Captain L. H. McNelly, a veteran of the Civil War and an officer in the Davis state police.

Captain McNelly was sent to DeWitt County in the spring of 1874 because of an outbreak of the Sutton-Taylor feud. On March 11 one of the Suttons and a man named Slaughter took passage on the steamer *Clinton* at Indianola. About one o'clock William Taylor and a companion boarded the ship, and shot Sutton and Slaughter to death in their cabin. The country seethed with excitement at this outbreak of an old feud and shortly armed men were riding or congregating in expectant groups about the community. On April 2 or 3, William Taylor was arrested in Cuero and sent under a heavy escort to Indianola. The train bearing Taylor was fired upon by unknown parties, supposedly Taylor's friends who hoped in this way to liberate him. At Indianola, Taylor was placed on the *Clinton* and taken to Galveston.[1]

It was the court trials growing out of this incident that caused General William Steele to send Captain McNelly with a special company of Rangers to DeWitt County. McNelly raised his company at Burton, in Washington County where he resided, and arrived at the town of Clinton, then the county site of DeWitt, on August 1, 1874. He reported: 'The citizens seem to be very much pleased with our presence and I will see that they are satisfied with our conduct while

[1] *Galveston News*, September 22, 1874.

CAPTAIN L. H. McNELLY

here.' He added that he would like to have more pistol ammunition and would need to have his horses shod.[2]

A few days later, Captain McNelly sent Sergeant Middleton and three men, accompanied by John Taylor, to escort an important witness from Yorktown, a village about twelve miles distant. The party secured the witness and had returned to within eight miles of Clinton when they were met in the road by fifteen armed horsemen.

'Who are you?' asked Sergeant Middleton.

'Who are you? *Que dow!*' (Look out!) 'Here they are, boys, give 'em hell.' With this the mob fired a volley, wounding one of the Rangers in the shoulder. Both parties concealed themselves as best they could, and the firing continued for fifteen minutes. During a lull the mob pretended to discover the identity of the Rangers, stopped firing, offered assistance to the wounded Ranger, and loaned the officers horses in the place of the wounded animals.

In the meantime the witness ran off, 'But I caught him this morning and have him in camp,' wrote the Captain. Captain McNelly said that the purpose of the mob was to kill the witness whose evidence would convict some of them of cold-blooded murders. 'At the first fire,' wrote McNelly, 'the witness fled and on their approaching my men their first words were, "By God, boys, he's gone. 'Twas he who ran off through the fields."' McNelly declared that the method of destroying unfavorable testimony in DeWitt County, one long in vogue, was to murder the witnesses. He was of the opinion that the road party was led by 'Old Joe Tumlinson.' [3]

On August 8, McNelly wrote that the grand jury was in session and would indict members of both the Sutton and Taylor factions, men who seemed to him 'all alike... turbulent, treacherous and reckless.' He was quite certain that the Tumlinson band, which numbered one hundred and fifty men, would not surrender to the sheriff. 'I saw him,' says McNelly, 'at the head of seventy-five well-armed men who have no interest but in obeying his orders; he is a man who has always righted his own wrongs and he tells me that the only way for this country to have peace is to kill off the Taylor party. He has never been made to feel that the civil law could and should be the supreme arbiter between man and man and I am satisfied that when the sheriff calls on me to serve papers on Tumlinson that he will resist or at least refuse to go into court without his arms and men as he has done heretofore.... I feel entirely able to whip Tumlinson with the men I have if it must be a fight but will need more men. Fifty men cannot over-

[2] McNelly to Steele, July 22 and August 3, 1874. A.G.P.

[3] *Ibid.*, August 3, 7, 8, November 30, 1874. A.G.P.

awe these people; they have been in the habit of over-riding the officers of the law so long that it will require more than I have to "bluff" them. We cannot expect help from the citizens; they had rather pay out half they own than obey the summons of the sheriff.' [4]

Captain McNelly was not sure as to the strength of the Taylor party, but he estimated that the Taylorites could also bring one hundred and fifty men into the field.

Between these two armed bands a state of constant warfare existed. Compromises and treaties had been so often broken that the confidence of one in the promises of the other was unknown. Between them the neutrals steered an unhappy and precarious course, and were obnoxious to both sides.

The trial of William Taylor was scheduled to begin at Indianola on September 24. On September 19, General Steele telegraphed McNelly, who had gone to Burton, to report at Indianola on the day before the trial. McNelly was unable to reach Indianola, but wired his sergeant to take the company there. The heavy rains and the swollen streams cut off the mail and the telegram was not delivered until four days after the trial was to begin. In the meantime the Tumlinson-Sutton party issued a public circular calling a meeting at Indian Motte near Clinton for the purpose of organizing a new company and selecting new officers. Their purpose was to go to Indianola 'to see that Taylor got justice.' The impression prevailed that Taylor would be killed before the end of his trial.[5]

In order to protect Taylor, Governor Richard Coke ordered General Steele to Galveston, where he mustered a company of the best infantry to escort the prisoner to the trial. The steamer *Harlan* arrived at Indianola on September 23 and the prisoner was marched to the jail in the center of a squad of soldiers. There was no disturbance at the trial.[6]

McNelly did not confine his activities to guarding prisoners and protecting courts. He established a system of espionage and sent scouting expeditions over the country in search of troublesome characters. When he heard that John W. Hardin and Jim Taylor would be in the county on a certain date, he declared that 'if they come I will kill all my horses or have them.' [7] He sent squads of from four to six men to scour the country in all directions, and instructed them to approach towns and country stores in as unexpected manner as pos-

[4] McNelly to Steele, August 7, 8, 1874. A.G.P.

[5] *Ibid.*, August 28, September 30, 1874. A.G.P.

[6] *Galveston News*, September 24, 1874.

[7] McNelly to Steele, September 2, 1874. A.G.P.

sible. To the Rangers this meant a whirlwind approach. 'I find,' he said, 'that it does a great deal of good to disperse congregations that usually meet at grogshops to have difficulties and concoct devilment; most of them being under indictment in some part of the State are in constant expectation of the approach of an officer and when they hear of my men coming, they scatter.' [8]

Early in November the United States marshal requested McNelly to aid him in serving twenty-seven writs from Galveston, calling for Joe Tumlinson and friends. McNelly hoped that the United States could lay its hands on old Joe and break him up. Papers were out in 'the case of that old negro they hung [and] gutted.' In conclusion McNelly expressed the opinion that these writs for the leading spirits of the Tumlinson party had been issued just in time, 'for old Joe has just joined the church and I think must be meditating the death of some preacher or some kindred amusement. I have been more on the alert than ever.'

At the end of November, Captain McNelly made a lengthy report covering his four months' stay in DeWitt County. The presence of the state troops there had been beneficial and their conduct exemplary. The peaceful citizens considered that their presence was an absolute necessity. Trouble would break out immediately upon their removal. Life had become more secure, not because of any change of the feudists' hearts, but because of fear engendered by the presence of the Rangers. 'Members of both factions would willingly witness a renewal of hostilities as peace leaves them without employment. These have nothing to lose and everything to gain by a return to open warfare and will do all in their power to promote discord.' The Rangers were closely watching the turbulent ones who were learning that their lawless course could no longer be pursued with impunity. Court would open again in December, both factions would be present, and trouble would be imminent. McNelly would have his men posted, and if trouble came he would try to see that not a single survivor escaped.

He turned again to the inefficiency and laxity of the local officers. 'I am satisfied that if a judge and state's attorney of probity, ability and nerve were sent down to hold court in December, they could effectually prevent a continuation of disgraceful scenes in and out of the halls of justice. With the present incumbents there is no hope.' [9] In his last report McNelly said that court was in session, going much quieter than in many years, but the officers had not improved. The district attorney was drunk most of the time, and 'when sober is of no

[8] McNelly to Steele, October 18, 1874. A.G.P.

[9] *Ibid.*, November 5, 1874. A.G.P.

earthly account.... Everybody curses him when they feel like doing so and he will resent nothing.'

To leave the impression that McNelly and his men cured the social ills of DeWitt County would be erroneous. Time only could heal the deep wounds that the feud had made. Moreover, McNelly was circumscribed in his action. He was known to be — and later proved to be — a hard man who resorted to vigorous action in enforcing the law, but Governor Richard Coke had warned him to be careful in dealing with citizens. One of his own men said in later years that Captain McNelly never claimed to have accomplished much in DeWitt County. A situation better suited to his particular genius awaited him on the Rio Grande.

2. *THE RED RAID ON THE RIO GRANDE*

In the spring of 1875 Captain McNelly was asked to organize another company of Rangers to perform special duty in the southwest, where cattle stealing was in progress on a grand scale. On April 18, 1875, General Steele received the following telegram from Sheriff John McClure of Nueces County:

> IS CAPT McNELLY COMING. WE ARE IN TROUBLE. FIVE RANCHES BURNED BY DISGUISED MEN NEAR LAPARRA LAST WEEK. ANSWER.

As Captain McNelly approached the border, he found the country overrun by bands of armed men who had assembled for the ostensible purpose of self-protection, but who could scarcely be distinguished either by appearance or performance from groups whose sole object was to plunder and raid. With his characteristic force McNelly struck down these organizations, Mexicans and Americans alike, as a necessary preliminary to the clean-up he planned. 'The acts committed by Americans,' he wrote, 'are horrible to relate; many ranches have been plundered and burned, and the people murdered or driven away; one of these parties confessed to me in Corpus Christi as having killed eleven men on their last raid. I immediately issued an order... disbanding the minute companies and all armed bands acting without the authority of the state; my order was obeyed, or agreed to be, without hesitation.... Had I not disbanded these companies it is possible...

and very probable that civil war would have ensued as the Mexicans are very much exasperated.' [10]

At Edinburg, Captain McNelly met Captain Neal Coldwell of the Frontier Battalion who seemed 'disinclined to take chances crossing the river.' Cortinas had made his appearance on the opposite side the day before McNelly arrived and had hanged an *alcalde* and another Mexican for killing one of his cow thieves.[11] In the latter part of May, McNelly moved to Brownsville, where he expected to remain during June. The people there were much alarmed about their safety. Even General Potter, commander of Fort Brown, admitted that the Mexicans had been crossing the river above and below Brownsville and that he had only one hundred and fifty men for defense and — McNelly added — these were negroes. Stealing had increased enormously, carried on by well-mounted and well-armed men. In conclusion — and McNelly's last sentences were often significant — he said, 'I think you will hear from us soon.' [12]

The increase in the theft of cattle was owing to the fact that the Mexicans had received large contracts to deliver beef to the Cuban market, and the boldness of the thieves was inspired by Juan N. Cortinas, now an important figure on the south side of the river, and the chief contractor for the Cuban market. When McNelly reached Brownsville, or Point Isabel, it was reported to him that a steamer was standing three miles offshore to receive a herd of four hundred cattle which were being held in Mexico at Bagdad. Two thirds of them bore American brands. Cortinas himself was in the vicinity with seventy-five men, half of whom were mounted on horses with American brands.[13] Cortinas had a band of his men in Texas after more cattle, and McNelly knew about it. The story of the Ranger's movements from June 5 to June 12, when he slew the thieves on Palo Alto Prairie, the scene of the first battle of the Mexican War, is most graphically told by McNelly in his official report which follows.

BROWNSVILLE, [TEXAS]
June —, 1875

GEN. WM. STEELE:

I have the honor to report that on Saturday the fifth I received information of a party of Mexicans, fifteen in number, who had crossed the river at [about] eight miles below Brownsville for the purpose of stealing cattle. I immediately ordered Lieutenant Robinson with eighteen men to proceed to the crossing of the Arroyo Colorado and send out scouts, to learn their whereabouts and report to me.

[10] McNelly to Steele, April 29, 1875. A.G.P.

[11] *Ibid.*, May 14, 1875. A.G.P.

[12] *Ibid.*, May (undated), 1875. A.G.P.

[13] G. A. Hall to McNelly, June 7, 1875. A.G.P.

On the morning of the eighth (8th) the Lieutenant reported that he had captured one of the raiders. I at once went to the company and learned from the prisoner, Rafael Salinas, that the party consisted of sixteen men under command of Camillo Lerma and Jose Maria Olguine, alias the Aboja (the Needles) and that they had been sent to [by] General Cortinas to La Parra neighborhood to get a drove of cattle for the Cuban market. He further stated that he had been left behind to remount and act as rear guard. I then sent a spy on their trail with instructions to follow them until they returned, at the same time keeping my men concealed and secretly guarding all the passes of the Arroyo Colorado for twenty miles in my front.

On Friday evening ... the eleventh we caught a Mexican called Incosnascion Garcia who was identified as one of the party. He told the same story as Rafael Salinas, as far as number, name and intention of the raiders, and said he was the advance guard and that they had about 300 head of cattle, and would cross the Arroyo that night, and try to drive to the river next day.

I stationed my men in a motte and remained there until two o'clock, when one of my scouts came in and reported that the thieves had passed four miles east of our post early in the night. I at once started to strike their trail, or get in their front by taking a near cut to Laguna Madre. About seven o'clock next morning I came in sight of them, about eight miles distant. They discovered my command about the same time and commenced running the cattle. They drove about three miles, and finding we were gaining on them, they drove the herd on a little island, in a salt marsh, and took their stand on the opposite side, and *waited* our approach for a *half hour* before we reached the marsh.

On arriving I found them drawn up in line on the south side of a marsh about six hundred yards wide, filled with mud and water, eighteen or twenty inches deep, and behind a bank four or five feet high. I formed my men as skirmishers and rode into the marsh, not allowing my men to unsling their carbines, or draw their pistols. As soon as we struck the water, the raiders commenced firing on us with Spencers and Winchester carbines. We advanced at a walk (a more rapid gait being impossible) and not firing a shot or speaking a word and keeping our line well dressed.

On our nearing the position they held, perhaps within seventy-five or one hundred yards, they wheeled their horses round, and galloped off at a slow gait. When we got out on hard ground we pressed forward and soon brought ourselves within shooting distance, fifty or sixty yards. The Mexicans then started at a full run, and I found that our horses could not overtake them. So I ordered three of my best mounted men to pass to their right flank and press them so as to force a stand.

And as I had anticipated, the Mexicans turned to drive my men off, but they held their ground, and I got up with four or five men, when the raiders broke. After that it was a succession of single hand fights for six miles before we got the last one. Not one escaped out of the twelve that were driving the cattle. They were all killed.

I have never seen men fight with such desperation. Many of them, after being shot from their horses and severely wounded three or four times, would rise on their elbows and fire at my men as they passed. I lost one man,... L. B. Smith of Lee County.... We captured twelve horses, guns, pistols, saddles, and two hundred and sixty-five head of beef cattle belonging in the neighborhood of King's Ranch, Santa Gertrudis.

James J. Brown, sheriff of this [Cameron County] with a posse of Mexicans were with us, in sight of the whole affair. But their horses were too much jaded for them to get into the fight. When it was over, I reported to the sheriff that the enemy had crossed the river... on the night of the fourth and that they had gone to the La Parra and gathered these beeves, that I had found them at the marsh, they had fought, and I would now place him in charge of their bodies. He knew most of them, his posse identified *all* of them as Cortinas men.... Camillo Lerma, Georgee Jimenes alias the 'Cyotee,' Telesforo Dias and Guadaloupe Espinoso are said to be Cortinas's favorite bravos and it is also said that he will be very indignant....

I find that the killing of those parties has developed a most alarming state of things on this frontier. The Mexicans on the other side of the river are very much infuriated and threaten to kill ten Americans for each of their Bravos. And then on this side the Mexican residents of Brownsville (that is the majority, the canaille or lower class)... are public in their denunciation of the killing and the attention given my dead soldier seems to have exasperated them beyond measure. I really consider the place in danger as Cortinas is known to have twelve or fifteen hundred men that he can muster in three or four days. The U. S. forces here only amount to about two hundred and fifty all told, officers, soldiers and servants — and they are negroes at that.... [14]

L. H. McNELLY
Captain, Company A, Vol. Mil.

One of McNelly's men has told the story of the Red Raid. This story is worthy of reproduction here because of its graphic quality and because it throws a brilliant light on the way of McNelly. It differs from the official account in some details, as in the disposition of the prisoners, but it coincides with McNelly's story in most respects. William Callicott now steps before the reader to tell how the Red Raid looked to a private in the Rangers.[15]

'In the early spring of 1875 Captain McNelly had orders to reorganize a company of forty Rangers to go to the Rio Grande to deal with the Mexican cow thieves and bandits that were coming from Mexico

[14] A.G.P. McNelly's letter is slightly amended as to punctuation and spelling.

[15] In searching for material for this book I located William Callicott in Houston and began correspondence with him. Though he was old and practically blind, he wrote in his own hand the account of his experiences in the Ranger force, first with Major Jones on the northern Indian frontier and then with Captain McNelly on the Mexican border. For him his task was one of great difficulty. He, like many of the Rangers, was not an educated man, but he set himself to the task and stayed with it as he stuck by McNelly. His eyes were so near gone that he could write only when the sun was shining and high in the heaven. It was his request that I correct his manuscript. This I have done without apology. What I have saved are his graphic style and his original mode of expression. Occasionally I have allowed him to violate some rules of composition in order to preserve the force and quality and character of the man. My regret is that he died before his account appeared in print.

into Texas, killing people and driving cattle into Mexico. Captain McNelly had orders to deal with these bandits and thieves in the same way that Major Jones dealt with the Indians — to kill those caught on this side of the river and take no prisoners. The Captain said he knew how to obey such orders, and as soon as he got his company in shape he made for the Rio Grande.

'We had not been there but a little while until we heard of a band of Mexicans who had come over after cattle. At the time we heard this only thirty men were in camp, the rest being out on a scout. Captain McNelly called for twenty-two volunteers which he readily got. Among them was Berry Smith, the youngest fellow in the company. Old Man Smith, who was with us, went to the Captain and asked him to let some other boy take his boy's place, said that Berry was the only child and if anything happened to him his mother would die of grief. The Captain told him that any of the Rangers would be glad to take Berry's place and he told Berry that if he wished he could stay in camp with his father.

'Berry said, "Captain, we have been out here some time and haven't had a fight yet and I would like to go if you will let me. If I get killed it will be no worse than for some of the other boys to get killed." The Captain told him that was the way he liked to hear a fellow talk, and to get ready to start. I will tell you later how Berry got killed.

'Another Ranger we had with us was Old Casuse Sandaval (Jesús Sandoval).[16] He was a Mexican who had a ranch on this side of the river. Several years before we went out there he and a white man caught four Mexican cow thieves and hung them all to one tree. After that the Mexicans on the other side swore they would kill him on the first chance. Casuse had not slept in his own house for over ten years because he was afraid of being killed. He knew the country well on this side of the river, knew all the Mexicans for miles around, and so the Captain let him join us, paying him the same that he did us, forty dollars a month. He gave him the same kind of arms we used, a Colt's 45 and a needle gun, and Casuse was proud of these weapons and made a fine Ranger. The way he helped us in handling spies will be told later.

'When on the Mexican border Captain McNelly used wagons instead of pack mules such as Major Jones used on the northern frontier after Indians. We did not need pack mules as we could buy grub from the ranches. Captain McNelly left seven or eight men, including a corporal,

[16] This Ranger's name appears on McNelly's muster roll as Jesús Sandaval or Sandoval. I have kept the spelling used by Ranger Callicott. The interpreter's name was probably McGovern and not Sullivan.

with the wagons, while the rest of us tied what little we had cooked to our saddles and started out to find the bandits.

'We hadn't been out but a day or two before we caught the first Mexican bandit spy. Captain McNelly marched his company so that it was hard for any prowling Mexican to escape him. Two or three men marched on each side of the company in the direction we were going and looked out for bandits and spies, and if they came across a Mexican that looked suspicious they would bring him to the company for Old Casuse to identify.

'Casuse would talk to the Mexican a little, and then tell Tom Sullivan, our interpreter, who was raised among the Mexicans at Brownsville, what the Mexican was. If the Mexican proved to be a citizen we let him go at once; and if he proved to be a bandit spy one of us would take charge of him and march along until we saw a suitable tree. The Captain would take Tom, the bandit, and four or five of the boys to the tree. Old Casuse would put the rope over the bandit's neck, throw it over a limb, pull him up and let him down on the ground until he would consent to tell all he knew. As far as we knew this treatment always brought out the truth.

'After the Captain had all the information he wanted he would let Casuse have charge of the spy. Casuse would make a regular hangman's knot and place the hangman's loop over the bandit's head, throw the end of the rope over the limb, make the bandit get on Casuse's old paint horse, and stand up in the saddle. Casuse would then make the loose end of the rope fast, get behind his horse, hit him a hard lick and the horse would jump from under the spy, breaking his neck instantly. Captain McNelly didn't like this kind of killing, but Casuse did. He said if we turned a spy loose he would spread the news among the bandits and we would never catch them. We caught several spies on that scout before we overhauled the bandits with the cattle, and Casuse dealt with all of them alike, showing no partiality — he always made them a present of six feet of rope.

'The last spy we caught was on June 11, Friday after twelve o'clock. The Captain turned him over to me to guard. He rode along with me until we stopped to get supper on a little creek. I had him tied with a rope so that he could not get away. I fixed a little supper for him and gave him all the jerked beef and bread that he could eat and good strong coffee, knowing that would be about the last meal he would have a chance to eat in this world. I gave him some cigarettes to smoke. He enjoyed it all.

'It was beginning to get late in the evening, all had had supper, and our horses had grazed for about two hours. As the sun was getting low, the Captain, Tom Sullivan, and two of the boys came over to where I was sitting down with the bandit smoking. The Captain said, "Bill, we will relieve you; we will take charge of the prisoner. Did you give him plenty to eat?" I told him he had all he could digest on six feet of rope.

'They took him out to a little motte about two hundred yards from where we were. Casuse took his old paint horse that he used for a trap-door gallows and I knew it was checking up time for the Mexican bandit spy. We at the camp could see all that was going on out there. They did not stay out there but a little while when the Captain and the boys came back to us, all except Casuse and the bandit. The Captain could stand death in any other form better than hanging. After Casuse had completed his job he came back to us and said, "He all right — he come backy no more." By that time it was sundown.

'We now prepared to go on after the bandits. The spy had told us all he knew, that seventeen Mexicans and one white man were driving two hundred fifty head of cattle in the direction of Palo Alto Prairie. He evidently told the truth. We planned to overhaul them in the night.

'I had on the only white shirt in the crowd. The Captain came to me and said, "Bill, from what the spy says we will be likely to overhaul the bandits tonight, and in the dark it will be a hard matter to tell our men from them if we get mixed up. I want your white shirt, but I will give you another when we get to a place where I can buy one." I told him the shirt made no difference to me, that the weather was warm and my undershirt was all I needed. I pulled off the shirt and the Captain tore it up and tied a piece around the left arm of each man. Berry Smith, the boy that was killed next day, still had the piece of white tied to his arm.

'After all was ready the Captain ordered us in line. He rode out in front of us and said, "Boys, from what the bandit told me, we are likely to overhaul them tonight, and when we do I will order you all in line of battle, and when I order you to charge them I want you tc charge them in line. Do not get ahead of each other and get mixed up with the bandits for if you do you are apt to kill one another instead of the bandits. Don't pay any attention to the cattle. The spy tells me there are seventeen Mexicans and one white man and that they are Cortinas's picked men, and Cortinas says they can cope with any Rangers or regulars. If we can overhaul them in an open country we will teach them a lesson they will never forget. If they should stampede, pick you out the one that is nearest to you and keep him in front of you and keep after him. Get as close to him as you can before you shoot. It makes no difference in what direction he goes, stay with him to a finish. That is all I have to say. Ready! Form in twos! Forward march!"

'Old Casuse took the lead and we rode all night in the direction which the spy told the Captain Palo Alto Prairie lay, and we got to the prairie about sunup. As luck would have it, we did not overhaul them in the night. If we had we could not have wiped them out.

'At the prairie we found their trail leading across it towards the Rio Grande. We followed it at a fast trot and lope, not wanting to overspeed our horses that had been under the saddle for twenty-four hours with but little rest and little to eat. We hadn't followed the trail farther than a mile or two before we came in sight of the bandits. The Captain knew we had them right where he wanted to overhaul them and he kept getting faster and faster. The bandits saw us, but thought, so the one that got away told after he got back to Mexico, that we were regulars and that they could stand us off.

'The bandits came to a big lagoon running out from the bay. It was about one hundred fifty yards wide with mud and water from knee deep to belly deep. They rounded up the cattle on this side of the lagoon, and then went over to the other side and dismounted in line of battle. When we came to the lagoon, Captain McNelly ordered us in line of battle about four feet apart and ordered us not to fire until we got out of the mud and water. The bandits opened fire on us from behind their horses, using their saddles for gun rests.

'As we were crossing the lagoon, the Captain happened to look off to the right and saw a skirt of timber about two miles away. He told Lieutenant Robinson to keep on across the lagoon and not to fire a shot until he got to where the mud and water were shallow enough to make a charge, and that he would take Casuse and six of the boys and keep the Mexicans cut off from the timber. The Captain took the right wing, going angling toward the timber. The bandits kept firing at us, but their bullets would pass over our heads, between us, or hit the mud and water before us. By the time we got out of the deepest mud and water the Mexicans, seeing that their bullets had no effect, mounted and away they went towards the skirt of timber. When they found themselves cut off by Captain McNelly and his men, they rallied and stopped, opening fire on Captain McNelly's squad. The Captain and his men killed one or two of them and the rest broke out full tilt across Palo Alto Prairie, with Lieutenant Robinson and us behind them and Captain McNelly and his men on the side.

'Soon we were all running in line of battle in case the Mexicans should turn to right or left or scatter in any way. We had the bandits

'SUCH AN UNEXPECTED LUNGE THAT HE WENT FROM UNDER MY HAT'

straight ahead of us going towards the Rio Grande. There was not a tree in sight, only now and then a little bunch of Spanish dagger.

'When we came within gun range Lieutenant Robinson shouted out, "Go for them, boys! Go for them!" Every man slapped spurs to his horse, giving him all the speed he had. I rammed both spurs to Old Ball who opened up his throttle with such an unexpected lunge that he went from under my hat and came near going from under me. We soon got up with them and the battle opened right. As fast as we overhauled one, we would shoot him or his horse. The last one we killed was riding the best horse in the bandit's crowd, and kept away ahead of any of the rest. The Captain and three or four of us were after him. We killed his horse from under him near a little Spanish dagger thicket and he ran into it on foot. The Captain ordered us to surround it, and then he dismounted, took his pistol out of his scabbard and started into the thicket. When he met the bandit they were about six or eight feet apart. The bandit had emptied his pistol and the Captain had only one ball left in his. The Mexican drew his Bowie knife and with a grin on his face, started to Captain McNelly, saying as he came, 'Me gotta you now, me gotta you.' The Captain leveled his pistol and placed the last shot he had between the bandit's teeth as if he had put it there with his fingers.[17] The Captain called, "Come in, boys." We dismounted and ran in to find the Captain standing over the bandit who had already checked up and breathed his last. The Captain took his knife and pistol. I untied his sash from around him,

[17] There is a story among the Rangers that McNelly resorted to a ruse. He called to his men to come to his aid, saying his gun was empty. The Mexican, hearing this and thinking he had an advantage, rose from his cover for the attack when McNelly killed him.

tying it around myself. It was the prettiest one I had ever seen, having the colors of Mexico, red, white, and green.

'Having put an end to the last bandit, we mounted our horses and started back over the trail of the dead. It was then about two o'clock in the evening. As we passed by I happened to come upon a dead bandit lying in the grass flat on his back with his hands and legs lying out straight from his body. He was shot through the head and I don't think he ever moved a muscle after he fell from his horse. His eyes were glared wide open, gazing at the hot June sun. His shaggy black beard was blood-stained and the blow flies were swarming over his face after blood and brains. Just back of his head, in the grass, lay a fine Mexican hat, bottom up. The high June sun was getting mighty hot on my head as I hadn't had a hat on since Old Ball made that awful lunge in the first charge that morning. So I eased down off Old Ball, picked up the hat, pulled up some grass, wiped off what blood I could, and put it on. Glad to get it. I then got on Old Ball and overtook the Captain and the boys. The Captain said, "Where did you get your Mexican hat?" I told him I got it off a dead bandit. He said, "It is a good one. With that hat and sash you could pass for a Mexican bandit in the dark anywhere."

'While we were going back over the trail and locating the bandits, Casuse and two Mexican ranchmen who had joined us during the fight began to gather them up. When they found one, they would fasten a rope around his neck, wrap the loose end around the pommel of the saddle and strike a lope to the road that was near the bandit trail. They put them all in one pile, Jack Ellis, the white man, included.

'Near the end of the trail we came upon Spencer J. Adams sitting on his horse, Sorrel Top, so called because his mane and tail were white. Adams had pulled off his shirt and had it wrapped around Sorrel Top's neck to protect a bullet wound from the flies. Adams was looking intently into a rush pond nearby.

'"What are you watching in that pond, Adams?" asked the Captain.

'"I am watching that bandit," said Adams.

'"How come him there?" inquired the Captain.

'"This morning when the fight started by the lagoon you all got ahead of me and Berry Smith and some of you shot the bandit off his horse and you thought he was dead. Berry and I saw him crawl into that Spanish dagger thicket you see there near the edge of this pond. We ran up to the thicket to shoot him again, but just as we got there he shot and killed Berry Smith, and shot at me and hit Sorrel Top in the neck. Later, after Berry was dead, he crawled out and got Berry's pistol, and a little while ago he crawled out to this pond of water. He is out about the middle of it — you can see the rush grass move when he crawls along. I think you broke his leg for he has not been on his feet today."

'When Spencer had told us this, the Captain said, "You boys surround this pond but don't get opposite one another. Use your guns, not your pistols, and if Adams hasn't let his bandit die on his hands, we will soon wake him up."

'The Captain did not do any shooting, but when the rush grass would move he would point to the spot and tell the nearest one to shoot. We had fired several shots without waking him up when finally one of the boys hit him. He floundered and kicked and sometimes his feet would go above the top of the rush grass. When he quieted down, the Captain said, "That will do — that shot checked him up. Ride in, Casuse, and bring him out." The inspection showed that he had been hit in many places. The Captain told Casuse to take him to the other bandits and come back as soon as he could.

'That made sixteen Mexican bandits and one white bandit, Jack Ellis, that we killed. One Mexican got away. We shot him off his horse and left him for dead, but he crawled out to where some Mexicans were cutting hay and hid in the hay.

'When Casuse got back to us, after taking in the pond bandit, we were all together except Berry Smith. We found him lying in four feet of the thicket stiff dead. He was only sixteen years old, had had no experience, and got too close to the bandit without seeing him. He must have been in six or eight feet of the Mexican as the thicket was not over ten feet wide anywhere.

'The Captain said, "Bill, do you know how to tie a dead man on a horse?"

'"Yes, sir," I said. He told me to tie Berry Smith on Old Ball and told one of the boys to help me. When it was done the Captain looked at the work and said it was a good job.

'"Bill," he said, "you must have done it before." I told him that was the first dead man, but I had tied all other kinds of packs on mules when I was with Major Jones's escort on the northern frontier.[18]

'Captain McNelly sent the two Mexican ranchmen back over the trail to get whatever they could in the way of horses, saddles, and bridles. He told them to kill any horses that were badly wounded, as he did not want them to stay out there in the sun and suffer for water. We captured only two horses. One was a big paint, the horse that Jack

[18] Mr. Callicott gave a detailed account of how he lashed the dead Ranger on the horse, but the account is omitted.

Ellis was riding, and the other was a little bay. We named the paint horse Jack Ellis and the bay one Cortinas.

'By this time we were ready to march. The Captain told me to ride Berry Smith's horse and to lead Old Ball with the dead Ranger tied on. We started towards Brownsville, a little town on this side of the river, to turn our Ranger boy over to the undertaker to have him prepared for the funeral. I marched in the rear.

'We hadn't gone more than two or three miles when we saw twenty-five or thirty men riding towards us from the river. The Captain said, "Well, boys, we are into it — with our horses all run down. We can't run them with the fix our horses are in. Ride your horses all in a ring, one behind the other." He told me to bring Old Ball in and I led him into the center with the dead Ranger tied on.

'He then told me and three other boys to go in a lope till we met the horsemen, and if they proved to be bandits we were to fire into them and come back to him as fast as we could. While we were coming back he and his men would shoot down their horses and we were to do the same when we got there. Then we would fight in the ring with our dead horses for breastworks. But it turned out that the strangers were Texans and Mexicans going out on a cow drive and we didn't have to kill our rundown horses that had served us true and faithful for twenty-four hours under the saddle without anything to eat and without rest.

'Four or five miles farther on we came to a Mexican stock ranch where Captain McNelly got a Mexican with a cart to take our dead Ranger boy into Brownsville. Four men went with the Mexican with orders to the undertaker and the sexton. Captain wanted everything ready for the funeral by three o'clock the next day.

'We marched two or three miles farther and camped on a creek where there was water and plenty of good grass for our horses, the first they had had for twenty-four hours. The Captain got us a little bread and beef from the ranch. We unsaddled our horses, put them to grazing under guard, and ate supper and rested.

'Between sundown and dark the Captain came around where I was lying down and told me that I was on first picket duty, and that he would act as corporal in locating the first pickets. I went to the herd, saddled Old Ball and reported that I was ready. The Captain said to me: "You haven't had any sleep in twenty-four hours. Do you think you can stand it without going to sleep?" I told him I could.

'"I guess you know the penalty where a picket goes to sleep on duty. It spells death.... Come on. I will locate you."

'If he had had Casuse along on his paint horse I would have thought they were taking me out to hang me as they had the bandit spy the evening before. To tell the truth, I looked like one with one dead bandit's hat on my head and another's sash around my waist. The Captain went about a half mile from camp to a thicket near the forks of two roads coming from the river.

'"Now you keep a close lookout," he said, "and if you see anybody coming from towards the river, ride out and halt them, and if they don't stop, fire into them and come back to camp as fast as you can. You will have to stand here four hours if you don't get killed before your time is up."

'He left me alone with the dead bandits' hat and sash. It was so dark I could hardly see my hands before my eyes. I had been raised near my old home graveyard which was within twenty feet of the house. I never had seen any ghosts or spirits and I didn't believe in them, but with all my strong belief in regard to such things, whenever I looked down on the ground I could see the dead bandit from whom I had taken the hat. He was lying just as he was four hours before with his eyes glared wide open and with his shaggy black blood-stained beard with flies swarming around his face. I could smell the fresh blood on the hat brim over my eyes. It made me feel a little strange. Still I would console myself as best I could, knowing it was only imagination.

'I was not particularly anxious to meet any bandits away out there by myself, but I would have liked for a few to come that way so I could have fired into them and then get the best speed Old Ball had back to camp. They did not come and I had to stay my four hours — the longest four hours' guard duty I ever stood in my life.

'I went to Kansas in 1871 when I was only a boy with a herd of cattle. I herded them at night when the storm would be blowing, thunder roaring, lightning flashing, and cows stampeding, but no four hours ever seemed as long as that. I was glad when the Captain came. We went back to camp together, but I didn't tell him what I had seen. I didn't tell any of the boys. I wore the hat for a long time, and wore it into Mexico on two trips when we followed the thieves over after cattle, but I never did see the dead bandit again as I saw him that night.

'The next morning bright and early we all started for Brownsville to attend the funeral of our dead Ranger boy. We got there early in the morning. The U.S. troops had sent a six-mule wagon out on the trail and hauled all the bandits that could be found into Brownsville and unloaded them in one pile on the public square. The Captain sent word for all to come and see how the Texas Rangers dealt with cow thieves. Here I saw the same old big fat Mexican that I got the hat from, and also the one I got the sash from in the Spanish dagger thicket.... When we got ready to go to the funeral I asked the Captain if I had not better get a different hat. He told me not, that that hat was about the best advertiser I could wear, and a fair warning to all bandits not to cross to the Texas side after Texas cattle.

'Captain McNelly told Lieutenant Robinson to take charge of us and keep us at the King House until time to go to the undertaker's department. He ordered that we leave our horses and go to the funeral on foot. He didn't want us to touch a drop of anything, said if we did it would spoil the whole thing.

'Lieutenant Robinson, Casuse and the balance of us marched to the undertaker's where we found the hearse ready with two fine black horses hitched to it, and two companies of U.S. regulars to march with us. We marched by a church and took him in and had his funeral preached, and then to the cemetery a little distance off. There people had gathered from far and near to see our sixteen-year-old Ranger boy laid to rest in the northwest corner of the Brownsville cemetery. The U.S. regulars fired a farewell shot over his grave and today our Ranger boy sleeps on the Texas bank of the Rio Grande.

'(Signed) WILLIAM CALLICOTT

'*April* 11, 1921.

'P.S. Everyone said it was the finest funeral that ever took place in the little town of Brownsville, located on the Texas bank of the Rio Grande.'

On June 16, Joseph P. O'Schaughnessy, United States marshal of Brownsville, swore that he went on Saturday, June 12, to Palo Alto Prairie with a detachment of United States troops to gather up the dead bodies of Mexican raiders who had fallen that day in a fight with Captain McNelly's command. They arrived at noon on Sunday and found the bodies of eight Mexicans which were placed on the two wagons and transported to Brownsville. 'These were all we could find, though not all that were killed.'[19]

Inspector of Cattle John J. Smith stated that the cattle captured by McNelly were turned over to him. There were two hundred and sixteen head. He listed thirty-four owners for ninety-seven head. The ownership of the other cattle could not be determined and these were sold for the 'benefit of whom it may concern.'[20]

There are discrepancies between the account written by Captain McNelly a few days after the fight and the one by William Callicott.

[19] Oath attested by F. J. Parker, Clerk, United States District Court, June 16, 1875. A.G.P.

[20] Statement of Inspector John J. Smith, June 17, 1875. A.G.P.

An important one is in reference to the disposition of the captured spies. McNelly would naturally make no mention of the strong measures he used to get confessions and accurate information. McNelly stated that he turned the spies over to Sheriff Brown. There is no other evidence to support this statement. Callicott's story is more in accord with the circumstances. McNelly cannot be condemned too severely if he did permit Jesús Sandoval to send the spies to eternity by way of his paint horse gallows. McNelly did not have men enough to guard prisoners — he needed all of them in the fight. Nor could he have turned the spies loose without defeating the purpose for which he was on the border. We are not dependent on Callicott's account alone for proof that McNelly dealt harshly with captured spies. General E. O. C. Ord testified in reference to the affair that 'The officer of the State troops in command had learned the whereabouts of this raiding party by means which I could not legally resort to, but which were the only means of getting at the actual facts. He had caught one of the members and hung him up until he was made to confess where the rest of the raiders were.' [21] Affairs on the border cannot be judged by standards that hold elsewhere.

[21] 'Texas Border Troubles,' *House Miscellaneous Document* No. 64, Forty-Fifth Congress, Second Session, p. 95. Serial No. 1820.

XIII

McNELLY AND THE WAR OF LAS CUEVAS

If McNelly is attacked by Mexican forces on Mexican soil do not render him any assistance.

Colonel POTTER *to Major* ALEXANDER

The American consul at Matamoros arranged for our surrender, as you will see by enclosed copy of telegrams, but I 'couldn't see it.'

L. H. McNELLY

Richard King: 'I know all about Las Cuevas.... It was settled by General Juan Flores and I understand he still owns it.'
Ranger: 'No, Captain, the other fellow owns it — we killed the general.'

XIII. McNELLY AND THE WAR OF LAS CUEVAS

1. McNELLY'S PLAN

Captain McNelly spent the time from June to October without a major encounter with the cattle thieves. During this period he instituted an effective spy system, and on many occasions learned of the plans of the thieves in time to break them up. The killing of the bandits on Palo Alto Prairie had made the Mexicans chary and they no longer hesitated to abandon their booty to escape him. His method of operation he told in a report of his efforts to intercept a party of raiders in the vicinity of Loma Blanca, eighty or ninety miles from Brownsville. He started the night he heard of them, rode forty miles, secreted his company, and sent scouts east and west. 'On the evening of the third day we found the herd. The Mexicans had heard of us and turned the cattle loose two days before we found them.'[1] Seventeen thieves, led by Alfonso Cono and Rafael Riojas from the Bolsa, abandoned the cattle, scattered, and crossed the river in twos and threes. McNelly said that he had spies with the thieves and kept posted on all their movements. He reported that they were disgusted with the country and were moving up the river.

As the thieves moved up the river, Captain McNelly did also. On August 4 he received a telegram that a band was expected to cross at Las Cuevas on the sixth. He knew the point of meeting, the Magotee of Don Juan, and the time they were expected to arrive. 'I left camp after dark and traveled by trails all night the fourth and fifth laying in the brush during the days; reached a point of timber on the morning of the sixth and remained there until the night of the eleventh [or seventh] when I learned from one of the spies that they [the thieves] had not come over.' News kept coming of a big raid, but the Rangers were doubtful. McNelly concluded by saying that if the party that had been making so much preparation to cross failed or backed out, 'there will be no further use for my company down here.'[2]

[1] McNelly to Steele, July 7, 1875. A.G.P.

[2] *Ibid.*, August 13, 1875. A.G.P.

Early in October, Captain McNelly went to his home in Washington County with chills and fever, and when he returned later in the month he learned that two hundred head of cattle had been stolen from Cameron County and sent to Monterey. 'I am in communication with my spies on the other side,' he wrote, 'and I feel satisfied that within a short time will be able to send you a good report. I have met Commander Kells of the U.S.A. Boat, *Rio Bravo*, and if he does as much as he says he will, you may expect some stirring news soon.' He had seen Kells's orders and his report to the Secretary of the Navy, and he considered that Kells had 'latitude enough for anyone,' and especially for a comrade of Walker of South American fame. McNelly asked for permission to act with the United States forces when called upon to do so.[3] Four days later he wrote that Attorney General George Clark had told him to go ahead and act with the United States forces, and he added, characteristically, 'Unless I get some instructions to the contrary you may confidently rely on hearing some stirring news before the 20 of this month.' The officials in Mexico were alarmed and were saying that they intended to stop the raiding, but McNelly thought they could not do it with cattle bringing eighteen dollars a head. The moon would be bright from the tenth to the twenty-fifth, and work plentiful. He had seen General Potter and Captain Kells, and from Potter's talk he thought General Ord had been 'stirring him up.'[4]

There can be little doubt that McNelly had some deep scheme in mind, and it seems that his purpose was to bring on a war with Mexico. There is some evidence that Captain Kells was in the conspiracy and that McNelly was making every effort to bring the army officers into it also. On November 12, McNelly wrote that he had seen the senior cavalry officer, Major A. J. Alexander, and had secured from him a promise 'to instruct his men to follow raiders anywhere I will go.' He had just learned that the purchasers of stolen cattle had contracted to deliver eighteen thousand head in Monterey within ninety days, and he hoped to be able to put Alexander to the test. 'I should think

[3] McNelly to Steele, October 31, 1875. A.G.P.

[4] McNelly to Steele, November 4, 1875. A.G.P. McNelly's relations with Captain Kells are touched upon in the testimony of John L. Haynes, Collector of Customs at Brownsville. On November 16, Haynes wrote that Kells informed him that he had been sent to the Rio Grande 'to bring this thing to a head.' He wanted Haynes to assist Judge Dougherty and others in having the gunboat *Rio Bravo* fired upon from the Mexican side. If the Mexicans would not do it, arrangements might be made to have McNelly's men do it. Another plan was to have McNelly drive a herd of cattle into Mexico and then the *Rio Bravo* could attack the nearest ranch. Las Cuevas was mentioned as the most desirable one. Haynes did not approve of the plan and claimed that nothing in Kells's instructions warranted such action. 'Texas Border Troubles,' *House Miscellaneous Documents*, No. 64, Forty-Fifth Congress, Second Session, Second Series, pp. 281–282. Serial No. 1820.

myself in bad luck if I don't find some of their party [thieves] on this or the *other side* of the river.'[5]

The next news from McNelly was a telegram.

> A PARTY OF RAIDERS HAVE CROSSED TWO HUNDRED AND FIFTY CATTLE AT LAS CUEVAS. THEY HAVE BEEN FIRING ON MAJOR CLENDENIN'S MEN. HE REFUSES TO CROSS WITHOUT FURTHER ORDERS. I SHALL CROSS TONIGHT IF I CAN GET ANY SUPPORT.

This was followed by a second telegram that night.

> I COMMENCED CROSSING AT ONE O'CLOCK TONIGHT — HAVE THIRTY MEN. WILL TRY AND RECOVER OUR CATTLE. THE U.S. TROOPS PROMISE TO COVER MY RETURN. LIEUTENANT ROBINSON HAS JUST ARRIVED MAKING A MARCH OF FIFTY-FIVE MILES IN FIVE HOURS.[6]
>
> L. H. McNELLY
> CAPT. RANGERS

While Captain McNelly is getting his men across the Rio Grande, we may examine the country around Las Cuevas, and sketch the events of the few hours previous to the sending of the telegrams. Las Cuevas Crossing of the Rio Grande lies some ten miles down the river from Rio Grande City, and the army post of Ringgold Barracks. Las Cuevas Ranch is situated three miles from the river in a sandy and brush-covered country. Between the village and the river there was, in 1875, another ranch known as Las Curchas or Cuchattus. Both ranches were surrounded by corrals for cattle, and Las Cuevas was guarded by a palisade. The approach from the river led through the thick brush which extended from the sand of the riverbank to the very corrals and palisade. Along this trail hundreds of head of Texas cattle had been driven dripping wet from the Texas side, for Las Cuevas was headquarters of Juan Flores, chieftain of the cow thieves of the border. Of all the cattle that had gone up that trail, none had ever come back. For Texas cattle it was a one-way road.

In order to understand the situation in Texas, it is necessary to resort to the triangle. The base of the triangle follows the river from Rio Grande City to Brownsville, a distance of about one hundred miles. The other two sides are made by drawing lines from Edinburg to Brownsville and to Rio Grande City respectively. At the time of the Las Cuevas affair, United States forces were at each of these three points. General Potter was at Brownsville in command of the valley; Major

[5] McNelly to Steele, November 12, 1875. A.G.P.

[6] *Ibid.*, November 18, 1875. A.G.P.

MANUEL FLORES, SON OF JUAN FLORES

A. J. Alexander had a force at Ringgold Barracks; Major Clendenin and Captain Randlett were at Edinburg with a detachment of cavalry. Captain McNelly's Rangers were 'somewhere in the brush' near Edinburg, and about fifty-five miles from Las Cuevas Crossing. They were resting, washing their clothes, grazing their horses, and tightening up the wrinkles in their stomachs on good King beef. In the absence of Captain McNelly, they were under command of Lieutenant George Robinson.

This was the situation on November 16, when sixteen or seventeen of Cortinas's men pushed a herd of some seventy-five head of cattle into the triangle thus described and drove them hard for Las Cuevas Crossing.

2. *ON THE TRAIL OF COW BANDITS*

About dark on the night of November 16, a Mexican ranchman rode into Captain Randlett's camp, Company D, Eighth Cavalry, and informed him that the cattle were headed for Las Cuevas and would probably cross the river on the next day. Randlett wired General

Potter at Brownsville that he would start at nine to intercept the bandits, and asked that soldiers from Ringgold be sent to co-operate with him. Potter ordered the scout from Ringgold and wired Randlett:

> IF YOU CATCH THE THIEVES, HIT THEM HARD. IF YOU COME UP WITH THEM WHILE THEY CROSS THE RIVER, FOLLOW THEM INTO MEXICO. McNELLY IN COMMAND OF STATE TROOPS IS NEAR EDINBURG. TRY TO CONNECT WITH HIM AND TAKE A SHERIFF OR DEPUTY WITH YOU.[7]

Instead of marching straight to the river, Randlett stopped to gather a contingent of Texans and Mexicans, and waited until a courier could communicate with the party that had been sent out from Ringgold. At noon the following day Captain Randlett was told by a customs inspector that the Mexicans were making for the river and would probably cross that night. 'We immediately mounted and started in pursuit. I then declared my object to Thompson to be to *get in the rear* of the thieves and catch them at the river.' [8] He sent another courier to inform O'Connor of his bold design, directing him to 'hit them without mercy on their right flank when they reached the river.'

The trooper struck the bandit trail at 2:30 and reached the river at 4:15. He had executed his second purpose — he was in the *rear* of the thieves, had caught them at the river, after they were across. Fifty head of cattle were bogged and were being dragged ashore by ropes when the United States soldiers rode up on the Texas bank. The soldiers killed two Mexicans, wounded a third, and ran the others into the brush. Instead of crossing at once, Randlett frittered the evening away. O'Connor arrived with thirty men. Night fell, dark and cloudy, 'Alud,' said Randlett, 'I was compelled to suspend crossing until the next morning.'

During the night General Potter ordered more troops out from Ringgold under Alexander, and Clendenin arrived half an hour before day as Captain Randlett was sitting down to breakfast. Clendenin approved everything that Randlett had done, but would not permit him to cross the river. That would be 'a warlike invasion of a country with which our country was at peace.' Besides this, Major Clendenin had written a note to the *alcalde* of Las Cuevas, and he thought it would show 'bad faith to cross the river after opening communications with the Alcalde.' Thus he let *his* opportunity go. Colonel Potter wired him to do nothing until Major A. J. Alexander arrived to take supreme command. 'General is afraid you have not men enough,' read the

[7] Potter to Randlett, November 16, 1875. A.G.P.

[8] Randlett's Report, December 1, 1875. A.G.P. Italics mine.

BILL CALLICOTT
1875

Potter telegram.[9] Clendenin, having brought about a complete paralysis of the United States forces on the Las Cuevas front, was superseded. While he was making preparations to return to Ringgold, affairs took a sudden turn.

About noon a tallish thin man of quiet manner, and with the soft voice of a timid Methodist preacher, rode out of the brush and into the camp of the United States troops, which now numbered at least one hundred men. McNelly came alone; his thirty Rangers were washing their clothes, resting, and grazing their horses fifty-five miles away. McNelly quietly announced that as soon as his men arrived he would go into Mexico after the cattle and bring them back if possible.

The story of the coming of his men is told best by one of them, William Callicott.

'The messenger from Captain McNelly reached our camp about 2:30 in the afternoon. Lieutenant Robinson called Old Casuse, our Mexican Ranger, and Tom Sullivan, our interpreter, and found out all about it. The Mexican said the bandits had a big herd of cattle, 75 or 100, and he thought they intended crossing near Las Cuevas. Casuse said Las Cuevas was sixty miles or more by the nearest way.

[9] Telegram dated November 18, 1875, Fort Brown, sent by order of Colonel Potter. A.G.P.

We got ready as quickly as we could, taking forty rounds of pistol cartridges and forty rounds of gun cartridges, and nothing more. As we fell into ranks, Lieutenant Robinson said, "Boys, this ride will have to be made in five hours or less. I want to beat them to the river if I can." He left guards with the wagons and ordered us to follow Casuse, who knew the way and took all the near cuts. We went at a fast gallop and a lope, making the sixty miles in a little less than five hours, but we got there too late — the Mexicans had crossed the cattle to Las Cuevas, headquarters for all cow bandits.

'A U.S. captain from some fort had followed them to the river and camped on this side. He had two Gatling guns planted. Captain McNelly was also there. He came to me and said, "Bill, you go to that near ranch and get two or three muttons and dress them for supper and I will step up and see the U.S. captain again about getting 100 of his men. You boys cook and eat all the mutton you want, and broil a chunk for dinner tomorrow; you won't need any breakfast — it will make us too late getting over. Have everything ready by twelve to-night; we will start crossing by one. I have made arrangements with a Mexican to cross us in a dugout of a canoe that will hold four men. It has a leak in it but one of you can keep the water dipped out so it won't sink. We will swim our horses one at a time. Loosen your flank girths, as a horse can't swim well with the flank girth tight, and take your guns in your hands so that if the horse drowns you won't lose your guns. Take your morral with your cartridges in it and your dinner. Do as I tell you and be ready to start by twelve. I will soon let you know what I can do with the U.S. Captain, and if I can get 100 of his men we are all O.K."

'When the Captain came back about twelve he said the U.S. captain couldn't let us have any men. He told us to get ready, that we were going over if we never come back. When we were in ranks, the Captain stepped out in front of us and said, "Boys, you have followed me as far as I can ask you to unless you are willing to go farther. Some of us may get back, or maybe all of us will get back, but if any of you do not want to go over with me, step aside. I don't want you to go unless you are willing to volunteer. You understand there is to be no surrender — we ask no quarter nor give any. If you don't want to go, step aside."

'We all said, "Captain, we will go."

'"All right," he said, "that's the way to talk. We will learn them a Texas lesson that they have forgotten since the Mexican War. Get ready. I will take Casuse, Tom Sullivan and myself first. We will take Casuse's horse. Then I want Lieutenant Robinson, John Armstrong, Sergeant George Hall and Sergeant George Orell to bring their horses, and the rest of you come as fast as you can."

'When these five horses were over, Captain came back and said not to take any more horses because they bogged down and had to be pulled out with ropes. He told us to bring nothing but our guns, pistols, and the morral with our cartridges and grub. The Captain said he wanted us all over by half past three, that it was two or three miles to the ranch and it would take hard walking to make it on time. So we went three at a time in the leaky Mexican boat, and it took one man to dip out the water to keep it from sinking.

'At last we got over and found ourselves all together again in Mexico. It was the 19th of November, 1875, and 4 A.M.

'The Captain said, "Boys, the pilot tells me that Las Cuevas Ranch is picketed in with high posts set in the ground with bars for a gate. We will march single file as the cowtrail is not wide enough for you to go in twos. The mounted men will go first, and when we get to the ranch the bars will be let down and I want the five men on horses to dash through the ranch yelling and shooting to attract attention and the rest of us will close in behind and do the best we can. Kill all you see except old men, women, and children. These are my orders and I want them obeyed to the letter." Captain always planned his battles before he went in and he expected everybody to do as he said. Then the Captain and the guide led the way up the cowtrail through underbrush and trees so thick that you could not see a rabbit ten feet away.'

At this point we may stop to inquire how Captain McNelly justified his apparently foolhardy action. He was under no misapprehension as to what he was going into. Though he was not the sort of a man who would take his own men to a slaughter, yet he was leading thirty Texas Rangers against ten times their number, against a foe that in the past had given small quarter to Texans. Captain McNelly expected, in case he took Las Cuevas, to be surrounded there and cut off from return to his own country.

The last statement needs support. In order to understand it, we must review the relations of McNelly to the federal troops on the border. We know that McNelly had Colonel Potter's assurance long before the fight started that the United States forces would go with him into Mexico after thieves. We know that Potter ordered Randlett to hit the thieves hard, but that later the red tape of the army rendered the United States forces all but impotent. McNelly wanted the help of the federal troops, and he set about to create a situation which would compel the army officers to cut through the red tape and come to him in

Mexico. To execute his plan he was willing to lead his men up a cow-trail to Las Cuevas, storm it at daylight when the Mexican eyes were heavy with sleep, take a house, barricade himself, and fight off his besiegers until the United States forces came to his rescue.

He told Clendenin exactly what he proposed to do, and secured Clendenin's promise to come to him. Proof of this is found in the words of both the army officer and the Ranger Captain. Clendenin wrote:

'During the day, Captain McNelly, a Texan Ranger, came to the camp from Edinburg and informed us that his company of Rangers would arrive that evening and that he would cross to the Mexican side.... After receiving the dispatches ... I went to McNelly and urged him to await the arrival of Major Alexander. He [McNelly] said he had received information that the cattle were in a corral on the other side and that he could recover them. I replied, "if you are determined to cross, we will cover your return ... cannot cross at present to help you." '[10]

On the same subject McNelly wrote:

'He [Clendenin] promised me that in case I was cut off in my attack on the Cuevas, he would come to my assistance.... I learned from my spies ... that the Cuevians had about two hundred and fifty or three hundred men at the Ranch, and was satisfied that the best I could do would be to surprise them — dash into the ranch and take possession of the first house and hold it until the U.S. troops could come to my assistance — *and so told the officers before crossing.* I also told them that not one of us could get back alive without the aid of their troops.'[11]

3. *THE RANGERS IN MEXICO*

Let us return to the thirty men who had threaded the brushy trail and stood at the gates of what they supposed to be Las Cuevas. Ranger Bill Callicott continues the narrative.

'We reached the ranch just at daylight. Just before we got to the bars, Captain waited for us, and as we came up he said "Halt." We all stopped. He walked up and down the line of only thirty of us three miles in Mexico afoot and looked each man in the face. "Boys, I like your looks all right — you are the palest set of men I ever looked

[10] D. R. Clendenin to Acting Assistant Adjutant General, United States Forces at Fort Brown, December 5, 1875. A.G.P.

[11] McNelly to Steele, November 22, 1875. A.G.P. Italics mine. McNelly wrote his report the day after he recovered the cattle, though he had probably not closed his eyes for three days and nights. The army officers wrote their reports about ten days later.

'AND AWAY THE FIVE WENT SHOOTING AND YELLING'

at. That is a sign that you are going to do good fighting. In the Confederate army I noticed that just before battle all men get pale."

'Then the Captain had the pilot let down the bars, and when we got there, he said "Stand to one side boys. Casuse has not had a chance to breathe Mexican air or give a yell in Mexico for over twenty years. We'll let Casuse wake them up." It was then between daylight and sunup. "Go through," said the Captain.

'Old Casuse pushed his hat to the back of his head, drew his pistol, rammed both spurs to his old paint horse, gave a Comanche yell, and away the five went shooting and yelling. The rest of us closed in behind them, and if the angels of heaven had come down on that ranch the Mexicans would not have been more surprised. We were the first Rangers they had seen since the Mexican War.

'The Captain had said kill all but old men, women, and children. Many of the men were on their woodpiles cutting wood while their wives were cooking breakfast on little fires out of doors. We shot the men down on the woodpiles until we killed all we saw in the ranch.

'Then the pilot told the Captain that he had made a mistake in the ranch. This was the Cachattus (or Las Curchas) — the Cuevas Ranch was a half mile up the trail.

' "Well," said the Captain, "you have given my surprise away Take me to Las Cuevas as fast as you can." We hurried on to Las Cuevas and just as we got in sight we saw 250 Mexican soldiers dash into the ranch on horseback. We formed a line and opened fire at 150 yards. Between us and the Mexicans was open ground with a tree here and there. The Mexicans were shooting at us from behind houses, but their bullets went wild over our heads.

'When the Captain had taken in the situation, he said: "Well, boys, our surprise is gone. The Mexicans have all the advantage as to number and houses to protect themselves in. There are 250 of them, not counting the bandits, and they may have artillery. It would be suicide to charge them with only thirty men — it would spell death to all of us and do no good. So we will go back to the river."

'We hit the trail the way we came. As we passed Cachattus Ranch there was nothing except the dead and they lay where they fell, on the woodpiles, and in the streets or roads. The women and children and old men were all gone. We went back to the river and put out pickets to await the coming of the Mexicans.'

The following is from Captain McNelly's official report:

'Before daylight on 19th I started for the ranch, found what I supposed was the Cuevas, charged it, found five or six men there, and they seemed to be on picket. We killed four of them and then proceeded on my way to Cuevas (a half-mile distant) and about three miles from the river; on getting within one hundred yards of the first house in the ranch, I found about two hundred and fifty or three hundred men drawn up in line. About one hundred mounted, the rest on foot, they occupied the ground and the corrals between me and the first house of the ranch. I at once saw the utter impossibility of taking a house by assault, as the firing at the other ranch had given them notice of our approach. After exchanging shots for about ten minutes, I fell back taking advantage of a few bushes on the side of the road to conceal my movements from the enemy. I left Sergt. Hall with four mounted men to hold them in check as long as possible. They made no attempt to follow us and we reached the river all right.' [12]

[12] McNelly to Steele, November 22, 1875. A.G.P. In his telegram of November 20, McNelly said he killed four men before reaching Las Cuevas and five afterwards. These may have been the ones killed at the river. Jennings states that Captain McNelly said that the ranch was a mile from the river. He also asserts that McNelly went five miles into Mexico. Jennings's book, *A Texas Ranger*, abounds in errors and in misrepresentations. Jennings claims that he was with McNelly at Las Cuevas, but George Durham and G. W. Tally say he was not, and McNelly's muster roll of 1875 does not reveal his name. It does not appear until 1876. The most grievous error is the fact that Jennings makes the events of three days occur in one. See Randlett's report of November 29; N. A. Jennings, *A Texas Ranger*. This volume was republished by the Southwest Press, Dallas, 1930.

Thus far McNelly had failed. He had not captured a house or recovered the cattle, and he had not induced the United States soldiers to come to him on Mexican soil. A less determined man would have hastened to recross the river and seek protection in the camp of the United States soldiers, but McNelly never did that which the enemy expected. In this case he retreated to the river, concealed his men and awaited developments. Let Ranger Callicott continue the story.

'We went back to the river and put out pickets. They were stationed in the brush and between them and us was an old field about one hundred and fifty yards across. Captain McNelly told Lieutenant Robinson and John Armstrong to keep a sharp lookout. The Mexicans would think we had taken a scare, stampeded, and were swimming the river back to Texas and that they could kill us while we were swimming. Suddenly we heard yelling and shooting towards the pickets, and pretty soon Lieutenant Robinson jumped his horse off the bank almost on top of us. Then Lieutenant Armstrong and Sergeant George Hall came in on foot. They had been sitting sideways on their horses when the Mexicans broke on them shooting and yelling and their horses jumped from under them and ran off. Sergeant Orrell made it to us with his horse and Casuse had his. We now had only three horses.

'When the Mexicans did not see any of us on the bank, they thought we were swimming the river, and so here they came, twenty-five horsemen led by General Juan Flores, owner of Las Cuevas. The Captain said, "Charge them, boys!" and we ran up the cowtrail to the top of the bank and formed a line. "Open up on them as fast as you can," said the Captain.

'We opened and they ran back to the thicket, but General Juan Flores fell dead from his horse in seventy-five yards of the thicket with his pistol in his hand and two needle-gun bullets in his body.

'The Captain said he thought the rest of the Mexicans had stopped in the thicket. He said, "Widen out in line of battle four feet apart, march across and fire into the thicket." We marched and fired volley after volley until we marched up to where General Juan Flores lay. The Captain stooped down and picked up the pistol; it was a Smith and Wesson, plated with gold and silver, the finest I ever saw. Casuse said it was General Flores who lay there, owner of Las Cuevas, headquarters for all cow bandits.

'The Captain placed the pistol in his belt and said that the open field we were in gave the Mexicans too much advantage. We went back to the river.'

While this firing was in progress, Captain Randlett crossed about forty soldiers into Mexico, justifying his action on the basis of Clendenin's orders 'not to cross... unless he saw plainly that McNelly was about to be massacred.' He stated that when the firing began, Captain McNelly was on the Texas side, and at once embarked in the canoe for the Mexican shore. When the firing became heavier, McNelly cried across the river, 'Randlett, for God's sake come over and help us.' Randlett wrote: 'I believed his command was in danger of annihilation, and at once crossed with two men in the boat, directing Farnsworth to command on this side and send over men as fast as possible. He sent me about half his company and half my own.' Without doubt McNelly's cry for help exaggerated his distress, and was made for the purpose of bringing the federal troops into Mexico.

Having maneuvered the federal soldiers into Mexico, McNelly's next purpose was to use them. 'I tried to induce the federal officers,' he said, 'to go with me to the ranch, but they refused.' Randlett was willing to stay with the Rangers by the riverbank until his superior officer, Major Alexander, arrived, but he could not be induced to go into the interior.

The question uppermost in all minds was what would Alexander do? Would he cross the river and go with McNelly after the cattle and the Cuevians? Or would he order Captain Randlett back to Texas and leave McNelly's men alone in Mexico? In the interval of waiting, from about eleven in the morning until five in the afternoon, the Mexicans made several charges, but were repulsed by the combined force of soldiers and Rangers.

In the meantime the Mexican forces were increasing, and when Randlett learned that two hundred troops had arrived in the Mexican camp, he decided to return to Texas. Just as he had made this decision a flag of truce appeared. He met the bearer and received a neatly written document 'purporting to come from the Chief Justice of the State of Tamaulipas.' The document was full of friendly assurances. It promised that the cattle would be returned to Ringgold next day, that every effort would be made to arrest the thieves, and it requested that the troops be withdrawn from Mexico. Though he had already decided to retire because of the concentration of Mexican forces in his front, Randlett now decided to remain because he saw signs of weakness in the demand which the Mexicans had made upon him. He wrote: 'The invitation for me to retire was so mildly put that I did not feel compelled to accept, and would only consent on my own terms to a cessation of hostilities against the Las Cuevas thieves until 9 o'clock the next morning.' His conditions were that the flagbearer and the two hundred Mexican soldiers who had just arrived from

Camargo should fall back three miles from his pickets, which were a hundred yards from the river, and leave the flag of truce flying on neutral ground. When he returned to the river just after sundown, he saw Major Alexander on the Texas side.[13] Alexander ordered him out of Mexico immediately.

McNelly makes an entirely different report of the whole flag-of-truce episode. He states that at about five o'clock the Mexicans sent a flag of truce and a note addressed to the 'Officer Commanding the Forces invading Mexico.' He refused to receive the note with such an address, and pointed out that when Captain Randlett received it he thereby assumed command. The note demanded that the troops vacate Mexico and promised to consider the Texas complaint afterwards. McNelly states that Randlett agreed to the terms, but he did not. 'I refused to recross until they delivered me the stolen cattle and the thieves.' The Mexicans then asked for a suspension of hostilities for the night. 'I also refused that unless they complied with my demands.' The Mexicans told McNelly that they could not deliver the cattle that night for the reason that most of them were in Camargo. McNelly then agreed to make no advance that night provided the Mexicans would bring in the two horses, saddles, and bridles which the Mexicans had captured that morning.

Then comes a revelation of the audacity of this man: 'I ... agreed to keep the white flag up for some hours, and *agreed to give them an hour's notice before I commenced active operations*.' These terms were accepted.

By six o'clock the thirty Texas Rangers were alone in Mexico, facing a growing combination of a Mexican army and a Mexican citizen mob. Captain McNelly had agreed to give this formidable aggregation an hour in which to prepare to defend themselves against thirty men!

Night came down on the river. Captain McNelly sent his horses back to Texas and went himself to procure bread to go with the goat meat. Bill Callicott resumes the narrative.

'The Captain came back with some bread stuff and told us to eat our mutton we had broiled the night before we started into Mexico. He said, "Boys, it's all off. The U.S. Captain won't let me have any of his men and I know of no other Rangers in Texas except Major Jones's Rangers on the northern Indian frontier and they are too far away to get here. We will stay here a while. They can't surround us and cut us off from forage and water, and they can't cut us off from grub because I have arranged with that Mexican in the leaky dugout to furnish us with all the mutton, bread, and coffee we need." And so we remained there all night.

[13] Randlett's report, December 1, 1875. A.G.P.

'The Captain did not like the place where we were because the bank was too high. We moved to another place where the bank was about four feet high with a slope to the water. The Captain sent two boys over after spades. They brought two spades and a shovel. The Captain then went down about halfway between the bank and the edge of the water and stepped off a trench forty feet long fronting Mexico. Then he stepped off about thirty feet at each end leading angling from the main trench to the bank. Then he told three of the boys to come.

'"Boys," he said, "I want this trench dug two feet deep and three feet wide; pile the dirt on the upper bank and pack it level. When the Mexicans charge us again, they will come in big numbers, and when they do, we will fight them from the thicket to the bank; and if we can't stand them off at the bank we will fall back to this trench and fight them to a death finish. I am willing to die with you boys and I expect as much from you. Now work. I will have three fresh men on every hour until it is finished." If ever you saw boys scatter dirt we did, for well we knew that if the Mexicans did charge over the bank that trench would be our death cell — for the Captain always meant what he said.

'We finished. The Captain came and looked at our work and said that the Confederate veterans couldn't have done any better in the way of trench digging. Then we went back to the bank to watch the Mexicans.

'That night after dark the Captain came to me and said: "Bill, it is your time to go on guard. I will locate you on the outside post and I want to tell you what to do before we go as we will be too close to them to talk after we get there. I am going to put you in that bloodweed patch about one hundred yards from the Mexican lines. When I get you to the place, I will press you on the shoulder and you sit down facing the Mexicans and keep a good lookout. If one man comes towards the river, halt him three times; and if he does not stop, shoot him and come to me at the river. One man will be a spy trying to locate us before they charge. Be sure you let him get up close enough so you won't miss him. If more than one comes, fire on them and come to me."

'When we got to the place, he pressed me on the shoulder and I sat down. I still had on the hat I took off the dead bandit in the Palo Alto fight. I had been on guard about an hour; had seen nothing or heard nothing. Then I heard dry bloodweeds breaking towards the Mexican lines. The noise was coming nearer. The night was bright with starlight and finally I saw the object and took it for a man. It came closer, but I could not see it clearly for the bloodweeds. It was very near. I said "Halt:" I said "Halt" again, but it came on and I felt my Mexican hat begin to rise on my head as I sat there expecting a thousand Mexicans to charge me. Just then it turned to the left and I saw that it was nothing but a cow. My Mexican hat settled down in place, but I could feel my heart thumping right under my collar. Soon the Captain came with the relief, and I returned with him to the river-bank. I told him how near I came to shooting the cow for a man, and he said, "Bill, I'm glad you didn't shoot for it might have woke up that U.S. Captain on the other side of the river and he would think the Mexicans were charging us and would turn the Gatling guns loose on us and we wouldn't last twenty minutes. I am more afraid of the Gatling guns than of the Mexicans."'

So the long starlit night wore through and the morning of November 20 came creeping over the sage-gray valley. On this day Captain McNelly sent General Steele the following telegram:

MEXICO NEAR LAS CUEVAS
NOV 20 1875

GEN WM STEELE
AUSTIN

I CROSSED THE RIVER ON THE EIGHTEENTH. ON THE NINETEENTH I MARCHED ON FAST TO RANCH LAS CUEVAS. KILLED FOUR MEN BEFORE REACHING THE RANCH AND FIVE AFTERWARDS. ON MY ARRIVAL I FOUND ABOUT THREE HUNDRED MEN. AFTER A FEW SHOTS I RETREATED TO THE RIVER AS THE U.S. WERE ORDERED NOT TO CROSS. THE MEXICANS FOLLOWED ME TO THE RIVER AND CHARGED ME. THEY WERE REPULSED AND AS THEY SEEMED TO BE IN FORCE SOME FORTY U.S. SOLDIERS CAME OVER. THE MEXICANS MADE SEVERAL ATTEMPTS... TO DISLODGE US BUT FAILED. UNITED STATES TROOPS WITHDREW TO LEFT BANK LAST NIGHT... THE MEXICANS IN MY FRONT ARE ABOUT FOUR HUNDRED. WHAT SHALL I DO?

L H McNELLY
CAPT RANGERS

138 COLLECT
715 AND 752 VIA
BROWNSVILLE

By this time the wires were singing with messages from Las Cuevas on the Rio Grande to Washington on the Potomac. General E. O. C. Ord at San Antonio had orders from Washington to dispose his troops 'as if ordinary cattle stealing only were going on,' to return private property, the seized ferryboat of Camargo, and to inform the Mexicans that the United States troops were under orders not to cross.

On the same day, Potter wired Major Alexander:

FORT BROWN NOV 20

TO MAJOR ALEXANDER, COMMDG IN THE FRONT.
ADVISE CAPT McNELLY TO RETURN AT ONCE TO THIS SIDE OF THE RIVER. INFORM HIM THAT YOU ARE DIRECTED NOT TO SUPPORT HIM *IN ANY WAY* WHILE HE REMAINS ON THE MEXICAN TERRITORY. *IF McNELLY IS ATTACKED BY MEXICAN FORCES ON MEXICAN SOIL DO NOT RENDER HIM ANY ASSISTANCE.* KEEP YOUR FORCES IN THE POSITION YOU NOW HOLD AND AWAIT FURTHER ORDERS. LET ME KNOW WHETHER McNELLY ACTS UPON YOUR ADVICE AND RETURNS.[14]

COL POTTER

The job at Las Cuevas was too big for the United States army to handle alone, and the State Department was called in and the consular service put to work trying to get McNelly out of Mexico. At 3 P.M. Thomas F. Wilson, consul at Matamoros, wired Lucius Avery, Commercial Agent at Camargo, as follows:

I UNDERSTAND McNELLY IS SURROUNDED AND TREATING FOR TERMS OF SURRENDER. IF SO GO TO HIM IMMEDIATELY AND ADVISE HIM TO SURRENDER TO MEXICAN FEDERAL AUTHORITIES AND THEN YOU GO WITH HIM TO THIS CITY TO SEE THAT NOTHING HAPPENS ON THE WAY. INSTRUCTIONS HAVE BEEN SENT FROM HERE TO AUTHORITIES IN CAMARGO TO ALLOW YOU TO ACT IN THE MATTER. ANSWER.

Avery secured a copy of his instructions at Ringgold and hurried to the front. Captain McNelly, in his inimitable manner, tells us how he dismissed the services of the United States Diplomatic Corps.

'After the U.S. troops were withdrawn from the Mexican side,' runs his report, 'we heard all sorts of reports of immense Mexican forces gathering in our front — and most of these reports were believed at this and other points on the river. The American consul at Matamoros arranged for our surrender, as you will see by enclosed copy of telegrams, but I "couldn't see it."'

With all this knowledge of his situation, which was hourly growing worse, with the constant pressure from the United States army to retreat and from the consular service to surrender, what would this man whose soul was a flame of courage do? Would the cattle still be important to him?

[14] E. O. C. Ord to General Steele, November 20, 1875. Colonel Potter to Major Alexander, November 20, 1875. A.G.P. The italics in the telegram are mine.

The reader will recall that he had promised to give the Mexicans an hour's notice before he attacked them. At four o'clock on the afternoon of November 20, he served notice on them that he was coming and that the only way they could escape was to comply with his demands! Read his words:

'So about 4 oclk (20) I notified them, that unless they accepted my proposition to deliver such of the cattle and thieves as they had on hand, and could catch, to me at Ranch Davis, without waiting for the tedious legal forms that always ended in our receiving magnificent promises, in lieu of our property, that I would at once make an advance. After a few moments' consultation they agreed to deliver me all the stock they had succeeded in recapturing, and as many of the thieves as they could catch, in Rio Grande City at ten oclock on the 21st. Upon that promise I withdrew my company, reserving the right, if I saw proper, to go to Camargo and take the cattle.'

4. THE COWS COME HOME

The scene now moves up the river to Rio Grande City which stands opposite Camargo. When McNelly reached Ringgold (the fort at Rio Grande City), he decided to let the Mexicans deliver the cattle on the Texas bank. This was no easy matter, but was finally accomplished. Several notes were exchanged, the delayers of the south resorting to their favorite tactics. McNelly asked for an interview with a Camargo official, who replied that he was very busy that day, and would have to deny himself the pleasure of seeing the Captain until noon of November 22. Then Diego García wrote: 'Because of excessive work on hand I do not send you the cattle today, but early tomorrow morning you will have them on the other side of the river.' [15]

McNelly answered at once, and his letter shows him a master of diplomacy and psychology. He repeated the agreement he had had with Dr. Headly and Señor Alberretti the day before, reminded the Mexican that the cattle were to be delivered at ten o'clock that day. Then came his master touch: 'As the Commanding Officer of the United States forces is here awaiting your action in this matter, I would be glad if you would inform me of the earliest hour at which you can deliver these cattle and any of the thieves you may have apprehended.' [16]

[15] Diego García to McNelly, November 21, 1875. A.G.P. Translation by Carlos Castañeda.

[16] McNelly to Diego García, November 21, 1875. A.G.P.

Though McNelly knew that all the United States forces were utterly powerless to help him, he was still using them. After pondering his letter, the Mexican official found that his business was not as pressing as he first thought, and, as he himself said, he shortened the delay. 'Because of the multiple official duties,' he wrote, 'I had ordered the cattle to be taken back tomorrow, but I have now shortened the delay and they will be on the banks of the river at three o'clock in the afternoon at your disposal.' [17]

It is significant that Señor García did not say which bank of the river. Bill Callicott now takes the narrative as cheerfully as he took guard duty in the bloodweed patch.

'The next morning the Captain took ten of us and went up to Rio Grande City to get the cattle. We stayed all day looking for them, but they did not come until four o'clock. And when they did come, the Mexicans in charge stopped on the Mexican side of the river. The Captain sent them word to bring them over. They sent word back that they couldn't cross the cattle to Texas until they were inspected. The Captain said, "Well, boys, we are in it again." There were twenty-five Mexicans with the cattle and ten of us. The Captain said, "Well, boys, twenty-five to ten. That's near enough. We will go over again, if we never get back. What do you say?"

'"We are with you, Captain," we replied.

'A Mexican had a ferry at the place and on the Texas side. The Captain said, "All Aboard!" We went over and found that the Mexicans had seventy-five head, rounded up in a close herd. The twenty-five Mexicans were armed with Winchesters and pistols and they all left the cattle and came to us. They stopped in ten feet of us. The Captain told Tom Sullivan to tell them that the Presidente promised to deliver the cattle on the Texas bank. The boss shook his head and said not until they were inspected. The Captain told Tom to tell him they were stolen from Texas without being inspected and they certainly could be driven back without it. The boss shook his head and said no.

'The Captain motioned Lieutenant Robinson and he ordered us to fall in ranks. We fell in. Instantly we loaded our guns and covered the Mexicans.

'The Captain then told Tom to tell the son-of-a-bitch that if he didn't deliver the cattle across the river in less than five minutes we would kill all of them, and he would have done it too, for he had his red feather raised. If ever you saw cattle put across the river in a hurry those Mexicans did it — and in less than five minutes, except one that was so exhausted she would not take the water. We roped her and pulled her

[17] García to McNelly, November 21, 1875 (translation). A.G.P.

on the boat and the Captain gave her to the Mexican boatman for taking us over and bringing us back.'

Captain McNelly does not say that he went into Mexico at Rio Grande City, but it is not improbable that he did.

There is still another account of the delivery of the cattle. It is by Major A. J. Alexander and does but little credit to that officer's sense of justice.

'After receiving your dispatch of the 20th,' he wrote, 'I advised Capt. McNelly to withdraw to this side which he did. I then proceeded to Ringgold alone reaching there at 1 A.M. the 21st. That afternoon the Mexicans delivered 76 head of cattle at Ringgold.... The return of the cattle shows the effect of this demonstration.' [18]

Alexander, supreme commander on the Las Cuevas front, not only assumes credit for the return of McNelly, but he also assumes full credit for the return of the cattle. Nowhere in the reports of any of the officers is there a word of faint commendation for McNelly and his men. In contrast to this is the attitude of Captain McNelly towards the federal forces. Nowhere does he condemn them, either directly or otherwise.

In justice it must be said that the soldiers were of great service to him, though he was not able to do with them all that he desired. Their presence at Las Cuevas doubtless held the Mexicans in check, and we have seen how he used the troops at Ringgold to bluff the Mexicans out of their delay.

The story of Las Cuevas raid has been told in some detail and from rich and varied sources. Had the action of McNelly there been in the cause of freedom, or under some banner of patriotism, it would have conferred glory on him and his thirty men. But that battle was fought for a herd of cattle, for the purpose of crushing banditry and making life safe for Texas cows on the Rio Grande.

Callicott relates an incident which throws light on the character of Captain McNelly, and shows the esteem in which he was held by the boys — and they were really only boys — who followed him.

'Captain McNelly was a man who seldom got mad and never did get excited. He always handled his men as a father would his children. I never heard him speak a cross word to one of them, but when he gave a command it certainly had to be obeyed. Something came up the night after we got the cattle that showed how he felt towards us. After we penned the cattle at Rio Grande City the Captain and three or four of us went up to the U.S. fort to get some forage for our horses. Captain McNelly and a U.S. captain were sitting on a wagon tongue discussing the trip into Mexico when one of the Rangers went up and

[18] A. J. Alexander's Report, November 29, 1875. A.G.P.

sat down by our Captain. The U.S. captain jumped up and said, "Captain McNelly, do you allow one of your privates to sit down by you?"

'"Yes, sir," said the Captain, "I do at any time. I haven't a man in my company but what can lie down and sleep with me if he wants to do so."

'The U.S. captain said, "We don't allow privates that privilege with officers."

'To this Captain McNelly answered, "I wouldn't have a man in my company that I did not think was as good as I am."

'That showed the kind of love Captain McNelly had for his men and he did not have a man in his company that wouldn't have stepped in between him and death. We all loved him as a father as well as a captain.

'After we got the forage for our horses, we spread our blankets in front of the gate of the corral where the cattle were penned and laid down all in a row. Before we went to sleep the Captain said: "I went into the Confederate army at sixteen and at seventeen I was made a captain of a company. I have been in many tight places where it seemed that neither I nor my men could get out, but I always got out with part of them. When we went into Mexico with only thirty men, three miles from the river with no hope of getting help was one time when there seemed little chance of escape. If the pilot had not made a mistake, and we had dashed into Las Cuevas instead of Cachattus we wouldn't be here tonight. Of course we could have taken the ranch, but the 250 Mexicans would have surrounded us and we would have had little show. If we had gone into the houses to protect ourselves they would have killed us with the artillery. That U.S. captain never would have come over to help us. God pity such a captain. I claim that to be the tightest place I was ever in for all to get out alive."'

Whether Captain McNelly said these things to his men as they lay on their blankets by the corral gate we shall never know. One of his devoted followers put the words in his mouth, and from what we know of him, we can be sure that he might have said them.

The next morning — November 22 — Captain McNelly asked for four volunteers to take the cattle belonging to his friend Richard King to him at Santa Gertrudis Ranch. Ed Pitts, George Durham, W. L. Rudd, and William Callicott volunteered. They found thirty-five cattle bearing the King brand, and these they started on the hundred mile journey. Captain McNelly's last instructions to them were to stay with the cattle, come what may.

'We reached Santa Gertrudis Ranch without losing a cow,' said

Callicott. 'We got there about 3 P.M. and sent the old Captain word that Captain McNelly had sent him some cattle from Mexico. Captain King came to us and said, "Well, boys, I am glad to see you. From the reports at one time I didn't think any of you would ever get back to Texas. How many men did the Captain have with him over in Mexico?"

'We told him.

'"What! only thirty men to invade Mexico with!"

'"Yes, sir," we said.

'"Were you mounted or on foot?"

'We told him five were mounted and the rest on foot.

'"And all afoot but five! And the ranches you attacked were Las Cuevas and Cachattus. Those are the two worst ranches in Mexico. They are headquarters for all the cow-thievin' bandits who steal from this side of the river. I know all about Las Cuevas, know when it was started. It was settled by General Juan Flores and I understand he still owns it ——"

'"No, Captain," we said. "The other fellow owns it — we killed the General." Then we told him all about it.

'"Well," replied Captain King, "I am glad you all got back alive. It was reported that you were surrounded, cut off from forage and water, that it would be a second Alamo with you, that you would have to surrender."

'"No, sir," we said, "the Captain told us when we went over that he wouldn't have any surrender. It would be death or victory or all get out together the best we could, and he meant what he said."

'"That was a daring trip," said Captain King. "There is not another man in the world who could invade a foreign country with that number of men and all get back alive. Captain McNelly is the first man that ever got stolen cattle out of Mexico. Out of thousands of head I have had stolen these are the only ones I ever got back, and I think more of them than of any five hundred head I have."

'He told a ranch hand to tell his boss to come with ropes, a saw, and two men. When the boss came he told him about the cattle and where they came from. He told him to saw off the right horn of each cow and turn them all on the big range for the rest of their lives. The old Captain stood at the gate and saw the work done, and then he told the boss to open the gate and let them go free as long as they lived. He wanted these thirty-five cattle to spend the rest of their days in peace.

'Captain King invited us to go up to the house, but we told him we were too dirty to go where there were ladies — we hadn't changed clothes in ten days. Then he told us to take our guns and pistols and go

THE ROAD TO LOS CUEVAS

MONUMENT TO GENERAL JUAN FLORES

to a room over the warehouse. There we found plenty of nice clean blankets, pillows, chairs, table, wash bowl, towels, water, candles, matches — everything nice enough for a St. Louis drummer. We made our pallets and about dark our supper came — ham and eggs, butter, cakes, pies, in fact, everything good to eat with plenty of fresh buttermilk and coffee. Captain King's two daughters who had just graduated from some school in Kentucky sent up two big poundcakes tagged

COMPLIMENTS OF THE TWO MISS KINGS

TO

THE McNELLY RANGERS

'Well, we hadn't had any dinner that day and we were all hungry and began to eat the good things set before us. George Durham, the youngest Ranger after Berry Smith was killed, did not have the first joint of his stomach gauged and he overloaded it. After we finished supper we went to bed and everything was all right until about twelve or one o'clock when George had the worst western nightmare he ever had. George was subject to nightmares. We were all sound asleep when he jumped up, pistol in hand, saying, "Shoot, boys! Here they are, boys, shoot!" We had no light and could not find him except by the sound of his voice. We caught him and disarmed him and kept his gun and pistol until day and all slept well.

'The next morning Captain King asked us if we needed fresh horses, and said we could take his and leave ours. We told him ours would do. He then asked if we needed money. We told him Captain McNelly had given us money for grub. He said he would furnish the grub, and he did — enough to last three or four days. We filled our wallets with good eatin' stuff, started back for the Rio Grande and the two Miss Kings waved at us as we raced away.'

General Juan Flores is deserving of some consideration. We have seen that the Rangers killed him as he led his men in a charge across the open field on the morning of November 19. To the Texas Rangers, to Captain King, and to Bill Callicott he was head of 'all the cow-thievin' bandits of the Rio Grande,' but on the south bank of the Rio Grande he bore a different reputation. There he was a great man — as great as Richard King. He was *mayordomo* of Las Cuevas which without doubt harbored the raiders. Las Cuevas stands today and probably has much the same appearance that it had in November, 1875. The trails from the river are still as brushy as they were when McNelly led his Rangers there. The home of General Juan Flores still stands, and

THE HOME OF JUAN FLORES

THE CORRALS OF LOS CUEVAS

crooked pole corrals may be seen everywhere as they appear around these patriarchal Mexican ranches. The children, grandchildren, and collateral kin still dwell in the village and dominate it as of yore, a colony of the rare blue-eyed Mexicans. There is a sandy road leading from the banks of the river at Rio Grande City through the age-old town of Camargo, down the river through the brush to Las Cuevas, better known now as San Miguel. Hardby the road, at the very entrance to the town where none can fail to see, stands an imposing monument fifteen feet high, surmounted by a cross and decorated with a wreath of faded flowers.

The inscription on the monument reads:

AL CUIDADANO
JUAN FLORES SALINAS
QUE COMPETIENDO
MARIO PER SU PATRIA
EL 19 DE NOVIEMBRE
1875

In translation the epitaph reads:

TO CITIZEN
JUAN FLORES SALINAS
WHO FIGHTING
DIED FOR HIS COUNTRY
NOVEMBER 19
1875

XIV

McNELLY'S SUCCESSORS: LEE HALL AND JOHN ARMSTRONG

I privately sent the Meanses word that the governor had sent me down here to stop all such things, and that the next man they killed in that quarrel, or in that manner, I would come down direct and ... shoot them in less than two hours after reaching that neighborhood ... and I don't know but I had better do it.

L. H. McNelly

Arrested John Wesley Hardin, Pensacola, Florida, this P.M. *He had four men with him. Had some lively shooting. One of their number killed, all the rest captured.*

J. B. Armstrong

XIV. McNELLY'S SUCCESSORS: LEE HALL AND JOHN ARMSTRONG

1. McNELLY'S LAST SERVICE

THE first months of 1876 passed quietly. Lieutenant Robinson reported that he sent ten men to a place called Runeon de Perro, 'a perfect slaughterhouse of stolen beeves.' The rancher there was arrested, tried to bribe the sergeant in command, failed, attempted to escape, and was killed.[1] The heavy rains of January interfered with the operations of both the Rangers and the thieves. In February a few cattle were stolen in Cameron County from near the banks of the river.[2]

In March, Captain McNelly returned from the interior to Santa Gertrudis by way of DeWitt County. There he reported a recurrence of the trouble between the Sutton and Taylor factions. Prior to his arrival, a sheriff from Henderson County came to Sinton with a writ for a member of the Taylor party named Allen, and summoned a posse of nine men from the Sutton party to assist him in making the arrest. The result was a fight in which a deputy sheriff of DeWitt was killed and young Allen and another man wounded. The Henderson County sheriff left on double-quick time without waiting to see who won the fight. A few days later, forty or fifty armed men went to Allen's house, carried him to Gonzales County and sent the Suttons word to come and get him if they desired. The invitation was accepted, but when the party found young Allen dying, they did not harm him, telling Captain McNelly that they had no ammunition to waste on dying men in Taylor's jurisdiction.[3]

On his arrival at the King Ranch, Captain McNelly received a letter from Sheriff William S. Halsey describing conditions in Nueces County. Cattle were being driven from the Devil's River to Kansas,

[1] Robinson to Steele, January 3, 1876. A.G.P.
[2] *Ibid.*, March 1, 1876. A.G.P.
[3] McNelly to Steele, March 8, 1876. A.G.P.

and to other points. The sheriff said that he was powerless without the aid of state troops and asked for twenty Rangers. McNelly sent the Halsey letter to General Steele with the statement that unless some action were taken, the state would have another DeWitt County affair, and worse, on its hands. 'I am satisfied that a pursuit of the cattle thieves would lead to a meeting with the Hardin gang, a consummation devoutly to be hoped for.' It was reported that the cattle thieves had hired John Hardin's gunmen to keep competitors out of the Devil's River country, the rendezvous of thieves. 'If this is so, we may have an opportunity of ridding the State of these pests for good and aye, for I should deal with them without mercy.' [4]

Important matters on the Rio Grande made the Devil's River expedition impossible at this time. Mexico was in turmoil and McNelly recorded through March and April the beginning of the rise of Porfirio Díaz to the dictatorship. Díaz began his career in Brownsville, Texas, and his first victory was the taking of Matamoros. McNelly watched events closely and with interest.

On March 19, he wrote from Brownsville: 'Gen. Díaz is here keeping house; receives a great many people, strangers, every day.' Pena was a league from Matamoros and it was thought by the knowing ones that the heroic city would go over to him without firing a shot. Things were still quiet on March 24, but trouble would come as soon as Díaz met success or defeat. In either case one side would be out of employment and would turn to cattle driving as the most remunerative occupation. Appearances favored the success of Díaz. The government had been afraid to arm the national guard (militia) and had kept federal troops at Matamoros. These were needed in the interior and if they were withdrawn the national guard would assume control, and the belief was general that the militia would surrender the city to General Díaz at once.[5]

On April 2 McNelly wired, 'Díaz captured Matamoros this morning.' In a letter of the same date he wrote: 'General Díaz attacked and took Matamoros this morning after firing for about half an hour. Casualties four killed and twenty-four wounded. The Government troops, National guards and regulars, made but one slight stand and then surrendered. In fact, most of them went over to Díaz as soon as he appeared. One company of artillery (regulars), when Díaz charged them, instead of firing on him, turned their guns on the regulars drawn up

[4] McNelly to Steele, March 8, 19, 1876. A.G.P.

[5] *Ibid.*, March 19, 24, 1876. A.G.P. Many prominent Texans assisted General Díaz in the beginning of his career. Among these was John S. Ford. See testimony of Julius G. Tucker, 'Texas Border Troubles,' *House Miscellaneous Documents*, No. 64, Forty-Fifth Congress, Second Session, pp. 224 ff. Serial No. 1820.

to support the battery, and opened on them, and so it was all through.'[6]

Twelve days later McNelly wrote that Díaz was in favor with the Mexican cattlemen, was trying to make soldiers of his men by strict discipline, and had just suppressed an incipient revolt by shooting eight men. He was planning to start for the interior in two weeks, and 'if he can take the border men (thieves) with him, we will have some rest.' On April 25, McNelly reported that Díaz was pressing men into his service and many were crossing into Texas to escape him. Some petty stealing was going on by the river, two or three cows, oxen, or horses at a time. His own horses were getting fat, his men were under good discipline and well drilled.[7]

Early in May, Captain McNelly received information that there would be raiding for beeves near Laredo, and that the thieves were to cross five hundred head. 'If they make the attempt, I will hear of it and will try to get to the driving ground by the time the thieves do.' On May 19 he sent the following report:

GRANDHAM, TEXAS
May 19, 1876.

GEN'L WM. STEELE,
SIR:

I have the honor to report that on the night of the 17th I followed a gang of raiders, numbering eight or ten, to the river at a point five miles above Edinburg.

It was very dark, 10 o'clock P.M., and my guide missed the trail, detaining us about thirty minutes, so that by the time we reached the river, they had succeeded in crossing all the cattle but seven or ten, and then there were but four men on this bank. Two of them were killed and one wounded badly. The other escaped. The firing commenced from the other side as soon as my men came in sight. For fear of accidents, I had instructed my men not to fire until they were close enough to make sure shot.

We got six horses, saddles, and bridles and their camp equipage, consisting of coffee pots, cups, blankets, ropes, etc. I at once wrote a note to Captain H. J. Farnsworth, 8th U.S. Cavalry, stationed at Edinburg, asking him to assist in recapturing the cattle. He came up next morning (18th) with fifty men, but refused to cross, and said he would assist me in recrossing if he was satisfied that I would be unable to get back without his help. But said he would regret the necessity of doing so, and advised me not to go. Some of my Mexican guides thought that a part of the cattle were just back of the ranch, the Sabinisto; so I crossed with three men and searched the fields adjoining the ranch, but found no cattle. Saw the trail leading straight to Reynosa, distant but one mile and a half; and as Capt. Farnsworth told me that Genl. Escobedo had a large force there, I recrossed.

[6] McNelly to Steele, April 2, 1876. A.G.P.

[7] *Ibid.*, April 14, 25, 1876. A.G.P. McNelly made the above reports from Brownsville.

I then went to Edinburg and sent for the Alcalde of Reynosa, told him of the affair, and asked for the return of the cattle as soon as they could be found, and of the thieves. He promised to return the cattle, and to arrest the thieves and have them punished. On my urging a compliance of my first demand, he promised to send the thieves over secretly, as he was afraid to do so publicly.

Capt. Farnsworth and the sheriff of Hidalgo County assisted at the interview. Captain F. told him that he intends to support me fully in everything I saw proper to do in the matter. This evening the Chief of the Rural Police told me that they were making a very determined effort to catch the thieves. Genl. Elcobedo [Escobedo] and staff were in Capt. Farnsworth's camp while these thieves were crossing the river and driving the beeves inside Escobedo's lines for breakfast. And Escobedo's band of twenty pieces that he had brought to Farnsworth's camp was playing in our hearing when we commenced firing on the raiders. I believe there is some correspondence going on between Genl. Escobedo and the U.S. authorities in Fort Brown in regard to the matter. We leave this [place] in the morning en route for Laredo. Would have reported yesterday, but was waiting to see what the Mexican authorities were going to do, though I was satisfied from the first that they would not return the cattle or arrest the thieves.

Very respectfully,
L. H. McNelly [8]

This letter records McNelly's last trip into Mexico. On May 31, he wrote from Laredo that he was leaving for the Nueces, where he hoped to catch a gang of twenty or twenty-five men. He would break his company into small squads and scout from Fort Clark to Oakville, a hard country where civil authorities were helpless and took no notice of any outrage. He would make Fort Ewell his headquarters and would do nothing that was not legally justifiable.[9]

On June 4 he wired that he had captured King Fisher and nine of his men. He took them to Eagle Pass only to have them turned loose by authorities, despite the fact that seven of them could be convicted of murder. He also recovered eight hundred head of stolen cattle, but could not induce the cattle inspector to inspect them or the sheriff to issue subpoenas for the arrest of the thieves. The cattle were turned loose also.[10]

McNelly now came to Austin and gave to the newspaper an interview on conditions in the realm of King Fisher who ruled the country between Castroville and Eagle Pass. Here more than a hundred outlaws had assembled to terrorize the country and seize the reins of

[8] Brief reports of this affair appeared in the *Galveston News*, May 19, 20, 1876.

[9] McNelly to Steele, May 31, 1876. A.G.P.

[10] Telegrams, McNelly to Steele, June 4, 8, 1876. A.G.P. For another account of this affair see Jennings, *A Texas Ranger*.

government. The civil authorities were powerless; the county judge of Maverick County did not dare sleep in his own home. King Fisher's men carried off much property in open daylight and the owners dared not follow them or attempt to reclaim what they knew to be theirs. One man with his two sons had followed his stolen horses and found them in a corral. A man was present and asked them in a friendly manner to dismount, and shot them to death as they were hitching their horses. Since then no one followed stolen property in all that country.

The thieves had enclosed pastures on the Nueces where they kept stolen stock until such time as they were ready to drive to market in the Devil's River country. The citizens were in great fear and would not inform on the thieves. The terror was not confined, but was spreading, and the settlers declared that they had not suffered half as much from the Indians as they had from the depredations of the outlaws.[11]

McNelly later reported that conditions were bad around Goliad where the large stock-owners had formed a company of regulators to run out transients and non-property-owners. On the night of August 28, the ex-sheriff of San Patricio County had been killed in the church door. Sergeant Armstrong was sent to investigate, but before he arrived the coroner had held an inquiry and decided that there was not sufficient evidence to warrant an arrest, although McNelly was certain that one of the —— committed the crime or had it done.

Each of the prominent stockmen had five or six bravos employed to kill any offending person. The killing was done in the most casual manner, while the victim was playing cards, eating supper, or riding along the brushy roads. Even the walls of the church offered no asylum against the assassin's rifles. Reverting to the San Patricio murder, McNelly stated that the ranch man brought his bravo to the church door, pointed out the victim, stood by to see the killing well done, and then rode home. The assassin was a stranger — was always a stranger — and it was impossible to reach the real murderer by the process of law. Some other agency would be necessary and McNelly appointed himself agent.

'I privately sent the Meanses word that the governor had sent me down here to stop all such things, and that the next man they killed in that quarrel, or in that manner, I would come down direct and... shoot them in less than two hours after reaching that neighborhood; that that kind of thing had gone as far as human patience could bear, and that it had to stop, and I don't know but I had better do it.' [12]

[11] *Galveston News*, June 20, 1876. For an account of King Fisher see W. M. Walton, *Life and Adventures of Ben Thompson.*

[12] McNelly to Steele, September 20, 1876. A.G.P.

McNelly's last recorded public service was rendered in October. At that time, he and five of his men went to Clinton for the purpose of escorting five members of the Sutton party to the Galveston jail to which they had been committed by Judge H. Clay Pleasants.[13]

McNelly now became too ill for further service and when the company was reorganized his name was omitted from the roll and Lee Hall was made captain in his place. The result was widespread criticism from the press and the people. General William Steele justified himself by publishing the statement that McNelly's medical bill constituted one third of the bill for the entire company. He commended Hall, who was 'in the full vigor of early manhood and health,' and asserted that the new company comprised the best men of McNelly's company and cost only half as much.[14]

Thus was McNelly, the frail man, who had done so much to bring peace and security to the Rio Grande and the southwest border, set adrift by the state as soon as the fatal disease contracted in the service of the state overtook him. His successors did excellent work, but they never equaled McNelly. He died at Burton on September 4, 1877, at the age of thirty-three.

2. *LEE HALL ON THE RIO GRANDE*

In the summer of 1876 the reports of J. L. Hall and John B. Armstrong begin to appear in the reports of the adjutant general. There may be noted at this time a distinct change in the nature of the work performed by the Rangers. When McNelly was called to the Rio Grande in 1875, he was first concerned with the Mexican bandits from across the national boundary. By the middle of the year 1876, the emphasis had shifted to the bad white men who were operating on the Texas bank and in the interior. The feud in DeWitt County flared up occasionally and a state of general lawlessness prevailed along the whole frontier. The special company under McNelly and Hall, and the Frontier Battalion under Major Jones, devoted an increasing proportion of their time to the gentlemen of the road, feudists, and thieves. The great cattle drives to the North were in full swing, offering a good outlet for stolen cattle and horses and casual occupation to all who could qualify as cowboys. The adjutant general compiled what was known as the 'Crime Book,' containing names and description of refugees and wanted men. This book was distributed to the Rangers

[13] *Galveston News*, January 6, 1877. [14] *Ibid.*, February 6, 1877.

CAPTAIN LEE HALL

and local peace officers; such a terrific drive was made on the criminal class that by the middle of the year 1877 a decrease in crime was noticeable and commented on by the press.

In August, 1876, Lee Hall, second lieutenant of the Special Force, was placed on detached service at Goliad for the purpose of ferreting out a recent bank robbery. He learned the identity of the robbers who had fled to the Mexican border. The county was in possession of armed bands, 'calling themselves vigilants.' These had killed two men and ordered others to disperse. Hall ordered the vigilants to disperse and reported that business, which had been almost entirely suspended, was reviving and the county again becoming quiet.[15]

The bad conditions in Goliad County and the good effects of Hall's presence were described by a Goliad citizen as follows: 'Through the inefficiency of our sheriff our town and county had become a rendezvous of escaped convicts, cutthroats, outlaws, and murderers riding

[15] Hall to Steele, October 4, 1876. A.G.P.

through our streets at night, shooting through business houses and private dwellings, imperiling the lives of our women and children. Human life had become frightfully cheap and this terrible realization had settled down on the hearts of our people completely terrorizing and stupefying them and rendering them as passively submissive as sheep driven to the shambles for slaughter.... Lieutenant Hall had come an entire stranger, had taken in the situation at a glance and applied the remedy which caused the bold bad men to flee to parts unknown.' [16]

In November, Hall was again in DeWitt County searching for the murderers of Dr. Brazzell, who had been dragged from a sick-bed, taken a few hundred yards from his home, and with his son shot down in cold blood, and without cause. The people were terrorized and trampled upon by cutthroats and assassins who had got their hand in during the early feudist trouble. These had now formed a vigilance committee who made it their business to kill witnesses and intimidate juries. Thirty-one murder cases were on the court docket and so many people were mixed in the crimes that no one wanted to see another punished for fear that his own record would come to light [17]

Three days before Christmas, Hall reported the arrest of five men charged with the Brazzell murder. The Rangers surrounded the house and interrupted a wedding celebration. 'We came very near having a fight in the house, but finally talked them into a surrender which was very fortunate, as it would have been a very bloody affair,' wrote the officer. He said he thought he had the fighting members and if they could be brought to justice it would help to restore quiet in DeWitt.[18]

With the arrest of these men, the wildest excitement prevailed. The accused were taken before Judge H. Clay Pleasants who sat with a guard of Rangers on either side of him. He refused the men bail and committed them to the Galveston County jail for safe-keeping. Hall's suspense in getting them out of the country is indicated by a telegram sent from Flatonia: 'The agony is over. Am here with Captain McNelly en route to Galveston.' As already mentioned, the escorting of these men marked the last public service of Captain McNelly.

Judge H. Clay Pleasants was threatened with death and was constantly in danger of assassination. In an anonymous lettter he was told that he had sent the wrong men to prison for the Brazzell killing. 'It was the Jermans that done it and the reason why they kill them

[16] E. R. Lane to Governor Richard Coke, October 22, 1876. A.G.P.

[17] Hall to Steele, December 10, 16, 1876. A.G.P.

[18] *Ibid.*, January 4, 1877. A.G.P.

was because the old man and his sons riten a hole lot of blackguard and put it all over the shilow church.... Now you know very well that thare is two things that has and must be done, and that is that you can send after those men and bring them back and allow them bale, or you [and four others]... have got to die.... There is over twenty-five men that have you all five pick out, and they will give you two weeks from the day this letter is mail to bring them back and allow them bale.'[19]

In spite of the threats, Judge Pleasants remained firm and the accused men were kept in jail for a long time. In June, 1877, they were in Austin and were conveyed from there to Cuero by Hall, who stated that he would not trust them to the sheriff.[20] Apparently these men were never convicted, but it is a current report among the Texas Rangers that they were kept in jail until their careers were broken up. It is said that the wife of one of the men brought some peaches to the jail and that her husband ate them and dropped the seeds out the window and that he remained in the same jail long enough to pluck through the bars fresh peaches from a tree that had grown from one of the seeds.

The Special Force was reorganized at Victoria, probably on January 26, 1877. Hall was made first lieutenant, John B. Armstrong second lieutenant, and McNelly's name was dropped. Prior to that time General Steele had instructed Hall to make reports direct to him rather than through Captain McNelly. Steele stated that he had retained the best men in McNelly's old company, a statement that was resented by McNelly's friends.[21]

In February Hall broke his command into small squads and sent them through the southwest with instructions to report to Austin. The men were moving so fast that he could not keep up with them. His force was crippled because he had to keep several men in DeWitt. Eagle Pass asked for Rangers during district court and let it be known that if Hall's men would come, the juries and witnesses would take courage and indict King Fisher and his followers. Hall reported that two of the boys had just come to camp with a murderer, that a thief had been arrested in Karnes, that the shotguns had arrived, and that he wanted five or six copies of the crime book.[22]

On March 2, Lieutenant Hall made a lengthy report of his activities

[19] Letter dated, Clinton, DeWitt, January 16, 1877, *Galveston News*, January 26, 1877.

[20] Hall to Steele, June 5, 1877; D. Beale to Steele, June 5, 1877, A.G.P.; *Galveston News*, June 26, 1877.

[21] D. Beale to Steele, January 26, 1877. A.G.P.

[22] Hall to Steele, February 8, 16, 1877. A.G.P.

from the time he took charge of the company on January 25. He had captured numerous fugitives, depositing them in convenient jails as he went along, but had been less successful with the cow thieves and skinners. In February he sent Ranger Hardy and two men to San Patricio County, where they captured twelve hundred and fifty stolen hides from different parties, but made few arrests because the sheriff, county attorney, and other officials were implicated.[23]

From John B. Armstrong, Hall learned that thirty miles from Eagle Pass a noted Mexican desperado and thief had a ranch on the Rio Grande which served as a resort for thieves and cutthroats from both sides of the river. At the time the Mexican was out of favor with the Mexican authorities and Hall had assurances that if he would drive the band into Mexico the Mexicans would assist in annihilating or capturing it. There was also a gang of white renegades in the same vicinity.[24]

Upon Eagle Pass the Rangers bore down in three squads and their sudden appearance there from April 9 to 11 caused a general stampede to the Mexican side of the river. District court was in session at Fort Clark. Hall sought out the grand jurors and assured them of protection. 'I am happy to state that upon these assurances and our presence they seem to be doing their full duty, as they have found bills against King Fisher and others who have gone scott free heretofore, though several grand juries have been held since they have been guilty of the most heinous crimes.' Before Hall arrived, Armstrong had arrested four men and driven four others across the river. Hall went with Lieutenant Armstrong and Sergeant Parrot to Piedras Negras to consult the Mexican officials and arrange for extradition. But, before seeing any official, the Rangers 'happened' upon the criminal on the main plaza, arrested him and later 'extradited him according to law.' On May 16, Hall wired that he had arrested King Fisher and others charged, along with Ben Thompson, with the killing of Wilson in Austin. 'My men are now engaged in guarding the jail, bringing in witnesses, and protecting them in appearing before the grand jury.'[25]

In the spring, reports began to circulate that the state would disband the Special Force as an economy measure. In May, letters began to pour into General Steele's office urging that Hall's company be continued in service. A DeWitt citizen wrote: 'If Hall and his men are disbanded the reign of terror and assassination will be renewed and those who have been prominent in bringing to justice those suspected

[23] T. H. O'Callaghan to Steele, February 17, 1877; Hall to Steele, March 5, 1877. A.G.P.

[24] Hall to Steele, February 22, 1877. A.G.P.

[25] *Ibid.*, May 16, 1877, letter and telegram. A.G.P.

of crime will be the first to suffer. This will produce anarchy by inducing rival organizations, and no one can predict the end.'[26] After some agitation the West Texas Stock Association assembled at Goliad and subscribed over seven thousand dollars to be used in keeping the Rangers in the field. Among the subscribers were such prominent men as H. Runge, W. A. Pettus, Coleman, Mathis and Fulton and Thomas O'Connor.[27]

By summer the border was feeling the effects of the revolution in Mexico. Valdez and Escobedo had disbanded their forces on the Rio Grande, owing to the success of Díaz, and a horde of thieves and cutthroats were at large among the people. There was a big camp twenty miles east of Eagle Pass which would be investigated.

Hall and Sergeant G. W. Arrington of the Frontier Battalion attacked Valdez's camp near Eagle Pass on August 3. The Mexicans and outlaws heard that the Rangers were coming and a hundred, mostly fugitives, escaped. Fifty were captured and such as could be identified as wanted men were held. Eagle Pass was surrounded and searched with the result that sixteen men were arrested — seven for murder and three for horse theft — and delivered inside the Castroville jail.[28]

August 21 found Hall at Rio Grande City, where McNelly had received the Las Cuevas cattle in 1875. Hall had come because on August 12 a band of outlaws had a 'jail opening' at Rio Grande City, liberating several prisoners, who accompanied their deliverers into Mexico. There was much excitement and many accusations of conniving and double-dealing from both sides. Hall sent spies into Mexico, consulted the consul at Camargo, and interviewed Colonel Price, commanding at Ringgold. He heard that the raiders were within three miles of the river and that the authorities of Camargo knew their whereabouts. When he called on Colonel Gómez, *commandante*, to arrest the criminals, Gómez replied that he was making every effort to do so. Hall did not believe him, intimated as much, and demanded that the jail-breakers be delivered in four days. Three of the least influential were delivered, but Hall wanted them all. Gómez reported to General Canales that Hall had threatened an invasion, something which the Ranger declared he was careful not to do. Hall believed that the Mexican officials made no attempt to carry out the terms of the treaty of 1868 regarding

[26] W. R. Friend to Steele, May 27, 1877. A.G.P.

[27] Proceedings of the West Texas Stock Association, Goliad, June 11, 1877, on file A.G.P. The counties represented were Goliad, Victoria, DeWitt, Refugio, Bee, San Patricio, Aransas, Calhoun, Jackson, Lavaca, Gonzales, Wilson, Live Oak, Bexar, Nueces, Duval, Karnes, Uvalde, Maverick, Frio, Webb, Cameron, Zapata, Starr. Hall to Steele, May 31, 1877. A.G.P.

[28] Hall to Steele, August 6, 15, 1877, letters and telegrams. A.G.P.

criminals, and that the entire population was in favor of the men who raided or annoyed the Gringos.[29]

Without doubt the Mexicans recalled McNelly's raid in November of 1875, and when it was reported that another invasion was pending, the effect was described as 'electric.' *The Mier Whip* declared that the news came like an electric shock at midnight. Fearful for the national dignity, the sons of Mier 'presented themselves mounted and armed to the first political authority.' By dawn of August 13, more than a hundred citizens, animated by the sacred fires of patriotism, were ready to 'sacrifice themselves for the independence and dignity of their country.' Battalion No. 11 and the cavalry under Major Regino Ramón marched forward as to a festivity, 'and said they went with pleasure to kill "Gringos."' Battalion No. 11 exerted itself so greatly in getting to Camargo that seventeen soldiers died of sunstroke and were solemnly declared to be 'victims of the Gringo politics.' The editor did not know where the trouble would end, but thought the government out to arm the people on the river.[30]

Since there was little more for him to do around Rio Grande City, Hall proposed to go to Nueces County where an organization was killing inoffensive sheep-herders and driving the Mexican laborers from the country.[31] For the remainder of the year Lieutenant Hall made few reports; we may now leave him and follow his second lieutenant, a man who had learned much from McNelly and was truly his successor.

3. JOHN B. ARMSTRONG THINS OUT THE BAD MEN

John B. Armstrong went with McNelly to the Rio Grande in 1875 and participated with him in the Palo Alto and Las Cuevas affairs. He became a sergeant, and was made a second lieutenant in January, 1877, when Hall was given command of McNelly's company. One does not have to follow John Armstrong's career very far to recognize that he was a man after McNelly's own heart. His methods were McNelly's methods and he never hesitated to administer extreme unction to those who could not be handled in a more gentle manner. It is only fair to say that he shared with Hall in the work of cleansing Southwest Texas. These operations have been followed at some length,

[29] Hall to Steele, August 29, 1877. A.G.P.

[30] Extract from *The Mier Whip*, sent by Hall to Steele. A.G.P.

[31] Hall to Steele, September 1; September 15, 27, 29. A.G.P. For an account of the killing of the Mexican sheep-herders see testimony of Julius G. Tucker, 'Texas Border Troubles,' p. 230.

LIEUTENANT JOHN B. ARMSTRONG

and the story will not be repeated. On many occasions, however, Armstrong worked independently and in his own way. The episodes for which he was solely responsible are so stirring that they deserve separate notice.

The name of King Fisher has occurred many times in the narrative, and in September, 1876, Armstrong went with a squad of men into King Fisher's realm. From Carrizo he sent Captain McNelly, then at San Antonio, a long telegram describing his activities for one night.

CARRIZO, TEXAS
October 1, 1876

CAPTAIN L. H. MCNELLY,
SAN ANTONIO, TEXAS

Owing to heavy rains I was unable to reach the Carrizo until last night. On my arrival I learned that a party of desperadoes were camped on the Espinoza Lake ten miles northeast of this place and that another party would pass the night at the Pendencia. I sent Corporal Williams with ten men and a number of citizens to the latter place. I started with the balance of the detachment for the camp of the Espinoza. When within sight of the camp, about twelve o'clock P.M., we dismounted and proceeded on foot, leaving two men to guard the horses and ——, a desperado whom I had captured on my way. Discovered their camp on the bank directly in front of us, advanced slowly to within twenty yards of them when two of them commenced firing on us with their six-shooters. We responded promptly and a lively little fight ensued, resulting in the death of three of them and the wounding of another in five places. We subsequently learned from the wounded man that there were but four of them in camp, the balance having left. They had received information of our coming and had left.

Learning that there was a 'bad' Mexican at Whaley's ranch, eight miles distant, we sent three men to arrest him. He refused to surrender and fought desperately until our men were obliged to kill him in self-defense. There are numerous bad characters in the country, but they keep hidden in the brush so that it is difficult to find them. King Fisher left about a week ago with a large drove of cattle. Porter is supposed to be with him.

The parties that were killed had about fifty head of stolen [stock]. That morning after collecting their arms [of the desperadoes] we returned to our horses where we were informed by the guard that while we were fighting, the horses became excited, calling their attention from the prisoner, who took this opportunity to attempt to escape, was ordered to halt three times but kept running and was fired upon and killed.

ARMSTRONG
Sergeant Commanding Scout

Here, certainly, was enough excitement for one night. The Rangers had had three fights, killed four Americans and one Mexican, and recovered a herd of stolen horses and cattle.[32] There can be little doubt that the prisoner died *a la ley de fuga*.[33]

In December, 1877, Armstrong was back in Wilson County, where John Mayfield, accused of the murder of Robert Montgomery in Parker County, was living. On December 7, Armstrong and Ranger Deggs went to arrest Mayfield. They were particularly anxious to have him because of a liberal reward offered for him. They found Mayfield in

[32] For an interesting account of this affair see N. A. Jennings, *A Texas Ranger*. Jennings claims to have shot McAlister.

[33] Angelin B. Key to Governor Hubbard, January 25, 1877. A.G.P.

his corrals, and when he resisted arrest the Rangers killed him. Mayfield had many friends in the community, and these came to the scene of the fight so rapidly and in such bad humor that the Rangers were compelled to withdraw in order to avert further bloodshed.[34] The body of Mayfield was taken away by friends and buried secretly with the result that the reward was never paid.

In February, 1877, Armstrong reported on the activities of the hide thieves in the country between Carrizo and Fort Ewell.

'We went out there and found numerous camps and carcasses scattered around all over the country, but the men had all left, apparently on short notice. We have since learned that one Mr. Jack Hanning went ahead of us from Pleasanton and informed them we were coming.' The skinning business had been carried on extensively, and the hides were sent to Laredo in carts, the tracks of which would be seen everywhere. Things were quiet at Carrizo. Not a single desperado had been seen since the fight at the Espinoza. Eagle Pass was quiet too, though a large trade was being carried on in 'wet stock'. Several herds left monthly going North, one belonging to Charles B. was stopped recently at Fort Clark and thirty-nine head of stock not inspected were cut out. King Fisher had come back to the Pendencia and was gathering a crowd around him again. They had many horses hobbled around their camp, but since they were from Mexico there was no way of getting at them. 'You could not persuade a man in this whole country to testify against King Fisher or any of his clan.'[35] Armstrong returned to Pleasanton on February 21 with five prisoners whom he had gathered in Frio, LaSalle, McMullen, and Atascosa counties. He said he had rounded up numerous cow camps and houses, sometimes standing guard around a place all night, only to find that the parties wanted were not there. The squad had traveled from thirty to thirty-five miles a day and had worn out their horses.

The most famous exploit of John B. Armstrong was his capture of John Wesley Hardin. Mr. J. B. Gillett remarks in his book, *Six Years with the Texas Rangers*, that whoever said that Texas had never produced a champion in anything overlooked John Wesley Hardin. Though there may be some doubt that this Texan could qualify as a champion, there is no doubt that he would rank high on any roll of crime. John Wesley Hardin was not a picturesque desperado, not of the type of Jesse James, Sam Bass, or of many less famous personages. Hardin was what western men call a killer, a wanton murderer, not a highway-

[34] J. B. Armstrong to Steele, December 9, 1876; L. B. Wright to Steele, December 10, 1876. A.G.P.

[35] *Ibid.*, February 13, 1877. A.G.P.

man or bandit. It is said that he killed twenty-five or thirty men, not counting Mexicans and negroes. He was the son of a Methodist preacher, and emerged into prominence out of the Sutton-Taylor troubles in DeWitt County. The Ranger reports mentioned him in connection with Bill Taylor, and he must have belonged to the Taylor faction.

In 1874, Hardin was described as a man of twenty-three or twenty-four years of age, five feet nine inches in height, with light blue eyes, light hair, and thin, sandy mustache, a shabby and indifferent dresser, reticent in speech, a notorious murderer and outlaw. Another description, written in 1877 by a Texas Ranger who guarded him, said he was five feet ten, 'what the ladies would call a blonde,' quite communicative about his terrible adventures, and fairly well educated.[36]

With Hardin's numerous crimes, we have nothing to do. It was the killing of Charles Webb, deputy sheriff of Comanche County, in the town of Comanche, May 26, 1874, that finally put the Rangers upon his trail, and kept them there until his capture and conviction three years later. Because of Hardin's numerous crimes, both Louisiana and Texas set a price upon his head.[37]

It seems that Hardin was captured in Louisiana in September after the murder in May, and returned to Texas, but escaped and dropped completely out of sight until August, 1877.

The four-thousand-dollar reward for John Wesley Hardin dead or alive served to set a thousand self-appointed detectives on his trail and to send officers on all sorts of false leads. Any stranger who assumed the rôle of a bad actor was suspected of being Hardin. One of these men appeared in the town in which John Armstrong was recuperating from an accidental pistol wound, and impersonated Hardin. Armstrong talked with the local officer and the two decided to take Hardin alive. They agreed to go to the saloon, invite Hardin to take a drink, and while he was at the bar the local officer would seize his right arm and Armstrong would cover him with his six-shooter. The man was captured without difficulty and lodged in jail, but to the chagrin of the officers he turned out to be an impostor whose courage had been stimulated by too much whiskey.

The incident aroused Armstrong's sporting blood, with the result that he applied to the adjutant general for permission to work on the Hardin case. A detective, John Duncan, was assigned to work with him. Duncan rented a farm adjoining a kinsman of Hardin — some accounts say it was his father — and settled down to make a crop. Duncan learned that the man had a wagon or team belonging to Har-

[36] *Galveston News*, September 8, 1874; October 7, 1877. [37] *Ibid.*, September 8, 1874.

din, and began an attempt to purchase it. The relative wrote to Hardin for permission to sell, and Duncan managed to see the envelope which was addressed to John Adams or Swain in Alabama.

Armstrong requested the adjutant general to issue warrants for John Wesley Hardin and for his *alias* and to send them to him, one copy by mail and one by express. When Armstrong and Duncan reached Alabama, they learned that Hardin had gathered about him a gang that menaced the railroad — a fact which caused the railroad to render valuable assistance to the Rangers—and that Hardin had just gone to Pensacola, Florida. Without waiting for the requisition papers, Armstrong and Duncan continued on to Florida, where they stopped at a small station outside Pensacola to await Hardin's return and revealed their purpose to some local officers who agreed to assist them. When the train pulled in, Hardin was sitting by a window facing forward with his elbow on the sill. It was arranged that Armstrong would enter the front of the coach facing the Texan, the local officers would come in at the rear, while Duncan would, if possible, grapple Hardin's arm through the window. Neither Duncan nor the Florida officers carried out their part, and Armstrong was left to handle five men alone.

Because of his wound, Armstrong was carrying a cane, and when he climbed onto the platform he shifted it to his left hand and drew his six-shooter, a Colt .45 frontier model with a seven-inch barrel. At that time this particular model was associated with Texas, where its use was popular. Hardin happened to be watching the door, and when he saw the long-barreled six-shooter, he exclaimed, 'Texas, by God!' and reached for his own gun. In the meantime Armstrong was coming down the aisle, six-shooter presented, and commanding the gang to surrender. Fortunately for him, Hardin's gun had hung in his suspenders, and in his effort to jerk it he almost pulled his breeches off over his head. Hardin's companion sent a bullet through Armstrong's hat, and the Ranger answered with a shot straight to the heart. The man jumped through the window, ran a few steps, and fell dead. Still determined to take Hardin alive, Armstrong grabbed his gun, and was kicked backward into the empty seat. On the rebound he struck Hardin over the head with his six-shooter and put him to sleep for two hours. He instantly disarmed the other three men and stuck their weapons in his belt.

The conductor put the train at Armstrong's disposal and he ordered it forward. At intervals he dropped three of his prisoners with their guns minus ammunition, and by the time he reached Whitney, Alabama, Hardin's home, he had John Wesley only. From this place he sent General Steele the first of a series of cryptic telegrams.

WHITNEY, ALABAMA
AUGUST, 23, 1877.

TO GENERAL WM. STEELE.

ARRESTED JOHN WESLEY HARDIN, PENSACOLA, FLORIDA, THIS P.M. HE HAD FOUR MEN WITH HIM. HAD SOME LIVELY SHOOTING. ONE OF THEIR NUMBER KILLED, ALL THE REST CAPTURED. HARDIN FOUGHT DESPERATELY, CLOSED IN AND TOOK HIM BY MAIN STRENGTH. HURRIED AHEAD THE TRAIN THEN LEAVING FOR THIS PLACE. WE ARE WAITING FOR A TRAIN TO GET AWAY ON. THIS IS HARDIN'S HOME AND HIS FRIENDS ARE TRYING TO RALLY MEN TO RELEASE HIM. HAVE SOME GOOD CITIZENS WITH [ME] AND WILL MAKE IT INTERESTING.

J. B. ARMSTRONG
LT. STATE TROOPS

Hardin's friends did threaten to rescue him, but Armstrong told them that if an attempt were made, he would kill John Wesley with his first bullet and then kill them as long as his cartridges lasted.

Armstrong was in a tight place among Hardin's friends and without warrant or requisition for his prisoner. When the train for which he was waiting at Whitney Junction arrived, he found an empty coach which the railroad company had supplied for him and his prisoner. A tall woodsman with a long-barreled squirrel rifle reported and stated that the president of the railroad had sent him to assist in handling the prisoner. Armstrong put him to guard one door while he took the other and thus they entered Montgomery early in the morning, where Armstrong placed his prisoner in jail to await the necessary papers. He sent General Steele this telegram:

MONTGOMERY, ALABAMA
AUGUST 24, 1877

TO GENERAL WM. STEELE.

ARRIVED THIS A.M. PRISONER IN JAIL. NO PAPERS WHATEVER RECEIVED BY GOVERNOR. WHAT IS THE MATTER?

J. B. ARMSTRONG
LT. SPL. STATE TROOPS

This done, he went to a hotel to catch some sleep. He had not been asleep long when he was awakened and ordered to appear in court, where he found his prisoner who had been taken from jail on a writ of habeas corpus. Armstrong had to do some real talking to show why he should be permitted to hold a prisoner for whom he had neither warrant nor requisition. He explained that the papers were on their way by mail and express, exhibited a telegram to prove it, and showed his commission as a Texas Ranger. He then described the character and reputation of the man he had captured and pleaded with the court to continue the case until the papers arrived. His success is shown by a second telegram of the same date as the one above:

TO GENERAL WM. STEELE.
HARDIN TAKEN OUT ON WRIT OF HABEAS CORPUS. CASE CONTINUED TO WEDNESDAY. SEND ANOTHER REQUISITION BY MAN OR EXPRESS. AM AFRAID IT WILL MISCARRY BY MAIL AS DID THE FIRST. ANSWER.

J. B. ARMSTRONG

In a third telegram he wired:

IF REQUISITION DON'T COME TONIGHT GOV. HOUSTON [OF ALABAMA] WILL ISSUE A WARRANT ON GOV. HUBBARD'S TELEGRAM SO I CAN LEAVE HERE AT SIX TOMORROW MORNING. HAVE ARRANGED TO HAVE BOWER CAPTURED.

J. B. ARMSTRONG

Shortly after the papers arrived, Armstrong read the warrant to his prisoner who still denied that he was John Wesley Hardin and claimed that he was John Adams. Armstrong then read a second warrant for John Adams and asked, 'Now do you surrender?' Hardin admitted his identity and cursed Armstrong all the way from Alabama to Texas. Judging from the telegram that the Ranger sent as he clattered over the rails with his four-thousand-dollar prisoner, the profanity did not dampen his spirits.

TO ADJ. GENERAL WM. STEELE.
IT IS ALL DAY NOW. ON OUR WAY. PAPERS O.K.

J. B. ARMSTRONG [38]

When Hardin reached Texas, he was kept under constant guard by the Texas Rangers, and kept shackled most of the time. It was reported that his friends would come to release him, but no one attempted suicide in that fashion. He was placed in jail at Austin, where he remained until his trial at Comanche, already referred to. While in jail, John

[38] The only official record of the Hardin affair is the series of telegrams quoted. These are in the A.G.P. For the details I am indebted to Mr. Tom R. Armstrong, of New York, and Mr. Charles M. Armstrong, Armstrong Ranch, Texas, sons of John B. Armstrong. Ranger Armstrong was a born entertainer, but he never talked of his own exploits, nor wrote about them, nor had them written about by others. Tom Armstrong states in a letter to his brother, July 30, 1934, that he heard his father relate the capture of Hardin only twice, once in 1905 and again in 1910, when the son came from Yale with two friends — Harry Caesar and Skip Simpson — to spend the holidays on the Armstrong Ranch. For another account, see *The Life of John Wesley Hardin*, written by himself. He states that his alias was J. H. Swain.

'GUARDED BY RANGERS, THERE IS NO POSSIBILITY OF THE PRISONER'S ESCAPE'

Wesley Hardin received scores of curious visitors, and the old-timers of Austin tell of calling on him at the Austin jail. The trial was held at Comanche, Texas, in the last week in September. A squad of Rangers commanded by Lieutenant N. O. Reynolds, of the Frontier Battalion, escorted Hardin from Austin to Comanche and guarded him day and night while there, not only alert to any effort on his part to escape or on the part of his friends to deliver him, but also to keep the friends of Charles Webb from taking the law into their own hands.

A Texas Ranger who composed one of the guards, a member of Lieutenant Reynolds's company, wrote under the name of 'Mervyn' the best account of the scene before the trial, which was published in the *Galveston News*:

COMANCHE CITY, *September* 29, 1877

Editors News:

Day before yesterday Lieut. Reynolds, commanding Co. E. of the Frontier Battalion, arrived at this place guarding John Wesley Hardin. The Rangers were five days on the road with their prisoner. Hardin deported himself with the utmost decorum, evincing no restlessness, though his patience was sorely tried by the gaping crowds who gathered at the noon and evening camps to stare him in the face with a curiosity that knew no sense of delicacy. He was quite communicative, talking freely of his terrible adventures, expressing regrets for what he termed his errors, and hopes for the future. He is what the ladies would call a blonde; about five feet ten inches high; and is fairly educated in English and the common school branches. He has suffered with one old bullet wound on the trip hither. He is confined in the jail at this place, heavily sealed on the inside with oak, containing an iron cage. He is also ironed and guarded by Rangers, who remain within the prison walls both by day and night. A company of Rangers are camped in the back yard of the prison, so that the public may rest assured that there is no possibility of the prisoner's escape on the one hand or suffering by mob violence on the other....

Your correspondent has heard many stories of John Wesley Hardin, and can not but believe that some of them were greatly exaggerated. Many have asserted that he is unable to sleep with any degree of comfort to himself or those within hearing of him; that, disturbed by appalling dreams, he is wont to spring, howling like a mad man, from his bed, to grapple with phantom foes or cower whimpering on the floor. One narrator tells of a St. Louis hotel clerk who goes limping on crutches from a pistol ball received by making too hasty a visit to the dreadful dreamer while a spasm, such as I have described, was on him. But I have guarded this wild man, the report of whose bloody crimes has caused so much shuddering, whose name was 'bug bear' to the timid tourist in Texas. Yes, I have guarded him at midnight, when the moonlight was reflected in the dew drops on the prairie sedge, and in the tangled brush that skirts the cow-house. Alone and standing among the sleeping rangers I have gazed on the face of him I guarded, John Wesley Hardin, the gentlest sleeper of them all. Sometimes a troubled look disturbed his countenance for an instant; once he murmured 'Johnny,' his little son's name, but in the main his sleep was calmer than the moonlit stream flowing past me to the sea. If any demons ever haunted his bedchamber, they kept aloof from his bivouac. Were the irons on his limbs the potent charms that awed them away, or was it the cold blue gleam of the sentinel's Winchester? Perhaps some spiritualists can answer.

MERVYN.[39]

The jury remained out about an hour, returned with a verdict of second degree murder, and assessed the penalty of twenty-five years in the penitentiary at hard labor. Hardin wept bitterly, saying the jury had been too hard on him, but said the trial was fair, considering that the jury was not simply trying a man charged with crime, but John Wesley Hardin.

On October 5, Lieutenant Reynolds wired from Huntsville that he had landed John Wesley Hardin safe within the walls of the penitentiary. Hardin was granted a pardon by Governor Hogg in 1893. While in prison he had devoted himself to the study of law, and upon

[39] *Galveston News*, October 3, 1877. The identity of Mervyn is unknown. He was a rather regular correspondent to the *Galveston News*; the above is a fair sample of what he could do.

XV

THE FRONTIER BATTALION: MAJOR JOHN B. JONES

One of those killed was a squaw, but [she] handled her six-shooter quite as dexterously as did the bucks.... One of them had the scalp of a white woman fastened to his shield.

JOHN B. JONES

The operations of the companies will be directed, more than has heretofore been the case, to the suppression of lawlessness and crime.... [Officers and privates] are required and expected to use unremitting diligence in hunting up and arresting all violators of the law and fugitives from justice wherever they may be or from whatever quarter they may come.

General Order 15

I find that Kimble County is a theafe's stronghold.... Llanos and all tributaries are lined with them.... thease men make forays into other counties and burn cattle beyond recognition.

A Ranger Report

XV. THE FRONTIER BATTALION

1. MAJOR JOHN B. JONES

WHEN after Reconstruction the Texas legislature cleansed itself of carpetbaggers, scalawags, and negroes, and went Democratic, one of its first acts was the abolition of the state police. Along with the Democratic legislature came Richard Coke, of long beard and broad expanse, as chief executive. The carpetbag governor, E. J. Davis, barricaded himself in the second story of the state house and undertook to hold his office by force until he could appeal to President Grant for military aid. The Democrats took the first floor and laid the would-be governor under siege, fully determined to oust him from an office to which in their opinion he had no longer a shadow of a claim. When President Grant refused to interfere further in Texas politics, Davis yielded and the people's representatives again took charge of their own public affairs. They immediately tore away everything that the Republicans had done, on the ground that nothing good could possibly come out of the Republican régime and from the *tabla rasa* they rebuilt their institutions after their own pattern.

One of the first subjects to claim the attention of the new government was the adequate protection of the frontier. We have seen that prior to the Civil War the Texans refused to create a permanent force of Texas Rangers on the ground that the duty of protecting the border belonged to the central government. The Civil War and Reconstruction had altered all relationships. If the Civil War emancipated the slaves, so did Reconstruction emancipate the Texans from dependence on the federal arm, it made them ready at last to protect their own borders. The people, resenting the presence of federal troops and hating the 'buffalo soldiers' in the army posts, were ready to call their Rangers and willing to pay them.[1]

In his inaugural address, Governor Coke spoke of the frontier need, and the legislature passed a bill providing for six companies of seventy-

[1] The Indians called the negro soldiers 'buffalo soldiers,' because the kinky black hair of the negroes reminded the Indians of the curly hair on the face of the buffalo.

MAJOR JOHN B. JONES

five men each. The force was to be known as the Frontier Battalion and was to be commanded by a major who was responsible to the adjutant general and the governor. The companies were lettered from A to F, officered by a captain, first and second lieutenant, and the usual contingent of non-commissioned officers.

On May 2, 1874, Governor Coke issued to John B. Jones of Corsicana a commission as major of the Frontier Battalion. It is doubtful whether there is in the history of the Texas frontier a more important document than this commission. It is quite certain that Governor Coke could not have found in all Texas a man more competent for the difficult job ahead.

John B. Jones was born in Fairfield District, South Carolina, on December 22, 1834. At the time he was called to command the Frontier Battalion, he lacked a few months of being forty years of age. His father came to Texas and settled first in Matagorda County, but later established a ranch in Navarro County about ten miles from Corsicana. Major Jones had another ranch near Frost which was devoted to the raising of blooded horses. 'As a horseman, I have never seen his equal,' wrote Mrs. Helen H. Groce. 'His steed and himself seemed to be one — in perfect rhythm and harmony in every movement. He was simply irresistible on horseback and such lovely high-spirited horses as he always rode, usually a rich deep bay or shining mahogany.... How well I remember those magnificent stallions. I always remember them with gold rosettes and fluttering blue ribbons at their ears, Gold Eye, Dellinger, Lion, and the equally splendid brood mares.'

Major Jones was of slight stature, about five feet and eight, and weighed about one hundred and thirty-five pounds, but it was said that there was so much of command and dignity in his manner that one never thought of him as small. His eyes and hair were as black as a raven's wing, contrasting with his fair though weather-beaten face. He had a fine forehead and nose with nostrils as sensitive as those of his thoroughbreds. 'I can see him now, the perfection of neatness; dark well-kept suit, white shirt, black bow tie, heavy black mustache and hair, smooth olive skin, piercing, twinkling, sparkling, penetrating black or dark brown eyes that seemed to see through your very soul, and seeing sympathized as he understood.'

His pre-eminent characteristic was great tact. His father was not so blessed, but was very outspoken, determined, and forceful. One of his sisters said that John Jones was the only member of the family who 'could do anything with Pa.' He would agree with any plan Pa offered, follow along while Pa explained until they struck the snag which John saw from the first and together abandon the project which no longer ap-

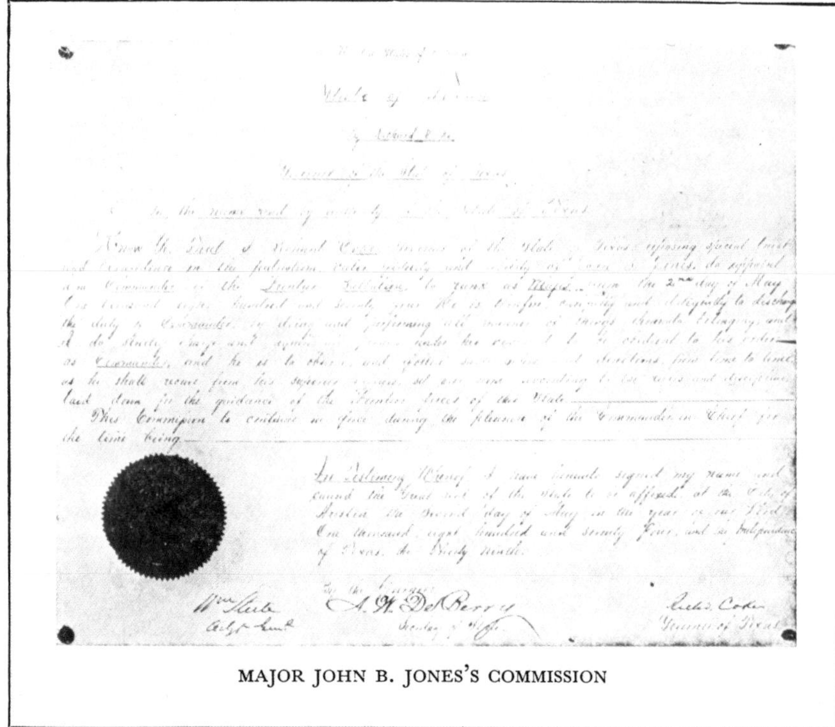

MAJOR JOHN B. JONES'S COMMISSION

peared feasible. It was this tact which enabled Major Jones to go into the most dangerous mobs or among feudists and bring peace where there had been war.

Along with his tact went that judgment born of a high intelligence, never better illustrated than in the period following the Civil War. His people and neighbors were hot-headed Southerners, and when the Confederacy failed they made up their minds that they would never live under Republican rule. They decided to found a colony in some South American country and migrate in a body, but were wise enough to send an agent to investigate. John B. Jones was selected and made the journey to Brazil, and probably to other countries. 'I shall never forget the night of his return,' wrote Mrs. Groce. 'He brought to us children a large wooden box of delicious candy.... This he opened with a little hammer and leaving it on the dining-room table, told us to help ourselves, while the grown-ups discussed their affairs in the adjoining sitting room. At the first chance I slipped into the sitting room and listened in. I heard him say, "No, Pa, we could never be happy there, that is a priest-ridden (I had never heard the word before) country." ' The envoy then described the conditions to which he objected, but the little girl sneezed, was discovered, and, as she expressed it, 'shunted from a conversation that was not meant for childish ears.'

He was a temperate man in all things and never touched tobacco or liquor, but loved sponge cake, the forerunner of angel food, and fresh buttermilk. He became addicted to coffee while riding the plains, where the only water for miles was from the stagnant green-scummed pools. This water was safer and more palatable when made into coffee, which he drank black.

John B. Jones had been prepared by training and experience for his work at the head of the finest force of Rangers that Texas has had. His education was begun at Matagorda, continued at Independence and Rutersville, and completed at Mount Zion College, Winnsboro, South Carolina. When the Civil War came, he joined Terry's Texas Rangers as a private and within a month was made adjutant of the Fifteenth Texas Infantry. In 1863 he was made adjutant of a brigade with the rank of captain, and in the following year was recommended for the rank of major, but the war closed before he received his commission.[2]

Governor Richard Coke knew him as a soldier and had confidence in his ability and character. The handsome, carefully groomed young Major Jones made striking contrast to the bluff and robust Dick Coke, who tucked a napkin in his collar to cover his broad expanse when he ate, and whose countenance after eating soup reminded the little girl of a geography map.

Of all the great officers of the Texas Rangers, John B. Jones's name is as yet the least known. He worked so quietly and so unostentatiously that he has not entered much into the tradition which has come down by word of mouth about the Texas Rangers. It is when one gets into the official records that one finds buried the measure of the man. He was very careful of records, kept copies of all his letters, even those written in camp and on the road under the most trying conditions, and it is from these records that the following brief account of the scope of his work has been written.

[2] For sketch and bibliography see *Dictionary of American Biography*. Mrs. Helen H. Groce wrote a sketch of Major Jones from which the above extracts were taken.

2. *CLEANING UP THE INDIAN TROUBLE*

Within less than thirty days from the time he received his commission, Major Jones had five companies in the field, and by July 10 all six were in service. Each company was ordered out in front of the county or counties in which it was organized. These men were raw, many of them wholly inexperienced; it required time, patience, energy, and intelligence to bring them into shape. Major Jones differed from all other commanders of the Texas Rangers in that he had a broad conception of his duty to guard the whole frontier from Red River to the Nueces. His point of view was that of a commanding general rather than that of a captain. In this he differed from McNelly, Ford, McCulloch, and even from Jack Hays; these were captains only, but Jones was a general.

To his credit it may be said that he did not undertake to direct his Rangers from a swivel chair in the state capitol. Escorted by twenty or thirty men, and accompanied by a wagon — commonly called an ambulance — he went into the field and patrolled time and again the entire length of the border, a territory four hundred miles long and a hundred wide. He moved his companies and detachments as a chess-player moves his men, provided them with supplies and equipment, and established with a firm but gentle hand strict discipline over officers and men.[3]

On June 13 he wrote from Kerrville that Captain Neal Coldwell's Company E had organized two days before and would move at once by way of the head of the Guadalupe to a permanent camp twenty-five miles southwest, where he would assume the protection of the country between the Nueces and the Llano. The men were short of small arms and Major Jones requested that twenty pistols and two thousand cartridges be sent to them at the first opportunity. On the same day Major Jones left for Captain Perry's camp in Mason County. July 10 found him with Captain G. W. Stevens's Company, twelve miles above Fort Belknap. He moved Captain Stevens twelve miles east to a camp on Salt Creek two miles from Graham. It was while here that Major Jones had his first and most important battle with the Indians.

On the morning of July 12, Lieutenant Wilson returned from a scout and reported a fresh Indian trail going down the east side of Salt Creek. Major Jones, Captain Stevens, Lieutenant Wilson, and twenty-four men started on the trail at a gallop. They followed the trail for fifteen miles

[3] Jones to Steele, December 1, 1874. A.G.P.

over the prairie and into the mountains about midway between Belknap and Jacksboro. The Rangers were now close upon the Indians who, upon entering Lost Valley, were joined by about fifty more, bringing the total force to one hundred warriors. Once in the mountains the Indians spread their trail and the Rangers separated to look for them. A squad of twelve men were attacked, but managed to retreat and the entire Ranger force concentrated and sought refuge in a depression or draw in Lost Valley while the Indians concealed themselves behind the rocks and brush of the adjacent hills. Here the white men were held in siege for the remainder of the day. While attempting to procure water, D. W. H. Bailey and W. A. Glass of Stevens's company were cut off and killed and Lee Corn of Coldwell's company and George Moore of Maltby's were wounded.

The Rangers realized that their situation was desperate, surrounded as they were in an open valley by four times their number, and without water. Their only hope was to steal away in the night or to send a messenger to the government fort at Jacksboro for help. The fact that they had lost twelve horses made it impossible to mount the men or carry away the two that were wounded. They decided to send a messenger for help and to hold their ground. The selection of horse and man for this task was of greatest importance.

One of the men volunteered to make the ride, but he was not sure that he could find his way to Jacksboro. Lee Corn, one of the wounded men, had an excellent horse and one, moreover, that knew where Jacksboro was. Corn directed the rider to mount this horse, point his nose towards Jacksboro, and ride, leaving the rest to the horse. Man and horse shot away and the Rangers waited in their improvised rifle pits. The rider got through; Captain Baldwin and a squad of negro troops arrived in Lost Valley before daylight. The combined force scoured the valley at dawn, only to find that the Indians had departed without leaving a trail. The dead men were rolled in blankets and carried to Jacksboro for burial; the wounded were left for medical attention. Three Indians were killed and three wounded. The Rangers captured one Indian horse and an assortment of bows, arrows, and moccasins. Major Jones reported that the Indians were armed with breech-loading guns, as the mortality among the horses would indicate, and that they were 'painted and decked out in gay and fantastic manner.'[4]

After this battle Major Jones continued his patrol northward. He stated that he would combine Companies B and C to watch for Indians

[4] Jones to Steele, July 14, 1874. A.G.P. This report was written from Flat Top Mountain, Young County, twenty-three miles west of Jacksboro; Grooms Lee, a participant in the fight, related in a personal interview the incident of the ride for help.

which he expected in large bodies. July 22 found him with Captain Ikard at Camp Eureka near the Big Wichita in Archer County. He thought this company was too far out and moved it to the southwest corner of Clay near Captain Stevens's Flat Top Mountain camp in northeastern Young County. Major Jones reported that two detachments had found the trail of the Indians who fought at Lost Valley and estimated the number between one hundred and one hundred and fifty. Lieutenant Campbell had found an Indian camp on the Big Wichita on July 11 and took from it forty-three horses.[5] On July 25, Ranger Israel with ten men of Maltby's Company E struck the trail of six Indians near the headwaters of the Clear Fork of the Brazos, killed two and wounded three, one of whom was captured and died later. The captive reported that the Indians left Fort Sill four days before the fight to go into the settlements after horses and scalps. The Rangers scalped the two Indians killed on the field, captured two bows, quivers, arrows, a shield, a Spencer rifle, two six-shooters, and one horse. They lost a horse and had one man wounded.[6]

Major Jones had spent the first three weeks on the upper frontier, and on July 31 he moved southward to Fort Griffin which was garrisoned by United States troops under General Buell. He soon reached a good understanding with the federal officer and instructed his captains to give Buell prompt notice of any Indians headed in the direction of Fort Griffin. From this point he moved to Captain Waller's camp on Sandy Creek in the southwest corner of Stephens County, where he found some of the men scouting and a half-dozen ill in camp. By August 9 he was at Captain Maltby's camp at the head of Home Creek in Coleman. He was displeased to find the captain and both lieutenants absent on one pretext or another. Captain Maltby had gone to Austin for some pistols and to visit. Major Jones was not aware that the emergency required the captain's presence in Austin. Pistols could have been sent to him. The lieutenant was reported to be ill, but had no surgeon's certificate. The Major would 'so inform both of them by letter from this place.' When Major Jones saw a letter from Maltby authorizing eleven furloughs to residents from Coleman and Brown and promising others to men from Burnet, he countermanded the permits and interdicted furloughs except in special and extraordinary cases. He stated that it was extremely difficult to make the men understand that they were not at liberty to go home when they pleased, or to get a brother or friend to substitute for them. 'I have established the rule, however, and am determined to maintain it, hoping that I will be sus-

[5] Jones to Steele, July 23, 1874. A.G.P.

[6] W. J. Maltby to Steele, July 28, 1874. A.G.P.

tained by the Governor and yourself, otherwise I can have no system or discipline in the Command.' [7] Thus did Major Jones let it be known that he would rule these young border Rangers — officers and men alike — with a firm though gentle hand.

September 5 found him with Captain Neal Coldwell on the head of the Guadalupe, the southernmost outpost of his command. He found the men in good condition, but the horses were worn down from scouting after Indians who had captured all the horses belonging to a party of bee hunters. Though the company was not well located, he could not move it because the whole country from the Llano *via* the head of the Guadalupe and Frio to the Nueces had been burned, and there were few places where water and grass could be found together. 'I have traveled a whole day at a time without finding any grass.'

Major Jones commended Captain Neal Coldwell as an active and zealous man who showed a disposition to discipline and control his men. Coldwell had relieved a private and sergeant for insubordination, and Major Jones upheld him by discharging the private and reducing the sergeant to the ranks. When a lieutenant named Nelson requested a transfer to another company on the ground that his life was in danger from some of the men in the command, Major Jones told him he would have to resign or go on with the command. He did this because he had formed the opinion that Nelson was not fitted for his position.

The same firmness which he exhibited towards his men served him against the influential citizens who demanded special favors. A Colonel Pickett wrote direct to General Steele requesting that Stevens's company be removed from Flat Top Mountain to White's Prairie, which was right in front of the Colonel's farm. Jones wrote that if this change were made, Colonel Pickett would have two companies of Rangers between him and the Indians while all of Jack and Young and a good portion of Parker and Palo Pinto counties would be entirely unprotected. Though Major Jones never resorted to sarcasm, he approached it in this letter. 'I have had many applications of this kind in regard to the proper disposition of the command and have long since learned that each man on the frontier thinks just in front of his farm or ranch is the best place to post a company or detachment, but never before have I found a man who wanted two companies.' He then recited the location of the various companies and pointed out that they were disposed so as to furnish protection on the entire line. 'Surely this ought to satisfy the people there that they have their full share of what little protection we have to give.' [8]

In order to tie the different commands together, he established a

[7] Jones to Steele, August 9, 1874. A.G.P.

[8] *Ibid.*, September 14, 1874. A.G.P.

line of couriers to ride from camp to camp at regular intervals for the purpose of carrying information and 'cutting' the trail of any Indians who might seek to come between the posts. The Major then made a rapid march up the line, and by October 3 he was again with Stevens at Jacksboro, and planning to leave for Ikard's post as soon as his horses were shod.

He had traversed the frontier and visited each of the companies three times. He was already tightening the reins over the organization that had never known much discipline, and was bringing the personnel to a realization that the Frontier Battalion was a military organization and not a holiday excursion at state expense. He was very gentle at first, and even by October had hardly made his influence felt.

On October 8 he left Jacksboro with one hundred men drawn from the different companies of the north, including his regular escort, for a scout to Pease River and the upper waters of the Big Wichita. He found no Indians and no fresh sign and reported that he believed the frontier was clear from the Brazos to the Red.

On his return he made a report on the Frontier Battalion as a whole. 'I am happy to report that the Battalion is now in good working order, the officers and men in fine spirits are doing their duty in protecting the frontier of the State from the depredations of the Indians as well as it can be done by so small a number of men.'[9]

At this point we may consider briefly a few engagements which the Rangers had with the Indians during the first two years that the force was in the field. In reality these accounts constitute a farewell to Indians in Central Texas, for their depredations were becoming fewer and of less importance.

Two minor engagements were reported for November. Lieutenant Millican struck a trail in Stephens County on November 17, and followed it into Shackleford, where he captured two horses and two mules. The next day Lieutenant Best of Maltby's company found one in Coleman, and followed it for twenty miles, overtaking the Indians late in the afternoon near Brownwood. Three Indians were killed, one was wounded, and the usual assortment of bows and arrows captured, including a six-shooter.[10] Three days later, November 21, Lieutenant Dan Roberts with a detachment from Perry's company and a part of Major Jones's escort under Lieutenant Beavert came upon eleven Comanches in southern Menard, followed the trail through the hill country towards Mason, and in a running fight killed five savages and captured a wounded one, who was sent to the governor at Austin.

By this time Roberts's horses were exhausted, but the detachment

[9] Jones to Steele, October 24, 1874. A.G.P.

[10] *Ibid.*, December 8, 1874. A.G.P.

from Major Jones's better mounted escort continued after the five live Indians. By the failure of horses, the pursuers were reduced to the lieutenant and two men, who drove the Indians into a cave, killed one, and wounded another. Only four of the eleven Indians escaped. The Rangers had three horses wounded and all broken down by the long race.[11] During December the Indians were numerous on the middle border, especially on the Brazos. They killed three men and ran off sixty or seventy horses.[12]

The next Indian engagement was in Lost Valley. On May 8, 1875, Major Jones learned that the Indians had driven a number of horses from Loving's ranch. He set out with about twenty men and struck the trail 'just where I entered the valley last summer, when in pursuit of Lone Wolfe and his party.' After a chase of four or five miles, the Rangers overtook seven Indians, and in a running fight killed five. These were armed with the best weapons and fought desperately, two of them continuing to fight after they were shot down. Major Jones wrote: 'One of those killed was a squaw, but handled her six-shooter quite as dexterously as did the bucks.... Another was a half-breed or quarter, spoke broken English, was quite fair, and had curly auburn hair.... One of them had the scalp of a white woman fastened to his shield.' Major Jones commended the Rangers because none of them stopped to scalp the Indians that were killed; all 'continued the rout without stopping until the last Indian in sight was killed.' He does not state what happened to the five Indian top-knots after the fight was over. Lieutenant Ira Long was especially commended for courage and coolness. When his horse was killed, the lieutenant hit the grass near an Indian who had just been dismounted. The Texan rose with clubbed gun, and probably would have finished the Indian on the spot had that savage 'not been expert in dodging.' [13]

The reports of the captains continued to mention an occasional brush with the Indians. In his report for August, Captain Dan Roberts stated that he struck the trail of Indians who had stolen herds in Mason County, followed four days, overtook the Indians on the Staked Plains one hundred and fifty miles west, killed one, wounded one, captured a Mexican boy and twenty-three head of horses.[14] This skirmish practically marks the end of the Indian troubles in Central Texas.

Major Jones summarized the results of the operations of the Frontier Battalion against the Indians. In the first six months the Rangers had

[11] Jones to Steele, November 24; December 2, 1874. A.G.P. In the first report the number of Indians is given as nine.

[12] *Ibid.*, December 23, 1874. A.G.P.

[13] *Ibid.*, May 9, 1875. A.G.P.

[14] Captain Dan Roberts, Report, August 31, 1875. A.G.P.

'THE LIEUTENANT HIT THE GRASS NEAR AN INDIAN WHO HAD JUST BEEN DISMOUNTED'

fifteen engagements with the Indians, killed fifteen, wounded ten, captured one, followed twenty-eight trails, and recovered two hundred cattle and seventy-three horses valued at five thousand dollars.[15] During the first six months about forty parties of Indians visited the frontier, about the average for several years. During the second six months twenty parties came, eight at one time during May. Rangers met them in five engagements, killed five and wounded one. For the next five months, May to September, only six bands had come. There had been one fight and several chases in which some horses were captured. From September, 1875, to February, 1876, no Indians had been on the border guarded by the Frontier Battalion.

There was a feeling of security as to Indians which had been unknown for a long time. Looked at in perspective, the operations of the Frontier Battalion after Indians were not important and will not compare in magnitude with the earlier work of Ford and others. It is quite clear, however, that Major Jones's force did bring the Indian troubles to a close; had the Indians been present in great numbers, he would have dealt with them more efficiently than did any of his predecessors. His great work as the peacemaker of the border was yet before him.

[15] Jones to Steele, December 1, 1874. A.G.P.

THE FRONTIER BATTALION

3. *OUTLAWS OF THE BORDER*

There is no doubt that the lawmakers intended that the Frontier Battalion should operate against the ordinary lawbreaker — the citizen thief and murderer — as well as against the Indians and Mexicans. The Ranger activities against the Indians have been followed through the later part of 1876. In this section we shall see with what results the Battalion dealt with the lawless white men.

To understand the problems that the Rangers had to solve, it may be well to describe the conditions that produced them for the period 1874 to 1880. It cannot be denied that Texas was then a lawless land. The Civil War had wrecked the country financially and had left behind a social débris in the place of an organized and well-ordered society. When the armies were disbanded, the Confederates drifted back to their homes with the war psychology still on them. For four years or less they had used firearms and become accustomed to bloodshed and to violent death. Then came Reconstruction which threatened to destroy whatever was left of self-respect, decorum, and fine morale. The carpetbaggers and scalawags, supported by the Union armies, were met by the Ku Klux whose strength was drawn from the majority of the population. During Reconstruction the Republicans asserted themselves especially in communities where they were fairly numerous. Between Democratic factions and Republican factions in such communities bitter feeling developed, and when both sides organized, the stage was fully set for feuds. In such feuds the local officials were powerless and of necessity belonged to one faction or the other. It became the duty of the Frontier Battalion to suppress these feuds and bring the murderers to justice or run them out.

A second contributory factor to the lawlessness was the frontier itself. Its position at the end of the Civil War, and for ten years thereafter, is fairly well defined by the location of the various companies of the Frontier Battalion and the line that Major Jones followed in his patrol from company to company. It is needless to recite the various reasons for lawlessness on the frontier. Fundamentally, it exists because the population there is so sparse that the ordinary forces of social control do not operate, and it is left to each individual to protect his own rights. Since these frontiersmen constantly faced danger from Indians, they carried arms at all times. Where all men are armed, conflicts among them are inevitable and the violent death of some is certain. The survivors became known as killers and some of them as murderers — there is a distinction. This indigenous class is recruited from the turbulent and adventurous men from the older settlements, refugees from justice. The Rangers were constantly searching for, arresting, or killing these men.

A third factor in the situation was the proximity of Texas to the Mexican border. The disorder there was so acute that a Special Force was organized under Captain McNelly to deal with it, and the story of this force has been told elsewhere.

A fourth reason for lawlessness arose from the fact that the cattle business was spreading over the Plains west of the location of the Frontier Battalion. By the beginning of the Civil War the frontier of farm settlement in Texas had arrived at the western extremity of the humid and timbered portion of the state. It had come to the edge of the Plains, to an environment new and strange. The frontiersmen had developed a pioneer technique suited to a humid and wooded country, but not to an open and semi-arid one. Consequently the advancing horde came almost to a full stop on the line separating the two great American environments. From 1850 to 1874 the farming frontier was almost stationary on this line. The open, arid country could not be fenced because there was no timber for rails and barbed wire had not been invented. Without fences there could be no farms and no farmers. Windmills were as yet almost unknown as a means of procuring a water supply, which could be found in only a few streams, in many cases intermittent. Had both barbed wire and windmills been available, farming could not have flourished because the principles of dry-farming had not been discovered, big machinery for the plains farms had not been invented, and the seed varieties that would stand the dry climate had not been imported from Africa and Asia or created by agricultural experiment.

In the period of waiting for these things to come to pass — a period of about thirty years — the turbulent conditions incident to a frontier existed in a given community for a much longer period than was commonly the case. That strip of country patrolled by Major Jones promised to be a permanent frontier. Moreover, while the frontier of farm settlement and orderly society was practically stationary, the more turbulent vanguard was constantly expanding over the Plains. It was in reality building there a permanent and new society in which farming had no place. The vehicle of this expansion, of this new form of American civilization, was the humble cow; the motive force which drove the cow was furnished by the horse, direction by the cowboy, and protection by the six-shooter. It was a powerful combination, this cow-horse-man-six-shooter complex of the Plains.

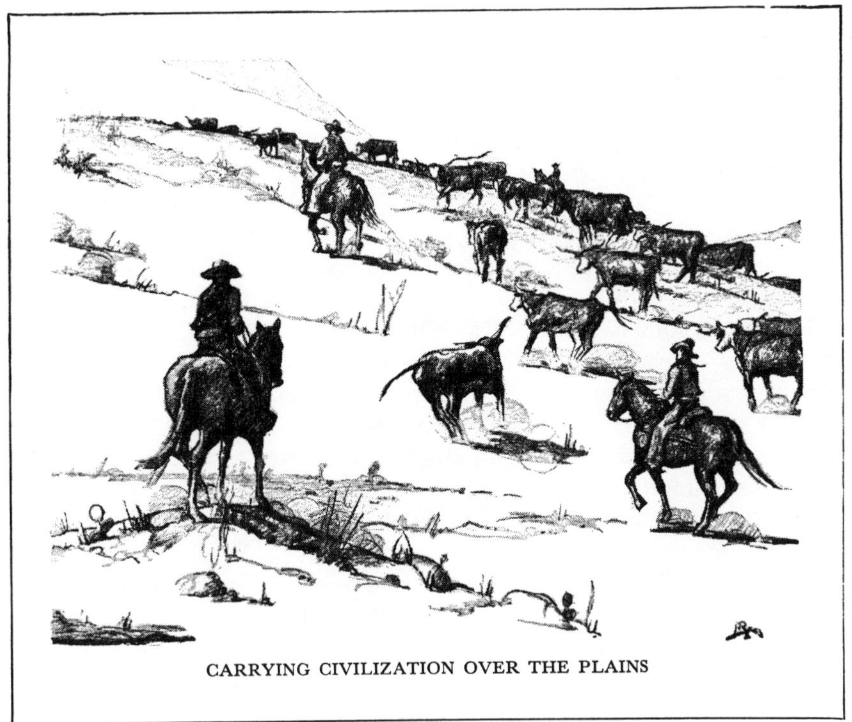

CARRYING CIVILIZATION OVER THE PLAINS

The story of the origin of the cattle kingdom has been told elsewhere. All the elements of it were brought together in the southern point of Texas when the young Texans took over the Mexican cattle of the Nueces Valley after the Texas Revolution. The movement of cattle in great herds northward began after the Civil War, in 1866 to be exact. The herds went to Abilene, Dodge City, Ogallah, Cheyenne, Denver, and Santa Fe in ever-increasing numbers and with them went the horses and men. By 1875, the cattle kingdom had been set up over all the grasslands of the Plains. A part of eighteen states became within ten years an occupied frontier where the ranch and not the farm was the unit of civilization. The frontier was no longer a line, but an area equal to two fifths of the United States.

The relation of Major Jones's Frontier Battalion of Texas Rangers to Texas society should now become clear. The Rangers occupied the line separating the two culture complexes. To the east of them were the farming belt and the region of settled homes; to the west was the cattle kingdom held by a group of fearless men, as dangerous and far more intelligent than the Indians whom they were supplanting.

Many duties of the Rangers grew out of the nature of the cattle business. There is no doubt that the cowboys themselves offered many problems. When a trail boss was making up an outfit to drive a herd northward, he was but little concerned with the moral antecedents of the men he took along. He wanted a man who knew how to handle cattle, horses, and guns. It made little difference to him what the man's name was or how many men he had killed. Many a criminal found occupation and even protection in the cow camps, and it is said that some outfits preferred men who were on the dodge, because they stuck closer to business, avoided the towns, and were always ready to fight their way out of a difficulty.

Moreover, the drifting herds offered a splendid outlet for stolen cattle and stolen horses. The Rangers were often called on to cut the herds for stolen cattle, a most ticklish job. Along the Mexican border many cattle were slaughtered for their hides alone, and in that section the Rangers might well have been called hide-thief-hunters. There are many records of brand burning, blotting, and blocking all over the cattle country.

Before the Indians were cleared out, the railroads began to be pushed across the Plains. The horsemen soon learned that they could rob a train and ride away to safety before the officers of the law learned of the deed. Along with the train robbery, stage robbery also flourished. From 1875 to 1890, the Texas Rangers always had one or more train robbers on their list, and during the period they killed or captured not a few of them.

With the invention of barbed wire in 1874 and the adoption of the well-drill and windmill, the farmers found it possible to move into the grasslands and fence the waterholes or their claims. The large cattlemen began to fence also; while some of them realized that the open range was passing, others resented the encroachment of barbed wire, farmers, nesters, and 'fool hoemen,' and began to cut the fences. The Texas Rangers were called to the scene and spent many weary nights 'lying on the fence' waiting for the wire-cutters to come.

For the first six months after the Frontier Battalion took the field, Major Jones devoted most of his time to the Indian problem, but not all of it. 'Besides the scouting for Indians,' he wrote in his December report, 'the battalion has rendered much service to the frontier people by breaking up bands of desperadoes who had established themselves in those thirty settled Counties, where they could depredate upon the property of good citizens, secure from arrest by the ordinary processes of law, and by turning over to the civil authorities many cattle and horse thieves, and other fugitives from justice in the older Counties.'

The Rangers had had 'two affairs with outlaws' in which two were killed and one wounded; they had arrested forty-five desperadoes and fugitives and delivered them to the civil authorities; they had recovered from the white thieves and restored to the rightful owners property valued at $9850, nearly twice the amount they had recovered from the Indians in the same period.[16]

In August, 1876, General Steele wrote Major Jones that the matter of lawlessness was becoming of more importance than anything else and that the governor desired the Rangers to do all they could to assist the civil authorities and to arrest known criminals. To further the work, General Steele was compiling a list of fugitives, a copy of which would be sent to each company. He had three thousand names on the list and others were arriving by every mail.[17] In November, 1876, Major Jones instructed the captains and officers to give a detailed report of all parties arrested, disposition made of them, fugitives pursued, prisoners escorted, jails guarded, and courts attended. They were also to report on Indian rumors, the weather, and the health and condition of men and horses.[18] In March, 1877, the officers were instructed to make no more scouts *westward* in search of Indians unless they were following a trail or acting upon definite information. 'The operations of the companies will be directed, more than has heretofore been the case, to the suppression of lawlessness and crime, will be confined mostly to the sparsely settled frontier counties and to the particular localities through which cattle will be driven during the spring and summer.' All cattle herds moving northward were to be inspected. Special attention was to be given to marks, brands, and blotching. Rangers were to report where a brand was changed: an S to an 8; U to O; and P to B or R. Officers and privates 'are required and expected to use unremitting diligence in hunting up and arresting all violators of the law and fugitives from justice wherever they may be or from whatever quarter they may come.'[19] Thus did the governor, adjutant general, and Major Jones cause the Texas Rangers, who had so long faced westward and fought Indians, to face about and direct their guns for the future against the white outlaws, thieves, feudists, highwaymen, murderers, and mobsters. This changed policy resulted in the death of scores, the arrest of hundreds, and the flight of thousands.

The first serious trouble with outlaws and thieves encountered by Major Jones's men developed on the southern end of the line in the

[16] Jones to Steele, December 1, 1874. A.G.P.

[17] Steele to Jones, August 23, 1876. A.G.P.

[18] General Order No. 13, November 24, 1876. A.G.P.

[19] Major Jones, General Order No. 15, March 20, 1877. A.G.P.

middle part of 1875. When the Frontier Battalion first went out, this region was occupied by Captain Neal Coldwell in charge of Company F. At the end of the first six months Coldwell's company had been disbanded in a reduction for the sake of economy. On May 19, 1875 Major Jones recalled Coldwell, and within eight days the company was full and stationed on Johnson's Creek, about twenty miles northwest of Kerrville. Five or six raids were made in that section between May 7 and June 1. Two of the parties were known to be Indians; and one was known to be white men.

'I am satisfied,' wrote Major Jones, 'there is an extensive organization of thieves on this part of the frontier.... All the stolen stock has been taken out this way. The Leon Springs robbers were going in the direction of the head of the Llano. The white man who was wounded in the fight died near here [Kerr County]. He confessed to being a member of an organized band of horse thieves and robbers. Had been in the clan but a short time and was not fully informed of their plans and operations, but thought there were sixty or seventy of them, that they carried the stolen stock out to the head of the Llano where it was left for some time, the brands and marks... changed, and then sent off to different places and disposed of. Many suspicious parties have been known to leave the settlements and go out in that direction and others have been seen passing from the head of the Llano to the head of the Nueces, where it was believed a branch of the clan is operating. I have reason to believe that their connection extends interior as far as Burnet, Austin, and San Antonio. Their camp is supposed to be in the vicinity of old Fort Terrett.

'I shall start tomorrow on a scout for them, will take a part of Capt Coldwell's company, and some thirty citizens from this and Kendall.... Will make a thorough search of all the country on the heads of the Llano and will break them up if they are there.' [20]

A week later, Major Jones reported from Menard County that he had scouted the country described, and though he found no organized bands, he did find suspicious persons who were doubtless confederates of the robbers and thieves. He interviewed these suspects, told them the Rangers would call on them occasionally to learn if they were harboring criminals or receiving stolen property. Major Jones reported that serious trouble was expected in Mason County and that he was sending Lieutenant Dan Roberts there to keep the peace while he continued to the northern end of the line.[21]

[20] Jones to Steele, N. W. Kerr County, July 1, 1875. A.G.P.

[21] *Ibid.*, July 9, 1875. A.G.P.

4. THE MASON COUNTY WAR

When Major Jones received by special courier instructions to send a detachment to Mason County, he abandoned his trip northward and went to the scene of trouble. On the Llano he came upon the first evidences of the disorders of the hill country. In passing Keller's place he was surprised to see fifteen or twenty men, armed with Winchesters, carbines, and six-shooters, rise from behind a stone wall in a fighting attitude. This aggregation of men, led by Sheriff Clark, who headed the German faction, was there because they had heard that the Gladden party of Cold Springs and the Beard party from Burnet were coming with about thirty men 'to burn out the Dutch.' Major Jones decided to investigate and end the trouble peaceably if it were possible.

'I turned back down the road and remained at this place at sundown. I find the houses closed, a deathlike stillness in the place and an evident suspense if not dread in the minds of the inhabitants. Every man is armed, but as far as I have been able to ascertain there is no body of armed men in or near the place at present. In fact there are scarcely any men here and as yet I have not been able to ascertain where they are. I shall remain here [Cold Springs] tonight with a view to learn the whereabouts of the Beard and Gladden party, having a friendly interview with them, and if possible, reconcile their difficulty and induce both parties to disband and return quietly to their homes.

'If I fail in this, then... I shall resort to other means to quiet the disturbance. My post office for the present will be Mason.' [22]

Major Jones's stop at Cold Springs gave the lawless element an opportunity to commit murder and spread terror in the town of Mason. Dan Hoester, while riding down the street, was shot by assassins concealed within a house. The murderers then fired into a hotel occupied by women and children, mounted their horses and made their escape. The sheriff and posse went in pursuit, which proved futile; Major Jones sent out three detachments, but stated that he had little hope of capturing men who had such a thorough knowledge of the country, were so well mounted, and had friends everywhere. The prejudice between Americans and Germans was so strong, he said, that there was small chance of learning the facts. Few of the Americans manifested any disposition to assist in the arrest of the murderers.[23]

[22] Jones to Steele, Cold Springs, Mason County, September 28, 1875. A.G.P.

[23] *Ibid.*, September 30, 1875. A.G.P. Major Jones named in this letter the three suspects.

Major Jones remained in Mason about one month — until October 28 — and before leaving he wrote an account of the origin of the Mason County disturbance. The feud was really between the Germans and the Americans, and was doubtless engendered during the Civil War and Reconstruction when the Germans espoused the cause of the Union rather than that of the Confederacy. The German faction was headed by Sheriff Clark and the more orderly element of the population. The American faction was led by John Beard, George Gladden, and Scott Cooley.

The immediate trouble began a week before Dan Hoester was killed, when two men of the American faction killed a man named Cheyney 'while he was arranging breakfast for them,' killed him in the presence of his family, then mounted, rode into town, and while eating breakfast at the hotel boasted that they had 'made beef of Cheyney and if somebody did not bury him he would stink.' They remained about town some time, and were not molested, though their guilt was of public knowledge. When Major Jones inquired of the justice of the peace why no warrants had been issued for them, the justice replied that no complaints had been made. After Hoester was killed, Sheriff Clark gave Major Jones warrants for the arrest of three men, but these had left the country and could not be found.

The justice of the peace and the sheriff belonged to opposing factions. When Major Jones asked Justice Hey for papers for any and all parties against whom indictments were pending, the justice reported that he had only one warrant, and that, said Major Jones, was for a trivial offense and could be executed by the constable or deputy at any time. The justice of the peace declared he had given Sheriff Clark no papers for several months 'and would never give him any more.'

The next day Justice Hey sent Major Jones papers for the arrest of ten men, *all of the opposing faction*, Sheriff Clark among them. The charges grew out of the acts of the posse which the sheriff had led in an attempt to capture the Hoester murderers. They were trivial — threatening to kill, false imprisonment, and attempting to kill. The ten accused men of the German faction surrendered to Major Jones and were brought before the justice. All were acquitted except Sheriff Clark, who gave bond in the amount of two hundred dollars.

In the November election Major Jones placed a Ranger guard in Mason at the request of the justice and another at Cold Springs 'on my own motion.' A few days later the American faction at Cold Springs sent Major Jones word that the Germans under Sheriff Clark had searched their houses. About the same time the American faction sent word that they were coming to Mason to make everybody take sides and kill all the Dutch. 'I immediately went down there with a detachment of men, succeeded in quieting their fears, prevailed on several who had run away to come back and stay home, and have kept a force there ever since until within the last few days.' [24]

While at Mason, Major Jones was confronted with the difficulties incident to dealing with factional strife. He first planned to use men from Lieutenant Roberts's company for the reason that they knew the country, but soon found that their very qualifications unfitted them for the service. One of Dan Hoester's murderers had been at one time a member of this company whose members were in sympathy with the American party. Major Jones discharged three of Roberts's men, sent the others away, and brought Ira Long's company instead, recruiting men from the interior who had no personal acquaintance with either party.

Letters were sent from Mason to the governor at Austin accusing Major Jones of partiality and of taking sides in the feud. The governor referred the complaint to General Steele, who wrote Major Jones without naming the complainant. Major Jones met the charge in the same honest manner in which he met friends, enemies, outlaws, or politicians. Incidentally, he shamed the governor for his lack of faith and put him in his place once for all. He wrote to the adjutant general:

'I am not surprised that reports have gone to the governor that I have taken sides with one or the other party to the terrible feud in this county, but am surprised that he should have taken notice of it. Having had some experience in troubles of this kind before, I knew the difficulties of steering clear of imputations of partiality and consequently was as careful as possible from the first to act in such a manner as to give no cause for suspicion even.' Though he had avoided personal or social intercourse with either side, he had not been in Mason ten days before each faction accused him of partiality to the other, and for that reason he could not determine which side made the complaint.

Then Major Jones very courteously informed the adjutant general that similar charges had been made against the governor, 'and I had to defend him against the charge on several occasions.' While the 'Dutch' had the upper hand, the American party appealed to the governor for aid, but received none. Then the Americans began to kill the Dutch, and just as they were coming into ascendancy by a process of judicious murder, the governor had sent the Rangers to put them down. A lawyer named Holmes made this complaint, not directly but by innuendo and 'they say.' Major Jones added: 'I suspect that he, if anyone, has made the complaint against me, from the fact that I have

[24] Jones to Steele, October 28, 1875. A.G.P.

on several occasions declined taking his advice and told him very plainly that I came here in the interest of no party, but in the interest of law and order and that in my management I would not be led by either party to the prejudice of the other.' [25] Here again was the firm hand of the man who was in the right. There is no record that either Governor Coke or his successors ever questioned the conduct of Major Jones again.

On the eve of his departure from Mason, the Major said that the county was quiet and had been since his arrival. The four weeks of peace were generally attributed to the presence of the Rangers. The people were begging him to remain, saying that trouble would start immediately he departed. He had some fears, but trusted that Lieutenant Ira Long — a discreet officer — would keep the peace. Both sides had accused him of acting harshly and with partiality, but 'I am conscious of having done all that I could and in the manner best calculated, from a moral as well as legal standpoint, to restore peace and quiet and enforce the law in this community. I must see what the companies above are doing....' And with all his plans disarranged by the German-American War in Mason County, the dapper peacemaker of the border set out for Lieutenant Foster's camp in Coleman County.[26]

5. THE KIMBLE COUNTY CLEAN-UP

The Frontier Battalion had no further important clash with white men in organized groups until the Kimble County trouble broke out in the early part of 1877. In the meantime every commander was busy with small things.

Lieutenant Pat Dolan related that between February 5 and 7 he had numerous squads combing the country for hide thieves. They captured many hides and at least eight men, while the ninth man 'came in and give up.' He took the prisoners to Uvalde, but the civil officers there would not receive all the prisoners. He started to Kerrville with four men, including one named Goodman, who complained of being sick and was left with the wagon under guard of Rangers Bowman and White. Goodman stabbed Bowman, took his horse and gun, and escaped, but the Rangers followed him to his home and were crowding him so closely that he left his horse and took to the brush. Sergeant O'Reilly and five Rangers 'remained out all night chasing him around — they shot several shots at him and run him in the river and he fi-

[25] Jones to Steele, October 20 1875. A.G.P.

[26] *Ibid.*, October 28, 1875. A.G.P.

nally froze out, as it was very cold and they brought him to camp in the morning.' Lieutenant Dolan added that Bowman was not badly hurt, that his horse and gun were recovered, and that the two Rangers neglected their duty. The country was full of cutthroats and thieves — 'This is the worst section of the country there is for men to work in and a better hiding-place for rascals than any other part of Texas. I had another man arrested yesterday for riding a stolen mule, but he showed beyond a doubt where he got the mule so I turned him loose.' Four days later, Dolan reported that his camp was constantly watched and all the movements of the Rangers were carefully noted by the law-breakers. He had arrested a man for theft of a six-shooter, but he believed he had a horse thief. He asked Major Jones to send him three pairs of shackles or leg irons for prisoners. In a postscript he said the prisoner had admitted that he was a horse thief. The man had a small sorrel Mexican pony with a white spot in his forehead and branded AR on the left thigh; the other was a dun horse stolen near Bluff Creek branded JL on the left thigh and 13 on the neck. In conclusion he asked, 'What shall I do with the horses?'[27]

In February the situation in Kimble County began to claim attention. Alarming reports came to Major Jones from citizens, local officials, and from officers of the Ranger force. Felix Burton urged that the Bear Creek Company of Rangers be permitted to remain at the junction of the Llanos, where it could suppress crime and arrest thieves, 'both of which our country is full and running over.' Horses, cattle, and hogs were being stolen almost daily, cattle from other counties were being driven in by tens, thirties, and fifties. Owners found their stock re-marked and re-branded and dared not reclaim it without help of the Rangers. Crime ranged from murder to the lowest grade of theft, and one man said, 'this county seems to be head quarter for men loaded with crime from all parts of the State.'[28]

Ranger H. B. Waddill wrote five days later: 'I find that Kimble County is a theafs stronghold.... Llanos and all tributaries are lined with them.... A man that isn't a thouraough expert at stealing has no show of holding his own... thease men make forays into other counties and burn cattle beyond recognition.... Everyone that is not known is looked upon as an enemy. John Joy sais that he has fed from 25 to 30 head of horses per night during the winter, the County is unsafe to travel through.' The people wanted Rangers at the junction of the Llanos or at the mouth of Johnson's Creek.[29]

[27] Dolan to Jones, February 15, 1877; February 19, 1877. A.G.P.

[28] Felix Burton to Jones, Kimble County, February 22, 1877. A.G.P.

[29] H. B. Waddill to Jones, Fort Mason, February 27, 1877. A.G.P.

In March matters became worse. Judge A. McFarland wrote letters on two successive days. The people were arming. Enormous demands were being made on the ammunition stores for Winchester and Sharps carbine cartridges, and the magazines were exhausted without fulfilling the requisition. Everything indicated an active season of cattle driving. The honest men were arming against the thieves and a crisis could not long be deferred. It would require speedy action to defer a conflict. 'Our working farmers and stock raisers are desperate and will resort to extreme measures soon.... I urge you to send a force to Kimble at the *earliest* possible *moment*.' [30]

Three days later, W. A. Blackburn, judge of the Seventeenth Judicial District, wrote from Lampasas that the situation in Kimble County was terrible. From forty to a hundred men could be raised in a few hours to resist the execution of legal processes and these had declared that no court could be held. The judge was scheduled to begin court the fifth Monday in April, provided he could leave Lampasas, and he requested a Ranger escort.[31]

Before Major Jones had received these last reports, he had decided to clean up Kimble County. For this purpose he planned to concentrate his forces at Junction. He asked H. M. Holmes of Mason to send him further information about re-branded cattle and about the complicity of the Kimble sheriff with the thieves. 'I have a letter written by the sheriff which I think will convict him.' He ordered Sparks to keep his main force at Lampasas, but to send two men to Lieutenant M. F. Moore at Bear Creek Camp in Kimble. The Major wrote Judge Blackburn that he was informed about conditions in Kimble, would have three companies there by April 15, and would probably be present himself. He hoped the judge would hold court in the interest of law and order. He thought the sheriff and county judge were both in league with the thieves and believed he could furnish proof by the time court convened.[32]

Without further delay, Major Jones began concentrating all his resources for the proposed drive on Kimble County. On April 11 he ordered Faltin and Schreiner to send supplies of corn, flour, bacon, sugar, beans, rice, salt, soap, pepper, candles, soda, and twelve gallons of pickles to Junction. He wanted the supplies delivered on April 20 or 21, 'not earlier or later,' and he did not want even the teamsters to know their destination until they left Kerrville. He ordered Lieutenant

[30] A. McFarland to Jones, March 26, 27, 1877. A.G.P.

[31] W. A. Blackburn to Jones, March 30, 1877. A.G.P.

[32] Jones to H. M. Holmes, March 31; to John C. Sparks, April 2, 1877; to W. A. Blackburn, April 6, 1877. A.G.P.

Moore to send three men, 'who know where everybody lives on both Llanos and Johnson's Fork,' to Junction on the evening of April 18, with two days' rations. The remainder of the company was to follow with ten days' rations, their movements so timed as to put them in Junction on April 20. He wrote Lieutenant Pat Dolan that he would be in his camp on April 16 and he wanted Dolan to be ready to go with him on a ten-day scout. He wrote General Steele that he had spies among the outlaws and knew where all of them lived.[33]

On April 19 he wired General Steele from Junction:

> APPROACHED THIS PLACE TODAY FROM SOUTH IN THREE DETACHMENTS. TWO NOT YET IN. WILL HAVE FIVE OUT NORTH TOMORROW. HAVE TWO PRISONERS. FIND NO ORGANIZED RESISTANCE.
>
> JNO. B. JONES
> MAJ. FRONT. BATT.

On April 22 he wired again:

> HAVE TWELVE PRISONERS AND MY SCOUTS ARE COMING WITH MORE. IS JAMES —— ONE OF THE GOLIAD ROBBERS?

The next day he wrote Judge Blackburn:

'I have been in this county three days, have had out from three to five scouting parties all the time, have four now out. Am scouring every hollow, hill and dale of this section of the country and will have all the active lawbreakers captured or driven off in a few days. We had captured twenty-six up to last night, and am quite confident of four more today. We are cutting out some work for your court next week and I shall remain here to help you make it up.

'The violaters of the law are mighty scared up and are "hiding out," while the honest law-abiding citizens are much gratified... and are doing all in their power to assist us in ridding the country of lawless characters with which it has been inflicted for some time past.

'I think one term of your court is all that is lacking now to make Kimble a civil and law-abiding county, safe for good people.'

Then followed a P.S. which read:

'One of my scouting parties has this moment come in with three more prisoners. J. B. J.'

On April 27 he wired General Steele that he had eight prisoners at Fredericksburg and others in Kimble for trial. He had caught thirty in all, wanted in eighteen different counties. The next day he wrote that he had disposed of the eight prisoners — horse thieves, cow thieves,

[33] Jones to Faltin and Schreiner, April 11, 1877; to Lieutenant F. M. Moore, April 11, 1877; to Pat Dolan, April 11, to Steele, April 12, 1877. A.G.P.

and escaped convicts. He needed a list of fugitives; he had let one murderer go free and another unmolested because he had no list.

He would go that day with Judge Blackburn to hold court in Kimble. If they could get honest jurors — and he believed they could — he doubted not that several representatives would be sent to Huntsville. By the next week, he hoped to have the Kimble community, 'I mean that portion of it that will be left, in a quiet and peaceable condition.'

On May 6, after court was done, Major Jones moved on to Fort McKavitt, from which place he wrote a full report of his activity in Kimble County. He told of assembling his forces on the headwaters of the South Llano on April 18, and sending them in four detachments down the tributaries of the Llano to converge on the little town of Junction in the afternoon of the next day. The next day Lieutenant Moore came from Lampasas, and on the following day five detachments of Rangers descended on Kimble County. Their coming was a complete surprise, but when the citizens learned of their arrival, they flocked to the camp, greeted the Rangers with cordiality, and offered any assistance which they could give. The Rangers caught every man against whom there were charges save three, who with a fourth had committed a murder three days before Major Jones's arrival. The fourth did not leave and was the first man caught. The Rangers made forty-one arrests — thirty-seven in Kimble County. The charges were murder, theft, forgery, assault, escaped convicts, and suspicion.

The presence of the Rangers enabled Judge Blackburn to hold court. A good grand jury returned twenty-five indictments, and would have found more but for lack of witnesses and time to procure evidence. All cases were continued because the jury commissioners could find only nine good, honest citizens, besides the grand jurors, who were qualified, but another jury list was made up and the criminals would be tried at the next term of court. Several indictments were returned against the sheriff and county judge, both of whom resigned. Lieutenant Moore would remain in camp on Bear Creek near Junction to keep the rascals from reorganizing and to run out any strays that were overlooked.

Major Jones warmly commended the conduct of his men in the unpleasant service. The work of shelling the woods for outlaws was fatiguing, as it had to be done mainly at night. Several parties were caught by surrounding their homes in the night and closing in upon the men at dawn. On these occasions the Rangers often came in contact with the womenfolk of the outlaws, from whom they received terrible tongue-lashings for searching their homes and arresting the men. Other criminals were caught around their camp fires in the woods.

No Ranger failed to come cheerfully and promptly up to his duty. Each man seemed to take a personal interest in catching everyone he was ordered to arrest. At the same time they gave proper consideration and good treatment to all with whom they came in contact. The expenses of such operations — telegrams, couriers, and extra forage for the hard-ridden horses — were necessarily heavy.

The little Major was on his way up the line to look into affairs in Coleman, Runnels, and Callahan counties, and wanted his mail forwarded to Fort Griffin.[34] He had cleaned up Kimble County, stronghold of the toughest of the tough, without shedding a drop of human blood. In fact, there is but one instance on record where blood was shed in any affair over which Major Jones had personal supervision, and that was in the killing of Sam Bass and Seaborn Barnes at Round Rock in 1878.

As Major Jones went up the line, the outlaws ran before him like frightened quail. On May 10 he wired from Coleman:

> JUST ARRIVED. CAUGHT TWO IN McCULLOCH YESTERDAY. TWO HERE JUST NOW.

Before he reached Brownwood he received a telegram from the sheriff, R. B. Wilson, stating that twelve men had broken the Brownwood jail, released six prisoners, and gone west. Major Jones spent several days scouting Brown and neighboring counties, but the records do not reveal that he caught anything more important than accomplices.[35] Judge J. R. Fleming wrote from the bench of the Twelfth Judicial District voicing regret that he could not join the Rangers with fifty or sixty men in prosecuting the good work. He hoped the Major would arrest all the outlaws or run them out of the country, and informed him that there was a good jail at Comanche which would receive any overflow from Brownwood.[36]

Major Jones went to Fort Griffin but found no game, and in early June he wired from Coleman that he was on his way to Austin *via* Brown, Hamilton, Lampasas, and Burnet. He had been ill for several days and had to be hauled part of the time in a wagon. When he reached Lampasas on June 14, it was to learn that a conflict had occurred between the Horrell and Higgins factions, in which two men had been killed and two wounded. He decided to remain there to see if he could quiet the disturbance and bring the offenders to justice.'[37]

[34] Jones to Steele, Fort McKavitt, May 6, 1877. A.G.P.

[35] Sheriff R. B. Wilson to Jones, May 11, 1877. A.G.P.

[36] J. R. Fleming, Stephenville, to Jones, May 19, 1877. A.G.P.

[37] Jones to Steele, Lampasas, June 14, 1877. A.G.P.

6. THE HORRELL–HIGGINS FEUD

The Horrell-Higgins feud seems to have started during Reconstruction when E. J. Davis sent some state police, negroes among them, to Lampasas. On March 19, 1873, Captain Thomas Williams and two or more men attempted to arrest Bill Bowen in a barroom, were fired into by eight or ten men with the result that Captain Williams and two of his men lay dead upon the floor. Both Thomas and Martin Horrell were wounded and the former was arrested. Very little is known of the Higgins faction other than that they were hardy and fearless men. The leaders were Pink Higgins and R. A. Mitchell. The tale is told that Old Pink Higgins was an awful hard man on transgressors. At one time he was hired as a range rider for the Spur and Matador, and told to stop the theft of his employer's livestock. He rode upon a man who had killed an animal and was preparing to skin it. He killed the man, cut the cow open, put the body inside, rode into town and told the officers that if they would go to a certain place on the prairie they would find the most freakish thing in nature — a cow giving birth to a man! After that, cattle theft was of rare occurrence on Pink Higgins's range. Again, when he met on the prairie the most dangerous gunman of the section, and won, he declared that when his vanquished foe fell, the devil gave a thirty-minute recess and set all hands to building a fire suitable to the deserts of the coming guest.

The first Ranger report of trouble between these factions was made by Captain John C. Sparks on March 30, just as Major Jones was preparing to make his drive in Kimble County. Just as court opened in Lampasas on March 26, at about ten o'clock, one of the Horrells came hurriedly in and reported that he and his brother had been ambushed and both wounded about five miles out as they were riding in to court.[38]

The next outbreak apparently came in June with the death of two men and the wounding of two others. On July 12 — two years from the date of the Lost Valley fight — Major Jones was back in Lampasas with a small squad of Rangers at his heels to break up the Horrell-Higgins feud. His tactics here were quite different from those used in Kimble. On July 25 he wrote that a man named Graham had been shot from the brush the night before in the northern part of the county. The dead man was supposed to have been a member of the Higgins-

[38] John C. Sparks to Jones, March 30, 1877. A.G.P. For an account of Pink Higgins, see C. A. Jones, 'Pink Higgins, The Good Bad-Man,' *Atlantic Monthly*, July, 1934. This account tells of the Horrell-Higgins feud, but gives the Horrells a fictitious name.

Mitchell party and to have died at the hands of the Horrells. The Major was starting with seven men — all he had — to investigate and if possible ascertain and arrest the perpetrators.[39]

Three days later, he wrote that at sunrise that morning he had arrested the entire Horrell party — fourteen in all — at the residence of Mart, ten miles below Lampasas. He had released all except Tom, Mart, and Sam Horrell. There was great excitement in the country and many feared that the Horrells would be released by their friends or taken and summarily disposed of by their enemies. Though the Major had only ten men and was holding six prisoners (he does not name the other three) without a jail, he was not apprehensive of losing his prisoners to their friends or foes. 'Have no doubt that I will hold them and protect them until they are disposed of according to law, and believe that both parties will submit quietly to the decision of the court.'[40]

Not only did he hold them, but three days later (July 31) he had in addition the three leading spirits of the Higgins faction and four others as well. There was more bitterness than he had expected, and he had called Company C from Brown County. On the way these Rangers had made six arrests and brought a notorious cow thief to deposit at San Saba.[41]

Major Jones's superb ability as a pacificator was never exhibited to better advantage than in dealing with the Horrells and Higginses. The details of how he managed these two sets of dangerous men are entirely lacking in the records, but the proof of his power as a mediator and the results are preserved in two remarkable documents which repose in the adjutant general's records. One document, signed by the three Horrells, is a proposal by that faction to bury the war hatchet, put up the guns, and bury the past with the dead; the second, signed by the three principals of the other faction — Pink Higgins, R. A. Mitchell, and W. R. Wren — is an acceptance of the Horrell offer. The witness to both documents is the distinctive signature of Major John B. Jones. There is so much of tensity of feeling, delicacy of expression, suppressed though burning emotions, and terrible significance in these documents that they are given in full.

LAMPASAS TEXAS
July 30th 1877

Messrs Pink Higgins Robert Mitchell and William Wrenn.

GENTLEMEN:

From this standpoint, looking back over the past with its terrible experiences both to ourselves and to you, and to the suffering which has been entailed upon both of our families and our friends by the quarrel in

39 Jones to Steele, July 12; July 25, 1877. A.G.P.

40 *Ibid.*, July 28, 1877. A.G.P.

41 *Ibid.*, July 31, 1877. A.G.P.

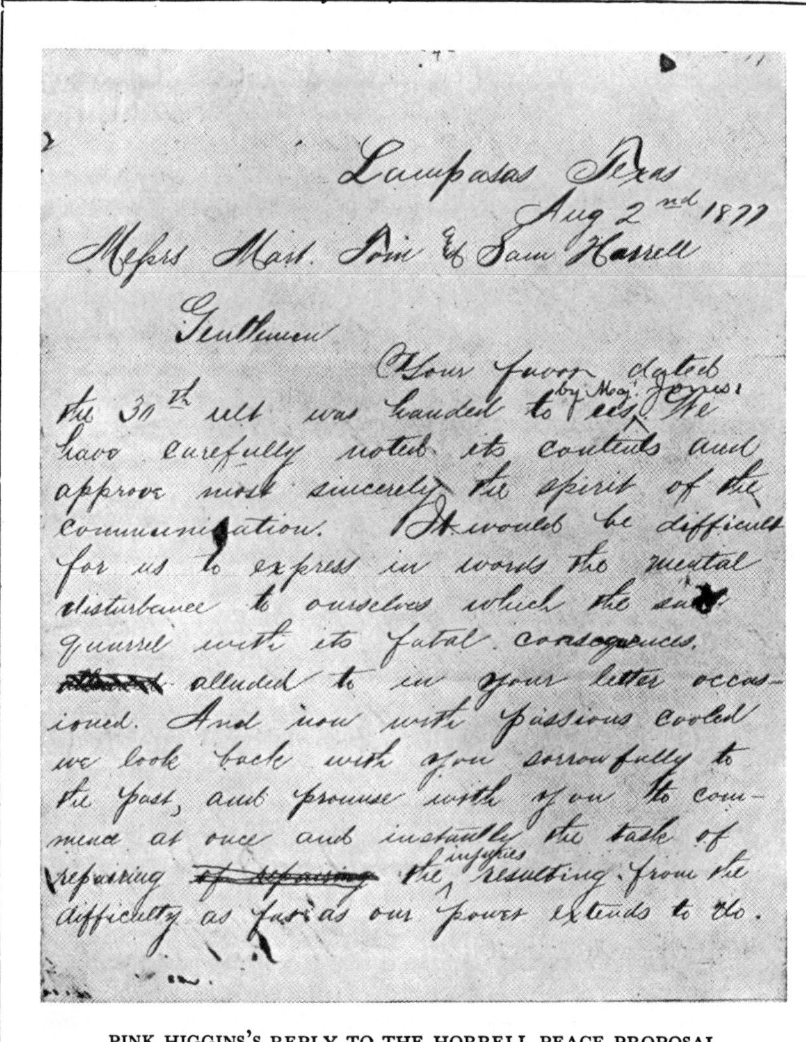

Lampasas Texas
Aug 2nd 1877

Messrs Mart. Horrell & Sam Horrell

Gentlemen

Your favor dated the 30th ult was handed to us by Maj. Jones. We have carefully noted its contents and approve most sincerely the spirit of the communication. It would be difficult for us to express in words the mental disturbance to ourselves which the sad quarrel with its fatal consequences, ~~[illegible]~~ alluded to in your letter occasioned. And now with passions cooled we look back with you sorrowfully to the past, and promise with you to commence at once and instantly the task of repairing ~~of repairing~~ the injuries resulting from the difficulty as far as our power extends to do.

PINK HIGGINS'S REPLY TO THE HORRELL PEACE PROPOSAL

which we have been involved with its repeated fatal consequences, and looking to a termination of the same, and a peaceful, honorable and happy adjustment of our difficulties which shall leave both ourselves and you, all our self respect and sense of unimpaired honor, we have determined to take the initiatory in a move for reconciliation. Therefore we present this paper in which we hold ourselves in honor bound to lay down our arms and to end the strife in which we have been engaged against

Certainly we will make every effort
to restore good feeling with those who
armed themselves in our quarrel, and on
our part we lay down our weapons with
the honest purpose to regard the feud which
has existed between you and us as a by
gone thing to be remembered only to be buried.
Furthermore as you say we will abstain
from offering insult or injury to you or
yours and will seek to bring all of our
friends to a complete conformity with the agreements herein
expressed by us.
As we hope for future
peace and happiness for ourselves and for
those who look to us for guidance and
protection and as we desire to take position
as good law abiding citizens and preservers
of peace and order we subscribe ourselves
Respectfully &c.

Witness
Jno B Jones
Maj. Frontier Battalion

J. P. Higgins
R. A. Mitchell
W. R. Wren

PINK HIGGINS'S REPLY *(continued)*

you and exert our utmost efforts to entirely eradicate all enmity from the minds of our friends who have taken sides with us in the feud hereinbefore alluded to.

And we promise furthermore to abstain from insulting or injuring you and your friends, to bury the bitter past forever, and join with you as good citizens in undoing the evil which has resulted from our quarrel, and to leave nothing undone which we can effect to bring about a complete consummation of the purpose to which we have herein committed ourselves.

PROVIDED:

That you shall on your part take upon yourselves a similar obligation as respects our friends and us, and shall address a paper to us with your signatures thereon, such a paper as this which we freely offer you. Hoping that this may bring about the happy result which it aims at we remain

Yours Respectfully,

THOS. L. HORRELL
S. W. HORRELL
C. O. M. HORRELL

Witness
JNO. B. JONES
Maj. Frontier Battalion

To this letter the opposing faction sent the following reply:

LAMPASAS TEXAS
Aug 2nd 1877

Mess. Mart. Tom and Sam Horrell

GENTLEMEN

Your favor dated the 30th ult. was handed to us by Maj. Jones. We have carefully noted its contents and approve most sincerely the spirit of the communication. It would be difficult for us to express in words the mental disturbance to ourselves which the sad quarrel with its fatal consequences, alluded to in your letter occasioned. And now with passions cooled we look back with you sorrowfully to the past, and promise with you to commence at once and instantly the task of repairing the injuries resulting from the difficulty as far as our power extends to do.

Certainly we will make every effort to restore good feeling with those who armed themselves in our quarrel, and on our part we lay down our weapons with the honest purpose to regard the feud which has existed between you and us as a by gone thing to be remembered only to bewail. Furthermore as you say we will abstain from offering insult or injury to you or yours and will seek to bring all our friends to a complete conformity with the agreements herein expressed by us.

As we hope for future peace and happiness for ourselves and for those who look to us for guidance and protection and as we desire to take position as good law-abiding citizens and preservers of peace and order we subscribe ourselves

Respectfully &C.

J. P. HIGGINS
R. A. MITCHELL
W. R. WREN

Witness
JNO. B. JONES
Maj. Frontier Battalion

It would be pleasing to record that this triumph of diplomacy, backed by a corps of Texas Rangers, established lasting peace in the hill country around Lampasas. Unfortunately it cannot be thus recorded. The Horrells and Higginses could sign peace pacts when they were prisoners and could doubtless regret the blood that had been shed — especially on their side. But they were, as Judge Blackburn wrote Major Jones, brave and reckless men, and their blood was too hot for them to live in peace. The Rangers returned time and again to Lampasas, but there were no more encounters there comparable to those that occurred just prior to the advent of the Rangers in June of 1877.

The summer of 1877 was one of comparative peace — a calm between the Lampasas storm and one that was gathering in El Paso. During this interval Major Jones was patrolling the frontier, rearranging the companies, and training his men by precept as well as by example.

Two incidents of the summer will illustrate the character of the work and of the times. One was a report that a gang of organized thieves was planning to make a concerted attack on the border, deliver all prisoners from the jails, and kill all the Ranger captains who had been making life miserable for them and their kind. They were planning, it was reported, to make certain of the death of Major Jones, John C. Sparks, John B. Armstrong, and Lee Hall. They had a secret code, that of the Knights of the Golden Circle. It was reported that a band of Mexicans would be formed in Frio Cañon to disguise themselves as Indians and depredate on the frontier in order to attract the attention of the Rangers. Should the first efforts succeed, and the criminals in frontier jails be delivered, the band would then try the Austin jail and the penitentiary at Huntsville. On their return to the west they would plunder towns and rob the banks. Efforts were being made to enlist members of the Ranger force in the plot, spies were kept in Austin, and saws were being smuggled to prisoners in the backs of books. The report originated from a convict, who related to Superintendent Thomas J. Goree that he had seen the whole plan set forth in a letter brought to the Austin jail where he was at the time in residence. General Steele asked the Rangers to investigate, but after doing so, they reported that they could find no evidence of any such plot.[42]

The second episode illustrative of the Rangers' work was the killing of Bone Wilson on September 15, 1877. On Monday morning, Sep-

[42] Thomas J. Goree's notes on interview with W. A. Bridges, W. A. Bridges to Steele, September, 1877. John B. Armstrong wrote from Cuero on September 28, 1877, that he had decided there was no line of couriers between DeWitt and Coleman and no organization for the release of prisoners from the Austin jail. A.G.P.

PINK HIGGINS AND HIS MEN UPON THEIR RETURN FROM A TRIP UP THE CATTLE TRAIL

Front row from the left:
Felix Castello, Jess Standard, R. A. Mitchell, John Pinckney (Pink) Higgins
Back row:
Powell Woods, Unknown, Buck Allen, A. T. Mitchell

tember 10, Sergeant Thomas M. Sparks set out for the Wilson home on Silver Creek, some thirty miles north of west from old Fort Chadburn. The Rangers reached Silver Creek Wednesday at midnight and camped in a large thicket near the Wilson home. A citizen reported that young Wilson was hunting buffalo and that his father was expected on Thursday with a load of hides. A Ranger watched from a mountain all day with field glasses, but no wagon appeared. Sergeant Sparks now changed his tactics, and sent three citizens and a Ranger bear-hunting with dogs. In the valley of Middle Oak Creek the hunters saw two horsemen approach a thicket where they were met by two men on foot. When the men saw the hunters, the two horsemen — Bone Wilson and his father — rode away and the others returned to the thicket. The hunters rode casually into the camp, inquired for buffalo and bear, and returned to the Ranger rendezvous with the information they had obtained. The Rangers broke camp that night at seven and by eleven were making their beds within a half-mile of the Wilson camp. An hour before dawn they stole to the Wilson camp, surrounded it, and at sunrise charged in to capture a cousin and brother of the man they wanted. From the prisoners they learned that Bone and his father had gone to the Wilson home and were expected back that day. Four of the best horses were left under saddle near the camp, the others concealed, one man went to the mountain to watch, and the others hid themselves. At three o'clock the signal came that men were approaching. Seven Rangers awaited the horsemen by the edge of the trail that led to the camp. Bone Wilson was riding ten steps ahead of his father with a fresh buffalo hide, his coat and gun in front of him, 'and when he got within twenty or thirty steps of the ambush all rose to their feet with seven guns presented at his heart and ordered him to hold up his hands and surrender. He stopped his horse and looked at the crowd as though trying to recognize some one.' When the demand to surrender was repeated, he threw the buffalo hide from him, caught his gun, and turned his horse which was instantly shot down. Wilson lay behind his horse, placed his gun in the saddle, and fired or attempted to fire, when the horse jumped up and ran away. Wilson then dodged behind his father's horse, and while attempting to fire under the animal, was struck in the right nipple by a Ranger bullet. He ran about five steps, fell, and died immediately. The sergeant added that the body was properly identified before the coroner and decently interred in the Stephenville Cemetery.[43]

While the Rangers of the Frontier Battalion were rendering the sort

[43] Sergeant Thomas M. Sparks, Company C, to Jones, September 22, 1877. A.G.P.

XVI

THE EL PASO SALT WAR

Don Louis Cardis was killed this moment by Charles Howard, and we are expecting a terrible catastrophe in the county, as threats have been made that every American would be killed if harm came to Cardis. Can you not send us immediate help, for God's sake?

S. SCHUTZ AND ALL CITIZENS OF FRANKLIN

The San Elizario mob has not disbanded.... Howard's bondsmen surrounded.... Can get no assistance here. United States troops ordered not to interfere.... I go there this moment to see.

MAJOR JONES

The mob have got together to arrest kill and plunder [*us*].... *Some eight or ten of us have got together and will fight till we die... send us help for the honor of the* Gringos.

HOWARD'S BONDSMEN

Shoot all the Gringos and I will absolve you.

BORAJO

When I give the word, fire at my heart. 'FIRE!'

JOHN ATKINSON, *Bondsman*

XVI. THE EL PASO SALT WAR

1. ISOLATION OF EL PASO

In order to understand the situation of El Paso at the time of the events about to be related, it is necesssary to realize that in 1877 the community was as isolated from the settled portions of Texas as Yucatan, Kansas, or Georgia. From Austin or San Antonio to the western extremity of Texas the distance is over six hundred miles, and from the outermost settlements of any consequence to El Paso was five hundred miles, an endless arid waste where water was almost as scarce as human habitation. In short, El Paso was beyond the reach of state protection, and in case of a disturbance there, thirty or more days would elapse from the time a company of Texas Rangers left the frontier until they arrived at the distant settlements of the upper Rio Grande.

No less important than this isolation were the racial antecedents of El Paso's inhabitants. Of the twelve thousand souls along the banks of the upper Rio Grande only about eighty were non-Mexican. Though these may be called Americans, they were a polyglot assembly representing many nationalities — Germans, English, Jews, Canadians, and a few native-born. It is not difficult to see that in a race war the handful of 'Americans' would have rough sledding with the Mexican horde.

Of the Mexican population about five thousand lived in Texas and seven thousand across the Rio Grande in Mexico. In reality, they were all one people. The river, instead of separating them, rescued them from the desert and bound them together; all depended upon it both for domestic purposes and for the irrigation of their meager crops; across its muddy channel the Mexicans intermarried, celebrated the same festivities, observed the same religious rites, rejoiced in the same feast days, and shared their sympathies, passions, and prejudices. As a writer of the day expressed it, 'They are in close business relation with one another, and more than all this, they are cemented together by that indissoluble bond of sympathy and fraternal feeling which springs from poverty and distress.'[1]

These Mexicans were gathered in little villages which were born on the river in pairs, almost identical twins they were. Beginning on the west and proceeding down the river, the traveler would find Franklin (now El Paso) in Texas with eight hundred people facing El Paso del Norte (now Juarez) in Mexico. Twelve miles farther, Ysleta, then the county seat of El Paso County and the oldest permanent settlement in Texas, sat opposite Sargossa. Four miles below was Socorro, six miles farther was San Elizario or San Ecleario, while on the southern bank were the companion villages of Loma Colorada, Guadalupe, San Ignacio, and smaller settlements.

Among the Mexicans on the north bank there was little or no sense of loyalty to the government under which they lived. On the contrary, they felt that Texas was by right a part of Mexico. Only a few of them had the faintest understanding of the form of government under which they lived, and they had not the slightest compunction about revolting against it if they thought they might succeed. They may have felt, and doubtless did feel, much resentment because the handful of Americans held practically all the political offices, and certainly the more lucrative ones. The Mexicans were, moreover, peculiarly susceptible to leadership. Under good leaders they were a docile and harmless people, but under evil guidance they were as bad as their leaders desired. As will appear, their leaders in the Salt War were not saints.

It may be said that the Americans were no more saintly than the Mexicans. They were border men — strong, dominating, sometimes domineering, and often brutal. There may have been some truly good men on both sides, but the good are not conspicuous in the story narrated here. The Americans were merchants, magistrates, a sheriff, bartenders, customs inspectors, and — fortune seekers. They possessed a high degree of intelligence, but were not too scrupulous in selecting the means to the ends which they earnestly sought.

2. *SALT IN POLITICS*

The Salt Lakes of El Paso lie in the desert one hundred and ten miles east of El Paso and about ninety miles from San Elizario. Ap-

[1] 'El Paso Troubles in Texas,' p. 53, *House Executive Document* No. 93, Forty-Fifth Congress, Second Session, p. 53. Serial No. 1809. Hereafter referred to as 'El Paso Troubles in Texas.' A detailed study of the El Paso Salt War was made by Charles F. Ward, *The Salt War of San Elizario, 1877*, M.A. Thesis, University of Texas.

parently they were discovered, or called to the attention of El Pasoans, about 1862. Prior to that time the people of the valley had secured their salt from the San Andreas Salt Lakes in Tularosa Basin in New Mexico, but some trouble developed there, and in 1863 the Mexicans of El Paso opened a wagon road to the lakes in Texas, often called the Guadalupe Lakes, or the Salt Lakes. The salt, which was free to all comers, was taken alike by Mexicans from the hither and yonder side of the Rio Grande. It was bartered in the interior of Mexico, and constituted about the most lucrative money crop for a large portion of the border population.

The road to the Salt Lakes left the Rio Grande — and water — at San Elizario, and in the dry season the patient ox-teams made the round trip of one hundred and eighty miles with no more water than that which the drivers carried in barrels set in the high two-wheeled carts.

The first step towards trouble came when the Texans undertook to acquire legal possession of the Salt Lakes, monopolize the salt, and collect a revenue upon each bushel or *fanega* that was taken away. At the time there were many land certificates issued for various public services, and the holder of one of these could 'locate' the acreage called for on any part of the public domain. Samuel Maverick, of San Antonio, located the first claim on the Salt Lakes about 1866, but his certificate did not cover all the salt country by several hundred acres. The people ceased taking salt for a short time, but they made no disturbance because they had not been long in the habit of taking salt there and did not greatly resent the interruption of a custom not yet well established. As soon as the news spread that all the salt had not been appropriated by Maverick, the oxen were again under the yoke bowing the creaking carts through the alkali to Guadalupe Lakes.

The second step towards trouble was taken in 1867–68 when a company was formed in El Paso County for the purpose of completing the monopoly on salt. In this company were A. J. Fountain, W. W. Mills, and others. The certificate, procured from B. S. Dowell, and known as the Jett certificate, proved defective and the company fell into two factions which carried the Salt Lakes into El Paso County politics.

Mills headed one group which continued its attempt to locate the land, and became known as the Salt Ring. Fountain, head of the other faction, pursued a different course, actuated no doubt by political motives, and offered to secure the land for the people of El Paso. He led the Anti-Salt Ring, won the election and was rewarded with a chair in the state senate.

Among those who worked with Fountain against the Salt Ring was Antonio Borajo, parish priest of San Elizario and Socorro. All who testified agree that this wearer of the cloth had an unbounded influence over the Mexican population — and the Mexican vote — but no one states that it was a good one. This Italian — for such he was — wove in and out of the shadows like an evil spirit transplanted from the age of the Medicis. It was only a few days after the election when Padre Borajo approached Senator-elect Fountain and asked him what he proposed to do about the Salt Lakes. Fountain answered that he intended to carry out his campaign pledges and have the state deed the land to El Paso County for the common benefit of the people. Borajo, who had delivered the Mexican vote that elected Fountain and therefore felt that he had a right to advise, now revealed his sinister plan. It was that Fountain should procure the Salt Lakes in his own name and impose a tax which Borajo would advise the Mexicans to pay. The proceeds would then be divided between the senator and priest.[2] The senator stated that when he declined Borajo's proposal, the priest became enraged, threatened him, and was ordered from the house.

Borajo now turned to another Italian, Don Louis Cardis, and gained his support in the fight for control of the salt. When Fountain went to Austin and introduced a bill in the senate to have the Salt Lakes delivered to the people, under the management of a board of trustees selected by them, he was surprised and chagrined to receive a protest signed by four hundred names to the effect that the El Pasoans wanted no legislation whatsoever on salt. There was nothing for Fountain to do but withdraw his bill. He learned that Borajo and Cardis had induced the Mexicans to sign the protest by telling them that if Fountain's plan should succeed their friends on the south side of the river could no longer get salt from the lakes, and that the senator was scheming to gain possession of the salt for himself.

The salt question had split the Republican party in El Paso County wide open, but inasmuch as an election was approaching, the bosses realized the importance of healing the breach in order to retain their power. Captain A. H. French, important member of the Mills faction, brought Louis Cardis and Senator Fountain together for a conference. Though Borajo was not present, he had sent a letter stating that Cardis acted for him and that he would endorse his action. This meant but one thing — that Cardis controlled the Mexican vote and was the political boss so long as he pleased Borajo.

Cardis, who was something of a Machiavelli himself, was neither slow nor modest in naming the terms on which the two factions of the Republican party could be reunited. Fountain was to be given the

[2] A. J. Fountain to Major John B. Jones, March 4, 1878, 'El Paso Troubles in Texas,' pp. 127–129.

lead because he was a senator and controlled the patronage. Customs Inspector Marsh was to be displaced by French and patronage was to be divided equally between the two wings. For himself Cardis asked to be made mounted inspector.

Thus far all was well, but Cardis now presented the demands of Padre Borajo who held the trump — the Mexican vote. Borajo asked for complete control of the public schools, the power to select the teachers, and some arrangement with Fountain with reference to salt. Evidently Cardis was not in full sympathy with Borajo as to the last, because he remarked that the priest 'had salt on the brain' and thought there was a fortune in it. Borajo's plan had not changed: Fountain would take the lakes and divide the proceeds. When Fountain suggested that under such an arrangement he might take all the proceeds, Cardis replied, 'We know that you would not do anything of the kind,' and added that the priest was determined to have the lakes and no one could enjoy them adversely to him.

Fountain refused the demands as to schools, as to the removal of Inspector Marsh, and as to salt; and in doing so he made the split in the Republican party permanent. 'Cardis, Borajo, and their faction at once commenced warfare on me, which lasted as long as I remained in El Paso County,' said Senator Fountain.[3] The truth is that the Republican régime in Texas was already over. El Paso, because of its peculiar situation, remained a fragment, a Republican island in a Democratic sea. The breach in the Republican party offered an opportunity to some Democrat who felt able to cope with the forces of racial and political antagonisms.

Into this breach came Charles H. Howard, American, Democrat, politician, a man of undoubted courage and as little scruple as the rest — and an excellent pistol shot. Howard at once conceived it to be his duty to bring El Paso County back to the political faith. To do this he had to have the Mexican vote which he could secure through an alliance with Cardis and a good understanding with Borajo.

Howard made some agreement with the two Italians as to salt, and became a partner with them in control of the Mexican vote. In the next election he became district judge and Cardis a member of the Texas legislature. Cardis soon perceived that Howard was coming to the head of the party, and he began to steal away Howard's influence. Howard avenged himself by whipping Cardis publicly on at least two occasions. It was the brutal and direct American way set against the subtle cunning of a Mexicanized Italian. Back of Howard was the handful of

[3] A. J. Fountain to Major John B. Jones, March 4, 1873, 'El Paso Troubles in Texas,' pp. 127–129.

DON LOUIS CARDIS CHARLES H. HOWARD

Americans and a few Mexicans and back of Cardis was a horde, an ignorant rabble under the direction of a greedy priest.

Howard broke whatever agreement he had made with Cardis and Borajo as to salt, and located the Salt Lakes in the name of his father-in-law, George B. Zimpleman of Austin. Not only did he refuse to divide his profits with the Italians, but he took vigorous measures to stop all traffic in salt that did not pay tribute to him. Howard claimed that he broke his agreement because Cardis and Borajo attempted to force him into some 'monstrous schemes.' He declared that they had forfeited all claim on him and were seeking to have him murdered in order to carry out their own plans.[4]

By this time Borajo was having trouble with the Church and was removed from El Paso and ordered into the interior of Mexico. Father Pierre Bourgade, parish priest of San Elizario, stated that when the order for his removal came, Borajo refused to go. The bishop came down to effect the transfer, and in the words of Father Bourgade, 'The priest met the bishop at Socorro on his way down here, and being much excited, called him hard names. The bishop was advised by the driver of the carriage to go no farther; that there might be danger from some men whom he thought the priest had posted on the road. But the bishop

[4] A. J. Fountain to Major John B. Jones, March 4, 1878, 'El Paso Troubles in Texas,' pp. 127–129.

came, nevertheless, and had to camp out, because the people were afraid to offer him hospitality.' The bishop failed to get possession of the parish and returned to Ysleta. Then Borajo made speeches inciting the people against the bishop and all the priests under him. He called them Protestants, *pelados*, and thieves. 'In all this he worked in perfect accord with Louis Cardis,' said Father Bourgade. Later Borajo withdrew, but continued to work with Cardis and had a hand in inciting the Mexicans against Howard.[5]

In the latter part of June, 1877, Howard went with Ward B. Blanchard, a surveyor, John E. McBride, and three negroes to survey the Zimpleman land. Three Mexicans who had been employed refused at the last moment to go. On the way out the party stopped at Quitman where Cardis owned a stage station. Here Howard assaulted Cardis, who escaped by running under a table. When asked why he did not kill Cardis then, the American replied that Cardis was too cowardly. Blanchard surveyed three sections of land, taking in all the Salt Lakes not owned by Maverick.[6]

Immediately upon his return, Howard posted notices that the Salt Lakes belonged to him, and warned the people not to take salt without paying a fee.[7] Hearing that two Mexicans had threatened to go after salt, Howard had them arrested and brought before Judge G. N. García for trial. When one Mexican disclaimed any intention of going after salt, Howard asked the judge to dismiss his case. When no evidence was produced to show that the other intended to go, Howard, struck with the humor of the situation, said: 'I reckon we will have to dismiss the case against him too.' The Mexican, who knew no English and thought Howard was making sport of him, jumped to his feet, declared that he had said he would go after salt and that he intended to go. The judge put the Mexican under a two-hundred-dollar bond and ordered the sheriff to take him in custody until the bond was made.

Violence began that night when the mob seized Judge G. N. García because he refused to issue a warrant for Howard's arrest. Howard, McBride, his agent, and the justice of the peace were also taken and held prisoners for three or four days. The justice of the peace and county judge were released on condition that they resign, but Howard's terms were much harder. He would have to relinquish all claim to the Salt Lakes, assign them to the people, and make a twelve-thousand-dollar

[5] Father Pierre Bourgade, Testimony, March 1–2, 1878, 'El Paso Troubles in Texas,' pp. 99–100. His name is variously spelled.

[6] Testimony of Ward B. Blanchard, February 11, 1878, 'El Paso Troubles in Texas,' pp. 69–70.

[7] Testimony of John P. Clark, Postmaster of San Elizario, February 4, 1878, 'El Paso Troubles in Texas,' p. 71.

bond to leave El Paso County never to return. In short, he was to be banished by Cardis, who thought in this manner to rid the country of his worst enemy.[8]

Howard signed his abdication with reluctance and amid a stormy scene. His bond was made and signed by Jesús Tobar, Tomás García, Charles Ellis, and John Atkinson. Father Bourgade acted as mediator, and when Howard departed from the presence of the infuriated crowd, it was with the good priest's arms about him as a protection from the many guns that were trained upon him.[9] He was arrested on October 1, and on October 6 he arrived at Mesilla, New Mexico. It may be said that he had no intention of staying out of El Paso County or of yielding possession of the Salt Lakes.

The departure of Howard did not quiet the Mexicans. District Judge A. Blacker wired Governor Hubbard on October 10:

> CIVIL AUTHORITIES POWERLESS IN EL PASO COUNTY. NO LEGAL AUTHORITY CAN TAKE ONE STEP WITHOUT MILITARY BACKING. LIFE AND PROPERTY STILL IN DANGER AND WILL BE UNTIL MILITARY PROTECTION IS AWARDED. MOB QUIET, BUT ORGANIZED AND UNYIELDING.[10]

Sheriff Charles Kerber, who was also held captive for a time, informed the governor that he could not find men for a posse, that only fifteen Americans were available, that the Mexicans were unreliable, that the twenty soldiers who had arrived refused to take part in a civil disturbance, and that Cardis was leading and telling the Mexicans that they had a right to arm themselves. 'None of the American citizens are safe so long as we have no troops here to enforce law and order.' [11]

At the same time, Cardis was writing the governor that the disturbance was over and 'everything seems to be quiet.' He assumed credit for the restoration of peace, but stated that the governor would receive reports to the contrary. He told the governor that he would send full particulars by mail, but the storm broke too soon and the particulars from his pen never came. One of Cardis's last acts was to call committees from the various communities for the purpose of harmonizing affairs. In spite of his manifold duties, Cardis kept a diary, and his last entry, dated October 7, reads: 'Rucker with twenty men and

[8] Testimony of G. N. García, 'El Paso Troubles in Texas,' pp. 106–108.

[9] Affidavit of Jesús Cobas, pp. 71–72; of Vidal García, pp. 72–74; statement of Father P. Bourgade, pp. 98–100, 'El Paso Troubles in Texas.'

[10] A. Blacker to Governor R. B. Hubbard, October 9, 1877, 'El Paso Troubles in Texas,' pp. 141–142.

[11] Charles Kerber to Governor R. B. Hubbard, October 10, 1877, 'El Paso Troubles in Texas,' p. 142.

Howard came in the morning. Captain Courtney advised me to be on the lookout, for Howard is making desperate threats at my life.' [12]

3. MURDER AND THE MOB

On Wednesday afternoon, October 10, between two and three, Louis Cardis entered the store of E. Schutz and Brother, and asked one of the clerks to write a letter for him. He was sitting in a rocker with his back to the door when Joseph Schutz saw Howard enter the front door with a double-barreled shotgun. In order to warn Cardis, Schutz said in a loud voice, 'How do you do, Judge Howard.' Cardis immediately rose, passed behind the clerk, and took a position back of the desk which concealed the upper part of his body. Howard emptied one barrel into the lower part of the Italian's body and legs and as the torso sank into view the second charge of buckshot penetrated his heart. Though Cardis was armed, and his six-shooter was found at full cock, he apparently made little effort to defend himself.[13]

Howard walked slowly from the room, reloaded his gun, and went to the custom house to seek the protection of the officials there. Deciding that El Paso would be too hot for him, he hitched his team to his buggy and, accompanied by two negro servants, set out for Mesilla, New Mexico.

The crisis was now at hand, the seriousness of which was fully understood by cooler heads. Joseph Magoffin wired Governor Hubbard:

> WE ARE UNDER GREAT EXCITEMENT AND FEAR THE WORST. HAVE MOVED MY WIFE OVER THE RIVER AND AM HERE AT THE CUSTOM HOUSE TO DO MY BEST TO PREVENT VIOLENCE.

Schutz wired General Edward Hatch:

> DON LOUIS CARDIS WAS KILLED THIS MOMENT BY CHAS. HOWARD, AND WE ARE EXPECTING A TERRIBLE CATASTROPHE IN THE COUNTY, AS THREATS HAVE BEEN MADE THAT EVERY AMERICAN WOULD BE KILLED IF HARM CAME TO CARDIS. CAN YOU NOT SEND US IMMEDIATE HELP, FOR GOD'S SAKE?

The telegram was signed by Schutz and 'all citizens of Franklin, Tex.' [14]

[12] 'El Paso Troubles in Texas,' pp. 61 ff.

[13] Statements by Jesús Gonzales, A. Krakauer, Leopold Sender, 'El Paso Troubles in Texas,' pp. 59–61.

[14] Joseph Magoffin to Governor R. B. Hubbard, October 10, 1877. A.G.P. S. Schutz and others to General Edward Hatch, October [10, 1877], 'El Paso Troubles in Texas,' p. 64.

Owing to the fact that Howard was gone and the mob without a recognized leadership, violence did not follow immediately, though its spirit was stirring. More and more Mexicans were filtering across the river to join the rabble. On October 20, 1877, Judge A. Blacker wired from Fort Stockton, where he was holding court, that the county was in the hands of the mob and that there was only such government as the mob would permit.[15]

Two days before Cardis was killed, Governor Hubbard asked General Steele about sending Rangers to El Paso. Steele told him that the nearest Rangers were five hundred miles from the scene of trouble and that it would require thirty days or more to put two companies there. The Rangers had no wagons to transport subsistence, and could find no food and little water on the route. Besides, they were badly needed where they were.[16] When Cardis was killed, Governor Hubbard ordered Major John B. Jones to go in person to El Paso and see what could be done to pacify the county. Major Jones left Austin on October 24, and went to Mesilla, New Mexico where he met Howard and Fountain on November 3. Four days later he wired the governor from El Paso:

> THE SAN ELIZARIO MOB HAS NOT DISBANDED. HAVE HOWARD'S BONDSMEN SURROUNDED NOW, THREATENING TO KILL AND PLUNDER THEM. CAN GET NO ASSISTANCE HERE. UNITED STATES TROOPS ORDERED NOT TO INTERFERE. MEXICANS ARE UNRELIABLE. NOT ENOUGH AMERICANS FOR A POSSE. I GO THERE THIS MOMENT TO SEE.[17]

Major Jones had doubtless seen the stirring letter from Howard's bondsmen and friends at San Elizario. The letter follows:

> To the Americans of Franklin
>
> Soldiers and Citizens
>
> The mob have got together to arrest kill and plunder Ellis, Cobos, Tomás García, Atkinson, Gregoria García [and others] — some eight or ten of us have got together and will fight till we die; we are in Atkinsons — send us help for the honor of the *Gringos*.
>
> To Charles Kerber:
>
> Help us Charlie for Christs sake, we will do our damndest in the meantime.
>
> ATKINSON, ELLIS, BALL
> COBOS, GARCIA and others
>
> *What do you think* CLARK and CAPT RUCKER
>
> SAN ELIZARIO, *Nov 6th* 1877, 8 P.M.

[15] 'El Paso Troubles in Texas,' p. 142.

[16] William Steele to Hubbard, October 8, 1877. A.G.P.

[17] Jones to Steele, El Paso, Texas, November 7, 1877, 'El Paso Troubles in Texas,' p. 155.

As Major Jones went down the river to the mob, he must have had advice from all quarters and great quantities of conflicting reports. Sheriff Kerber wrote him from Ysleta on November 8, 'Be on the lookout, Major, these greasers are very treacherous.' [18]

Upon his arrival at the scene, Major Jones wired that the trouble was serious. 'Think I can control the mob a few days; in the meantime will organize three months' minute company.' He later decided to recruit a detachment for Company C, Frontier Battalion, and place it under John B. Tays, a local man, with the rank of lieutenant.

4. MAJOR JONES QUIETS THE MOB

Major Jones approached his delicate task at San Elizario with his usual intelligence. He secured the able support of Father Bourgade and at once got in touch with the leaders of the mob. When he asked them if they intended taking the bondsmen, they evaded an answer and produced a copy of the constitution to show him that they had a right to assemble and bear arms. 'The Major said to them,' wrote Father Bourgade, 'they should obey the law and go quietly and disband themselves; and further that he did not come to settle the salt question, but only to keep the peace; that if their rights to the salt lakes had been invaded, the courts would settle the question, and they ought not to appeal to arms. They said they had a right to collect the bond.' The Mexicans declared that Howard had forfeited his bond by returning to El Paso, that they had no hope of collecting it in court, and that they had a right to collect it by force. They finally promised Major Jones 'to keep quiet, disband, and go to work, and not give cause for any further complaint.' The Mexicans held another meeting that night and asked Major Jones, through the priest, to attend.

They were alarmed because they had heard of the military company that was being raised, objected to having any Mexicans enlisted in it, and asked for one of their own. Major Jones did not yield to their request, and again elicited from them a promise to hold the peace and await the action of the courts. Father Bourgade added that he doubted the sincerity of their promises because of side remarks and private talk which he heard in the assembly.[19]

Numerous letters and telegrams show that Major Jones was in constant communication with Howard, who was intent on returning to El

[18] The plea from San Elizario and the Kerber letter are in the A.G.P.

[19] Testimony of P. Bourgade, March 1, 2, 1878, 'El Paso Troubles in Texas,' pp. 90–106.

Paso County at the first opportunity. Before Major Jones arrived in El Paso, Howard had written General Steele that El Paso County was quiet because nobody opposed the mob and that the Americans were afraid to open their mouths. He did not wish to see general punishment visited on the rioters who were ignorant as mules and misled, but thought that the leaders should be punished and made to respect the law. He wanted to return to El Paso, expressed his irritation because no aid was sent, and declared that 'If the governor don't help us, I am going to bushwhacking.' [20]

While in New Mexico, Howard undertook to enlist some men to accompany him to Texas, but found few fitted for the service because they were either drunkards or criminals. A letter which he wrote Major Jones had in it much sound advice, as well as an excellent appraisal of the nature of the Mexicans and the character of Ranger Tays.

Among other things he told Major Jones not to rely too much on the promises of the Mexicans who in their present state were entirely unreliable. To try to reason with them 'is like talking to a lot of Jacks, all braying at once... some of the people have a good deal of hell in them.' The priest knew them better than anybody. There should be about fifteen or twenty Mexicans added to the Ranger force. Captain García could pick good men. '...John Tays is a good man, but he is very slow.' The governor could not do anything at all in the Salt Lake matter.... That question could be settled only by the courts.... 'On the salt question I shall evince [yield] nothing. If they steal salt I will endeavor to have them punished.' He could not imagine more unpleasant work than the Major had before him, work which would require not less than forty men. He would come to El Paso when the Major was ready for him.[21]

When Major Jones had pacified the mob and mustered in the Ranger detachment, he met Howard and brought him down and put him under bond for appearance at the March term of court. This was done without incident, and on November 22 Major Jones left for Austin, trusting the situation in the hands of Lieutenant John B. Tays and Sheriff Kerber. Meantime Howard had gone back to New Mexico.

About the first of December, sixteen carts and wagons, all in charge of Mexicans, left San Elizario for the Salt Lakes. They were expected back on December 12. When Governor Hubbard heard this, he wired the Mexican leader, Chico Barela, and others, to obey the laws. When Howard heard of it, he stubbornly held to his intention to prosecute and made preparations to sequester the salt. On the day the carts

[20] Howard to Steele, October 25, 1877, 'El Paso Troubles in Texas,' p. 154.

[21] Howard to Jones, November 23, 1877. A.G.P.

were expected, he instituted suit. Father Bourgade, who did indeed understand the situation, was greatly alarmed and on the day before the carts were due, wrote Major Jones a long and interesting letter.

Though he had made up his mind to remain silent on the state of the unfortunate country, considerations of humanity made it necessary for him to give what information he had. The situation was worse than it had ever been. 'Some of those rioters are actually at the salt lakes,' he wrote. They had gone to see if they would be arrested and thereby get another chance 'to achieve what is yet but half done.' On the other hand, three fourths of them were starving in consequence of their bad crops and the blocking of the salt trade, and were determined to get something from the salt or fight to death. They were at fault, but too ignorant or too malicious to see it.

It was doubtful if any dependence could be placed in the company of Rangers whose members were animated by the desire to 'make some easy living and have no interest at all in supporting the law here with peril of their lives.' Moreover, the Mexicans did not trust them, but thought they were employed and paid by Howard.

The good father thought that the only way to prevent blood from being shed, to protect Americans and some Mexicans and 'save our country from a total ruin,' would be to send an official fully authorized by the governor with a hundred men. This official should come with a good deal of 'show and displaying,' and remain until court convened. The leaders of the Mexicans should be tried and punished or pardoned and all made to stand by the law. If this were not done, and quickly, 'you ought not to be surprised at your receiving some news from here you do not anticipate.'

The good priest assured Major Jones that he did not speak for himself or from selfish motives. He was not a citizen, had no claim on the state, and did not feel that he himself was in much danger. He spoke for those who were law-abiding. If misfortune came to them, they could not say that he had not used the influence 'that I am supposed to have.' [22]

The turn of events on this day rested with Howard who had said, 'If they steal salt I will prosecute them.' Armed with sequestration papers, he left El Paso in company with four Texas Rangers whom Lieutenant Tays had sent to escort him to the Ranger camp at San Elizario. About noon Father Bourgade came to the Ranger camp and reported that 'there was a big excitement up the road, and... armed men all along the road.' Tays and twelve men started to meet

[22] Unpublished letter from Father Bourgade to Major John B. Jones, December 11, 1877. A.G.P.

Howard and on the way met Chico Barela with eighteen men, some from Mexico. Tays immediately sent a messenger to Captain Thomas Blair, U.S.A., at El Paso, asking him to come to his support with the regular soldiers.

Captain Blair's part in the events that followed is a subject of dispute, but his conduct certainly can never stir in his descendants much ancestral pride. Ranger Tays said that Blair had promised to come to his support in case men from Mexico were present in the mob. Howard expressed doubt as to whether Blair would keep his word.

'I have every confidence in him,' said Tays.

'I am afraid he won't,' answered Howard.[23]

Howard and Tays reached the Ranger quarters in San Elizario about six o'clock, and were soon put under siege by the mob. Meantime Blair had received the call for aid and started for the scene with fourteen men. He reached the vicinity of the besieged between nine and ten o'clock, but was intercepted by the mob, which he estimated to number one hundred or one hundred and twenty men. The leaders accused him of coming to protect Howard. This he denied by saying that he cared nothing for Howard, and would not intervene in the salt question. Later he assured the Mexicans that he would not interfere with them at all, and marched back to El Paso.[24]

Practically all witnesses agree that Blair could have gone through the mob, which was as yet small and unorganized. Had he done so, all trouble would probably have been averted because the Mexicans would not have dared to fire on United States soldiers. This much is certain, seven days elapsed with the mob howling around the besieged Howard, his friends and bondsmen, and the Rangers, while the United States troops made not the slightest effort to relieve them.

'I am well satisfied,' wrote Lieutenant Tays, 'that if Captain Blair had marched on, there would not have been a shot fired from the mob, as there were but few in the place that evening. Had he been there with his men, we could have held the place until assistance came, and more likely would not have had to fire a shot.' When the Mexicans learned definitely that the United States forces would not interfere with their plans, they went wild with joy. They felt that they had a free hand to deal with the Rangers and Howard as they chose.

But let us return to the mob. In the first hours of the siege on Wednesday night, Tays put out a double guard, and Howard, after receiving some of his friends, went to the store of Ellis near the Ranger quarters to spend the night. Howard came back to the Ranger quarters

[23] Testimony of J. B. Tays, 'El Paso Troubles in Texas,' pp. 108–109.

[24] Thomas Blair's testimony, 'El Paso Troubles in Texas,' p. 106.

and reported that Ellis had stuck a revolver in his boot and started out, but had not returned. This first victim was brought in from the sand hills two days later in a gunny sack, with his scalp, eyebrows, and beard cut off, his throat slashed from ear to ear, and twice stabbed in the heart. There was some speech-making among the Mexicans followed by an ineffectual charge. There was much jubilation among them when they heard that Captain Blair would not come through their lines. Chico Barela, leader of the mob, told Captain Blair that they had nothing against him, but would kill him if he attempted to come through. Barela said the captain left very quick.[25]

Thursday morning daylight revealed to the beleaguered men that their quarters were surrounded by three lines of pickets with squads of cavalry or horsemen stationed in groups beyond. The besieged had stretched ropes across the opening between the building and cut port-holes in the adobe walls. John Atkinson, one of Howard's bondsmen, came into the Ranger quarters with eleven thousand dollars. Captain Gregorio García, who held Ellis's store, sent for more men. Atkinson, who spoke Spanish, had a parley with Cisto Calciedo in which the Mexican told him that unless Howard were delivered within three hours they would shoot Howard and burn Atkinson's house for interfering with their business. Sergeant Mortimer was shot and fatally wounded as he passed from one building to another. He fell in open ground and was brought in by Lieutenant Tays under fire. Soon the firing became general and at such close range that the Rangers dared not appear on the roofs. About four o'clock the justice of the peace came with a flag of truce, saying that the Mexicans did not want to fight; he brought a request that firing cease for the night. The truce was granted, but came to an untimely end when Santiago Cooper went to the roof to get some blankets and had his hat knocked off and his coat perforated with a shower of bullets. The Rangers opened more portholes in the walls and placed men in each room of the building. During the night firing almost ceased.

On Friday morning the Mexicans charged Captain García's detachment in Ellis's store, and kept up an intermittent fire all day. There was little change in the situation on the fifteenth and sixteenth, except that the Mexican lines were drawn tighter, Captain García was driven from Ellis's store, and all the besieged, including some women and children, were gathered in the Ranger quarters.

Towards the last, a deputy sheriff, Andrew Loomis, from Pecos

[25] The above account is based largely on the report of Lieutenant Tays, 'El Paso Troubles in Texas,' pp. 157–158. The Barela episode is based on an unsigned account by one of the Rangers, dated December 28, 1878. A.G.P.

County, insisted that he be permitted to leave. Tays sent out a flag of truce and Loomis left to become a prisoner of the mob. The Mexicans sent Lieutenant Tays word that they wanted to parley with him. It is an axiom in Texas history that when a Texan fights a Mexican he can win; when he parleys he is doomed; and so it was in this case. The Mexicans secured from Tays an agreement that firing should cease for the night, pending a conference in the morning. They kept their promise as to firing, but used the time to build fortifications and dig rifle pits; when Tays met them in the morning, they informed him that if he did not surrender Howard they would blow up his quarters with gunpowder which they had placed under him during the night, but if Howard would come down of his own will and relinquish the Salt Lakes, they would spare his life.

When Tays brought this word, Howard realized that his end had come. 'I will go, as it is the only chance to save your lives, but they will kill me,' he said. He gave his personal effects to John McBride, told his companions good-bye, and went out to the mob with Lieutenant Tays. Tays claimed that he told Howard not to go and that he would protect him; others say that Howard heard murmurings against him by the besieged men.

When the two Americans reached the Mexicans, there was no one to interpret and they sent for Atkinson, but when Atkinson arrived, he was guarded in another room and not permitted to see Tays. Atkinson now took matters into his own hands and made some arrangements with the mob — Tays says he betrayed him. He returned to the Ranger quarters and told the men that Tays had sent orders for them to come down with their arms, that everything had been peaceably arranged. The besieged men complied, marched down into a corral or room, where they were disarmed and herded into a dirty room. They were so worn out with the long strain that several of them fell asleep, among them McBride, Howard's agent. Meantime Chico Barela came into the room with Howard and Tays, and embraced Howard after the Mexican fashion.

5. DEATH TO THE GRINGOS

Though the fate of all was uncertain, that of Howard and his close associates was not long in doubt. The mob, elated by success, demanded blood. Atkinson gave up the eleven thousand dollars — only a thousand less than Howard's bond — on condition that all be permitted to go free, and Chico Barela swore by the Holy Cross that he would faithfully carry out the terms of the agreement. Atkinson apparently believed him, and replied dryly, 'Well, you have received a better price for us than we would bring at public auction.' Some said that Chico Barela intended to keep his word until he received a message from Borajo, 'Shoot all the Gringos and I will absolve you.'

Howard, Atkinson, and McBride were selected for execution; and Howard, as the most important, went first to the shambles. He walked erectly with his hands behind him; as he faced the mob, he told them in broken Spanish that they were about to execute three hundred men. The firing squad was drawn up in line. A deathlike silence encompassed the scene. Howard struck his breast and said 'Fire!' and the silence was punctured by sharp reports. Howard kicked and squirmed on the ground and Jesús Telles ran with a *machete* and struck at the body, but Howard turned just then and the Mexican cut off two of his own toes. The body was then hacked and mutilated.

Atkinson and McBride were brought to the same spot. McBride was very melancholy (*triste*) and had nothing to say. He was killed instantly but Atkinson addressed the mob in excellent Spanish, reminded them of their pledge, and asked them if they intended to violate it. Shouts of '*Acábenlos!*' went up, meaning 'Finish them!'

'Then there is no remedy?' said Atkinson.

'No, no!' shouted the Mexicans.

'Then let me die with honor. I will give the word.' He removed his coat, opened his shirt to lay bare his breast, and said in a cool manner:

'When I give the word, fire at my heart — *Fire!*'

Five bullets struck him in the belly, reads the account. He staggered, but did not fall. '*Más arriba, cabrones!*' (Higher up, you ——!) he shouted. Two more shots were fired and he fell, but he was not dead. He motioned towards his head, and Desidero Apodaca placed a pistol there and finished him.[26]

The mob howled and danced at the excellent work, and in it were more than a hundred men from Mexico.

While these events were happening, the Mexicans were plundering the houses and stores, hauling wagonload after wagonload of household goods and merchandise to Mexico. When the firing squad had finished, the mob cried to know what should be done with the other Americans. Most of them agreed that they should also be killed. Death to the Gringos, blood, blood! Then came Chico Barela, the

[26] Tnis account was given by Juan Nep. García, 'El Paso Troubles in Texas,' pp. 96–98.

'WHEN I GIVE THE WORD, FIRE AT MY HEART — *Fire!*'

leader, who told them that if they killed another man he would turn his men on them and kill them all. The Rangers slept under a strong guard, their fate to be decided in the morning. Next morning there was a review, and maneuvering, and speech-making. Two speakers from Mexico made a strong plea to kill all Americans. The mob was agreeable, but again Chico Barela stood out and had his way. Even the Rangers gave him credit for saving their lives. The men were given their horses, but not their arms, and were permitted to depart for Franklin, where they arrived that day. Tays concludes his report, written December 20, 'When I arrived here [that is, at Franklin] the greatest excitement prevailed and found Capt. Blair making preparations to start to my assistance with his command some time next spring.'[27]

On December 18, the Rangers arrived at Franklin. While they were catching up with their sleep, Sheriff Charles Kerber set himself to the task of finding them pistols and rifles to replace the arms taken from them by the mob. The sheriff commanded Schutz to supply them with

[27] Lieutenant Tays's report is published in 'El Paso Troubles in Texas,' pp. 157–158. Tays's stricture against Captain Blair was not printed, but is taken from the original letter in the A.G.P. at Austin.

pistols and carbines, and telegraphed to Las Cruces for breech-loaders. He also undertook to gather reinforcements from all quarters. Captain Moore came with twenty colored troops and others were expected. Appeals were sent to New Mexico, which was well populated with fighting men. 'I expect 50 citizens from Silver City,' wrote the sheriff, 'and then I will drive the scoundrels before me like sheep.' [28]

Preparations were rapidly made for the return of the Rangers and citizens to the scene of the mob. In the meantime the Silver City men, led by Kinney and Tucker, had arrived, some on foot and some without arms. On the whole they were a pretty hard set; Tays denied responsibility for them by saying that 'they were not mixed with my outfit.'

On December 22, the Rangers and Kerber's posse, including the Silver City men, set out for San Elizario and with them went a wagon bearing coffins in which to bury the bodies of the mob victims. There can be little doubt that the men, whether of the Rangers or posse, conceived it to be their duty to avenge in blood the death of Howard, Atkinson, and McBride. One Ranger declared that these men died bravely, 'fully believing that we would avenge them: and we will.... The boys are wild and wooly and will yet be heard from.' [29]

The party first went to Ysleta, where Sheriff Kerber ordered the Rangers to 'round up' a house on the outskirts. They found here some old guns which they smashed, and arrested a Mexican and an Indian. They camped for the night at Ysleta, and when they left for San Elizario next morning, the mounted men went in front and the wagon followed with the two prisoners sitting on the coffins. Tays reported that the prisoners jumped from the wagon and were killed by the guards when they refused to halt. The bodies were left in the road where they fell, and were viewed by General Edward Hatch, who reported that the men were murdered. There can be little doubt that *la ley de fuga* was invoked.

Sheriff Kerber ordered the arrest of the owner of the first house in Socorro. The Rangers surrounded the house, killed the man, wounded the woman, and justified their deed by claiming that they were fired upon. In the village lived Jesús Telles, who had cut off his toes while striking at Howard. Five men were sent for him, killed him, and for good measure killed a Mexican whose name is not recorded. General Edward Hatch now appeared on the scene, and reported that the road

[28] Sheriff Charles Kerber to George B. Zimpleman, December 19, 1877, *Galveston News*, January 6, 1878.

[29] An account of the fight by 'one of the Rangers,' A.G.P. The letter, dated December 28, 1877, is addressed to the Editors, *Independent*, a Mesilla newspaper. The name O. H. Matthews is written on the letter, but there is no other evidence of its authorship.

SCENES OF THE SALT WAR

Upper: The mob's headquarters
Lower: Corrals where fighting occurred

SCENES OF THE SALT WAR
Upper: The place where Howard was killed
Lower: The Salt Lake

to San Elizario was lined with armed men lying in the mesquite. He advised Tays to go no farther and the Rangers returned to Ysleta.

The Christmas holidays had passed before the work was done. 'On the 28th,' wrote Lieutenant Tays, 'I went to San Elizario and buried Atkinson [and] McBride in the graveyard. We put Howard in a coffin and fetched him to Franklin next day. The bodies had been dragged from where they were shot about 1/2 mile by ropes and horses and then thrown in an old well. They were all naked except Howard who had on his shirt and socks. He was mutilated, one side of his thigh was gone and his bowels were torn out. No people in the town except a few of our friends.... The Mexicans have all left and taken their families, trouble is anticipated.' [30]

Thus ended the Salt War in El Paso County. Small disturbances followed, but the main trouble was over, and a semblance of order was restored. The aftermath came in the form of an investigation brought about through the members of Congress from Texas and in response to a request from Governor Hubbard. The basis for the demand was that Texas had been invaded by armed forces from Mexico. On January 3, 1878, President Hayes appointed Colonel John H. King of the Ninth Infantry and Lieutenant Colonel William H. Lewis of the Nineteenth Infantry to act with a third member appointed by the governor of Texas. Governor Hubbard designated Major John B. Jones for the important task. The board was ordered to assemble at Fort Bliss on January 16, or as soon thereafter as possible. Major Jones did not receive his commission until February 9 and arrived on the scene on February 18 after the investigation had begun. The final report was made on March 16, 1878.

Major Jones approved the recommendations of the majority, but objected to some of the opinions expressed in the report and made a minority report in which he incorporated additional recommendations. For one thing, he objected to the wide range of the inquiry, which he insisted should have been confined to the international phases of the question. He objected to the investigation of the conduct of the Rangers, but the other members overruled him and investigated everything.

The board estimated the money loss to Texas at $12,000; Major Jones made further inquiry and put the amount at $31,050. The committee recommended that a permanent military post should be established in the vicinity of El Paso County, garrisoned by two hundred men, including fifty cavalry. Such a force would prevent further trouble over salt and would tend to prevent trouble over the use of the water from the Rio Grande for irrigation. Mexico was to be required to honor extradition papers for fugitives from Texas and on presentation of proof, to make reparations for damages committed by the rioters from Mexico. Mexico was to punish its own citizens who had participated in the riot, but if punishment were not possible

[30] J. B. Tays to Major Jones, December 30, 1877. A.G.P.

in Mexico, those legally charged with murder were to be delivered for trial in the United States. It is doubtful if any of these measures, depending in any way on Mexico, were carried out.[31]

Lieutenant Tays remained for some time in charge of the Rangers in El Paso. The records do not reveal that he was a successful man, or that he had many qualifications for the service in which he was engaged. Why Major Jones, ordinarily unerring in his judgment of men, did not perceive that Tays was not a Texas Ranger is hard to understand. The man lacked resourcefulness, initiative, and that combination of dash and judgment so essential in a crisis. It is quite certain that Jones, McNelly, Lee Hall, John Armstrong, and many other officers whose names figure in the service, could have come out of the El Paso riot unscathed and with honor.

[31] For an account of the investigation and Major Jones's minority report, see 'El Paso Troubles in Texas,' pp. 1–31.

XVII

SAM BASS: TEXAS'S BELOVED BANDIT

The world is bobbing around.

SAM BASS

Major Jones is quite sure that Ware killed Seaborn Barnes.... The coroner's jury decided that George Harrell, another Ranger, fired the shot which proved fatal to Sam Bass.

Galveston News, July 21, 1878

XVII. SAM BASS: TEXAS'S BELOVED BANDIT

Sam Bass was born in Indiana — that was his native home
And at the age of seventeen young Sam began to roam.
He first came out to Texas a teamster for to be
A kinder-hearted fellow you scarcely ever see.

THIS bit of biography of the Texas bad man was the first poem the writer learned outside the home circle, learned it at the age when it was a great privilege to be permitted to pad along in the freshly plowed furrow on a West Texas farm at the heels of the hired man. Sam had roamed over the mesquite flats roundabout, outwitted a sheriff, and whipped a posse. To all the hired men and small boys of that country, Sam Bass was a personable young man who rode fast horses, robbed banks, stage-coaches, and railway trains, outwitted detectives, whipped United States soldiers, and, for a time, outran the Texas Rangers. Hired men and small boys sighed over his untimely end at the gun muzzles of the Texas Rangers, and consigned Sam's betrayer to the nethermost chunk of an orthodox hell. In those days in Texas the legend of Sam Bass yielded nothing to Robin Hood, Dick Turpin, Claude Duval, or Jesse James. Every old Texan along the frontier either saw, chased, or entertained — in most instances unawares — this ubiquitous wraith, this knight of the road, this generous and open-handed highwayman. Sam supped in every home, sat at every camp fire, and scattered the new minted gold of the Union Pacific robbery wherever he went. The only thing against him was that he came out of the North at a time when all southern children still believed that all Yankees wore hoofs and horns. But Sam overcame this stigma and was perhaps the first Yankee to gain popularity in Texas after the Civil War. So much for the legend; now for some facts.

Sam Bass was born on a farm two miles from Mitchell, Indiana, on July 21, 1851. Both parents died while he was young and he was reared by an uncle who gave him no schooling. Sam left home in 1869, and from St. Louis floated down the great river to Rosedale, Mississippi, where he remained for a year. By the end of the year he had taken his first steps as a card player and become a proficient pistol shot. With this preliminary training he came to Texas, arriving at Denton in the latter part of 1870. For a time he was employed as a farmhand and teamster by Sheriff W. F. ('Dad') Eagan, who later spent so much time hunting him. It was said that the young man was thrifty and economical, that he never paid more than five dollars for a suit, and that when Dad Eagan sent him to Dallas to transact business, he had to warn him against working his team and himself on short rations.

In 1874, Sam became the owner of a 'little sorrel mare.'

Sam used to deal in race stock,
One called the Denton mare;
He matched her in scrub races
And took her to the fair.

If the Denton mare was not the speediest thing in Texas — where life often depended more on a fast horse than a just cause — she was fleet enough to carry Sam into the sporting world and to win enough money to cause her owner to leave Dad Eagan. After 1875 there is no record that Sam stained his hands with toil. He began to frequent the saloons, to make the acquaintance of evil companions, and to perfect his skill at cards.

Sam always coined the money
And spent it very free;
A kinder-hearted fellow
You scarcely ever see.

Shortly after leaving Dad Eagan in March, 1875, Sam went to Fort Sill and from there into the Indian Territory where the sorrel mare won a herd of Indian ponies. The Indian refused to yield the stakes, but under cover of darkness Sam collected the ponies with some which he had not won and headed for Texas, arriving at San Antonio about Christmas time. He remained thereabout until August when he joined Joel Collins in making up a herd of cattle to drive to the northern market. Collins and Bass drove the cattle to Kansas and from there shipped them to Sidney, Nebraska, in order to escape some inquisitiveness as to title. From Sidney they drove the herd to the Black Hills, where the discovery of gold had made Deadwood notorious. Bass and Collins invested their cattle money in wagons and teams and engaged in freighting between Dodge City, Yankton, and the Hills, but when winter closed the roads, they sold their teams and opened a pleasure resort devoted to liquor, cards, and dissolute women. Instead of sticking to this conservative business, the partners purchased a mine out of which Sam expected to make a fortune. They went broke instead, and in order to recoup their losses and procure money with which to pay their debts in Texas, they robbed seven stages which connected the Black Hills with the outside world. In this enterprise they were joined by Jack Davis and a man named Nixon, supposedly a Canadian.

Jack Davis had come from California with the news that large quantities of gold were being shipped over the Union Pacific to the East, and it is thought that he suggested the robbery of one of these gold trains. Joel Collins perfected the plan and led the enterprise. Two other men were taken in, Bill Heffridge who came up with the cattle herd, and James Berry from Mexico, Missouri. The place selected was a water station at Big Spring, Nebraska, and the time was the night of September 19 at ten o'clock.

The plan worked perfectly, and the six men rode away from the eastbound passenger train with three thousand new twenty-dollar gold pieces and some change taken from the terrified passengers. All the gold pieces had just been coined and bore the date, 1877, a fact which had important consequences in the pursuit of the men.

Shortly after leaving the scene, the men divided the booty, and separated to travel in pairs. Joel Collins and Bill Heffridge were killed September 26 by a sheriff named Bardsley and ten United States soldiers at Buffalo Station on the Kansas Pacific Railroad. About twenty-five thousand dollars in gold was found on their pack-horse.

James Berry was shot and captured about the middle of October near Mexico, Missouri, and $2840 recovered. He gave the names of all the men engaged in the robbery, and stated that Nixon went to Chicago. It was presumed that he went from there to his homeland in Canada, and nothing more was heard from him.

Bass and Jack Davis traveled southward, and in order to hide their identity, they purchased a hack, stored their gold under their scant luggage, and drove to Texas. Bass reported that they traveled for a time with officers who were hunting for them. Jack Davis now dropped out of the story and little more than rumor was heard of him. Bass came to his old haunts in Denton County with more money than anyone there had seen in ten years.[1] He explained his prosperity with stories of successful mining operations in the Black Hills, and began to gather about him the congenial spirits from the ranches, barrooms, and creek bottoms. The thickets, creek and river bottoms of Denton County furnished ideal concealment, the prairie made good roads for hard riding, and the railroads that radiated from Dallas offered un-

[1] The facts are taken from *Life and Adventures of Sam Bass*, published shortly after Bass's death in Dallas. In the same year the *Authentic History of Sam Bass and His Gang* was published in Denton. The facts are about the same in both accounts. Jim Murphy's statement is not the same as the one bearing his signature in the adjutant general's records.

limited opportunities for a repetition of the Big Spring adventure. If Sam had learned that three of the men in that affair had died in their boots, the news did not disturb him.

Bass must have reached Denton County in the late autumn, but nothing was heard from him until Washington's Birthday when he opened the biggest season of train robbing that Texas has ever known. Within fifty days he and his men held up and robbed four trains within a radius of twenty miles of Dallas.

The Texas Central was robbed at Allen Station on February 22 and again at Hutchins on March 18. The Texas and Pacific was treated in like manner at Eagle Ford on April 4 and at Mesquite on April 10. The procedure in each case was about the same and the belief was widespread that the robberies were all directed, if not executed, by the same mind. In every case the horsemen rode off towards Denton County.

Texas was accustomed to crime in those days, but wholesale train robbery was until that time unknown. The wildest excitement prevailed because the robbers were now striking at the great corporations — railroads, express companies — and the United States mail. Though all the robberies succeeded, none of them yielded any considerable returns. At Mesquite the robbers ran into so much gunfire — from officials, express messengers, passengers, and a camp of convict guards nearby — that several of them went away with minor buckshot wounds which later led to their identification.

The public exhibited a morbid interest, not wholly unsympathetic, in the robbers, and gave them the name of Sam Bass and Company. Newspaper men swarmed into Dallas and Denton counties and furnished the state more exciting news than it had known since Lee surrendered. The whole country was agog with rumors and expectations. Business men and bankers loaded up their shotguns and Winchesters and placed them conveniently behind the counters and by the doors.

It was said that the robbers organized as a regular train crew. Bass was called the 'conductor' because he 'went through the train.' Frank Jackson, whose business it was to take possession of the cab, was the 'engineer.' Other members of the crew were Seaborn Barnes, Thomas Spotswood, Arkansas Johnson, Henry Underwood, Sam Pipes, and Albert Herndon. Bass and Barnes participated in all the robberies, Jackson in three, Johnson in two, and the others in one.[2]

It was not until after the last robbery that Major Jones and the Texas Rangers were called to the scene. On April 12, General Steele

[2] *Galveston News*, May 5, 1878

wired Major Jones to take charge of the bandit hunt in North Texas. The Major arrived in Dallas on the night of the fourteenth and immediately got in touch with Colonel E. G. Bower. As no Ranger companies were near, Major Jones was ordered to organize a detachment in Dallas as a part of Company B; he offered the command to June Peak, former deputy sheriff, city marshal, and at the time city recorder. 'I think Mr. Peak is the best man that can be gotten for the position. He has been raised here, is very popular, is regarded as a terror to evil doers, is a man of fine courage, active, energetic, and efficient in arresting violaters of the law... ' Recorder Peak obtained a thirty-day leave of absence and was mustered into service as lieutenant of the Frontier Battalion with authority to raise thirty men. On June 1, Peak was made a Captain of Company B, and remained in the Ranger service for several years.[3]

At the time of Major Jones's arrival, the wildest excitement prevailed in Dallas and Denton counties. The city of Dallas had become headquarters for all the detectives and bandit hunters of the country. United States Marshal Stillwell H. Russell was quartered at the Windsor Hotel with nineteen special deputies, but Major Jones stated that everybody knew who they were and where they were going every day. William Pinkerton, son of Allan, had a flock of his men at the LeGrand, and not a day passed that one or more Pinkertons did not make a trip to Denton to see if Bass was still there. 'Sam seems to be their meat,' declared a reporter, 'and they will roll him over should they get the drop on him, as one of them said he is worth $8000 up north.' In addition, the express companies and railroads had their secret service men and special agents on the ground. To add to the confusion there were numerous self-appointed detectives who were ambitious to win the large rewards. It was estimated that not less than a hundred and fifty Bass hunters were in and around Denton County, and that they had to be alert to keep from being shadowed and arrested by their fellows.

Rumors were flying everywhere. Some said that the gang numbered sixty men with eight or ten participating in each robbery. They had their rendezvous in Denton County and had spies on the trains to signal them as to danger from armed guards. There were also friends and spies in Denton and these kept the robbers informed as to the movements of every stranger.[4]

Despite the feverish activity, not a single member of the train-robbing gang had been apprehended, nor had the identity or whereabouts of

[3] Jones to Peak, May 29, 1878. A.G.P.

[4] Jones to Steele, April 16, 1878. A.G.P.; *Galveston News*, April 18, 1878.

one been learned, when Major Jones reached Denton County, *incognito*, on April 14. It is not strange that the location of the robbers was unknown because Sam Bass had chosen a perfect rendezvous for himself and men. A reporter — and they were almost as numerous and far more noisy than the detectives — wrote: 'When you strike the cross timbers up here and get in Elm and Hickory Bottoms, you see four or five Chickahominy swamps all boiled down into one. The foliage is dense — the vines hang in masses and it is not good daylight until 12 noon. Now, Bass, Underwood, and Company know these "bottoms" thoroughly.' The writer declared that the bottoms to hide in and the grand prairie, found to the east and to the west, to run in — when running was in order — afforded an ideal place for the operations of a small force of armed and desperate horsemen.

Major Jones conducted his campaign for about one hundred days and by the end of that time two of the gang had been sentenced to prison, three had died from Ranger bullets, one had gained immunity by betraying his companions only to die by suicide before the year closed, and the others had fled never to be heard from in Texas again. The records of the adjutant general's office, comprising scores of letters and telegrams, show beyond doubt that it was Major Jones who planned and executed the entire campaign. With his gun-fighting Rangers at his heels, and with the co-operation of the federal authorities, he played with Sam Bass and Company from Elm and Hickory bottoms west to Stephens County, east to the federal courts in Tyler, and south to the finale of gunfire in the streets of Round Rock.

The story of the hundred days follows. Major Jones's first step was to have as many of the men as possible arrested on federal charges and sent at once to Tyler, one hundred miles east of Dallas. This was arranged through United States Marshal Stillwell H. Russell and Judge Duval of Tyler. Owing to the absence of Judge Duval, this plan was not perfected before Albert Pipes and Henry Herndon, two of the principals in the Mesquite train robbery, were caught by Peak and his men in the Collins settlement near Denton. This arrest was made on April 22 before daylight. Major Jones's next plan was to arrest all accomplices, including lawyers. On April 23 he caught Scott Mays for harboring train robbers. On April 24, Pipes and Herndon, who were held on state charges, were released on a $2500 bond without knowledge of Major Jones and during the sheriff's absence. Jones wired Stillwell Russell at Tyler to authorize their re-arrest on federal charges. 'Whole business is spoiled unless they can be re-arrested at once and [held] in confinement some weeks at Tyler under Judge Duval's order.' Stillwell H. Russell expressed astonishment at the action of the Dallas commissioner, and ordered the men re-arrested and sent to Tyler forthwith. They were re-arrested on April 26. Major Jones wired General Steele that they would not be freed, even if bond was made, because orders were coming that night to transfer them to Tyler. If they could be kept in jail, he thought he could catch others; if they were freed, further arrests would be doubtful.[5]

On May 31, the federal grand jury at Tyler indicted eight principals and six accessories to the train robberies. 'I have good evidence against them and will get more,' wired the Major from Dallas on May 1.

Meanwhile Captain June Peak and Sheriff Eagan of Denton County had been beating the brush for the remainder of the gang whose identity was now known. Major Jones asserted that they would 'catch them or chase them out of the country.' On May 3, Lieutenant Peak wired Major Jones from Decatur:

> FROM INFORMATION THE PARTIES HAVE GONE TO JACK COUNTY. EAGEN IS WITH ME. SHALL I FOLLOW? IF SO HOW FAR?

Major Jones answered from Dallas:

> FOLLOW AS LONG AS YOU CAN KEEP TRACE OF THE ROBBERS.

On May 12, June Peak's men, together with a sheriff's posse, ran on to Sam Bass's party on Salt Creek in Wise County. They killed Arkansas Johnson and killed or captured all the horses, setting the bandits afoot.[6] Bass and his men remounted themselves on stolen horses and made their way back to Denton County.

The Salt Creek fight ended the campaign of the Rangers in North Texas. Captain June Peak was called to Dallas on May 17 and his company reduced from thirty-one to fifteen men and he was ordered to remain near the city. The people could not understand why the Rangers had quit the hunt, as it was well known that Bass was still in the country. The reason the Texas Rangers dropped out of the active chase will become clear in the sequel.

Meantime Bass and Company were reported upon from all quarters. On May 28, Bass was reported to be surrounded on Caddo Creek in Stephens County by Sheriff Berry Meadows and posse. The sheriff had gone to Breckenridge for reinforcements and severe fighting was

[5] Series of telegrams between Major Jones, Stillwell H. Russell, and General William Steele, May 22, 23, 24, 25, 26, 1878. A.G.P.

[6] Peak to Jones, May 14 (Decatur), 1878. A.G.P. The newspaper accounts state that the Salt Creek fight occurred on May 12. Peak's telegram implies that the fight took place on May 13.

CAPTAIN JUNE PEAK

expected.[7] It is quite probable that Bass was there, but the only result of his presence was a humorous account by a Breckenridge town wit of how a local lawyer, whom we will call Bill Sebasco, '*took* Sam Bass.' On Saturday night before June 4, Sam was reported to be at McIntosh's store on Dillingham Prairie in Young County with six-shooters, Winchesters, and plenty of gold. On June 3 he and his men were supposed to be in camp at Black Springs, eighteen miles from Jacksboro, where they were buying ammunition and provisions in generous quantities, paying in gold. Eighteen Rangers had them surrounded and were

[7] *Galveston News*, May 29, 1878.

only waiting for daylight to attack them, but the bandits 'skipped out during the night, their trail leading off into the mountains.' On the same date it was reported that Bass was twelve miles southwest of Graham in Young County.[8]

In the early morning of June 6, five men, supposed to be Bass, Jackson, Underwood, Carter, and Barnes, rode to Work's livery stable in Denton and demanded the two horses which had been captured from them. Hostler McDonald refused to saddle the horses as instructed and was promptly clubbed over the head with Frank Jackson's six-shooter. The horses were then saddled and bridled and the men dashed out of town followed by fifty irate citizens.[9] Later Bass was reported to be in the rocky portion of Wise County but needless to say he was not found there. It is assumed that he left the northern part of the state about June 15, and it is known that he and three companions rode South.

In order to understand the inactivity of the Texas Rangers after May 17, it is necessary to shift the story to the federal court at Tyler where the cases against the various principals and accessories were scheduled to be heard on May 21.

Among those who had been arrested for harboring Sam Bass was James W. Murphy and his father Henderson Murphy of Denton. Jim Murphy's betrayal of Sam Bass is set forth in his sworn statement of July 23, parts of which follow:

'I hereby certify that on or about the 21st of May 1878, whilst in Tyler... for trial as an accomplice of Sam Bass and other train robbers, I proposed to Maj. Jno. B. Jones through Walter Johnson and Capt. June Peak that I thought I could assist in the capture of the Bass party by joining them and putting them in a position where they could be captured. The Major then sent for me to come to his room where I had a long talk with him in the presence of Capt. Peak and Walter Johnson Deputy U.S. Marshall, after which he told me to wait there until he could have a talk with Judge Evans U.S. District Attorney.... He returned in half an hour and said he had made an arrangement by which he could have the case against me dismissed. The agreement was that I should go off secretly the next morning before Court met when it would be announced that I had run away, and forfeiture would be taken on my bond, but the District Attorney would protect my bondsmen...'

It was further agreed that Murphy would, after joining Bass, communicate with Major Jones, or Walter Johnson, or Captain Peak, who was to remain at or near Dallas. Major Jones agreed that if any

[8] *Galveston News*, June 4, 1878. [9] *Ibid.*, June 7, 1878.

of the party was caught, Murphy's case would be dismissed, or if he did his part and the robbers could not be captured, he would receive full credit on his trial. Murphy wrote:

'I then begged him [Major Jones] to have the charges against my father dismissed also, as the old man did not have anything to do with Bass or his gang. He promised to talk to the District Attorney about it and have the case dismissed if he could. I then went to Denton and went to work to get in touch with them. When my father came home he told me his case was dismissed but my bond was forfeited. I told him Major Jones had promised to try and get his case stopped and not to be uneasy about the bond, that Major Jones would attend to that.

'I lay in the bush two weeks, but did not find Bass until he returned from Wise County, after the Salt Creek fight, when I sent him word to meet me at my house where I intended to give him away to Johnson....'

Murphy then related several efforts to betray Bass, all of which failed for one reason or another. The last attempt was made when Bass went to Denton and stole a horse from Billy Mount's stable. Murphy's story continues with the flight of the men from Denton.

'We then left Denton, and the party was so suspicious of me and watched me so closely — having heard that I was a spy — that I had no opportunity to communicate with anyone who could arrest them from the 11th of June until we reached Belton on the 13th of July, when I wrote to Everhart [Sheriff of Grayson County who had been let into the secret] and directed my letter to Wm. Everhart or Walter Johnson, telling them we were on the way to Round Rock to rob the bank or the Rail Road and begged them for God's sake to be there in time to prevent them from doing it.

'At Georgetown I had another opportunity to write and wrote to Major Jones that we were coming to Round Rock where we would rest our horses four or five days and then rob a bank or the Rail Road unless he could get them in time to prevent it and that unless he did come I would have to help them rob the bank or train or they would kill me and begged him to come for God's sake....' [10]

Very little of an authentic nature is known of the trip made by Sam Bass, Seaborn Barnes, Frank Jackson, and Jim Murphy from Denton to Round Rock save what appeared in the biographies of Bass which were published shortly after the chase was done. The following

[10] J. W. Murphy's sworn statement was taken in Austin on July 23, and sworn to on July 24. Accompanying it is a memorandum dated May 21, 1878, signed by United States District Attorney A. J. Evans, agreeing to protect Murphy's bondsmen, and to dismiss his case if he was instrumental in the arrest of any one of five robbers. A.G.P.

unless he could get there in time to
prevent it and told him he must come that
I would have to help them rob the
bank or train or they would kill me
and begged him to come for God's sake
as I did not want to do that. After
we got to Round Rock we went into
the Bank twice to look at the place
under pretence of getting money changed
and agreed to rob it at half past three
o'clock Saturday evening the 20th I
was on the look out and expected to see
Maj. Jones or communicate with him
on friday or Saturday & let him know
the time & plan but the boys went in
friday to get some tobacco & take another look when the fight came off
accidentally and Bass & Barnes were
killed. I did not get to see Major
Jones until he was running through
old Round Rock going back after
Bass & Jackson but would have gone
to Round Rock to see him before the
time came to attack the bank

J. W. Murphy

The State of Texas } This day personally appeared
County of Travis } before me the undersigned authority J. W. Murphy and after being introduced to me
by Maj. John B. Jones signed the foregoing instrument in writing, and after being by me duly sworn
on oath stated that all the allegations & statements set out in the foregoing instrument
are true. Witness my hand and the
seal of the District Court of Travis County

LAST PAGE OF MURPHY'S SWORN STATEMENT ABOUT THE BASS AFFAIR

is an account of the meeting of Bass and Murphy after the latter's return from Tyler.

'Well, old fellow,' said Bass, 'how do you like to play checkers with your nose?'

'Not at all,' said Murphy.

'That's nearly hell, ain't it, Jim?' said Bass. 'Well, old fellow, you had better come with me and you won't have to play checkers with your nose.'

The prison bars made the checkerboard referred to by Bass. Bass now gave Murphy fifty dollars to change and waited for him to get ready. Both Jackson and Murphy made their brothers 'swap horses' with them so that they could have good mounts. Both brothers 'kicked a little' at such arbitrariness, but Bass said, 'Boys, it's no use to kick, for we must have good horses in our business.' Then the four started on the journey south. They came by Rockwall, Terrell, Kaufman, Ennis, Waco, Belton, Georgetown, and to Round Rock.

In Dallas County they stopped at a farmer's house, where they passed themselves off as June Peak's Rangers. The farmer declared that he 'thought a heap of Bass,' although he had never laid eyes on him. This pleased Sam, who, after he had gone to bed, said, 'Well, it wouldn't take much to make this old man solid with me.' Farther along they came to a store where farmers were discussing the crop failure. One farmer boy said that he had it in mind to quit farming, hunt up Sam Bass and go to robbing trains which was more profitable than farming. This created general laughter. The boy had some peaches, and, turning to Sam, said, 'Stranger, if you will give me some candy I will give you some peaches.' The trade was made. Later Sam said, 'What do you think that fool would have said if I had told him I was Bass and showed him a few twenties? I'll bet I could have broken his eyes off with a board! I'll bet he hasn't had twenty dollars this year.'

There was much banter and merrymaking on the way south, for Sam always seemed in good spirits. At Waco they went to the Ranch Saloon for beer, and it was on that bar that Sam threw his last twenty-dollar gold piece of '77.

'Jim,' he said, 'there's the last piece of '77 gold I have. It hasn't done me the least bit of good, but that is all right. I will get some more in a few days. So let it gush! It all goes in a lifetime.'

From a hill where they camped near Belton, Sam looked down on the village and gave it as his opinion that the officers there were bad medicine. Barnes thought they were no worse than Dad Eagan of Denton and declared that 'when we throw red-hot balls at them...

you will see them pull on the bridle reins until their horses can't get out of a walk.... They blow like h — l, but when they have to face the music they pull on the bridle reins and swear their horse is give out.'

In the discussion of the many rewards out for them, Sam said that he would be worth a thunder-mug full of money to any man who could take him alive, but since it would be death, anyway, he would never give up but would 'die afighting.' They also speculated on how much money they could 'draw' from the various banks with their six-shooters.

Jim Murphy's experience from the time the party left Denton until after the fight in Round Rock was no pleasant one. Soon after he joined Bass in Denton County, Henry Collins came into the camp with a stranger and notified Bass that Murphy was a spy. A council was called and Murphy was told that he had to die. There was long and earnest conversation while the man's life hung in the balance. Murphy convinced Frank Jackson that he had sold out to Major Jones to fool him and to get out of a bad scrape. Though there are accounts of Jackson's friendship for Murphy, the most authentic record of it is to be found in a letter written in Murphy's own hand to Major Jones pleading leniency for Jackson.

> Well, Major Jones, I received a message from frank Jackson this morning, he wants to no of me if thare is any thing he can do to get his self reprevd he ses that he will lay the plan to catch Underwood and all of the rest of the crowd if I will have him turned loose... ses he was persuaded into it and is tired of that kind of life....if it haden bin for frank jackson I would of bin killed shore and that is the reason I want him repreved.[11]

Not only did Murphy have to contrive to escape death at the hands of Bass, but he had to take care to escape the local peace officers, who had no knowledge of the part he was playing. It is reported that when Bass found him in the post office, just after he had dropped a letter into the box, his suspicion was again aroused, and Murphy had to agree to take the lead in any robbery they might undertake.

While the robbers were riding south, Major Jones was attending the trial of Pipes and Herndon at Austin. When he received Murphy's note, he was doubtless surprised that the outlaws would come almost under the shadow of the capitol to commit this crime. He had only a few Rangers at Austin, and dared not send all away for fear that the state treasury would be taken. The nearest force which he could call was the company under Lieutenant N. O. Reynolds at San Saba. Major Jones sent Corporal Wilson with orders for Reynolds to report at Round Rock. According to Gillett, Wilson killed his horse in making the sixty-five-mile ride to Lampasas, where he caught the stage in the early

[11] J. W. Murphy to Jones, August 27, 1878. A.G.P.

T. W. DAUGHERTY

BANKER

AND EXCHANGE DEALER

Denton, Texas, augs 4th 1878

well Major Jones I received
amesage from frank Jackson this
morning he wants to no of
me if thare is any thing tha
he can do to get his self repre
he ses that he will lay the plan
to catch under wod and all
of the rest of the croud if I
will have him turned loose I tol
him that I would right to you a
see what could bee dun he se
that he was pur suaded in to it
and that he is tired of that kin
of life and will do any thing in the wor
to get repreved and I am sadis
fied that him and his brother ca
work up a job on the hole croud
let me heare from you soon

J. W. Murphy

ONE OF SEVERAL LETTERS WRITTEN BY JIM MURPHY TO MAJOR JONES. IT PROVES THAT FRANK JACKSON SAVED MURPHY'S LIFE

Denton Aug [illegible]

[illegible] Sir

if it haden of bin for frank Jackson I would of bin killed there and that is the reason that I want him repreve to me for if than is any chance for him to com to me right away an he will go to work I haft to have A letter from you to sadis fy them that every thing is all right I talk to frank through his brother Willian Jackson what ever billey ses I can rine lion

JIM MURPHY TO MAJOR JONES (*continued*)

morning for a fifty-mile ride to San Saba. Wilson arrived in the Ranger camp about dark on the night of July 18. Lieutenant Reynolds detailed eight men and the best horses for the trip to Round Rock. He was too ill to make the hard ride on horseback, but rode in a light spring wagon which was whipped over the road by tough and rangy mules. With the mules in the lead, the party traveled at a fast trot and lope all night, waking the settlers as they passed. Jack Martin, merchant of Senterfitt, told his customers the next day that hell had broken loose somewhere as he heard the Rangers pass his place in the night on a dead run. At sunrise the Rangers made breakfast on the San Gabriel Crossing, forty-five miles from their destination. They arrived at Round Rock in the afternoon some ten minutes after the fight was over.[12]

At the time Major Jones sent Corporal Wilson to San Saba for Reynolds, he sent three other Rangers — Dick Ware, Chris Connor, and George Harrell — to Round Rock. He himself was in Round Rock on July 18 as revealed by identical telegrams from there to railroad agents at Hearne and Austin to 'Guard trains against robbers.' He secreted the three Rangers in a building on the main street with instructions to keep out of sight until the robbers showed up. He took Morris Moore (evidently M. F. Moore), a former Ranger, but at the time a Travis County peace officer, with him, and he let Deputy Sheriff Grimes of Williamson County and Albert Highsmith into the secret.

While these preparations were being made Sam Bass, Seaborn Barnes, Frank Jackson and Jim Murphy were in camp near the cemetery out beyond Old Round Rock. They had looked over the Round Rock bank twice and decided to rob it on Saturday, July 20. They came in on Friday afternoon in order to look over the situation a third time. On the way in, Jim Murphy managed to drop out in Old Round Rock, but the other three rode in and hitched their horses in an alley on a side street. They crossed the main street to the Kopperel store which stood beside the bank. Deputy Sheriff Grimes and Morris Moore saw them and decided that one of them was armed. When the officers entered the store, Bass and his companions were purchasing tobacco and talking with Simon Jude, the clerk. Grimes placed his hand on Barnes and asked him if he had on a gun. Grimes was killed instantly for his inquisitiveness, and Moore was shot through the lungs and disabled. Bass received a shot in the hand, but otherwise the robbers were unhurt.

As the robbers dashed from the store and ran for their horses, the Rangers came from their hiding and opened fire on them as did several

[12] J. B. Gillett, *Six Years with the Texas Rangers*, chapter IX.

'THE RANGERS CAME FROM THEIR HIDING AND OPENED FIRE.'

citizens. Major Jones came on a run from the telegraph office and joined in the firing. One bandit fired at him, but the bullet went high and was embedded in the stone wall to his rear. Just before the outlaws reached their horses, Seaborn Barnes fell with a gunshot through the head. Bass was mortally wounded, but with the aid of Frank Jackson, gained his saddle and the two men rode out under a fusillade towards Old Round Rock.

Murphy is quoted as saying: 'I was sitting in a door at Old Round Rock as they came by, and Frank was holding Bass on his horse. Bass looked pale and sickly, and his hand was bleeding, and he seemed to be working cartridges into his pistol. Jackson looked at me as much as to say, "Jim, save yourself if you can."... I then saw Major Jones go by, and hallooed to him, but he did not hear me. I then went into the new town; there was a good deal of excitement, and someone asked who the dead man was. I said... it must be Seaborn Barnes. Someone asked how they would know. I said he has got four bullet holes in his legs — three in his right and one in his left leg, which he got at Mesquite. They found the wounds, and was going to arrest me, when Major Jones came up, and shortly after recognized me, and I went

The State of Texas

To Rich'd. C. Hart.

Date, 1878		$	Cts.
July 22	To Cot sheet and pillow furnished Sam Bass while wounded at Round Rock and held as prisoner by State Troops	5.20	
		5.20	

I Certify that the above Account is correct and just.

Jno. B. Jones
Maj. Front. Batt.

Received, at Round Rock the day of 187 of **WM. STEELE,** Adjutant General, the sum of Dollars in full of above account.

Rich'd C. Hart

BILL FROM RICHARD HART FOR COT, SHEET, AND PILLOW FOR SAM BASS

down with him and identified the dead body as that of Seaborn Barnes.' [13]

The search for Bass and Jackson was halted by nightfall, but was resumed early the next morning. Bass was found under a large tree in the edge of the prairie north of town. As the men approached, he

[13] (Anonymous), *Life and Adventures of Sam Bass*, pp. 81–82.

held up his hand, saying, 'Don't shoot. I am the man you are looking for. I am Sam Bass.' He had torn up his garments to bind his wounds.

He was brought to Round Rock and Dr. Cochran was called to tend his wounds. Jim Chatman was employed as nurse, and every attention was given him by Major Jones. Bass lingered until Sunday, conscious to the last. Major Jones was with him, or had others with him, all the time, and made every effort to learn from him the identity and whereabouts of his confederates; all his statements were written down. Bass steadfastly refused to give information, though he talked freely of the men who were killed, and of the facts that were well known.

On Sunday Bass's death became a certainty. Major Jones again tried to gain some information.

'No,' said Bass, 'I won't tell.'

'Why won't you?' asked Major Jones.

'Because it's agin my profession.... If a man knows anything he ought to die with it in him.' And he did. When Dr. Cochran told him the end was near, he said, 'Let me go.' And, as he went, he said:

'The world is bobbing around!'

Sam Bass had led an active campaign from September to July. He died the day he was twenty-seven, yet he made in Texas a reputation as a bandit that has never been surpassed. He struck the human imagination, and carried it with him, but he was no match for Major Jones and his experienced Texas Rangers.

He and Seaborn Barnes sleep the long sleep in the little cemetery at Round Rock. A monument stands over each grave. The one that marks Bass's grave is the third that has been erected — the two earlier ones having been chipped away by souvenir hunters. It bears the inscription:

Samuel Bass

Born July 21, 1851
Died July 21, 1878

At Barnes's head is a simple slab of Texas sandstone. The inscription is a classic in epigraphy:

Seaborn Barnes

Died July 19, 1878

He was right bower to Sam Bass

Frank Jackson alone rode away from Round Rock. He went back to Denton, and then rode out of history. The rumor persists that he lived his natural lifetime on a ranch in New Mexico.

Jim Murphy! 'In personal appearance he is of quiet manner, slow gait, heavy cast of features, rather dull expression. Underneath all he carries a comfortable ease and looks as though it would be hard to rouse his 200 pounds of flesh. He wears a red mustache and chin beard and has small blue eyes.' Murphy led a miserable existence, writing pitifully ignorant and servile letters to Major Jones, and living in constant fear of dying at the hands of Frank Jackson or some other friend of Sam Bass. So great was his fear that he often asked to be permitted to sleep in jail. On June 7, 1879 — less than a year from the date of the Round Rock fight — he died in great agony of poison administered by his own hand.

The trial of Pipes and Herndon began in Austin on July 8, 1878, while Sam Bass and his three companions were making their way south to Round Rock. It was concluded on July 22, when the two young men were convicted and sentenced to prison. On August 27, 1878, Henry Collins, while at the home of his cousin, Joel Collins, ten miles south of Sherman, was shot by a Grayson County posse led by Deputy Sheriff H. H. Haley. As a result of his wound his leg was amputated. It is not known that he participated with Sam Bass in any of the robberies.[14] Henry Underwood disappeared after the Salt Creek fight and was heard from no more.

The pen-fighters of the Texas border have used a stock of paper and the village historians of the curb have whittled away many soft-pine boxes and expended much breath in trying to decide whether Dick Ware or George Harrell killed Sam Bass. The prying historian must take away the mystery because the contemporary and official documents agree that the honor belongs to George Harrell. The *Galveston News* stated that 'Major Jones is quite sure that Ware killed Seaborn Barnes, as he was very near... and looking at both of them at the time. The coroner's jury decided that George Harrell, another Ranger, fired the shot which proved fatal to Sam Bass.'[15]

Lieutenant Reynolds, in his official report for July, stated that 'private Ware killed Seeb Barnes and Herrold wounded Bass but he made his escape with Frank Jackson.'[16] The coroner's verdict, as given by the *News*, and the lieutenant of both men agree that George Harrell fired the fatal bullet.

[14] *Galveston News*, August 28, 1878. [15] *Ibid.*, July 21, 1878.
[16] N. O. Reynolds, Report for July. A.G.P.

SAM BASS

If this study makes anything clear, it is the fact that Sam Bass was a prey to the superior intelligence of the diminutive major of the Frontier Battalion. It was the mind of Major Jones which landed Sam and two of his companions on some other shore. The mind of the great officer encompasses that of the outlaw.

XVIII

THE END OF THE INDIAN TRAIL: THE RANGERS IN THE FAR WEST

I am sorry we could not have tried a round with old Vic for I flatter myself we should have sent you some wool as a trophy.

Captain GEO. W. BAYLOR

Hoy! Esta las Indios.

PUEBLO GUIDE

I demanded their surrender, announcing at the same time that we were Rangers, but they attempted to draw their guns, and the fight opened in full.

Corporal KIMBALL

I found... a mob nearly ready to do their dirty work. I am camped in the Courthouse and have no fears of being attacked.
Am going after one of Millen's bad men... reached Fort Griffin and jailed my prisoner.

Fragments from Captain G. W. ARRINGTON'S *reports*

XVIII. THE END OF THE INDIAN TRAIL: THE RANGERS IN THE FAR WEST

By the year 1878 the frontier of Texas had moved definitely and arrogantly into the far western portion of the state. After Charles Goodnight established his ranch in the Palo Duro in 1876, other cattlemen crowded into the Panhandle to take the free range. In 1880, Ranger Bradley, writing from Arrington's camp on Blanco Canyon, said that the range was crowded, yet many more herds were coming, and those who were bringing them swore that they would have their share of grass and water even if they had to fight for it. Following the cattlemen came the farmers, nesters, and the railroads with their wild camps and camp followers. The horse thief and cow thief were in evidence on all sides.

In response to this situation the state found it necessary to station companies of Rangers farther west than they had been before. In their remote camps on the western rim of the state, the Texas Rangers fought their last battles with the Indians who came from Old Mexico under Victorio, from New Mexico, and from the Reservations in the Indian Territory. This chapter undertakes to tell something of the services of George W. Baylor at El Paso, of C. L. Nevill at Fort Davis, and of G. W. Arrington, in the Panhandle.

1. GEORGE W. BAYLOR AT EL PASO

George W. Baylor, son of a United States Army surgeon, was born in the Cherokee Nation in the present state of Oklahoma on August 24, 1832. After the Salt War he was appointed to succeed Lieutenant Tays, who resigned to enter the customs service. On August 2, 1879, Lieutenant Baylor set out from San Antonio with his wife and two young daughters for the six-hundred-mile trip to El Paso. A large wagon drawn by mules hauled a square piano, other household goods, and on the rear a family of game chickens, consisting of a rooster and four hens. A second wagon carried rations for the men and provender for the animals. Mrs. Baylor, her sister, and the two girls, aged four and fourteen, occupied a mule-drawn hack or ambulance; two men on their way to New Mexico followed in a two-wheeled cart. This party, protected by six mounted Texas Rangers, one of whom was Sergeant J. B. Gillett, spent forty-two days on the road, arriving at Ysleta in September. There they were joined by nine Rangers of Tays's Company, and there they made headquarters for a number of years.

At the time, Lieutenant Baylor was in his prime, forty-seven years of age, six feet two inches, a fine type of the frontier gentleman. He had a fair education, a flair for writing for newspapers and an inclination to fill his official reports with historical allusions. Though a courageous individual fighter, he lacked reserve, was a poor disciplinarian, and an indifferent judge of men.

Baylor and his command had been in El Paso about a month when the first Indian trouble developed. At midnight of October 5, a Mexican messenger came to camp with a note from Captain Gregorio García of San Elizario — one of the men who participated in the Salt War — stating that five Mexican haycutters had been killed by Indians fourteen miles north of La Quadria stage station. Within an hour Sergeant Gillett and ten men were in the saddle with five days' provision packed on two mules, headed for the scene of the massacre. By daylight the party reached the Hawkins stage station, now Fabens, where they found a Mexican who claimed to be the sole survivor of the disaster.

The Mexican related that some twenty-five or fifty Indians attacked him and his four companions, and with tears rolling down his leathery countenance, he told of seeing his poor papa fleeing into the chaparral followed closely by an Indian who was in the act of driving a lance through his vitals. The Rangers hurried on to the ranch where the families of the haycutters lived, and the first man they saw was the *pobrecito* papa of their first informant. The old man told the Rangers, with tears running down his more leathery face, that his son and all the others were killed and that he alone had escaped. It turned out that all the Mexicans had escaped, but each thought that all the others were slaughtered.

Though the Mexicans had escaped, the hay camp was found in a messy condition. Sugar, salt, beans, and coffee had been poured on the ground because the Indians wanted the sacks that contained them. The Indians had broken all the pots and pans, cut the precious water barrel to pieces with an axe, taken all the blankets, and started towards the mountains.

The Rangers followed the trail to the Rio Grande, crossing near the Mexican town of Guadalupe, where a party of Mexicans recruited by the *alcalde* joined in the chase. Twenty-one miles south on the Chihuahua road, the Indians killed a herder on Don Ramon Arranda's ranch, and relieved the stage company of four horses and sixteen Spanish mules.

The Rangers reached this ranch at sunset, and having ridden their horses seventy-eight miles that day, they spent the night, but were on the trail with additional Mexican allies the next morning by daylight. About eleven o'clock the trail led into a dark and awesome gap in the mountains with dangerous rocks on either side. Here the Apaches awaited their pursuers, and as the Rangers and Mexicans approached cautiously, they were fired upon. Desultory firing went on all day with only one casualty to the Indians and none to the Americans and Mexicans.

The Rangers and Mexicans withdrew near night to Don Romano Arranda's ranch, where there was feed for horses and milk and cheese for the men. At Guadalupe Lieutenant Baylor 'made a treaty' with the *presidente*. The Mexican official agreed to permit the Rangers to come into Mexico in pursuit of Indians and to join them when they came. 'I generously extended to him,' wrote the Ranger to his superior, 'the privilege of coming over on our side and killing all the Reservation Indians he could find and agreed to join him in the good work.' [1]

The last serious Indian trouble in the El Paso region was caused by the Mescalero Apache chief, Victorio, who quit his reservation in the fall of 1879, with one hundred and twenty-five warriors and a hundred women and children. The old Apache's knowledge of the mountains and of the location of water, grass, and wood, and his ability as a commander made him formidable and dangerous to Americans and Mexicans. From New Mexico he came down to Santa María in Chihuahua and established himself on the fresh ranges in the Candelarias — so called from the candle-like peaks — which rise to great heights from the middle of an extensive plain. From this eagle's nest, Victorio commanded a fine view of the country all around for twenty or thirty miles and could see the wagon trains that plied their way from El Paso del Norte to Chihuahua.

Six or seven of Victorio's best horse thieves — and none were better — slipped into the village of San José and retreated swift as coyotes with a herd of Mexican ponies. Fifteen Mexicans from that village and Carrajal (or Carrisal) followed the trail. Victorio saw them coming and sent his men to wait for them in a pass, where every Mexican was killed. When the first party did not return, thirty-five more men — all the

[1] George W. Baylor to Jones, October 10, 1879. A.G.P. For more detailed account see Gillett, *Six Years with the Texas Rangers*, chapter XII.

fighting men of Carrajal — set out on the trail only to fall into the same slaughter pen.

This disaster caused all the border towns to organize for the purpose of driving out the Indians, finding, and burying the dead. Contingents were raised in El Paso del Norte (Juarez), Guadalupe, San Ignacio, Lucero, and Carmel, and a runner was dispatched to invite the aid of Lieutenant Baylor and his Texas Rangers. The combined force amounted to about one hundred and eighty men.

The supreme command was offered to Lieutenant Baylor, but he had judgment enough to know that this was a courtesy and contented himself with second place. Near the vicinity of the Candelarias this motley army of border fighters found Victorio's trail, now two days old, and soon they came to the mountain pass, the scene of the massacre of the Mexican citizens. Baylor described what they saw in graphic manner:

'The scene of the conflict was perfectly horrible. I saw in one little narrow parapet which the beleaguered Mexicans had hastily thrown up seven men piled up in a space 6 × 7 feet. The Indians had shown great cunning as they have through all this campaign. The trail passed between, and [was] commanded by, three rocky peaks. The Mexicans were fired on from one side just as they reached the crest of the mountains. They had evidently dismounted and run into the rocks on the opposite side when the Indians began killing the horses that they had tied and opened fire on them from nearly overhead and [from] a peak out on one side. They were all killed. A letter written by them asking for help was found outside their breastwork near the body of two men who had evidently attempted to escape but were riddled by balls.' Twenty-six bodies were buried. Gillett declares that they were well preserved by the high altitude and cold, and that not one had been touched by wolf or bird.[2]

Baylor's Rangers returned from the Mexico expedition late in November to pass the holidays in camp at Ysleta. On January 19, 1880, nine or ten Rangers under Gillett began a hundred-mile ride to a stage station at Crow Springs to rescue a shepherd dog that for fifteen days had held the place alone. Early in January, two mining engineers, J. P. Andrews and W. P. Wiseall, stopped at the Ranger camp on their way from Colorado to San Antonio. They had a new ambulance drawn by fine horses, a saddle pony, all sorts of modern firearms, and a fine shepherd dog. Against the advice of the Rangers the men chose to travel by the old Butterfield stage route by Hueco Tanks, Alamo Springs, the Cornudas, and Crow Flats instead of the safer route by Fort Davis.

[2] Baylor to Jones, December 3, 1879, A.G.P.; Gillett, *Six Years with the Texas Rangers* chapter XIII.

They made it safely to Crow Flats, where they camped at an abandoned stage station. Here the Indians attacked them and drove off all their horses, leaving them afoot seventy-five miles from the Pecos settlements on the east and one hundred miles from the Rangers at Ysleta. They decided to try for the Pecos, and in order to deceive the Indians they rigged up two dummies as guards and left the dog with a side of bacon and a sack of corn to guard the place and give it the appearance of being inhabited. On the first night they traveled twenty-five miles, and at daylight found themselves at the Guadalupe Mountains, where they were attacked by a large band of Indians, estimated at one hundred. They took refuge on a peak and managed to hold off the Indians all day, but as dusk approached, the Indians were known to be creeping upon them from both sides. About dusk the watcher on the west side of the mountains saw an Indian mop appear over a large boulder, and proceeded to drive a bullet through it. The boulder was dislodged, and as it went thundering down the mountain the two engineers followed in its wake, running over the kicking Indian as they went. During the night they made their way back to the stage station, where they found the dog still on guard.

After resting a while the men tied their feet in gunny sacks, their shoes having worn out, and set out for the hundred-mile walk to Ysleta. On January 18, they walked into camp more dead than alive and asked the Rangers to go rescue their dog and bring in their ambulance.

Sergeant Gillett and eight men made the round trip in one week. When they reached the stage station, the shepherd dog challenged them boldly from a position which he had chosen on top of the wall, where for fifteen days he had fought off the coyotes and other varmints. He had eaten all the bacon and most of the corn. When he recognized the horsemen as friends, his joy was unbounded. 'The Rangers,' wrote Sergeant Gillett, 'were as much delighted as if it had been a human being they had rescued.' [3]

Baylor anticipated that, with the coming of spring and the rise of fresh grass in the desert valleys and mountain coves, Victorio would again be on the march. It was not until midsummer, after the rains had set in, that Victorio moved into Texas. From Lake Guzman in Mexico he moved by Boracho Pass to the Rio Grande and across it into Texas. The Mexican government notified General Grierson at Fort Davis who in turn warned Baylor at Ysleta. On August 2, 1880, Baylor and fourteen Rangers left the camp for a two weeks' campaign. Two days later Baylor, at Fort Quitman, received instructions from Grierson: 'Scout

[3] Baylor to Jones, January 18, 1880, A.G.P.; Gillett, *Six Years with the Texas Rangers*, chapter XIV.

towards Eagle Springs and look close for Indian trails.' The Rangers set out for Eagle Springs, and on the following morning came to a place where the United States troops had just fought the Indians. There they saw many dead cavalry horses on the field, bullet marks on the rocks, as well as the fresh blood of the soldiers. They saw where Grierson and seven men had fought from a strong fortified position in a small rocky parapet which commanded all approaches and water as well. The Ranger captain exhibited his learning by declaring that Alexander could not have ousted the few federal troops from this position without loss of half his men.

Soon the Rangers came to the place where the Indians had waylaid the stage, killed the driver and passenger, and mutilated the dead by stuffing the torn letters from the mail sacks into the wounds of their victims. On August 6, they came to Victorio's trail made by one hundred and eighty animals, half of which carried riders. Victorio had torn down the military telegraph line, dragged off the poles, or knocked off the insulators, causing Baylor to remark, 'Vic is becoming scientific as well as warlike.'

While Victorio was following the road, the stage driver from Van Horn topped out on a ridge, and, seeing the Indians before him, decided that the mail could not go through and turned back to Van Horn. All the men at Van Horn were out after the Indians, and the only help available was the man who drove the water wagon for the town. When night fell, the stage set out for El Paso with the water wagon as an escort. Just as this formidable party reached the place where the Indians were seen, some Scotch terriers dashed down the road barking furiously and everybody thought the Indians were upon them. The stage 'put off at Gilpin speed for Eagle Spring,' while the water wagon whirled and went towards 'Van Horn at a 2:40 gait.' The incident reminded the Ranger Captain of John Hood's story about the meeting of the man with the lion: 'The man ran with all his might and the lion with all his mane.'

The Rangers did not find Grierson at Van Horn, and could learn nothing of him; but beyond Van Horn they met a negro soldier who had orders to take a message to Grierson at Van Horn. The Rangers told him that they had just left Van Horn, and that Grierson was not there. To this the negro replied that he was ordered to go to Van Horn, 'and thar Ise gwine.'

Baylor found Grierson's trail leading north, and soon overtook Captain Livermore's supply train, which was guarded by an escort and a Gatling gun. The train was traveling fast and the Rangers remained in striking distance in the hope that the Indians would attack and the

Rangers could witness 'such a gitten up the mountains as never was seen' when the Gatling gun began to play on the Indians in an open country. The combined party overtook General Grierson at Rattlesnake Springs, which is about twenty miles from the Zimpleman Salt Lake. Grierson had beaten Victorio to the water hole and driven the Indians from their camp in the Diablo Mountains.

One day was spent in scouting the mountains only to find that Victorio had gone west in apparent haste, and fearing that the Indians would sweep the stage line, the troops set off for Eagle Springs. The Indians beat their pursuers to Quitman canyon, met the stage and killed the only passenger, General Bynum, former United States Marshal from Galveston. Strange to say these men had only one gun, and for it only one cartridge, which caused Baylor to marvel that men could be so blind when their lives hung on their Winchester's muzzle. When the driver met the Indians, he whirled his stage, regained the road, and set out full-speed for the station with the red men in pursuit. The passenger received a fatal wound in the thigh 'within an inch of a wound he received at Gettysburg'; and another bullet entered his body low down and ranged upward into the abdomen. Baylor said: 'We buried him (a mixed crowd of Confederates, citizens, and U. S. soldiers) and fired a couple of volleys over his grave.'

The Apaches headed for the river, stopping only long enough to kill a sheep herder and souse his head in some hot tallow which he had been rendering. When they crossed the river, they took one hundred and sixty head of Texas cattle. The Rangers reached the river in time to find forty head mired in the sands; and from these unfortunate animals the Indians had cut chunks of beef and left them in their misery. The federal troops did not at that time have authority to enter Mexico, and the Rangers dared not follow Victorio alone. In closing his report, Baylor said: 'I am sorry we could not have tried a round with old Vic for I flatter myself we should have sent you some wool as a trophy.'[4]

Neither the American nor Mexican government could permit the ferocious and cunning Victorio to run at large, and so they agreed to send co-operative expeditions to rout him out of his mountain stronghold in the vicinity of Lake Guzman, ninety miles south of El Paso. General Buell was to come down from New Mexico with five hundred and fifty cavalry, one hundred infantry, a Hotchkiss gun, and two hundred Apache scouts, while General Joaquin Terrasas of Mexico with three hundred and fifty soldiers was to approach from the west

[4] Baylor to Jones, August 26, 1880, A.G.P.; Gillett, *Six Years with the Texas Rangers*, chapter xv. There is some discrepancy in the spelling of the proper names by Baylor and Gillett. Gillett spells the name of the man killed on the stage as Byrnes.

by way of Gallinas. The plan was to strike Victorio, if possible, on the morning of September 25.

This proposed move aroused the suffering little border towns along the Rio Grande, and they decided to send contingents of volunteers under Don Ramon Arranda, who owned the rancho at San José. On the night of September 16, Lieutenant Baylor received from his friend Don Ramon an invitation to join once more in the hunt with his Texas Rangers, and on the next morning Baylor with fourteen men set out for the rendezvous at the Arranda Ranch, where a force of perhaps a hundred men had assembled. The reports on the movements for the next few days are so confused that they cannot be followed, but they were of the character of a seven-league game of hide-and-go-seek through a mountainous and desert country, principally around the little town of San José.

On the morning of October 3, General Terrasas appeared with two hundred cavalry armed with Remington pistols and carbines and mounted on strong horses of uniform size, and also a hundred Indian infantry from the interior, wearing rawhide sandals and carrying Remington muskets and double cartridge belts with two hundred rounds of ammunition. Their only food consisted of ground parched corn carried in a canvas bag. A spoonful of this, sweetened with sugar and mixed with a little water, constituted a meal. Gillett declared that these light soldiers easily kept up with the cavalry, and in the mountains could outmarch them.

On October 6 the force was further increased by the arrival of United States cavalry under Lieutenants Shaffer and Manney, and sixty-five Apache scouts under Captain Parker.

When two days later it was found that Victorio had turned to the southwest, heading deep into Chihuahua, General Terrasas, who distrusted the Apache scouts, told the American officers that their presence in Mexico was objectionable, and asked them to withdraw. Thus, on October 9, the Rangers and regulars set out for Texas and within five days the Rangers were in camp at Ysleta after a twenty-nine-day scout.

The day after the Americans left, General Terrasas's scouts reported that Victorio was at Tres Castillos, some small hills about twenty-five miles southwest of Los Pinos Mountains. It seems that Victorio had full knowledge that the Mexicans were approaching, but waited to give them battle. On October 14, General Terrasas made the attack, killed Victorio, sixty warriors, and eighteen women, and took sixty-eight prisoners with a loss of three killed and twelve wounded. Though the Apaches could not recover from this blow, they sent one more expedition to Texas, which was destroyed almost completely in what is doubtless the last real Indian fight on Texas soil.[5]

Shortly before Victorio was killed, a party of twelve warriors deserted and with four women and four children made their way through the mountains to Texas, where they began to depredate on small detachments of soldiers, isolated herders, and travelers along the transcontinental road. Early in January, 1881, the Apaches attacked the stage in Quitman Canyon and killed the driver, Morgan, and a gambler named Crenshaw. Major Jones wired Captain Baylor to investigate, and on January 16, Baylor left Ysleta with fifteen men to determine whether the murder had been committed by Indians or white men.[6]

At Quitman the trail was found bearing to the southwest towards the Hot Springs, on the Rio Grande. The Rangers followed the trail into Mexico, finding it marked by the gambler's kid glove, the stage-driver's boot-top, a pair of moccasins, a camp on a high bare hill, and a horse that had been killed for food. The trail led back to Texas, and headed for the Eagle Mountains. In a canyon leading into the mountains was a freshly abandoned camp where the Indians had left blankets, saddles, baskets, 'and many things of use to them.' They had just killed and piled up in camp two horses and one mule, had the blood in vessels, and a mule tongue stewing as if in preparation for a war dance. There was a five-gallon can of mescal on the ground and fifteen or twenty gallons more in a horsehide sunk in the ground. Here was the mate to Morgan's boot, a bag made from the leg of the passenger's trousers, express receipts, postal cards, and other mail taken from the stage.

Though the sign was hot, the Rangers were for a time completely balked. It was intensely cold and the ground was frozen so hard that the Indians made no track and moved no stone as they fled to the mountains. The three Pueblo scouts, Bernardo Olgin, Domingo Olgin, and Amaseta Duran, were trained in the ways of their Apache enemies, but they could not find the trail. The Rangers turned back towards Mexico, intending to pass around Eagle Mountains on the west, strike Eagle Springs, and seek information from the stage-drivers as to whether they had seen the trail.

On the day that Baylor lost the trail, Nevill found it on the west side of Quitman Canyon where it led across the plain from Eagle Springs to Diablo Mountains. On January 24, Nevill and his Rangers joined Baylor and provided supplies with which to continue the chase five days

[5] Baylor to Jones, October 28, 1880, A.G.P.; Gillett, *Six Years with the Texas Rangers*, chapter xv. For an account of Victorio's remarkable career see 'Apache' in Hodge, *A Handbook of the American Indians.*

[6] Baylor to Jones, January 16, 1881. A.G.P.

more. The trail led by Chili Peak, a noted landmark, to Rattlesnake Springs, and to the edge of the Sierra Diablos. In these mountains the Indians took their first sleep by a horrible gorge which offered them refuge in case of an attack. They killed a horse for food and for water they melted the snow with hot rocks. That they were traveling more leisurely now was shown by the fact that camps were closer together. On the morning of January 28, the Rangers found the carcass of a horse, a carcass so freshly killed that when they lifted a dismembered leg the blood dripped. Baylor wrote: 'The chase was getting to be exciting and we felt that our chance to avenge the many outrages committed by this band was near at hand.' The trail bore north and west, and before night the Rangers came upon the noon campfires of the Indians still burning. From this place the Indians turned up a dark canyon and passed over the brow of Devil Mountains. The evidence indicated that most of them were afoot, and that the few horses they had were worn out. The Rangers knew that if they moved over the crest of the mountain, they would be discovered. The Indians were only two hours ahead, or less, and the flocks of doves flying overhead indicated that water was near; this the Indians would not pass. So the Rangers made a dry camp in the gorges below and waited for daylight.

'The morning of the 29th January we were awakened by the guards and noiselessly prepared for the march and passed over the mountain brow before daylight.' It was hard to follow the trail, and the captain, the lieutenant, and the three scouts could be seen with backs bent and faces close to the ground as they followed the trail which led north along the rocky crest. Soon the Pueblos said in a low voice, 'Hoy! Esta las Indios,' and the Rangers saw the campfires not over a half-mile away.

The horses were left with a guard of five grumbling men and the other nineteen Rangers advanced on foot. Seven men and a sergeant made a detour while the main body of Rangers crept forward Indian style among the dagger thickets to within one hundred yards of the Indians, who were getting out of bed. Just as the sun rose in all its cold mountain splendor, the men deployed to right and left, knelt and with careful aim sent their messengers of death among the astounded Indians. Baylor reported that 'The Apaches ran like a herd of deer, making very little resistance and each one for himself, unlike our Comanches who will always turn at bay no matter against what odds.' The Rangers killed four warriors, two women, and two children, and wounded many more. One Indian, whom the Rangers named Big Foot, ran four hundred yards in full view while not less than two hundred shots from Winchesters and Springfields were fired at him. 'One

'... AND THE RANGERS SAW THE CAMPFIRES NOT OVER A HALF-MILE AWAY.'

warrior stood his ground, principally because he got the gable end of his head shot off early in the action.'

The warriors were the first to run off, and the result was that the women and children were the chief sufferers. Baylor explained that it was a bitterly cold, windy morning, and as the Indians all wore blankets, it was impossible to tell women from men. 'In fact,' he added, 'the law under which the Frontier Battalion was organized don't require it.' A squaw and two children were captured. The squaw had three bullet wounds in the hand, and a baby was slightly wounded in the foot. The woman got into a hole and was not found until after the fight. She left her baby on the ground, where it received the wound in its foot. Lieutenant Nevill, who took the prisoners to the hospital at Fort Davis, wrote: 'Every time it hears a gunshot, since then, it begins to scream.' As the Rangers rushed down the mountain side, they saw the little Indian girl, and one of them motioned to her to sit down. This she did and remained there until the Rangers came back.

The Rangers captured seven mules, nine horses, two Winchesters, one Remington carbine, one United States Cavalry pistol and six Cavalry saddles, thought to have belonged to the negro soldiers killed at the Hot Springs. In addition they recovered an American saddle, a Mexican saddle, and one hundred and fifty yards of calico. Of such spoils as they did not want, and of the camp equipage, they made on top of the Diablo Mountain the last grand bonfire of the kind that Texas has seen.

The Indians had camped by two holes of water, but as they ran away they left so much blood in the larger pool that it was not fit to drink, and there was barely enough in the smaller one for the Rangers to make their coffee. A fire was started — or the Indians' fire rekindled — and the Rangers took breakfast, which is well described by Captain Baylor.

'We took breakfast on the ground occupied by the Indians which all enjoyed as we had eaten nothing since dinner the day before. Some of the men found horse meat pretty good whilst others found venison and roasted mescal good enough. We had almost a boundless view from our breakfast table: towards the north the grand old Cathedral Peak of the Guadalupe Mountains; further west the San Antonio Mountains, the Cornudas, Las Almas, Sierra Alta; at the Hueco Tanks, only twenty-four miles from our headquarters, the Eagle Mountains. The beauty of the scenery [was] only marred by man's inhumanity to man, the ghostly forms of the Indians lying around.'

At Eagle Springs Captain Baylor and Lieutenant Nevill separated, the one returning to Ysleta and the other to Fort Davis, where the captive squaw and two children were placed in the post hospital on February 7.[7]

2. *NEVILL AT FORT DAVIS: PECOS OUTLAWS AND BIG BEND INDIANS*

The establishment of a Ranger camp at Fort Davis was made necessary in 1880 because of the outlaws who had collected on the Pecos, a halfway station between the gangs that operated on the frontiers of Texas and those who carried on the Lincoln County War in New Mexico. In May something akin to a reign of terror was inaugurated at Fort Davis in a series of fourteen or fifteen robberies which culminated in the daylight holdup of Sender and Siebenborn in which the merchants were relieved of their money and the customers of their watches. County

[7] Baylor to Jones, January 16 and February 9, 1881; Lieutenant C. L. Nevill to Jones, February 8 and 10, 1881; Nevill to Neal Coldwell, February 9, 1881, A.G.P.; Gillett, *Six Years with the Texas Rangers*, chapter XVII.

Attorney John M. Dean, in an urgent appeal to Governor Roberts, described the manner in which the highwaymen operated. 'On entering a store they present their guns and pistols and order everyone to hold up their hands and then one of the robbers ransacks the premises and searches the persons of the proprietors.' [8] A few days later, G. M. Frazer wired Major Jones from Fort Stockton that the robbers were in force on the Pecos near by, and that Ace Carr, thought to be a Pegleg Robber, had been captured and the others set afoot. The citizens were in great fear and anxious for the Rangers to come.[9]

Ten Rangers, commanded by Sergeant E. A. Sieker of Company D, had come from Captain Roberts's camp in the hill country and reached Stockton on June 6.

On July 1, Sergeant Sieker made a scout towards Presidio del Norte, and when within about eighteen miles of that place discovered four men with pack-horses going towards the mountains. When the Rangers advanced, the horsemen opened fire and at the same time retreated up a steep mountain side and took refuge behind some rocks.

Ranger George Bingham received a bullet in the heart and Ranger Carson had his hat shot off, his stirrup leather cut, and his horse wounded. In return he wounded one of the robbers, who was determined to sell out and kept throwing bullets close around the heads of the Rangers. 'When I saw him stick his head out to shoot,' wrote Sieker in his report, 'I shot him between the eyes.' The sergeant continued: 'We charged the party and took their stronghold; then we had the advantage for the first time and then they surrendered. Had I known Bingham was killed at that time I should have killed them all. But we had disarmed them before we knew it. Then they prayed for mercy.'

The Rangers were compelled to remain with the dead on the mountaintop during the night of July 3 while a Mexican went to Presidio for a coroner. Sergeant Sieker wrote: 'It was a sad sight... to see the two bodies covered with blankets [and] prisoners tied with ropes lying by a little brush fire.... I got a Mexican to go to Del Norte for a coroner. He got back the morning following, but Bingham's body wouldn't admit of moving far, so we buried him on the side of the road, and our little squad showed him all the respect we could. We formed and fired three volleys over his grave, and with saddened hearts we wound through mountain passes to Davis, arriving safely with our prisoners. The people are happy over our success and will have Bingham's remains buried here.' The Rangers reported that the citizens would pay them twelve

[8] John M. Dean to Governor O. M. Roberts, May 21, 1880. A.G.P.

[9] G. M. Frazer to John B. Jones, June 3, 1880. A.G.P.

or fourteen hundred dollars for putting an end to this group of predatory men.[10]

Lieutenant C. L. Nevill, commanding Company E, arrived at Fort Davis on August 5 and relieved Sergeant Sieker, who took most of his detachment back to Captain Roberts's company at Fort McKavett. Nevill with thirteen men found it necessary to guard the jail where Carr and the other prisoners were confined. He reported that the prisoners were desperate and making every possible effort to escape.[11] Six days later, on August 12, he joined with Baylor and the United States troops in chasing Victorio's Apaches out of Texas. He got back to Fort Davis on August 25 to find that his prisoners had been very restless. Lieutenant Nevill had intercepted a letter to Billy the Kid asking him to come and rescue them. They told Billy the Kid that they were 'in a damned tight place,' that there were fourteen Rangers guarding them, but ten were on a scout, and that Billy would either have to rescue them or meet them at Huntsville.[12]

On September 1, Nevill reported that the prisoners had attempted to tunnel their way out of the jail with a spoon. Corporal Harris caught them after they had dug a hole the depth of a man's arm. Shortly after, one of the men 'played being stricken with paralysis in one leg and arm, said he would die if he did not get to stay out in the air. I thought I would try him last Sunday and he forgot himself on several occasions while being watched. He would cross the paralyzed leg and once when the violin was being played and on change suddenly from a waltz to a jig he went to patting his foot pretty lively.... I had him locked up again.... He is not dead yet but getting well very fast.' [13]

On September 15, Lieutenant Nevill moved his camp to a canyon about six miles south of Fort Davis on the government road, but left five men to guard the jail. The removal of the horses from Fort Davis permitted the Rangers to devote all their time to the prisoners. The jail, which had only one entrance, was surrounded by a twelve-foot wall. The prisoners were kept on the ground floor; the Rangers occupied upper quarters from which position they could have a full view of the walls and of the prisoners. At night a suspended light shone down on the guarded men.[14]

The tedium of camp life was broken when Corporal R. G. Kimball

[10] E. A. Sieker to John B. Jones, July 12, 1880; to D. W. Roberts, July 12, 1880. A.G.P.

[11] Lieutenant C. L. Nevill to Adjutant General John B. Jones, August 8, 1880. A.G.P. Nevill was promoted from sergeant to second lieutenant and given command of Company E on September 1, 1879.

[12] C. L. Nevill to Adjutant General John B. Jones, August 26, 1880. A.G.P.

[13] *Ibid.*, September 1, 1880. A.G.P.

[14] *Ibid.*, September 28, 1880. A.G.P.

and a small squad of men from Company D rode into Fort Davis on October 20 with a badly wounded prisoner for deposit in the jail hospital. The story that the corporal told was that he had left Captain Roberts's camp on September 25 to take the trail of some horses stolen from Fort Terrett. He and six men followed the trail to the Horsehead Crossing on the Pecos, where four men dropped out because their horses were exhausted. Corporal Kimball and Bill Dunham secured fresh mounts from a ranch and continued up the Pecos sixty miles to the J. W. Carter Ranch, where they changed horses again and were joined by a Mr. Bill Smith. They were now within sixty miles of the New Mexico line, and in order to overtake their horses before they crossed into New Mexico they made a hard night ride to Pope's Crossing, only to learn that they had passed their quarry in the night. They turned back the next morning, October 8, and after riding about six miles, met two mounted men on the open prairie. 'I demanded their surrender,' said Corporal Kimball, 'announcing at the same time that we were Rangers, but they attempted to draw their guns, and the fight opened in full.' Both men continued to fight until they were shot from their horses. One man, who was shot through the lungs, died at a nearby ranch, but the other was brought to Fort Davis, where he finally recovered.[15] In pursuit of these two men the Texas Rangers rode fourteen days and traveled probably five hundred or more miles.

On December 7, James A. Tays, deputy collector of customs, requested Lieutenant Nevill to assist him in capturing some smugglers. The Rangers found the camp about eighty miles south of Fort Davis and took possession of twenty-five hundred cigars, eleven mules and *aparajos*, four horses and saddles, two Winchesters, one pistol, and three swords, all of which were confiscated and delivered to the customs officer. About this time the Ranger guard withdrew from the Fort Davis jail, with the result that the prisoners knocked out the floor and made their escape to the mountains, taking with them a Winchester and over a hundred dollars in money.[16]

For more than a year Nevill continued to hunt Indians in the Big Bend country south of his camp. The account of some of his expeditions and the closing days of his service will be briefly related.

In the latter part of the year 1881, Lieutenant Nevill had the unique distinction among Texas Rangers of operating on the water. He ac-

[15] R. G. Kimball to *Galveston News*, October 27, 1880, published November 5, 1880; C. L. Nevill to J. B. Jones, October 23, 1880. A.G.P.

[16] Nevill to Jones, December 20, 1880. A.G.P.

companied the Gano surveying party on a boat trip down the Rio Grande. Apparently the Indians did not expect the Rangers to come in boats and allowed themselves to be seen on three occasions. In the first instance the Rangers captured and killed nine horses, while four Indians fled into Mexico. On January 18, the boatmen spied eight Indians who had just crossed from Texas, but they did not permit the Rangers to come within shooting distance. The following day an abandoned camp was found at the mouth of Marivillas Creek, but no Indians were near.

Lieutenant Nevill found the navigation of the Rio Grande in boats more dangerous than riding the plains and mountains after outlaws and Indians. One boat turned over on December 23 and another wrecked on a snag 'in a very swift riffle' on the last day of the year. 'I barely escaped drowning as I had on my pistol and belts, coats and boots. I lost my Field Glass and 300 rounds of ammunition.' [17]

Though Lieutenant Nevill remained in the service until November, 1882, there is little more of interest to record of him. He was primarily an Indian hunter and really continued to hunt Indians after they were all gone from Texas. Even in his last report, written in November, 1882, he talked more of Indians than of white men. That the white thieves and robbers gave his men a wide berth is shown by a letter which was found on the Southern Pacific near Malone Station.

In the Hole June 20th 1882

FRIEND DAN.

I put the money and the five watches under the black rock 22 steps from where we eat dinner Sunday on the bank. I seen two rangers yesterday on a scout so I took a skip at once Dan meet me in El Paso on the 29th without fail and we will go to Frisco and see how it will win for us we will all get together in El Paso

Yours etc

FRANK J——

P. S. Dan do as I tell you and your day will be bright as J—— used to say

The development of the West made great demands for strong men. Nevill had acquired ranching interests and formed a partnership with J. B. Gillett. In November he was elected sheriff of Presidio County in which Fort Davis is situated, and on November 25, 1882, he retired from the Ranger service to take up the duties of his office.

[17] Neville to King, February 4, 1882. A.G.P.

3. GEORGE W. ARRINGTON: THE IRON-HANDED MAN OF THE PANHANDLE

Any history of the Texas Rangers that did not give some account of Captain G. W. Arrington, the first Ranger captain of the Texas Panhandle, would be incomplete. Captain Arrington was born at Greensboro, Alabama, December 23, 1844. Like so many of the Rangers of this period, Arrington had been a Confederate soldier. He entered the army at the age of sixteen, and after some experience with the regular force proved himself sufficiently daring to become a member of Mosby's guerrillas. When the South was overwhelmed, he went to Mexico to join Maximilian, and in 1867, went to Central America, but soon returned to the states. At the time Major Jones organized the Frontier Battalion, Arrington was living in Brown County and following the only pursuit then open to Brown County boys, that of a cowboy. He enlisted in the Ranger force under Lieutenant Foster and remained in the service for eight years. From the first he distinguished himself for his ability and judgment, and began to rise from the ranks — sergeant, lieutenant, captain. He saw active service from one end of the frontier to the other, and continually received expressions of confidence from his superiors by being assigned difficult missions.

When Major Jones recommended his promotion from sergeant to first lieutenant, effective December 25, 1878, he wrote that Sergeant Arrington had been in the service nearly three years and the greater part of the time under his personal observation. 'I have tested him thoroughly in the management of men, in commanding detachments, and in his capacity for business, and think him well qualified for this business.' [18]

Arrington proved in later years to be one of the strictest disciplinarians among the Ranger captains, an attribute acquired perhaps while riding with Mosby's guerrillas. Major Jones recognized this trait, and warned Arrington not to be too strict over the men of Company C at first, as they were strangers to him and had been under pretty slack rule. 'As you become better acquainted with them, you can draw the reins tighter and gradually bring them to proper discipline and duty.' [19]

Lieutenant Arrington took command of Company C at Coleman, succeeding Captain Sparks, resigned. In May he went to San Saba to protect an attorney who had killed a saloon keeper over a local option

[18] Jones to Steele, December 29, 1877. A.G.P.

[19] Jones to Arrington, January 8, 1878. A G.P.

CAPTAIN G. W. ARRINGTON

election. 'The lives of the officers of the San Saba County are hanging by a thread,' said the county judge. With ten men Lieutenant Arrington made a forced march, arriving at San Saba in the early morning of May 25. 'I... found the entire community in a great state of excitement and a mob nearly ready to do their dirty work.... I am camped in the Courthouse and have no fears of being attacked.' [20]

In July he was ordered to Fort Griffin, where armed conflict had broken out between two factions. John Larn and John Sellman were the leaders of a party of some sixteen men who were riding through the settlements at night and firing their guns in the dooryards of the

[20] Jonathan I. Guion to 'any Detachment of State Rangers,' May 23, 1878; G. W. Arrington to J. B. Jones, May 25, 1878. A.G.P.

grangers. The farmers had organized a vigilance committee to protect themselves, apparently with good effect. John Larn was hanged by a mob and Sellman escaped through warning brought to him by Hurricane Minne, so called because of her alliance with a bad man known to the border as Hurricane Bill.

In the winter of 1878–79 the Indians from the reserves in the Indian Territory and New Mexico were reported to be in various parts of the Panhandle in large numbers. On Christmas Day, Arrington received permission from Major Jones to scout for the Indians, and on New Year's Day he led seventeen men towards the Pease River country where the Indians were reported to be raiding. The Rangers were snowed up several days at O'Brien's ranch, but on January 15 found a trail of twenty Indians leading north. Within two miles the Rangers overtook a small party and killed one Indian. Farther on they came to a camp of fourteen lodges and one hundred and fifty ponies. They succeeded in cutting the Indians off from their horses and were preparing to attack when nine soldiers of the Tenth Cavalry appeared as the escorts and protectors of the Indians who had come to Texas to hunt.

The practice of the federal government of permitting Indians to come to Texas was bitterly resented by the cattlemen and settlers. The inclination of the Texas Rangers to kill these Indians was displeasing to the government. The friction that developed led to a clash between Captain Arrington of the Rangers and Lieutenant-Colonel J. W. Davidson in June of 1879.

In response to news that Indians had been depredating in the Panhandle, Captain Arrington and twenty men left Fort Griffin with forty days' rations and on June 12 struck camp on Sweetwater Creek in Wheeler County near the government post, Fort Elliott.

Wheeler County had just been organized over the vigorous opposition of Lee and Reynolds, the post traders, who wished to keep all the business at Fort Elliott. The sutlers had induced Colonel Davidson to forbid the soldiers going into the new town of Sweetwater and let it be known that they would discharge any of their employees who went. One of these employees caused the trouble between the army officer and the Ranger captain. The incident, which well illustrates the unyielding courage of Arrington, was related by the Ranger officer in his report of June 18, 1879.

'On my arrival, I had hardly unsaddled before an Irish shoulder-hitter, who is kept by the suttler, rode up and asked me in a very loud gruff voice if I had charge of these men, and on being answered, said, "Gen. Davidson wants to see you, he says you are going to attack the

Indians." I replied that he seemed to know a great deal about my business and if I had time might possibly call the next day. This man Donnelly had hardly got out of sight before Gen. Davidson drove up and seemed to be in a terrible passion, and after being seated, asked me what my orders were in regard to Indians. I told him that my orders were always to give protection to life and property and preserve the peace whether from Indians or white men. He then asked me if I would kill Indians should I find any. I replied that I most assuredly would if they were armed, and after a good deal of random talk, he left.'

Captain Arrington said that he found out later the cause of Colonel Davidson's concern. He knew that Indians were in the country, chasing citizens, taking food, killing hogs and cattle, and robbing men of their horses on the prairie. He even sent them word that the Texans were in the country and as a result all parties of Indians were making for the line, saying 'Texas soldiers no buenos.'

On the morning he wrote his report, Arrington heard, through John Donnelly, that Colonel Davidson had said that if the Rangers killed or molested the Indians in the Panhandle he would order his men to fire upon the Rangers. Arrington went at once to the heart of the trouble and sent Colonel Davidson the following note:

SWEETWATER, WHEELER CO., TEXAS
June 18th 1879

Lieutenent-Colonel Davidson 10th Cavalry,
Commanding Post Fort Elliott.

SIR

One John Donnelly a clerk in the Post Traders store has said in substance as follows. That you would fire upon me and my men or put us in irons if we should kill or molest any Indians in the Panhandle. This man Donnelly is the one whom you honored as a messenger to me on the day of my arrival here, and for that reason I think his talk should be noticed.

I therefore desire to know whether or not Donnelly expressed your intentions in policy, not that I have any fears of you in the execution of the enterprise, but for the purpose of laying the matter before the Governor and the Legislature of Texas which is now in session.

Though Colonel Davidson made no reply to Arrington's note, he did round up John Donnelly, who issued on the same day a written statement designed to exculpate the army officer. Colonel Davidson sent Governor Roberts a copy of Arrington's letter, together with Donnelly's statement so that, if Captain Arrington made the complaint threatened, the 'antidote may go with the poison.' [21] Though

[21] Arrington to Adjutant General John B. Jones, June 18, 1879; Arrington to Colonel Davidson, June 18, 1879; statement by John Donnelly, June 18, 1879; Colonel J. W. Davidson to Governor Roberts, June 25, 1879. A.G.P.

nothing further came of this incident, it served to give Arrington the reputation of a man who, in the performance of what he considered his duty, was willing to challenge the United States Army officers and fight them if necessary.

After remaining in Wheeler County for ten days, Captain Arrington set out for a scout farther west to investigate depredations committed during the winter on Charles Goodnight's ranch. Goodnight told Arrington that if he were not given protection, he would raise seventy-five fighting men and protect himself. From Goodnight's the Rangers marched south along the foot of the Plains through Briscoe, Floyd, and Motley counties to find that new ranches were on all the streams, and that more settlers were coming every day. To protect this far country from the bands of Indians and outlaws that frequented it, Arrington recommended that a Ranger company be established on Tasker's ranch. The men could construct winter quarters of sod, have plenty of water and wood, and get supplies through Fort Griffin, whereas if they remained at Fort Elliott in Wheeler County supplies would have to come from Fort Dodge, Kansas.[22]

This recommendation was accepted, and on September 2 the Rangers broke camp at Fort Griffin, and, after a seven-day march over a parched and desolate country, made a permanent camp in Crosby County on Catfish Creek, some eight miles from Blanco Canyon. The station, known as Camp Roberts, was the first to be established in the Panhandle.[23]

From September until January, Captain Arrington and his men scouted the country for a considerable distance around their camp, and acquainted themselves with the location of the different lakes found on the High Plains — Double Lakes, Cedar Lake, Rich Lake, and Silver Lake. Occasionally they would find an Indian trail which usually led to the west to disappear among the numerous cow and horse tracks of the High Plains. These trails to the west induced Captain Arrington to believe that water could be found somewhere between his camp and the settlements of New Mexico. There was a legend about the Lost Lakes which lay about midway of the desert, a two-day march in any direction from other water. Arrington knew that if he could find the Lost Lakes, he would be able to intercept there the Indians who came across the desert from New Mexico to raid on the stockmen of the Plains.

Captain Arrington now determined to go in search of the Lost Lakes, but in order to avoid the disasters that had befallen other at-

[22] Arrington to Jones, July 12, 1879. A.G.P.
[23] *Ibid.*, September 11, 1879. A.G.P.

tempts, he made the most careful preparations. He ordered his wagon to bring supplies and four ten-gallon water kegs to Double Lakes, where a temporary camp was established near the Yellow House caves. From George and John Causey, buffalo hunters, he secured two buffalo hides, and fashioned each hide to carry two water kegs on a stout pack-mule. Leaving five men and the supply wagon in the temporary camp, Arrington set out with ten men and the pack-mules for the west, spending the first night, January 12, 1880, at Silver Lake. His plan and experience may be given from his own account.

'My plan,' he said, 'was to make a two days' march from Silver Lake in a due southwest course into the desert, hoping... to intersect the Indian trail we had left at Double Lakes and possibly to find the Lost Lakes which tradition said were somewhere out there in the desert. I believed that by steady marching for twelve hours a day I could within two days make from 80 to 100 miles, and if I failed to find water within that time, I intended to refill all canteens from the four kegs of water we had with us, and give the remainder to the horses and retrace my steps.

'At sunrise [January 13, 1880] we fell in line and taking our course by a small compass we started at a brisk walk into the unknown region. ... At the end of about thirty miles march, we came suddenly in sight of the real desert. This consisted of low sandhills, extending north, south and west as far as the eye, aided by powerful field glasses, could discern, absolutely barren of vegetation, almost white as snow; certainly by far the most desolate and uninviting region that I ever beheld.

'We knew the reputation of this desolate region for bewildering the brain, choking the throat, parching the lips, and swelling the tongue of man and beast,... but we did not swerve from our course. We approached it, plunged into it, and traveled on and on.

'Night came on, with not the slightest change in the face of the surrounding country, and we camped in one of the wildest and most desolate spots imaginable.... On the following morning, as soon as it was light enough to see the needle on the face of the compass, we were again on the march. The sun came up and as it climbed higher and higher and cast its glistening rays down upon the white sands, we were entertained continually with nature's most wonderful picture show, the Desert Mirage.

'Miles away appeared a lake of water on whose margin stood beautiful groves of trees, so natural that one could scarcely believe they were not real; but the picture would only last for a moment, when the scene would shift, change, and finally disappear....

'All the day long we held to our steady course, never varying, with only the billowy white sand extending... in every direction, the whole pervaded by an awful silence — a silence that you could almost hear. The stillness seemed to affect the men and not a dozen words were exchanged among them during the day.'

Captain Arrington then relates that late in the afternoon of the second day, the nature of the country began to change. The ground became more firm under the tired horses' feet. The men rode to the top of a hill just as the sun was sinking and to their surprise and joy beheld a dry salt lake. Captain Arrington knew that throughout the Plains country fresh water could usually be found, if found at all, on the west side of the lakes. The riders moved forward, around the north end of the lake, and there, sure enough, they found some springs of fresh but brackish water. Around these springs was much Indian sign showing that the red men made this water their rendezvous when crossing the desert. There were ashes of many fires and the skeletons of four or five horses which had had all the flesh cut from the bones. Of most interest to the Ranger captain was an Indian 'sign board' which was propped up on the bank near the largest spring.

Upright in the ground was the bleached shoulder blade of a giant buffalo, an enormous fan-shaped bone fourteen to sixteen inches long, ten inches wide at one end and two inches at the other. On the smooth face of this white blackboard of the Plains, the Indians had inscribed in green, yellow, and red messages for their companions. Near the left edge of the bone were some Indian tipis, trees, and an Indian standing near a fire apparently cooking. Approaching this camp and trees was another Indian leading a pony with a travois loaded with baggage. Behind the travois, near the right edge of the bone, were two sets of *large shod* horse tracks, not pony tracks. The Rangers interpreted the writing, together with the trail that led southwest, to mean that the Indians had moved camp farther out to a place where there were trees, and had moved because they knew that men on shod horses were after them.

The Rangers spent the night here, giving the water the name of Ranger Lake, which it still bears, and the next morning they marched west eighteen miles, where they found four more lakes arranged on a north-south axis. This was the real camping place as indicated by cattle carcasses. Each skull had a round hole in front where the Indians had removed the brains to use in tanning hides. The Rangers camped here on the night of January 16, but returned the next day to Ranger Lake to await the full moon when Captain Arrington expected to intercept Indians as they rode in from their raids on the Texas plains. The captain secreted his men in the hills, his horses in a deep draw near the lake where they could graze, started one man to the Causey Brothers to procure rations and another to Camp Roberts to bring the five extra men. He must have sent these couriers out on January 20, for there is a report in the adjutant general's office, written on that date from the 'Camp on Sand Hills,' in which he mentioned the courier to Causey's and to the Yellow Houses. The Rangers lay in the sand hills for fifteen days. At first they were reduced to half-rations of bacon, flour, and coffee without sugar, but soon the bacon gave out, and there was no meat save what they killed. There was plenty of antelope, but the men did not dare use their precious ammunition acquiring it. The full moon passed and no Indians came. On the last day of January, the Rangers broke camp and started the desert journey to Silver Lake and the Yellow Houses.

The first day was clear and sunny and the hungry men had no trouble in following the trail. They managed to kill an antelope, which was entirely eaten at one meal. At five o'clock the next morning, February 1, a snowstorm came from the northeast and by the time the men took their saddles the ground was covered. Of this experience Captain Arrington wrote:

'It would be hard to imagine a more forlorn aspect than the little squad of men and horses presented that morning as they fell in line and took up march facing that terrible blizzard, already half famished with not a morsel of food; the horses, almost exhausted, reeled as they walked; the men gaunt and haggard from starvation, their faces drawn and pinched until their most intimate friends would not have recognized them. I knew that 50 or 60 miles northeast was the Yellow Houses and Causey Brothers Buffalo Camp and that there was relief if we could but reach these points. But I also knew that if we should miss these points, there was little chance for us in this terrible storm. I got my course as best I could and struck out facing the storm with the men and pack-mules following.... Those who know anything about a blizzard on the north plains of Texas may have some idea of our situation. Night came on and there was no relief in sight. The snow by this time was twelve or fourteen inches deep.'

To make matters worse, one of the men announced that he could go no farther because his horse had given out. When he attempted to dismount, he found that he was paralyzed with cold. There was no horse that could carry two men, for their hardships had equaled those of their masters, but fortunately Captain Arrington had picked up an Indian pony that was now pressed into service. The Ranger was tied on the Indian pony and the procession again moved forward. Within ten minutes the snow stopped, the clouds rose and parted, and a single

THE BLIZZARD MARCH

'I got my course as best I could and struck out facing the storm with the men and pack-mules following.'

star appeared directly in front of them. Taking the star for a guide, Arrington bore on and within half an hour came to the breaks of a canyon. By this time all the stars were out, and the Rangers descended beneath the level of the plain into the gracious shelter of the Yellow Houses, near the place where they had concealed their wagon.

A hundred feet above the wagon was a cave large enough to shelter the entire squad, and here the men had left some mesquite roots which were now covered with snow. They dug out the roots, cut up the frame of a pack-saddle for tinder, and built a fire.

The next morning, February 3, men were sent with pack-mules to Causey Brothers' Buffalo Camp, and soon returned with food. By this time the men were so weak from hunger and exposure that they could scarcely stand, and the food was issued to them at first in small amounts. The Rangers left this camp on February 4, reached the home station, Camp Roberts, on February 6, after an absence of forty days in which time they had marched, including side trips, eight hundred and twenty miles.

Captain Arrington had indeed found the Lost Lakes in the desert. As soon as the newspapers published an account of his trip, Lieutenant Colonel John T. Hatch wrote to Major Jones from Fort Sill for information as to the location of the lakes. He stated that the soldiers had long known such lakes existed, but had never been able to find them because they were two days' march from water. He said that the Comanches knew nothing of them until Mackenzie's campaign in 1872, when the Apaches informed them. Captain Arrington believed that Ranger Lake was in Gaines County, but we know now that all the lakes are in New Mexico.[24]

To follow Arrington through the Panhandle for the two years after the discovery of Lost Lakes would be good entertainment, for he was there preserving peace when the whole country was throbbing to the tread of cowmen, horses, cattle, and nesters, all flavored with the toughness of the frontier. He was present at the birth, or soon after, of every rowdy cow town, and throughout he was the same stern and unyielding master. When he was called to Seymour, he found it quiet for want of whiskey, but he added that 'a new supply is expected soon.' Spring was at hand, for it was April and May, one hundred and fifty cowboys would be in town, and if the whiskey arrived in time things would be lively.

In the summer of 1880, a Colonel A. B. Norton came to the Panhandle to survey the Capitol Reservation Lands, and displeased Arrington by requesting the Rangers to hunt water for the surveyors. He was more displeased, however, by a 'spiritual deadbeat' named Howard who had ingratiated himself into the good will of Norton and converted him to spiritualism. Arrington's puritanical repulsion overflowed in a letter written to Captain Neal Coldwell on July 2. 'Norton has about gone crazy on spiritualism.... Two years ago the spirits told him that he would be appointed to inspect State lands and after that to retire to private life, ta, ta.' His disgust of Howard was so great that he would not talk to him. 'This old fellow, the boys say, is a free lover, says that if his wife was living she might habitate with anyone, that virtue is a fraud.... Howard says the spirit [of] an Indian Chief has been with him on the whole trip to guard him from raiders. I wish a bunch of Comanches had struck him... he would have found out his little mistake. They don't talk to me as I cut it off short.... I'm no free lover.'

On November 27, Arrington led his Rangers to Teepee City where

[24] Arrington wrote two reports on this expedition. The first was written from the Sand Hills, January 20, 1880, and sent out by the courier; the second was written on February 9, 1880, shortly after reaching Camp Roberts. The account from which the long quotation is taken was written years later. See L. F. Sheffy, 'The Arrington Papers,' *Panhandle-Plains Historical Review*, 1928, pp. 30–66.

the cowboys had indulged in another shooting spree, and from there to Doan's Store on Red River where the Texas Cattle Trail crossed. Three families lived there and others were opening farms between Doan's and the mouth of Wanderer's Creek. Eagle Flat, south of Doan's, gave promise of becoming a hard place; it had two saloons and one fancy house, whatever that might be. His circle brought him to 'so-called Pease River City' of one house set in a desolate country a mile from the river, and then to Teepee City where 'a fellow who rides the mail' had fired six shots into his camp and left for Odom's ranch. The cowboys were reported to be planning to charge the place on Christmas night and fire at everything in sight. He would make them sorry; 'I want to check their time the first break they make.' That was about all the news except that some of the horses had the epizootic, and the plains north of the canyon had burned off, and the canyon itself would have burned if his boys had not fought the fire all night.[25]

The reports for the year 1881 show that Captain Arrington covered the entire Panhandle: Mobeetie, Tascosa, Fort Elliott, Fort Griffin, Doan's, and all the rest. If his direct methods were not already apparent, they could be sensed in such expressions as the following: 'Reached Fort Griffin and jailed my prisoner'; 'Am going after one of Millett's bad men'; 'One of my men got drunk and I calaboosed him.' That was Arrington, iron-handed ruler, who took the shortest route to the goal he sought.

Arrington was not blind to the business opportunities about him. A part of his savings went into ranch lands, and on July 1, 1882, he filed his resignation to take effect on August 31. In addition to his own ranching interests, he was made manager of the Rockingchair, and shortly after his resignation he was practically drafted as sheriff of Wheeler County.

From what has been said of Captain Arrington, it is easy to understand that he made bitter enemies as well as staunch friends. He was a strict disciplinarian, never took his men into his confidence, and discharged them for infraction of his rules. Many of them disliked him because of his unyielding nature. It is said that he lived in expectation of being assassinated by his enemies. He had a friend who was in a similar state; the two men made an agreement that if either of them was killed the other would at once kill the murderer. This insurance was so effective that both died natural deaths.

Captain Arrington continued to enforce the law, and joined that distinguished leader of the Panhandle, Colonel Charles Goodnight, in a war on cattle thieves. When a firm, which we call Baker and Shields,

[25] Arrington to Jones, December 13, 1880. A.G.P.

shipped sixteen cars of cattle to market, the inspectors cut out four cars as stolen stuff. The cattlemen got out warrants for the arrest of the big men Baker and Shields, but when Baker, who was known as the Deacon, heard that he was wanted, he scurried off to his home in Massachusetts where he had better standing and his neighbors fewer cattle. Captain Arrington was handed a warrant and told to go after him. When the ex-Ranger captain reached New England, he had considerable trouble in getting to his man, but finally decided to see the governor, who happened to be Ben Butler, elected in 1882. He had almost as much trouble getting to Ben Butler as he had in getting hold of the Deacon. Finally, however, he broke through the guards and got to Butler. It so happened that Butler had a personal and political dislike for this Texas cattle king, and as he signed the extradition papers he remarked that he had never signed a paper with more pleasure than he did the one that would send the Deacon back to Texas. Arrington now captured the Deacon and took the train for Texas. He knew that if he followed the regular train route, he would lose his prisoner through habeas corpus and all the legal dodges known to the lawyers of rich men. Therefore Arrington changed trains frequently and zigzagged his way back southward without losing his man. His story of the trip might have closed with his favorite laconic expression, 'I jailed my prisoner.' The Deacon finally came clear by paying all costs including the expenses of Arrington's trip to New England. Colonel Goodnight has earned the just title of father of the Texas Panhandle; Arrington — the iron-handed — is known as the first and greatest peace officer.

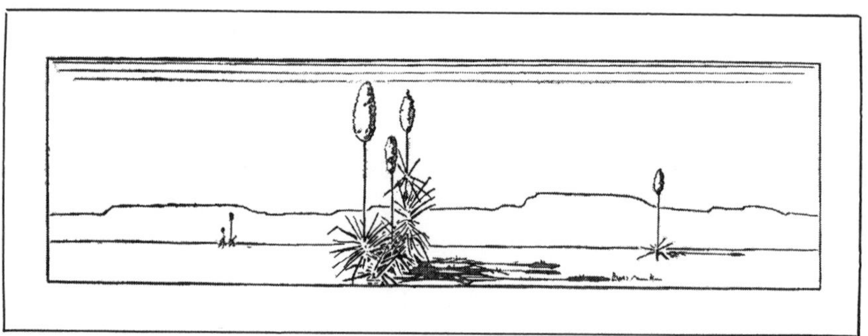

XIX

THE CLOSED FRONTIER: LAST SERVICES OF THE FRONTIER BATTALION

What we want is about three good Rangers.

JOHN N. GARNER

I am now staying with a man who is suspitioned of cutting wire and have almost gained his confidence.... He and I stold a stake rope a few days ago and expect to kill a beef.... Then if he knows who the wire cutters are I think he will tell me.

Ranger Report

Nothing will do any good here but a first class killing and I am the little boy that will give it to them if they dont let the fence alone.

Ranger IRA ATEN

These are my last fence-cutters whether I catch them or not.... We have had to tell ten thousand lies and I know we won't get away without telling a million.

Ranger IRA ATEN

XIX. THE CLOSED FRONTIER: LAST SERVICES OF THE FRONTIER BATTALION

When Baylor's and Nevill's Rangers made their breakfast on top of El Diablo with the dead bodies of Indian men, women, and children lying about them in the cold mountain air, they performed a rite which brought to an end the history of the Texas frontier. Never again was a Texas Ranger to shed the blood of an Indian; never again was an Indian to scalp a settler or burn his cabin. The long fight with the Comanches and Apaches, which began in the seventeenth century, was at an end and Texas belonged to the whites. As already noted, the scene was changing in Texas so rapidly as to defy description. The cowmen had within five years following 1877 covered the Western Plains, taken the Panhandle, and the arid and broken spaces that are drained by the Pecos. Behind the cowmen came the farmers to fence the water holes and turn the prairie sod. By 1882 the Southern Pacific and the Texas Pacific had reached El Paso on their way to the Pacific coast.

We have already noted the break-up of the Frontier Battalion by the resignation of the principal captains which took place about 1881, the year that Major Jones died. A new generation was assuming control of the destinies of the state, men who knew but little of the days of the Civil War.

In reality the Frontier Battalion should have been disbanded with the death of Major Jones, not because of his death, but because the frontier was gone. Though the organization continued for twenty years longer, it did not operate as a frontier force. No longer could one draw a line from Ranger camp to Ranger camp, a line extending from the Red River south, and say: here is the frontier where the Rangers stand guard between savagery and civilization. Civilization had overtaken the Rangers, encompassed them, and made them an interior police force. It was only on the Rio Grande border that they faced the criminal who was not of their own blood and nationality.

Since 1881 the Texas Rangers have had no battle front, and therefore no program or plan of campaign. They have been 'trouble-shooters,' a state police — though God forbid the name! — whose function it has been to handle situations beyond the control of local peace officers. We find them hunting cow or horse thieves, protecting negroes from mobs, aiding judges in holding court, 'laying on fences' to capture wire-cutters, or fighting Mexicans along the border.

1. THE FENCE-CUTTERS

The invention of barbed wire in 1873 made it possible for the first time to fence the western, or plains portion, of Texas. The fencing was well under way by 1880, and was practically complete by 1890. Though the day of free grass was about over, many men — long accustomed to believe that the Great Plains could not be used by farmers — were loath to believe or accept the fact. When they saw all the lands going under fence, they seized their wire-cutters and used them in the determination to keep the free range. The result was a fence-cutters' war between the fence men and the free grass men. In Texas the trouble became so acute that Governor John Ireland called the legislature in special session in 1884 to pass a law making fence-cutting a felony. The law also provided that the big pasture men should leave gates every three miles and forbade them 'fencing in' the nesters who were spotting the west with shanties, dugouts, and large families.

From the first, the Texas Rangers were called in wherever fence-cutting was prevalent. The crime was particularly hard to handle because the fence-cutter carried no evidence of his deed. The horse thief was caught with the horse and the cow thief with the cow, but the fence-cutter rode away from the curling steel tendrils with no evidence upon him. He had to be caught on the job through detective work.

JOHN GARNER WANTS THREE RANGERS

It would require a volume to tell the story of fence-cutting in Texas between 1880 and 1900. Some idea of the trouble, and the difficulty of its remedy, may be gleaned from the letters and petitions that poured in on the governor and adjutant general, from reward notices in the newspapers, and from reports made by Texas Rangers who were sent to stop the work. The best that can be done here is to give the reader samples from these very human documents. The first one given came from a young county judge of Uvalde County who later became Vice-President of the United States. On November 13, 1893, John N. Garner wrote General W. H. Mabry in part as follows:

'I write at the request of several of the most prominent citizens of this county to inform you of violations of the law in this county and to ask your assistance.

'Francis Smith & Co. some weeks ago fenced their pasture on the Nueces River with a splendid four wire fence. It had only been up some four weeks when *our entire side* was cut between every post. They rebuilt it at once and in less than ten days it was cut again. They rebuilt it again and last Friday night it was cut a third time just as before. ... What we want is about three good Rangers to come here and catch these law breakers. They can catch them within a week or ten days.' [1]

Sheriff J. C. Wall and other county officials wrote Governor Culberson from Brady, McCulloch County:

'There is in a portion of this county a lawless class of people who cut fences, burn houses, etc. The grand jury, which has just adjourned, can not get sufficient evidence to indict guilty parties.

'It will take some detective work to get evidence sufficient to punish the guilty and check the lawlessness. We think it advisable for you to quietly send one or two Rangers here to go and stay among the lawless element and find out who the guilty parties are. The local officers can not find out.' [2]

From Brown County came the following:

'We have two small pastures near Brownwood. The fences around these pastures have been cut and broken down 50 times during the last 5 months. We have been notified by letters (signed "White Cappers") that the stock in the pastures would be poisoned. That we would be killed. That our homes would be blown up with dynamite. And that the grass would be burned. The grass has been set on fire three times in last ten days and a large part burned. We would like to have a man sent here... to try and capture the perpetrators. We think that one man of the proper kind would be sufficient.... We have been informed that you have the proper kind of men among the Rangers.' [3]

A petition to the Governor of Texas signed by a number of women showed the terrible conditions in Waller County. The petition prayed for protection from a band of lawless men who were cutting fences.

'This combination of lawless men is so strong that the sheriff of Waller County has failed to give us protection.... They cut our fences and threaten us with death if we dare to repair them. They have overawed the officers of the law who fear to incur their enmity. They have fired shots into the houses of our good citizens at night in the attempt to as-

[1] John N. Garner to General W. H. Mabry, November 13, 1893. A.G.P.

[2] J. C. Wall to Governor C. A. Culberson, April 27, 1897. A.G.P.

[3] R. W. Low and A. E. Noel to Governor C. A. Culberson, September 19, 1898. A.G.P.

sassinate them or to overawe them. They have openly and in the day time rode up in squads to citizens engaged in repairing cut fences and pushed the muzzles of guns against their persons and threatened them with instant death if they continued their work.' [4]

Governor Culberson offered a reward for the detection and capture of the depredators, and it was not uncommon to see such notices as the following in the newspapers:

$100
REWARD

I WILL PAY THE ABOVE REWARD FOR INFORMATION WHICH WILL LEAD TO THE CONVICTION AND INCARCERATION IN THE PENITENTIARY OF THE FELON WHO MALICIOUSLY CUT THE HAMILTON PASTURE ON THE BANDERA ROAD LAST NIGHT

W. G. HUGHES

BOERNE, AUGUST 6, 1889.

The manner in which the Rangers worked is told briefly by John R. Hughes in a letter to General L. P. Sieker, written from Richland on May 26, 1888.

'I am now staying with a man who is suspitioned of cutting wire and have almost gained his confidence. He talks freely to me about stealing cattle. He and I stold a stake rope a few days ago and expect to kill a beef as soon as we eat up what he had on hand when I came. Then if he knows who the wire cutters are I think he will tell me.'

SERGEANT IRA ATEN AND THE DYNAMITE BOMBS

The story of the experiences of two young detectives who were sent to work among the fence-cutters in Navarro County is graphically told in a series of five letters which Ira Aten, Sergeant of Company D, wrote from camp and field to his superior officer at Austin. These letters — written in pencil on rough paper — are worthy of preservation because of their quaint humor and their revelation of a singularly original and audacious character. They give the Ranger's attitude, not only towards fence-cutters, but towards grangers, manual labor, matrimony, superiors, shotgun law, mob law, and dynamite.

Sometime in August, 1888, one might have seen a plain farm wagon drawn by a horse and mule making its way slowly into Mexia. On the spring seat of the jolting vehicle were two young men roughly clad as

[4] Miss Alwina Roehl and others to Governor C. A. Culberson, September (n.d.), 1898. A.G.P.

farm laborers. Behind them in the wagon bed were some crude cooking utensils, an axe, some spare clothing, and such other equipment as might be of use to hard-working and simple-minded country boys in search of honest employment. A casual examination might have uncovered two or three six-shooters, a pair of Winchesters, and perhaps a shotgun, such weapons as travelers in Texas carried at that time. There was nothing to indicate that these two young men were Jim King and Ira Aten, Texas Rangers in search of the fence-cutters of Navarro.

YOU MAY HEAR OF A KILLING

They stopped at Mexia only to learn that the sheriff of Navarro and posse had captured some of the fence-cutters. They concealed their camp in a thicket near Mexia, and while Jim King remained with the wagon, Sergeant Aten took the train to Corsicana to make some preliminary investigation. His letter reporting activities follows:

'Corsicana, Texas
August 20, 1888

'Captain L. P. Sieker,
Quartermaster Front. Batt.,
Austin, Texas.

'Dear Sir:

'Seeing in the newspapers when I got as far as Mexia where the Sheriff of Navarro County and a posse had waylaid a fence and caught some fence-cutters in the act of cutting Judge Frost's pasture fence, I thought it prudent to run up here on the train and learn full particulars.... I have seen Judge Frost and Mr. West today and they say the parties that were captured was not in the neighborhood of where they want us to work, and they were not bad men at all like the ones they want us to work after. The ones that were captured was only petty cutters.... It is a question now whether the fence-cutters will let up on their midnight work or not. Judge Frost thinks they will cut all the more now, but I am unable to say what they will do....

'I left J. W. King and our outfit concealed near Mexia in the brush. I will go back to Mexia tonight and then we will proceed on our journey to where we want to stop at, which is some 15 or 20 miles from Mexia. We will do our best although it may be a failure....

'I will ask it as a special favor of the Adjutant General's office never to ask me to work after fence-cutters again under any and all circumstances for it is the most disagreeable work in the world and I think I have already done my share of it for the State of Texas and her people. ... I would rather be at the camp and only get $30 per month than get $50 per month and have to work after fence-cutters. If it was any other detective business besides fence-cutting where I would not have to be as guilty of the same crime as [the criminals] themselves, I would like it. However, being I have consented to try these villains, I will ask for plenty of time, etc., so dont get out of patience with me if we dont do anything right away....

'You may hear of a killing if everything works right up here, but it may be some time yet. I dont know when I will have a chance to write again....

'Remember me kindly to all in the office.

'Yours very Respt'ly,
'Ira Aten
'*1st Segt. Co. D, Rangers.*'

TEN THOUSAND LIES

'Richland, Texas
Aug. 31, 1888

'Capt. L. P. Sieker,
Austin, Texas.

'Dear Sir:

'We are among the fence cutters in the best shape of the world. My plans have so far worked as I expected and we are here without the shadow of suspicion as far as we are able to tell.

'We came through Wortham and up to Richland and inquired the way to Kauffman Co., so everybody in Richland thinks we are going to Kauffman. However our wagon tyre run off about a mile on the other side of Richland and in a little rough place our wagon wheel broke down and of course we didnt have money enough to get it fixt. Besides, the blacksmith (as luck would have it) had went to Corsicana on a spree and never came back for a week and of course we could not get our wagon wheel fixt if we had wanted to but we didnt want to very bad.

'After our wagon broke down soon came along another wagon and the man helped us to move our wagon out of the road and sympathiz with us very much owing to it looking so reasonable of breaking itself down. However, I had a hard time pounding off the tyre and then had to break the wheel with an ax. This was about 4 o'clock in the morning 22nd inst. I came on back to Richland then on the mule and made a pitiful talk and all seemed to sympathiz with us in our break down.

RANGER TYPES OF 1888
Wood Saunders
Walter Durbin

'I went back to where I left Jim King and the wagon and fell in with a noted fence cutter and he told me where he thought we could get work making hay. We went by our wagon and took a good look at things etc. We camped at our wagon that night and the next morning drug it back to Richland on a pole and a large crowd of the fence cutters all seen us and I dont think any of them suspicioned us being detectives for a moment.

'We stayed around Richland all day and established camp under some trees close by. We had most of the names of the fence cutters and we would know them and when one was called we would locate him right then and there.... They would talk very freely about fence cutting and didnt seem to care who was around, but I guess they thought we were all fence cutters.

'That night they had a meeting of indignation in regards to the fence cutters... caught cutting the fence by the sheriff and posse.... The meeting was about six miles from Richland at the little station called Angus. Lots of these fence cutters went and they made big war talk against the pasture men, Sheriff, and everybody that would try to stop fence cutting etc....

'The next day I went over to see if I could get work making hay where the noted fence cutter told us he thought we could. However they had already got a supply of hands and didnt need any more.... The next day I went over to see the gin man that run the gin right in Richland. Well, I got Jim King a job a baling cotton for the season and I took a job a picking 35 acres of cotton out for the son of the man that runs the gin and he is under bond now for fence cutting.

'We have been working all this week building a rock furnace around the gin boiler. It has been awful hard work handling the rough and large rocks but we never grumbled in the least but went at it like we were raised to it. Jim King says he would not work at it for less than $5 per day only under these circumstances. We got our furnace job done yesterday and wont have anything else to do but odd jobs until cotton picking time.

'We got to see lots of the fence cutters every day as they came to Richland and often came down to the gin. We are slowly getting acquainted with the villians but it will take a long time to get their confidence sufficient to cut fence with them as I have heard them say often that their crowd didnt need any help to cut fence and an outfit was a fool to take in any outsiders to help them. Lots of such talk I have heard them make.

'These fence cutters are very near as hard as my Brown Co. fence cutters and when they once suspicion us they will no doubt try and murder us but we will be at the killing, etc. I dont feel any uneasy-ness as long as we are not given away by our friends unintentionally. Should they give us away I will leave the Co. in disgust and say they dont need any assistance for they cant keep their mouths shut long enough for it to be given to them.

'The fence cutters here are what I would call cowboys, or small cow men that own... from 15 head all the way up to perhaps 200 head of cattle and a few cow ponies etc. Some have 100 acres of land and some more and some not so much and perhaps a little field in cultivation etc. They hate the Grangers as they call them for it is the Grangers (or farmers) that have the pastures with the exception of Frost & Barry and a few others. In fact they hate anybody that will fence land either for farming or pasture. They are a hard lot of men in here and they are thieves as well as fence cutters. They are talking about going to Corsicana in arms and taking them fence cutters out of the jail etc. That is all talk, they wont go. They had another indignation meeting over at Angus night before last.... The most of these men that are holding these meetings etc. are villians of the deepest dye and death would be to good for them....

'Now for the good citizens, what do they deserve? I will simply state this that a great many good citizens that dont own one-half as much as the parties that has been the instigator of all this fence cutting in this section have had their fence cut from around their little horse pasture and even in several instance have had it cut from around their cultivated lands where corn and cotton was planted. They have quit cutting from around fields now but there are not a pasture of no kind up on the west side of the Houston & Texas Central Railway in this section where these wild and wooly wire cutters operate.... Small pastures have been cut time and again until the owners have not the means to put up the wire any more and now all pastures are down and this is called the free range country.

'Many have took down their wire and rolled it up to save it from being cut etc. The fence cutters themselves have told me that while a man was putting up his fence one day in a hollow a crowd of wire cutters was cutting it back behind him in another hollow back over the hill. They delight in telling all such things and most of it is true also....

'I have dropped on another plan to catch the villians much sooner I think than working in with them. That is this, to have two or three of these good citizens put up their fence and I with one of the pasture men ... watch the fence every night with double barrel shotguns and if they cut the fence arrest them if possible and if we cant do that take them the best way we can etc....

'These are my last fence cutters whether I catch them or not. I dont want to make a failure in this but when I see that nothing can be done rest assured I will report such to the Adjutant Generals Office for I would rather be in h——l than here. We have had to tell ten thousand lies already and I know we wont get away without telling a million. Here-after it will take more than $50 per month to get me to go out and see how many lies I can tell or to be placed in a position so that I will have to tell them to keep from being murdered.... Nothing will do any good here but a first class killing and I am the little boy that will give it to them if they dont let the fence alone. I wish I had Hughes to lay with me on the fence for it is awful risky business....

'Perhaps you will get tired reading this lengthy letter but thought I would give you the outline of what we have done although it is very little. Jim King's fiddle comes in very handy. He draws large crowds very near every night and we make lots new acquaintances by it.

'Will close
'Yours Very Respt
'Ira Aten'

SUSPICION LAYS UPON US

The Ranger-detective's next letter was written on September 17, 'By the Big Spring, Navarro County.' His plans had been upset because the sheriff, who did not know the identity of the two young laborers, had remarked that Governor Ross had sent detectives into the county with the result that the wire-cutters had become more wary and ceased for a time to use their pliers. To make the situation more discouraging, suspicion had fallen on the two strangers. Aten can tell the story best.

'King and myself have given up our Cotton Contracts ... and went to work (or pretending to work) for the Love ranche about two miles west of Richland and about 3 miles of the fence that they have been cutting mostly. The Love ranche is run by two good men and they know who we are etc.... They only had about three miles of wire fence and when the villians cut they cut down the three miles and it is still down. They will put it up whenever I say so but I dont deem it a wise idea for them to put it up yet awhile, owing to us just going to work for them, and already slight suspicion lays upon us. Why the rascals would smell a rat... they would never cut the fence.

'But if these good men 3 and 6 miles distant... puts up their fence, the rascals would never once think that we would go that distant to guard a fence, but that's what we are doing every night.... We have a double barrel shotgun apiece and if the villians cut the fence we are guarding and they dont surrender when called upon somebody will most likely go away with their hand on their belly.

'We have an excellent place to watch. Its at what is known as the Cross lanes where four pastures come together.... We can hear them cutting on either of the 8 strings of fence from a half to 3/4 of a mile... If such a thing is possible I want to take the villians without killing them but I think a little more of my life than theirs and I will stand a trial for murder before I will stand up and be shot down like a fool.

'I expect some of these days to stand up before a fire and shake off my sixshooter and Winchester, kick them in and watch them burn and go up in the Panhandle and settle down upon a little farm, go to nesting, be a better boy, and read my bible more. When I am called upon by an officer to assist him in making an arrest I will go out to the barn and get the pitchfork or the hoe and follow in behind the officer like old Grangers do. So I dont want to kill these rascals and have any more deadly enemies on my trail than I have already got.

THE DYNAMITE BOMB PLAN

'Should I fail to get these rascals by watching the fence,... I am agoing to try and get these fellows to try my dinamite boom [bomb] racket.... I cant explain it to you by writing but dont you forget but what it can be done if a man can get the dinamite in the right shape. I think it would be against the law to use it, but I wouldent mind going to the penitentiary for a few years just to get to know some of these villians had been caught up with in their rascality....

'I wish you would look up the law, Captain, and see if a man has a right or not to put dinamite along on his own fence and on his own land for its protection. It seems like a man ought to have that right whether the law gives it to him or not. Dont get frightened... for I havent invested any money in dinamite yet, but I have invested some money in about 15 cartridges each one loaded with buckshot and they will be better than dinamite booms if the rascals will only go to work as they have done heretofore.

'I dont want to lay on a fence two or three years just to catch a few villians while dinamite booms would always be there ready for them whenever they took a notion to cut. But I havent got the dinamite in the right shape and dont know how I could get it unless I go up to Chicago and join the anarchist and get them to fix it for me.

'Well, I [will] quit writing none-sence... I know you will have a big laugh over my idea about the dinamite booms.... This is a lengthy letter for me to be writing up to headquarters but having nothing to do this eve but to sit down by the Spring and think and I have written my thoughts....

'Yours Very Resp'ly
'Ira Aten

'P.S. I have laid on the ground and written this letter so if poorly written you will know the cause.

'Ira'

OF COURSE COCK THE GUN

CORSICANA, TEXAS,
Oct. 8, 1888.

'Capt. L. P. Sieker,
Quartermaster Front. Batt.

'DEAR SIR:

'I have only one more chance with any hopes of stopping fence cutting in this section and that is with my dynamite [5] boom as I call it. I have had the law examined and it dont say anything about a man having the right to protect his property by the use of dynamite or by the use of a shotgun either. So I have come to the conclusion if it was not against the law to guard a fence with a shotgun to protect the property it certainly would not be against the law to use dynamite for the same purpose. There-fore I have *invested* some money in *dynamite* and will in a few days set my *dynamite booms* upon the *few* fences that have been put up recently....

'Should the Gov. or the Genl. disapprove of this, all they have got to do is to notify me to that effect etc. They sent me here to stop fence cutting any way I could and to use my own judgement etc. how to do it. And that is what I am doing and if they will let me alone the balance of this month I will have my booms set and when the fence is cut why they will hear of it at Austin.

'The dynamite boom is entirely safe unless the wire is cut or fence is torn entirely down. Stock in rubbing against the post or wire *will not explode* the boom, but should they break all the wires where the boom is then of course it will explode.

'I can not explain the working of my boom thoroughly but can give you an idea of how it works etc. It is simply taking an old shotgun or musket, put some powder in it as if for shooting, then slide down a *dynamite cap* on the powder and then the dynamite on top of cap until you think you have enough. Put cap on gun ready for shooting, fasten wire to triger and then to the bottom of a post that is not in the ground, place gun in a box made for the special purpose and place the box just under the ground and cover up so it cant be seen. Of course cock the gun when you put it in the box and a fellow will have to handle it carefully.

'So you see by this post being very crooked and not in the ground,.. when wires are cut or torn down the post will fall and the end will fly

[5] The reader will observe that Ranger Aten in this letter spells dynamite correctly. He had purchased the explosive and evidently improved his orthography by reading the wrappers.

up giving the wire at the bottom end of the post a jerk sufficient to shoot the gun off. The powder explodes the dynamite cap and the cap explodes the dynamite and then small pieces of shot gun will *be found all over Navarro Co.* Well, if it dont kill the parties that cuts the fence, it will scare them so bad they will never cut another fence, thinking it was a mere scratch that they did not get killed.... When one of my booms once explodes all fence cutters will hear of it most likely and then all a pasture man has got to say to secure the safety of his fence against these midnight depredations is: "I have dynamite booms on my fence."...

'We have quit guarding the fence and now I am going to put on my boom... and see what success I can have in that way....

'Keep your ears pricked, you may hear my dynamite boom clear down there.... I will use the greatest precaution ... and see that no innocent man gets hurt with them. They are dangerous in setting them unless a man is awful careful. However, if I get blowed up, you will know I was doing a good cause.... Not necessary to write more.

'Yours Very Respt'ly,
'Ira Aten
'*Co. D Ranger*'

The last letter in the fence-cutting correspondence was written from Corsicana on October 15. Ranger Aten's proposal to use dynamite aroused Austin authorities and brought him strict orders to desist and to come in. The doughty Ranger declared that he was glad to get the order which he had expected to receive. He had taught the fence men how to make the bombs and set them, and now they could take steps for their own protection. The order, he said, did not close his mouth or keep him from explaining how to work the dynamite bombs. 'You will see yet my boom racket having the effect to put a quietus on fence cutting in Texas.' There is no record that bombs were ever set in Texas, but there is a tradition that Ira Aten's 'boom racket' had much influence in putting fear into the hearts of fence-cutters and in stamping out the illegal use of the nippers.

2. FROM THE RIO GRANDE TO THE RED

This section relates incidents of the Ranger service in the last two decades of the nineteenth century. It will be noted that the Rangers were operating from the Rio Grande to the Red River, and from the Panhandle of West Texas to the pine forests of East Texas. Most of the action occurred, however, along the international border and in the sparsely settled region of the Pànhandle where frontier conditions still prevailed.

A CORPORAL AND THE NOW DECEASED

On June 5, 1889, Corporal C. H. Fusselman, Company D, made a report to General W. H. King of which the following is an extract:

'Yesterday morning while in discharge of my duty... killed one Mexican name Donaciano Beslanga. I will explain.

'Sunday eve as I road into Alpine I met Capt. Gillespie who had a telegram from Haymond station stating that the now deceased had the town terrorized... had shot one man... and was riding through town shooting.... well we took the 8:52 train and when we arrived... the now deceased had gone to Maxan Springs... got a hand car and went down but did not find him.... we returned to [Haymond] on 3:20 train.... I borrowed a mule and went again to Maxan Springs found he had left at sunrise. I lay and watched his wife until 10 at night when a heavy storm blew up which drove now deceased in to his home for shelter. I run on him but he slipped me as it was so dark and as I was looking under the tank for him lightning flashed and he shot at me.... I run towards him and returned the shot... I lost him as it was so dark and raining so hard. Next morning I got a rifle and took his trail at daylight when about 3/4 miles from Station I heard him cough. I went towards him and the instant I saw him he saw me and sprang to his knees. I could see that there was no chance for his giving up as he had a bad expression on his face so I fired as he did... witness said that the two shots were so near together that they could just be distinguished.

'Then about 15 shots were exchanged.... I emptyed my gun run in on him grabbed his gun and shot him once with pistol before he would give up. he was hit 8 times 5 shots were fatal he would have fought ten minutes longer if I had not grabbed his gun and took it away from him I wired Gillespie who came at night with Justice and held inquest... officers say I am justifyable in killing as it was in self defense in the discharge of my duty please excuse this long explanation

'Very respectfully

'C. H. FUSSELMAN' [6]

TRAILING TRAIN ROBBERS

Captain Frank Jones's chase after bandits on the Rio Grande is related in his own words. It seems that early in September the Southern

[6] Corporal C. H. Fusselman to Adjutant General W. H. King, June 5, 1889. A.G.P.

COMPANY D IN UVALDE COUNTY. CAPTAIN FRANK JONES, 1886 OR 1887. NOTE WATER KEGS, DUTCH OVENS, SADDLES, ETC.

Pacific train was robbed in Val Verde County. Captain Jones and five men left their camp (Camp Hogg, probably near El Paso) on a special car and arrived at the scene of the robbery, where they were joined by five citizens. They immediately took up the trail which led off in the direction of Mexico.

'I followed the trail to the Rio Grande that evening and tied up our horses without any grass at all. The next morning as soon as it was light enough I found where they had crossed into Mexico and there was 5 of them as each horse track showed plainly in the sand all of them shod all round. They took a southeast course after crossing the river for about ten miles and then all scattered. I followed a single horse trail. ... About eight miles from where they separated they came together and burned quite a lot of papers, as the ashes showed, and unshod their horses. The trail then led back to the river and recrossed to this side and again scattered. We again followed one track and found where they came together and camped. We followed the trail in this way, they separating every few miles and going across the roughest country on the route, always leading up the Rio Grande.

'On the 5th day we found where they had reshod their horses and then they staid together. On the 6th day we found their camp in a dense cane brake on the Mexican side of the river. One of their men out as a scout looking after stock discovered us about 4 miles below their Camp and although we chased him he had too much the start and got into camp and gave the alarm. After we chased this man we continued on up the river until we came to the cane brake and some dogs came out to meet us. We then scattered out and tried to look through the cane but I soon saw it was too dense and was besides very dangerous. I then surrounded the brake as well as I could and set fire to it in several places and closed in as it burned. We then located the camp and closed in on it but the men had mounted fresh horses and fled. I found a camp that had evidently been there for several months with quite a lot of plunder. There was 3 extra saddles in the camp of men who must have been murdered. This was the camp of a man named John —— who has some stock on this side of the river. The only way for the Mexican authorities to get at his camp would have been to cross to this side. We found a great many stolen cattle there and letters that prove they were regulars in the business.

'After leaving their camp I trailed them to this side and then back into Mexico at a point a few miles higher up the river where they left their horses and again went into the cane. I spent three days in beating and burning out the brakes on both sides but failed to ever catch them.

'There is no Mexican settlement anywhere in that region.... If we had not found the robber camp we would have been without rations for several days. I demolished their roost entirely and am satisfied hunger will drive them from the River.

'Now Genl I wanted you to know through me that I... crossed into Mexico and chased these men.... Of course I would not cross into Mexico where there are settlements and [where there] would be any danger of stirring up international trouble. You would do me a favor by stating this matter to Gov Hogg as it really is as he might hear through the papers of my crossing. My horses are completely broken down. I returned to camp today. The robber camp is about one hundred miles from here.

'Respectfully
'FRANK JONES
'*Capt. Co. "D" F. B.*'[7]

[7] Captain Frank Jones to General W. H. Mabry, September 11, 1891. A.G.P.

That Captain Frank Jones did not give up John ——, who was lost temporarily in the cane brakes fringing the Rio Grande, is indicated by a telegram stating that with the deputy sheriff and two citizens of Val Verde County, he struck the robbers' trail seventy-five miles north of Del Rio, overtook them fifty miles above Howard's well, killed one and captured three.[8]

This telegram was supplemented by a letter giving brief details of the chase. Captain Jones left El Paso on a freight with seven men from Comstock, struck the trail of the robbers above Del Rio, and followed them to Crockett County. 'They ran and we pursued, firing on them, and killed one of their horses. Two of them were badly wounded and were captured within a mile of where we started. One of them had his horse shot and had to stop and we captured him. The other ran about eight miles, and after being wounded, blew his brains out.... We buried him as well as we could and then came back.' [9]

DEATH ON PIRATE ISLAND

When Captain Jones was ordered to El Paso County to quiet disturbances along the river around Ysleta and San Elizario, he wrote: 'If I am sent back to El Paso County, I hope you can allow me to take more than four men. Old "residenters" say that four men will simply be murdered and will do no good... there must be fully fifty men in the gang that has caused so much trouble and they are well organized too. They are part of the mob who murdered Howard some years ago.' [10] Just six weeks later, Captain Frank Jones fell on Pirate Island at the hands of the gang to which he referred. At the time he had five men.

Pirate Island is an island only by definition. When the United States and Mexico established by treaty the boundary line between the two countries, it was determined that the line should be the *then* bed of the river. The Rio Grande overruled the international agreement, and in 1854 shifted its channel southward, leaving a part of Mexico on the north side of the river, and leaving an irregular area — Pirate Island — several miles long and six miles wide between the new bed and the old one.

The 'island,' covered with such brush and herbage as grow in the valley of the desert river, soon became the rendezvous of a lawless element. The Mexican law hardly dared cross the Rio Grande to this cut-off territory and Texas authorities had no legal jurisdiction

[8] Frank Jones to General W. H. Mabry, October 22, 1891. A.G.P.

[9] *Ibid.*, October 24, 1891. A.G.P.

[10] *Ibid.*, April 16, 1893. A.G.P.

there. In this no man's land resided some three hundred Mexicans, among them a set of desperate characters known as the Olguin family. The little ranch in which this family lived was known as Tres Jacales — the Three Huts.

At the head of this patriarchal tribe was old Clato Olguin whose fighting days were over. He had been a real border man in his time, but age had slowed him up until he could do no more now than stand in his *jacale* door and scowl in surly manner at the agents of the law who dared worry his breed. His three sons — Jesús María, Antonio, and Pedro — were in their prime and had made some progress in the family's chosen profession of crime. Jesús María had been charged with cattle theft and indicted for resisting arrest.

It was the unsuccessful attempt of Deputy Sheriff R. E. Bryant to arrest Jesús María and his son Severio for cattle theft that brought Captain Frank Jones and the Rangers to Pirate Island. On June 29, 1893, a squad consisting of Captain Jones, Corporal Karl Kirchner, Privates F. F. Tucker, E. D. Aten, J. W. Saunders, and Deputy R. E. Bryant left Ysleta with writs for the arrest of Jesús María Olguin and his son Severio. The party camped that night five miles below San Elizario and at daybreak the next morning, rode 'straight across the Island for the Olguins Ranch,' some five miles from their camping place. They rounded up the ranch, but found no one save old Clato, some women and a boy. The men they wanted had evidently crossed the international border to the house of Antonio.

The Rangers continued up the river by a road that crisscrossed the boundary in such a way that the traveler never knew whether he was in Texas or in Mexico. After riding about three miles, the men spied two mounted Mexicans who, at sight of the officers, wheeled their horses and ran, with the Rangers in pursuit.

After a chase of three hundred yards, the Mexicans arrived at a little settlement of four houses, three on the right and one on the left. The two fleeing Mexicans — one of whom was Jesús María — quit their horses and dodged into one of these houses.

By the time the Rangers reached the second house where five or six Mexicans were congregated, Corporal Kirchner was in the lead, and as he passed a volley was fired on him putting the magazine of his Winchester out of action. Saunders came next, followed by Aten, who fired the first shot by the Rangers, using his six-shooter. When Captain Jones came under fire, he halted within thirty feet of the door and returned the fire with his Winchester. In the meantime Kirchner, Saunders, and Aten whirled their horses and returned to him. Bryant and Tucker were also close by. During this time the Mexicans

THE DEATH OF CAPTAIN FRANK JONES

were firing on the Rangers from the door of the adobe hut, from a porthole, and from a wall which flanked the house.

The second volley fired after the Rangers dismounted broke Captain Jones's thigh, causing him to fall. He straightened his broken leg out in front of him and fired two or three more shots when a Mexican ball struck him just over the heart. Tucker stood over him as he fell.

'Captain, are you hurt?' asked the Ranger.

'Yes, shot all to pieces.' A moment later, when the fatal bullet struck him, he said, 'Boys, I am killed,' and fell back dead.

The reports do not reveal what happened in the few minutes following Captain Jones's death. Since Severio Olguin had received a broken arm and Jesús María had been shot through the right hand, it is not improbable that the Mexicans, taking advantage of the excitement caused by Jones's death, quitted the scene.

Bryant told the Rangers that they had crossed the line into Mexico, were within a mile of the main plaza of Tres Jacales, and that a courier had sped to Guadalupe to fetch soldiers and men who would be upon them in fifteen minutes.

'My first decision,' wrote Corporal Kirchner, 'was to stay with our dead Captain and kill or capture the Mexicans, but after waiting about forty-five minutes, I saw from the appearance of everything we would be overpowered and murdered [and] so we retreated to this side and thence to San Elizario where I found it impossible to get a single white man to assist me.'

Kirchner wired the Rangers at Ysleta to come and bring all available help. The Rangers came, bringing three citizens, and the sheriff brought a posse of sixteen men from El Paso by special train. The Texans now went to the state line and demanded the body of Captain Jones, which was delivered on July 2 by order of the authorities at Juarez.

In the meantime Colonel Martínez of Juarez, while on his way with Sheriff Simmonds to deliver Captain Jones's body, met Jesús María Olguin and Antonio, the ex-convict, in a short bend of the road. The Mexican escort arrested them and at Tres Jacales captured Severio, and placed them in jail at Juarez. The records do not show what disposition was finally made of them, though it is a safe guess that they went free.

At the time of the fight, a detachment of Rangers was stationed at Alpine under Sergeant John R. Hughes. Sergeant Hughes came to Ysleta and assumed command of the Rangers. He succeeded in recovering most of Captain Jones's effects, including a Winchester, watch, spurs, belt, and money. Corporal Tucker lost his horse, saddle, and handcuffs. All were recovered save the captain's pistol and the corporal's handcuffs. Sergeant Hughes succeeded Captain Jones in command of Company D and for many years continued to render service in the Trans-Pecos country.[11]

PUGILISM IN EL PASO

In February, 1896, practically the entire Ranger force was sent to El Paso to prevent a prize fight between Bob Fitzsimmons and Pete Maher, promoted by Dan Stuart and similar men of the El Paso sporting fraternity. Captains Rogers, Hughes, McDonald, and Brooks went with General Mabry to El Paso and observed the unloading of the ring paraphernalia. A captain with one or two men dogged the heels of Fitzsimmons, Maher, and Dan Stuart, wherever they went. The promoters put out the report that Bat Masterson was coming with a hundred fighting men to see that the contest came off on schedule. Bat was present, but he made no attempt to have a showdown with the Rangers.

When it became evident that the fight could not be held in Texas,

[11] Corporal Karl Kirchner to W. H. Mabry, July 2, 1893; George W. Baylor to Mabry, July 9, 1893; John R. Hughes to Mabry, July 1, September 4 and 6, and November 24, 1893. In addition to these there are a number of letters and documents in the A.G.P. bearing on the international phase, but these are of little importance in this account.

TEXAS RANGERS AT EL PASO TO PREVENT FITZSIMMONS-MAHER PRIZE FIGHT, FEBRUARY, 1896

Pete Maher developed acute ophthalmia as an excuse for the delay, and in the meanwhile a search was begun for some neutral strip such as Pirate Island where the fight could be held, but the Rangers made it plain that there could be no fight on neutral ground. Another plan was to cross the state line and allow the gamblers to change their money in New Mexico, but the United States government refused the use of the territory; they then talked of Old Mexico, but the governor of Chihuahua blocked that plan.

Finally bag and baggage were loaded on the train and the entire party set out for the East with the Rangers on board. Pete Maher's eyes improved so much that by the time the train reached Langtry, near the border of Coahuila, he was in condition to fight; the party crossed the river and held the contest, while the Rangers remained on the American side. To discredit the Rangers the report was sent out that they too had crossed, but this was emphatically denied by General Mabry.

There was no clash anywhere between the Rangers and the touts of the square ring. Even the great Bat Masterson saw fit to observe the polite decorum that is customary between armed men. There is a report that Bat forgot his manners at Sanderson, where the train stopped for lunch in the desert. A Chinese waiter was unable to serve the large crowd that flowed from the train into the wayside eating joint. Bat became impatient and began abusing the Chinaman and this was all right with the Rangers; but when Masterson picked up a castor as if to hit the Chinaman, McDonald protested in his usual mild manner. Masterson, more exasperated, no doubt, by the Rangers than by the Chinaman, challenged McDonald with —

'Maybe *you'd* like to take it up.'

'I done took it up,' was the quiet answer.

It is needless to say that an awkward move on the part of either man would have made plenty of excitement. There is no intimation that Bat Masterson was afraid, but neither were the Texas Rangers, who carried the law to the worst gunmen that ever trod the arid reaches of West Texas

BANK ROBBERS SWING HIGH

While all the Texas Rangers were in El Paso to prevent the Fitzsimmons–Pete Maher prize fight, a gang of men led by Kid Lewis made a raid on the City National Bank of Wichita Falls, killed the cashier, Frank Dorsey, wounded the bookkeeper, secured six hundred dollars in gold and silver, mounted their horses and rode for the creek bottoms. McDonald received a telegram on the train asking him to come to the scene, and when he reached Wichita Falls two hours later, he found horses waiting for him and his five men. The citizens who gave chase to the robbers wounded one horse, but permitted the fugitives to escape. The Rangers took the trail, and even though it was February, they followed it through stream and thicket and finally captured two men and a sack of money.

When the Rangers arrived at the jail, they found a mob waiting to take charge of the prisoners who after some strategy were landed in jail. McDonald now made preparations to take the prisoners to Fort Worth for safe-keeping, but this move was objected to by the district judge.

For some reason, which is not quite clear, McDonald refused to stay at the jail. In his reports to the adjutant general and the governor, he declared that he was suffering from wounds which he had received in the Matthews fight, that it was not his business to guard prisoners, and that he had many calls to duty elsewhere that could not be ignored. At any rate Captain Bill pulled out, taking all the Rangers with him. That night, February 25, 1896, the mob hanged the murderers and bank robbers to the telegraph poles adjacent to the bank where they had committed their crime.

The protests about McDonald's actions were so vigorous that General Mabry requested him to make a full report. A part of his letter is given to show with what vigor he could express himself, even when his cause was not, on the face of things, the very best. His letter ran in part as follows:

'I would like very much to say, were I not writing to my superiors in office, that I have no apologies to make, as I did my whole duty in the Wichita Falls affair. We ran the bank robbers down, caught them and turned them over to the jailer who was deputy sheriff.'

He then related that twenty-five deputies were sworn in, and he told how Judge Miller cursed and abused the sheriff for not being present and for not protecting the prisoners under his care. 'I told the Judge that if he was to abuse me that way he would certainly get action, and he said I was not as trifling as M—— and of course I would not take it.... I don't boast about what I would do, but I certainly would not allow anybody to curse and abuse me in that manner and I was not mealy mouthed about so stating at the time.... But General there must always be some one to attach all the blame to and when they can not find any one else the poorly paid Ranger, who dares open his mouth, gets all the blame and some of us can stand a reasonable amount of abuse (at long range.)' [12]

DEAD HORSE THIEVES ON DAVIS MOUNTAINS

On September 24, 1896, W. R. Martin, division superintendent of the G. H. & S. A. Railroad, received a telegram from J. B. Gillett stating that some horse thieves were camped fifteen miles north of Altuda and were making plans to rob a train. The superintendent asked Captain Hughes to take his men on the train to Alpine and break up the plan. The Rangers loaded three horses and a pack-mule on the baggage car at 10:30 P.M. By daylight the next morning Captain Hughes, Thalis T. Cook, and R. E. Bryant unloaded their horses, mule, and saddles in Alpine, where they were joined by a man named Combs who had lost a fine race horse and by Deputy Sheriff Jim Pool of Presidio County, and by an expert trailer, Jim Stroud, whose scent for the trail had been made keener by the loss of a prize stallion.

[12] McDonald to W. H. Mabry, April 4, 1896. A.G.P.

RANGERS OF THE EIGHTIES

This photograph shows J. H. Rogers (second from left in top row) and J. B. Brooks (fourth from left) before they became officers. Captain Will Scott is between them.

It was the morning of September 27 before the trail of mounted men was found leading out of the Glass Mountains. Though it rained all day, the hunters managed to keep the trail which, on the morning of September 28, led into the pasture of McCutchen Brothers. The Rangers feared that if they continued on the trail with the pack-mule, the men whom they were pursuing would see them from the mountains, recognize them as Texas Rangers, and quit the country. Consequently they resorted to the strategy of sending McCutchen's cowboys out with the ostensible purpose of hunting cattle. Each cowboy was accompanied by a Texas Ranger who could pass for a cowboy anywhere.

Cook and party found a trail in the Star pasture which they followed into a little side canyon where two men raised up with guns aimed and ordered them to turn back if they did not want to be killed. Cook, who lacked nothing in courage, bantered with them and asked them if they were not joking. The spokesman cursed Cook and told him that seven guns were trained on the Rangers who would be killed if they advanced. Cook tried to persuade his companions to charge, but they decided to go for help instead, and left him to hold the bandits while they rode seven miles to the ranch and back. Cook took cover and attempted to hold the enemy at bay until reinforcements could arrive.

After a time Cook retired towards the ranch and met Captain Hughes and men coming to his rescue. As they rode back, Cook and Hughes laid out the plan of battle. Three men were to charge at full-speed to a protected position within firing range of the concealed men, while the others were to scatter and come in from the sides. When Cook and Hughes came within about three hundred yards of a small peak which rose some two hundred feet above the plain, a shot was fired and a bullet whizzed by.

'Where was that shot?' asked Cook.

'From that mountain top,' answered the Captain.

'We ran our horses almost to the top of the mountain,' wrote Captain Hughes, 'when the fight was so hot that we dismounted. Here McCombs got a bullet through the ear. We drove them off the mountain top to the side where two of them were killed.'

When one of these had received two wounds, he yelled, 'I have got enough.'

'Hands up then, and come out,' demanded Thalis Cook. Instead of obeying, the man fired again and thereafter he was beyond the power of surrender. A third man made his escape into the valley 'dodging and shooting.' The Rangers called to him to surrender, but he continued shooting, and finally mounted a horse and got away.

In the camp were found five horses, including Combs's race horse and Stroud's stallion. The two dead men were identified, hauled to Fort Davis in a buckboard supplied by McCutchen, and 'given a decent burial.'

Captain Hughes, in his official report, related an incident of the fight which is worthy of preservation. The story is told in Hughes's own words, slightly amended as to punctuation.

'When we were saddling up at the ranch a pale-looking man came to the fence and said if he had a horse he would go with us. I offered him a horse and told him to come on. He could only find a pistol, and I did not try to find him a gun as he looked like he was not able to carry one. When we made the charge on the mountain, he was right with us, and using his pistol. When the heat of the fight was over I looked and saw the boy by my side *with a gun.*

'I asked where he got the gun and he said he got it from "that man," pointing to a dead man.

'I asked him if he had plenty of cartridges. He said he had not, but [that] there was a belt full on the dead man.

'I told him to get them. He did so and returned to me and asked me what to do.

'After everything was over, I asked who the boy was and learned his name was Arthur McMaster. He had been sick and was staying at McCutchen's ranch.' [13]

It is needless to say that this invalid could have had a place in the Ranger camp at any time his health would have permitted.

VACCINATION WITH THE SIX-SHOOTER

Along the middle border of the Rio Grande, conditions were quiet in the last two decades of the nineteenth century owing to the dictatorial rule of President Díaz. The iron rule of the dictator did not prevent the smallpox from breaking out each spring nor keep it from spreading among the Mexicans on the Texas side of the river. When the local health officer undertook to establish a quarantine, put all the smallpox patients in what the Ranger in his report termed the 'pest house' and vaccinate those not yet infected, he ran into strong resistance. The Mexicans preferred to enjoy their smallpox undisturbed. A call for help was sent to Captain J. H. Rogers, Company E, who came with Ranger A. Y. Old to assist Dr. Blunt in establishing the quarantine regulations.

On March 19, 1899, the two Rangers set out with the physician to remove the smallpox patients from their homes. They found the streets crowded with excited Mexicans who became riotous when the officers broke down the doors behind which the smallpox victims had barricaded themselves. Later in the day the Mexican mob attacked the local officers with stones and firearms, and wounded one policeman. The Rangers came to the scene and managed to restore order, but the physician was compelled to cease operations while Captain Rogers wired Sergeant Dubose at Cotulla to bring all available Rangers to Laredo.

On the morning of March 20, Sergeant Dubose and two men came in on a freight train and were met at the station by Captain Rogers, who sent them to the Hamilton Hotel to await developments. Captain Rogers and Ranger Old went with the local officers to the eastern part of the town to search for arms which were reported to be concealed by the Mexicans. They encountered the first resistance at the home of Agipito Herrera, where a number of armed Mexicans had congregated, some of whom attempted to pass across an alley to a vacant house. When they were ordered back, two of them obeyed. The third

[13] Report of John R. Hughes, October 4, 1896. A.G.P.

attempted to shoot, but Rogers shot first and the Mexican, to quote the report, 'disappeared.' Herrera made his escape from the local officers — Mexicans, who made no effort to support the Rangers — but soon reappeared with several companions armed with Winchesters. The Mexican shot Captain Rogers through the right shoulder before he fell with a shot in the breast and two in the head. Refugia Herrera, sister of the dead man, was wounded in the arm and Santiago Grinaldo 'was shot through the bowels.' The Rangers, having driven the enemy to cover, retired from the place under a shower of stones hurled by the women.

In the meantime the Rangers at the hotel came to the place to find a hundred Mexicans, twenty-five of them armed, surrounding the body of the dead Mexican. As the Rangers turned into the street, the firing was resumed on both sides and ended with the Rangers in possession of the field. Four wounded Mexicans were captured, four crossed the river into Mexico, and others escaped to the brush. The trouble ended with the appearance of the United States troops under Captain Ayers.[14]

There are many stories among the Rangers of their services in smallpox epidemics along the river. One is about a big Ranger whose knowledge of the sixshooter was superior to his knowledge of therapeutics. He was instructed to go to a certain Mexican hut which had been occupied by a smallpox patient and fumigate it with formaldehyde. The Ranger had had no experience with formaldehyde, and he understood that he was to fumigate the inhabitants as well as the contents of the *jacales*. The Mexicans were easily persuaded to remain in the cottage while the Ranger lighted the candles and withdrew to let the fumes do their work. In a short time he was joined by coughing, sneezing Mexicans. He ordered them back to the house and they went obediently enough, but were soon out again, and no persuasion could induce them to return. Orders were orders, and finding all methods of persuasion useless, the big Texan seized two or three of them and dragged them bodily into the house and shut the door, determined to hold them until the fumigation was complete. It took him but a short time to develop great sympathy with the Mexicans, so much, in fact, that tears began to stream from his eyes, and he, with the Mexicans at his heels, burst into the open. It is 'norated' in Ranger camps that he reported to his captain that he fumigated the houses, but was unable to do a very good job on the inhabitants.

[14] Sergeant H. G. Dubose to General Thomas Scurry, March 28, 1899. A.G.P.

3. THE DISSOLUTION OF THE FRONTIER BATTALION

The existence of the Frontier Battalion for nearly twenty years after the frontier had been closed made of it an institutional anachronism. Its primary function had long been to guard the border people from Indians, Mexicans, and border outlaws. The companies were always stationed on the fringe of settlement, and operated mainly in regions where local authority was non-existent or too weak to cope with the lawless element.

The basis upon which active opposition to such a force was founded was the unfriendly attitude of the Anglo-American towards a centralized police power. The people of Texas were frequently reminded of the Reconstruction days when the state police exercised arbitrary powers. The resentment of the criminal class to the Texas Ranger can be counted upon at all times. This group is augmented by the criminal's relatives and friends, who have constituted an influential part of many communities at times. Another source of opposition has come from local peace officers, who often resent the implication that they are not competent to handle local situations. As long as the counties were unorganized, the Rangers had a free hand in controlling crime, but with county organization it was essential that the Rangers work in co-operation with sheriffs and other officers. In some instances the peace officers were in league with the criminals, and joined with them in opposition to the Rangers.

The criminal lawyer, with his pecuniary interest in crime, could be counted on to throw every legal obstacle possible in the way of the Ranger force. There is no way of tracing the subtle influence of this class in shaping Ranger legislation for the past forty years, but it has no doubt been considerable.

The Rangers, after they became primarily an interior force, were often subject to just criticism because of their own bad conduct and indiscretion. The organization has throughout its history, with the exception of comparatively brief periods, had exceptionally good men in it. Unfortunately, it has also had men who reflected no credit on it. If a man is inclined to be a rowdy or braggart, overbearing or malicious, he has no business with the commission, the prestige, and the arms of a Texas Ranger. If a little liquor is mixed with any of these bad qualities, it is certain to expose them to view and to subject the individual and the organization to general criticism. On the whole, however, the men were of exceptional character. The immediate reason for the decline of the prestige of the Frontier Battalion, and for its final dissolution, was the fact that the Rangers had practically worked themselves out of a job by destroying the forces of crime that supported them.

It was after the Frontier Battalion had performed this great service that some shrewd lawyer took occasion to read the law creating the force in 1874 and discovered a way to paralyze the effectiveness of the Rangers. The part of the law over which the issue was raised read as follows:

> Each *officer* of the battalion... shall have all the powers of a peace officer, and it shall be his duty to execute all criminal process directed to him, and make arrests under capias properly issued of any and all parties charged with offenses against the laws of this State.[15]

Anyone except a lawyer would have recognized that the intent of the framers of the law was that every Ranger in the Frontier Battalion was an officer, and that as such he had all the powers of a peace officer. The lawyers saw that they could make other lawyers see that *only the officers* of the Frontier Battalion had such powers and that the privates had no such powers. Therefore, any private who arrested a criminal was guilty of false imprisonment and subject to arrest and prosecution. When this technicality was discovered, many charges of false imprisonment were made against the Rangers in different parts of the state, and warrants were issued for their arrest. The fact that they had been operating under the law for more than a quarter of a century, during which time they must have imprisoned thousands of criminals, had no effect on the situation. The question was submitted to Governor Joseph D. Sayers, who asked his attorney general for an opinion, which was rendered by T. S. Smith, May 26, 1900. The attorney general's ruling effectually destroyed the authority of every private and non-commissioned officer and in reality destroyed the Frontier Battalion. In part the opinion reads: 'My conclusion is that the non-commissioned officers and privates of the frontier batallion... referred to... as "rangers" have no authority... to execute criminal process or make arrests, and that only the commissioned officers of that organization have that power.' [16]

The force that Governor Richard Coke had called into being and

[15] Adjutant General Thomas Scurry, General Order No. 24, May 26, 1900. A.G.P. Italics mine.

[16] Adjutant General Thomas Scurry, General Order No. 24, May 26, 1900. A.G.P. In the reorganization of the Rangers' force in 1935 the legislature apparently made the same error that it made in 1874. Section 11 reads in part: 'The officers shall be clothed with all the powers of peace officers, etc.' If the ruling of the attorney general in 1900 is accepted, then the courts must declare the law of 1935 defective since it confers the powers of peace officers on the captains only.

that Major John B. Jones had organized and developed into a fighting machine to drive out the Indians, hold back the Mexican marauders, stop the feuds, and break up the gangs of cow and horse thieves, of stage and train robbers, and kill or capture murderers, was no more. The Frontier Battalion had pushed the frontier from the Nueces to the El Paso section of the Rio Grande; it had gone with the cattle from central Texas to the Palo Duro and even to the farthest corner of the Panhandle. It had made Texas a fairly safe place in which to live. Now its members were asked to lay down their arms, apparently because some lawyer had for a criminal's fee read the law and learned that the privates in the Frontier Battalion were not officers, but in reality, because there was no longer a frontier. Though the Battalion followed the frontier into the past, it left behind a tradition of courage and heroic individual action which is unsurpassed by any organization in any country in the world. To the names of Jack Hays, Ben McCulloch and Samuel H. Walker, who founded the tradition, and of Rip Ford who upheld it in the middle period prior to the Civil War, must be added the names of John B. Jones, L. H. McNelly, Lee Hall, John B. Armstrong, N. O. Reynolds, G. W. Arrington, Dan Roberts, George W. Baylor, C. L. Nevill, June Peak, and many others, including privates whose names cannot be given.

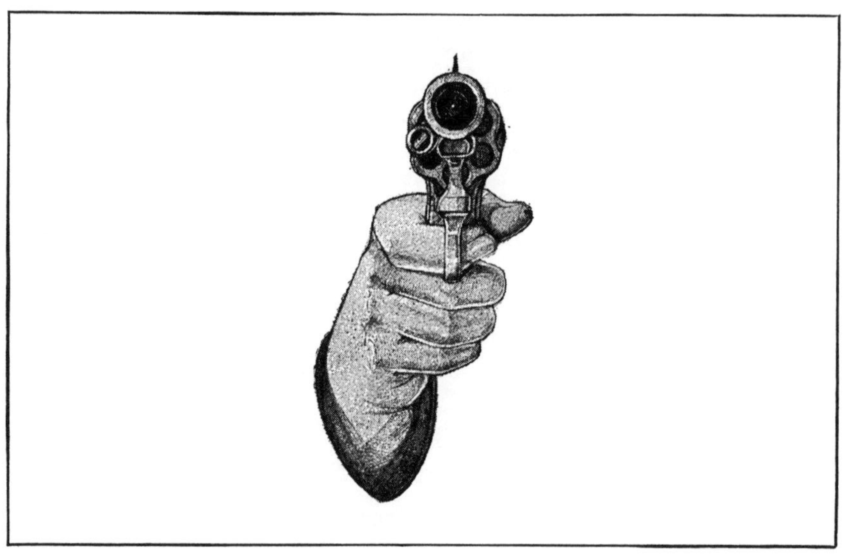

XX

THE TEXAS RANGERS IN THE TWENTIETH CENTURY

No man in the wrong can stand up against a fellow that's in the right and keeps on a-comin'.

Captain BILL McDONALD

The fact that the Rangers are kept on the move has a wonderfully deterrent influence over thieves, who are unable to keep trace of them and constantly fear being surprised and captured by them.

Adjutant-General's Report

My men are crack shots and I am not afraid of them getting the worst of anything.

Captain J. A. BROOKS

We got him and I chained him up. There is no way of holding a prisoner here except to chain him with chain and lock. It is very unpleasant for one Ranger to have to police a tough place like this.

Captain J. A. BROOKS

XX. THE TEXAS RANGERS IN THE TWENTIETH CENTURY

THE governor did not view with equanimity the prospect of abolishing completely the organization which had done so much to restore order in Texas. The attorney general rendered a second opinion which permitted a reorganization on a temporary basis, until the legislature could amend the defective law of 1874. The Battalion was reduced to four companies of six men each, three officers and three privates to a company. All arrests had to be made by a commissioned officer, but he could summon the privates to assist him.

This skeleton organization functioned from June 1, 1900, to July 8, 1901, when the law creating the new Ranger force became effective. By this law the governor was 'authorized to organize a force to be known as the "ranger force" for the purpose of protecting the frontier against marauding or thieving parties, and for the suppression of lawlessness and crime throughout the state.' [1]

The arms, equipment, and regulations of the new Ranger force were not materially changed from what they had been with the Frontier Battalion. The captains were permitted to choose their own men, but were admonished to select only men who were courageous, discreet, honest, temperate, and of good families. The Rangers were still mounted men, though they frequently traveled — often with their horses — on the trains which now penetrated all parts of the state. They furnished their own horses and horse equipment; but they wore no uniform and carried no badge.

1. THE FOUR CAPTAINS

The new Ranger Force comprised four companies of not more than twenty men each. The four captains and the quartermaster with the rank of captain were appointed by the governor. Each captain selected his own men and nominated his sergeant, the only minor officer.

[1] Adjutant General Thomas Scurry, General Order No. 62, July 3, 1901. A.G.P.

The officers were the men who had already won distinction in the Frontier Battalion. Captain J. A. Brooks was given Company A with headquarters at Alice; Captain W. J. McDonald continued with Company B at Amarillo; Captain J. H. Rogers commanded Company C at Fort Hancock; Captain John R. Hughes had charge of Company D at El Paso; and L. P. Sieker, quartermaster, was at Austin. Each of them was as courageous as the tradition required; all had their mettle of courage tested many times. They were equal to their opportunities, but with the passing of the frontier, the chances for gaining distinction had diminished.

Of the four, Captain W. J. (Bill) McDonald is most widely known, not because he was more deserving than the others, but because he had the ability to stage himself before the public; he capitalized the tradition, perhaps unconsciously, and made himself the symbol of all it had been. He was himself a frontier phrase-maker and coiner of epigrams, and was so picturesque and daring that others coined phrases about him. He called himself a 'brother-in-law of the church' because his wife was a member; if a man wanted to fight, Bill invited him 'to fly at it'; and he once declared that he could stand a lot of abuse — at long range. He was responsible for the story, now a worn-out chestnut, about the call for a company of Rangers to quell a mob. When a lone Ranger got off the train — Bill McDonald, of course — there was vigorous protest from the citizen committee at his inadequacy to control the situation. 'Well, you ain't got but one mob, have you?' he inquired sweetly. Though there is some basis for the story, there is no basis for anyone's ever telling it to a Texas Ranger because each one has had to laugh at it a thousand times. It seems to be the only story that the public remembers about the Rangers.

When Captain Bill started out alone to talk to a mob of strikers, someone protested at the danger. Bill replied that he was 'a pretty good single-handed talker.' When Captain Bill and one Ranger, according to his account, marched into Fort Brown, and made twenty negro soldiers who had their weapons trained on him 'put up them guns,' an army officer was said to have declared that 'Bill McDonald would charge hell with a bucket of water.'

There were other circumstances which added to Captain McDonald's reputation. He was stationed in the interior while his three companions were on the border. He had good social qualities, plenty of salty talk, and a wide acquaintanceship with newspaper men and politicians. Moreover, Bill McDonald dominated his men, kept himself in the foreground and used them for a background, while other captains were willing to direct their men and keep themselves out of the public eye

CAPTAIN JOHN R. HUGHES, AFTER HIS RANGER DAYS

as much as possible. Bill was always on hand at Democratic conventions, went wolf-hunting in Oklahoma with Theodore Roosevelt, and at the suggestion of Colonel E. M. House, had his biography written by Albert Bigelow Paine. Not caring particularly for Republicans, Bill made Roosevelt pay for his company on the wolf hunt with a letter about it — and Bill — which was reproduced on the fly-leaf of the book.[2] The two men had much in common.

To his other gifts Bill added a good fighting Scotch name, a fine

[2] Albert Bigelow Paine, *Captain Bill McDonald, Texas Ranger: A Story of Frontier Reform.* This sketch of McDonald is based on this volume.

face lined with sun, wind, and character, a pair of mild blue eyes, a soft voice, and a 'suddenness' — things that made him irresistible to friend or enemy. In every sense of the word, Bill McDonald was what athletes call a natural. The philosophy that supported him, and had supported all the great Rangers before him, Bill McDonald articulated in striking phrases: 'No man in the wrong can stand up against a fellow that's in the right and keeps on a-comin'.'

Brooks, Hughes, and Rogers, though lacking McDonald's showmanship, were his equal in every respect as officers, and in the opinion of many, were superior. They were quiet, unobtrusive men — not good single-handed talkers, not colorful or spectacular, but dependable, intelligent, and wise in the ways of criminals. Captain Brooks served for many years as county judge of Brooks County, which was named for him; Captain Hughes became president of an Austin bank, but continued to reside in El Paso. Until his death Captain Rogers served at intervals in the Ranger force. Throughout his life he was noted for his deep religious nature, and, as a staunch Presbyterian, he was much more than a 'brother-in-law to the church.' He frequently served as president of the Sunday School, and on more than one occasion he was called from church to 'go after' a criminal or restore order in a disturbed community. His six-shooter and Bible were his constant companions, but he was heard to remark once that he thought more of the Bible than he did of the gun. He was exceptional in this respect.

A citizen of the border has summed up the border's opinion of three of the captains, comparing them with McNelly, whose name still lives on the river.

'McNelly was always the ideal. He seems not to have had a single weakness. For McNelly, the man, as well as for McNelly, the officer, the border had the utmost respect. The reputation he bore, among the Americans and Mexicans alike, was that of a gentleman always, but possessed of keen insight and comprehending mind; just, cool, and courageous; daring, but — and even more important for his border reputation — always considerate of the safety and well-being of his men, and of the moral rights of his prisoners.

'Brooks, a generation later, stood, in his way, equally well, although there was always a distinction in the border's regard for these two captains. By this, I mean that while the reputation of both McNelly and Brooks was that of strong, just, and fearless men, Brooks had not McNelly's reputation for insight into the hearts and minds of men.

'Rogers... was regarded almost as well. There was just one quality that the Border held against Rogers, and that was one which would have added to his reputation in another portion of the state. He was a bit too much the Presbyterian — the Sunday School man — to wholly please the Border....

'Hughes had a mixed reputation. With many of those who knew him, he took a place next to McNelly amongst border captains and peace officers. Others... rated him... below Brooks and Rogers. Their charge against him was that he was susceptible of being influenced by clever stories and lacked the ability of McNelly, Brooks, and Rogers to distinguish, in this regard, between the true and the false.' [3]

The miscellaneous activities of the Rangers during 1900 and 1901 appear in the following facts gleaned from the annual report. On November 1, 1900, Captain Brooks and two Rangers escorted eight railroad machinists from San Antonio to Yoakum, where a strike was on. On November 4, McDonald took his company from Amarillo to Cotulla to preserve order during an election. November 24 found Captain Rogers and two Rangers protecting prisoners from a mob in Hempstead, and in December, Captain L. P. Sieker went to Tucson, Arizona, and returned with a man accused of forging a pardon for a life-termer in the penitentiary.

On January 20, 1901, Captain Brooks and three Rangers went to Houston and Galveston to arrest the prize-fighters, Choynski and Johnson. The Rangers appeared at the ring in disguise, their identity known only to Judge John Lovejoy. In the third round Johnson was knocked out and the Rangers arrested the men, but because of public sentiment, no indictments could be secured.

The Rangers' influence — over and above their acts — were described by the adjutant general in his report of 1901–02: 'The fact that the Rangers are kept on the move has a wonderfully deterrent influence over thieves, who are unable to keep trace of them and constantly fear being surprised and captured by them.' [4]

2. *SOME BORDER EPISODES*

COW THIEVES AND MIGRATORY LABOR

In December, 1902, Company D was moved from Fort Hancock in El Paso County to Alice in Nueces, with a detachment at Brownsville. There was little to do at Alice except to watch for stolen stock that might be driven there for shipment.

[3] Harbert Davenport to W. P. Webb, December 26, 1934.

[4] Adjutant General's Report, 1901–02.

'At Brownsville we found entirely different conditions,' wrote Captain Hughes. There were reports of cattle being stolen all the time. 'At one time we brought in 100 head of cattle to Brownsville.' Most of this stock was identified and claimed by citizens of the town and country thereabout. There were many calves among the herd, stolen from the milk pens. The citizens brought their children, little boys and girls, down to the corral where the Rangers held the cattle. 'The children went into the corral, called the calves by their names, caught them and led them out and home.' Many of the cattle were branded, but the brands had been burned by the thieves.

At another time the Rangers brought twenty-five head from Starr County. Sixty complaints were made against one man, but only twenty-four indictments were found.

Captain Hughes spoke of the migratory laborers who had begun to cross the river and go north in Texas for seasonal work. Among them was a numerous and an increasing number of criminals who did not go to chop or pick cotton, but to gamble, peddle mescal, and steal. About the time they started from the Rio Grande, reports would begin to come in of horses and cattle being stolen from both sides of the river. When cold weather drove them south, reports of a like nature would come from the interior. 'We have captured a great many of these people and returned the stock to the owners, but so long as the farmers in the interior of Texas continue to employ these people, the conditions will exist and the Rangers will be needed to catch them.'[5]

AMBUSH AT BROWNSVILLE

In 1902, Captain J. A. Brooks had to deal with a very serious situation which grew out of the theft of cattle from the King Ranch. In May, 1902, Sergeant A. Y. Baker, Ranger Harry Wallis, and Ranger W. E. Roebuck were sent to scout the King pastures and catch the thieves. While riding out El Saenz pasture, the Rangers came upon a *vaquero* whose business it was to watch the fence line. The fact that the fence rider was three miles from a fence caused the Rangers to suspect that either he was acting as a lookout for the real thieves or that he was himself searching for unbranded calves; they immediately tied him to a tree and left him there until their work was finished.

On the following morning, May 16, at about nine o'clock, the Rangers found two or three unbranded calves tied to bushes or trees, and, feeling sure that their game was near, they scattered to search the brush. Sergeant Baker soon came upon a Mexican who was in the act of

[5] John R. Hughes to General John A. Hulen, September 5, 1904. A.G.P.

'WHILE THE HORSE WAS FALLING, BAKER SHOT THE MEXICAN IN THE HEAD'

branding a calf. The Mexican, armed with two six-shooters, fired at Baker, but the Ranger's horse shied at the click of the weapon and received in the head the bullet which otherwise would have struck the rider. While the horse was falling, Baker shot the Mexican in the head with a soft-nosed Winchester bullet. The dead man was recognized as Ramon De La Cerda whose family owned a small ranch adjoining the King estate.

The killing of young De La Cerda caused intense excitement and led directly to three more killings. Though the inquest indicated that Baker had acted in self-defense, the Mexicans and their sympathizers were not satisfied; six days after the body was buried, it was secretly disinterred for a second inquest in which 'evidence' was produced to the effect that De La Cerda had been dragged and otherwise maltreated. Public sentiment was sharply divided between the Rangers and those who for personal or political motives opposed them. The findings of the secret inquest, together with the wild rumors growing out of it, only served to inflame the minds of De La Cerda's supporters. Captain Brooks reported that Baker made bond in the sum of ten thousand dollars, and that he was supported by such people as the Kings, Major John Armstrong — McNelly's lieutenant — and Lyman Brothers.

The killing of De La Cerda was taken up by the Red Club, and inflammatory speeches condemning the Rangers by name as official murderers were published in a small Mexican newspaper.

The Rangers, stung by the abuse heaped upon them and by the threats made against their lives, dealt harshly with their enemies. Ranger Puckett whipped a Mexican with his quirt for stealing his trousers, and Ranger Wallis slapped a customs inspector who was supporting the paper that had been abusing the Rangers. Word came to A. Y. Baker that Alfreda Cerda, younger brother of Ramon, was seeking an opportunity to avenge his brother's death. Captain Brooks was present through all the trouble, and in one of his reports said: 'My men are crack shots and I am not afraid of them getting the worst of anything.'

The summer wore through before further serious trouble occurred. It came on the night of September 9 when an attempt was made to assassinate A. Y. Baker from ambush. Baker, Roebuck, and Jesse Miller, a cowboy from the King Ranch, were riding from town towards their camp in Judge J. B. Wells's 'little pasture' when they were fired upon from the brush by men who were using shotguns and Winchesters. Roebuck, who was riding Baker's horse that night, was killed by a single buckshot that cut the blood vessels of his neck; Miller's horse was killed by a charge of buckshot in the head, while Baker escaped with a slight wound from a single buckshot in the leg.

The excitement was now terrible in Cameron County and more trouble was expected. The district court was suspended and nothing was talked on the street save the murder and its probable outcome. Captain Brooks, who had in the meantime come to his men in Brownsville, began an investigation which resulted in the arrest of six men, including Alfreda De La Cerda, brother of Ramon who had been killed in the King pasture. While the men accused of murdering Roebuck were in jail, the Rangers heard that a mob was forming to lynch them, and reported to Captain Brooks, who promptly sought out the leaders and told them that they could not take the prisoners, the suspected murderers of his own men, without killing him and every Texas Ranger in Brownsville.

Alfred De La Cerda was released from jail on bond, and on October 3, he was killed on Elizabeth Street by A. Y. Baker against whom he had been making threats. Three days later Herculano Berbier, an important witness for Baker, was killed by unknown parties.

As a result of all this trouble, Governor Joseph D. Sayers ordered

General Thomas Scurry to Brownsville to make an investigation. General Scurry made his report on November 11. He did not find ground for censuring the Rangers, though he readily admitted that they had cuffed some of the Cerda crowd without gloves. The grand jury in its report to Judge Stanley Welch commended the Rangers for their services and especially commended Captain Brooks. In protest against the removal of Captain Brooks's Company Judge Welch wrote: 'All the ills of the Cerda killing have settled themselves, and I believe that with the aid of the Rangers under Captain Brooks, crime can be eliminated from Cameron County.... The local constabulary cannot reach the outlaws.' The only change that the judge wanted was an increase in the number of Rangers.[6]

WITH CHAIN AND LOCK

Since 1917 the Texas Rangers have often been called to restore order in the new oil towns. It is of interest that Captain Brooks rendered a similar service as early as 1904. A gas well at Batson had run wild and the gas had killed a number of horses, cattle, hogs, and three men. The destruction was stopped by setting the gas well on fire, but Captain Brooks found much trouble of another nature. He wrote that he had been compelled to take a hand in keeping the peace, which was constantly disturbed by fighting and the discharging of firearms. 'There is,' wrote Captain Brooks, 'bad feeling between the officers and the men who work in the oil field and it will be only a few days before they have it in for me as I have notified all of them that I hoped to keep this place quiet as long as I remain here.' On the night of February 7 one of the gang killed a man who was on his way home, and the next night 'one of the same crowd put on two six-shooters and went out to the west side and run some of the women out, fired off his pistol, and caused some little stir. We got him and I chained him up. There is no way of holding a prisoner here except to chain him with chain and lock. It is very unpleasant for one Ranger to be compelled to police a tough place like this.... The sheriff has not asked for Rangers and I don't think he will.'

In reply General Hulen wrote: 'Your letter... regarding the lawless conditions there gives some insight as to the situation, but you do not suggest or request additional Rangers. I will order as many Rangers

[6] The account of the trouble at Brownsville is based on numerous letters and reports on the affair. The chief sources are as follows: General Thomas Scurry to Governor J. D. Sayers, November 11, 1902, together with a report of his investigations; numerous letters from Captain Brooks to General Scurry; Grand Jury Report, September 18, 1902; Stanley Welch to Governor J. D. Sayers, November 8, 1902; and clippings. A.G.P.

to Batson as you may request. I certainly do not want you to jeopardize your life.' [7] There is no record that Captain Brooks called for additional help.

Captain Brooks resigned from the Ranger service on November 15, 1906. The high esteem in which he was held is attested by the letter written him by Adjutant General W. H. Mabry. After stating that Governor Lanham accepted his resignation with regret, the letter continues: 'The Governor, as well as myself, deeply regrets that it becomes necessary for you to leave the service. You have been a Ranger since 1883, during which time you have served from private to captain; having served as Captain since May, 1889. You have made an enviable record, and the loss of your experience to the State cannot be estimated. You have always most faithfully and excellently performed your duties, and you can and doubtless will, look back upon your long service as an officer of the State with pride and satisfaction.'

HELL AND A BUCKET OF WATER

The incident that brought much renown to Captain Bill McDonald was his courageous investigation of a raid made by negro soldiers on the town of Brownsville on the night of August 13, 1906. It seems that these troops were in a surly mood before they reached Texas because rumor had come to them that they were not wanted there. Their resentment grew when they came into the Jim Crow section and found themselves segregated in cars reserved for their race. The negroes arrived in Brownsville on July 28 and began to drink and conduct themselves in an obnoxious manner. A series of clashes occurred, each of which increased the tension.

The riot came on the night of August 13, a fortnight after the negroes reached Brownsville. Shortly after midnight the signal shots were fired and immediately ten or twenty men — the number was never determined — advanced from the fort and into the town, firing into houses, saloons, and at the officers who came to investigate. They killed a bartender, wounded the chief of police in the arm, and killed his horse. After marching nearly three blocks, they hurried back to the barracks, put up their guns, and returned to their bunks. The raid was over in ten minutes.

Naturally the town of Brownsville was wild with excitement, comparable only to that which existed when Cortinas made his night raid there nearly fifty years before. Major C. W. Penrose began an inves-

[7] Captain J. A. Brooks to General John A. Hulen, January 24, 1904; February 9, 1904; General John A. Hulen to Brooks, February 13, 1904. A.G.P.

tigation and was soon joined by a Major Blocksom, under orders from Washington. The investigation moved slowly, no one was arrested, and to the citizens it seemed that nothing was being accomplished. Numerous telegrams for relief went out to Washington and to Austin, and once more citizen guards patrolled the streets in constant expectation of further trouble. Captain McDonald reached Brownsville on August 21 in company with two of his men, W. T. McCauley and Ryan. Blaze Delling and Sam MacKenzie had come over from Harlingen and were assisting the citizens in patrolling the town and in preserving order.

The Rangers and the citizens' committee had gathered valuable information which was imparted to McDonald, who spent most of the night in making further investigations and in giving the third degree to a colored ex-soldier who ran a saloon and had knowledge of the raid.

The next morning, according to McDonald's account in his biography, he was ready to tackle the negroes in Fort Brown. Leaving three of his Rangers as reserves, he set out with W. J. McCauley for the fort. The citizens protested that the men there were under arms and excited, and that without an order from Major Penrose, the Rangers would be shot down if they attempted to enter. To this Captain McDonald is reported to have replied: 'I'm not going to get any order from Penrose. Them niggers have violated the laws of the State, and it's my duty to investigate the crime. I never yet had to have an order to go any place my duty called. I'm going into that fort, and the only pass I want I've got right here.' The 'pass' was an automatic shotgun.[8]

At the gates of Fort Brown the two Rangers came face to face with twenty negro soldiers, whose rifles were leveled on them. Though the soldiers ordered the two men to halt, the Rangers advanced into the muzzles of the guns. 'You niggers hold up there! I'm Captain McDonald,... and I'm down here to investigate a foul murder you scoundrels have committed. I'll show you niggers something you've never been use' to.' And then, with an assurance that only a man of supreme courage can show, he barked: *'Put up them guns!'* It was this act which led Major Penrose to say that Bill McDonald would charge hell with a bucket of water.

The story of McDonald's struggle with the United States Army and Government over the negroes cannot be told in detail. He did compel or persuade the army officers to let him make an investigation in which the officers assisted, and, as a result of this investigation, he had Judge Stanley Welch issue warrants for the arrest of twelve soldiers and one

[8] This account is based on A. B. Payne, *Captain Bill McDonald: Texas Ranger*, chapters xxviii–xxix. The quotations are from the book.

CAPTAIN W. J. (BILL) McDONALD

ex-soldier. He did not attempt to take the negroes from Fort Brown, probably because he realized that such an effort would result in failure.

He soon perceived that preparations were on foot to move 'his' prisoners.

Judge Wells heard of the order, which came on August 23, and he is reported to have said: 'They are going to take your prisoners away, Bill, and you can't help yourself.'

'The hell I can't!' said Bill.

McDonald wired Governor S. W. T. Lanham for support and assistance, and the army officers issued a statement that they could find no one connected with the crime. In the meantime all the political bigwigs of the border had come to Brownsville to advise and give counsel, among them Congressman John Garner.

McDonald soon found himself in opposition to the citizens, even those who had welcomed him so warmly. Judge Stanley Welch demanded that McDonald return the warrants which had been issued, but the Ranger refused to comply on technical grounds.

The closing scene, according to McDonald's account, occurred in the Miller Hotel and was witnessed by a large crowd from the balcony. The wiry McDonald, with shotgun across his arm and three or four Rangers at his back, faced Judge Welch, who was supported by a motley collection of peace officers and the important political figures of the border. The judge charged that the Ranger would cause trouble by his action; the Ranger replied that the row came before his arrival and that all had been quiet since. He paid his respects to the judge's militia by telling him that they 'looked like fifteen cents in Mexican money.' John Garner suggested that further action on both sides be suspended until Captain McDonald received more definite instructions from the governor. The telegram came before the conference broke up, and cut all support from under the Ranger by ordering him to act under the direction of the district judge and the sheriff. On the following day the prisoners were transferred to Fort Sam Houston at San Antonio, while all other negro soldiers were sent to El Reno, Oklahoma. None of the negroes were convicted, but President Theodore Roosevelt disbanded the three companies involved.

The citizens of Brownsville do not accord to Captain McDonald much credit for his action in the negro riot. Their view of the affair is given in the words of Judge Harbert Davenport as follows: 'It so happened... that the Rangers' part in this affair was wholly in the newspapers. The riot occurred between midnight and daybreak; and when the dawn came, it was all over. There was nothing for the Rangers, or anyone else, to do but to allay the uneasiness of Brownsville inhabitants.... What remained to be done was for the army and not the police — either state or local.' [9]

[9] Harbert Davenport to W. P. Webb, December 26, 1934.

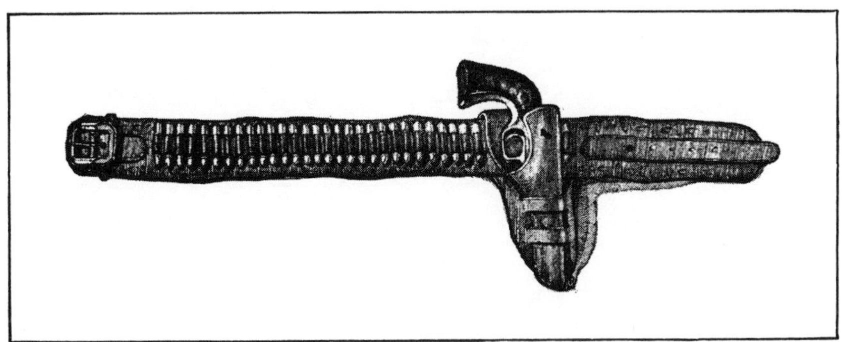

XXI

REVOLUTION, WORLD WAR, AND PROHIBITION

The Rangers claimed that they fired about fifty rounds and that there were four or five dead Mexicans on the sandbar in the river and on the bank of the river.... I went on the river where the fighting had taken place.... On the Mexican side I could see several dead horses and several large Mexican hats.... [But] if there were any dead Mexicans on the sandbars, the river evidently washed them down stream. These Rangers are all good men, and the way things looked to me, there evidently must have been some Mexicans killed.

Captain CHARLES F. STEVENS

And as I got out in the corner of the yard — this Mexican... jerked his horse up, and he hollered at his men to kill all the Americans. And as he said it, I shot, and he didn't, of course, holler no more.... When the shot was fired it sounded like it busted, everyone shot.... I thought so at least from the way the bullets were whizzing.... I only got in three shots until I was knocked down.

SAM H. NEILL

The Rangers killed the patrons of his school, the wolves caught his goats, the hawks killed his chickens, and a Mexican ran off with his wife.

Colonel Langhorne's report on a border school teacher

We knew what we were going up against when we seen a bunch of Comanches; there were two things to do, fight or run. You meet a bunch of Mexicans and you don't know what you're up against.

E. W. NEVILL

They got away.

An unofficial report.

XXI. REVOLUTION, WORLD WAR, AND PROHIBITION

1. BACKGROUND OF THE BANDIT TROUBLE

THE activities of the Texas Rangers from 1910 to 1920 were determined primarily by problems growing out of Mexican revolutions, the World War, and prohibition. Prohibition was national, the Mexican problem was international, and the World War was universal. The part played by the Rangers in each was therefore comparatively small, though important enough in Texas to merit some attention.

The story of the Mexican revolutions must begin with Porfirio Díaz, the strong man of Chapultepec, the only man who has ever preserved order for any appreciable period in Mexico. We have seen that Captain McNelly reported the beginning of the Díaz revolution at Matamoros in 1876, and its later successes on the northern Mexican border. In 1877, Díaz established his supremacy and for almost thirty-five years he held Mexico in his iron hand. The conditions under his rule have been described as follows:

'A force of "rurales," comparable with the Texas Ranger force or mounted police of Pennsylvania, maintained law and order throughout the Republic, while their number did not exceed 1200 at any one time. Americans were welcome wherever they went in Mexico and their financial assistance was sought in opening up all the resources of the country; and during their visits they were welcomed with equal hospitality at the palace of the rich "hacendado" or hut of the humblest peon. In short, there was no such thing dreamed of as an anti-American feeling of Mexicans toward Americans. Over the world, in every civilized country, Porfirio Díaz was regarded as an honorable, honest, patriotic, upright ruler, practically an autocrat or dictator, but devoted to his country and his people.' [1]

[1] 'Investigation of Mexican Affairs,' *Senate Document* No. 285, Sixty-Sixth Congress, Second Session, p. 3338. Serial Nos. 7665–7666.

This stable period in which Mexico made great progress has been called the 'abnormal period' of Mexican history. In 1910 normalcy was resumed in the Orozoco-Madero revolution which overwhelmed the strong man of Chapultepec, and led to his resignation in 1911. The briefest history that can be written of Mexico for the next ten years is a list of the eleven presidents, all of whom succeeded to office through revolution and some through murder. In the period of four years, 1911 to 1915, Mexico had nine presidents, one of whom served twenty-eight minutes.

The repercussions of the revolutions were not seriously felt along the American border until 1912, when there was some fighting in Juarez opposite El Paso, and later opposite Presidio. The crisis, so far as the United States was concerned, came because President Wilson refused to recognize Huerta on account of the murder of Madero. In 1914, the United States seized Vera Cruz, an act which caused most of the Americans in Mexico to flee for their lives. In the general fighting that followed, Carranza came to the top, but in so doing he split with Villa. Because the United States seemed to favor Carranza, Villa became infuriated, and initiated the raid on Columbus, New Mexico, March 9, 1916, and at other points along the border. These raids led to the Pershing punitive expedition into northern Mexico, which had no other result than to stir the resentment of the Mexican people against 'El Fantasma,' the Specter of the North. Although the United States recognized Carranza as *de facto* President of Mexico on October 6, 1915, this did not make Carranza a friend to the Americans. In fact, the preponderance of evidence indicates that he held his followers together by his anti-Americanism, that he supported numerous plots against the United States, and that he was strongly pro-German.

The second factor affecting the relations of the United States and Mexico, and of the Texas Rangers to the Rio Grande border, was the World War. It was but natural that both the Allies and the Central Powers would take all possible measures to enlist the support of the other nations of the world. From the beginning of the conflict the drift of public opinion in the United States was towards the Allies; and since Mexico was strongly anti-American by that time, it drifted towards Germany. Germany was not slow to seize the opportunity to foment discord between the neighboring countries. That Germany had gone far in her program before America entered the war is indicated by an abundance of evidence. Shortly before war was declared, Germany's purpose was clearly revealed in the Zimmermann note. German agents were scattered all over Mexico, German army officers were teaching military science and tactics to Mexican soldiers and revolutionists, and a powerful wireless station in Mexico City was sending information from the United States to the Central Powers. When the bandit troubles were at their worst on the border, complete immunity was granted to Germans. To combat the activities of the Germans, the United States also had its agents on the border and its spies in Mexico.

The third factor affecting the duties of the Texas Rangers and the relations between Mexico and the United States was national prohibition which became effective in 1919. At the bottom of this problem is the fact that Mexico was wet and the United States was theoretically dry. There has always been smuggling on the border, but never until prohibition went into effect was smuggling so profitable or so easily engaged in by those of limited means. A small band of Mexicans could load a dozen pack-horses with liquor that cost them a hundred pesos, make a run to the numerous customers in Texas, and recross the border with a thousand pesos or more. Since Texas was also dry, the Texas Rangers were assigned to the duty of curbing the liquor traffic. In the performance of this duty — which none of them particularly liked — they had many a brush fight.

These three factors — Mexican revolutions, World War, and prohibition — served to accentuate Mexican antagonism to Americans and kept the Texas border in a constant uproar from 1912 to 1920.

What is known as the bandit troubles in Texas may best be presented against the background of Mexican affairs during a decade of turbulence. A vivid, though biased, account of the suffering of the Americans, both in Mexico and on the border, is set forth in thirty-five hundred pages of evidence taken by the Senate investigating committee of which A. B. Fall was the chairman and the leading spirit. There can be little doubt that Senator Fall was intent upon bringing about intervention. Certain internal evidence shows the anti-Mexican spirit of this committee. It is also a fact that A. B. Fall was interested in oil in Mexico, and was compelled to go on the stand and testify as to his relations with the Mexican oil situation. Captain W. M. Hanson, then senior captain of the Texas Rangers, was also a member of the committee. Hanson had been part owner and manager of a large Mexican estate, but when the revolution broke out, he was captured and sentenced to be shot. Though the sentence was revoked, Hanson was deported and his property confiscated.

The committee compiled a list of murders and outrages committed by the Mexicans against the Americans, both in Mexico and along the border. There was placed in evidence a map prepared by the National Association for the Protection of American Rights in Mexico showing the geographic location of the murders. This map is called the Murder

Map of Mexico. According to the figures on the Murder Map a total of 550 Americans lost their lives in the Mexican troubles between November 20, 1910, and September 30, 1919. In Mexico 365 civilians and 59 soldiers lost their lives; along the border on the American side, 62 civilians and 64 soldiers were killed. The total list of killed, wounded, and outraged is given as 785, and the partial property loss to American citizens is estimated at $50,481,133. The total losses, including deaths, injuries — personal and corporation — were estimated at more than five hundred million dollars.

Despite its bias, the Fall report is a gripping human document, unfortunately hidden in the mausoleum of official publications. More than two hundred and fifty people came to testify, most of them against, but some for, Mexico. Among them were suave diplomats, ignorant negro soldiers, Protestant preachers, Texas Rangers, Catholic priests, a one-legged Villa bandit, timid nuns, audacious spies, cautious propagandists, rough-clad ranchmen, lordly oil tycoons, and army officers. Their story is a composite of murder, pillage, and rapine all over Mexico.

Mrs. Moore told of the murder of her husband, and of the looting and burning of houses in the Villa raid on Columbus, New Mexico. Her account was supplemented by that of a Mexican boy who was captured in the Villa raid. The boy's father, driven from home by the Carranzistas, fled to Villa's camp for protection and became a member of Villa's staff. The boy joined Villa's band in order to be near his father, lost a leg at Columbus, and was captured by the Americans. Michael Spellacy came before the committee to tell how a Carranza officer gained recruits. 'Look at me,' said the officer to the peons. 'A few months ago I had nothing. Now I have a thousand pesos and I have assaulted twelve or fifteen or twenty girls.' Mike had forgotten the exact number of girls, but he remembered that, on the strength of the appeal, the officer gained four recruits. Mother Elias of the Barefooted Carmelites related that the Carranza soldiers carried the nuns into their mountain camps, but permitted them to return later, seeking refuge in hospitals to become mothers.

In contrast is the amazing story of success told by Edward Lawrence Doheny, oil operator, friend of A. B. Fall, member of the Teapot Dome conspiracy. He went from Leavenworth, Kansas, in 1873, 'with a bunch of shave-tail mules,' pack-mules for Lieutenant Wheeler to use in surveying the boundary between Arizona and Mexico. He related his interest in prospecting which resulted in the development of an oil empire in Mexico. His account is a revelation of the intellectual powers and the native force of the oil tycoon who contacted presidents, hired college professors by the score, controlled a dozen oil companies, and figured in millions of dollars.

For several hours Michael J. Slattery, owner of gold mines, mills, and other properties, unfolded his story of life in Mexico from 1901 until August, 1914, when he went out with a band of refugees on freight cars while mobs swirled about the train crying 'Death to the Gringos!' This robust Irish-American bitterly recalled that the Mexican experience had broken his wife's health completely, that she had tried to extract from him the promise that he would kill her before permitting her to fall into the hands of the Villa bandits. He denounced in unmeasured terms the American policy, the Democratic party, and the newspaper reporters who discounted all stories told by refugees. It shamed him to admit that on one occasion he had protected the Americans by hoisting over them the Irish flag.

He was amazed by the indifference of the American people and struck by their mad quest for pleasure and wealth as he saw it with Jim Gibson, an old Texas sheriff who was with him in Mexico. Mike and Jim went to a New York restaurant for lunch, and the first thing they knew they found themselves in the midst of dancing people, not all young people but middle-aged business men.

'I called the waiter over,' said Mr. Slattery. 'I had been out of the country a long time. I said to him, "What is this going on here? Dancing right in the middle of the floor of the restaurant and at three o'clock in the afternoon?"

'He looked at me as if I was... escaped from the asylum, and he said, "This is the business men's dance."

'I said, "The what?" and he said, "This is where these men come out and relax for an hour, from three o'clock to four."

'Then, when I saw the kind of dancing... this tangoing, as they call it, I will never forget the remark of Jim Gibson. It was very characteristic, and... a summing up in his mind the attitude of the American people. He said, "By God, the patriotism of the American people has gone to their feet."'[2] It was 1914. War in Europe. Murder and outrage in Mexico. Dancing in restaurants at three o'clock in New York.

2. *DEAD MEN ON THE RIO GRANDE*

More of these stories — pertaining to the general Mexican situation — cannot be told here. Our concern is with what happened on

[2] 'Investigation of Mexican Affairs,' pp. 2025 ff.

the Texas border as a result of Mexican revolution, German propaganda, and American prohibition. The Murder Map presents with fair accuracy the loss of American life there, but it tells nothing of the economic losses or of the death of hundreds of Mexicans, many of them innocent, at the hands of the local posses, peace officers, and Texas Rangers. In short, the Mexican revolutions tended to overrun the border and to produce in southern Texas and New Mexico conditions similar to those that existed in Mexico itself. The number killed in the entire valley has been estimated at five hundred and at five thousand, but the actual number can never be known. The situation can be summed up by saying that after the troubles developed the Americans instituted a reign of terror against the Mexicans and that many innocent Mexicans were made to suffer. The Americans found sufficient cause in the raids, murders, and thefts for vigorous action, but when they learned that the Germans were supplying the Mexicans with arms and ammunition, the I.W.W. with incendiary literature, that Japanese were accompanying some of the bands and manufacturing crude bombs for them, and that plots were being made by the Mexicans, with the aid of Germans and Japanese, to take Texas and other Southwestern States, their anger was lashed into fury. Of bandits they asked no quarter and gave none. In the orgy of bloodshed that followed, the Texas Rangers played a prominent part, and one of which many members of the force have been heartily ashamed. The reader would not be interested in a list of a hundred or more clashes, raids, murders, and fights that occurred between 1915 and 1920. Of more interest are the first-hand accounts of participants who gave testimony before the Fall committee.

On October 18, 1915, a band of Mexicans crossed the river and wrecked a train north of Brownsville. They pulled the spikes, removed the fish-plates, and as the train approached at about thirty miles an hour, they pulled the rail from the cross-ties with a wire, causing the engine to go over on its side. An account of the wreck was given by John I. Kleiber. 'I noticed that the train began to bump... and slow up. Well, I felt it slacken speed, and... it listed to one side.... At that moment the train stopped. Scattering shots and then irregular volleys broke out and increased in volume; and cries, shouts—"Viva Carranza!" they cried. "Viva Luis de la Rosa!" "Viva Aniceto Pizana!"

'It was a warm night and the windows were up,... and everyone went to the floor—went in between the seats. You could hear bullets whistling through the car.... Dr. McCain and Mr. Wallace [Wallis], and... the boy... took refuge in the toilet.

'I could hear them [the bandits] getting aboard the train and passing to and fro. I had only been lying there a very few minutes when I saw

... Brashear... stick his head out into the aisle.... I saw a look of intense terror come into his face... He threw his hands up and his eyes became set and he gasped. Just then I saw the mouth of a rifle go by, and I saw the flash, and I saw blood spurt, and he fell. This listing... of this car continued, and I laid there; and the firing continued.

'Finally... the blood from Brashear had come down in a pool and I was covered with blood. I had on a light suit... blue serge coat and ... linen trousers....'

Judge Kleiber told of the killing of Dr. McCain, Corporal McBee, the death of Engineer Kimball, and the wounding of Wallis and Brashear. The bandits robbed the passengers and took all the military tan shoes, including Judge Kleiber's. Two merchants saved themselves by claiming that they were Germans. This sparing of Germans was very significant, especially when it was learned that this band had been organized among Carranza soldiers who were under General Emiliano Nafarrate at Matamoros. The leaders were Luis de la Rosa and Aniceto Pizana.[3]

The murder of two Americans on September 1 or 2 by a band of twenty-five Mexicans under Aniceto Pizana was told by S. S. Dodds. Mr. Dodds had a gang of men putting in a pumping plant about eight miles from the river when twenty-five Mexicans, armed with German Mausers and American Winchesters, approached and captured them.

Q. Now, ... what occurred ... after these men threw their guns on you?

A. Why, we were in a deep excavation and we came out and they took our valuables and lined us up — we thought to shoot us — and one of this bunch had worked for me ..., and would not stand for them executing us at this time, and we waited around a little while, and they burned the house that I had there and destroyed more or less property and an automobile.

Q. An automobile?

A. Yes, sir; and we were down between two levees of a new irrigation canal ... and Donaldson drove up on a farm wagon going to town for a load of lumber; ... and they surrounded him and cut his team loose and drove us down the canal right of way; ... for a couple of miles and milled around ... to about noon ... [and] Smith and Donaldson were executed and ——

Q. By whom?

A. By four of the gang — four of the bunch. From there we went into a little clearing, ... and a steer was tied there and a bunch of jerked beef, and an oat sack full of tortillas, and we had lunch... and we stayed around there two or three hours and started out... on the old Alice road, and at that point a posse of civilians and soldiers intercepted the gang,... and during the fight that ensued I escaped.

Q. Any casualties during the fight?

[3] 'Investigation of Mexican Affairs,' pp. 1269 ff.

A. I understand that one Mexican was killed.... I was busy getting away.

Q. What were the circumstances in the execution of Smith and Donaldson?

A. There were no circumstances; they just were out of luck and had no friends. They happened to be Americans.

Q. They just lined them up and shot them?

A. They took them out in the brush, probably thirty feet from the edge of the clearing, and shot them.... It may be of interest to this committee to know that before these men were shot they were asked if they were Germans.

Q. They were?

A. No, sir; they were not. The Mexicans asked them if they were 'Alemanes.'...

Q. And their answer was what?

A. No; they did not know at the time that it might have saved their lives.

Q. Did they tell what nationality they were?

A. No, sir...; they just shook their heads.

Q. And then they were shot?

A. Yes, sir.[4]

The suffering of the women on the Texas border may be seen in Mrs. Nellie F. Austin's account of the murder of her husband and son at Sebastian, Texas, August 6, 1916. The bandits captured the men while they were working on a corn-sheller near the house. Mrs. Austin was warned of the approach of the bandits to her house by the sound of creaking leather and rattling chains. After robbing the house of all the guns and valuables, and taking the Austin horses, the bandits went away with their two prisoners, A. L. and Charley Austin. Mrs. Austin was not much frightened because her husband and son had assured her that everything would be all right.

Mrs. Austin: After they had gone through the gate they closed it very carefully after them, and I could see our horses plunge and jump.... I was so pleased to think they had gone.... I had been writing a letter to my son and I thought I would add a postscript and tell him that the bandits had been there and robbed the house — I stood up to go to the table to write, and I heard this volley.

Q. Firing?

A. It was.... I knew what it was — and I think for a moment I must have gone crazy. When I came to I was standing at the same place; my dog had come into the house and was jumping up in my face, lapping it with his moist tongue, brought me to. I knew enough to get my hat and to start after them to find them — and I kept feeling my heart give out.... I saw Elmer Millard coming back.... I asked him where my boys were. He said: 'They have shot them, Mrs. Austin.'... I went down and there were two roads.... I got but a few feet in the other road when I could see

[4] 'Investigation of Mexican Affairs,' pp. 1250 ff.

my husband's feet in the roadway. He wore white trousers.... I had to pass.... I got to my husband first... I saw that Charley [her son] was dead; one of his eyes that I could see was open; then I picked my husband up and turned him over; blood was flowing from his mouth, but there was no other mark on his face. I talked to him and talked to him; I knew he was alive for his eyelashes moved — or eyelids — but he couldn't speak.... I went to Charley and I couldn't move him for he was like a piece of stone; he was lying in a pool of blood.... I thought if we could get a physician we could save my husband. Elmer said, 'Oh, no; Mrs. Austin, they are dead.'... Coyotes were howling not very far away and I was afraid to leave my dead and go and try to let them know where I was; but after a while I went....[5]

A vivid picture of the conditions brought about by the numerous raids and murders, together with the difficulties of the Americans in finding the causes, was painted by Lon C. Hill, border man, ranchman, and capitalist.

Q. Now, what was the general condition about that time among the citizens on the border down there — did they feel safe under the protection of their flag?

A. No, sir; no. They were just in this fix, gentlemen: All the Americans ... the biggest part of them, were going this way [indicating].

Q. Which way?

A. Up north, up the railroad, getting out of that country. And all the Mexicans were going that way [indicating towards Mexico], and the people, they came into town and lived — the people that lived out in the country.... They brought their women and children into town, and a great many just got on the train, left their chickens and hogs and cows, and everything else, and just went to Corpus and San Antonio, and went from there to Canada — just scattered all over the country....

Q. What were the objects of those raids?

A. Well, Senator,... that is a question that bothered us down there for a good little while. What were they up to? Now, when the thing first started we couldn't understand... why those fellows there would want to come over there and steal a few cows... and run across the river.... We got to investigating... and we found out that they had been sending off a lot of money through the post office... and they sent a world of money to Los Angeles, California,... to a firm known as the Magnon Bros.

Q. Ricardo Magnon?

A. I think he is the fellow. Well, they sent worlds of money over there, and they had all kinds of literature from California on this I.W.W. stuff.... Well, now, they would send this money off, and then they would order guns and ammunition... lots of it... and it... got noised around... that they were trying to take that country... and they said they were going to run all of the Gringos out of there.... Well, to my mind and to the other fellows', that was absolutely inconceivable... how a bunch of Mexicans would take a fool idea in their heads that they were going to kill all those Americans and take all that country...; it was just laugh-

[5] 'Investigation of Mexican Affairs,' pp. 1312 ff.

able to us... that they really meant it. But they were coming... they would tell us... coming... in bunches and take your horses and burn up your houses and kill you and then, after a while, they were just going to come over in a great big army and take the whole country....

Well... the inside dope... we could never get it from the leaders... but we would get hold of some fellow, and they would tell us... and ask them what in the name of goodness is the matter with you Mexicans; are you all going crazy here? Well, what are you up to; what are you going to do?

'Well,' they said, 'we have organized, and we have got some foreigners going to help us, and we are going to take all the land back that you Gringos stole from us before the constitution of 1857.'

Q. What term did they use to describe these foreigners?

A. Well, 'enrejados' — something like that.

Q. Extranjeros?

A. That is it; that is the name.

Q. Do the Mexicans... by the term 'extranjeros'... mean Mexican citizens?

A. No; they don't.

Q. Do they mean Americans?

A. No; they don't; them fellows didn't; they meant Alemans, to come out and tell you the right of it.

Q. Aleman means a German?

A. Aleman means a German. They would tell you they had instruction not to kill any Germans and not to molest any Germans and... there was a whole raft of Germans came down there and lived down there, and on both sides of that river, too.... They... would say that they were going to take the country between the Rio Grande and the Nueces....

Q. And they were going to take it back?

A. Yes, sir; and the Aleman was going to help them, furnish them ammunition, money, and everything.[6]

The testimony of Lon Hill indicates the confusion that existed in the minds of the Americans when the Mexicans began their inexplicable raids. There were strange rumors of great plans that were on foot to take Texas, but as Hill said, it was inconceivable 'how a bunch of Mexicans would take a fool idea in their heads that they were going to kill all those Americans and take all that country.' The mystery was deepened when the Americans learned that some of their own Mexicans, people who had lived in close harmony with them for years, were joining the raiders.

Caesar Kleberg also spoke of the mystification of the Americans over the Mexican activities. He said that they had never had trouble over the Mexicans banding together, that they could not understand it, and that the Texas Mexicans could not comprehend it either. Before the Norias raid on the King Ranch, the bandits captured Manuel Rincones, one of Mr. Kleberg's Mexicans, and kept the old Mexican for three

[6] 'Investigation of Mexican Affairs,' pp. 1253 ff.

MEXICAN FIGHTING MEN OF THE BORDER

days. Manuel made a statement as to the leaders and told how the band was organized. His evidence indicated that the leaders were Carranza soldiers and that they were encouraged by Carranza's representative at Matamoros, General Nafarrate.[7] Charley Armstrong, who was in the midst of the raids, relates that the people could feel that something mysterious and terrible was impending, but they could not learn what it was. The Mexicans — the good Mexicans — felt it but could not express it. Something was wrong. Shrugs. Gestures. Strange horsemen riding through the brush. The grapevine of the border, transmitting strange messages among ignorant but simple-hearted and kindly people. Mexicans who had always been tractable became timid or sullen. No wonder such men as Lon Hill would ask, 'What in the world is the matter with you Mexicans; are you all going crazy here?'

Slowly it dawned on the border people that the raids were not sporadic outbursts of irresponsible bandits; they became convinced that the disturbances had behind them a purpose, an intelligence greater than that of the bandit leader or of his ignorant followers. Two years later,

[7] 'Investigation of Mexican Affairs,' pp. 1282 ff.

in 1917, the Zimmermann note revealed the plan of Germany to unite Mexico and Japan with Germany in a general war on the United States for the purpose of restoring the Southwest to Mexico and giving the Far West to Japan. Zimmermann's plan of 1917 bore a striking resemblance to the amazing Plan of San Diego, Texas.

It was in January, 1915, that Tom Mayfield, deputy sheriff of Cameron County, arrested a man in McAllen by the name of Basilio Ramos, *alias* B. R. García. It is important to give Tom Mayfield credit for this arrest because the agents of the federal government assume all credit for the act and do not mention Tom Mayfield's name. Basilio Ramos had in his possession many papers, and among them the Plan of San Diego, Texas. United States Marshal T. P. Bishop and Special Agent Frank J. McDevitt took Ramos and the papers to Brownsville and turned them over to Inspector E. P. Reynolds for investigation. On January 29, 1915, Special Agent E. C. Breniman of the Department of Justice filed complaint before United States Commissioner E. K. Goodrich, charging Basilio Ramos and other signers of the Plan of San Diego with conspiracy against the United States Government. At the time, Ramos could not make bond and was placed in the Cameron County jail to await preliminary trial.[8]

According to the sworn testimony of Basilio Ramos, the Plan of San Diego was made in the jail at Monterey, Mexico, on January 6, 1915. Ramos, who was twenty-four years of age and single, testified that he was born at Nueva Laredo, Tamaulipas, that he had been placed in jail at Nueva Laredo because he was a Huertista, and that he was released on May 29, 1914, on the condition that he would leave Mexico at once. He immediately crossed the river to Laredo, Texas, where he remained about a month without work, but later found employment at San Diego as an agent for the Royal Brewing Company of Kansas City. He left this position on December 29, 1914, and started to Tampico, Mexico, but was again arrested and remained in jail at Monterey until January 7 or 8, 1915.

Ramos stated that the Plan of San Diego was drawn by 'a friend of ours,' who had been in jail, and that copies of the document in Spanish were smuggled into the jail by the servant who brought the prisoners their meals. Among the eight signers of the Plan were a lawyer, a saloonkeeper, and a commission man, all Huertistas.[9]

[8] Copies of the papers found in possession of Ramos are on file in the Adjutant General's papers at Austin. See E. P. Reynolds to Supervising Inspector, Immigration Service, Laredo, Texas, February 9, 1915. The Plan of San Diego is published in 'Investigation of Mexican Affairs,' pp. 1205 ff.

[9] Sworn statement of Basilio Ramos taken by Inspector Reynolds, Brownsville, Texas, January 28, 1915. A.G.P.

The Plan of San Diego provided that on February 20, 1915, at two o'clock in the morning, the Mexicans were to arise in arms against the United States and proclaim their liberty and their independence of Yankee tyranny. At the same time they would declare the independence of Texas, New Mexico, Arizona, Colorado, and California. The army would be the 'Liberating Army for Races and People'; and the red flag with its white diagonal fringe would bear the inscription 'Equality and Independence.' Funds would be provided by levies on captured towns, and state governments would be set up in the state capitals.

Every North American man over sixteen would be put to death as soon as his captors could extract from him all his funds or 'loans'; every stranger found armed should be executed regardless of race or nationality; no leader should enroll a stranger in the ranks unless he were Latin, negro, or Japanese. The Apaches of Arizona and other Indians were to receive every guarantee and have their lands returned to them.

The five states were to be organized as an independent Mexican republic, which at an appropriate time would seek annexation to Mexico. When success had crowned the initial effort, six more states north of those named — evidently Oklahoma, Kansas, Nebraska, South Dakota, Wyoming, and Utah — were to be taken from the United States and given to the negroes who were to select a suitable banner for their republic. This buffer negro state would lie between the Mexicans and what one of the signers of the Plan called 'the damned big-footed creatures' of the north.

Ramos had papers authorizing him to organize lodges or *juntas* and to give commissions in the five states named. There was also a letter from the secretary, A. S. Garza, in reference to General Nafarrate whose name appears more than once in the story of the border. Garza believed that such individuals as Nafarrate should accept 'with fervor, abnegation, and respect an idea so sublime'; if it was not the grandest idea in America, it was at least 'a challenge unto death of decapitated Latin America to the white-faced hogs of Pennsylvania.' Garza could send Basilio no funds because he had given them all to the brother of General Santos and had to pawn his watch in order to get across the river and pay his room and board in Laredo. Despite his low financial state, he was not discouraged. He was working with good results; everyone accepted his idea; and he believed that much could be accomplished in a short time. Near the end of this letter he became highly emotional over the 'crimes of the damned big-footed creatures against our poor race.' The letter closed thus: 'To be quiet would be a crime against one's country because it is the homesick hour of the weak....

I wish you happiness on the arid rocky road which we shall traverse. Equality and Independence, Your friend, A. S. Garza.'[10]

The authorship of the Plan has never been revealed, but it does not have the marks of Mexican composition. Some say that it was prepared by the Germans who hoped to bring on trouble in Mexico. Others say that a prominent border character who later held a responsible position in Texas designed it in order to overturn the Carranza government and regain a ranch that the revolutionists had taken from him.

3. THE RANGERS AND THE BANDIT TROUBLES

There has never been a time in the history of the force when the Texas Rangers had a greater opportunity for distinguished service than they had during the bandit troubles. That they did not distinguish themselves is not so much the fault of individual men as it is of their political superiors. James E. Ferguson became governor in 1915, and almost from the time that he entered office he was engaged in bitter political strife. Both Ferguson and Hobby used the Rangers for political purposes, or were accused of so doing. Neither of them gave the Rangers that superior leadership that the crisis demanded. Some of the Rangers were good and efficient; but some of them were totally unfitted for the service.

It is not the purpose here to indict individual Rangers or companies or to tell of the excesses that they committed during the bandit troubles. In fairness to them, it may be added that they had the support of many citizens of the Valley. In passing judgment one must not forget the psychology of fear and racial antagonism that made the Rio Grande a battle-line and the border a battle-field. On one side of the river the slogan was 'Kill the Gringos'; on the other it was 'Kill the Greasers.'

THE KIDNAPING OF CLEMENTE VERGARA

The kidnaping of Clemente Vergara occurred early in 1914, antedating the real bandit troubles by about a year. The case is of unusual interest and is discussed whenever border men talk of border troubles. Every teller of the tale is convinced that the episode, which occurred at a time when relations were strained, came near causing trouble between the United States and Mexico.

[10] A. S. Garza to Basilio Ramos, January 15, 1915. A.G.P.

Forty miles above Laredo the three-house town of Palofox is held in the crooked arm of the bending river, and just opposite is Hidalgo in Mexico. These outposts of contrasting racial cultures, surrounded by barren hills, appear to dwell in eternal peace one with the other. In reality they have been the scene of many stirring events. That nature did not design this land for a numerous people was indicated by the following conversation between a Texas Ranger and a customs inspector as the two descended the winding road that leads from the hills to Palofox by the river.

'This country is developing fast,' said the customs inspector.

'What makes you think that?' inquired the Texas Ranger doubtfully.

'Well, two fellers drove a big herd of sheep in here not long ago,' was the reply.

'They won't stay,' argued the Ranger.

'No,' admitted the inspector, 'they won't stay — and I'll get the sheep.'

Getting the other fellow's sheep, cattle, and saddle horses has been a profitable occupation on the border, an occupation conducted in feudal manner under great clouds of pistol smoke, amidst feuds, and with funerals.

For several years a Ranger camp was maintained at Palofox, held by two to four men. It was there that Ranger W. M. Molesworth added something to the Ranger tradition by taking the town of Hidalgo single-handed. At the time the incident occurred, a state of intermittent war existed between the inhabitants of Palofox and Hidalgo.

Just prior to the Christmas holidays, the Mexican gunmen sent the Texas Rangers word that they would come to the river bank at a certain time and fire two shots as a challenge. If the Rangers wanted a fight, they could come down on their side and shoot it out across the river. The signal came at the time stated, the two Rangers trotted down with Winchesters, but the Mexican riflemen did not appear. They later sent the Rangers word that if one of them ever appeared in Hidalgo, he would be shot.

On Christmas day, Ranger Molesworth and one companion, whose name will not be mentioned because he is still a customs inspector, decided to take the dare. They crossed the river in a boat and made their way cautiously into the town. By this time the customs inspector had imbibed a little too much and the whole procedure was left to Ranger Molesworth. The first man the Ranger met was the *cabo* who had charge of the Rurales. The Ranger embraced the Mexican, and with his arm about him, conducted him to one *cantina* after another. Encountering no resistance, the Texan decided that perhaps the bad men did not know of his presence, and so he signaled them. Though all the

CLEMENTE VERGARA

shooting was directed at hairless dogs and saloon signs, the marksmanship was perfect, and when the reverberations had died and the smoke had lifted, the only visible inhabitant was the *cabo.* All others had retired behind the adobe walls, and the place was as quiet as it seems when viewed from the Texas hills. The Ranger, with some assistance from the *cabo,* got his companion into the boat and rowed to his own side of the river. Though this act was not officially reported, it has become a part of that great body of Ranger and river lore and Ranger Molesworth came to be known as the man who took a Mexican town single-handed. Such are the tales of the border. Some are true and some are legend, but all are veracious in portraying the character of border men — such men as Clemente Vergara.

Clemente Vergara did not live in one of the three houses of Palofox; he lived above the town in a quaint stone ranch house which stands on a bluff overlooking the Rio Grande. From his house door he commanded a fine view of the shelving Mexican bank, and of the large brush-covered island, set like an irregular diamond in the broad stream. Isla Grande lies nearest the north bank, and was used by Clemente Vergara as a trap for saddle horses.

THE VERGARA RANCH HOUSE

SCENE OF THE KIDNAPING

On the morning of February 12, 1914, about nine o'clock, a Mexican came to the stone ranch house and told Dolores Vergara that some Mexican federal soldiers had driven her father's horses from Isla Grande into Mexico. Dolores saw that it was true, saw the Mexicans drive eleven head towards Hidalgo, and she sent a messenger to carry the news to her father, who had gone early that morning to Palofox.[11]

[11] Signed statement of Dolores Vergara, March 11, 1914. A.G.P.

Vergara immediately crossed the river in a skiff and talked to Nito Sierra and Andrew Rodriguez, who told him that nothing could be done about the horses until the return of the commander Juan Garza Galan. The negotiations were without results, and at night Vergara returned to the ranch.[12] On Friday, February 13, the Vergara family were astir early. By seven o'clock horses were hitched to the buggy which was to go to Laredo to meet Señora Vergara, who was coming from San Antonio. Clemente was busying himself while waiting, doubtless, for Dolores to get ready, by branding some calves in the corrals near the house when three men approached the Mexican bank and Nito Sierra called out to Vergara that if he would come to the Mexican side, Apolonio Rodriguez would settle with him for the horses. The ranchman and his nephew got into the skiff, and, unarmed, rowed to the Mexican shore. As the boy jumped out to beach the boat, one man entered it and seized Vergara, and another caught the boy, who jerked away and hid himself in the brush, which is very thick there.

This pantomime was witnessed by Jesús María la Cruz, Juanita del Rio, and Cecilio Gueverra, who, in the words of Dolores, 'came to the house and told me that the Federals were beating my father and I ran with these people to the river bank. I called to my father to come back to this side. There were three men in this party, all mounted and two of them were riding my father's horses. These men made my father walk before them and went toward Hidalgo.'[13]

On the morning of February 14 the mother and daughter crossed the river at Palofox, proceeded to Hidalgo and to the barracks where they found Vergara. The girl said: 'He was confined in a room in the barracks with a guard at the door. My father had two cut places on his head, a cut on the nose, and a bruise on the left side of his face. The wounds had never been dressed and the blood was clotted in his hair.... We were not allowed to talk with him about what had happened. We remained with my father until ten that night.'

Mother and daughter spent the night in Hidalgo with friends. Early the next morning a federal soldier came with the baskets of food and the bedding which they had brought, and told them that Vergara had been sent to Piedras Negras by the captain, Apolonio Rodriguez. The women returned to the barracks to see the captain, but were told that he was not there, and then they returned to Texas.[14]

Thus far the story of Clemente Vergara is as plain as the outlines of a desert landscape on a clear and sunny day, but from the time that the

[12] Affidavit of Marceo Villareal, March 9, 1914. A.G.P.

[13] Statement of Dolores Vergara, March 11, 1914. A.G.P.

[14] Affidavit of Dolores Vergara, March 11, 1914. A.G.P.

wife and daughter left the barracks at Hidalgo on February 15 until Vergara's body was delivered on the Texas bank some time in the night of March 7, his whereabouts and fate were shrouded in mystery comparable to that which encompasses the same scene when bathed in the dim light of a desert new moon. Once again the border stirred with the activity and suppressed excitement which comes when an American citizen 'crosses the river.'

The conditions in Mexico were so turbulent that the authorities in Texas were at a loss as to a method of procedure. This time the revolution was between Federalists led by Victoriano Huerta and Constitutionalists under the banner of Venustiano Carranza. Both parties had set up a government in Nuevo Leon, but neither was well established and neither had been recognized by the United States, for as David F. Houston expressed it, President Wilson was looking around for another bandit. Governor O. B. Colquitt asked his attorney general, B. F. Looney, for an opinion as to the charges that could be brought against the horse thieves and kidnapers. Looney rendered an opinion which stated that the only crime committed in Texas was that of horse theft, but he pointed out that by the treaty of February 22, 1899, this was an extraditable offense. He suggested that since the Huerta forces controlled the country around Hidalgo, negotiations should be opened with the Huerta government; but inasmuch as the real authority was uncertain, negotiations should also be begun with Carranza. Warrants should be issued for the arrest of Apolonio Rodriguez and such of his companions as could be identified.[15]

Governor Colquitt also wired William Jennings Bryan, Secretary of State under President Wilson, asking him two questions. Which government did the United States recognize? Would the United States consent to the sending of a body of Texas Rangers into Mexico in pursuit of lawless men who committed crimes in Texas? Bryan replied to the first question by saying that requests for extradition should go to the governor of Nuevo Leon, but nullified this by adding that it would have to go to the chief executive authority. Who this was, he did not say. As to the Rangers, Bryan was more explicit: they were the same as any other armed force and could not invade Mexico.[16]

Men of the border are not greatly concerned with the delicate considerations which trouble governors and peace-loving secretaries. Warrants were issued for the arrest of Captain Apolonio Rodriguez, Nito Sierra, Juan Castillon, and Andres Rodriguez. Consul Garrett of Nuevo Laredo bestirred himself in Mexico, working in co-operation with the

[15] Attorney General B. F. Looney to Governor O. B. Colquitt, February 27, 1914. A.G.P.

[16] *Dallas News*, March 1, 1914.

local officers and with Captain J. J. Sanders of the Texas Rangers. Numerous rumors were afloat, published in the papers, and passed by word of mouth along the river. On February 25, a report was published that Vergara had been hanged on the morning after his capture, that the body was still hanging, and that it would be viewed by Consul Garrett and S. J. Hill, Vergara's brother-in-law.[17]

The Vergara case broke, so far as the fate of the man was concerned, on the night of March 7, when the dead body was delivered to the Texas bank near Palofox, but the mystery was deepened because no one seemed to know who had delivered it.

On March 8, Governor Colquitt received the following telegram from Ranger Captain Sanders:

> HAVE JUST RETURNED FROM HIDALGO. HAVE THE BODY OF CLEMENTE VERGARA ON TEXAS SOIL.

If Colquitt realized the serious implications of the telegram — that the Texas Rangers had gone to Hidalgo in defiance of William Jennings Bryan — he gave no indication of the fact, as revealed by the records. The telegram was published, and the reports went out that the Texas Rangers had secretly invaded Mexico, exhumed the body, and brought it across the Rio Grande in the night. In short, the Texas Rangers had invaded a foreign country at a time when the tension between it and the United States was at the breaking point. The United States began to put pressure on the governor of Texas and the governor passed it on to the Ranger captain.

Though Captain Sanders was in a hole, he had company in the person of Consul Garrett who was with him on the night that the body was discovered. The two men found it necessary to think their way out of the difficulty, and to explain the 'error' in the telegram of March 8. Their explanation was most ingenious, but since it saved the face of the chief executives at Austin and at Washington, it was not questioned too closely, and was secretly welcomed, probably, at both capitals.

The officers' story was that on March 7, Captain Sanders and Consul Garrett went from Laredo to the Vergara Ranch accompanied by Rangers Hines and Phelps, Customs Inspector L. Petty, and Constable Warner Petty of Minera. From Palofox the party went to the Coleman Ranch to spend the night. 'During the evening,' wrote Captain Sanders, 'we were told that if we would go to a designated point on the Texas bank of the Rio Grande, at a certain time, on the morning of Sunday, the 8th, we would find the body of Clemente Vergara.'

On Sunday morning, according to the story, the party went down the

[17] *Dallas News*, February 25, 26, March 1, 2, 1914.

'THEY POINTED SIGNIFICANTLY TO AN OBJECT WHICH LAY UPON A STRETCHER'

river and at the designated place came upon a driftwood fire around which eight or ten Mexicans were warming themselves. These men pointed significantly to an object which lay upon a stretcher that stood by the edge of the water — the body of Clemente Vergara! The captain asserted that neither he nor any of his Rangers set foot on Mexican soil.

The explanation of the 'error' in the telegram is almost too plausible. It was that the Ranger and the consul returned to Laredo tired and exhausted from their exciting labors. Both had to make reports of the day, Garrett to Washington and Sanders to Austin. Garrett wrote his report first, but instead of saying that he had returned *from Palofox,* as would have been the truth, he said that he had returned *from Hidalgo.* He justified this variation from the truth on the ground that the State Department knew about Hidalgo because he had been there before; but he feared that the officials in Washington would not know of such a small place as Palofox.

Immediately after Garrett had finished his telegram, Sanders asked him to write the report which he would dictate to the authorities at Austin. Sanders dictated, according to his explanation, as follows:

HAVE JUST RETURNED *TO LAREDO.* RECOVERED CLEMENTE VERGARA'S BODY ON TEXAS SOIL.

But Consul Garrett, whose mind apparently was still on his own message with its harmless misstatement of facts, wrote from Sanders's dictation:

HAVE JUST RETURNED *FROM HIDALGO.* HAVE THE BODY OF CLEMENTE VERGARA ON TEXAS SOIL.

The Ranger captain was so tired that he did not notice the error, and so the misleading telegram went through to Austin. Both officers agreed that this was the correct explanation, and everybody concerned was glad to find such an easy way out of the difficulty.[18]

Despite the flimsy explanation, there is other evidence that the Texas Rangers did not enter Mexico. On March 11 the *Dallas News* reported that the party was organized by S. J. Hill, led by a Mexican, and guided by another Mexican who had witnessed the murder and burial. A daughter of Clemente Vergara, in relating the story to M. B. Brown, stated that the party was composed entirely of Mexicans, eight in number, and that Juan Garza was the leader. There can, however, be little doubt that both Captain Sanders and Consul Garrett had complete knowledge of the whole plan and in all probability they were near by to see that it was executed successfully.

The following account of the recovery of the body appeared in the *Laredo Times* of March 9, 1914:

> One of the most sensational, dramatic, and daring incidents to occur on the Texas border at a time when the complicated conditions already existing between the United States and Mexico have become about as intense as possible was the work of ten men, fully armed and determined, who at about 2 o'clock yesterday morning left the town of Palofox,... crossed the Rio Grande, proceeded to the Hidalgo Cemetery... and recovered from a shallow grave the body of Clemente Vergara....
>
> Some time during Saturday night a party of ten men, comprising parties from the Vergara Ranch and Palofox, assembled in the latter place, fully armed themselves and proceeded to a point on the river front a short distance away, crossed the stream and... wended their way to the cemetery on the outskirts of Hidalgo. They surreptitiously entered the cemetery and proceeded to a spot... where the night before... a man had gone and located the grave of Vergara. One member of the party had with him a spade and at once began the removal of the earth.... When recovered the only clothes on the dead man consisted of an undershirt, pants, and socks.... Reaching the river the party placed the body in a skiff,... making their landing on the American side at a place known as Winter's crossing....

[18] Sanders to Colquitt, March 14, 1914; undated memorandum in A.G.P., initialed H (Hutchings), T. A. G. (T. A. Garrett); *Dallas News*, March 14, 1914.

The records show that only one of the stolen horses was recovered. They fail to show that any of the thieves, kidnapers, or murderers were punished. There is a rumor, however, that two of them were captured farther up the river by the Texas Rangers, but they were never delivered inside prison walls. They made a break for liberty which seems to have been successful. Having lost their prisoners, the Rangers made no official report of the capture, but stated unofficially that 'they got away.' Perhaps the river knows, the river that conceals its mysteries more effectually than the graves along its banks conceal the bones of men.

THE GOAT WAR AT SAN JOSE

From June, 1917, until the end of the year the region around Eagle Pass was in constant turmoil because of extensive cattle theft from Mexico. On August 27, Newman P. Blocker, vice-consul at Piedras Negras, made a long report to the Secretary of State at Washington in which he set forth in an interesting manner the conditions and their causes.

He stated that from June until the end of August the cattle thieves had operated continuously from Esquillas to a point forty-five miles south of Piedras Negras, a distance of almost two hundred miles of river front. The American side of the river was occupied by ranches owned by American citizens and corporations, the grass was good, and water sufficient; the Americans had developed their herds with Hereford and Burmah stock and were supplying the packers with an abundance of beef cattle yearly.

The opposite side of the river was equally good for cattle, but, owing to revolutionary condition and fear of seizure, much livestock had been withdrawn into the interior, much shipped to the United States, and that which remained had been depleted by the warring factions. Consequently the price of meat had advanced outrageously south of the river and the Mexicans were unable to purchase it for their consumption.

Knowing that fat cattle, such as were grazing in a stone's throw on the American side, would bring fabulous prices in Mexico and seeing no officers near the river bank, the Mexicans had taken to stealing by the wholesale.

One of their methods was to watch the river bank in the afternoon from three to five when the cattle came down to drink. A man hidden in the underbrush, which was thick on the Mexican side, would shoot the drinking cattle down with a high-powered rifle, and after dark a party of five or six men would ford the river, skin and cut up the animals, sell the hides in Piedras Negras, Las Vacas, or Guerrero, divide the meat among the inhabitants, and leave the American ranchman minus several steers worth thirty or forty dollars each.

On June 27, Mexicans from Guerrero and San Jose raided the Indio Ranch, eighteen miles above Eagle Pass, and drove off twelve head of cattle. On August 10, they made another raid on the same ranch, crossing several head; and on August 15, they drove off fifteen more. In July, fifteen horses were stolen near Comstock, and a beef was killed below Eagle Pass opposite the Mexican town of Jiminez.

A. H. Allen, manager of the Indio Ranch, reported the theft to the Mexican officials, and furnished them with the names of the thieves. Though river guards and inspectors were thick on the Mexican side, they could not find any thieves or make any arrests. Manager Allen wrote Blocker: 'It is impossible to do anything with these officers as they all *se tapan con el mismo fresada*' (cover with the same blanket).[19]

The tension produced by raids, theft, and official duplicity reached a breaking point in December when it was reported that two American citizens employed by W. E. Wethersbee, American owner of San Gregorio Hacienda, had been killed while deer-hunting on the hacienda. The murdered men were Lee Sharpe and Speck Sellers.[20] Mexican officers sent out detachments with orders to shoot the murderers without trial. Consul Blocker was of the opinion that Sharpe was killed because he interfered with the plans of thieves who were depredating in Texas.[21]

This was the situation around Eagle Pass when the thieves decided to quit stealing cattle and begin on the goats of the Indio Ranch. At 6.30 P.M. of December 29, 1917, the telephone rang at Ranger headquarters in Eagle Pass. Captain K. F. Cunningham, Company M, answered the call which was from Manager Allen at the Indio. Allen told the captain that one hundred and sixty head of his goats had been driven into Mexico. In a short time the few Texas Rangers at Eagle Pass, and three troops of cavalry with a machine gun were en route to the Indio Ranch. The Rangers arrived at 10 P.M. and the soldiers four hours later.

By daylight twelve Rangers and citizens were at the goat pens prepared to follow the trail of the stolen animals. They found that the goats had been crossed at a blind crossing. The sign indicated that guards had stood in the gulches where they had left tracks and the print of gunstocks in the sand. Special Ranger Eugene Buck reported

[19] A. H. Allen to American Consul Blocker, September 3, 1917. A.G.P.

[20] Blocker to Secretary of State, December 8, 1917. A.G.P.

[21] *Ibid.*, December 22, 1917. A.G.P.

that on the previous night he had seen signal fires opposite, indicating that more men were waiting there. The Rangers now sent for Major E. C. Wells, in command of the troops, and when he arrived, the combined force of soldiers, Texas Rangers, and citizens crossed into Mexico and followed the goat trail about a mile to the village of San Jose.

As the force, numbering one hundred and fifty men, approached the house of a Mexican river guard, who was supposed to prevent smuggling, they found a piece of fresh goat meat, a quantity of rawhide string, and an old Mexican who would not talk. In front of the house was a cow tied to a tree, hobbled, belled, and branded with the Indio brand. Several slaughtered goats were hanging in trees. Near by were two Mexicans, a man and a woman. The Ranger captain halted them, but the woman ran and screamed, and at the same instant the Texans were fired on from both sides. The Mexicans fired from the brush where they had concealed themselves in a semicircular line eight hundred yards long. When the soldiers had dismounted and begun firing by platoons in V formation, the Mexicans retreated and some of them took refuge in a house farther in town, from which place they continued shooting. The machine gun was now brought into action and when it began to sputter lead through the walls, the house became silent and the Mexicans who were able fled the town.

On their return, both the Ranger captain and the army officer reported that six were known to have been killed. Later the number was raised to twelve, but Major Wells learned that there were seventeen burials in Piedras Negras and three at San Jose immediately after the fight. In addition a few were wounded, and were evading the officers by claiming to have smallpox. The Mexican authorities were naturally enraged at this invasion and charged the Americans with having killed a woman. The officer expressed his regret for the fact, if true, but excused the deed by saying that those who keep bad company often suffer. Both army officers and Rangers agreed that the punishment would have a salutary effect. Captain Cunningham reported that the governor of Coahuila had organized a Ranger company similar to the Díaz Rurales, and that these men were doing good work in cleaning up the border. They had executed a few of the bandits and placed others in the penitentiary. The invasion of Mexico, which occurred on December 30, 1917, lasted three hours.[22]

[22] Blocker to the Secretary of State, December 31, 1917; Captain K. F. Cunningham to General James A. Harley, December 31, 1917; Cunningham to Harley, January 30, 1918. A.G.P.

BANDIT TROUBLES IN THE BIG BEND

El Pourvenir and Pilares, two little Mexican settlements in a tiny arc of the Big Bend, are completely isolated from the uplands of Texas by a mountain cord so rugged and steep that it can be crossed only by pack-mules and sure-footed ranch horses. The inhabitants of this remote region are Mexicans whose relations are much closer to the people of Mexico than they are to those of Texas. Just across the river — more easily crossed than the mountains — the Cano brothers — Chico, Jose, and Manuel — headed a gang of bandits who preyed on the stockmen of the border. 'They were not Carranzistas, they were not Villistas, they were not anything;... whoever is in charge on the border... they are with,' said E. W. Nevill. Their sovereignty was complete on their side and extended to the Mexicans at Pilares and El Pourvenir. The Texas border men referred to them as the Chico Cano bunch of bandits.

Chico had a long record with Texas officers — customs men, Rangers, sheriffs — and ranchmen. He especially hated Joe Sitters of the customs service. On January 23, 1913, Sitters and his companions captured Chico and started out of the mountains with him. They were waylaid by Cano's gang and in the fighting Jack Howard was killed, and Harvis and Sitters were wounded. Chico made his escape and swore that he would have Sitters's scalp.

His opportunity came on May 24, 1916. Ranger Eugene Hulen, son of the adjutant general at that time, Charlie Craighead, Sug Cummings, —— Trollinger, and Inspector Joe Sitters had made their camp at a water hole in the mountains about seven miles from Pilares. During the night they heard horses going by; the colts were nickering and Mexicans were talking. When the men examined the trail the next morning, they saw that the ropes of the animals were dragging the ground, a ruse to throw the Texans off their guard. Sitters, who was in charge, ordered the men to saddle their horses, pack the mules, hide them in a canyon, and follow the trail, which soon led into a sharp deep canyon. Sitters ordered three of the men to follow the trail, while he took Eugene Hulen and went along the side in the hope of seeing the men with his field glasses. The Texans ran into an ambush. Sitters and Hulen were killed, and the other three lost their horses. They managed to get back to their mules, stripped off the packs and rode them bareback out of the canyon to the Bill McGee Ranch. There they sent a note to John Pool, who telephoned to Marfa for help. A posse of eleven men, among them Inspector R. M. Wadsworth, left Marfa and reached the Pool Ranch that night, where horses were waiting for an all-night ride to the McGee Ranch. There they met Craighead, Trollinger, and Cummings, who told of the waylaying and said that they believed that Sitters and Hulen were dead. The story of the rescue is told by R. M. Wadsworth: 'So we started to where this waylaying happened, went in a round-about way to get into the canyon, afraid they were laying still another trap for us, and looked over and saw where the shooting happened, and finally found both bodies, Hulen and Sitters's bodies.'

Senator Fall inquired as to the condition of Sitters's body, to which Wadsworth replied: 'He was in a very bad condition.... I was right there. I helped to put him on a pack-mule myself. He was lying on his back in sort of a cramped position; looked like he died in great agony, his knees drawed up, cramped up, his hands and fingers like that, drawed up over his face; you could see where his flesh had been knocked off his knuckles with rocks; his left eye in his head had been caved in. The rock was lying a little bit to one side; I judge it weighed about 20 pounds. He had eleven bullet holes in his body.' [23]

The men's clothes, boots, watches, money, six-shooters, and rifles were all gone. The ordeal of bringing those naked bodies out of Pilares Canyon was one that left a deep and bitter impression on all who participated in it. The men recall that the pack-mule on which the customs inspector's body was carried became sick and vomited. Old man Zapata made his brag in Ojinaga that he was with the raiders. He had four sons with the Chico Cano gang.

The Brite Ranch raid of Christmas morning, 1917, was another link in the chain of bandit troubles on the upper border. The ranch is located in Presidio County about twenty-five miles from the international border. Sam H. Neill, who had lived on the border since 1873 and served many years with the Rangers and in the customs service, went to the ranch with his wife to spend Christmas with their son, Van Neill, and family. Christmas is Christmas, even in the Big Bend during bandit troubles. There were five children in the house and they were hustled to bed early. There were women there, and, in the words of Mr. Neill, 'They fixed up their little old Christmas tree that night.' The next morning the ranch was surrounded by bandits. Let this veteran who had lived on the border sixty-five years tell the story.

'Well,... the women folks claimed they wanted to get up early, so I have always been an early riser, and I got up and went into the kitchen for my coffee; my breakfast was always coffee, that is all I ever eat, and started me a pot of coffee... and I came back... in my son's room, to make a fire. They had no kindling — we were then surrounded

[23] R. M. Wadsworth in 'Investigation of Mexican Affairs,' pp. 1532 ff.

by those fellows, but I didn't know — I take the basket and went to the woodpile, about sixty yards from the house, and got the kindling and made the fire. I went back to the woodpile again and got other kindling and made one in my wife's room....

'When I got back to the kitchen the coffee was ready, the cook had come in and fixed a cup of coffee. I turned from the stove and set in the window drinking the coffee, when I looked down the Candelaria Road, coming from the river, and I saw six men abreast, riding fast. I looked at them for a few seconds and I called her attention to it, and she looked and... says, "What can that be?"... As they come around two big circular tanks... I saw them reach and pull their guns. I dropped the cup and saucer and run through his room.'

'Your son's?'

'Yes, sir. He was still in bed; I hollered and says, "We are surrounded by bandits and have got to fight." I doubled in my wife's room and got a gun, a six-shooter —— '

'You mean your rifle?'

'Yes, sir. And as I got out in the corner of the yard — this Mexican ... jerked his horse up, and he hollered at his men to kill all the Americans. And as he said it, I shot, and he didn't, of course, holler no more.... When he hollered that, they jumped from behind the walls and tank dumps like a bunch of quail flushed from behind adobe walls. ... When the shot was fired it sounded like it busted, everyone shot.... I thought so, at least from the way the bullets were whizzing. I fought them from the corner of the house. I only got in three shots until I was knocked down.'

The bandits — about forty-five in number — captured two Mexican boys who had gone to the milk pens. They sent one of them in to tell the Texans that if they did not surrender the house would be bombed. The Neills sent them word to bomb away. They asked for a truce, a cessation of gun-firing. They said that all they wanted was the saddle horses. Mr. Neill said that they were going to refuse that, but his wife 'put in' and advised her son, foreman of the ranch, as follows: 'There ain't but two of you boys and lots of them, they will get you after a while; you better agree to that.' And so the firing ceased.

The bandits in the meantime took possession of the Brite Ranch store, where they remained for five hours. While they were there, Micky Welsh, stage-driver, came up with two Mexican passengers. They shot the Mexicans, took Micky inside, hanged him to a rafter, cut his throat, and wiped the bloody knife on the dead man's shirt. They plundered the store, packed all they could on their horses, and set out for the mountains with four men, supposedly dead, lashed to

VAQUERO

the horses. Just as they dropped off the rimrock, a body of Colonel Langhorne's troops came from Marfa, guided by Inspector Grover Webb. Another troop came from Rudiosa and another from Candelaria.

A short distance from the Brite Ranch the soldiers found the body of the Mexican leader who had been killed by Mr. Neill. The Mexican had on the coat of a Carranza uniform. His companions had partially buried him by placing him in a gully and caving the bank in on top of him. The raid was attributed to Chico Cano's gang.[24]

On March 25, 1918, about fifty bandits attacked the E. W. Nevill Ranch which lies along the river thirty-five miles south of Van Horn. They shot Nevill's son and mutilated the body. They looted the house of everything save the boxes, empty trunks, and the bedsteads; they killed the Mexican woman at the ranch, but spared her three children. This party was pursued by Colonel Langhorne who caught them at Pilares and killed several.[25] It seemed that all trails led to Pilares, all

[24] Testimony of Grover Webb, 'Investigation of Mexican Affairs,' pp. 1526 ff.

[25] Testimony of E. W. Nevill, 'Investigation of Mexican Affairs,' pp. 1510 ff.

stolen horses went that way. The raiders were led by Carranza troops, and back of the raid was Chico Cano.

It is no wonder that these raids and murders — of which these are samples — created consternation among the Texas ranchmen and caused them to take strong measures against the inhabitants of El Pourvenir and Pilares. As Ranger or Inspector Nevill expressed it, 'it was pretty squally.' He declared that conditions were 'worse now than when we had to contend with the Comanches every light moon. We knew what we were going up against when we seen a bunch of Comanches; there were two things to do, fight or run. You meet a bunch of Mexicans and you don't know what you are going up against.... That is the way I look at it.'[26]

All the ranchmen of the sunswept uplands were certain that much of their trouble came from the Mexicans who lived at El Pourvenir. John Pool, owner of thirteen sections, said: 'The Mexicans who live in small settlements along the river on the Texas side have no means of livelihood and do not own land or stock and only have small patches in corn as an excuse for remaining on the river. It is a well-known fact that they act as spies and informers for the thieves and bandits from the Mexico side of the river, and when they locate the best horses and other stock in the ranches on this side they furnish the information to the desperate characters along the river in Mexico and lead them to our ranches.' Raymond Fitzgerald, owner of sixty-eight sections, gave further testimony as to the character of the El Pourvenirians: 'Their standing as thieves, informers, spies and murderers has been well known in this section for two or three years. They used this El Pourvenir ranch as headquarters,... but stayed in Mexico during the day and occasionally came over at night. Several of these people were cousins to the noted Chico Cano bunch of bandits who were known all over this section of Texas as being one of the worst gangs the Citizens and officers had had to contend with during the last few years.'

To meet this situation, Captain J. M. Fox's company of Texas Rangers was sent into this region in the fall of 1917, and began work in co-operation with the federal agents. Rangers and citizens made a preliminary visit to Pilares and El Pourvenir and found the Mexicans wearing Hamilton Brown shoes taken from the Brite Ranch store. The result was the organization of an expedition to find out how the Mexicans had acquired this unusual footgear in place of their customary rawhide sandals. The party was organized at the Fitzgerald Ranch and was comprised of eight Texas Rangers under Bud Weaver and four citizens, Buck Pool, John Pool, Tom Snider, and Raymond

[26] Testimony of E. W. Nevill, 'Investigation of Mexican Affairs,' p. 1550.

Fitzgerald. John Pool went as a guide; Fitzgerald said, 'I went to see if I could find any of my stolen stuff.' Buck and Tom sayeth not, but men of the border understand that their reasons were sufficient, for border men are brothers under the skin.

The party left the Fitzgerald Ranch after dark and reached its destination about two in the morning. The men left their horses in charge of one or two guards, and, as Bud Weaver expressed it, 'rounded up the houses.' The roundup netted about twenty-five Mexican men. While they were gathering evidence — Crystal White soap, Hamilton Brown shoes, and barlow knives — the Texans were fired upon from the brush. Rangers and ranchmen threw themselves to the ground and returned the fire. They reported that their horses stampeded, but they recovered them and also recovered Joe Sitters's saddle. Ranger Bud Weaver wrote the report in which he stated that they did not remain on the ground and did not know, therefore, 'how many, if any, were killed.' The ranchman John Pool, who had no official record to mind, wrote: 'I do not know whether we killed anyone or not, but it was reported that there were about fifteen dead Mexicans there the next morning,' and he named eight of them, but Chico Cano was not among them.

The incident had serious consequences for the Rangers and led to the dismissal of Captain Fox and his entire company. Colonel Langhorne, whose men were close enough to hear the guns — if they were not actually in the party — made out a strong defense for the Rangers and a strong case against the citizens of El Pourvenir. He stated that he had known of the bad reputation of the El Pourvenirians since he first came to West Texas. In fact, he was sent there by General Funston to run down the murderers of Sitters and Hulen. The army officer gave a long list of crimes committed by the El Pourvenirians, and closed his letter with an amusing account of the one American resident of the place. This American was a school-teacher. His salary was eighty-five dollars a month which he received for teaching one pupil — his own son. This hard-working teacher had married a Mexican, deserted her, took another Mexican woman, and employed his former wife as a nurse for his child. He lived as the Mexicans lived and advised them to keep other 'white' men away. Though his name appears in the Ranger records, it will not be given here. In spite of his influence over the Mexicans, he was not without his troubles. He complained — evidently after the Ranger visit — that 'The Rangers killed the patrons of his school, the wolves caught his goats, the hawks killed his chickens, and a Mexican ran off with his wife.' [27]

[27] Undated statements by Ranger Bud Weaver, Raymond Fitzgerald, and John Pool;

Despite the unanimous agreement among the Rangers and ranchmen as to the culpability of the Mexicans, El Pourvenir was not a closed incident. When Mr. Canales initiated his investigation of the Ranger force about a year later, he based his most serious charge on the killing of the Mexicans. Captain Fox, in an effort to protect his men, asked to be held solely responsible and requested that he, and not they, be discharged. The adjutant general refused to discharge him, but later the governor discharged the entire company. Mr. Canales asserted that this was done, not because the Mexicans were killed, but because Fox supported Jim Ferguson instead of Will Hobby for governor, and Hobby was elected.

4. WORLD WAR AND THE LOWER BORDER

With the entry of the United States into the World War, conditions on the border became more complicated. In addition to dealing with bandits, who continued to infest the river, the Rangers and other officers were called upon to apprehend German spies, run out propagandists, and catch slackers who sought to evade the draft by going into Mexico. The border swarmed with officers, federal and state, and hummed with feverish activity. Hardly a day passed without its exciting event. Today a raid was pending; tomorrow a soldier, a Texas Ranger, or a number of Mexicans were killed on the river; and the next day a suspected German spy was captured and quizzed. The Texas Mexicans often became involved in plots on behalf of the warring factions in Mexico; they were often suspected of being in league with a German spy system supposed to extend from the United States into Mexico, thence to Cuba and Germany. Every citizen was expected to prove his loyalty by acting as informant on suspects.

The Ranger captains who were most active in the lower border were Captain Will L. Wright at Laredo and Captain Charles F. Stevens at Brownsville. Captain Stevens arrived at Brownsville on January 2, 1918, in charge of Company G and remained in that region until July. Immediately upon his arrival he interviewed the Mexican consul, J. F. Garza, the military officers, and other government agents on both sides of the river. In company with the Mexican consul, he went to Matamoros to talk with the military commander and customs officials and to give them the names of two Mexicans who were accused of killing a foreman on the King Ranch and wounding a man at Ray-

Colonel G. T. Langhorne to W. M. Hanson, March 18, 1918. See also J. T. Canales's Charges Against State Ranger Force, Art. 11, February 3, 1919. The affidavits of a number of the widows of the El Pourvenir incident are in the Canales Report. All papers are in A.G.P.

mondville. While at Matamoros, Captain Stevens called on the American consul, G. C. Woodward, who was astonished to see a Texas Ranger on Mexican soil.

Captain Stevens was convinced that the lower border was full of German spies and propagandists. He reported that two suspects, Colonel Eugenio Cuellar and Lieutenant Lorenzo Lopez, were in jail at Brownsville. More important than these, he thought, was a Spanish multi-millionaire, Señor Inigo Noreiga, who was then in Cuba. General Juan Andrew Alamazan was operating with his bandits along the border and was probably receiving protection from two Mexican merchants of McAllen.[28]

By the middle of January, Captain Stevens had decided that much of the trouble was due to 'talk carriers' who were doing 'a whole lot of ribbing on both sides of the river.' He was warning the good Mexicans to beware of German propaganda.[29] March — the days when the famous German drive was on in Europe — found him at Brownsville, where General Slocum had called a meeting of citizens to inform them that General E. Nafarrate had proclaimed himself provisional governor of Tamaulipas, and was planning to make an attack on Brownsville. Two Rangers and two river guards were watching the river at night. A man named Betancourt was organizing another movement about Brownsville.[30] 'The way I figure things out here,' he wrote, 'it seems that some of the Germans want intervention, knowing that it would take so much of our army away from the European War.... If they get to fighting in the state of Tamaulipas, we will have to keep a very close watch for raids because Nafarrate is not friendly to the American people.'[31] In April he reported that Nafarrate had been killed at Victoria. If the report were true, it was a good thing because Nafarrate had planned to make Matamoros the capital; he was anti-American, and a friend to all the bandits of the Tamaulipas border.[32]

In March and April, the Rangers were busy in pursuit of German spies and propagandists. Captain Stevens reported that a German doctor or professor, sent by his government to study insects, was living five miles north of Mercedes. 'I think the government is having him watched but in my opinion the best place for this man to be is in some

[28] Captain Charles F. Stevens to General James A. Harley, January 5, 1918. A.G.P.

[29] Captain Charles F. Stevens to Major Walter Woodul, January 13, 1918. A.G.P.

[30] For an account of the activities of F. R. Betancourt, see 'Investigation of Mexican Affairs,' p. 3014. Charles E. Jones, newspaper man and spy, testified that he followed Betancourt from San Antonio to California, where he went to secure aid from Governor Estaban Cantu of Lower California.

[31] Captain Charles F. Stevens to General James A. Harley, March 19, 1918. A.G.P.

[32] Captain Charles F. Stevens to Major Walter Woodul, April 14, 1918. A.G.P.

jail.' The menace of the pink boll worm, which had come from Mexico, indicated that it would be easy for these 'shrewd fellows' to import insects for the destruction of American cotton. When this German left his farm, 'making for the Rio Grande with the intention of crossing into Mexico,' Captain Stevens wired Colonel Sears, who arrested the German as he was procuring a boat. The Rangers searched his house, took his papers, and arrested a Reverend Rooper, former Lutheran minister. The Ranger felt confident that two links in the chain of spies had been removed.[33] A few days later, the Rangers arrested three German-Americans and charged them with treason for assisting in the attempted escape of the German entomologist. 'According to my view,' wrote the Captain, 'this section is a hot bed of German spies and German propaganda and I am taking a good many up.... The Military and Federal officers are co-operating with us in all matters and we with them.' [34]

The war on German suspects went on with the arrest of a German horticulturist and alien enemy, and an expert machinist who formerly worked on the Stover Ranch, owned by the Busch family. Though these men were questioned for two days, they were so 'smooth' that they could not be led to incriminate themselves. The distribution of checks among the ministers of various denominations for missionary work with the Mexicans was investigated by the Texas Ranger, the postmaster of Mercedes, and Van V. Curtis of the Department of Justice. The Captain thought the checks were tips or feelers used to open the way for German propaganda through the churches.[35]

While the evidence is conclusive that German influence was operating among the Mexicans, there can be no doubt that many Germans were picked up on trivial charges. All who bore a German name or spoke with a German accent were suspects, and if one expressed sympathy for Germany, the government agents were sure to be upon him. On July 12, Captain Stevens arrested a German because he had expressed himself, according to the *Brownsville Herald*, as follows: 'We have men and officers on the other side training troops. We can blow up these river pumps when the time comes.... We will show the —— who we are. General C. has more sense than all the Americans have.... Don't you think there is a half million men over there, for the German submarines have got at least half of them.' [36]

The excitement along the river was by no means confined to German suspects. There were constant clashes between the American soldiers

[33] Captain Charles F. Stevens to Major Walter Woodul, March 27 and 31, 1918. A.G.P

[34] *Ibid.*, April 6, 8, 1918. A.G.P. [35] *Ibid.*, April 23, 1918. A.G.P.

[36] *Ibid.*, July 20, 1918; clipping from *Brownsville Herald*. A.G.P.

and the Mexicans. On December 30, 1917, Lieutenant George E. Smith of the Thirteenth Cavalry, while relieving outposts on the river near Hidalgo, discovered a number of Mexicans who were acting suspiciously. Several men disappeared in the brush, but one took two rifles into a boat and started across the river. The troops ordered him to halt, but he fired on them, and when last seen he 'was disappearing below the water.' On May 19, 1918, a military patrol saw a number of Mexicans crossing the river and ordered them to halt. The Mexicans killed an American sergeant and the Americans killed Vicente Loredo. Captain Stevens reported that the Mexicans were either cattle thieves or Caballero revolutionists who had retreated to the United States.[37]

On June 9, near Mercedes, several American soldiers were swimming their horses near La Feria Pump when one of the men slipped from his horse and drowned. Failing to recover the body, the men left the river to report, and a larger detail came to the river and continued the search. While making the search, Lieutenant Schale and four soldiers crossed the river. The lieutenant was murdered and his men were made prisoners by Carranzistas.[38]

On June 10, Ranger Jesse Perez and companions arrested General Benjamin Lopez and his two sons, as they crossed the river into Texas. General Lopez was second in command in the Caballero revolutionary movement against Carranza, and the sons were active in fighting Carranza. The Mexicans reported that they had been captured, and had been condemned to execution, but had made their escape.

Captain Stevens made the following report on the trouble that was developing at the time between Carranza and Obregon: 'I have heard it whispered around that General Obregon is getting sideways with Carranza. If he does, there will be trouble in Mexico. Obregon is a Yakqui Indian, and that would mean the uprising of some of the western states of Mexico. He is one of the strongest men in Mexico at this time.... I cannot get a great lot of information on this Obregon affair, this not being the right part of the country for Obregon news.' [39]

On June 12, the Rangers, while at La Feria Pump, heard the guns of a battle between Carranza soldiers and revolutionists in which sixty men were reported killed. Four days later, the Carranza soldiers pursued some Mexicans who were drowned while swimming their horses across the Rio Grande. The Captain thought they were loaded 'with something very heavy,' as the men of the river were excellent

[37] Captain Charles F. Stevens to Major Walter Woodul, May 20, 1918. A.G.P.

[38] *Ibid.*, June 10, 1918. A.G.P.

[39] Jesse Perez to Captain Charles Stevens, June 11, 1918; Stevens to Major Walter F. Woodul, June 11, 1918. A.G.P.

swimmers. Whether he thought they were bringing over the sixty thousand dollars in gold which, according to reports, had been taken in a Mexican train robbery, or whether they failed from a more common cause, singing bullets, he did not say.[40] Lead sinks more men in the Rio Grande in a year than gold does in a decade.

The Rangers were also busy with the Mexicans of Texas birth who were trying to evade military service. The Captain wrote: 'In the last few days I have been picking up some of the slackers and delivering them to the Military authorities.... Most all these young Mexicans who are born on the American side try to evade registration on the grounds of being Mexican citizens.... [They] are baptized on the Mexican side, and they try to claim exemption from draft by getting a certificate from the church of their baptism.'[41] He was also suspicious of a Mexican organization, The Union Nacional, which had chapters at McAllen and other border towns. 'In my judgment it is no good for the peacefulness of this border.'[42]

In their zeal Captain Stevens's men disarmed some of the Mexicans on the border and found themselves in conflict with the sheriff of Cameron County, who threatened to file charges against them for robbery with firearms. The most serious charge against them was that of murdering Florencia García on the Piper Plantation. Three Rangers, who were sent to investigate cattle-stealing there, arrested eight or nine men, took some of them to jail at Fort Brown, and released the others. Among those released was Florencia García. Shortly after this a dead body, supposed to have been that of García, was found near the river. Stevens defended his men from the charges, stating that the opposition to the Rangers did not arise from 'the finding of a dead Mexican,' but was due to their activities in breaking up German propaganda and spy work, or to a desire to hurt Governor Hobby's candidacy for governor.[43]

On the night of August 21, 1918, Rangers Joe Shaw and Chavez were scouting near the farm of Tefilo Solis, two miles from Brownsville, when they saw some men in the field. Shaw approached the Mexicans, but sent Chavez to cut them off from the river. There was shooting, and Chavez saw the Mexicans running away. Shaw was found in the field, shot in the breast and back. Captain Stevens arrested Tefilo Solis and learned that Shaw had shot one of the Solis boys in the face and head with birdshot. Three rifles and a shotgun were found concealed in the field, two pairs of shoes by the river bank, and the print

[40] Captain Charles F. Stevens to Major Walter Woodul, June 14, 18, 1918. A.G.P.

[41] *Ibid.*, June 12, 1918. A.G.P.

[42] *Ibid.*, June 26, 1918. A.G.P.

[43] *Ibid.*, May 23 and 25, 1918. A.G.P.

of bare feet in the sand. It was supposed that the Solis boys were attempting to evade the draft.

It is not a trivial offense to kill a Texas Ranger on the border. Three days later — August 24 — Rangers O. E. Walters, John Sitters, and the three Saddlers — John, George, and Len — fought some Mexicans on the river bank by the Piper Plantation. The results were told by Captain Stevens as follows:

'The Rangers claimed that they fired about fifty rounds and that there were four or five dead Mexicans on the sandbar in the river and on the bank of the river.... I went on the river where the fighting had taken place.... On the Mexican side I could see several dead horses and several large Mexican hats. When the fight occurred, the river was very low, barely running, but the same night there was a rise, and if there were any dead Mexicans on the sandbars, the river evidently washed them down stream. These Rangers are all good men, and the way things looked to me, there evidently must have been some Mexicans killed.

'I expect we will have a lot of trouble with these slackers. And since the age limit has been changed, there will be hundreds of them trying to get across the river, and after once on the Mexican side. and they cannot get work and nothing to eat, they will be coming to this side stealing and giving us a lot of trouble.' [44]

In the vicinity of Laredo and Rio Grande City, Captain Will L. Wright and his company were having trouble with Mexican draft evaders, horse thieves, and bandits. On March 3, 1918, Captain Wright and six men left Laredo for Hebronville, where they camped in quarters furnished by Henry Edds, and turned their horses out to graze and rest. At four o'clock on the following morning, a Mexican rider woke the Rangers with the news that the Tom East Ranch, thirty-five miles away, had been raided by bandits. Though the Mexican was not certain as to the particulars, his story indicated that the inhabitants had probably been killed. In order to reach the scene as soon as possible, Captain Wright threw the saddles in a truck, loaded his men in automobiles, and set out for the East Ranch. There he mounted the men on horses that were furnished by a citizen, and took the bandit trail.

The trail led to the San Antonio Viejo Ranch, which had also been robbed, and thence towards Roma, which lies on the Rio Grande a few miles above Rio Grande City. The Rangers and three citizens followed the trail twenty-five miles and came upon the Mexicans in

[44] Captain Charles F. Stevens to Major Walter Woodul, August 26, 1918. A.G.P. The fight occurred about dusk.

the brush near El Javali Ranch. The brush was so thick that the Rangers were within twenty feet of the bandits before they saw them.

'They were all on the ground,' wrote the Captain, 'their horses standing by them. They commenced shooting at us as they got on their horses, and before you could snap your finger they were all running and we after them. After they ran a short distance they scattered in bunches and the men also scattered to follow them.' Eight of the bandits stayed together and these were pursued by Captain Wright, Ranger Pullin, and the three citizens. The Rangers and ranchmen crowded the Mexicans so hard as to cause them to throw away or lose most of the booty taken from the ranches as well as their pistols and rifles. The Texans killed one Mexican, knocked another from his horse, and wounded others. The leader of the raiders was riding a grain-fed horse, a fine pinto, taken from the East Ranch. The Rangers were never able to overtake this horse, but found him at the river. Seven horses, two mules, saddles, bridles, pistols, and rifles were captured. The Rangers in this fight were Captain Wright, Rangers Hutchinson, Pullin, W. C. Wells, Munroe Wells, and J. P. Perkins; the citizens were Henry Edds, Oscar Thompson, Tom Moley, Dudley Stillwell, John Draper, and a man named Franklin.[45]

In the fall of 1918 one of Captain Wright's men, Sergeant J. J. Edds, was involved in two incidents which led to criticism of the Rangers. The first was the killing of Jose María Gomez Salinas, better known around Rio Grande City as Jamaica. This Mexican was suspected of having stolen horses from local ranchmen, Eduardo Yzaguirre and L. D. Eldridge. On the morning of September 1, Antonio Perez reported the loss of a horse and notified Sergeant Edds at Rio Grande City. Edds advised the ranchmen to put their cowboys on the trail while he would take the Rangers to the river to cut the thief off from Mexico. The cowboys captured Jamaica before he reached the river and notified the Rangers but Edds could not take the prisoner to Hebronville because he was summoned to appear in court at Rio Grande City. Arrangements were made, however, to send the prisoner to jail in charge of Sabas Ozuma and Frederico Lopez, *vaqueros* on the Yzaguirre Ranch. The prisoner was handcuffed and put on a horse, and sent toward Hebronville. Sabas Ozumas has told all that is known of what happened on the road: 'Everything went all right until we arrived within four miles of Hebronville, the prisoner riding in front and Frederico and I a few steps behind. As we passed some brush, he looked around and at the same time put spurs to his horse

[45] W. L. Wright to Adjutant General, March 7, 1918. A.G.P.

BRAVO

and dashed into the brush, when we fired at him, killing him. We only fired one shot each, hitting him in the back.... He fell dead from his horse... about fifty feet from us. The Mexicans exonerated Sergeant Edds of all blame, saying that the only orders Edds gave them was to take the prisoner to jail safely, but to watch him closely. They considered it their duty to kill him rather than to let him escape.'[46]

About a month after the killing of Jamaica by the two Mexicans, Sergeant Edds killed Lisandro Munoz on the Sanchez Ranch, near Roma in Starr County, under the impression that he was dealing with Alonzo Sanchez, a deserter. This unfortunate incident came

[46] Statements of Sabas Ozuma, Eduardo Yzaguirre, Captain W. L. Wright, and Sergeant J. J. Edds are in A.G.P. See also Captain W. L. Wright to James A. Harley, September 7, 1918. The fourth charge of the Canales investigation of the Texas Rangers was based on this incident.

about under the following circumstances. On the bulletin board in the post office at Rio Grande City the name of Alonzo Sanchez was posted as a deserter and the officers were on the lookout for him. The officers received word that on the night of October 5, Sanchez would be at his father's ranch in Star County, and Edds asked Captain Wright for permission to capture him.

Three Rangers left the camp after two o'clock in the morning of October 6 and reached the house of Jesús Sanchez before dawn. One man was left to guard the front, while Sergeant Edds and Ranger Wells went along a net wire fence, looking for a gate that would admit them to the rear yard. Wells remained on the outside where he could command a view of the rear, while Edds passed into the yard where he spied two men sleeping on separate cots. The deserter had been described as a man wearing a small black mustache. One of the men suited the description which led Sergeant Edds to conclude that he was Alonzo Sanchez, the deserter.

The Ranger called the sleeping man several times and finally aroused him.

'Quien es?' asked the Mexican.

'The Rangers — John Edds,' the sergeant answered.

'He eased off the cot towards me in a crouching position,' said the Ranger, 'and I told him in Spanish to sit down, that I wanted to talk to him, and kept asking him his name.... He did not reply, but suddenly sprang towards me, catching my Winchester.... I told him to turn my gun loose, that I was not going to hurt him, but he did not do it, and we scuffled back towards the fence about fifteen feet.... He kept trying to wrench the gun out of my hands, and was a more powerful man than I. He was about to get the gun and I pulled the trigger and the ball hit him in the leg.... He lived only a few minutes, as the ball had cut an artery, and he bled to death.'

By this time the other Mexican, Zaragosa Sanchez, brother of the deserter, was awake. He asked what was the matter and Edds told him that he had shot Alonzo.

'Is he dead?' asked the Mexican. Edds answered that he did not know, and ordered him to examine the body, stating that if the man were not dead, they could call a doctor.

The Mexican made the examination and exclaimed: 'This is not Alonzo, but Lisandro.'

'What Lisandro?' asked the Ranger.

'Lisandro Munoz, my cousin,' was the answer. Zaragosa Sanchez stated that Alonzo had been over to Texas that night to attend a dance, but he had evidently crossed the border before day. As there were no witnesses to the shooting, no one could dispute Edds's story and no legal action was brought against him.[47]

5. *POLITICAL FIRE*

As long as the World War continued, there was little probability that the Texas Rangers would be severely criticized for any action, regular or irregular, that they might take against revolutionists, German spies, draft evaders, or any others who interfered with the single purpose of victory against the Central Powers. In fact the war had the effect of strengthening the hand of the Rangers and increasing their number. A law was passed increasing the force to a thousand men, and most of these emergency Rangers were stationed on the border. This increase permitted the enlistment of men who were inexperienced, and in some cases incompetent. The Ranger service was also affected by the fact that the state was split politically into Ferguson and anti-Ferguson factions. Both factions used the Rangers for political purposes at a time when the force really had a great opportunity for distinguished service. O. B. Colquitt seems to have been responsible for introducing the spoils system into the Ranger Force, but Ferguson and Hobby went further in sinking the Rangers in the mire, and their vicious policy has been followed by succeeding governors without exception.

Another thing that created opposition to the Rangers was their effort to enforce prohibition under the Dean Law. Local officers often resented the raids made by the Rangers in their jurisdiction. All bootleggers in the state — and their numbers increased constantly — were bitterly opposed to having their places raided unceremoniously and unexpectedly by such men as Captain Frank Hamer, Captain Tom Hickman, and others.

It was not until the World War closed that the growing opposition to the Ranger force reached a climax in a sweeping legislative investigation. It is not strange, in the light of incidents related in the chapter, that the attack came from a citizen of the Rio Grande Valley and a man of Mexican blood. This was Mr. J. T. Canales of Brownsville, representative in the legislature. Many people are under the impression that Mr. Canales was intent from the first on the abolition of the force, but this seems not to have been his purpose.

[47] Account based on sworn statement of J. J. Edds, Zaragosa Sanchez, Jesús Sanchez (father of Alonzo), Ranger Munroe Wells, October 18, 1918. A.G.P.

Mr. Canales introduced a bill into the legislature providing that the pay of the Rangers should be increased in order that more desirable men might be attracted to the service. The bill further provided that each Ranger should give bond to the amount of one thousand dollars and that ex-service men should be given preference in the appointments. The purpose of the bond was to eliminate bad characters and to prevent the politicians from paying their debts with Ranger commissions. The bill was reported favorably by the Military Committee and came to the house for debate. 'On the floor of the House,' wrote Mr. Canales, 'the attack was made on the bill and in the course of the debate the facts came out that the then Ranger force was honeycombed with undesirable characters and in great need of reorganization. The Rangers during 1915, 1916, 1917, and 1918 had committed many outrageous acts, that is to say, would arrest persons and after the persons were arrested they would be shot by the Rangers unceremoniously... without a chance to prove themselves innocent.' These charges caused Barry Miller to suggest a thorough investigation which was provided for in a concurrent resolution.

The investigation began at Austin on January 31, 1919. Mr. Canales presented eighteen, or more, charges against the Rangers, some of them dating back two or three years. The Rangers were charged on three counts with the murder of eighteen or twenty prisoners. Other charges alleged wanton killing, flogging and torture of prisoners, drunkenness, and assault. Captain W. M. Hanson, inspector, was accused of making sham investigations designed to exonerate men who should have been punished, and the adjutant general was charged with using the Rangers for political purposes. The burden of Mr. Canales's complaints, however, was against the Rangers for the maltreatment of Mexicans.

Despite the severity of the charges and the strenuous efforts of Mr. Canales to prove them, he never went so far as to demand the abolition of the force. In response to a recent inquiry as to his attitude towards the men and his purpose, he wrote as follows:

'Not only myself but all my family have been always friendly to the Ranger force, especially when we had such captains as Captain Rogers, Captain Brooks, and Captain Hughes, all of whom had been stationed at Alice... and our ranch which was located thirty miles south of Alice was used by the Rangers as a station to change horses. We usually supplied them with fresh horses and gave them guides when they would go south into the countries of Starr, Hidalgo, and Cameron. At that time the Rangers were used to protect cattle men from cattle thieves, desperadoes, and other bad characters. Later on the Ranger force was used for political purposes.... Governor Hobby had appointed a republican politician as senior captain of the Ranger force. I had known —— for a number of years as a corrupt republican politician and was surprised to have a republican placed at the head of the Ranger force. —— began to fill the Rangers with cutthroats and murderers and the result was the outrages brought out at the hearing. ... I wanted to clean the Ranger force of such undesirable elements and to get —— discharged as I believed him to be the cause of the trouble... I did not want to destroy the force or impair its efficiency.'

In answer to the question as to how the Mexican citizens of Texas look upon the Rangers, Mr. Canales said: 'I wish to say that we believe the Texas Ranger force is an element of safety in the enforcement of laws if such force can be kept free from politics as the original force was; but it is a dangerous element and a menace to the citizens if the Ranger force is used for political purposes by the governor as it was used by Governor Hobby, and Governor Ferguson.' [48]

The investigation lasted nearly two months and resulted in about two thousand pages of testimony. On the whole it seems to have been conducted with much less prejudice than the Fall investigation which followed soon after. The Mexicans at least had their day in court, though the preponderance of the testimony was in favor of the Rangers. One of the most interesting witnesses was William G. B. Morrison, who compared the effectiveness of the Rangers with that of the soldiers. He stated that during the serious bandit troubles as many as thirty-five thousand troops were stationed in Hidalgo and neighboring counties, but in spite of numbers, the bandits would slip into the camps, shoot down the guards, and 'get away with it.' They considered the soldiers a joke and would run into them at every turn of the road. If the cavalry patrol started down the river, the bandits could hear the clatter-clatter, crunch of leather, and rattle of accouterments for a mile, and step into the brush. But when the Rangers were out, the case was different. The Mexican seldom tampered with a Ranger unless he had him dead to rights and could shoot him in the back. 'When the Rangers come in, the little grape-vine telegraph system that exists among the Mexican goes along in the underbrush, God only knows how.' The Mexicans know that the Ranger is 'used to that country, used to tracking, used to Texas and the roads, and he knows the Mexicans, and you are just as apt to run slap-bang into him without seeing him as not.' [49] He stated that the enemies of the Rangers accused them of killing from five

[48] J. T. Canales to W. P. Webb, January 11, 1935.

[49] Transcript of the evidence in A.G.P.

hundred to five thousand men, but he added that the citizens killed as many as the Rangers.

As a result of the investigation, the law of March 31, 1919, was passed, reducing the Ranger force to four regular companies of not to exceed fifteen privates, a sergeant, and a captain. In addition there was to be a headquarters company of six men in charge of a senior captain. A sixth officer with the rank and pay of captain was to serve as quartermaster. The provision in Mr. Canales's original bill requiring a bond was thrown out by amendment. The new law provided that any citizen could make complaint against any Ranger for any offense, and it instructed the adjutant general to investigate the charge and institute legal action if the evidence warranted.[50] This provision represents the chief direct result of the Canales investigation. An indirect benefit came from the general shakeup and perhaps from the resignation of the high officer whom Mr. Canales believed was responsible for the abuses he complained of.

[50] *General Laws of Texas*, Thirty-Sixth Legislature, pp. 263–266.

XXII

FRANK HAMER: MODERN TEXAS RANGER

I made up my mind to be as much like an Indian as possible.

I sure felt good that morning going up and down the long slopes with that thief ahead of me.

XXII. FRANK HAMER: MODERN TEXAS RANGER

It is not uncommon to hear that the Texas Ranger force has deteriorated and that it does not now attract the high type of men that it once did. It may be admitted that the modern force has not produced men whose reputations will compare with some of those whose deeds have been related, but this admission is no reflection on the modern force. The fundamental fact is that the present-day Ranger has no frontier upon which to paint an heroic picture of daring and courage. The Ranger of the old order belonged to a primitive and highly individualistic society which offered him great opportunities. The modern, complex society has reduced his proportions, but it has not changed his nature.

Captain Frank Hamer has been selected as the prototype of the modern force. He would probably be named as the first choice by most of the men who have served on the force and by a majority of the people of Texas. If all criminals in Texas were asked to name the man that they would most dread to have on their trail, they would probably name Captain Frank Hamer without hesitation. There is not a criminal in Texas who does not fear and respect him.

Frank Hamer's service has covered that period of transition in Texas from frontier simplicity and directness to modern complexity. He started his official life on horseback in pursuit of horse thieves, cow thieves, and train robbers. He was trained by men of the old tradition, Captains J. H. Rogers, John R. Hughes, and others who learned in the school of Major John B. Jones's Frontier Battalion. Today he finds himself in a different crime world, that of the automobile, the radio, the acetylene torch, a world in which crime is organized on a capitalistic basis with its bankers, fences, mouthpieces, and what not. From the study of boot-heel prints and horse tracks, Frank Hamer graduated to the Bertillon system and hotel registers. He has seen crime change from a rural to an urban occupation. He started by riding from thirty to fifty miles a day over the Plains of Texas after a criminal who rode no farther; and he has come now to following men who travel a thousand miles in the same length of time. Few men have been able to

CAPTAIN FRANK HAMER

make this transition from one school of crime to another so entirely different.

The great peace officer must have three qualities: courage, intelligence, and character. Courage alone never made more than an average Ranger, because the quality is so common among Rangers that it affords no distinction. It is the superior mind which gives knowledge plus unswerving integrity which gives character that distinguish the great officer. Such a man cannot be scared, bought, or fooled. Hamer may have been deceived on occasions, but even his worst enemies — and he has bitter ones — have never intimated that he has price or fear.

Captain Hamer's father, Frank Augustus Hamer, came from West Virginia to Texas in 1870. He married Lou Emma Francis, whose father was a Virginian and whose mother was from Tennessee. At an early date the Hamers settled in Wilson County, where Frank was born near Fairview on March 17, 1884, but in 1890 the family moved to San Saba County where Frank grew to manhood. Here he attended such schools as the country afforded, but even at this early date his whole interest was in the outdoor life. While in school he read a book which has had considerable influence on him, Josiah Wilbarger's *Indian Depredations in Texas*, a book that abounds in thrilling stories of Indian depredations, massacres, and thefts. It also tells of the way in which the Texas Rangers and Indian fighters tracked down and killed the Indians or were killed by them. It would be logical to assume that the book would arouse in an adventure-loving boy the desire to be like the Texas Ranger, but it did not have this effect on Frank Hamer. 'I made up my mind,' he said, 'to be as much like an Indian as I could.' It may have been this desire that caused him to become such a close observer of nature and all its manifestations.

When he was a small boy, he would make expeditions alone into the woods, excursions which would last from one to six weeks. He took only his rifle, fishing tackle, and knife; he slept on the ground and lived on the game and fish which he took from the then unspoiled forests and streams of the beautiful hill country of Texas. On these excursions, he formed an intimate personal acquaintanceship with the insects, the birds, and the animals. The flight and signal call of birds, and especially the peculiar antics of the mocking bird, which takes a fighting attitude towards all the carnivora, told him where to look for predatory animals. He learned the habits of small animals, how to track them, and where to find their homes. He studied the bird-calls and the animal cries and practiced imitating them until he could call them to him. Almost anyone can call crows, but Frank Hamer can call quail, deer, road runners (piasanos), fox-squirrels, and hoot owls; and of all these he thinks the hoot owl the most comical. One must sit very still when calling the denizens of the forest to him. Nature became an open book to Hamer and he became more and more like an Indian. Every type of human being reminds him of some animal, of something in nature. The criminal is a coyote, always taking a look over his shoulder; a cornered political schemer is a 'crawfish about three days from water'; an officer going down a railroad track to meet a killer barricaded behind a pile of cross-ties, lifting his legs gingerly, reminds him of a sand-hill crane walking up a river-bed. The merciless murderer is 'as cold-blooded as a rattlesnake with a chill.' But sometimes his allusions are Biblical. A red-headed cowman from West Texas is 'Sandy Samson from the slippery slopes of the salty Pecos.'

Needless to say these trips into the forest developed the marksmanship of which Hamer is a master. With a rifle he can kill a deer running at full speed and birds in full flight. His skill with the pistol may be illustrated by the following incident which happened shortly before this account was written. Sheriff John Graham of Kimble County offered to eat a peckerwood that was hammering high up on a pecan tree if Captain Hamer would shoot its head off while it was in motion, but the sheriff had to back down on account of a weak stomach. As a knife-thrower Captain Hamer can equal a Mexican. In the hill-country of Texas are many armadillos, clumsy animals with the shell of a terrapin and the head of an opossum. The Captain hunts these animals only with a knife, which he throws with such force and accuracy that he not only kills the animal, but in many instances pins it to the ground.

A boy cannot grow up in the San Saba country without knowing and loving good horses. Frank Hamer began to ride early and continued in the saddle until paved highways and automobiles made the horse impractical in the pursuit of criminals. But his love of horses is still deep, as one can see when he talks of Bugler, a powerful bay animal that was his favorite and a real companion. He handled his horses gently, but with the hand of a master, and can make you believe that a horse and man can come to understand each other perfectly if associated on long journeys, provided both have horse sense. He believes that the endurance of a horse on long or hard journeys depends more on the rider's knowledge of how to ride than on his weight. Though Hamer weighed nearly two hundred pounds, he could help the horse in such a way that he could hold with those of lesser burden. One must sit deep in the saddle, bear a part of his weight on the stirrups, and catch the rhythm of the animal. If the ride is long, there must be no

FRANK HAMER AND BUGLER IN THE LLANO COUNTRY, 1914

galloping, but only the trot and walk. The cinch must be neither too loose nor too tight. Long hills must be taken at a walk, and, if time permits, with loose cinch for easy breathing.

Hamer's sensory powers — sight, smell, hearing — may not be as acute as those of the Indian, but they are certainly far sharper than those of the average man. He doubtless inherited keen senses, but these he has cultivated and developed until his world of sense perceptions extends far beyond the horizon that bounds most mortals. The stories about them may seem incredulous, but are true nevertheless. Two incidents that occurred during the hundred-and-two-day pursuit of Clyde Barrow may be used to illustrate his power of smell and hearing. When Captain Hamer came into Austin, he would call a few of his friends to his home for his chief diversion, a game of no-ante poker. The chase was nearing the end; he knew it and every sense was alert. 'Did some one burn himself?' he inquired. One of the players had struck a match which stuck to his finger. Hamer was the only one that had caught the odor of scorched flesh. On the same evening, he remarked that an airplane was passing, yet it was a half-minute before the sound was audible to the others.

As for sight, his feats with guns prove that it is excellent, but even these do not reveal the full measure of his visual powers. He has spent much time on the rifle ranges, and on one occasion when the target was too far to see where the bullets hit, he sat by the rifleman and called the shots *before they hit*. He can see the bullet, which looks like a bee, enveloped in a tiny cloud of heat waves produced by friction between lead and air. The discharge from a shotgun 'looks like a swarm of gnats.' A discussion of this little-known subject may be found in a treatise on ballistics.

Hamer uses his eyes for observation as well as for seeing. There is a distinction. He is a close observer of human ears, and declares that no two persons have ears alike. Were he ambitious, he could make a national reputation by promoting this original idea. It would be a simple matter for crime bureaus to make imprints of criminal ears which could be used to check with finger-prints. When there is excitement he knows almost by intuition *what* to look for. An automobile backfired like a pistol shot, the crowd began to peer, a group gathered. Hamer interrupted his conversation long enough to say: 'When you think you hear a gun in a crowd, don't look for the gun. Watch the crowd, and if you see some fellow coming so fast that his vest pocket's dipping sand, you'll know it was a gun.' To Hamer such a one is just a human mocking bird giving a danger signal.

By the time the San Saba youth was seventeen, he had reached a height of six feet two with an inch to grow, but as yet he was in no way formidable. At seventeen he went 'on his own,' working as a cowboy on the ranches. Naturally, he wore the cowboy attire — boots, soft felt hat, spurs, and belt — all of good quality. On one occasion he came about noon to a country store south of Brownwood, where he stopped to eat some sardines and crackers and feed his horse. He noticed a crowd of toughs, such as congregated in those days around such places, but went about his business. He hung the nosebag on the horse, bought and ate his lunch and made ready to continue his journey. By this time the toughs were commenting on his appearance and particularly on his good clothes. It was decided that one would take his spurs, another his hat, a third his belt, while the others would remove his boots and with them administer such punishment as the occasion seemed to require.

The boy paid no attention, except that he drew his knife from his pocket and began to whittle a toothpick out of a match. The crowd moved towards him, and a self-selected leader emerged and approached with his eye fixed on the knife. The boy made no move either forward or back, but as usual, he did the unexpected thing. He did not move his hands, but began to gather saliva in his mouth, and when the man paused to decide on his next step, Hamer spat in his face. The man hesitated, some one of the crowd asked if he were 'going to take it.' He looked at the knife, wiped the back of his hand over his face, and withdrew. With studied deliberation, the boy slipped his bridle on his horse, mounted, and rode away. Captain Hamer said that he knew that he must do something wholly unexpected, and something that would win at least a part of the crowd to his side. 'Had he reached for me I would have made two pieces out of him,' said the Captain in conclusion.

When Hamer was growing up, the Texas Rangers were doing a great deal of work in Western Texas, and since there were no Indians to join in outdoor life, he decided that the next most desirable organization was the Texas Rangers. It was while he was on the Carr Ranch between Sheffield and Fort Stockton that two horses, saddles, and bridles were stolen. Hamer took the trail and followed the thieves to the Crockett County line, where he captured men and horses.

Hamer was often alone at the Carr Ranch and spent much time hanging on the new community telephone to hear the news that traveled over the wires from one isolated ranch to another. One night he heard Sheriff D. S. Barker telephoning Charlie Witcher, his former deputy, asking him to intercept a horse thief who was coming that way on a stolen horse. Witcher was busy, did not want to get mixed up in the courts, and declined to do any more thief-catching. At this point Hamer broke into the conversation and volunteered to take the job, since the thief would have to pass his ranch on his way out.

'Who are you?' asked the sheriff.

'I am Frank Hamer and am working on the Carr Ranch.'

'Well, if you'll catch him, that will be fine. I'll describe him.'

'No need to,' said Hamer. 'I heard you describe him to Charlie.'

Hamer knew that the man could not reach the ranch until about daylight and that he would stop at the windmill, as there was no water on the road for miles back. He got up at three o'clock, saddled his horse, and waited with Winchester and pistol near the water tank. The man showed up on the stolen horse about daylight, and, as Hamer had calculated, rode straight to the windmill to water the horse. Suddenly he found himself covered by a Winchester, and a little while later he was headed back the way he had come with a young cowboy about twenty feet behind him.

'Believe me,' said the Captain, 'I sure felt good that morning going up and down the long slopes with that thief ahead of me. Finally, after riding sixteen miles, I saw Dud Barker top out on a hill two miles off.

'I SURE FELT GOOD THAT MORNING . . . WITH THAT THIEF AHEAD OF ME.'

He was driving a couple of fast horses to a light buggy and they were sure stepping. I wouldn't have sold out very cheap that day.

'While we were going back, Sheriff Barker asked me how I'd like to join the Rangers. Shortly after that, Captain J. H. Rogers wrote Barker to have me report to Sergeant Jim Moore at Sheffield. I enlisted on April 21, 1906. I was twenty-two years old.'

After serving more than two years as a Ranger, Hamer resigned to become city marshal of Navasota, where he remained from November 1, 1908, until April 1, 1911. This appointment, at a much larger salary than he received as a Ranger, came because of his services there with John Dibbrell when a lawless element was causing trouble. Dibbrell was offered the place, but refused it and recommended Hamer. The citizens thought he was too young, but finally took the risk. Navasota lies in the dark plantation belt of the Old South, and on Saturdays and holidays the negroes were so numerous that a white woman hardly dared walk on the sidewalk. In a short time the situation changed and the women found plenty of room to go where they pleased. The negro's attitude towards the young officer was expressed by a porter in an Austin barber shop. A customer brought in a number of pictures of the Texas Rangers, and one of the barbers held up Hamer's picture for the porter to see.

'Do you know that man?' asked the barber.

'Yes suh,' said the porter with a broad grin, 'an' when I sees him comin' I jes' steps aside.'

Hamer antagonized an influential element in Navasota by killing a pet bulldog that belonged to a prominent citizen, the proprietor of the leading hotel. Though the dog was dearly loved by his own family, he was a terror to others and a menace to other dogs equally dear to their masters. His powerful undershot jaw, strength, and the courage of his breed made him master of the canine family. The city council ordered the young marshal to watch for the dog and to see that his master kept him off the streets. It was not long before Hamer knocked the dog insensible with his six-shooter to make him release a throat-hold on a fine bird dog. He ordered the hotel man to keep the dog muzzled, and told him that if the dog attacked other animals, he would be killed. It was not long, however, until the dog was out, and this time he killed a bird dog belonging to Herbert Terrell. The hotel man managed to get his prize pup into the hotel before the marshal appeared, but this did not save the dog, for Frank Hamer's word was out. He walked straight into the hotel and killed the dog in the lobby.

The town split into Hamer and anti-Hamer factions with the hotel man leading the anti-Hamer group which was recruited from saloon toughs, some of whom had felt the heel of the Hamer boots — and some the toe. The young marshal's struggle for supremacy was desperate, and in the course of time more of the toughs made contact with his boots. The situation was one that would permit no compromise, one in which the officer could show no weakness without complete loss of prestige. The details of the struggle cannot be given, but if related, would read like a chapter from the life of Wyatt Earp. This does not mean that anyone was killed, but some were pretty well marked for future identification.

From Navasota, Hamer went to Houston, where he served as special officer for Mayor Baldwin Rice from April 1, 1911, until April 20, 1913. He was detailed to work after a gang that had killed a number of Houston policemen.

From Houston, Hamer went to Junction, in the hill country where he had grown up, to work after wire-cutters, horse and cow thieves. It was while here that he took the trail of a horse thief that was headed towards the west. He called the sheriff of Sutton County, telling him to look out for his man. When he reached the Allison Ranch, he found a telephone call from the sheriff, who was a good sheriff despite the fact that he stuttered. The conversation ran as follows:

'Hello, Sheriff, what is it?'

'Hello, F-Frank... F-F-Frank, I-I-I got him.'

'Y' did. Well, that's fine. Tell me about it.'

'C-C-C-Come on in, Frank, you c-c-can r-r-r-ride it b-b-b-before I c-c-can tell you.'

Hamer re-entered the Ranger service on April 1, 1915, and spent one year on detached service. He was then cattle inspector for more than a year when he returned to the Rangers on October 1, 1918, as a member of Captain W. W. Taylor's company, which was stationed in the lower Rio Grande Valley. Within a few days he was engaged in a fight in which his best friend, Sergeant Delbert Timberlake, was killed. The curious thing about Timberlake's death was a premonition of it. Shortly before the fight he spoke to Hamer about this premonition, and said that he had some letters that he wanted to destroy. He went to a trunk, took out a package of letters, and made a fire of them in the camp yard.

The prohibition law was in effect and the Rangers were having much trouble in keeping Mexican liquor out of Texas, and in their effort to do so were working in conjunction with Sheriff W. T. Vann of Cameron County. There was a Mexican named Incarnacion Delgado who was a cart man operating between Matamoros and Brownsville. To outward appearances he was as inoffensive as any cart man should be, but the officers believed that he was using his humble occupation, which gave him a passport for six days in the week, to cover his smuggling of opium, mescal, and tequilla.

Sheriff Vann and the Rangers had information that Delgado was planning to cross the river; they knew his probable route and his signal to his confederates — the bleat of a goat. The officers planned to conceal themselves near the intersection of two trails, one of which they felt the smuggler would follow. The sheriff led the party which consisted of Captain Taylor, several Rangers, and two customs inspectors. On the way out, the officers in charge agreed that if anyone approached, the command to halt would be given, and if not obeyed the men were to fire. Ranger Frank Hamer, though a private, vigorously objected, stating that Delgado was a dangerous man, who would not surrender, and that he would kill someone if possible.

'I am in favor,' he said, 'of giving him the works first and the orders afterwards.'

'We might kill an innocent man,' said one of the officers.

'No, we won't kill an innocent man because no innocent man is going to be on this trail at this time of night,' said Hamer. His judgment was overruled.

As the men rode to the place of concealment, Hamer found himself by Timberlake, and noticed that he was carrying a shotgun, a weapon which Texas Rangers rarely use except at close range and for mob-quelling.

'Tim,' said Hamer, 'what kind of a gun is that?'

'A shotgun,' answered the sergeant.

'What do you mean by coming out on a deal like this with a shotgun?' asked Hamer.

'Well, Pancho' — which is Mexican for Frank — 'the way I feel to-night, one gun will do me about as much good as another. I have a feeling that I'll get mine any way you take it.'

The men had been in position about two hours when they heard the twigs breaking under catlike tread, the bleat of a goat, and the brush scratching leather boots that were coming along the trail. Hamer and the sheriff rose quietly to their feet, leveled their guns, and the sheriff gave the command, 'Halt!' Delgado held his pistol in his right hand and fired instantly. The ball struck the ground eighteen feet from Timberlake who had not risen, ricocheted, and penetrated his body. Timberlake went over, saying, 'Cap, he got me through the guts.' Vann and Hamer fired at the flash of the pistol, and as successive plumes of flame burst from the Ranger's Winchester, one man remarked, 'Good God, watch Frank use the pear-burner on him.' The Mexican ran a few feet and fell dead with his forty-five pistol clenched in one hand and a dozen pistol cartridges in the other. He was wounded in the hand and had two Winchester bullets in the body. At this time the Ranger force had been greatly enlarged as a war measure, and W. M. Hanson was inspector. He reported that Sheriff Vann fired all the shots that took effect. Captain Hamer states that he carried the automatic rifle and Sheriff Vann had a shotgun. Captain W. W. Taylor verifies the statement. Therefore the official report by the inspector is in error.

Sergeant Timberlake's companions took him to a Brownsville hospital, where he lingered until seven o'clock the next morning. The surgeons informed him that he could not live; he 'remained calm and collected and met his death with great courage,' runs the official report.

Frank Hamer, who succeeded him as sergeant, was by him to the last.

'Pancho,' said the wounded man, 'there's no chance for me, is there?'

'No, Tim, there's not a chance for you.'

'Did he get away?' asked the man on the bed.

'No.'

'That helps a whole lot,' said the Ranger. Then a tremor passed over him and Hamer pulled the white sheet over the face of his companion and went out to a group of fellow officers who stood by the window.

'Well, he's cashed in,' was the way he informed them.

'Hamer,' said one of the officers, 'if we had followed your advice, things would have been different. We made a mistake.'

'Yes,' he assented, nodding to the white sheet that could be seen through the window, 'and there is your mistake.' And thus do the Texas Rangers go straight up to death.[1]

From April 11, 1920, until September 21, 1921, Hamer was in the United States prohibition service, where he found plenty to do in catching stills and trying to shut off the illicit liquor trade from Mexico. He became noted for the vigor with which he struck the bootleggers and liquor runners. It was while in this service that he sent his superior to the penitentiary for four years by uncovering evidence of his complicity in violating the law that he was being paid to enforce.

He left the prohibition service — some say because he enforced the law — in September to become captain of Company C, Texas Rangers, with headquarters at Del Rio. On January 1, 1922, he was transferred to Austin as captain of the Headquarters Company, which position he held continuously until November 1, 1932. In this interval he saw service in all parts of the state, while his reputation continued to grow. He led his men in cleaning up the oil towns of Mexia, Ranger, and Borger; he assisted in defending the rights of Texas in the contest with Oklahoma over the Red River boundary; and it was in this period that he showed his powers as a detective by unraveling a number of difficult cases. He solved the Engler murder case, but could not secure an indictment because a Travis County grand jury would not accept the evidence of a ballistic expert. He built up circumstantial evidence that was all but conclusive in the Corpus Christi bomb case, but again was unable to secure a conviction. He unraveled the Leahey case, and furnished evidence which sent Leahey to the electric chair.

Yet this man, who has made his name a terror to the lawless, barely escaped becoming an outlaw himself. 'Had I not gone with the law,' he said, 'I would have gone against it.' The incident that almost made him a bank robber occurred when he was about nineteen. At that time he was employed to help deliver a herd of horses to a buyer at San Angelo. In his outfit was an experienced criminal who, because of his age and personality, had considerable influence on the younger men.

[1] Inspector W. M. Hanson to General James A. Harley, October 15, 1918. A.G.P. The official account is supplemented by Captain Hamer's oral account and the statement of Captain W. W. Taylor.

As the cowboys held the horses near town while the details of the trade were being completed, this outlaw suggested that it would be a simple operation to raid the bank and use the funds to establish a ranch in Old Mexico. Frank Hamer, among others, accepted the suggestion, and plans were hastily made. The men had moved to the head of the street that led by the bank and were about ready to make their play, when the foreman appeared and ordered them to take the horses to the delivery ground. This interruption no doubt saved the man who has left his mark on the tradition of law-enforcement in Texas. With a little time to think, Hamer realized what a fool he might have been and from that time forward he has done his own thinking. 'It was the adventure, and not the money, that appealed to me,' said the Captain. 'Had I gone into it, things would have been different.'

His instinctive sense of the right thing to do is illustrated in his experience in breaking up a ring of car thieves and recovering fifty automobiles in one community in Texas. He knew who the thieves were, but he could not recover all the cars because they had been sold all over the county. While eating chili in a café, he overheard a waitress remark that she would give ten dollars to see a telegram that the Ranger was reading. On inquiry he learned that she was the sweetheart of one of the men who knew the possessors of the stolen automobiles.

Hamer returned later for another bowl of chili, and in drawing his handkerchief from his pocket, let a folded telegram fall unnoticed to the floor. 'As I went out the door, I cut my eye around and saw that gal land on that telegram like a duck on a junebug,' he said. The telegram, signed by the adjutant general, read:

> DO NOT PROSECUTE INNOCENT PURCHASERS WHO TURN IN CARS. ARREST ALL OTHERS AND HOLD IN JAIL FOR CRIMINAL PROSECUTION

The next morning the stolen automobiles were pouring in on Captain Hamer faster than he could write receipts for them. He had written the telegram.

Apropos of Hamer's inflexible adherence to right, or to what he thinks is right, is one remarkable experience that he had on the Mexican border. No dates and few names can be given in connection with this story, but the story is this: A revolution was in progress in Mexico (and that certainly fixes no date). The revolutionists were depending on confederates and sympathizers in Texas for arms which were smuggled across the border by men who smuggled for profit rather than from patriotic motives. The United States government finally established an embargo on arms and all forces were put to work to prevent smug-

A BORDER AGREEMENT

gling. At first the Texas Rangers were ordered to assist the government in this work, but for a reason that is not clear they were later instructed to pay no further attention to them.

Frank Hamer believed that the smuggling of arms to revolutionists was wrong and refused to obey the order. Moreover, he knew that when the Rangers were withdrawn, the bandits would come from the other side and clean up the Texas ranches. Therefore, he continued to make it interesting for smugglers and thieves.

He was not discharged for the probable reason that his superiors knew he would talk, and it is barely possible that they feared he might make the issue personal. Therefore, some other way had to be found to handle this contrary fellow. All the Rangers save one were withdrawn, and Frank Hamer was left alone to patrol ninety miles of a dangerous international border. If his body should be found in the brush or floating down the Rio Grande, the assumption would be that the smugglers and thieves had killed him for meddling with their affairs. Realizing that he could do little alone, Frank Hamer sought out the Mexican officer who had charge of the south bank and suggested to him a way by which the theft of property and smuggling of arms could be stopped. As a result of this conference, Hamer crossed the Rio Grande and became the virtual head of a large squad of Mexican soldiers who combed ninety miles of border. When stolen property or stock was located and identified, the possessors were invited to back up against an adobe wall about thirty feet from a military firing squad, and the stolen goods were assembled and returned to their owners in Texas.

It requires one sort of courage to hold ninety miles of Texas border against gun smugglers, thieves, and politicians, but it requires an entirely different kind to wage war single-handed against the Texas Bankers' Association in defense of bank robbers. Captain Frank Hamer conducted such a war because he was convinced that the bankers were in the wrong; he won it because he was able to prove to the public that the bankers were paying five thousand dollars each for the killing of innocent men. His war on the Texas Bankers' Association was fought in the spring of 1928, and a record of it will be found in the newspapers of March and April.

The Texas bankers had become exasperated at the numerous robberies that were being committed, and equally impatient with the failure of the courts to convict or to punish the robbers. Consequently, they adopted strong measures designed to rid the country of bank robbers and to save the delay and expense incident to court trials. In every member bank large placards were posted which read as follows:

REWARD

FIVE THOUSAND DOLLARS FOR DEAD BANK ROBBERS

NOT ONE CENT FOR LIVE ONES

Whether this reward discouraged bank robbing is not known, but that it did not stop it is certain. Within a few months numerous banks were robbed, and at Clarksville Captain Tom Hickman and some fellow officers shot down two robbers as they emerged from the bank with handbags containing the bank's currency. Captain Hamer and Captain Tom Hickman learned of a plan to rob another bank, and they were on hand, determined to make the bandits pay for their folly. They saw the bandit car cruise by the bank a number of times and were somewhat mystified because the strike was not made. They saw the reason in a lanky country boy who was standing by a telephone pole directly in front of the bank with a gun, which he had brought to town to have repaired. The robbers could not afford to take the risk of creating a disturbance on the street, nor could they be sure that the man with a gun was not a guard ready to shoot them down. The country boy did not realize that he had saved more than one human life.

Shortly after the reward was posted, Captain Hamer noted that a great many bank robbers were being killed by local officers, and that practically all the killings were done in the night. Having a very suspicious nature, as well as a thorough knowledge of the mental processes of both officers and criminals, he began to ask himself why so many bank robbers were killed at night and so few in banking hours. After some investigation he came to the amazing conclusion that the men who were being killed were not real bank robbers, but simple-minded, half-drunken boys who had been induced to join pretending bank robbers, and lured to the spot where they were shot down by officers who had been tipped. The officers then collected from the bankers the five thousand dollars, which they divided with the pretending bank robbers. In short, Frank Hamer learned that two or three men were making a profession of framing robberies for the purpose of killing men at the rate of five thousand dollars a head.

When Captain Hamer undertook legal action against the men who were engineering the killings, he could get no support from the local officers, who refused to believe that the jobs had been framed, or from grand juries that were dominated by these officers. He next approached the Bankers' Association, but with no better luck. The bankers refused to withdraw the reward, or even to modify it. Their position, and that of some officers, was that any man who could be induced to participate in a bank robbery ought to be killed. Frank Hamer does not believe in bank robbery, but he does believe in what he conceives to be right, and he holds steadfastly to the theory that every man, even a crook, is entitled to justice.

Hamer was for a time at his rope's end. He knew that there was some way to break up the murders, but he also knew — and this gave him much concern — that other murders were being planned and that he must hurry to prevent them. He did something then that he had never done before and that he has never done since: he turned to the press. On the afternoon of March 12, 1928, he handed to the reporters in the press room of the State Capitol a signed statement containing a complete exposé of what he termed the bankers' 'murder machine.'

On March 13 the story appeared on the front page of every large daily, and was given prominence throughout the country. Editorial comment demanding that his charges be investigated followed, and public sentiment was aroused to such a pitch that two of the ringleaders were indicted. Hamer immediately arrested these men and secured from them written confessions. The bankers were not indicted, but their reward was modified.

When someone reminded Hamer of the danger he was facing in antagonizing the greatest aggregation of wealth in the state — the bankers —

San Antonio Express

SAN ANTONIO, TEXAS, TUESDAY MORNING, MARCH 13, 1928—TWENTY-TWO PAGES.

Robber Reward Killings Framed Ranger Charge

Murder Machine Already Pockets Part of Bounties for Dead Bank Bandits, Hamer Says, Urging Change in Policy.

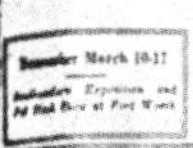

The Dallas Morning News

VOL. XLIII. NO. 165 DALLAS, TEXAS, TUESDAY, MARCH 13, 1928—TWENTY-TWO PAGES 5c PER COPY

Victims 'Framed' to Collect Robber Reward, Says Ranger

Hamer Claims Full Proof of 'Murder Ring'

Says Weaklings Induced to Commit Crime, Then Shot Down.

Eight Men Killed

Two Robberies Now Being Planned, Captain Asserts.

he replied characteristically: 'When you go fishing, what kind of fish do you like to catch, little ones or big ones? The bigger they are, the better I like to catch 'em.'

Hamer's signed statement, somewhat condensed, was as follows:

THE TRUTH ABOUT THE BANK BANDITS AND THE REWARDS

'The purpose of this article is to lay before the people of Texas, and the bankers of Texas, certain facts that they ought to have about the dead bandits and the rewards that have been paid for them. I agree that bank robbing should be stopped, that bank robbers should be shown little consideration, and should be killed when caught in the act of robbing a bank. But I do not agree that the method adopted by the Bankers' Association of Texas is either wise or just, because it is adding the crime of murder to the crime of robbery.

'There has come into existence in this state a murder machine. Here are the conditions, as I see them, out of which that machine sprang and in which it is permitted by the public to exist:

'The first condition or fact is that bank robbing has become widespread in the last few years, not only in Texas but in other parts of the United States. There is a group of criminals who make bank robbing a profession.

'A group of bankers representing most of the wealth of Texas combined through their association to offer a reward of $5000.00 for dead bank bandits. For one taken alive they would not pay a cent.

'This reward has aroused the greed and desire of a small group of men who have more love for money than for human life, and who are besides unscrupulous enough to do anything that will bring them money without too much risk of personal danger.

'There is another group of men, usually young men, drifters and loafers, whose principal traits are weakness of character combined with a certain reckless spirit. These are the men who are lured by the unscrupulous ones mentioned above into bank robbery only to be shot to death by officers who have been tipped off to the robbery.

'Finally, there is the public which, because of ignorance of the true situation, gives its support to the killing of these men, not knowing the circumstances under which they are killed.

'Here is as perfect a murder machine as can be devised, supported by the Bankers' Association, operated by the officers of the state and directed by the small group of greedy men who furnish the victims and take their cut of the money. If what I have said above is true, and I shall give the facts below to prove it, THEN THE SITUATION THAT HAS COME

ABOUT IN THIS STATE IS A DISGRACE TO TEXAS AND TO CIVILIZATION, AND SHOULD NOT BE TOLERATED.

'Supposed bank bandits have been killed since this reward was offered at Stanton, Odessa, Rankin, and at Cisco. The Cisco job, it will be remembered, was a daylight job, and was pulled off by real bank robbers. One of the men was killed, and it will be noted that three others were taken alive. Every peace officer and citizen in Texas should commend the good work done at Cisco, and they do commend it. But what about the other three?

'The Stanton job needs no discussion. Unfortunately the "noble" bandit killers were better plotters than they were marksmen, and failed to kill one of the men. It was admitted that the two Mexicans were picked up, offered work, and told to wait in front of the bank, and then shot down there in the hope of collecting $15,000.00 from the Bankers' Association.

'Here are some of the facts about the Odessa job where two men were killed and the reward of $10,000 paid. The job was pulled off at night. Now it so happens that it is not a capital offense to rob a bank at night — that is, without firearms and without endangering human life. We have a private organization bringing about the execution of men by illegal means and for money. The fact that the bandit must be taken dead, and therefore tells no tales, only makes it easy for plotters to be present when the killing is done and get away under cover of darkness. This they have done, and are planning to do again as I shall show later.

'The two men who were killed in the Odessa job had nothing with them that would enable them to get into the vault of the bank, once they were inside the building. The tools that were by them were "planted" there after they were killed by a man well known to me whose name I am ready to give to the proper authorities at the proper time. This man shared privately in the reward paid by the bankers.

'The men who were killed at Odessa have been identified, and so far as finger-prints and other investigations show, there was nothing against either of them. They were not professional bank robbers, nor were they even experienced criminals. They were but the weak characters who have been lured to their death in the way I have explained.

'These men did have in their possession an acetylene torch of the kind used by experienced bank robbers, but it was impossible to find, either on the person of the dead men, or anywhere about, tips for this torch. Without these tips the torch was as useless to them as a flashlight without battery or bulb, as a gun without ammunition.

'The acetylene tank that was a part of the torch was stolen from a certain place which I know. The man who stole the tank left tracks made by high-heeled boots. This can be proved. But the photographs of the two dead men, copies of which I have in my possession, show that both men had on well-worn shoes. Where was the man with the boots? Was he probably not the "expert" who was to use the torch?

'The reward for the Rankin job was shared in by three men. But I have in my possession facts to prove that at least one other man shared in it privately. This fourth man is the same one who had a private cut in the Odessa money, is the man who has brought about the death of four men, not one of whom was an expert professional bank robber, and for this work the bankers have paid $20,000.

'In conclusion, I want to address a few words to the President of the Bankers' Association of Texas who heads the organization that is paying these rewards. I do not believe that the bankers of Texas or the people of Texas want to be a party to such cold-blooded murders as are being committed. The men who are dead cannot be brought to life, but my purpose is to prevent the death of others. I KNOW IT TO BE A POSITIVE FACT THAT THE MAN WHO SHARED IN THE ODESSA AND RANKIN REWARDS IS NOW FRAMING TWO MORE BANK ROBBERIES TO BE PULLED IN THIS STATE IN THE NEAR FUTURE NOT FOR THE MONEY THAT COMES FROM THE BANK ROBBED BUT FOR THE MONEY THAT WILL COME BY WAY OF REWARD FOR MEN KILLED.

'Furthermore, the reward offered by the Bankers' Association has not stopped bank robbing by the professional bank robbers. Since the reward was offered, the following banks have been robbed: McCauley, Sylvester, Killene, Copperas Cove, Mullen, Grove, and Meridian. Here are seven robberies in addition to the three at Cisco, Odessa, and Rankin.

'As a duly constituted officer of the law I want to lay before the bankers of Texas a proposition, a challenge which I do not see how they can refuse to accept.

'I challenge the Texas Bankers' Association to appoint a committee of any number of their own members and let me put the facts before them that I have, and I will lay any wager that the committee will agree with me that no reward should have been paid either in the Odessa or in the Rankin job.

'I extend this appeal to the peace officers, to the press, and to the people of Texas in the hope of stopping organized murder in this state.'

THE TAKING OF CLYDE BARROW AND BONNIE PARKER

On May 23, 1934, the news was flashed over the wires that Clyde Barrow, Texas bandit number 1, had come to the end of his trail in the pine forests of Louisiana at the hands of Captain Frank Hamer and five associates. Until that story went out, very few people knew that Captain Hamer was on Barrow's trail. At the time he was not a member of the Texas Ranger force, having resigned before the Fergusons returned to the governor's chair in 1933. In view of the erroneous and misleading stories which appeared in the newspapers about the taking of Barrow and his companion, Bonnie Parker, Captain Hamer finally agreed to give as much of the story as he could without violating confidences which he received in the one hundred and two days that he followed the trail. While the story is not in the exact words of Captain Hamer, it is from notes taken in a two-hour interview on July 4, 1934, and is told in the first person as the most economical medium.

'On January 16, 1934, between daylight and sunup, four prisoners were delivered from the Eastham Prison Farm, which is a part of the Texas penitentiary system at Huntsville, Texas. One of the guards, Major Crowson, was killed, and four convicts, Joe Palmer, Henry Methvin, Raymond Hamilton, and Hilton Bybee, escaped to an automobile with unknown confederates, who from a concealed position held off the guards with machine-gun fire. It was soon learned that the delivery was planned and executed by Clyde Barrow and one or more companions.

'A few weeks later, on April 1, 1934, two state highway patrolmen, E. B. Wheeler and H. D. Murphy, saw a car parked on a side road near Grapevine, Texas, and when they stopped to investigate, or to give aid if needed, they were shot and brutally murdered by a dark-haired man and a red-headed woman. Description by people who saw the couple, together with finger-prints found on a whiskey bottle, indicated that the work was done by Clyde Barrow and Bonnie Parker. These murders brought the total number charged against Barrow to fourteen, shortly raised to fifteen. As a result of these repeated crimes, the whole state was aroused and every peace officer and highway patrolman was on the lookout for the pair.

'I was not in the state service, having resigned from the Texas Rangers on November 1, 1932, because Mrs. Miriam A. Ferguson and her husband were soon to take charge — for the fourth time — of the governor's office. About February 1, 1934, Lee Simmons, superintendent of the penitentiary, came to Austin and asked me if I would be willing to take Barrow's trail and follow it to the end. I agreed to try it, and was issued a commission as a state highway patrolman. The fact that I was after Barrow was known to only a few people before we caught him.

'On February 10, I took the trail and followed it for exactly 102 days. Like Clyde Barrow I used a Ford V8, and like Clyde I lived in the car most of the time.

'I soon had valuable sources of information, but these cannot be revealed without violating confidences. The fact that I never betray a confidence, even from the criminal, has resulted in bringing me inside information which every successful officer must have. I soon learned that Barrow played a circle from Dallas to Joplin, Missouri, to Louisiana, and back to Dallas. Occasionally he would leave this beat, but he would always come back to it as most criminals do. One time he and Bonnie went as far east as North Carolina for no other purpose, it seems, than to visit a cigarette factory. Again they would go to Indiana, Iowa, or New Mexico, but like wild horses, they would circle to their old range. The thing to be decided was whether to set the trap in Texas, Missouri, or Louisiana. I decided that Barrow could be most easily caught in Louisiana, because he was "hot" in Texas and in Missouri, having killed men in both states, but he had killed no one in Louisiana, and would probably make that his hiding-place.

'It was necessary for me to make a close study of Barrow's habits. I had never seen him, and never saw him until May 23, but I interviewed many people who knew him, and studied the numerous pictures of him and of his woman companion. I knew the size, height, and all the marks of identification of both Clyde and Bonnie. But this was not enough. An officer must know the mental habits of the outlaw, how he thinks, and how he will act in different situations. When I began to understand Clyde Barrow's mind, I felt that I was making progress. I learned that Barrow never holed up at one place; he was always on the go; and he traveled farther in one day than any fugitive that I have ever followed. He thought nothing of driving a thousand miles at a stretch. Barrow was also a master of side roads, which made his movements irregular. Around Dallas, Joplin, and in Louisiana, he seemed to know them all.

'Before the chase ended, I not only knew the general appearance and mental habits of the pair, but I had learned the kind of whiskey they drank, what they ate, and the color, size, and texture of their clothes. I first struck their trail at Texarkana. At Logansport they bought a half-gallon of whiskey; near Keechi they bought gasoline, and then went in the night to a negro house and had the negroes cook them some cornbread and fry a chicken. In Shreveport they bought pants, underwear, gloves, and an automatic shotgun. In their camp on the Wichita River, near Wichita Falls, they lost or threw away some bills for goods bought in Dallas. From the clerk I learned the size, color, and pattern of one of Bonnie's dresses, and the kind of Ascot tie and belt buckle she wore. A description of these was sent to Ed Portley of Joplin, Missouri, with information that Clyde and Bonnie were probably hiding in some abandoned mines near by.

'But the trail always led back to Louisiana, where I located their hideout on February 17. I cannot give the name of the parish because of what followed. Because I was out of Texas, it was desirable for me to take the local officers into my confidence. I learned that the sheriff of this parish could not be trusted, and so it was arranged to have Barrow's hideout moved into a parish where the officers were more reliable. In a comparatively short time the hideout was established in Bienville Parish at a place well known to me.

'The next task was to catch Clyde when he was "at home." On several occasions I went alone to this secret place. It was my hope to take him and Bonnie alive; this I could do only by finding them asleep. It would have been simple to tap each one on the head, kick their weapons out of reach, and handcuff them before they knew what it was all about. Once the plan came near succeeding, and would have succeeded but for one of those accidents which will happen over which the officer has no control. There was always plenty of sign in the camp: stubs of Bonnie's Camels — Clyde smoked Bull Durham — lettuce leaves for the white rabbit, pieces of sandwiches, and a button off Clyde's coat. I found where they had made their bed.

'The end would have come two or three weeks earlier had not some local and federal officers made a drag on Ruston, Louisiana, and when Clyde heard of it, he quit the country and I had to wait for him to return.

'I traveled alone until shortly before the middle of April. On April 10, I called Chief L. G. Phares of the Highway Patrol to tell him that Barrow had used a Pontiac sedan to make his getaway after killing Constable Cummings and kidnaping the chief of police of Commerce, Oklahoma. I gave Chief Phares the license and engine number of this car and also the numbers on extra license plates from Oklahoma and Louisiana which Clyde carried in his car. Chief Phares told me that the Highway Department had decided to hire an extra man to travel with me. I asked for B. M. Gault who had served with me in the Headquarters Ranger Company. Gault met me in Dallas on April 14, and traveled with me until the chase ended on May 23.

'Bob Alcorn and Ted Hinton, from the sheriff's department of Dallas, gave me information, and were members of the party that met Barrow. In Louisiana I made contact with Sheriff Henderson Jordan of Bienville Parish, and after I had informed him of my plan, he agreed to assist me and pay no attention to other officers, state or federal. He brought with him Deputy Oakley.

'We did not find Barrow in his hideout but at his "post office." All criminals who work in groups must have some way of communicating with one another when they get separated. I learned that Clyde had his post office on a side road about eight miles from Plain Dealing, Louisiana. It was under a board which lay on the ground near a large stump of a pine tree. The point selected was on a knoll from which Bonnie in the car could command a view of the road while Clyde went into the forest for his mail.

'By the night of May 22, we had good reason to believe that Clyde would visit this mail box within a short time. About midnight we drove out of Gibsland, secreted our cars in the pines, and made arrangements to furnish him more news than he had ever received at one time. No detail was neglected. The road here runs north and south, and the knoll over which it rises is made by a spur or point which slopes from east to west. The stump that marked the location of the post office is on the west side of the road. We therefore took our position on the opposite, and higher, side so that we could look down on the car and its occupants. Within an hour after we reached the place, which was about 2.30 in the morning, we had constructed a blind from pine branches within about twenty-five or thirty feet of the point where the car would stop.

'We expected Barrow to come from the north, or from our right as we faced the road. The six men were spaced at intervals of about ten feet, parallel to the road. I held the position on the extreme left, and next was Gault, Jordan, Alcorn, Oakley, and Hinton in the order named. Gault, Jordan, and myself were to take care of the front seat, Oakley and Alcorn of the back seat, if occupied, while Ted Hinton at the end of the line represented the reserves. If the car got past us, Hinton was to step out and bust the engine with a Browning Machine Gun. Jordan and I had automatic shot guns, three had Winchesters, one a machine gun, and all carried revolvers or automatic pistols.

We agreed to take Barrow and the woman alive if we could. We believed that when they stopped the car, both would be looking towards the post office and away from us; such action on their part would enable us to escape observation until we demanded their surrender.

'With everything ready, we had nothing to do but wait about seven hours, without breakfast or coffee. Waiting is about the hardest thing an officer has to do. Many men will stand up in a fight, but lose their nerve completely if required to wait long for the excitement. On this occasion I did not detect the slightest nervousness on the part of a single man.

'As daylight came a few cars passed, and occasionally a logger's truck; and the sun came up at our back, which was in our favor. It was probably about 9.10 when we heard a humming through the pines that was different from that made by the other motors. A car was coming from the north at a terrific speed, singing like a sewing machine. We heard it when it must have been three miles away.

'Finally, it came into view at a distance of a thousand yards, and though it was still coming rapidly, it began to slow down as it climbed the hill towards us. We first recognized the color of the car, a gray Ford sedan, then the license number; we saw two persons, a small black-headed man and a small red-haired woman. We recognized Clyde and Bonnie, and knew there was no mistake. The speed continued to slacken under the brakes and the car came to a full stop at the exact spot that we had previously decided it would.

'When Barrow brought the car to a standstill, he pressed the clutch and slipped into low gear with the engine idling. Just as we had figured, both he and the woman peered with all their attention towards the stump.

'At the command, "stick 'em up!" both turned, but instead of obeying the order as we had hoped, they clutched the weapons which they either held in their hands or in their laps. When the firing began, Barrow's foot released the clutch and the car, in low gear, moved forward on the decline and turned into the ditch on the left. I looked at my watch and it was 9.20.

'There can be no question raised as to who fired the first or the fatal shots. All fired as we had agreed to do and every man in the squad did everything that he was supposed to do. It was not a pleasant duty, but it was a duty which no one shirked. Should I ever go on such another case, I hope that I shall have the help of such men as the five who were with me that day.

'An examination of the car revealed that the shots had been accurately placed, most of them ranging from the position of the driver's feet upwards at an angle that would take into account the entire body. The examination also revealed that the car was nothing but an arsenal on wheels. The inventory included:

3	Browning automatic rifles	Cal.	30
1	sawed-off shotgun	Gauge	20
1	sawed-off shotgun	Gauge	16
1	Colt automatic pistol	Cal.	32
1	Colt automatic pistol	Cal.	380
1	Colt revolver, double action	Cal.	45
7	Colt automatic pistols	Cal.	45
100	machine gun clips of 20 cartridges each.		
3000	rounds of ammunition scattered all over the car.		

'As soon as possible, I called Chief Phares at Austin and told him that the job was done.'

The public set in at once to lionize the man who had at last rid Texas of the merciless killer. The moving pictures offered him a large fee to appear before the talkies and tell the story. A promoter flew from Oklahoma City to Austin to induce him to go with the car to the Chicago World's Fair, with the view of setting up a concession. Hamer not only refused to commercialize the Barrow affair, but he stopped others from doing so. Some man who had more business acumen than caution acquired the Barrow Ford and began a tour of the state which ended abruptly in Austin. Hamer, accompanied by Gault, entered the place of exhibition and told the promoter that the show and the lies would have to stop. The showman hesitated and the officer swung with his open hand and slapped him across the room. When the man rose Hamer, standing over him, gave some definite orders. 'And,' he concluded, 'if you ever use my name again, even if you are in South America, I will come to you if I have to crawl on my hands and knees.' The Austin newspaper reported the next morning that the show had folded up and departed for an unknown destination. Friends in Austin undertook to have a dinner in honor of Hamer, but he stopped the dinner by letting it be known that he did not consider it appropriate and that he could not attend. For the time he spent in pursuit of Clyde Barrow, he received the munificent sum of one hundred and eighty dollars a month and a promise of expenses, but when he submitted his expense account, the state refused to pay for telephone calls amounting to about fourteen dollars, because he had not taken receipts. The state lost sight of the fact that for him to have revealed his identity might have spoiled all his plans.

The reader may inquire whether the subject of this sketch has any faults. Indeed he has, plenty of them. For one thing, he is utterly lacking, so his friends say, in 'policy.' He frequently does things and says things that are not calculated to promote his interests with the powers. He is also very stubborn. He refused to allow his friends to have a dinner in his honor for running down Clyde Barrow. He will not attend social functions, always claiming that he 'has a date with a man downtown' at that very hour. In short, he never permits anyone to take charge of his mind or to direct his activities, preferring, as he expresses it, 'to run in a herd by myself.'

Ordinarily he tells the truth, and, where crime is concerned. always. The bigger and more influential the criminal, the plainer he makes it, so that everybody can understand. This makes him unpopular with those who have something to hide. He has been known to misrepresent some official facts. Once he was hunting bootleggers near El Paso on the road that leads east. He was then a sergeant and had two or three men with him. A high-powered car would not stop, and the men shot off the tires. One of the occupants showed fight and Hamer slapped him to the ground with his open hand. When the man arose, he was somewhat dazed, and reached for his handkerchief — a bad move. Tony Apadocha misunderstood the man's intention and whacked him on the head with something that left a mark. Tony made a mistake, but in a good cause. Hamer reported that when he slapped the man down, he struck his head on the running-board of the car.

He has been known to disobey instructions when he thought they were wrong, or in the interest of wrong, as for example when he sent his superior in the federal Prohibition service to the penitentiary, and when he continued his war on gun smugglers after he had been ordered to quit.

Another very serious fault is that he loves to play poker, which is his one diversion. The poker club meets about once a week in his dining-room, and the game is played in the presence of his family, but not a penny changes hands. The poker chips are the best that money can buy, the kind that are used in professional gambling houses. They bear the initials of a wealthy Texan who undertook to run a gambling house near Houston and did so until Captain Hamer raided the house, broke up the equipment, and kept the chips as souvenirs.

These poker games show Frank Hamer at his worst. He has been known to practice deception by acting as if he held four aces when in reality he held nothing more than two deuces. Quite often he acts with such convincingness as to steal practically everything on the table, but he claims that he was taught by that great mentor, Captain J. B. Wheatley, who, it must be said, continues occasionally to teach him something. Both of these men have spent many years in reading the human countenance and detecting the truth behind all that hides it, and they persist in carrying this training to the dining-room table with terrible results for their opponents. The legislature should investigate them and pass a law of restraint. It would meet with the hearty approval of such members as Best, Gault, Green, Smith, and — others.

By way of conclusion, it may be stated that Captain Frank Hamer's natural gifts are such as would have made him distinguished as a Texas Ranger at any time during the history of the force, whether fighting Indians, Mexicans, or bandits. Whatever his achievements — and they are sufficient to extend his reputation over the nation — they are small as compared to what they might have been had greater opportunities offered themselves. In much of his work he has been handicapped by the political considerations of those in power; and he has seen much of his effort thwarted by the technicalities of the courts and the manipulations of lawyers as shrewd and unscrupulous as they are able. He has rarely had a free hand in enforcing the law, and he has never had an opportunity to organize and direct the Ranger force as he would have done in the midst of the great dangers that once threatened the state.

Though Captain Hamer is probably the poorest politician in Texas, he is a power for law and order, and politics should not deprive the public of his service.

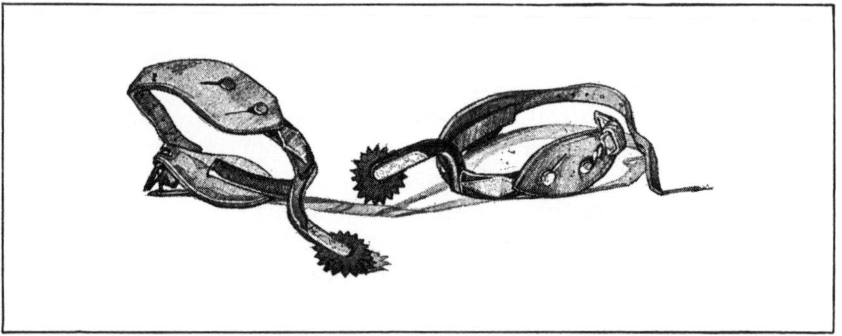

XXIII

SOME ADVENTURES OF A RANGER HISTORIAN

I missed him but he cut down on me and hit a rock right by me, stinging my face with fine gravel. I said 'Good God, I've got to shoot,' and I went down on them sights ——.

Captain W. L. WRIGHT

The other day we run on some horsebackers and one of them thought he would learn me how to shoot, so I naturalized him — made an American citizen out of him.

A Ranger report

The coroner came out and told us they were dead.

ARCH MILLER

XXIII. SOME ADVENTURES OF A RANGER HISTORIAN

FROM 1915 to 1918 much publicity was given to the activities of the Texas Rangers, and especially to their work along the Mexican border. From many quarters there was criticism that the Rangers were participating too much in politics and in some instances abusing the powers they held as peace officers. This criticism culminated in a legislative investigation led by Representative J. T. Canales of Brownsville and resulted in the reorganization of the force, as narrated in an earlier chapter.

It was the agitation preceding the Canales investigation that suggested the need for a history of the Texas Rangers.

Soon after the work was begun, I realized that if I were to understand the genius of the force and the psychology of the men, it could be done only through contact with those who had been in service. By attending the meetings of the Ex-Texas Rangers' Association at Menard, Weatherford, and Ranger, I made the acquaintance of many veterans of the Indian wars. France Peveler, for example, was a Ranger before the Civil War, one of the men who tried the murderer of Major Robert S. Neighbors 'without judge or jury.' To these meetings came Sam Gholson, the Sieker brothers, W. M. (Major) Green, and such captains of the Frontier Battalion as Dan W. Roberts and June Peak. There was also Mrs. Dan W. Roberts, whose life in the Ranger camp at Menard has been described in her booklet, *Six Years in Camp with the Texas Rangers.* In Austin I met Captain J. H. Rogers, Captain J. J. Sanders, and saw, on one occasion, Captain Bill McDonald. I also made the acquaintance of Captain McNelly's wife, Mrs. W. T. Wroe. In 1929, I met Captain J. H. Brooks, county judge of Brooks County, which was named for him. From each of these men, and from many others, I gleaned some insight into the spirit of courage which has become a tradition of the Texas Rangers. Each of them supplied a bit of information that has entered into this narrative.

In addition to knowing the ex-Texas Rangers, I wanted to know the force as it operates at the present day. I first visited Captain Tom Hickman, who was then at Fort Worth with Company B. Captain

CAPTAIN TOM R. HICKMAN

Hickman has been stationed for the most part in the interior, and has been especially active in preserving order in the oil fields and the boom towns that grow up near them. Outside of Texas he is widely known as a judge of stock shows and rodeos. He has judged rodeos all over the West, and in Chicago, New York, and London.

I felt that any study of the Rangers would be incomplete without visiting the border camps that lay along the Rio Grande from Point Isabel to El Paso. In the summer of 1924 the opportunity came through the kindness of Captain R. W. Aldrich, quartermaster of the force. Captain Aldrich, like so many Rangers, has been to far places. He went to the Boer War with a shipload of Missouri mules, fought through the Spanish-American War, was once a banker in Oklahoma, a cowboy on the Catarina Ranch, and a border Ranger with Captain Sanders.

For several years he has maintained a country home near Austin. He has the largest private collection of rare books and the largest private library in the city. Not only does he collect books, but Indian relics, firearms, plants, and animals. His spacious grounds are like a botanical garden, and his animals — coyotes, deer, skunks, snakes, javelinas, raccoons, prairie dogs, black bear, peacocks, parrots, pigeons, doves, squirrels, rats, and monkeys — attract scores of visitors to his place, which is kept open to the public.

In August, 1924, Captain Aldrich took leave from his desk in Austin, and we set out in a T Model Ford for a tour of inspection of the Ranger camps. Adjutant General Thomas F. Barton issued me a Ranger commission while Captain Aldrich supplied the 'jewelery' — a cartridge belt and a forty-five calibre double-action Colt revolver. We took bedding and chuck-box preparatory to spending the entire time in the open.

Our first objective was San Antonio, where we found some thirty Rangers in charge of Captain B. C. Baldwin. Governor Pat Neff had sent the Rangers to San Antonio for the purpose of stopping liquor traffic and other infractions of the law. The political element in San Antonio resented the presence of the Rangers and fought bitterly to have them removed, but Governor Neff, equally stubborn, maintained them.

These men were quartered in an old residence at 331 Garden Street, south of the Alamo. On the whole they appeared to be the biggest men I had ever seen in one group, and they were about the most miserable. They spent their time between liquor raids in skylarking, a gay mask behind which to hide their longing for the home ranges.

Captain Aldrich had authority to detach one of them to accompany us, and his choice fell on J. A. (Arch) Miller of the Texas Big Bend. This selection was more than agreeable on both sides: to us it meant a guide who had first-hand knowledge of the upper border, a congenial companion, and a friend who can never be forgotten; to Arch it meant escape from city life, which he heartily detested, and a return to his home, the Big Bend.

Arch Miller stands about six feet and two inches, and at that time weighed about one hundred and ninety pounds. He appeared to be about thirty years old, and was a picture of health and vigor. He is evidently of Irish ancestry, as indicated by a broad, open countenance, slightly wavy russet hair, and Irish blue eyes.

We left San Antonio at eleven o'clock and drove into Laredo at six in the afternoon. The car had hardly come to a halt before W. W. Sterling, later Ranger captain and adjutant general, placed his boot

GENERAL W. W. STERLING
Former Captain of the Rangers and Adjutant General

on our running-board, covered our window with his Stetson hat, and told us that a report had just come in that Captain Will L. Wright had been killed by Mexican smugglers down the river. After an hour of telephoning, it was found that the report was erroneous.

We spent the night in Laredo and early the next morning set out to find Captain Wright, who was in the chaparral thirty miles down the river. Upon leaving Laredo, I buckled on the six-shooter, less conscious of it than I expected to be for the reason that nearly every American on the border carries one when out of town. It had been arranged that we would pass through Mirando City, a shack oil town in the desert, and pick up Bill Sterling whose association with the Rangers from boyhood made it impossible for him to refuse our invitation. As justice of the peace, Bill preserved order in the oil town by methods learned from the Texas Rangers and other border officers. On an unpainted pine shack, dimensions ten by ten, we found a large sign suggestive of Roy Bean's temple of justice at Langtry:

W. W. Sterling, Justice of the Peace
The Law on the Tex.-Mex.

Near by was a boxcar in which the judge held his occasional prisoners by means of generous lengths of trace chains and padlocks. Soon Judge Bill came striding out of the forest of derricks and told us that he was ready to go.

Arch Miller pushed the Ford around the laboring oil trucks, through the derricks, and by a sandy winding road into the chaparral where Captain Wright was hunting his human game — dangerous horseback smugglers, who were running liquor over the rimrock to fast automobiles that carried it to San Antonio, Dallas, Oklahoma City, and St. Louis. At an abandoned ranch we found the Rangers in their noon camp and there we appeased our hunger on fresh beef, sourdough biscuits, pinto beans, boiled coffee, and stewed wild plums gathered from the brush.

The equipment of this camp might have been handed down direct from the old Frontier Battalion, or from the Rangers of the Texas Republic. The cooking equipment comprised a coffee pot, Dutch oven, enamel-ware plates, iron cutlery, tin cups for coffee, and a tin dishpan for washing dishes. Bed-rolls were spread on the ground for the noon rest; saddles lay under the trees with sweat blankets spread over them, and near by were the queer-looking wooden pack-saddles. Winchesters were everywhere. Of special interest were the ropes, lariats, tie-ropes, and particularly the horsehair rope that the Captain put around his bunk at night in order to keep rattlesnakes from climbing into bed with him and warming themselves against the small of his back. The only modern note was the small truck used to haul chuck-box, bed-rolls, and water-keg.

Saddle horses, tied to the trees, were eating from nosebags, but

A RIO GRANDE CAMP AT NIGHT

the wiry pack-mules ran free and gazed at us with a combined air of insolence and impudence. Pack-mules — formerly used by all the Rangers — are now found only on the border, and are indispensable to work in the range country. They are trained to follow the horses; this they do with that singular devotion that the hybrid bears to its nobler ancestor. When carrying the pack, the mules make due allowance for brush or limbs. Captain Wright told of an incident, which occurred when some Northern men were on a scout with him. The party came to a pass in a canyon through which there was barely room for a riderless horse to go because of overhanging rocks. One of the visitors suggested that the packs would have to be removed from the mules, but the Rangers knew that it was not necessary. The mules walked up to the pass, 'looked at the rocks above, and began to figure distance.' When the horses went through, the mules 'stooped,' crouched, or whatever a mule should do under such circumstances, and cleared their packs.

Dinner over and the smokes finished, Captain Wright asked us to go with him to the place near by, where he had met the smugglers in the Las Animas fight on December 18, 1922. As the way led through

ARCH MILLER

thick chaparral, it was decided that we should go on foot. We were near the river and on a favorite route of the horsebackers; every man seemed to feel that there was danger of running on smugglers at any moment. I noted that none of them went far from his firearms. As a tenderfoot I began to wonder whether these men might plan to initiate me by letting me 'smell powder smoke' in a sham brush battle, but I kept such thoughts to myself. My apprehension grew when, after we had gone a half-mile, Bill Sterling suddenly exclaimed, 'By George, I forgot my gun!' He had unbuckled his belt before dinner and had forgotten to buckle it on again. Knowing that Bill was a veteran capable of handling a gun in an emergency, I felt that I should let him have mine even though I would be disarmed and an easy victim to any prank that the men might have in mind. I remembered that two or three men had remained in camp, sufficient to stage 'an attack' from ambush.

With some misgivings I volunteered to let Bill have my gun, explaining why I thought he should have it; after the proper hesitancy, he accepted it. I made up my mind that if any shooting started, I would get as close to one of the Rangers as possible, and stay by him regardless of what happened. I determined to show no more concern than I could help because I held a commission as a Texas Ranger and could not afford to tarnish the record. Moreover, there was something about these fellows that inspired courage.

The trail we followed led us out of the brush to the sloping edge of a great natural amphitheater — a horseshoe made by a desert hill — with the open part facing the Rio Grande two miles to the south. The declivities within the horseshoe, barren save for small rocks and scant herbage, met in the center to form a wash or playa through which the waters of the basin drained out between the hills that overlooked the river. A heavy growth of sage, catclaw, creosote, and ratama brush masked the draw and the sandy stream-bed which offered a fair road for horsebackers.

It was into this covered road that Captain Wright and five men had trailed three Mexicans with fifteen horses. The Captain knew that it would be dangerous for him or his men to show themselves on the barren ridges because the smugglers always went heavily armed with high-powered Mausers and Winchesters, and since they considered their situation as desperate when Rangers appeared, they shot on sight. Captain Wright planned his attack so as to cut off the smugglers' retreat to the Rio Grande and to drive the men to the open ridges. He sent two men to the east side, went with another to the west, and sent one or two on the trail below to flush the game and drive it over the barren ridge on the north.

In half an hour the disposition was made, and when the Winchesters began to crack in the brush, out came the bootleggers to the heights where they were caught between the cross-fire of the four waiting Rangers. Captain Wright showed me where he stood in a rifle duel with the Mexican 'general,' one hundred and fifty yards away.

'I missed him,' said the Captain, 'but he cut down on me and hit a rock right by me, stinging my face with fine gravel. I said "Good God, I've got to shoot, and I went down on them sights ——." '

That ended the story, but the Captain's presence there on the hill told who was victor. Later one of the men told me that the 'general' went down with a broken neck.

We descended into the brush to search for the broken bottles and for the skeleton of the horse that had been killed that day. It was with difficulty — so dense was the thicket — that we found the bleached bones and the fragments of a hundred bottles. I was fortunate enough to stumble upon them first, and felt that I had perhaps gained a little prestige among the border men.

Three Mexicans were shot down in the fight and left where they fell until, as Arch Miller remarked, 'a coroner came out and said they were dead.' The Rangers captured fourteen or fifteen horses and eight hundred bottles of liquor — tequilla, sotol, and imported Scotch and rye — for the Christmas trade. The Mexicans had unpacked their horses, and, despite the fact that many of the bottles were broken, the Rangers were unable to repack the remainder on the Mexican horses, including those of the riders who lay on the hills. A Texas Ranger is no equal to a border Mexican in the art of loading pack-horses.

A BOOTLEGGER PACK TRAIN CAPTURED BY CAPTAIN W. L. WRIGHT'S RANGERS

About a year prior to the fight at Las Animas, November 22, 1921, Captain Wright fought the liquor runners on the Bernenia Ranch in Webb County. In this engagement he captured thirty-seven horses and three thousand quarts of tequilla. It was in connection with a fight similar to these that a private in the Rangers made the following report to Captain Aldrich:

> Dear Captain:
> The other day we run on to some horsebackers and one of them thought he would learn me how to shoot, so I naturalized him—made an American citizen out of him.

After we had returned from this excursion, and no effort had been made to haze me, I felt better acquainted with my companions and told them of my apprehensions when I let Bill Sterling have my gun. Their comment was that, where men go armed and in expectation of danger, practical jokes are out of order.

From Laredo we headed up the river for the next camp, which was at Del Rio. In order to make this trip, we had to double back on the

San Antonio road and turn west at the village of Artesia or Artesian Wells into a country road that led through the Catarina Ranch, a wild country still ruled by cowboys. By this time I was beginning to appreciate the unfailing wit and humor, as well as the intelligence and physical prowess of Arch Miller. After we had gone perhaps six or seven miles, we came to a cross-road store in front of which a rusty cowboy sat astride a sweaty ranch horse, eying us with a well-simulated air of suspicion. Chubedaro — as we later dubbed him because he had worked for a ranch by that name — assumed a tough role as he leaned forward on his horse, elbow on horn, hairy chin in hand, and gazed at us as if he had never before seen anything like our Ford car or its contents. To Arch Miller's civil question as to the condition of the road to Asherton, he said: 'I don't know. I ain't been over there in fifteen year.'

'That's a long time,' said Arch, with cheerful indifference and, opening the car door, he unwound six feet and two inches of bone and muscle as he stepped out to make some examination of the car. That much man made a difference to Chubedaro, whose little eyes did not miss anything that Arch wore — boots, belt, gun, or hat. He became helpful, and we found his road information accurate.

At Del Rio we found Captain C. J. Blackwell with five or six men quartered in the edge of town. Arch Miller was getting into his own territory now, and that night he was out with Captain Blackwell's men after the liquor runners. I was not invited to go, but I learned something of what happened from the conversation next day.

From Del Rio, we came back to the highway and made our next stop at Marathon, Arch Miller's home town. Here we found Lee Trimble and also Arch's partner — Rangers work in pairs on the border — John Hollis, known to the border as Ricochet John. The story of how he got the name is this. A local ranchman lost a horse and John took the trail, which he followed like an Indian. Just before he reached the river, he came in sight of the Mexican thief who was in a canyon with all chances for escape in his favor. John returned with the horse and apologized for the accidental death of the thief. He had not meant to kill him; he fired to scare him and make him stop, but the bullet struck a rock, ricocheted, and killed the Mexican. Ever after, John's name has been Ricochet.

From Marathon we jumped off early in the afternoon for the ninety miles' drive south into the wildest and most picturesque portion of Texas, the Big Bend. Captain Aldrich, Ricochet John, and I rode in our Ford, while Arch Miller and Lee Trimble led out in Arch's Ford with a saddle laced on the hood. The Big Bend from Marathon south was the Rangers' own country, and the welcome they received as they went along showed what they meant to the people. At one place, men were repairing a windmill tank that supplied water for the cattle; Arch stopped, helped with the work, and exchanged notes on the conditions of the country. There was only one ranch house on the road, and here Arch was greeted by men, women, and children as if he were son and brother. It was more than frontier cordiality; his greeting was not unlike that given in the old days to the Rangers who kept the Indians out of the settlements. Again we passed someone whose auto was giving trouble; with a few magic touches Arch set the motor humming. It seemed that he could take a tin can, pocket knife, pliers, and a piece of baling wire and repair any Ford on four wheels; and as for driving one, he could, in the words of Will Rogers, simply make a Ford lie down and turn over. If one needed moving, Arch merely reached for an axle and set it around as if it were a cracker box. If a tire had to be removed, Arch deflated it, and stripped it from the wheel without tools. All these things he did with the zest of one who has a great love of life.

Along with the work went a running fire of witty comment and observation. If we stopped for rest, a little pistol shooting, or, as Arch called it, 'can rolling' was in order. A lone horseman without visible occupation was 'a cowboy without any cows'; and when the Ford was humming over the road at top speed, we were 'skipping through the dew.' The vegetation of the desert, new and strange to one who has lived in a more humid climate, was as familiar to Arch as turnips and spinach. He explained the practical uses of the different plants: how the Mexicans made ropes, morrals, and baskets from the fiber of the lecheguilla; how men procured water and food from the great bulb in the heart of the maguey; how rubber was manufactured from the gayule; and how wax for Russian church services was made from the candalia — candle plant.

The plant that gives a weird character to the desert is the ocatillo, the dozen sinuous, thorn-covered spines of which reach up to a height of eight or ten feet. Viewed from a distance it reminds one of a vase full of those wavy swords — blades up — that come from Borneo or the Philippines.

'And what do they make from the ocatillo?' I inquired.

'Well,' Arch replied solemnly, 'I don't know what they make from it, but I know that if you hit a bad Mexican down the back with it, you can make him strike a long lope.'

On the road we met many Mexicans. Some rode horses, some burros, and some were in wagons drawn by four, six, or eight burros. These

Mexicans were classified by the Rangers as good, bad, and uncertain. Arch usually interviewed them and spoke a kindly word to the good ones. Occasionally he would motion one out of earshot, and, after some conversation in Spanish, each would go his way. Arch missed no opportunity to gather information as to the state of the Big Bend.

Soon after we left Marathon, we saw the lofty Chisos Mountains — now a state park — loom before us, and for two hours we drove straight towards them without appearing to get nearer. Finally we left them on the right, and dropped down Tornillo Creek, so named from a variety of the mesquite that produces a bean resembling a screw. The name 'tornillo' is no more appropriate for the bean than for the winding dry creek or the spiral road, which hunted along hogbacks to head some canyon only to reverse itself for a mile or two in search of a ford.

About dusk we drove into the camp at Glenn Springs where lived one American family — W. D. Burcham's — in addition to the Rangers. In this place one senses the isolation that the Rangers experienced in the old days. All supplies were hauled ninety miles by truck over a mountain road; gasoline sold at forty cents a gallon; the mail came once a week. The country across the river was so remote from civilization that the Mexicans who dwelt there got their mail, even that from the interior of Mexico, at Glenn Springs. The Mexican mail carrier came on horseback to meet the mail truck, his large-roweled spurs, bighorned saddle, and ornate bridle contrasting with the simpler horse gear used by the Texans.

The four Rangers had their camp in a small cottage where we found Bob Summerall, Lee Trimble's partner and as perfect specimen of the thin-flanked cowboy as I have seen. These four men — Lee, Bob, Arch, and Ricochet John — concealed their pleasure over being together again by much solemn banter. The three who had remained at home listened with grave credulity to the wild tales that Arch unfolded of his experiences in the great city of San Antonio. Occasionally one called him a liar, more often they did so by agreeing with him too readily, but Arch assured them with much gravity that he was telling the truth. As they cooked the evening meal, *sans* shirts, to the accompanying thump of boot heels on bare floors and the gay jingle of Lee's and Bob's spurs, they conversed half in Spanish and half in English, but if one burned himself on a hot skillet handle or dropped a tin cup, he expressed his sentiments in the more musical language.

The evening meal finished, we sat on the porch and watched the night come up the Rio Grande. The scenery about Glenn Springs, and throughout the Big Bend, is as wild, and as beautiful in its way, as any in America. All the afternoon, as we rode south, we had been dazzled by the gorgeous El Carmen Mountains far over in Mexico. Though the name suggests color, it cannot even suggest the rich tones, the varying hues, the ineffable palpitating beauty of El Carmen as seen under the splashing rays of an August sun. El Carmen, we were told, is a great screen of solid rock, a sheer precipice of splendid dimensions, upon which the western sun produces its marvelous effects.

As the sun set behind us, the colors disappeared, but the outlines of the mountains made a remarkable silhouette against the clean desert sky. It was a masculine human form outstretched in perfect repose, feet thirty miles from head, hands folded over chest, good chin, straight nose, and fine brow. The Rangers had named the figure the War God of the Rio Grande.

The whole effect as we sat under a million stars, the desert silence broken by coyotes yip-yipping to each other from distant hills, was not that of war, but of tranquillity and peace. Yet the cottage had a blood-stained and tragic history. In 1915–16, when the Mexicans were making their worst raids, those on Columbus, New Mexico, and Glenn Springs, Texas, this cottage was occupied by a man named O. G. Compton and his three children, a girl of eleven and two boys, ages seven and four. Just in front of the cottage, not fifty yards away, were army tents occupied by nine soldiers, who had been sent to watch the crossings and guard the settlement. One night in May the bandits came without warning and in great numbers. They killed five soldiers and would have killed four more had these not been fast in taking to the hills. Compton hurried to the bed where his three children were sleeping, but succeeded in getting only the girl out of the house before the Mexicans entered. It is supposed that they shot the smaller boy to stop his screaming. The older boy, a deaf mute, could not hear the guns or the yells of the raiders, and did not scream. The bandits apparently thought him *muy bravo*, and left him uninjured; or they, like the Indians, had a prejudice against killing a deaf mute.

When news of the raid went out to the upland ranches, all the men and boys of the Big Bend flocked to Glenn Springs and among them was Arch Miller, then about twenty. When Arch saw the destruction, the dead, and the bloody prints left by small hands on the floor and walls of the cottage, he joined the Rangers.

On the next morning, we pushed farther down the river to the little town of Boquillas, wholly abandoned save for Jim Teague, who lived in an adobe house near the banks of the Rio Grande. The tubercular germs were fighting desperately with air and sun for what was left of Jim Teague. The Rangers often fed him, but on this occasion, we ate his beans and bacon with cheerful pretense.

BOB SUMMERALL

LEE TRIMBLE

The excuse for Boquillas was a silver mine which lay just across the river in the twin town of Boquillas, Mexico. Our visit brought out more stories of bandit days prior to the time that President Wilson sent General Pershing after Pancho Villa. The stories aptly illustrate an important principle, namely, that the American who falls into the hands of Mexican bandits can escape death only by outthinking his captors.

Two or three Americans were over at the Boquillas mines with a truck when the bandits swooped down and captured them, truck and all. The Mexicans were determined to have the truck, and since they did not know how to drive, they let one of the Americans serve as chauffeur. The captives felt confident that it would be only a question of time until they were put to death, and they set their wits to work devising some means of escape.

Their first purpose was to create delay in order that they might remain as near the border as possible. A sandbed offered them an opportunity to stall the truck; this they did and no measures that were tried could get it forward. Though the Mexicans were greatly exasperated, they could not afford to kill the Americans without losing the truck. It was finally suggested that some of the Mexicans cross the mountains and bring horses, mules, or oxen with which to pull the truck out of the sand. Eventually the Mexicans agreed to go and thereby reduced the number of guards. With this much accomplished, the Americans decided that perhaps they could get forward if everybody would push on the car while the engine raced — in neutral — as hard as it could. The Mexicans declared that they were soldiers, not peons, and they refused, at first, to demean themselves by pushing an American truck out of a Mexican sandbed. The Texans did their best, and as they pushed and heaved, the driver engaged the clutch and moved the car forward a little — but not too much. The water boiled in the radiator, the engine roared, and the Americans shouted and swore earnestly at one another. The Mexicans, struck by the sincere efforts of their captives and the possibility of success, came to their assistance. There was more pushing, heaving and shouting until every Mexican was leaning his weight to the truck and pawing sand to keep his footing.

Suddenly a leather-lunged Texan sang 'Let 'er go!' The driver shot the gas, the car jumped forward with a great lurch, and as the Mexicans were thrown off balance, each Texan seized a gun, and clubbed a bandit. In an instant the Texans had full possession of the whole outfit. They hastily turned the truck and soon crossed into Texas with their captives. According to the story, the Mexicans were tried in a Texas court and sent to the penitentiary for robbery with firearms.

'Arch,' I said when the story was ended, 'how could they send Mexicans to the penitentiary in Texas for a crime committed in Mexico?'

'Well,' Arch replied, 'you see, we kinda have to stick together down here. Of course it was wrong — they ought to have killed 'em.'

A second story concerns Ray Miller, Arch's brother, better known as Pinochle. As we went out of the Big Bend, we met Pinochle in charge of a gang of Mexicans, who were building a highway, 'manicuring the road,' Arch said. At the time of Pinochle's adventure, his father owned the silver mine at Boquillas, Mexico, and as he was negotiating the sale of the mines or ore — which was brought across the river on a wire — he sent Pinochle over to get ore-cuttings and to make pictures of the mining equipment.

While Pinochle was filling his morral with ore samples and making pictures, the bandits fell on the town and captured him. As he was a Gringo, they decided, as Arch put it, to ' 'dobe wall him.' With the formalities disposed of, Pinochle found himself backed up against a clean white wall with a Mauser squad in the immediate foreground. Just as the commander was ready to give the signal, Pinochle made his play by bringing his little camera into position as if to take a picture of his own execution. The Mexicans could see no reason to hurry, and so they waited until he had finished. Pinochle could tell that the commander felt slighted, and he tactfully suggested, with much circumlocution, that the general have his picture made. The general was agreeable. In fact, the Mexicans were so interested by this time that Pinochle made singles, doubles, and groups of the entire party, and that despite the fact that his films had long been exhausted.

Pinochle had lost his hat, and so he emptied the ore out of the morral, which he fitted turban fashion on his head as protection from the sun. He could plainly see that he was making headway by his good nature and his audacious unconcern as to his fate. In order to promote further good will, he amiably suggested that everybody take a drink on him. No Mexican can refuse a courtesy, even from a man who is about to be shot. Pinochle ordered the *cantinero* to roll out the sotol keg. The potency of sotol, brewed from a plant of that name, has never been determined, but in comparison with it, straight American whiskey is a pink tea and raw tequilla a weak toddy.

By the time two drinks of sotol had gone around, the Mexicans were ready for more pictures with new poses. The artist suggested that some striking results could be obtained by photographing the men while they were firing their guns. The happy idea called for another drink while it was being considered, and for another after it was accepted.

FOUR ACES OF THE BORDER
Left to right: Pete Crawford, Ray (Pinochle) Miller, John Poole, Arch Miller

Targets were set up and more pictures made to the accompaniment of gunfire and in the midst of clouds of acrid powder smoke.

Pinochle decided that the time for him to start for Texas would be when the Mexicans had reached a state where they were too drunk to make a sure shot on purpose, but not sufficiently drunk to kill him accidentally. So he arranged the grand finale — a picture in which the entire party were discharging their guns. When he thought the last gun had cracked, he made a flying leap to a near-by horse, and, as Arch told it, 'Pinochle hit the Rio Grande so hard that he knocked it dry for fifty feet.'

From Boquillas we went up the river, around the Chisos to the west, and climbed out to the rimrock at Alpine. Thence we drove thirty miles to Marfa, the home of J. B. Gillett. When we struck a county seat, we made the sheriff's office headquarters, and the sheriffs, many of whom had served as Rangers, always offered us the hospitality of the jail. Jeff Vaughn was the sheriff. He had formerly been a Ranger and he has since been a captain of Rangers.

When Jeff Vaughn was a young officer, he was handed a warrant and told to 'go get' a certain bad Mexican that had been terrorizing the country. Vaughn disappeared for some days, but finally rode into town with a pack on the front of his saddle. He threw off the pack in front of the jail and reported, 'there he is.' Such literal interpretation of orders gives men prestige in a border country.

On inquiry, we learned that Captain J. B. Gillett was at the Davis Mountains camp meeting, held yearly at Skillman's Grove. We turned our Ford in that direction and reached the camp ground in time for the evening meal with Captain Gillett. That night we slept on Lobo Flat and on the following day struck the river at Presidio, a settlement that dates back to the seventeenth century.

This old border town was controlled by Captain Jerry Gray, who had quit the Ranger service to care for the irrigated farm which he had acquired near the bank of the river. From Presidio we went on to El Paso and then by the most direct route to Austin, where we arrived three weeks after our departure.

It was several years later that I completed the trip along the Mexican border by traveling from Brownsville to Laredo with J. Evetts Haley. At Brownsville we met Judge Harbert Davenport and the inimitable Joe Wells, whose historical knowledge of the border is unsurpassed. They accompanied us to Point Isabel, over the battle-fields of Palo Alto and Resaca de la Palma, where Samuel Walker rendered service in the Mexican War. We found Palo Alto Prairie just as it appeared on June 12, 1875, when Captain McNelly chased and killed the bandits, as related in another chapter. In Brownsville we saw the streets over which Cortinas had ridden in search of his enemies.

Judge Davenport accompanied us up the river to Rio Grande City, where Ford, Tobin, and Heintzelman met Cortinas. Under the guidance of Señor Longorio, friend of Mr. Davenport, we crossed to Camargo and drove to San Miguel, or Las Cuevas, the place attacked by Captain McNelly on November 19, 1875. We saw the monument erected to General Juan Flores and had, from old men, the broken recollections of McNelly's raid.

We passed through Roma, visited Mier, and continued to Laredo. In company with W. E. Maberry, a former Texas Ranger, Inspector Petty, and M. B. Brown, I visited the Vergara Ranch and saw Isla Grande and the place where Vergara was kidnaped in 1914. Thus was the tour of the border complete.

FAREWELL TO THE TEXAS RANGERS

While this book was going through the press, an act was passed by the legislature which practically closed the career of the Texas Rangers as the chief law-enforcement body of Texas. The New York *Herald Tribune* of August 4, 1935, published the story, entitled 'Texas Rangers Lose Name, Keep Glory.' In part the story runs: 'Famous in tradition as the Southwest's most picturesque and most fearless law-enforcement group, the Texas Rangers as now constituted will pass out of existence August 10. To a large extent their duties will be perpetuated under a new law which combines the Rangers and the State Highway Patrol in a Department of Public Safety.'

The law creating the Department of Public Safety does not actually abolish the name of the force, but it reduces the number of companies to two mounted companies and a headquarters company — a total of forty men. The same law increases the Highway Patrol to one hundred and forty men. It is safe to say that as time goes on the functions of the un-uniformed Texas Rangers will gradually slip away and that those of the Highway Patrol will increase. Curiously enough this practical abolition of the force has occurred exactly one hundred years after the force was created by a revolutionary body on October 17, 1835.

BIBLIOGRAPHY

SECONDARY WORKS

Anonymous. *Life and Adventures of Sam Bass*, Dallas Commercial Steam Print, Dallas, 1878.

Anonymous. By a Citizen of Denton County, Texas. *Authentic History of Sam Bass and His Gang*, Monitor Job Office, Denton, Texas, 1878.

Anonymous (Compilation). *General Taylor and His Staff*, Grigg, Elliot and Company, Philadelphia, 1848.

Barker, Eugene C. 'Journal of the Permanent Council,' *The Quarterly of the Texas State Historical Association*, vol. VII, July, 1903–April, 1904, Austin, 1904.

Barker, Eugene C. *The Life of Stephen F. Austin*, Cokesbury Press, Nashville, 1925.

Brackett, Albert Gallatin. *General Lane's Brigade in Central Mexico*, H. W. Derby and Company, Cincinnati, 1854.

Brown, John Henry. *The Indian Wars and Pioneers of Texas*, L. E. Daniell, Austin (n.d.).

Carleton, James Henry. *Battle of Buena Vista*, Harper and Brothers, New York, 1848.

Chatfield, W. H. (Compiler). *The Twin Cities of the Border*, E. P. Brandao, New Orleans, 1893.

Duval, John C. *The Adventures of Big Foot Wallace, the Texas Ranger and Hunter*, J. W. Burke and Company, Macon, Georgia, 1871.

Duval, John C. *Early Times in Texas*, H. P. N. Gammel and Company, Austin, 1892.

Erath, George Bernard. *Memoirs of Major George Bernard Erath*, Texas State Historical Association, Austin, 1923.

Ewell, Thomas T. *A History of Hood County, Texas*, The Granbury News, Granbury, Texas, 1895.

Gammel, H. P. N. *Laws of Texas*, vols. I, II, III, and VI.

[Giddings, Luther.] *Sketches of the Campaigns in Northern Mexico by an Officer of the First Ohio Volunteers*, G. P. Putnam and Company, New York, 1853.

Gillett, James B. *Six Years with the Texas Rangers, 1875 to 1881*, Von Boeckmann-Jones Company, Austin, 1921.

Green, Thomas J. *Journal of the Texian Expedition against Mier*, Harper and Brothers, New York, 1845.

Greer, James K. (Editor). *Buck Barry: A Texas Ranger and Frontiersman*, The Southwest Press, Dallas, 1932.

Grinnell, George Bird. *The Fighting Cheyennes*, Charles Scribner's Sons, New York, 1915.

Haltom, Richard W. *History and Description of Nacogdoches County, Texas*, Nacogdoches News, Nacogdoches, Texas, 1880.

Henry, Captain W. S. *Campaign Sketches of the War with Mexico*, Harper and Brothers, New York, 1847.

Hitchcock, Ethan Allen. *Fifty Years in Camp and Field, diary of Major-General Ethan Allen Hitchcock, U.S.A.*, edited by W. A. Croffut, G. P. Putnam's Sons, New York, 1909.

Jennings, N. A. *A Texas Ranger*, Reprint, Southwest Press, Dallas, 1930.

Johnson, Willard D. 'The High Plains and Their Utilization,' *Twenty-first Annual Report of the United States Geological Survey*, Part IV. Continued in the *Twenty-second Annual Report*, Part IV, Government Printing Office, Washington, 1901 and 1902.

Kendall, George Wilkins. *Narrative of the Texas Santa Fe Expedition* (2 vols.), Harper and Brothers, New York, 1856.

King, W. H. 'The Texas Ranger Service,' in Dudley G. Wooten (Editor), *A Comprehensive History of Texas*, vol. II, William G. Scarff, Dallas, 1898.

Kittrel, Norman G. *Governors Who Have Been and Other Public Men of Texas*, Dealy-Adey-Elgin Company, Houston, Texas, 1921.

Lamar, Mirabeau Buonaparte. *The Papers of*, vols. III; IV, Part I; V; Von Boeckmann-Jones Company, Austin.

[Maltby, W. J.] *Captain Jeff or Frontier Life in Texas with the Texas Rangers*, Whipkey Printing Company, Colorado, Texas, 1906.

McHenry, Roy C. 'Hand-Gun History,' *The American Rifleman*, August 15, 1923, Washington, D.C.

Montgomery, Cora. *Eagle Pass; or, Life on the Border*, George P. Putnam and Company, New York, 1852.

Morrell, Z. N. *Flowers and Fruits*, Gould and Lincoln, Boston, 1872.

Noel, Virginia P. *The United States Indian Reservations in Texas, 1845–1859*. M.A. Thesis, The University of Texas, June, 1924.

Nunn, William Curtis. *A Study of the State Police During the E. J. Davis Administration*. M.A. Thesis, The University of Texas, Austin, 1931.

Olmsted, Frederick Law. *A Journey Through Texas*, Dix, Edwards and Company, New York, 1857.

Oswandel, J. J. *Notes on the Mexican War, 1846–47–48*. Philadelphia, Rev. Ed., 1885.

Payne, Albert Bigelow. *Captain Bill McDonald, Texas Ranger*, Little and Ives Company, New York, 1909.

Pierce, Frank C. *A Brief History of the Lower Rio Grande Valley*, George Banta Publishing Company, Menasha, Wisconsin, 1917.

Polk, James Knox. *The Diary of James K. Polk*, vol. III, Milo Milton Quaife, Editor, A. C. McClurg and Company, Chicago, 1910.

Ramsdell, Charles W. *Reconstruction in Texas*, Columbia University, New York, 1910.

Ramsdell, Charles W. 'Texas in the New Nation,' *The South in the Building of a Nation*, vol. III.

Reid, Samuel C., Jr. *The Scouting Expeditions of McCulloch's Texas Rangers*, G. B. Zieber and Company, Philadelphia, 1848.

Reports of the Committee of Investigation sent in 1873 by the Mexican Government to the Frontier of Texas, Baker and Godwin, Printers, New York, 1875.

Richardson, Rupert Norval, *The Comanche Barrier to South Plains Settlement*, Arthur H. Clark Company, Glendale, California, 1933.

Rose, Victor M. *The Life and Services of Gen. Ben McCulloch*, Pictorial Bureau of the Press, Philadelphia, 1888.

Ripley, Roswell Sabine. *The War with Mexico*, vol. I, Harper and Brothers, New York, 1849.

Smith, Justin H. *The War with Mexico*, vol. I, The Macmillan Company, New York, 1919.

Smithwick, Noah. *The Evolution of a State*, Gammel Book Company, Austin, 1900.

Stevens, Brevet-Major Isaac I. *Campaigns of the Rio Grande and of Mexico*, D. Appleton and Company, New York, 1851.

Sullivan, W. J. L. *Twelve Years in the Saddle*, Von Boeckmann-Jones Company, Austin, 1909.

Walton, William M. *Life and Adventures of Ben Thompson, the Famous Texan*, Privately printed, Austin, 1884.

Ward, Charles Francis. *The Salt War of San Elizario, 1877*. M.A. Thesis, The University of Texas, Austin, 1932.

Webb, W. P. *The Great Plains*, Ginn and Company, Boston, 1931.

Wilbarger, Josiah W. *Indian Depredations in Texas*, Hutchings Printing House, Austin, 1889.

Yoakum, Henderson K. *History of Texas, from Its First Settlement in 1665 to Its Annexation to the United States in 1846*, vol. II, Redfield, New York, 1856.

DOCUMENTARY SOURCES

TEXAS

General Laws of the State of Texas, 36th Legislature, 1919.

Republic of, *Annual Report of the Secretary of War*, November, 1839. Whiting's Press, Austin.

Journals of the Fourth Congress of the Republic of Texas, 1839–1840. Vols. I and III. Edited by Harriet Smither.

Journal of the House of Representatives of the Republic of Texas, Fifth Congress, First Session, Appendix. Seventh Congress, Appendix.

Reports of the Adjutant General of the State of Texas (Biennial), 1870–1932.

UNITED STATES

Congressional Globe, Part I, 1857–1858.

House Executive Documents, 4. 29th Cong., 2nd Sess. Serial No. 497.

House Executive Documents, 60. 30th Cong., 1st Sess. Serial No. 520.

House Executive Documents, 1. 30th Cong., 2nd Sess. Serial No. 537.

House Executive Documents, 52. 36th Cong., 1st Sess. Serial No. 1050.

House Executive Documents, 81. 36th Cong., 1st Sess., 1859–1860. Serial No. 1056.

House Executive Documents, 93. 45th Cong., 2nd Sess. Serial No. 1809.

House Miscellaneous Documents, 64. 45th Cong., 2nd Sess. Serial No. 1820.

Senate Executive Documents, 1. 30th Cong., 1st Sess. Serial No. 503.

Senate Executive Documents, 14. 32nd Cong., 2nd Sess. Serial No. 660.

Senate Executive Documents, 2. 36th Cong., 1st Sess. Serial No. 1023.

Senate Documents, 285. 66th Cong., 2nd Sess. Serial Nos. 7665–7666.

MANUSCRIPT SOURCES

Adjutant Generals' Military Papers, 1835–1935, State Capitol, Austin.

Caperton, John C. Sketch of Colonel John C. Hays, Texas Ranger, Transcript, Archives, Library, The University of Texas, Austin.

Ford, John S. Memoirs of Archives, Library, The University of Texas, Austin.

Frontier Papers, State Library, Austin.

Governors' Letters, Files of, State Capitol, Austin.

Indian Office Letters Received, volumes for 1855 and 1856. Transcript, Archives, Library, The University of Texas, Austin.

BIBLIOGRAPHY

Indian Affairs Papers, State Library, Austin.

Neighbors, Robert S. Papers, Archives, The University of Texas, Austin.

Sumpter, Jesse. The Life of, the Oldest Citizen of Eagle Pass, Texas, 1906, Archives, Library, The University of Texas.

NEWSPAPERS

Brownsville Herald, 1902, Brownsville, Texas.

Daily Austin Republican, 1870, Austin.

Daily Democratic Statesman, 1873, Austin.

Daily Picayune, 1849, New Orleans, Louisiana.

Daily State Journal, 1870–1873, Austin.

Dallas News, 1914, Dallas.

Flake's Daily Bulletin, 1871, Galveston, Texas.

Galveston Daily News, 1871; 1874; 1878; 1879, Galveston, Texas.

Lampasas Dispatch, Lampasas, Texas.

Norton's Union Intelligencer, 1873, Austin.

San Antonio Herald, 1855, San Antonio.

San Antonio Ledger, 1855, San Antonio.

Telegraph and Texas Register, 1838; 1839; 1840, Columbia, Texas.

Texas Democrat, 1846; 1849, Austin.

Texas State Gazette, 1849; 1850; 1852; 1853; 1871, Austin.

True Issue, 1855, LaGrange, Texas.

Key to Abbreviations in Footnotes.

A.G.P. Adjutant General's Papers.
G.L. Governor's Letters.

INDEX

INDEX

INDEX

INDEX

INDEX

INDEX

INDEX

INDEX

INDEX

INDEX

INDEX

INDEX